A HISTORY OF

ENGLISH PLACENAMES

AND WHERE THEY CAME FROM

'We do not make history – history makes us'

Martin Luther King

A HISTORY OF
ENGLISH
PLACENAMES
AND WHERE THEY CAME FROM

JOHN MOSS

PEN & SWORD
HISTORY
AN IMPRINT OF PEN & SWORD BOOKS LTD.
YORKSHIRE – PHILADELPHIA

First published in Great Britain in 2020 by
PEN AND SWORD HISTORY
An imprint of
Pen & Sword Books Ltd
Yorkshire – Philadelphia

ISBN 978 1 52672 284 3

A CIP catalogue record for this book is available from the British Library.

Typeset in Times New Roman 10/12 by
Aura Technology and Software Services, India.
Printed and bound in the UK by TJ International.

Pen & Sword Books Limited incorporates the imprints of Atlas, Archaeology,
Aviation, Discovery, Family History, Fiction, History, Maritime, Military, Military Classics,
Politics, Select, Transport, True Crime, Air World, Frontline Publishing, Leo Cooper,
Remember When, Seaforth Publishing, The Praetorian Press, Wharncliffe Local History,
Wharncliffe Transport, Wharncliffe True Crime and White Owl.

For a complete list of Pen & Sword titles please contact
PEN & SWORD BOOKS LIMITED
47 Church Street, Barnsley, South Yorkshire, S70 2AS, England
E-mail: enquiries@pen-and-sword.co.uk
Website: www.pen-and-sword.co.uk

Or
PEN AND SWORD BOOKS
1950 Lawrence Rd, Havertown, PA 19083, USA
E-mail: Uspen-and-sword@casematepublishers.com
Website: www.penandswordbooks.com

Contents

Foreword

In my earlier book, *Great British Family Names and Their History*, I wrote that while many families are named after places, some placenames come from the people who founded them. It seemed logical, therefore, that this book would follow, and that while it comes from a more-or-less opposite direction, it complements the first, bears out the original premise and completes the picture.

This is a book about the derivation of many English cities, townships, villages and hamlets – placenames whose origins lie shrouded in history; names that come from the days when Celtic tribes occupied these islands and were later overtaken by Romans, Angles, Jutes, Danes and Saxons, as well as the Norman French invaders of 1066. These immigrant cultures were all assimilated, and from them emerged the common placenames we recognise today, even though the passage of time may have obscured their origin.

I began this project after taking early retirement, at a time before online resources were commonplace. My research entailed many months spent in Manchester Central Library, making copious long-hand notes. In those days there were no smart phones, laptops or tablets – my well-worn Schaeffer fountain pen, a pot of black ink, a notebook and the empty silence of a library full of books were the only resources at my disposal.

I found several printed publications of particular value, and I have made great use of them. First, William the Conqueror's *Domesday Book,* sometimes referred to as the Great Survey of 1086, originally called *The Book of Winchester*, and specifically the excellent complete translation of the survey by Dr Ann Williams and Professor G.H. Martin. This immense resource is the ultimate reference work and my book would have been almost impossible to complete without it. Second, I must mention Anne Savage's scholarly translation of the *Anglo-Saxon Chronicles*, which offered essential information regarding anything pre-dating the Norman Conquest. A.D. Mills' *Dictionary of British Placenames* also proved a most useful starting point, in its comprehensive, if brief listings of over 17,000 places in Britain.

Then, given the profusion of material now in the public domain, thanks to the exponential growth of online resources, I feel obliged to make a passing reference to the Internet. While its factual information is voluminous and its accessibility has enabled almost anybody to publish anything, no matter how trivial or fatuous, the veracity of much of its content is frequently dubious, trivial or erroneous. The reader should tread warily and guardedly, and the maxim should always be 'let the reader beware'.

It is a fortunate and convenient fact that nowadays almost every town, city, village and parish in England has its own website, as do most local history societies, each extolling the pride and virtue of their particular place. These have proved an invaluable boon and I have found that, for the most part, they are rich veins of trustworthy information. This is particularly true of official local authority and council websites, who have direct access to their community records of history, charters, grants and foundations, and I have used some of these sources in compiling this work.

The interpretation of the meaning of English placenames is not an exact science. Often there are several possibilities as to an exact translation, especially when dealing with old Saxon words, many of which were not written down, or if they were, it was at a time before the English language, as we understand it, was formally fixed. This being so, it is not surprising that spellings vary and explanations of name derivations differ from one authority to another. This is to be expected; ancient placenames are often ambiguous and it is impossible to be absolutely certain of their true meaning or origin, so that a fair amount of educated guesswork as well as traditionally accepted interpretations are called upon to make sense of them.

Many medieval words have long fallen out of common usage and their significance is almost lost. This is particularly true of land measurements referred to in the Conqueror's survey of 1086, where the meaning of ancient words like carucate, hide, bovate and sokeland are lost to most contemporary readers. In an age before measuring tapes and rulers existed, when the general populace was neither literate nor numerate and precise units of measurement were unknown, such calculations had to be based on rather more subjective criteria. Therefore, I have included a glossary at the beginning of this book in explanation of the most frequently occurring terms.

Of course, there are far too many townships and villages in England to deal with all of them in the degree of detail they might deserve, or to include every possible name. So, what follows is a selection of around 2,000 English placenames – a purely personal choice.

As to my definitions, in general terms, for the purpose of this book, I define a town as a fully operational entity with its own council, public services and elected councillors; a village is identified as a suburb of a larger town's local authority which will normally have a church at its centre, and a hamlet as a small collection of dwellings with no church. However, as many great cities began life as small hamlets, I have used the word 'townships', as a generic term for all such embryonic settlements, no matter how big, small, or important they were to become.

What follows, therefore, are some of the explanations and derivations of many placenames in England. And, while much of the material that I have included may be available elsewhere, in this book I have attempted to produce a valuable, concise and eminently readable reference document.

John Moss
September 2019

Glossary

This glossary is included here to assist the reader in the further study of the *Domesday Book*, in which many of these old and antiquated terms are to be found, and in the hope that it promotes a better understanding of life at that time.

Acre
An old imperial unit of land area measurement, measuring 43,560 square feet (i.e. approximately 4,000 square metres or forty per cent of a hectare). Defined in the Middle Ages as the amount of land that could be ploughed in a day by one man and one ox.

Advowson
A Middle English word introduced from the French '*avoeson*' by the Normans. Technically meaning to vow, acknowledge or admit, but in common eleventh century usage it meant rights given to a patron (an avowee), usually related to a diocesan bishop and within his right to hold or convey. These were valuable assets, giving the holder (the avowee), influence and manorial rights, and usually included use of a house, rectory or parsonage, as well as income from tithes or other local rents and taxes.

Almsland
Land leased or granted to a religious institution like a church or monastery in exchange for prayers and masses to be said for the donor.

Alodiary
Sometimes spelt 'allodiary'. A practice widespread in south-east England, especially in Kent, in medieval times. Technically, an alodiary is a person who owns a plot of land (known as an alod). Initially, an eleventh century Anglo-Saxon system whereby land or estates were the absolute and outright possession of the alodiary (the owner), not liable for chargeable tenure or payment of fees or tithes during his lifetime. Upon the alodiary's death, the land reverted to the king. The modern concept of an allotment may have begun here.

Anglo-Saxon Chronicles, The
An historic document and an early record of events in Saxon England, probably begun during the reign of Alfred the Great, some time around 890AD and added to by others until the twelfth century. Originally written in Old English with later entries in Middle English.

Arpent
An old French unit of land area measurement. One square arpent is equivalent to just over three-quarters of an acre. or approximately 3,300 square feet.

Balliwick/Bailiwick
A district or jurisdiction under the supervision or authority of an elected or appointed bailie or a bailiff.

Berewick
A portion of detached farmland that belonged to a manor and reserved for the lord of the manor's own use.

Bordar
A smallholder of low social rank, who held a cottage in return for menial work.
From the old French word 'borde', referring to a wooden hut or lowly habitation. Similar to a cottar. Both were cottagers of some kind and were frequently interchangeable terms.

Borough
An urban settlement, often fortified (from the Old English 'burh', indicating a stronghold), and administered by a burgess.

Bovate
A bovate was a measure of land which could be ploughed by one-eighth of a plough (or carucate). A medieval form of a Latin word *'bovata'*, referring to a bullock or an oxen, generally used in those days to pull a plough.

Burgess
A local official, whose title originally meant a freeman of the borough. Later it became an elected member of the local town council, or a local representative sent to Parliament.

Bushel
A bushel is an ancient measure of capacity equal to eight gallons (equivalent to 36.4 litres), used for corn, fruit, liquids.

Carucate
Derived from the Latin word for a plough (*'caruca'*), commonly used in northern England under Danelaw (lands governed by the Danes), and equivalent to an area of land that could be ploughed in a day by one team of oxen.

Chantry/Chantry House
The word chantry comes from the French verb *'chanter'*, or the Latin *'cantare'*, meaning to sing. Before the Reformation, endowments or licences were founded to pay for priests to sing masses or to pray for the souls of the departed. Their residences were known as 'chantry houses'. Many large churches had Chantry Chapels attached.

Chapel of Ease
An alternative church building, which though not a parish church as such, was deliberately built within the parish for those who could not make to the parish church (i.e. the sick, lame or elderly), and for whom it was more convenient, nearby, or 'easier' to attend for worship.

Cester
Sometimes spelt 'sester', this was a medieval measure for liquids, especially wine or honey. Before pints and quarts, this measure varied between twenty-four and thirty-two ounces. Sometimes it was used as a dry measure for things like grain, and was equivalent to about twelve bushels, (about fifty-six imperial pounds or thirty-six litres).

Cinque Ports
A confederation of coastal channel ports in Kent and Sussex, formed for military and trade purposes. The name comes directly from the French and means 'five ports'. Their introduction can be traced back to Saxon times though the name only came into being in the twelfth century. It was their duty to provide ships and crew for service to the monarch for two weeks every year. The five ports were originally Hastings, New Romney, Hythe, Dover and Sandwich, though other towns contributed to the confederation. These were known as 'limbs' and included Lydd, Folkestone, Faversham, Margate, Deal, Ramsgate and Tenterton.

Civil Parish
The lowest unit of local government, falling somewhere below a county or a district. Whereas a Parish was traditionally an ecclesiastical division administered by the church, a Civil Parish was administered by locally elected officials independently of the church.

Cnut
Cnut was king of England from 1017–35, who was often commonly known as Canute. He was born c.995 in Denmark, the son of Sweyn I (known as Forkbeard), but embraced the Anglo-Saxon culture of England and was widely respected as a wise ruler. His accession was recorded in the *Anglo-Saxon Chronicles* in 1017: 'Cnut received all the Kingdom of England, and divided it into four, with himself in Wessex, Thurkill in East Anglia, Eadric in Mercia and Eric in Northumbria'.

Colibert
A term most commonly used in the West Country for a free man. Often simply referred to in Domesday as an Englishman. A free man was not bound to a manor or estate and could transfer himself and his land from one lord to another.

Cottar
A tenant, usually a farm labourer, who occupied a cottage (or cotset), in return for labour. Many male slaves had been ploughmen before the Conquest and invariably free men. As enslaved workers under Norman occupation, they were often designated a small modest cottage – a cotset.

Cotset
A cottage occupied by an estate labourer, often a Saxon slave. Distinctions between terms like cottars and bordars are hard to define, as both referred to the occupants of cottages, and were frequently interchangeable.

Danegeld
Tribute or protection money paid by Saxons to Danish Vikings to keep them at bay and save their lands from being ravaged.

Demesne
From the Old French *'demeine'*, meaning 'belonging to the lord'. Land attached to a manor, kept specifically for the owner's use. The terms 'in demesne' or 'held in demesne' indicated land belonging or adjoined to the manor house or its estate, occupied by the owner but worked for him by a tenant.

Dicker
A medieval quantity of ten (a corruption of the Latin word for ten: *'decem'*). The Latin *'decuria'* referred to 'a parcel of ten', a unit of barter and trade used on the Roman frontier. The German word *'decher'*, meaning a 'set of ten things' has a similar origin.

Dissolution of the Monasteries
Sometimes referred to as the 'Suppression of the Monasteries', following the Act of Supremacy in 1534 and Henry VIII's break with the Church of Rome. Upon his orders, between 1536 and 1541 all monasteries, priories, abbeys, friaries and convents were forcibly disbanded in England, Wales and Ireland. Their income, estates and assets were usually appropriated as income for the Crown, with significant amounts sold off to fund the king's military campaigns.

Domesday Book

Also called the Domesday survey and the Great Survey. Originally known by its Latin name *Liber de Wintonia* (the Book of Winchester), it was commissioned by William the Conqueror as a detailed audit of the properties, lands, livestock and all tangible and taxable assets of Britain. The *Anglo-Saxon Chronicles* describes William's commission of the survey at Gloucester in 1085 thus: 'the king had great deliberations... with his counsellors about this land, how it was occupied and by what sort of men... [and] how many hides of land were in the shire; what the king himself had in land, and in livestock on the land; what dues he had from the property each twelve months from the shire... also he let it be written down'.

The survey audit was also used as a basis for the redistribution of land amongst his Norman knights and other supporters following his Conquest of 1066. Lands and properties previously freely owned by Saxons were confiscated and granted as rewards to Norman knights and clergy. The survey was completed in 1086, a year before William's death. It was known as Domesday insomuch as it was compared to the Last Judgement. The name also takes its name from the Old English word 'dom', meaning 'assessment' or 'audit', because it assessed the assets and potential wealth of King William's newly acquired realm.

A later survey, known as *Little Domesday*, was carried out to include those parts of the country omitted in the first volume of the Great Domesday Book of 1086. These included Essex, Norfolk and Suffolk and several other northern districts and townships which were overlooked in the original survey.

Enclosure

In medieval times an enclosure was, as the word suggests, any area of enclosed or fenced land, at a time before land was routinely enclosed. It might have included arable land, pasture or paddocks, and may have been enclosed with bushes, hedges, pole fences, surrounded by water or marsh and rarely in stone. Land enclosure as we might understand it formally began in the thirteenth century, separating private land from what may previously have been common or open land. The practice became widespread during the sixteenth century and by the nineteenth, apart from rough pastures and mountainous areas, virtually all land in England had become enclosed in one way or another.

Englishmen

A descriptive term which Norman overlords used for common Saxons, to discriminate them from Frenchmen (Normans).

Feld

The Saxons used the word 'feld' or 'felda' to describe open tracts of land that had been cleared of woodland for farming. The word is clearly related to the modern word 'field', but had quite different connotations; today we might think of a field as a plot of land bounded by hedges or fences, but the opposite was true of the Saxon 'feld', where an individual's piece of land would be marked only by a narrow separating strip of pathway. In Old English, 'feld' meant 'open land'.

Ferding

Another measure of land used in Domesday, whose exact dimensions are unclear, but a ferding probably consisted of a few acres.

Free Borough

A 'free borough' was a township or manor granted special liberties and privileges by the Crown. These might include the right to hold fairs and markets, and on rare occasions to create merchant's guilds and hold their own borough courts.

Free Man
A man who was free, that is not bound in servitude to a lord as such, but while able to hold land under the feudal system, might owe some periodic service to the lord of the manor. A Frenchman, usually a Norman settler of non-noble status, had an equivalent status to a free man.

Frenchmen
A generic term used by Normans to describe common men from France or Normandy, usually immigrant settlers, who were not Norman aristocrats or of noble birth. These tended to be tenants and free men, but worked alongside Saxons. Nevertheless they were regarded by the Normans as of superior status to Englishmen.

Friary
A building where friars lived. Unlike monks, who often belonged to a closed religious order based on prayer and meditation, friars tended to live among the local community, often tending the sick or founding hospitals.

Furlong
A furlong is an old imperial measure of distance equal to one-eighth of a mile (i.e. 660 feet, 220 yards, forty rods, or ten chains). In metric terms one furlong is 201.168 metres. It now survives only in horse racing, where distances are still measured in furlongs.

Geld
From the Danish word '*gaeld*', also known as 'man price', taken generally to mean the value or price of a property (or a person, as slavery was common). In medieval England, it became synonymous with the word 'money', or could sometimes mean 'rent', 'debt', or 'indebtedness'.

Glebe
Glebe was a portion of land within an ecclesiastical parish provided to support a parish priest and yielding profit to supplement his income.

Great Survey
An alternative name for the *Domesday Book*, William the Conqueror's great audit of England, completed in 1086.

Hidate
To divide a shire or a borough into hides, or to calculate how many hides there were in an estate, usually for taxation purposes. Such manors were said to be 'hidated'.

Hide
Originally, a hide was an Anglo-Saxon word that simply meant 'family', but it came to mean a land-holding sufficient to feed or support a family. The *Domesday Book* frequently used it as a measure of land for calculating taxes. It was roughly one hundred and twenty acres, depending on the quality of the land.

Hundred
A sub-division of a shire or a county used for administrative purposes. A secular term, related to a district or region, as opposed to the religious division of a parish. Known in northern England as a wapentake and in the south-east as a rape or a lathe.

Hundred Rolls
The Hundred Rolls were a census of England in the late thirteenth century, which included land holdings and details of land occupation, and often referred to as 'The Second Domesday Book'. Although they were in many ways more comprehensive than Domesday, only a few survive, mostly in the Midlands and in East Anglia.

Justicar

In medieval England, a Justicar was a monarch's chief minister, roughly equivalent to a prime minister. It originally referred to any officer of the King's Court (a *Curia Regis*), but gradually came into wider usage as denoting any minister of the Crown holding subordinate authority to the monarch and often acting on his behalf or in his place when he was absent.

Lathe

An administrative subdivision of the County of Kent, which probably originated in the sixth century. Similar to a Hundred, though slightly larger in area, it was still in local use until the early twentieth century. Similar to a Rape in Sussex.

Lead Vats

Large containers, such as tubs, barrels or tanks, used for storing or holding liquids. Several lead vats or tanks from the middle or late Anglo-Saxon period are known to exist and may have been very common at that time.

League

An old unit of length in medieval times, originally, the distance a man could walk in an hour, roughly about one and a half miles. At sea it was a distance of three nautical miles.

Little Domesday Book

A later more detailed survey of the counties of Essex, Norfolk and Suffolk, significantly smaller than the main Great Survey. The document concludes, in Latin: 'This survey was made in the year one thousand and eighty-six from the incarnation of the Lord and the twentieth of the reign of William, not only throughout these three counties but also throughout others.'

Lorimer

From the French '*lorein*' or '*loreyn*', meaning a strap or a harness, the name was commonly applied in medieval times to a saddle or harness maker.

Mainou

A variation on the word 'Manor', used occasionally in the Domesday survey. See: 'Manor'.

Manor

An estate, usually under the control of a baron, the lord of the manor. A typical classification in medieval times, favoured by the Normans, where their predecessors, the Saxons, usually preferred parishes, which were under the control of the church.

Mark

A medieval unit of currency worth the equivalent of thirteen shillings and four pence, or about seventy pence in modern coinage. It was introduced by Edward III in 1344 and was sometimes called a 'gold noble'.

Messuage

A dwelling house with outbuildings and curtilage (an enclosure).

Middle English

Spoken and written in England from the time of the Norman Conquest of 1066 until the fifteenth century. It was a gradual synthesis of Old English and Norman French, and laid the foundations of modern English.

Minster

In Anglo-Saxon times, a minster was the church attached to a monastery. Derived from the Old English '*mynster*', meaning monastery, itself coming from the Latin '*monasterium*', signifying a group of clergy living in a community. Usually founded by the Crown, later it grew to mean any large church.

Mitta/Metta/Mittae

A mitta (or metta) was equivalent to four bushels or two hundredweight or a horseload, used more typically for large measures of salt, especially in the Midlands, where Droitwich was a major producer of salt. 'Mittae' is the plural form of 'mitta'.

Mixed Measures

A term used by Domesday to define arable land that was identified neither as pasture, meadow nor woodland, but grew a variety of produce, including fruit and vegetables. In other words, 'mixed produce'.

Modi/Modii

From the Latin, '*modus*', an old Roman unit of measure for dry goods, especially grain, almost equivalent to an Imperial Peck, or 8.1 litres. The term is thought to come from a form of Roman cylindrical headdress which resembled a grain measure, which was often found on representations of classical deities.

Moneyers

Individuals who were officially permitted by the state to mint coinage.

Motte and Bailey

An early form of castle or fortification, favoured by the Anglo-Saxons, and temporarily copied by early Norman invaders following the Conquest of 1066. Initially they comprised a simple ditch and wooden palisade surrounding an enclosed courtyard (the bailey), and a raised earthwork mound (the motte). Such earthworks were easy and relatively quick to build. Later they would be consolidated in stone, as exemplified by the many stone castles which the Normans built throughout Britain.

Old Cornish

An ancient Celtic language, similar to Welsh and to a lesser extent, to Gaelic. Only spoken in Cornwall, where it is considered endangered. As a language with numerous dialects, it was only in 2008 that a standard form was agreed; this is now taught in some Cornish schools and the Cornish Bible is now read in some local churches.

Old English

Sometimes called Anglo-Saxon English. It arrived with Anglo-Saxon settlers during the fifth century and continued to be written and spoken in England until the twelfth century. It was a complex language that contained significant Germanic inflexions and influences, and bore little resemblance to modern English. It was gradually replaced by Middle English.

Oxgang

Another unit of medieval land measure, similar to a bovate, but more commonly used in Scotland and measuring approximately thirteen acres. It depended on the quality of the land, and may have included land not suitable for ploughing, therefore probably not taxable. In Yorkshire it was defined as the amount of land needed to sustain one draught ox or two goats and a kid.

Pannage

The right to feed pigs and other animals in woodland, especially where acorns and chestnuts were plentiful. The practice has been largely abandoned but is traditionally still carried out every autumn in the New Forest National Park.

Parage

From the old Norman French '*perage*'. Technically indicating equality or parity of status. It was a medieval form of land tenure, whereby persons of equal status, usually of the same blood, or siblings, were granted equal rights in land ownership, despite having otherwise unequal inheritance. It was common for the firstborn to possess an inherited or bequeathed estate in its entirety. Parage operated separately from this tradition.

Parish

An administrative part of an Anglican or Roman Catholic diocese, with its own church and parish priest. In medieval times, ecclesiastical parishes roughly corresponded to county or shire boundaries and were a common form of land division in Anglo-Saxon times. See also: 'Civil Parish'.

Plough

A method of assessing the value of an estate based on the number of eight ox plough teams needed to cultivate the land. Domesday rated land as one, two, two and a half ploughs, and so on, referring to the number of teams of oxen required to work the estate. This measure was also used to assess the estate for taxation purposes. Sometimes known as 'ploughland'.

Pontage

From the French '*pontage*', meaning 'bridge-building'. In medieval times it probably referred to the upkeep and maintenance of strategically important bridges, a responsibility usually borne by the local council or burgesses, and for which they were granted privileges, in exchange for allowing toll-free passage across a river.

Portreeve

Sometimes called a Portwarden, this was an official possessing political or administrative authority over a town or borough. The 'port' element of the title does not necessarily apply to a seaside town with a harbour as such, but usually referred to a market town or a walled town. Another function of a port reeve was to act as returning officer in local elections. The role tended to be subordinate and supportive to a mayoral function, although in time the two functions of reeve and mayor were combined.

Prebend

A stipendiary payment drawn upon the parish by a prebendary, who would be asenior member of the clergy, such as the canon of a cathedral or collegiate church. From the Old French '*prebende*', meaning a salary or a pension.

Radman/Radknights/Rodknights

Translated loosely as 'road knight' or 'riding knights', radmen were serving men usually functioning as mounted escorts or bodyguards for a lord of the manor. They were usually free men, tenants under the medieval feudal system, and who could be required to offer other services, such as ploughing, when the need arose.

Rape

A traditional administrative sub-division of land in medieval Sussex, known long before the Norman Conquest in England, and largely replaced by them with such units of measurement as hides and carucates.

Reeve
Sometimes known as a port reeve, borough reeve or a shire reeve. A reeve was given authority directly by the Crown and was often responsible for running the town or district, and frequently acted as chief magistrate. The Shire Reeve was an official post of some importance in Anglo-Saxon England and was contracted to 'sheriff' in Norman times, when the office was significantly demoted, and usually held by a man of low rank, appointed by the lord of the manor to oversee peasants.

Riding
The Danes divided Yorkshire into three district regions, part of their territory called Danelaw, which we now call 'Ridings' – these included the East Riding, the North Riding and the West Riding. The word comes from the Old Scandinavian 'thrithjunger', meaning a 'third part'. These regions were effectively abolished in 1974, though the East Riding was reinstated as a unitary authority in 1996.

Sake and Soke
A legal mechanism denoting jurisdiction over a court, whereby in legal disputes, typically over landownership, those granted sake and soke could retain or intercept fines and other profits that might otherwise go to the king.

Salt Pans
Sometimes known as salterns or salt ponds, these are shallow artificial ponds whose purpose is (and was) to extract salt by evaporation of natural brine or sea water. These were much prized resources in medieval Europe, where salt was a scarce commodity that commanded a high price.

Serf
An agricultural labourer bound by the feudal system who was tied to working on his lord's estate. A person of low social class, owned by the lord of the manor, inherited along with the land, and ranked only one level higher than a slave.

Sester
See: 'Cester'.

Shieling
A roughly built animal shelter or field hut for securing and protecting animals overnight while out to pasture, and also frequently served as an overnight shelter for shepherds and herdsmen. It can also be used as a description of an area of pasture itself.

Shilling
A very old unit of imperial currency, equivalent to five New Pence. There were twenty shillings to a pound. It was abandoned in favour of decimalisation in England in 1971.

Sokeman
A freeman class of tenants who as part of their tenancy were obliged to render service of some kind to the lord of the manor. These often involved occasional agricultural, or even military service. The legal term for this kind of tenancy was known as 'socage' and the tenanted property as 'sokeland'.

Staller
Originally an old Norse term carried into Anglo-Saxon, a staller was a royal official, equivalent to a constable or a standard bearer, who was also often master of the king's horse. The concept was introduced by King Cnut, who reserved the position for his closest confidantes – usually wealthy thegns or earls.

Subregulus
A petty prince, a baron or medieval vassal ruler, authorised to act on behalf of the monarch.

Sulung
The specifically Kentish term for a unit of land measurement of about 120 acres, corresponding to a carucate or hide.

Swannery
The right to keep and breed swans, reserved for specially privileged persons. Following Edward IV's Act Concerning Swans of 1482, which declared swans to be the property of the Crown, a royal Swan Master was appointed to count and mark swans. From early medieval times the kidnapping and eating of swans was considered to be a treasonous crime, and apart from royalty, only those specifically given leave by the Crown were allowed the right of swannery.

Tale
A medieval form of the word 'talent', referring to a talent-weight, used as a measure of money, especially of silver or gold.

Thegn
An Anglo-Saxon order of nobility, equivalent to the Norman barons which replaced them and usurped their estates. Sometimes spelt 'thane', 'thayne' or 'theign'.

Thegnland
Land granted to a Saxon thegn, honouring his status, either by the king, the church, or the Norman earl who was lord of the manor.

Tithes
An Old English word, simply meaning 'a tenth'. A tax of one tenth of annual produce or earnings, taken to support the church and its clergy within a parish. This may have been paid in coinage or produce, so that most parishes had a tithe barn to store and keep what was rendered.

Vill
A shortened version of the French 'ville', which in a modern sense means a city, town or village. In Norman times the term applied specifically to a small village or hamlet.

Villan
Sometimes spelt villain or villein, it was a term used in feudal England to denote a peasant villager or serf, having more rights than a slave, but less than a free man, and usually tied to the land of the lord of the manor.

Virgate
A measure of land of approximately thirty acres.

Wapentake
A northern term for the land measurement of a Hundred, used more commonly in the Danish held part of England known as Daneland.

Warren
Sometimes known as 'free warren'. This was a right granted by the sovereign to hunt hare or fox. Hunting rights were jealously guarded in medieval England, though many members of the clergy were allowed exemptions to hunt 'beasts of the warren', predominantly small

game like foxes, rabbits and hares. The hunting of 'beasts of the chase' (notably wild boar and deer), was a privilege otherwise reserved for the monarch.

Waste/Wasta

Land which was either unusable, not fit for agricultural use - fallow, scrubland or uncultivated meadow, and therefore not liable to be taxed. Referred to in Domesday as '*wasta*'. Sometimes this 'wasta' was the result of William the Conqueror's punitive ravaging of the north, at others it simply meant land that was not taxed for some reason and rendered no dues to the lord of the manor or to the king.

Waste Houses

Usually uninhabited and valueless properties which were too poor to render anything by way of rent or tax, and probably fit only for demolition. They also included houses which might be cleared by Norman overlords to provide additional land for fortifications or castles.

Yoke

A medieval area of land measurement amounting to about fifty acres, or a quarter of a sulung, which could be ploughed by a yoke of oxen. Most commonly used for assessing tax in Kent.

Part One

Common English Placename Elements
From Old English, Old Scandinavian,
Middle English and Celtic

This section has been included so that readers might be able to work out the origin of some of the meanings of the names of English towns, villages and hamlets that have not been included in this book for themselves. The following lists are not exhaustive, but contain most of the more commonly found placename elements.

OLD ENGLISH

ac	oak tree
aesc	ash tree, aspen
ald, eald	old
baece, bece	brook or stream
beacen	signal, beacon
bece	beech tree
bel	funeral pyre, beacon
beorc	birch tree
berg, beorg	mound, hillock, tumulus
bere	barley
bere-wic	barley farm, sometimes just 'farm'
blaec	dark, black
bothl, bold	special building, dwelling or house
brad	broad
brer	briar, wild rose
broc	brook, stream
brocc	badger
brom	broom tree, thorny bush
brycg	bridge
bucc	buck, stag
bucca	male deer, billy goat
bula	bull
bur	cottage
burh, burg	fortified dwelling or stronghold
burna	stream
bury	manor house (fortified)
byge	river bend
caerse	water cress
cal	cabbage
calc, cealc	chalk, limestone
cald	cold

calu	bare, bald hill
camb	ridge, hill-crest
carn	cairn, heap of stones
ceap, ceping	market
ceorl	peasant, freeman
cese	cheese
cirice	church
claeg	clay
cloh	deep ravine
cnoll	hilltop
cocc	cockerel
cofa	cave chamber
col	coal, charcoal
copp	hilltop, summit
cot	cottage, hut, shelter
cran	crane, heron
crawe	crow
croft	enclosure
croh	saffron
cruc	hill, barrow, mound
cumb	combe, valley
cu	cow
cwen	queen
cyne	royal, regal
cyning	king
dael	valley, hollow
denn	woodland pasture for pigs
denu	long shallow valley
deop	deep
dic	ditch, dyke
draeg	portage slope
dun, din	hill fort, hill
ea	river
earn	eagle
ecg	edge, escarpment
edisc	enclosed land
eg, ieg	island, dry land
elfitu	swan
ende	district of an estate
ened	duck
eofor	wild boar
eorl	nobleman
eowestre	sheepfold
eowu	ewe
ersc	ploughed field
faeger	fair, pleasant
faesten	stronghold
fald, falod	fold, animal enclosure

feld	open land cleared of trees
fennig	marshy, muddy
fleot	estuary, creek, inlet
folc	folk, people, tribe
ford	shallow river crossing
fugol	fowl, bird
ful	foul, dirty
funta	spring, water spout
fyrh	woodland
gat	goat
geard	enclosed yard
geat	gate, pass, gap
gifu	gift
gos	goose
graef	trench, ditch
graefe, graf	grove, copse
groet	gravel
haeme	dwellers, inhabitants
haer	heap of stones
haesel	hazel tree
haeth	heath, heather
hag-thorn	hawthorn
halh	corner, recess or nook of land
halig	holy
ham	homestead, village
hamm	land enclosed by water, river meadow
ham-tun	home farm, settlement
hangra	sloping woodland
har	grey, hoar
hara	hare
heafod	headland, promontory
heah	high
hearg	heathen or pagan shrine
hecg	hedge, hedgerow
heg, hieg	hay
helde	slope
hengest	stallion
heorot	stag, hart
here	army
hid	hide of land
hind	hind, doe
hlaw	tumulus, mound
hlose	pig-sty
hoc	nook or corner of land
holt	wood, thicket
hop	enclosure in a marsh or moor
horu	filth, dirt
hramsa	wild garlic

hreod	reed, bullrush
hrither	oxen, cattle
hund	dog
hunig	honey
hunta	huntsman
hwaete	wheat
hyrst	wooded hill
hyth	landing place or inland port
ieg	island
inga, ingas	people, family or followers of
iw	yew tree
lacu	watercourse, stream
laece, laecc	stream, bog
leac	leek, garlic
leah	woodland clearing, meadow or glade
maed	meadow
maegden	maiden
mael, mel	cross, crucifix
mearc	boundary
meos	moss
maere, mere	small lake, pond, pool
mersc	marsh
munuk	monk
mutha	estuary, river mouth
myln	mill
mynster	monastery, large church
mythe	river confluence
naess, ness	headland, promontory
ofer	river bank, shore
oxa	ox
paeth	path, track
penn	animal pen or enclosure
pirige	pear tree
plega	to play games or sports
pol, pull	pool, tidal stream
port	harbour, market town, gate
preost	priest
pyll	tidal pool or stream
read	red
refa	bailiff, reeve
ric	strip of land
rodu	clearing
ruh	rough
ryge	rye
sae	inland lake
salh, sealh	sallow, willow
sceaga	small wood, copse

sceap, scep	sheep
sceat	angle or corner of land
scela	temporary hut or shelter
scene, sciene	bright, beautiful
scir	shire, district
scucca	demon, evil spirit
Seaxe	Saxons
sele	house, dwelling
sic	small stream
sid	deep
slaed	valley
slaep	slippery place
sloh	mire, slough
staeth	landing-place
stede	religious site
stan	stone, rock, boundary stone
stapol	post, pillar, column
stede	enclosed pasture
steort	tongue or spur of land
stig	narrow path
stoc	outlying farm or remote homestead
stocc	tree trunk or log
stod	herd of horses
stow, stou	religious site or assembly place
straet	Roman road, paved thoroughfare
swin	pig, swine
thing	assembly, meeting
throp	outlying farm or remote hamlet
thyrne	thorn tree
ticce	kid, young goat
torr	rocky hill, outcrop
tote, tot	lookout place
treow	tree, wooden post
tun	enclosure, manor, settlement, farmstead
twisla	fork in a river
uf	owl
wad	woad
waed, gewaed	river crossing
wald, weald	high forested woodland
walh	Briton
weard	watch, protect
weorc	fortification, work
weg	way, road, path
wella	spring, well or stream
weorc	building, fortification
wer, waer	wier, dam
wic	farm, dairy or industrial settlement

wiell	well
woh	twisted, crooked
wudu	wood, forest, timber
yfer	brow or edge of a hill

OLD SCANDINAVIAN/NORSE

akr	cultivated arable land
askr	ash tree
austr	east
bekkr	stream
berg	hill
blakr	dark, exposed
boli	bull
bolstathr	dwelling, homestead
bondi	peasant, landowner
both, buth	temporary shelter
brekka	hill slope
brunnr	spring, stream
buth, both	temporary shelter
by, byr	farmstead, settlement, village
dalr	valley
eik	oak
elptr	swan
erg	hill pasture, shieling
ersc	ploughed land
ey	island
ferja	ferry
fjorthr	firth, sea inlet
garthr	enclosure
geit	goat
gata	road, street
gil	deep ravine
goltr	boar
grar	grey
griss	pig, swine
haugr	mound, tumulus
holmr	island in a marsh
hulm	island, water meadow
hvin	gorse
kaldr	cold
kalfr	calf
kamber	crest
karl	peasant, freeman
kelda	spring, water spout
kirkja	church
kjarr	overgrown marsh
klovr	clover
konungr	king

hrafn	raven
kringla	circle, ring
krok	river bend
kross	cross
lundr	grove, small wood
marr	marsh, fen
melr	sandbank
myrr	mud, swamp, bog
ra	roe deer
saete	settlers, dwellers
saetr	hill pasture, shieling
scelf, scylfe, kialf	ledge, shelf
skali, skili	temporary shelter
skogr	wood, woodland
slakki	shallow valley
thorp	outlying district, remote settlement
thvelt	clearing, meadow
toft, topt	building plot
tun	farmstead, enclosure
vagr	creek
vath	ford, shallow river crossing
vik	bay, inlet
vithr	wood, forest
yr	yew tree

MIDDLE ENGLISH/OLD FRENCH

bigging	building
brend	burnt clearing
bury	manor, manor house
mont	hill, mount
side	hillside, land alongside a river
toun	village, estate, manor
ville, vill	town, village

CELTIC

breh	hill
cadeir	lofty place, high chair
carn	cairn, heap of stones
ced	woodland, forest
crug, cruc	mound, tumulus
din, dun	hillfort
egles	Christian church
lan	enclosed yard
lindo	pool, lake
penn	end, hill
ros	moorland, heath, promontory
torr	hilltop, rocky peak
tref	hamlet

Part Two

Migrations and Invasions

The Celts, Romans, Anglo-Saxons, Danes and Normans

The Celtic Tribelands

Although the British Isles had been occupied since prehistoric times, the earliest of its identifiable inhabitants were Celtic-speaking Britons, distant ancestors of the Welsh and Cornish, who probably arrived on these shores around 5,000 years ago. It would be an over-simplification to say that the Celts were one people; they were made up of different tribes. The Romans referred to them collectively as Belgae, people of Indo-European descent who shared a common gene pool element and had migrated westward from central Europe to the Atlantic coast during the Mesolithic period (sometimes called the Middle Stone Age).

Some of the earliest written Greek sources describe these aboriginal Britons as *Keltoi,* and the Romans called them *Celtae*. Initially, the new arrivals probably spoke a variety of Germanic languages, related to ancient Dutch or Frisian. Later, these developed into a variety of proto-Gallic dialects, one form of which was Brythonic, (or Brittonic), which gradually became better known as Celtic and elements of which survive almost intact in modern Welsh.

The Celts left little by way of language; ancient British placenames survive in only a few places in England. Notable examples are in Cornwall and Devon, whose county names derive directly from the Cornovii and Dumnonii tribes, whose territories they were. But there is little else, largely because names were hardly ever written down. What survives of the Celtic tongue exists in Brythonic Welsh, Irish Erse, Scottish Gaelic, Manx on the Isle of Man and a few places on the west coast of Cumbria.

In the main, the Celts left us monuments – stone circles, henges, barrows and hill forts. Most of their placenames have either been lost to us or replaced by the Latin names which the Romans overlaid on their settlements.

The Roman Occupation

The Roman legions, led by Julius Caesar, first arrived on the shores of Britain and landed in the Isle of Thanet, Kent in 55BC. It is not clear why they came; some believe it was for tin and copper, others that it was to trade and yet others that it was little more than to expand the empire. Whatever the reason, the Celtic-speaking Britons did not welcome them. Caesar's stay was brief and saw him fleeing back to Europe after a shocking military defeat. He tried again a year later, this time successfully, and is thought to have advanced well into Kent and Middlesex as far as the River Stour. His campaigns were few and short; Julius Caesar's attempts at invasion ultimately failed and he returned to France leaving behind no occupation force.

It was not until 43AD, under the Emperor Claudius, that a new landing took place, followed by the subsequent Roman conquest of the land they called Britannia. Their legions immediately set up fortified encampments, brought with them Roman culture and bestowed Latin names upon their settlements. They named places like *Aquae Sulis* (Bath),

Eboracum (York), *Camulodunum* (Colchester), *Deva* (Chester), *Mamuciam* (Manchester), *Salinae* (Droitwich), and many others. There are also the innumerable placename references to Roman settlements and military establishments that bear variations on the Latin word 'ceastre', including townships like Horncastle, Castlethwaite, Bicester, Lanchester, Godmanchester, Chesterfield and Caister, to name but a few.

Roman culture and law dominated the British province for 350 years, before their withdrawal in 410 in order to defend Rome from the threat of the Visigoth invasions. In the political and security vacuum that followed, Britain lay militarily unprotected and Pictish tribes from Scotland seized the opportunity and began systematic raids against northern England. With the Romans gone, Britain was prey to any who fancied their chances.

The Anglo-Saxon Invasions

When the Roman legions left Britain, the insecurity created by their departure was soon seized upon by warring tribes from the near continent: Angles, Saxons, Frisians and Jutes. These various tribes are generally grouped into one single entity and for historical purposes they have been called Anglo-Saxons. According to Bede, the Saxons first arrived in Britain around 449, though other accounts place it a few years earlier. In a text by the sixth century Welsh monk and historian Gildas, entitled *De Excidio et Conquestu Britanniae* (The Overthrow and Conquest of Britain), written around 540, he described how the sinfulness and wickedness of British nobles had brought down the wrath of God and presaged the arrival of heathen Saxons, to help protect Britain, thus:

> 'The barbarians (the Saxons)... introduced as soldiers to the island, to encounter... any dangers in defence of their hospitable entertainers, obtain[ed] an allowance of provisions which for some time, being plentifully bestowed, stopped their doggish mouths. [But, they went on to] break the treaty and plunder the whole island. In a short time, they follow[ed] up their threats with deeds'.

Gildas' religious fervour often overshadowed his objectivity, but in general terms his narrative was borne out by actual events. Weak leadership and feudal wars from British tribal chieftains did indeed see them initially inviting Saxons to Britain as mercenaries to assist in keeping the Pictish and Scottish tribes from the north at bay. But other uninvited Saxon invasions soon followed, as did successive migrations of yet more Germanic tribes like the Angles, Jutes, Francs and Frisians. The Saxon guests had become invaders, and there followed a period often called the Dark Ages, when according to Gildas, these warlike European tribes ravaged and pillaged their way across much of eastern Britain. Gildas' account goes on to describe the virtual genocide of its Celtic people, while those that survived were driven to western extremities of Britain – to Cornwall, Wales, Cumbria and Scotland.

However, not all Saxon incursions were aggressive, and many would eventually settle, intermarry and become assimilated, so that over time a gradual but dramatic change in the linguistic, genetic and cultural demography of Britain took place. Its people had become Anglo-Saxons. This led to the development of the many Saxon placenames that exist throughout England today; it would be true to say that the majority of towns, villages and hamlets contain several, if not all elements of the Saxon language, which we call Old English.

Saxon Britain was far from a united nation. Although a distinct Anglo-Saxon identity and language became well established, at least in the eastern half of Britain, its disparate petty kingdoms were often in dispute with each other, particularly with regard to territorial boundaries. The Saxons were also largely illiterate and left behind little written history. Also, they seemed to have little interest in the far south-west of England – Devon and Cornwall were subject to only a few incursions by them, and consequently, many Old Celtic placenames still exist there.

The Danes and Danelaw

By the eighth century, separate kingdoms existed in Sussex, Wessex, Mercia, Northumbria, Kent and East Anglia. These piecemeal political and territorial divisions and the lack of a single authoritarian rule prompted invasion by Scandinavian raiders from Norway, Sweden and Denmark; the Saxons knew them as Danes – many called them Norsemen or Vikings.

Most commentators agree that the Danes first invaded Britain in 793, when Vikings raided the monastery at Lindisfarne, the holy island located off the north-east coast of England, slaying its priests and looting its treasures. By 866, the Vikings had arrived in York, (which they called Jorvik). At that time it was the second biggest city in the country after London. In the years that followed, Danes systematically advanced south and westwards, establishing a territory that became known as the Danelaw. Saxon settlements paid protection or tribute money, known as Danegeld, to avoid destruction and bloodshed. Prayer books at that time bore the bidding words 'God save us from the Northmen'. By the late-ninth century the Vikings had taken all of England except the Kingdom of Wessex. Wisely, its king, Alfred, made an uneasy peace with them, paying a large sum in order to effect a compromise.

The Kingdom of Wessex was the last remaining independent Anglo-Saxon part of Britain. Its capital at Wintancaester (Winchester), stood out against the inexorable advance of Danish occupation. Alfred, commonly known as Alfred the Great, was determined to stop their advance. Matters came to a head when Wessex came under Danish attack in 870; a year later Alfred's army defeated a Danish army at the Battle of Ashdown in Berkshire.

Alfred saw the need for the unification of the whole nation in defence of the realm, and urged other petty kings to put aside all differences and work to create a single new nation – England. He reorganised his army and built a series of well-defended and fortified settlements, or 'burhs', to protect what remained of England from the inexorable Danish advance, work that was continued by his daughter Aethelflaed along with her brother and Alfred's successor, Edward the Elder. In the event, the Danes were finally stopped in 910 at Wodensfeld (Woden's Field, now called Wednesfield, in the West Midlands) – sometimes known as the Battle of Tettenhall. The battle was recorded in the *Anglo-Saxon Chronicles* thus:

> 'The English and the Danes fought at Tettenhall, on August 6th, and the English took the victory... They put the force to flight and killed many of them. King Eowils was killed, King Healfden, Eorl Ohter, Eorl Scvurfa, Hold Athulf, Hold Benesing, Anlaf the Swart, and many more. The same year, Aethelflaed built the burh of Bremesbyrig [thought to be Bromesberrow, near Ledbury in Herefordshire].'

Initially, the Danes had few intentions of settling in England; their interest lay in obtaining tribute or protection money. In 1006, it was recorded that King Aethelred paid 36,000 pounds of silver in tribute, and by 1012, the annual amount had risen to 48,000 pounds.

King Alfred had been a devout, cultured and literate man who fostered the translation of books from Latin to Anglo-Saxon, personally making many translations and setting up schools of learning. By the 890s, his laws, charters and coinage referred to him as 'King of the English'. A treaty of Alfred and the Danish King Guthrum had been ratified in 886, which defined the boundaries of English and Danish territories, creating an uneasy peace between the two peoples, albeit with frequent treaty violations.

Alfred's grandson, Athelstan quite brilliantly took personal control of the minting of the nation's coinage, controlling the number of moneyers that each borough and township could support, granting official licences and having his likeness stamped onto every coin that was minted. This single act demonstrated Athelstan's handle on real power; the effect was to create a sense of unification and nationhood, in a way that Alfred had hoped to achieve. Around 890, the term 'Engaland' was being used to describe what was rapidly becoming a unified nation. Athelstan went on to invade Scotland, Wales and Cornwall, whose kings swore him fealty; still a far from united kingdom, but he had created a virtual empire.

Athelstan, in common with the other immediate heirs and successors of King Alfred, had established a powerful ruling dynasty, that oversaw a land that was prosperous and well governed for best part of a century. However, that all changed when Ethelred II ascended the English throne in April 1016. Commonly held to have been one of the weakest, poorly advised and potentially most disastrous kings of England, Ethelred's reign saw the re-emergence of Viking incursions. In 982, the *Anglo-Saxon Chronicles* recorded that:

> 'Three ships of Vikings came up into Dorset, and ravaged in Portland the same year. Also that year, London was burnt, and two eorldormen passed away.'

Despite peace offerings and treaties, Danish incursions occurred almost yearly between 997 and 1014, with villages in Kent, Sussex and Essex burnt to the ground and people put to the sword. In 1013, King Swein (Forkbeard) of Denmark landed 'with a heathen force' and declared himself King of Northumbria and eastern England. Finally, events came to a head at the Battle of Ashingdon, when the English army, led by Edmund Ironside, was defeated and utterly destroyed by a Danish army lead by Cnut, King of Denmark.

Danish Kings
The merging of English and Danish culture was effectively finalised when in September 1015, Cnut (sometimes known as Canute), acceded to the English throne. His first act was to banish or execute any potential Saxon rivals and threats. However, his accession saw him transformed from a hitherto ruthless Viking warrior into a wise and respected ruler with a shrewd grasp of government and administration, upholding codes of law that had been established by the Saxon kings before him. Added to this, his fortuitous marriage to Emma, the widow of the Saxon King Ethelred, saw Danish and Saxon conflict all but suspended.

In the years that followed, like the Saxon invaders had done before them, the Danes became settlers and farmers and were assimilated into the English culture, so that during the first few decades of the eleventh century the country achieved relative peace and a viable Anglo-Norse accommodation had been established.

The influence of the Scandinavian language is still evident in many placenames, particularly in the eastern counties of England. Places like Grimsby, Wetherby, Selby and Whitby bear witness to a Danish legacy, as the Old Norse suffix 'by', indicated a village, farmstead or settlement, very much as did the affix 'thorpe' in placenames like Scunthorpe, Mabelthorpe and Cleethorpes.

In 1042, Cnut died, and with all his natural lineage at an end, Edward the son of King Ethelred and grandson of King Alfred inherited the throne as Edward the Confessor, and became the penultimate Anglo-Saxon King of England.

Unlike his forebears, Edward was not a soldier, but was a pious, studious man. The real power behind the throne lay in the hands of the somewhat unscrupulous Saxon Earl Godwin of Wessex, who had gained influence during Cnut's reign, and who for a while occupied an important role as chief counsellor and mentor in Edward's court. However, in time, Godwin's corrupt ambitions found disfavour and Edward banished him, along with his family.

Most villages and townships in Anglo-Saxon England kept little or no records, and at a time when language tended to be passed on by oral tradition, their meanings are lost to us. What little material that was written down tended to be on a local parish by parish basis, with churches and monasteries forming the mainstay of historical records. Unfortunately, most of this information treasure store was destroyed along with the convents, friaries and other religious houses in Henry VIII's sixteenth century Dissolution of the Monasteries.

During the Confessor's reign, the rudiments of English were firmly established, with common elements found in placenames throughout England. Places like Rotherham, Nottingham, Birmingham, Cheltenham and Grantham, for example, all bear the affix 'ham', a recognised Old English word for a village or homestead; townships like Portsmouth, Falmouth, Exmouth, Yarmouth, Avonmouth, Weymouth and Bournemouth all derive from the Anglo-Saxon word 'mutha', meaning a river mouth or estuary; towns and cities like Bury, Salisbury, Banbury, Canterbury and Aylesbury refer to fortified places or strongholds, ('burhs'), as do Peterborough, Loughborough and Middlesbrough, variations on the original Old English word. Saxon England seemed set fair for peace and prosperity, until the Confessor's death in January 1066, and the arrival of Duke William from Normandy.

It is commonly believed that during an earlier visit by his cousin William, Edward may have promised him the succession of the English crown; this is certainly what William claimed. However, when Harold Godwinson inherited the function of royal adviser in 1053, he effectively became the real power behind the throne as Edward spent his time in prayer and studying the scriptures. When Edward died and was buried in Westminster Abbey, Harold took the crown of England that same day.

The Norman Conquest

Harold's assumption of the English throne in January 1066 was done in great haste and even many of his own countrymen regarded him as a usurper; there were other more legitimate claimants to the crown. Among them were the young boy Edgar the Atheling, Harald Hadrada of Norway and Duke William of Normandy. William was sorely vexed at being overlooked, especially as the matter had been decided in his absence and with an importunate degree of urgency so that he was determined to claim what he saw as his right to the English throne.

The Norman Conquest of England that began later that year was protracted and bloody; the Saxons did not take kindly to their new overlords. Especially so, in that they were foreign – they spoke Norman French while the general populace spoke Saxon English. Further, the Normans founded very few new settlements but undertook the systematic confiscation of the manors and estates of the Saxon earls and thegns. William also gave manorial grants to those knights who had supported him in the invasion, and this further fomented nationwide unrest. The northern counties were particularly fierce in their opposition, so that William saw fit to put down all uprising and dissent with vicious retribution. Towns, villages and crop fields were razed to the ground or put to the torch. Men, women, children and all cattle put to the sword. In 1087, the *Anglo-Saxon Chronicles* described William's treatment of subjugated Saxons and even his own family members:

> 'A hard man he [William] was, and fierce; no man dared against his will. He had eorls in chains, who went against his will; bishops he deposed from their bishoprics and thegns he sent to prison. Next he did not spare his brother Odo; he was a very powerful bishop in Normandy – Bayeux was his bishopric – and he was the foremost man next to the king.'

William, Duke of Normandy was crowned King of England in Westminster Abbey on Christmas Day 1066. Yet William was never English and neither were his chief ministers. Norman French was the language of nobility and power – Saxon English was only spoken by commoners. Even so, over time, the influence of the French language made itself known in placenames throughout the new Norman Kingdom of England. Norman usurpers proceeded to add their own family names to confiscated manors and estates. Townships like Shepton took on the Malett family name to become Shepton Mallett; the Old Manor of Wootton had the Bassett name appended and it became Wootton Bassett; Leighton had the Busard (or Buzzard) family name appended to it to become Leighton Buzzard. Places like Ashby became Ashby de la Zouch, after their new Norman lords of the manor. There were others: Chapel-en-le-Frith, Ashby-de-la-Launde, Naughton Beauchamp, Beaulieu, Redmarley D'Abitot, Little Hautbois, Stanstead Mountfitchet – all derived directly from their French places of birth or their family names.

The Conqueror's Great Survey of 1086 did much to set England's placenames down in writing, and would be responsible for the many variants on the names of places. It comes as no surprise that the commissioners charged with making the audit were Norman French, and their interviewees were mainly Saxon, so that language barriers and misinterpretations were inevitable. Also, most Saxons would have been illiterate and would not have known how to spell the name of their village – names would have been passed on by oral tradition, and probably in a local dialect. The upshot was a plethora of name variations. To take just a few as examples, Pickering in Yorkshire was recorded in the *Domesday Book* as both Pickeringa and Picheringe; Great Oakley in Essex was written as Accleia and Adem; Hainton in Lincolnshire was entered as Gaintone and as Haintune. There are countless other examples.

Over time, a gradual synthesis of Old English, Scandinavian and Norman French took place, to emerge as Middle English, which in a rudimentary way began to resemble something akin to the Modern English we speak today.

KEY TO THE ENGLISH COUNTIES

AV = Avon
BE = Bedforshire
BER = Berkshire
BUC = Buckinghamshire
CAM = Cambridgeshire
CD = County Durham
CH = Cheshire
COR = Cornwall
CU = Cumbria
DE = Derbyshire
DEV = Devonshire
DOR = Dorset
ES = East Sussex
ESS = Essex
GLO = Gloucestershire
GRL = Greater London
GM = Greater Manchester
HAM = Hampshire
HE = Herefordshire
IOM = Isle of Man
IOW = Isle of Wight
KE = Kent
LA = Lancashire
LE = Leicestershire
LI = Lincolnshire
M = Merseyside
N = Northumberland
NORF = Norfolk
NOR = Northamptonshire
NOT = Nottinghamshire
OX = Oxfordshire
R = Rutland
SH = Shropshire
SOM = Somerset
ST = Staffordshire
SUF = Suffolk
SUR = Surrey
TW = Tyne & Wear
WA = Warwickshire
WI = Wiltshire
WM = West Midlands
WO = Worcestershire
WS = West Sussex
YO = Yorkshire

The counties and regions of England referred to in this book.

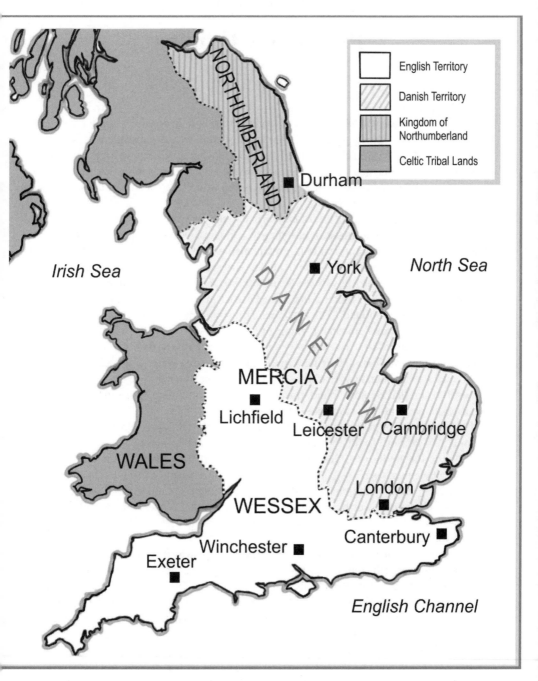

	English Territory
	Danish Territory
	Kingdom of Northumberland
	Celtic Tribal Lands

NORTHUMBERLAND

Durham

Irish Sea

York

North Sea

D A N E L A W

MERCIA

Lichfield

Leicester   Cambridge

WALES

London

WESSEX

Canterbury

Winchester

Exeter

English Channel

Britain at the time of King Alfred's death.

Part Three

Placename Origins

Celtic Placenames

Some of the most ancient of British placenames were laid down several millennia ago by the Celtic peoples who occupied these islands. Most were lost, as subsequent invasions and migrations tended to adapt, change or replace them, so that only a few vestiges remain. The names which the Celtic peoples gave to places would have been in simple descriptive terms: 'the tribe who live on the hill', 'the settlement in the wood', 'the people of the valley', and so on.

These names tended to take one of two forms. In the main they were either topographical names which described the place, or else they were possessive names taken from the founder or chieftain of a settlement. It is a term greatly disliked by many authorities, but the people who are sometimes referred to as the 'Ancient' Britons bequeathed names to many of our mountains and rivers. The Malvern Hills of Worcestershire are one example – a Celtic name meaning 'bare hill'. Then there is the Lake District mountain of Helvellyn, whose name meant 'pale yellow moorland'. The Quantock Hills of Somerset derive their name from the old British word 'cantuc', meaning 'ridge' or 'edge'.

Similarly, many Celtic river names survive to the present day, including the River Thames ('dark'), the Tyne ('flowing'), the Calder ('rushing water'), the Derwent ('oak'), the Mersey ('river boundary'), and so forth. Lakes were known to them as 'meres', and many still retain that element: Windermere, Grasmere, Buttermere, Mere and Ellesmere are notable examples, but there are many others.

The descriptive typographical name element 'cumb' (which is closely related to the Brittonic Welsh word 'cym', meaning 'valley'), is found in places like Ilfracombe and Salcombe in the south-west, Seacombe in Cheshire and Bowcombe on the Isle of Wight. The ancient element 'pen' or 'penn' was the word the Celts applied to hills, headlands and promontories, and is commonly found in the West Country, Cumbria and in Wales, with examples including Penwortham, Penrith, Pendleton, Pendle, Penge, Penketh and Penistone.

Roman Placenames

The Romans gave their own names to their settlements, which were in the main military garrisons, but only made minor changes to the existing placenames which they came across. When they withdrew from Britain, indigenous Britons adopted Latinised names for these former military installations, adopting the element 'caestre', signifying a fortified Roman town or encampment, and resulting in a plethora of towns and cities around Britain which still echo their Roman origins. Places like Chester, Towcester, Tadcaster, Winchester, Castleford, Lancaster, Doncaster, Leicester, Bicester and Castlethwaite are just a few of many.

The Romans created roads. Many tended to be based around existing tracks, which they paved and strengthened to cope with the infrastructure and logistics of large armies and rapid communications. They built new roads as straight as possible to connect their outposts and settlements. These 'straets' as the Saxons called them, survive today as Watling Street, Ermine Street, Ichfield Street, Chester-le-Street and Stane Street; the word has also come down to us in common use as the 'streets' in every town and city in the British Isles.

Anglo-Saxon and Scandinavian Placenames

The term 'Anglo-Saxon' is frequently used nowadays as a somewhat generic term for a series of Germanic tribes, who made their mark on the new territories which they settled. For example, the Angles gave their name to the East Anglia region where most of their settlements were established. They would also give us the name of the nation – 'Angleland' as it would have been called after the Angles, a name that later evolved as 'Engaland', or England as it is now. The language that was developing was a synthesis of Saxon with European and Danish additions, so that by the end of the ninth century, the effects had become recognisable as Anglo-Saxon, a form we now know as Old English.

The Frisians gave names to many of their settlements which contain a placename element reflecting their own origin: places like Frisby, Friston, Friesthorpe and Freston – all on the east coast of Lincolnshire, Leicestershire, Sussex and Suffolk, where they settled.

Saxon heritage is reflected in the counties of south-east England: Essex means 'East Saxons'; Sussex means 'South Saxons'; and Middlesex, the 'Middle Saxons'. Even Alfred's Kingdom of Wessex harked back to a time when it would have been the territory of the West Saxons.

Apart from topographical and tribal name elements, the Saxons often included animal references in their placenames. For example, Swinton in Greater Manchester means 'swine village (or settlement)'; townships like Gateshead mean 'goat's promontory'; Gosfield means 'field where geese are found'; Hartlepool and Harlebury both make references to harts (deer or stags), and so on.

The personal names of people are also most common placename elements. The name given to the town of Dudley in the West Midlands, for example, described a 'leah', or woodland clearing belonging to a man called Dud or Dudda; Birmingham was probably founded by a man called Beorma; Adwick was a farm owned by Adda; the North Yorkshire village of Giggleswick was named after a man called Gichel or Gikel, and 'wic', indicating a dairy farm. Hence, 'Gikel's dairy farm'. Levenshulme translates as 'Leofwine's island'; the North Yorkshire town of Pickering was probably named after an early settler called Picer or Picher.

Words like 'hulme' or 'holme', derived from the Old Scandinavian word 'holmr' are most common in placenames, and referred to 'islands', most typically higher or raised dry ground surrounded by marsh, water or wetlands. Among their number are places like Davyhulme and Hulme in Manchester and Balkholme in East Yorkshire. The Old English word 'eg' or 'ieg', (commonly corrupted to 'ey'), had a similar meaning and is found in places like Nunney in Somerset, Oaksey in Wiltshire, North Hinksey in Oxfordshire and Putney in Greater London.

Features of the natural world are also common elements in the naming of places. The Old English word 'burna', indicating a brook or stream, (a 'burn' as it is known in Scotland), is a common placename element, as in towns like Blackburn, Glyndebourne, Otterburn, Burnley and Slaidburn. Tree and plant species are found in the names like Ashburton, Astbury and Ashton-under-Lyme, where the Saxon word 'aesc' means 'ash tree', and garlic is found in placenames like Ramsbottom, Ramsey and Ramsden, where 'hramsa' was the Saxon word for that plant species. Old English affixes like 'ac' or the Old Scandinavian 'eik' signified oak trees or acorns, with townships like Acle in Norfolk, Acomb in Northumberland and innumerable places called Acton containing this element in their placenames.

Early settlements that developed around churches and other religious houses were commonly referred to by the affix 'mynster', and exist today in places like Westminster, Axminster, Beaminster, Leominster and Kidderminster. Early Christian settlements like Morwenstow, Hibaldstow, Fulstow, Chepstow, Felixstowe and Padstow all contain the Old

English element 'stou', which referred to a religious meeting site, or latterly to a church. Many others named their settlements after early Christian saints and missionaries, many of whom came from Ireland to convert Saxon pagans and establish churches: these include places like St Ives, Bury St Edmunds, St Asaph, Chalfont St Giles and St David's. Saints placenames are particularly common in Cornwall.

Alfred the Great and his son Edward's many townships and settlements which they had fortified against Danish incursions, reflect their new characteristics by the addition of the affix 'burh', signifying a stronghold or fortified dwelling, or one of its later variations: these include the towns and cities of Edinburgh, Guisborough, Wappenbury, Bury Thorpe, Bury St Edmunds, Peterborough and Middlesbrough, as well as three towns in England simply called Bury,

The word 'mutha', which translates as 'mouth', was applied to river estuaries and appears at places where rivers meet the sea, as in Portsmouth, Falmouth, Exmouth and Dartmouth.

Norman Placenames

From 1066, the Normans added another ingredient into the mixing pot of the emerging English language. French elements began to appear in some placenames, especially where there were several places of the same name: the 'le Street' affix to Chester-le-Street distinguished this place from Chester; the 'de la Zouch' suffix distinguished Ashby de la Zouch from all the other townships called Ashby, and so forth. The Normans were fond of adding their family names to newly acquired manors and estates in order to mark the new territories that King William had so generously doled out to those who had supported him in the Conquest.

The Conqueror also reserved huge tracts of land as his personal possessions, and the affix 'King's' was commonly added to such places as Kingswinford, King's Lynn, King's Norton and Kingston-upon-Hull. The princes of the church and various religious houses also benefitted from the king's beneficence; these included places like Bishop Aukland, Bishop's Stortford, Bishopthorpe and Bishopsbourne, as well as Churchlawton, Church Stretton and Church Brampton. Then there were the priories and abbeys such as Newton Abbott and Norton Priors. The 'Priors' element of Ditton Priors was appended when the manor came into the possession of Wenlock Priory. The Manor of Upton Bishop was given to the Bishop of Hereford. King Stephen granted the village of Hawkshead in Cumbria to the Cistercian monks of Furness Abbey.

Some former Saxon manors and estates were even donated to religious houses in France: for example, the Herefordshire township of Monkland was given into the possession of Conches-en-Ouches Abbey of Saint-Pierre of Castellion in Normandy; the Manor of Much Marcle in Herefordshire was granted to the Abbey of Sainte-Marie of Lyre; other estates went to Cluny Abbey in Normandy... and there are many more such examples. Numerous places bear the mark of a one-time priestly ownership: Prestwich, Preston, Prescot and Prestbury, all of which incorporate the Old English word 'preost' (a priest), places meaning 'priest's dairy farm', priest's farmstead', priest's cottages' and 'priest's stronghold'.

The Emergence of Modern English Placenames

The development of English placenames is perfectly illustrated by the changes that occurred to the city of York over the centuries. It began as a small Celtic settlement, known to them by the name Eborakon. The Romans modified and Latinised the name to Eboracum in 71. Later, the Saxons renamed the settlement as Eoforwic. When Danish invaders took it into their possession in 866, they renamed it Jorvik, and the Normans recorded the placename as Euruic in the *Domesday Book* of 1086. This gradual absorption of the spoken and written tongues of immigrant cultures created the language which the world eventually recognised as English.

Common Placename Elements

Apart from those townships whose placenames ended in 'cester' or 'chester' (marking early Roman forts), and those terminating in 'burgh' or 'borough' (the Anglo-Saxon fortified settlements), probably the four other most common placenames endings 'ton', 'ham', 'feld' and 'ville'.

The first of these is derived from Old English 'tun' (which eventually developed into 'ton'). It was a word used by Saxons and Danes alike to identify an enclosure or a farmstead; an enclosure as we might understand it differed from the Saxons' perception of the word. Theirs was a time before land was commonly fenced in, or enclosed, a practice that really began in the twelfth century. Before that, the Old English word 'feld' (or 'felda') indicated open landscape, and not an enclosed area of farmland or meadow, or a 'field' as we might understand it. Such enclosed places must have stood out as exceptional in Saxon times. Many survive in townships like Beaconsfield, Fallowfield, Sheffield, Driffield and Cuckfield.

The word 'tun' was used by both Saxons and Danes to indicate a wider range of settlements including villages, manors and estates. These include place like Allerton, Netherton, Adlington, Wellington and Bridlington.

Another Anglo-Saxon word, 'ham', is marginally different from 'ton', but covers many of the same kinds of settlements and includes homesteads, dwellings, manors and estates. Places like Birmingham, Eltham, Nottingham and Durham fall into this category. The similar and easily confused Saxon word 'hamm' (with a double-'m'), signified an enclosure, either enclosed by water or marshland, rather than a dwelling or a homestead.

There are also combinations on both name-end affixes; 'ham-tun' for example, signified a home farm or enclosure, or the land on which the homestead stood. Wolverhampton, Kilkhampton, Southampton and Northampton are typical of this concatenation. There is also 'ham-stede', where the word 'stede' represents the site or location of a dwelling. Hampstead Heath is a perfect example of this word combination, as is Berkhamstead in Hertfordshire. Technically, the expression means 'homestead (or dwelling) and its place (or site)', and included the dwelling-house, its land and outbuildings – what Domesday referred to as a 'messuage'.

The word 'vill' was in the main a Norman French expression, (which has developed into 'ville' in common usage). They also classified a certain type of peasant's status as 'villan' (sometimes 'villain' or 'villein'), and the village where they lived as a 'vill'. But the word had much wider connotations and could have been used for any settlement, no matter how large or small. Such placename suffixes still survive in English placenames like Pentonville, Morville, Turville and Bournville.

It is not coincidental that while many European languages tend to use a single word to describe all their townships, both great and small, a drive through the French countryside reveals that almost every habitation, whether it is a major city like Paris or Toulouse or the smallest village, will have a road sign pointing to 'Centre Ville'. Conversely, because of the many languages that have contributed to modern English, there are many words we use for them, and each has a specific connotation. A hamlet is recognised as quite a different sort of habitation to a city for example, and a town is easily distinguished from a village.

The many diverse cultures that have settled in Britain over the past 3,000 years have created a veritable panoply of words at our disposal, and while their origin may be largely lost to us, their meanings have become infused into the names of the places where we live.

Part Four

Land Ownership and Tenancy

Earls, Thegns, Free Men and Serfs

In medieval times, with few exceptions, land belonged to men; Anglo-Saxon society depended largely upon the governance of earls, the ruling nobility of the English shires and answerable directly to the king. It was not an hereditary right, and they were usually chosen from a few outstanding families. Below them were thegns, who received grants of land from them in exchange for service, often of a military nature.

Then there were commoners, known as free men, who held land and did not pay rent to a lord; these were the skilled craftsmen of the time – the blacksmiths, masons and armourers. The remaining group, commonly known as serfs, had no property and worked the land for their overlords in exchange for food and lodgings. Below them were slaves.

The Monarchy and Norman Aristocrats

Following the Conquest and the redistribution of sequestered Saxon lands to Norman barons, the old shires and parishes were effectively redrawn, as new territorial boundaries, or manors came into being. The largest, wealthiest and most profitable manors (about twenty per cent), invariably went to King William himself and to his immediate family. Odo, his ill-fated half-brother and Archbishop of Bayeux was made Earl of Kent and given some of the richest pickings, as was Robert, the Count of Mortain, another half-brother through his mother's side, whom he created Earl of Cornwall and granted extensive lands throughout England.

Many English places show evidence of Crown ownership: King's Norton in Birmingham is just one of many examples; others include Kingswinford in the West Midlands; King's Lynn in Norfolk; and Kingston upon Thames in Greater London, among several dozen other places bearing the mark of the monarch. Then there are those that had the Latin affix 'regis' attached (meaning 'of the king'), to show royal connections, Rowley Regis in the West Midlands and Bognor Regis in West Sussex. Some simply had the word 'royal' attached: places like Royal Leamington Spa and Royal Tunbridge Wells. Queens also laid claim to extensive land holdings; their possessions were often clearly marked in their placenames: Queen Charlton and Queen Camel, both in Somerset are examples, as is Queenborough in Kent. Places like Princes Risborough in Buckinghamshire and Princetown in Devon show the same royal connections.

Norman aristocracy soon followed suit and staked claim to manorial estates by appending their family names to new acquisitions. Places like the village of Hemingford Grey in Cambridgeshire was granted to the de Grey family, Leighton Buzzard in Bedfordshire was held by the Busard family, Milton Clevedon belonged to the de Clevedons, and Redmarley d'Abitot in Gloucestershire had been the country seat of the d'Abitot family since 1066.

Prince Churchmen

Next came the princes of the church – about twenty-five per cent of all English manors went to religious houses. The religious did very well out of William's Conquest, with ten per cent of all produce given to them directly as tithes for their personal consumption and upkeep. While many lower classes suffered hunger and deprivation in times when the harvest failed, Norman churchmen grew fat on provisions freely given to them.

Apart from the Archbishoprics of Canterbury, Lincoln, York, Durham, Exeter and Winchester, among many others, manorial estates were granted to religious houses in Normandy. Among them were Bishops of the Church of Sainte Marie in Rouen, the Church of Mont-Saint-Michel, as well as Bishops of Coutances, Caen and Rheims. William's beneficence to the church stemmed from a profound sense of guilt brought about by his often savage repression of Saxon opposition, and in keeping with the deeply pious attitude to the church and the promise of a heavenly afterlife set against the perils of fire and eternal damnation. In this way, William kept the church happy and onside, as well as securing himself a place in heaven, as all good medieval monarchs sought to do.

The church's influence still remains today in the placenames that reflected their land acquisitions: places like Bishop Auckland in County Durham; Bishop's Caundle in Dorset; Bishop's Stortford in Hertfordshire; and Bishop Norton in Lincolnshire are just a few of the many places that fell under their ownership. Other places found their local church attached to the name: places like Church Langton in Leicestershire; Church Minshull in Cheshire; and Church Stretton in Shropshire are typical. Larger townships added the Old English element 'mynster', signifying a religious settlements – Kidderminster, Westminster and Leominster are just a few – there are many more.

Females and Land Ownership

Although women held an almost equal status to their menfolk in Anglo-Saxon England, they had few if any rights of land ownership or inheritance. This was invariably passed down through the male line. With few exceptions, women are not known by name and are notoriously absent from manorial and estate ownership. Those who are specifically named in records tend only those of the very highest social status or royal personages.

Consequently, the names of men of significant status feature largely in village placenames: innumerable chieftains', founders' and early settlers' given names were incorporated into the names which were given to early settlements. However, only a handful of places in England derive their names from women. Among these few are Epsom, which was named after Ebbe, its probable female founder; Aldaed was a woman thought to have founded Alderley Edge in Cheshire; Wolverhampton was named after Wulfruna; the Warwickshire town of Kenilworth received its name from an obscure woman called Cynehild; and Royston in Hertfordshire was named after Rohesia.

The Normans were no better at recording land ownership of women. Contemporary accounts record that following the Conquest of 1066, Saxon women were so disenfranchised that many fled to nunneries to avoid forced marriage with Norman soldiers. Even the comprehensive *Domesday Book* named only a few women with significant landholdings as in general, following the Conquest, apart from a handful of female nobles, women had very low status and their possessions invariably passed as dowries to their husbands.

Of those landholdings recorded in the Great Survey, over 200 places in England were retained as a courtesy by Queen Edith of Wessex, (known in Saxon English as Ealdgyth), the widow of Edward the Confessor; she was said to be the richest woman in England at the time of her death in December 1075. Then there was the mother of King Harold and widow of Earl Godwine of Wessex, Countess Gytha (Thorkelsdottir), who was one of the most important female landholders at the time of the Conquest. As a niece of King William, she received special favour and held great tracts of land in the south of England.

North of the Thames, especially in Middlesex, Buckinghamshire and Yorkshire, significant estates and manors were in the possession of Countess Judith de Balliol of Lens, the widow of Earl Waltheof and another niece of William. The Conqueror's own wife,

Queen Matilda of Flanders, was also a major beneficiary of the redistribution of English land and received several mentions in the Great Survey. Other women noted for their land possessions were Countess Godgifu (also known as Godiva, sometimes 'Goda', Countess of Mercia and daughter of Ethelred), as well as Ethelred's wife, Countess Aelfgifu.

Edith (known as 'Swan-neck'), the former mistress and later wife of King Harold, had been a major landholder before the Conquest, but her lands were given to the Earl Alan of Richmond (known as 'Alan the Red'). Cristina, daughter of Edward the Exile and Princess of the West Saxons, managed to retain estates in Warwickshire and Gloucestershire. She was a nun at the time of Domesday, but had substantial holdings in Oxfordshire and Warwickshire.

Tenants and Sub-tenants

Around 170 Norman manorial estates were overseen by appointed tenants-in-chief, usually barons, each handpicked by the sovereign, and supported by a sheriff (or 'shire reeve'), who administered the estate, its accounts and its courts. In exchange for grants of tenancy, barons were expected to supply men, cavalry and arms to the king's service when called upon.

Below the barons were under-tenants (or sub-tenants), who paid rent ('geld') to the overlord for their land tenancy and were required to provide some form or work like ploughing, harvesting, animal husbandry and other general labouring. Occasionally, in the absence of ready money, rents were paid in kind or in produce.

Finally, a lower serf class were granted small plots of land for their own use provided they worked the lord's lands or paid rent. These included bordars, cottars and free men. The system was oppressive, draconian and controlled, and the lower classes were tied to the land in a feudal system within which they lived and served, with no right to wander freely. Thus was the social order of England set in place – an order that would exist for several centuries thereafter under Anglo-Norman rule. It also laid the foundation of what many describe as the English class system, which essentially followed this early hierarchy, as the upper class, the middle class and the working class, divisions which were effectively still in place until the end of the twentieth century, and vestiges of which survive in some form to the present day.

Part Five

The North-East

County Durham, Northumberland, Tyne and Wear, and Yorkshire

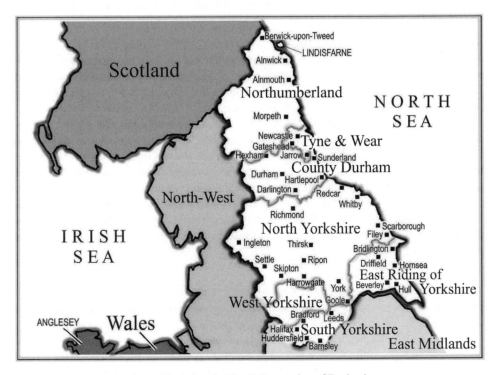

A map depicting the North-East region of England.

Acaster Malbis

This Yorkshire village derives its placename from three sources. First, 'a', from the Old Scandinavian meaning 'river'; second, the Old English word 'ceaster', meaning 'fortification', (often the remains of a Roman military settlement); finally the affix 'Malbis', after the Malbis family who held the manor in 1252, and attached their family name to distinguish the place from the village of Acaster Selby a few miles away. The placename therefore translates as '[place near] the fortification on the river belonging to the Malbis family'. The river in question was the River Ouse. The place was recorded in the *Domesday Book* as Acastre, listed as a very small estate, with land for two ploughs, supporting just three families in the Ainsty Hundred of the former West Riding, held by Robert Malet in 1086, having been the property of a Saxon man called Alsi before the Norman Conquest. By the twelfth century the placename had been written as Acaster Malebisse.

Adlingfleet
According to the placename of this Yorkshire village, there is a local connection to royalty, as it translates into modern English as 'water course [or stream] of the prince'. The name comes from the Old English words 'aetheling', meaning 'prince' or 'nobleman', plus the affix 'fleet', meaning 'water channel', 'water course' or 'stream'. In 1086, the place was recorded as Adelingesfluet, listed in the Staincross Hundred (then in the West Riding), held by Geoffrey de la Guerche, it having belonged previously to a Saxon called Siward Barn. The manorial estate included land for three ploughs, one league of woodland, a furlong of mixed measures, a church with its own priest and a mill, altogether valued in 1086 at one pound and five shillings.

Adwick le Street/Adwick upon Dearne
These two townships in the ancient Strafforth Hundred and a district of Doncaster both share a common ancestry; they were recorded by the single placename of Adeuuic and refer to their probable founder, a man called Adda, and the Old English element, 'wic', signifying a dairy farm. Domesday uses three other spellings of the name: Adewic, Adewinc and Hadewic. The 'le street' part of the first placename, like many other townships with similar affixes, refers to its location on a Roman road (in Old English, 'straet'). The road in question runs from Doncaster to Tadcaster. Hence 'Adda's farm on the Roman road'. In 1086, it belonged to Nigel Fossard with Count Robert de Mortain as its tenant-in-chief. Six carucates of the estate were also sub-tenanted to three named men: Swein, Gluniarnh and Arnketil.

Adwick upon Dearne locates it near the river of that name. In 1066, this settlement was held by two men, Regnvald and Wulfheah. By 1086, it had been granted to Roger de Bully (sometimes known as Roger de Busli), a Norman baron who had accompanied William in the conquest of England.

Agglethorpe
This small North Yorkshire hamlet derived the first part of its name from a Danish man called Acwulf, who may have been its founder or an early leader. It demonstrates the inroads that Scandinavian migrants made into north-eastern England, having originally arrived as opportunist invaders during the eighth century, but eventually putting down roots, intermarrying with indigenous Saxons and developing peaceful settlements. The second element of the placename comes from the Old Scandinavian word 'thorp', which signified an outlying farmstead or remote settlement. The placename therefore translates as 'remote settlement [or farmstead] belonging to Acwulf'. By the time of the Domesday Book, the place had been recorded as Aculestorp, listed within the Hundred Land of Count Alan (of Brittany) in the North Riding, having belonged to Thorkil before the Norman Conquest.

Allendale Town
It is unusual to find an English town placename which actually contains the word 'town', but the township of Allendale in Northumberland is one of the few. The name comes from the River Allen on which it stands, a Celtic name, (or perhaps even older), whose meaning is obscure. Two other affixes complete the name: 'dalr' was one of several words that Scandinavians used to describe a valley, and 'tun', an Anglo-Saxon word that in this case meant 'village' or 'settlement'. Hence, 'valley settlement of the River Allen'. The placename was written as Alewenton in 1245.

Allerton Bywater
This district of Leeds in Yorkshire has a placename that means 'farmstead where alders grow beside water'. It comes from the Old English words 'alor', meaning 'alder (tree)' and

'tun', which signified a farmstead. The 'bywater' affix was appended sometime in the late fourteenth or early fifteenth centuries, and self-evidently places it by water, in this particular case, beside the River Aire. Domesday recorded the place as Alretune, and listed it as a large manor supporting forty-three villans, twelve smallholders and three priests, in the Skyrack Hundred of the former West Riding, held in 1086 by Ilbert de Lacy, having belonged to Earl Edwin before the Conquest.

Alnwick
Recorded in 1178 as Alnewich, from the Old English 'wic' (a specialised farm, like a dairy), indicating a farmstead beside the River Aln, this Northumberland township dates back to the seventh century, though its beginnings are much earlier. Alnwick Castle, begun by Gilbert de Tesson (sometimes 'de Tisson'), William the Conqueror's standard bearer, was the seat of the Earls of Northumberland. By 1096, it belonged to the de Vesci family, before it passed to the Percys, who became the principal landowners for the next seven centuries. The placename was recorded as Alnewich in 1178.

Altofts
Altofts is a village district in Wakefield in West Yorkshire whose name probably comes from a combination of Saxon and Norse words, the Old English word 'ald' meant 'old', and the Old Scandinavian 'toft' referred to homesteads or dwellings. Hence, the placename means 'old homesteads [or dwellings]'. An early record of the placename was around 1090, when it was written as Altoftes.

Angram
This small hamlet near Harrogate historically lay within the former West Riding of Yorkshire and derived its name from the Old English word 'angrum' or 'anger', meaning 'grassland' or 'pasture'. It was recorded in the thirteenth century as Angrum.

Annfield Plain
A relatively recently created placename, first recorded in 1865, the first word of the name of the township of Annfield Plain in County Durham identifies it as a field, (or more properly 'open country'), that once belonged to a woman known as Ann. The second word refers to the slopes, known locally as 'planes', up which wagons were hauled during the construction of the Stanhope and Tyne Railway in 1834.

Appleton Wiske
As you might have expected, the North Yorkshire village of Appleton Wiske was historically associated with apples. The Old English words which make up the placename are 'aeppel', self-evidently referred to an apple, a 'tun' was a farmstead, and 'wisc', a marshy meadow; in this case part of the flood plain of the River Wiske. The placename may therefore be interpreted as 'farmstead where apples grow beside the marsh-meadow [of the River Wiske]'. Domesday listed the village as Apeltona, within the Allerton Hundred of the North Riding, held in 1086 by King William.

Aske
Aske is a township in the Parish of Easby, near Richmond in the North Riding of Yorkshire. The Aske family held the land as tenants from the Earl of Richmond following the Norman Conquest of 1066. Formerly, the manor and its estates had belonged to a Saxon named Thor.

According to the *Domesday Book*, the estate was then known as Alreton, 'in the hundred of Land of Count Alan', and had just 'five villagers, three smallholdings and four ploughlands'. The placename is derived from the Old Norse word 'askr', which translates as 'the ash tree', and probably describes a specific location, possibly a special place or a district boundary of some kind. In early times, the ash tree had mystical significance and was often planted at the outskirts of a settlement or at an important meeting place.

Askham Bryan

Unsurprisingly, this Yorkshire village takes part of its name from a one-time owner, a man called Brian or Bryan. As for the first part of the placename, it comes from the Old English word 'aesc', meaning 'ash tree', and either 'ham', a settlement, or 'hamm', an enclosure. Hence the name means 'Brian's settlement [or enclosure] where ash trees grow'. The 'Bryan' affix distinguishes the place from the nearby village of Askham Richard. Domesday recorded the place as Ascham, in the Ainsty Hundred of the West Riding, held in 1086 by Count Alan of Brittany, having belonged to Earl Edwin of Mercia before the Conquest.

Askrigg

Like Askham Bryan previously, the 'Ask' element of this North Yorkshire placename comes from 'aesc', or the Old Scandinavian 'askr', the ash tree, but with the Old English suffix 'ric', meaning 'ridge'. Therefore the placename means '[place by] the ridge where ash trees grow'. Domesday listed the village as Ascric, in the North Riding Land of Count Alan. Before the Conquest, its lord had been a man called Arnketil, and by 1086 his son Gospatric had become a tenant of the manor.

Austwick

Located firmly within the Danish territory of Danelaw, unsurprisingly, the North Yorkshire village of Austwick derives the first element of its placename from the Norse language. The Old Scandinavian word 'austr' meant 'eastern', which along with the Saxon word 'wic' which signified a specialised farm or a dairy, produces a placename that probably translates as 'eastern dairy farm'. The 'eastern' element is thought to be relative to the nearby settlement of Clapham. The place was listed as Ousteuuic by Domesday and listed in the Amounderness Hundred of the old West Riding, held in 1086 by King William, having belonged to Thorfin of Ravensworth before the Conquest.

Aysgarth

Aysgarth appears in the *Domesday Book* as Echescard, a name made up entirely of the Old Scandinavian elements 'ieki' or 'eiki', meaning oak, and 'sckarth' or 'skarth', an open space, gap or clearing (usually in a woodland, in this case Wensleydale Forest). Taken together, the name means 'open space where oak trees grow'. The Great Survey places the township in the 'Hundred of Land of Count Alan [Rufus, of Brittany]', in the North Riding of Yorkshire, whose Lord of the Manor at that time was Geoffrey of Swaffam, having been held by Cnut in 1066 and previously valued at just four shillings.

Balne

Balne is a hamlet in North Yorkshire whose placename comes directly from the Latin 'balneum', meaning 'bathing place', a probable reference to one of several pools in the area that were historically used for bathing. An early record of the placename as Balne was some time during the twelfth century.

Bamburgh

Originally known as Bebbe's Stronghold, this Northumbrian village was named after Bebbe, the wife of King Aethelfrith. Sometimes known as the first true King of Northumbria, Aethelfrith united the two separate kingdoms of Bernicia and Deira. The second element of the placename derives from the Old English 'burh', signifying a fortified place or stronghold. By the eighth century the placename had been recorded as Bebbanburge.

Barnby Dun

The township of Barnby Dun in the Doncaster region of Yorkshire provides yet more evidence of Danish settlements in north-west England when it was part of the territory known as Danelaw. It was named after a Dane known as Bjarni, which along with the Old Scandinavian affix 'by', signifying a farmstead, village or settlement, translates as 'Bjarni's farmstead [or settlement]'. The final word is derived from the River Don, on which the village stands. Domesday recorded the place as Barnebi in 1086, lying within the West Riding Hundred of Strafforth, part-held by Roger de Bully, William de Percy and Robert, Count of Mortain. Before the Norman Conquest, three Saxon men, Ketilbert, Oswulf and Ulfkil had held the manor.

Barnsley

The South Yorkshire town of Barnsley most likely derives its name from a man thought to have been called Beornmod or Beorn, probably of Danish or Scandinavian origins, with the Old English suffix 'leah', indicating a woodland clearing or glade. Hence, 'woodland clearing belonging to Beornmod'. An alternative explanation has been offered by some, in that the Anglo- Saxon word for a barn or storehouse is 'berne', and that the placename might mean 'barn in a clearing'. The place was recorded in the *Domesday Book* as Berneslei in the Staincross Hundred and the Manor of Tanshelf, held in 1086 by Ilbert de Lacy (sometimes de Laci or de Lace). Other towns of this name also exist in Gloucestershire and in Hampshire.

Bawtry

The name of this town near Doncaster in Yorkshire is based on two Saxon words – 'ball', meaning exactly as you might expect, and 'treow', a tree. Hence, unsurprisingly, the placename means '[place by the] ball tree'. A ball tree is a tree or shrub that has been rounded into a ball shape, a practice common nowadays for a particular kind of topiary used on the standard box tree. By the end of the twelfth century, the place had been recorded as Baltry.

Beal

The placename of the village of Beal in North Yorkshire signifies a 'corner of land at a bend in the river'. It comes from two Old English words, 'beag', meaning 'circle' (here used as a synonym for 'bend' or 'curve'), and 'halh', meaning 'nook [or corner] of land'. The river in question was the River Aire a short way north of the original settlement. Domesday recorded the place as Begale, and listed it as a very small estate supporting just four households in the Osgodcross Hundred of the former West Riding, and held in 1086 by Ilbert de Lacy. Before 1066, the manor had belonged to Barth, identified as the father of Gamal.

Beauchief

Beauchief is a district in the Yorkshire City of Sheffield, whose name comes from the Old French 'beau', meaning 'beautiful', and 'chef', meaning 'head', as in a headland, a promontory or a hill-spur. Hence, 'beautiful headland'. The placename was recorded as Beuchef in the twelfth century.

Beck Hole

Sometimes written as one word, Beckhole is a village in the Borough of Scarborough in North Yorkshire, that was known as Amerholm until the sixteenth century. The placename derives from a shallow river crossing on the Eller Beck where it meets with the West Beck to become the River Esk. The name derives from the Old English word 'baec' or 'bece', meaning a small stream or brook. The 'Hole' element of the name reflects the fact that the place is set within a deep valley. So deep and steep was the incline that in times past, stage coaches had to be hauled up by ropes and pulleys to get them out of 'the hole'.

Bedale

The North Yorkshire township of Bedale was recorded by this name in the *Domesday Book* in 1086. The name derives from a man called Beda, who probably founded the original settlement, plus the Old English affix 'halh', signifying a small valley, nook or hollow. Hence the placename might be taken to mean 'small valley belonging to Beda'. Before the Norman Conquest, Bedale was held by Tori (sometimes Torphin or Thorfinn), and afterwards was in the possession of Count Alan Rufus (also known as Alanus Rufus, Alain le Roux and Alan the Red), and tenanted by a man called Bodin. According to the Great Survey, the manor was part of the Catterick Wapentake and had at least one mill.

Belsay

Two possible explanations have been offered for the interpretation of the name of this village in Northumberland. One has it meaning 'hill-spur [or promontory] used for a warning beacon or a funeral pyre', and the other as a hill-spur belonging to a man called Bil. The Old English word 'ho' or 'hoh' meant 'hill-spur' or 'ridge', and 'bel' indicated a warning beacon. The Belsay estate was first recorded as Bilesho in 1163, as Belesho in 1171 and as Beleshou in 1270, at which time it was a possession of Sir Richard de Middleton, who was Lord Chancellor to Henry III.

Ben Rydding

This village in the Ilkley district of Bradford in Yorkshire was unknown until the mid-nineteenth century when it first appeared on maps. It was named after a man called Ben with the additional Old English affix 'rydding', meaning 'clearing'. Hence, 'Ben's clearing'. The present-day township grew up around Ben Rhydding Hydropathic Establishment, which had opened in 1844, as the first purpose-built hydro in the United Kingdom. The place had formerly been known as Wheatley, and old name meaning 'clearing where wheat grows', from the Anglo-Saxon 'hweate' and 'leah'.

Berwick-upon-Tweed

The placename comes from two Old English words, 'bere, and 'wic', meaning 'barley' and 'farm'. Hence, 'barley farm'. Recorded in 1167 simply as Berewich, by 1229 it had become known as Berewicum Super Twedam (the Latin for Berewick-upon-Tweed), reflecting its location on the River Tweed. Berwick was founded as an Anglo-Saxon settlement during the time of the Kingdom of Northumbria, which was annexed by England in the tenth century. The town is the only part of England which is sited on the north bank of the River Tweed, at the most northerly point of Northumberland, a mere three miles from the Scottish border. For this reason, its ownership has been frequently fought over by the English and the Scots and it changed hands at least thirteen times before finally becoming English in 1482. In 1502, a treaty between Henry VII of England and James IV of Scotland acknowledged Berwick as lying within, but as a separate and independent state from the Kingdom of England, a position that continued until 1836 when Berwick-upon-Tweed was made a county in its own right. It was amalgamated into the county of Northumberland in 1974.

Bessacre

The name of the Doncaster district of Bessacre in Yorkshire illustrates the changing nature of language. The name comes from the Old English words 'beos', which means 'bent grass' or 'rough grass', and 'aecer', a cultivated plot of land, (related to the modern word 'acre'). The thing is, nowadays so-called 'bentgrass' is very fine grass specifically used on lawns, golf course and bowling greens, and is not rough at all. Nevertheless, the original placename means 'cultivated plot of land where bent grass is grown'. It was recorded in 1182 as Beseacra.

Binchester
The last affix of the name of this hamlet in County Durham reveals a former existence as the site of a Roman fort or military garrison, based on the Saxon word 'caester'. The first element derives from 'binnan', meaning 'within' or 'inside'. Hence, '[settlement] inside the Roman fort'. The fort in question was known as Vinovia and the village name was recorded as Bynceastre in around 1040.

Birkby
This small North Yorkshire hamlet has an ancient history that is steeped in Danish culture. The placename comes from two Old Norse words, 'Bretar', referring to indigenous Britons, and 'by', which signified a farmstead or village settlement. Hence, 'farmstead of the Britons'. Clearly, both British and Danish settlers lived side by side, in the territory known at that time as Danelaw. By the time of Domesday, the place was recorded as Bretebi, and listed as a berewick of Northallerton in the Allerton Wapentake of the king's lands in Yorkshire.

Bishop Auckland
The country seat of the Bishops of Durham since the twelfth century, Bishop Auckland grew up around the castle and the Bishop's Palace, which was known earlier as Auckland Palace. It is situated at the confluence of the River Weaver and the River Gaunless and was known as Alcitt (or Alcleat), around 1040, derived from Celtic and meaning 'rock or hill on the Clyde river'. Clyde is an older name which native Celts called the River Gaunless. It has been suggested that the Auckland placename derives from the Old Norse, meaning extra or additional land, a name that emerged later as a probable hangover from the earlier Danish occupation, and a reference to land which King Cnut granted the Bishop of Durham some time around 1020. The prefix 'Bishop' was added later to reflect the permanent residence of Bishop Pudsey in the town in 1183, when he established the manor house, which eventually developed into the castle.

Blanchland
The Northumbrian village of Blanchland inherited its name directly from the Old Norman French words 'blanche', meaning 'white', and 'lande' a woodland glade, heath or clearing. Hence, 'white woodland clearing or open land'. It was recorded in 1165 as Blanchelande.

Booth
The East Yorkshire village of Booth probably took its name from a family of that name, who may have originated in nearby Boothby, a name which derives from the Old Scandinavian words, 'both', meaning 'shelter' and 'by', a farmstead, illustrating the presence of Danish settlers in Yorkshire before the Norman Conquest. Hence, the placename means 'farmstead with shelter[s]'. In 1550, the village name was recorded as Botheby.

Boynton
Before the Conquest, the Manor of Boynton in the old East Riding of Yorkshire, belonged to Torchill of Bovington (itself a variation on the placename). The name comprises three elements, of which the first refers to an early settler or chieftain called Bofa, plus the Old English affixes, 'inga', meaning the 'people or followers', and 'tun', a settlement, dwelling place or farmstead. Hence, the placename may be taken to mean 'farmstead [or settlement]

of the followers of a man called Bofa'. The *Domesday Book* recorded the place as Bouintone, Bouinton and Bouintorp, 'in the Land of the King in Yorkshire', where eight and a half carucates were his personal possession and two more carucates of land were held in demesne; another three carucates were rented to three Saxon men by the name of Ulf, Arnketil and Knut. The Norman knight Bartholomew de Boynton became Lord of the Manor after 1066, and his family descendants continued to hold the estates well into the sixteenth century.

Bradford

A common Old English placename, simply signifying a 'broad ford', which referred to a crossing of the Bradford Beck at Church Bank below the site of Bradford Cathedral, around which a settlement grew in Saxon times. It was recorded as Bradeford in 1086. After an uprising against William the Conqueror's brutal subjugation of the north in 1070, the *Domesday Book* describes the Manor of Bradford as laid waste ('wasta'). It then became part of the Honour of Pontefract and was ceded to Ilbert de Lacy for his service to William, after which time it passed to his family, who built a castle. It remained in the de Lacy family until 1311. Thereafter, the manor passed to the Earl of Lincoln, John of Gaunt, and then back to the Crown, before finally passing into private ownership in 1620.

Brafferton

The North Yorkshire village of Brafferton (not to be confused by the place of the same name in Darlington), derives its placename from three Anglo-Saxon words: 'brad', meaning 'broad', 'ford', a shallow river crossing (or ford), and 'tun', a farmstead. Hence, 'farmstead by (or near to) a broad ford'. The place was recorded as Bradfortune, Bratfortune and Bratfortone in the *Domesday Book*, listed in the Bulford Hundred of the North Riding, part-held by King William, Count Robert of Mortain and Gospatric, the son of Arnketil. Gospatric had owned the lion's share of the estate before the Conquest, but by 1086 his portion had been greatly reduced.

Bridlington

This township on the Holderness Coast of the North Sea, in the former East Riding of Yorkshire, was recorded in the 1086 Domesday survey as 'Bretlinton... in the land of the king in Yorkshire... with two berewicks, are thirteen carucates to the geld'. It has also been known as Brellington, Britlington and Bretlington and as late as the nineteenth century it was often referred to as Burlington. The township was probably named after a person called Bretel (or Berhtel), with the suffix 'tun' indicating a settlement or farmstead. Hence, 'the settlement of Bretel'.

Brough

The East Yorkshire hamlet of Brough gets its name directly from the Anglo-Saxon word 'burh', which referred to a stronghold or a fortified manor. The word is pronounced 'bruff'. There were several variations related to fortified settlements, including placename affixes like '-borough' and '-burgh', all of which have the same meaning and origin. The stronghold in question was the Roman settlement which they knew as Petuaria. The place was known as Burg around 1200 and only became formalised as Brough in 1868. There are three other places of the same name in Derbyshire, Nottinghamshire and Cumbria.

Bubwith

At the time of the 1066 Conquest, this East Yorkshire village name was recorded as Bobewyth. The name came from a man called Bubba who owned woodland, or as the Saxons called them, 'vithr', a word coming from Old Scandinavian language. Hence, originally, 'Bubba's wood'. At that time many placename elements in Yorkshire fell securely under Danish rule in the territory known as Danelaw, and the final element, 'wic', which meant 'dwelling', seems to have replaced the earlier Old English ending. Hence, latterly, 'Bubba's dwelling'. Domesday recorded it as Bubvid, in the East Riding Hundred of Hessle, whose chief tenant in 1086 was Gilbert Tison. In 1066, the estate had been held by two Saxons, Alwin and Ketil.

Bulmer

Bulmer is a North Yorkshire village which was known in 1086 as Bolemere, a name derived from two Old English words, 'bula', meaning 'bull' (or its plural form, 'bulena', meaning 'bulls'), and 'mere', which signified a pool or small lake. Hence, the placename may be interpreted as '[place by the] pool where bulls come to drink'. Domesday listed the village in the Bulford Hundred of the old North Riding, held in 1086 by Count Robert de Mortain, having been the property of two Saxons named Ligulf and Norethmann during the reign of King Edward.

Burnopfield

The County Durham village of Burnopfield was locally known in the nineteenth century as 'the Leap', or 'the Loup', after an area called Bryan's Leap. On face value it appears to be a strange name, whose origin is more a result of local oral tradition than reliable historic evidence. The placename probably comes from the Old English meaning 'field [or open land] by the valley stream'. Tradition has it that the placename emerged after an abortive Scottish invasion, when people resisted by burning crops in the fields to stop their advance. However, the 'burn' element of the name is more likely to have come from the Old English word 'burna', meaning 'stream' or 'brook'.

Burton Agnes/Burton Constable

Burton is a very common English placename with at least fourteen other hamlets, villages and towns of that name. It comes directly from the Old English words 'burh' and 'tun', the former indicating a fortified mansion or stronghold, and the latter a farmstead. Hence, it may be taken to mean something like 'a farmstead belonging to [or near] a fortified manor house'. Before the twelfth century, the village would simply have been known as Burton. As to the second half of the placename, 'Agnes' distinguishes and identifies it from the others (e.g. Burton Dassett in Warwickshire, Burton Joyce in Nottinghamshire, Burton-upon-Trent in Staffordshire, and so forth). The village of Burton Agnes in the former East Riding of Yorkshire simply translates as 'the farmstead at the fortified manor house [or stronghold] of Agnes'. The lady in question was Agnes de Percy, who held the manor in the twelfth century. The building alluded to has subsequently been identified as Burton Agnes Manor House, and is now a Grade I Listed Building maintained by Historic England.

It was recorded in the *Domesday Book* as Bortona and Burtone, in the Burton Hundred, and amounted to twenty ploughlands held by King William. The survey identifies Burton Agnes as comprised of three berewicks, Gransmoor, Harpham and Boythorpe. In 1066, it had been held by Earl Morcar of Northumbria, when it was valued at twenty-four pounds, but by 1086, it had been described as 'waste' and brought in only ten shillings to the king's coffers. Burton Constable was gifted to Ernburga de Constable shortly after the Conquest – his family title became appended to the place some time during the thirteenth century. The term 'constable' derives directly from the Old French word 'conestable' (or 'cunestable'), which comes from the original Latin word 'comes', signifying a count or person of other noble status, and 'stabuli', meaning a stable. Hence, 'an officer of the Count's stable'.

Butterwick

As the placename suggests, this North Yorkshire village produced butter in a specialised dairy farm, known in Old English as a 'wic'. There are places of the same name and presumably of the same origin in County Durham and Lincolnshire. The name was recorded as Butruic in 1086, listed it as a small estate supporting three households in the Burton Hundred of the East Riding, held at that time by Hugh FitzBaldric having belonged to Orm, the son of Gamal before the Norman Conquest.

Camblesforth
Somewhat idiosyncratically, although this North Yorkshire placename suggests that a ford is present in the locality, no such ford seems to exist. That being so, the placename translates as '[place by the] ford associated with a man called Camel'. Domesday recorded Camelesforde, Canbesford and Gamesford, in the West Riding Hundred of Barkston. It had several entries in the survey and was part-held in 1086 by Ernwin the Priest and Ralph Paynel, having belonged to Merleswein the Sheriff and a man called Grucan before the Norman Conquest.

Catcleugh
Catcleugh is a small hamlet in Northumberland whose placename means 'deep valley where wildcats are seen'. The name derives from the Old English words 'catt', meaning 'wildcat', and 'cloh', a ravine or gully. The place was recorded in 1279 as Cattechlow.

Catterick
The township of Catterick in the Swale Valley of North Yorkshire has ambiguous origins. One opinion is that it derives from the ancient Celtic language and originally meant 'battle fort' or 'battle earthwork', in reference to the Battle of Catraeth (c.598), which is thought to have taken place nearby. Another cites it as a corruption of the Latin word 'cataractia', meaning 'cataract' or 'waterfall'. The Roman fort at the crossing of the Swale was known as Cataractonium. Domesday recorded the placename as Catrice in 1086 and originally part of the North Riding; it had been held by the Saxon Earl Edwin of Mercia before 1066 and was valued at eight pounds. It was populated by just eleven households and a priest who tended its one church. There was land for twenty ploughs.

Cavil
By the middle of the tenth century, this hamlet in the East Riding of Yorkshire was already known as Cafeld. The placename comes from the Old English word 'ca', meaning 'jackdaw', and 'feld', signifying open unenclosed land. The name translates as 'open land where jackdaws are found [or seen]'. Domesday recorded the place as Cheuede, and listed it as a very small settlement supporting just five households within the Howden Hundred. The estate was assessed with forty ploughlands, sufficient for twenty men's plough teams. There was woodland measuring three leagues long and one league broad and a church with its own priest. Before 1066, the manor and its estates had belonged to King Edward, but by the time of the survey they had been granted to the Bishopric of Durham Cathedral, at which time the manor was valued at twelve pounds.

Cheviot Hills
The precise meaning of the name of the Cheviot Hills on the Northumberland border with Scotland remains shrouded in mystery. In its earliest form, it was probably known to the Celts as a single hill, and it is thought that they may have called it simply 'the Cheviot', possibly related to the Welsh word 'cefn', meaning 'ridge'. In 1181, the name was written as Chiuiet.

Corbridge
The Northumberland township of Corbridge began life as a river crossing near the Roman fort of Corstopitum, which was created as a storage and supply depot for the building of Hadrian's Wall. The name was derived from the native Celtic and may have been known to

them as Coria, which fell within the tribeland of the Votadini (sometimes Otalini) people. Following Roman withdrawal from Britain in the fifth century, the place was known as Corchester, the 'chester' element derived from the Latin word 'caestre', signifying one of their forts or military settlements. The bridge alluded to in the placename was built much later, over the shallow ford crossing had existed across the River Tyne for centuries. By the mid-eleventh century it had the Old English Saxon element 'byrig' attached (meaning 'bridge'), and was recorded as Corebyricg.

County Durham
Named after the county town of Durham, it was an ecclesiastical centre during the Middle Ages, largely on account of the tomb of St Cuthbert in Durham Cathedral. The Bishop of Durham was granted extensive powers with the effective status of a prince and ruler of the County Palatine of Durham. The Diocese of Durham, traditionally in the Province of York, is one of the oldest in England. County Durham is the only English county whose name includes the word 'county'.

Coxwold
Coxwold is a North Yorkshire village whose name stems from Saxon times, when 'cucu' referred to a cuckoo and 'wald' meant 'woodland' or 'forest'. The placename was recorded in the mid-eighth century as Cuhawalda, and means 'woodland where cuckoos are heard [or seen]'. Domesday listed the place as Cucualt, in the Yarlestre Wapentake of the West Riding, 'in the Land of Hugh FitzBaldric', where in 1086 a man called Kofse had ten carucates of land 'to the geld'.

Craster
The Northumbrian village of Craster grew up on the site of an old Roman military fortification, a fact that is reflected in the placename. It was known in the mid-thirteenth century as Craucestre, based on two Old English words, 'crawe', meaning 'crow', and 'caestre' or 'ceaster', which referred to a Roman fort or fortification. Hence, the placename translates as 'old fort where crows live [or are seen]'.

Danby Wiske
Danby was once a Danish settlement in the Danelaw, a detail recorded in 'Danir', the first element of the placename. The second element also comes from the Old Scandinavian language where 'by', meant 'village' or 'farmstead'. Finally, the location of the village on the River Wiske produces a placename that may be interpreted as 'village of the Danes on the River Wiske'. Domesday recorded it as Danebi, listed in the land of Count Alan of Britanny in the North Riding of Yorkshire, it having previously been the property of a man called Kofse, who also held a tenancy in nearby Coxwold. In the thirteenth century the placename was recorded as Daneby super Wiske.

Darlington
From the eleventh century, spelt variously as Dearthingtun and Dearnington, the Yorkshire town of Darlington probably derives its name from a settlement belonging to the family of a man called Deomoth or Derning. The Old English word element 'inga' in a placename often refers to a people or extended family. Hence, 'the settlement of Deomoth's people'. The town was probably originally known as Deathington, derived from the Anglo-Saxon and later, by Norman times, as Dearnington. In an early document dated in 1003, a man called Styr, son of Ulphus, granted land in the 'vill of Dearthingtun', as well as other lands in Cockerton, Coniscliffe and Haughton-le-Skerne, under licence from King Ethelred, to

the See of Durham. This ceremony was witnessed to have taken place in York Minister. By 1457, the township was known as Derlynton. The present name of Darlington was introduced some time around 1577, when Robert and William Darlington appear in local records, having taken the surname from the township.

Dinnington

Three places in England share this placename – in Yorkshire, Newcastle upon Tyne and in Somerset. This district of Rotherham in South Yorkshire was probably founded by a man called Dunna who gave his name to the place. Two other Old English name elements, 'inga' and 'tun', respectively mean 'people' or 'followers' and 'farmstead' or 'estate'. The placename therefore means 'farmstead [or estate] of the people of Dunna'. In 1086, the place was listed as Dunintone and Domnitone.

Doncaster

This South Yorkshire town was known in 1002 as Donecaestre, and by the time of the Domesday survey it had been recorded as Donecastre, the name taken from the River Don, on which the township stands, and the Latin word for a military fort or settlement, 'caestre'. Hence, 'Roman fort on the River Don'. The name 'Don' is an old Celtic word for 'river'. Roman occupation of Doncaster began around 71, when they built a fort at a crossing place at the River Don on the Great North Road (also known as Watling Street), and called it Danum. Some authorities identify Doncaster the place that the ninth century writer Nennius called Cair Daun in his *History of the Britons*. Domesday records Doncaster thus in 1086: 'Donecastre three bovates; Bentley, near Doncaster three bovates', all in sokeland belonging to Wheatley.

Driffield

The *Anglo-Saxon Chronicles* recorded Driffield thus in 705: 'Aldfrith, King of Northumbria [sometimes known as Alfrid the Wise], passed away on December 14 at Driffield, and his son Osred received the kingdom'. A plaque in the church at Little Driffield marks the place where Aldfrith was laid to rest, reputedly after being seriously wounded in battle at Ebberston. The East Yorkshire township of Driffield appears in Domesday as Drifeld, based on the Old English word for dirt: 'drif' or 'drit', and 'feld', a field or open land. Hence, simply, 'dirty field', although some interpret the name as meaning a 'field of scrubland' and others as 'manured field'. The survey distinguishes between Great Driffield (Drifeld) and Little Driffield (Drigelinghe).

Durham

By the eleventh century, Durham was known as Dunholme, a name derived from the Old English word 'dun', which stands for a hill, and the Old Scandinavian word 'holme' or 'holmr', which signified an island or a promontory surrounded by water or by fenland. Hence, in its original sense, the placename means 'hill on an island [or on higher ground]'. The hill in question is the location of Durham Cathedral and castle, which are located on the River Wear, no doubt the waters implied in the original Scandinavian word 'holmr'. Over time the place has also been spelt as Dunhelm and Dunholm. Unlike many English counties whose names are based on their main or capital cities (e.g. Lancashire, Yorkshire, Staffordshire, Worcestershire, etc), there never has been a Durhamshire, the county opting instead to be known as County Durham.

Easingwold

This North Yorkshire township appears twice in the Domesday survey of 1086 as Eisincewald and Eisicwalt, in the Burford Hundred, having belonged to Earl Morcar before the Norman

Conquest and afterwards to King William. It was assessed as twelve carucates of land with two leagues of woodland pasture, a manor house and a church with its own priest. In 1066, the estate had been valued at thirty pounds, by in 1086 at being only worth twenty shillings. The placename comprises three Old English elements: 'Esa', probably the name of the man who founded the settlement, 'inga', signifying 'the people, followers or tribe', and 'wald', a high forested area. Therefore we may take the combined elements to mean 'high forest belonging to the people of Esa'.

Eccup

Eccup is a district of Leeds in the County of Yorkshire and its placename comes from a man called Ecca, who may have established the original settlement or been its leader, and the Old English word 'hop', which signified an enclosed valley. Hence, 'Ecca's enclosed valley'. Domesday recorded the place as Echope and listed it in the Hundred of Skyrack, held in 1086 by Count Robert of Mortain. It was a small estate at that time with land sufficient for one plough, three acres of meadow and woodland measuring three by two furlongs, altogether valued at just five shillings.

Edmundbyers

This village in County Durham was named after a man called Eadmund, who might have been its founder or an early chieftain in Anglo-Saxon times. The settlement was well established by the eleventh century, though little else is known about its early history. The Old English word 'byr' or 'bur' referred to a barn, and the placename means 'Eadmund's barn [or byre]'.

Ellingstring

This is another example of how the Old Norse and Old English languages coalesced into an early form of Middle English, in the way that this North Yorkshire village placename incorporates both. The Saxon words 'ael' or 'el' signifies an eel, and the 'ing' element implied an association of some kind, while the Scandinavian word 'strengr', translates as 'watercourse'. Hence, one interpretation of the placename is 'watercourse at a place where eels are found [or caught]'. Another suggestion is that it is an association with a person called Ella or Eli, in which case the name could mean 'watercourse at a place associated with Ella'. Both seem equally possible. By the end of the twelfth century, the placename had been recorded as Elingestrengge.

Escrick

Escrick is another example of the synthesis of Saxon and Danish cultures and placenames in North Yorkshire. The Old Scandinavian word 'eski' signified the ash tree, and the Old English word 'ric' inferred a raised strip of land or a narrow ridge. Taken together, these produce a placename that means 'narrow strip of land where ash trees grow'. The Great Survey listed the village as Ascri, and assessed it as a very small estate supporting two households within the East Riding Hundred of Pocklington and held by Count Alan of Brittany. Before the Conquest the manor had belonged to Earl Morcar.

Felling

Felling is a township located around a mile south of Gateshead, historically part of Durham. Its placename is contentious; many argue that it is related to local fells or hills, and others that it relates to the felling of trees in the locality. Until the last century, it was often known as 'The Felling', but when the two original villages of Low Felling and High Felling merged, the placename became just 'Felling'. In about 1220, it was recorded as Fellyng and some maintain that it may have derived either from the Old English word which referred to a woodland clearing, or possibly 'felging' which signified fallow land.

Filey

This North Yorkshire seaside town was named in the *Domesday Book* as 'Fluelac... sokeland... in the land of the king in Yorkshire'. It also records that 'in Grisethorpe and Filey in [the] Dic Wapentake the king had eighteen carucates of land'. By the twelfth century, the town was known as Fivelai, with a parish church dedicated to St Oswald. Opinions differ as to its derivation, but one has it coming from the Old English words 'fifel' and 'eg', meaning 'a rocky outcrop [or island] shaped like a sea monster', while another prefers 'fif', meaning 'five', and 'leah', a clearing in a wood, thereby possibly meaning 'five clearings in a wood'.

Flawith

Flawith is a small hamlet in North Yorkshire whose name has three possible meanings. The first depends on the Old Scandinavian word 'flagth', referring to a witch or female troll, and the second sees it derived from 'flatha', meaning 'flat meadow'. A third explanation might come from the Old English word 'fleathe', which signified water lilies. Finally, the last element of the placename is a Norse word meaning 'ford'. Hence, the village name could mean '[place near the] ford of a witch', or '[place at a] ford by a flat meadow', or even '[place at a] ford where water lilies grow'. Either would seem equally possible. By the end of the twelfth century the placename had been written as Flatwayth.

Gateshead

Gateshead is a large town in Tyne and Wear, whose name comes from two Old English words 'gat' and 'heafod', together meaning 'goat's headland'. Spelt Gateshevet and Gatesheued during the late twelfth century and as Gatishevede in a legal record dated 1430, Gateshead lies at the head of an extensive Celtic trail, a major route north into Scotland. The township was first mentioned in the Latin translation in Bede's *Ecclesiastical History of the English People* as *'ad caput caprae'*, which can be translated as 'at the goat's head'. Bede also writes: 'Adda was brother of Utta, a well-known priest and Abbot of Gateshead'. The site of the monastery is not known although there are several prints of the ruins of Holy Trinity Church which are captioned 'Gateside Monastery'. The older part of this building, formerly St Edmund's Hospital chapel, was built about 1250.

Gilberdyke

This township in the East Riding of Yorkshire was known simply as Dyc in 1234 and had become Gilbertdike by the late fourteenth century, probably after the Gilbert family who became substantial landowners at that time. The Old English word 'dyc' means a ditch or dyke. The placename might therefore be taken to mean 'estate or land by the ditch [or dyke] belonging to the Gilbert family'.

Giggleswick

This North Yorkshire village name comes directly from Old English, named after a man called Gichel or Gikel, and 'wic', indicating a specialised farm, typically a dairy. Hence, possibly, 'Gikel's dairy farm'. It appeared in 1086 as the Manor of Ghigeleswic in the Craven Hundred of the West Riding, held as chief tenant by Roger de Poitou; the estate had belonged to a Saxon man called Fech, who seems to have retained a sub-tenancy, paying rent on four carucates of land which he had previously owned outright before the Conquest.

Goathland

Despite appearances to the contrary, the name of this North Yorkshire village has nothing whatever to do with goats. That first element refers either to a man called Goda, or else it comes from 'god', the old Saxon word for 'good'. The final element, 'land', is fairly self explanatory except that it referred specifically to cultivated or arable land. Therefore the placename translates either as 'Goda's cultivated land' or as '[place by the] good cultivated land'.

Goole

Goole has no entry in the *Domesday Book*, though it is located within the medieval Osgoldcross Wapentake, which at that time was considered to be in the West Riding. One of the earliest recorded references to the placename is in 1362, when it was known as Gulle, from the Middle English word 'goule', meaning 'stream' or 'channel', although some opinions translate the meaning as 'open sewer'.

Gosforth/Goswick

Gosforth (not to be confused with the place of that name in Cumbria), is a northern suburb of Newcastle-upon-Tyne, known in the mid-twelfth century as Goseford. The placename comes from the Old English words 'gos' or 'gese', meaning 'goose' or 'geese', and 'ford', a shallow river crossing. Hence, 'a river crossing or ford where geese are found'. The river in question was the Ouse, known at that time as the Ouseburn, which in itself may even be a corruption of 'goose burn', where the old Saxon word 'burn' signified a small river or stream. The Northumbrian hamlet of Goswick, like Gosforth, contains the same reference to geese, but with the alternative suffix 'wic', indicating a specialised farm of some kind. Hence, 'a farm where geese are kept'. In 1202, the placename was spelt Gossewic.

Great Ribston/Little Ribston

Historically located in the ancient Burghshire Hundred of the West Riding, the first written record of the place is as the single settlement of Ripestan in 1086. The placename comprises two Old English elements: 'ribbe', referring to the ribwort, a flowering plant in the plantain family, and 'stan', a rock or stone. Taken together they mean 'a rocky place where ribwort grows'. Some time before 1837, the township had been separated into Great Ribston and Little Ribston, both in the Claro Registration District of West Yorkshire.

Gristhorpe

A village in North Yorkshire bearing distinct Danish influence; in Old Norse, 'griss' stands for 'pig' or 'piglet', and 'thorp' signified an outlying or remote farmstead. The placename may translate as an 'outlying or remote farm where pigs are reared'. An alternative explanation has also been offered, in that Griss might have been a man's name, in which case the placename may mean 'Griss's remote farm', although it is more likely that this second explanation refers to the hamlet of Girsby, which is entered in the 1086 survey as Grisebi. The Domesday Book places Grisetorp in the Dic Hundred of the ancient North Riding of Yorkshire, a small village of some eighteen carucates of land belonging at that time to the Crown, having previously been held by Tostig, Saxon Earl of Northumbria and brother of King Harold Godwinson. The manor included several tracts of sokeland, including Scagetorp, Eterstorp and Rodebestorp.

Guisborough

Originally within the ceremonial county of North Yorkshire, and since 1974 located in the unitary authority of Redcar and Cleveland in the Tees Valley, Guisborough was recorded in 1086 as Ghigesburg. The spelling of the name is based on an old Scandinavian personal name, Gigr or Gaegr, and the Old English word 'burh', signifying a fortified place or stronghold. Hence, 'Gigr's stronghold'. Domesday's three entries offered several variations on the spelling of the placename, including Ghigesburg, Chigesburg and Ghigesborg, and placed it in Langbaurgh Wapentake, where 'Ultkil [held] one carucate [of land] to the geld... [and]

land for half a plough'. The entry continues elsewhere: 'In Guisborough and Hutton Lowcross [are] twenty-five carucates to the geld, and there could be fourteen ploughs'. The Count of Mortain held twenty-five carucates 'in the same place', which had previously belonged to Uctred. A man called Leysingr is also recorded having held three carucates of land and two bovates for rent.

Halifax
Halifax is a town in the Metropolitan Borough of Calderdale in West Yorkshire, which has been a centre of woollen manufacture since the fifteenth century. The town's name was recorded in 1095 as Halyfax and probably comes from the Old English 'halh-gefeaxe', meaning 'area of coarse grass in the nook of land'. This is not the only interpretation of the name however; another has it derived from the Old English words 'halig', meaning 'holy', and 'feax', meaning hair. This refers to the 'holy hair', a sixteenth century myth that the head of John the Baptist is hidden somewhere in the town – an explanation rejected by most contemporary authorities as pure fancy (of course). It is thought that there may have been a hermitage dedicated to St John the Baptist on the banks of the River Hebble, dating from the seventh century, or possibly a later Saxon church linked with the Parish of Dewsbury, but both theories remain conjectural.

Haltemprice
When Augustinian monks founded a priory at Cottingham in 1322, and later moved it to Newton, as this place was then called, it was declared to be 'a high or noble enterprise'. In French, 'haut' meant 'high' and 'emprise' meant 'undertaking' or 'enterprise'. This district of Hull in East Yorkshire then became known as Hautenprise, which translates into modern English as '[place of] high enterprise'.

Hamsterley
Despite appearances, the name of this village in County Durham has nothing whatsoever to do with hamsters or other small furry rodents. The Old English word 'hamstra' actually referred to the corn weevil, and the 'leah' affix signified a clearing in a wood. Therefore, the placename means '[place in the] woodland clearing full of corn weevils'. By the late-twelfth century, the village name had been recorded as Hamsteleie.

Harbottle
The Northumberland village of Harbottle gets its name from the Old English words 'hyra', meaning 'hireling', and 'bothl', a special building or dwelling. Hence, 'building or dwelling of a hireling'. The place was recorded as Hirbotle around 1220.

Harrogate
The name of the North Yorkshire town of Harrogate stems from the Old Norse words 'horgr', referring to a stone, stones or a cairn, and 'gata', a road or pathway. Hence it might mean 'the road to the cairn [or heap of stones]'. Recorded in 1332 as Harwegate, by 1399 it was held by the Duchy of Lancaster.

Hartlepool
Some time around 640, a woman named Hieu founded a monastery on the site which would in time become Hartlepool. Soon a fishing village grew up nearby. Danes destroyed the monastery in the ninth century, but the village survived and continued to thrive through the centuries. Its first written record was in 1153, by which time the township had grown into a small but busy port. In the late twelfth century, the Church of St Hilda was built. Recorded in 1170 as Hartlepl (later as Herterpool), the name is derived from three Old English words,

'heorot', referring to a hart or a stag, 'eg', signifying a bay or an island, and 'pol', meaning pool. Hence, 'the pool near the bay (or island) where stags are found'. In 1201, King John gave Hartlepool its first charter.

Haworth

This little Yorkshire village near Bradford is probably best known as the birthplace and home of the Brontë sisters, Charlotte, Emily and Anne, who lived at Haworth Parsonage. By 1029, the place was recorded as Hauewrth, from the Old English 'haga', a hedge, and 'worth', signifying an enclosed field or paddock. Hence, 'enclosure with a hedge'. Pronounced 'How-erth', it is also the destination for the restored Keighley and Worth Valley Railway, with a station in the village. The Brontë Way, a forty-three-mile long footpath, passes by the Lower Laithe Reservoir at Stanbury to the Brontë Waterfalls, across the moors to Ponden Hall at Top Withens, one of the likely settings for Thrushcross Grange in Emily Brontë's novel *Wuthering Heights*.

Hebden Bridge

Originally known only as Hebden, the modern placename developed on account of its iconic hump-back bridge over Hebden Water, a cascading stream in West Yorkshire that runs down from open moorland and, since the late eighteenth century, has joined the Rochdale Canal. The name translates as 'valley where brambles grow', from 'heop', meaning either a bramble or sometimes a rose-hip, 'denu', meaning a valley, and later, 'brycg', signifying a bridge. In 1086, it was known simply as Hebedene, in the Barkston Wapentake of the land of Osbern d'Arques, 'where Dreng had four carucates of land and two bovates to the geld'. By the end of the fourteenth century, the place had become known as Hepdenbryge.

Heckmondwike

The Great Survey of 1086 recorded this town in the Kirklees region of West Yorkshire as Hedmundewic, a name derived from a man called Heahmund along with the old Saxon word 'wic', which referred to a specialised dwelling or farm (like a dairy). Hence, 'Heahmund's specialised farm'. By the thirteenth century the placename had become Hecmundewik.

Hepburn

The Northumberland village of Hepburn derived its name from two Anglo-Saxon words: 'heah', meaning 'high', and 'byrgen', which signified a burial ground. Hence, 'burial ground in a high place'. In the mid-eleventh century, the word 'dun', indicating a hill, had been added and the village placename was recorded at that time as Hybberndune.

Hepple

Hepple is a village in Northumberland whose placename means 'corner of land where rose hips (or brambles) grow'. The name comes from 'heope' or 'heopa', which represent rose hips and brambles, and 'halh', the Old English word for a corner or nook of land. In 1205, the name was recorded as Hephal.

Hessle

This East Yorkshire township may have been surrounded by hazel trees in its distant past, as the placename, Hessle, comes either from the Old English word 'haesel' or the Old Scandinavian 'hesli', both of which translate as hazel, or hazel trees. The placename may be read as '[place at] the hazel tree [or trees]'. It was recorded in 1086 as Hase in the Hessel Hundred of the East Riding, whose Lord of the Manor was Gilbert Tison. The estates comprised 'four ploughlands, one lord's plough team, [and] three men's plough teams'. It was operated by seventeen villagers, two smallholders and a priest who was in charge of a church within the manor. Before 1066, it had belonged to two Saxons, Alwin and Ketil.

Hexham

There has been a settlement at Hexham since Saxon times. Many variant spellings of the placename have existed, including Hutoldesham, Hestoldesham, Hextoldesham and as Halgutstades Ham by around 1120. Several derivations of the name have been offered, but the most likely is that Hagustald was a man's personal name, and the Old English suffix 'ham' suggests it was originally his homestead. Therefore, possibly, 'the homestead of Hagustald'. Before it was incorporated into the County of Northumberland in 1571, Hexham was an ancient shire and known as 'Hexhamshire'.

Hornsea

Hornsea in the old East Riding of Yorkshire was recorded in 1086 as Hornesse and Hornessei. The placename comes from the Old Norse words 'horn', 'nes' and 'saer', which taken together mean a 'lake with a horn-shaped peninsula'.

Huggate

Huggate is yet another settlement bearing the marks of Danelaw in its decidedly Scandinavian placename. The first element comes from the Old Norse word, 'hugr', indicating earth mounds, tumuli or possibly burial barrows, and the second from 'gata', meaning a road or pathway. Hence 'road near or to the mounds', a clear reference to the road that leads out of the village to the ancient mounds on nearby Huggate Wold. This old East Riding township was recorded as Hugete in the Great Survey, part of the Warter Hundred part-held by Erwine the Priest, having previously belonged to Ingrith. A second entry lists eight ploughlands held by the king, having belonged to Barth, father of Gamal, before the Conquest. Both parts of the estate are listed as 'wasta' in the survey.

Hunderthwaite

In all probability, it was a Danish man called Hunrothr who gave his name to the early settlement or foundation of this hamlet in County Durham. The remaining element of the placename comes from the Old Scandinavian word 'thveit', meaning 'clearing' or 'meadow'. Hence, possibly 'Hunrothr's clearing (or meadow)'. An alternative explanation is that the first name element may be related to the Old English area of land measurement, the 'hundred', and indicating a large meadow covering most of the hundred. Domesday identified the place as Hundredestoit, listed at that time within the West Riding lands of Count Alan in Yorkshire.

Hunmanby

This North Yorkshire placename comes directly from the Scandinavian 'hunda mann', referring to houndsmen and sometimes to huntsmen (men who kept dogs or hounds), with the suffix 'by' indicating a farm or village settlement. Hence, 'farmstead or settlement where huntsmen keep dogs'. As with many placenames in the region known as Danelaw, Scandinavian elements are prevalent. Domesday recorded the name as Hundemanbi in Torbar Hundred whose chief tenant in 1086 was Gilbert of Ghent. He had been granted the land as a reward for his support of the Conqueror at Hastings, and for his part in subduing rebellious Saxons in what became known as 'the harrying of the north', when huge swathes of land were laid waste. Before the Conquest the manor and its estates had belonged to a Saxon called Ketilbert.

Hutton Cranswick

Hutton appears in placenames throughout England, and in isolation means 'farmstead on the ridge [or spur] of a hill', from the Old English words 'hoh', meaning 'hill ridge', and 'tun', a farmstead. There are around eighteen hamlets, villages or towns with this as part of their placename, but with a second identifier to distinguish each from the others (e.g. Hutton Conyers, Hutton Sessay and Hutton-le-Hole (Hutton in the Hollow), all in North Yorkshire, and Hutton Magna in Durham, as well as many others).

Hutton Cranswick's second element probably refers to an early settler called Cranuc with the addition of the Old English word 'wic', signifying a farm. Hence, the complete placename might be interpreted as 'Cranuc's farmstead on the ridge of a hill'. In 1086, the placename was simply Hottune, in the Driffield Hundred of the East Riding, held as Lord of the Manor at that time by Hugh, son of Baldric. Before the Conquest it had been held by the Saxon, Gamal, son of Karli. It had twelve villans at the time of Domesday, with land for four ploughs and one more for the Lord of the Manor. In 1066, it had been valued at three pounds, but by 1086 was worth only one pound.

Ilkley

In 79, the Romans called this West Yorkshire township Olicana, and by 972 the Saxons knew the place as Hillicleg. In 1086, it appeared under several different spellings in the *Domesday Book*, including Ilecliue, Illecluie and Illicleia. The placename is thought to derive from a man called Illica or Yllica, with the added Old English affix 'leah', signifying a woodland clearing or glade. Hence, the placename probably means 'woodland clearing belonging to Illica'.

Ingram

There are two explanations as to the meaning of this Northumberland village placename. The first element of the name is 'anger', an Old English word meaning 'grassland'. The second element could be either 'ham', meaning 'homestead', or 'hamm', signifying an enclosure. Therefore the placename may mean either 'homestead in the [or with] grassland' or 'enclosure in the [or with] grassland'. Either seem equally possible. In 1242, the placename was written as Angerham.

Issott

Issott is a rare surname, with many families bearing the name today either live or appear to have roots in Yorkshire. Surname reference books and internet sites disagree over the name's origin. There is a theory that the name is derived from the given name, Isolde. A romantic family tradition in the south west of the country has it that the Issotts (and various other surnames such as Izatt and Izzard), all stem from Isolde the wife of Tristan, nephew of the King of Cornwall of Arthurian legend. There is another theory claiming the name could be a corruption of an old Germanic word 'ishild', meaning 'ice battle', or even from other very early personal names such as Izod or Ysolt. But perhaps a Yorkshire variation could stem from the West Riding placename Ossett. The *Domesday Book* refers to Ossett as Osleset and was later written as Ossete. Tradition has it that the place belonged to a chieftain named Osla, but some maintain the name comes from an Old Norse word for a ridge or chain of hills. Given a strong regional dialect and a French scribe's mistranslation in the audit, little wonder that the spelling of the surname and placename might easily be confused.

Jarrow

The earliest records of Jarrow date from the seventh century when Bishop Biscop (also known as Biscop Baducing), was granted forty hides of land by King Ecgrith of Northumbria to found the monastery of St Peter in Wearmouth (sometimes known as Monkwearmouth) in 674. Then, in 681, he gave permission for the establishment of St Paul's Monastery in the settlement at Jarrow and in 686 Ceolfrith was established as its Abbot. It was in these two monasteries that Bede spent most of his life and wrote his major work, *Historia Ecclesiastica Gentis Anglorum* (The Ecclesiastical History of the English People) which was completed in 731. The early Anglo-Saxon settlers knew the settlement in about 716 as Gyrwe (pronounced Yeer-way), an old tribal name, which over time was corrupted to Jarrow. The name translates as '[settlement] of the fen dwellers', taken from the Old English 'gyr', which referred to a marsh, a fen or mudflat.

Keighley
The settlement at Keighley, in the former West Riding of Yorkshire, was founded by a Saxon man called Cyhha, which accounts for the first element of the name. The Old English affix 'leah', signified a woodland clearing; therefore the placename means the 'woodland clearing of Cyhha'. By 1086, it had been recorded as Chichelai, in Langbaurgh Wapentake, where 'Ulfkil and Toli and Hrafnsvartr and William, [have] six carucates [rented] to the geld'.

Kelfield
This North Yorkshire village has a name that translates as 'open land where chalk is spread'. It comes from 'celce' and 'feld', two Old English words which respectively mean 'chalky place' and 'open land'. Domesday recorded the place twice, as Chelchefeld and Chelchefelt, and listed it in the Pocklington Hundred of the East Riding, part-held by Hugh, the son of Baldric, and Count Alan of Brittany. In 1066, the manor had belonged in part to Earl Morcar and in part to Gamal, identified as the son of Karli. The manorial estate supported around six households and in 1086 was valued at one pound, as it had been before the Conquest.

Kelloe
Kelloe is a village in County Durham whose name is derived from the Old English words 'celf', meaning 'calf' or 'young cow' and 'hlaw', a hill. Hence '[place by a] hill where calves graze'. The placename was recorded as Kelfau in around 1170.

Kexby
If more evidence of Danish settlements in Yorkshire were needed, the village of Kexby is a prime example. It derived its placename from the Old Scandinavian words 'Keikr', a Dane's personal name and the affix 'by', indicating a village or a farmstead. Hence, the placename means 'Keikr's village [or farmstead]'. The earliest record of the written name was as Kexebi in the twelfth century.

Kingston upon Hull
Commonly known simply as Hull, the place has no entry in the *Domesday Book*. Earliest records date from the twelfth century when the monks at Meaux Abbey built a port at a place where the River Hull meets the Humber, and from where they could export their wool. The river name derives either from the Old Scandinavian word 'hul', meaning 'deep water', or from the Celtic meaning 'muddy [water]'. The township later developed into a major fishing and whaling centre and market town. Named by Edward I in 1299 as Kyngeston (Kings-town) upon Hull.

Kirby Grindalythe
Kirby is a common placename in England, which along with the close variant 'Kirkby' accounts for at least twenty villages and townships with one or other title; both versions

indicate a village with a church, and come from the Old Scandinavian 'kirkju-by'. With few exceptions, most are distinguished from others by an additional affix (places like Kirby Bredon in Norfolk and West Kirby on the Wirral, or Kirkby Lonsdale and Kirkby Stephen in Cumbria).

In this particular village, the Grindalythe element refers to cranes or herons, and is comprised of three separate parts: the Old English 'cran', which means 'crane', and 'dael', signifying a valley, along with the Old Scandinavian word, 'hlith', meaning 'sloping ground'. Hence, 'slope of a valley where cranes are found'. Taken together, the two placename elements might translate as '[the] village church on a valley slope where cranes are found'. Domesday recorded three entries for the place as Chirchebi, in the Toreshou Hundred of the East Riding of Yorkshire: one ploughland valued at five pence was held by King William, having previously belonged to Uglubarth; a second had been granted to Nigel Fossard with Count Robert de Mortain as its chief tenant and having been previously in the possession of Ketilbert before the Conquest, and a third entry named Thorfin of Ravensworth as part owner before 1066. All three entries record the estate as 'wasta'. In the mid-fourteenth century, place had been recorded as Kirkby in Crendalith.

Knaresborough

Knaresborough was referred to in the *Domesday Book* as the 'Mainou of Chenaresburg ... in the land of the king in Yorkshire'. It was recorded thus: 'In Chenaresburg, six carucates, with eleven berewicks ... it was worth six pounds and now renders twenty shillings [as rent or tax]'. Later the survey records it being formerly held and cultivated by Erneis. After the Conquest, William gave the land to Serio de Burgh. As for the origin of the placename, Knare (or Cenheard), may have been the name of an Anglo-Saxon chieftain and the 'borough' element, a derivation of 'burh', the old word for a fortress. Hence, 'Knare's fortress'. An alternative explanation cites the Old English word 'knar', meaning a rocky outcrop, giving the place a meaning of 'fortress on the rocky place'.

Knitsley

The name of this small hamlet in County Durham comes from the Old English words 'cnycc' (or the Middle English 'knicche'), meaning 'knitch' or 'faggot' (bunches or bound bundles of wooden sticks collected as fuel for fires), and 'leah', a clearing in woodland. The placename therefore translates as 'woodland clearing where knitches are obtained'. In 1303 the placename was recorded as Knyhtheley.

Leeds

The *Domesday Book* makes only a passing reference to Ledes, as a small habitation apparently of little value. It had been known as Loidis or Leodis since the early eighth century, when Bede included it in his *Ecclesiastical History* and perhaps it was known even earlier as Ladenses. The name probably derives from the Brythonic Celtic word 'Ladenses', meaning 'people of the fast-flowing river', in reference to the River Aire that runs through the city, although it has also been suggested that it might stem as a derivative of Welsh word 'lloed', simply meaning 'a place'.

Lesbury

An early record of the Northumberland village of Lesbury was as Lechesburi during the twelfth century. The name comes from 'laece', the Old English word for a leech (commonly used as a euphemism for a doctor or a physician), and 'burh', representing a fortified mansion or structure. Hence, the placename translates as 'fortified mansion [house] of a physician'.

Lindisfarne

Lindisfarne, sometimes referred to as Holy Island, is a tidal island joined by a low-tide causeway to the north-east coast of Northumberland. It has become famous for its connection with Bede, sometimes called the Father of English History. The placename derives from an Irish Gaelic word 'lind' (or 'lindis'), meaning lake or stream, and 'ferran', meaning 'land'. Hence, 'land [beside a] lake or stream', probably in reference to the flowing tidal waters which separate the island from the mainland. It was already known as Lindisfarnae by the middle of the eighth century.

Middlesbrough

Known in Saxon England as Mydildburgh, possibly after its founder or chieftain, a man called Mydil, whose 'burh', or fortress, it was; or it may derive from the Old English word 'midlest', meaning middle, in which case, the placename may be taken to mean 'middlemost stronghold or borough', which on balance, seems most likely. Around 1165, the placename had been recorded as Midelesburc.

Monk Bretton

This district of Barnsley derived its placename from two Anglo-Saxon words, 'munuc', meaning 'monk' and 'Brettas', a reference to what are sometimes called the 'Ancient Britons'. Hence the placename may be taken to mean '[estate or farmstead of the] monks of the Britons'. This is thought to be a reference to the monks of Bretton Priory. Domesday recorded the place as Brettone, a very small settlement estate in the Staincross Hundred of the old West Riding of Yorkshire, where there was land for just one plough. The manor had been granted to Ilbert de Lacy, and according to the account a Saxon man called Wulfmer had held the estate before the Conquest. In 1225, the place was recorded as Munkebretton.

Morpeth

Morpeth is an ancient market town situated on the River Wansbeck and is located fourteen miles north of Newcastle. By the beginning of the thirteenth century, it was known as Morpath, from two Old English words, 'morth' and 'paeth', possibly meaning 'murder path', more properly indicating 'a path where a murder took place'. It has also been suggested that the placename might equally be interpreted as a corruption of 'moor path', (that is, a path or track leading to the moors). Around 1200, the place had been recorded as Morthpath.

Muggleswick

Muggleswick is a small hamlet in County Durham whose placename had been well established by the end of the twelfth century. It was recorded in 1195 as Muclincgwic, but may have been much older, dating back to Anglo-Saxon times. The name came from a man called Mucel, its possible founder, plus the Old English affixes, 'ingas', meaning 'people', 'family' or 'associates', and 'wic', a specialised farmstead like a dairy. The placename in its entirety translates as 'Mucel's specialised [dairy] farm'.

Muker

The North Yorkshire village of Muker has decidedly Scandinavian origins as its name comes directly from the Old Norse language, where 'mjor' meant 'narrow' and 'akr' represented a piece or plot of land, a word closely related to the modern English word 'acre'. The placename simply means 'narrow plot of land', and was recorded in 1274 as Meuhaker.

Muscoates

This hamlet in North Yorkshire must have had a serious vermin problem at some point during early Norman times, as the placename means 'cottages overrun with mice'! The named comes from the Old English words 'mus', meaning 'mouse, and 'cot', cottage or cottages. The earliest record of the placename was around 1160.

Mytholmroyd
An ancient settlement in the Calder Valley of West Yorkshire, the first element of the Mytholmroyd placename comes from the Old English word 'mythe', which is related to 'mutha', meaning 'confluence', as in an estuary or mouth of a river. The second element derives from 'rodu', another Saxon word for a clearing or woodland glade. Hence, the name may be taken to mean '[place at a] clearing at the confluence of rivers'. The two rivers in question are the River Calder and Cragg Brook. In the thirteenth century, the placename was written as Mithomrode.

Myton-on-Swale
As the placename suggests, this North Yorkshire village stands at a place where the River Swale joins the River Ure. In fact the first word, 'Myton', comes from 'mythe', which meant 'river junction' in Anglo-Saxon times. The word may be related to the modern English word 'mouth' (as in the mouth of a river). The additional name element 'tun', which signified a farmstead or settlement, produces a placename that means 'farmstead at the junction of the River Swale'. The meaning of 'Swale' is very ancient and thought to mean 'rushing water'. The village was known as Mytun in the late-tenth century and was recorded in Domesday as Mitune, in the Bulford Hundred, held at that time by King William.

Nether Poppleton
The Old English 'nether' and the 'tun' elements of this Yorkshire village placename are fairly straightforward, as they respectively mean 'lower' and 'farmstead'. The 'popel' element is also Anglo-Saxon and means 'pebble'. Hence, in total the village name means 'lower farmstead on pebble [soil]'. The 'Nether' element also distinguishes the place from nearby Upper Poppleton. The place was recorded in around 972 as Popeltune, and in 1086 by the *Domesday Book* as Popeltone, a very small manor supporting just two households in the Ainsty Hundred of the former West Riding, held at that time by Osbery d'Arques, having belonged in 1066 to a man called Oda, described as 'the Deacon'.

Newbiggin-by-the-Sea
The first part of this Northumberland port and seaside resort derives its name from the Middle English words 'niwe', meaning 'new', and 'bigging', a building. Hence, the placename means 'new building by the sea'. It was recorded in 1187 as Niwebiginga. There is another place called Newbiggin in Cumbria, with the same meaning.

Northumberland
The county was already known as Northumberland by the early twelfth century, a name originally derived from the Northhymbre tribe who occupied the wider territory before Anglo-Saxon times. The Saxons knew it as the Kingdom of Northumbria. The name means 'territory of the Northhymbre', referring to people who lived north of the River Humber.

Nun Monkton
Ostensibly, it's rare to come across a place that has both nuns and monks in its name, but the North Yorkshire village of Nun Monkton has both. A fair interpretation of the placename might be 'nun's farmstead [on the estate] of the monks', where 'tun' signified either a farmstead or an estate. In 1086, the manor was simply known as Monechetone, located in the Burghshire Hundred, part of the estates granted by King William to Osbern d'Arques. According to Jane Wray, in her *History of Nun Monkton*, 'The name is of ecclesiastic origin,

as there had previously been a monastery which was destroyed by the Danes in 867 AD. The site of this monastery is not known, but it probably stood where the present church now stands'. A nunnery was founded on the estate land in the twelfth century, which led to its present-day placename.

Newcastle upon Tyne

The Romans knew this early settlement as Pons Aelius, which translates as 'bridge of Hadrian'. Soon after the Normans arrived in Britain, William the Conqueror had a wooden castle built on the site, the so-called 'new castle', to defend England from warring Scottish and Pictish incursions. The 'upon Tyne' extension was added later to distinguish it from other townships called Newcastle (notably Newcastle in Shropshire and Newcastle-under-Lyme in Staffordshire). The name of the River Tyne dates from early Celtic times and is believed to mean 'flowing [or fast-flowing] river'. Hence the town's placename means '[the] new castle on the fast-flowing river'.

Osmotherley

The Civil Parish of Osmotherley in the old North Riding of Yorkshire has been known variously from the early thirteenth to the sixteenth centuries as Asemunderlawe, Osmoundrelawe and Osmunderley. The name seems to be a combination of Old Norse and Old English origin. Probably named after a man called Asmund, 'hlaw' meaning a hill or possibly a burial mound and 'leah', signifying a woodland clearing. It may therefore be reasonably interpreted as 'Asmund's burial mound in a woodland clearing'. Domesday recorded the place as Asmundrelac in the Allerton Hundred held at that time by King William. By 1088, it had been written as Osmunderle.

Ovington

There are half a dozen places called Ovington in England, with examples in Essex, Hampshire, Norfolk, Durham and Northumberland. The village of Ovington in County Durham owes its name to a man called Wulfa, who was its probable founder. Additionally, the two Old English elements 'inga' and 'tun' taken respectively mean 'people or followers' and 'estate' or 'farmstead'. The complete placename may be interpreted as '[place of the] followers [family or people] of Wulfa'. Domesday identified the place as 'Ulfeton, in the land of Count Alan', then listed in the North Riding of Yorkshire as partly wasteland ('wasta').

Pateley Bridge

The first mention of a bridge at this place across the River Nidd in North Yorkshire was during the fourteenth century; a shallow river crossing or ford had existed there before this time. The first part of this township's placename comes from two Old English words, 'paeth', meaning 'path' or 'track', and 'leah', a woodland clearing. The placename is traditionally thought to mean '[place where] paths meet by the bridge in a woodland clearing'. The paths in question are thought to be the present roads from Knaresborough and Ripon, that meet here to cross the River Nidd. In 1202, before the bridge had been built, the place was recorded as Pathlay, and in 1320 (after the bridge), as Patheleybrigg.

Pickering

The North Yorkshire market town of Pickering, historically a civil parish in Ryedale district within the former North Riding, was recorded in the *Domesday Book* as Picheringa or Picheringe, probably named after an early settler called Picer or Picher with the additional Old English suffix 'ingas', signifying his people, family or followers. Hence '[place of the] people of Picer'. Another somewhat mythical account cites an event surrounding King Peredurus, when around 270 BC he is said to have lost a ring that was found later in a fish that was served for dinner (in this case, a pike); when cut open, the ring was found in the fish's stomach. This supposedly led to the town adopting the name 'Pike-ring'. However unlikely this version might be, the image still appears on the town's coat of arms.

Pocklington

Located in the old East Riding of Yorkshire, the Pocklington placename contains three Old Saxon elements: first, 'Pocela', the name of its probable founder, 'inga', meaning the people or followers and 'tun', an estate of settlement. The placename may therefore be taken to mean 'the settlement of Pocela's people'. The settlement can be traced back to the Iron Age when it had been the territory of the Parisi tribe. Domesday identified the place as Poclinton in the ownership of King William and worth eight pounds in 1086, having belonged to the powerful Earl Morcar of Northumbria before 1066 and had been valued at fifty-six pounds; at that time it was a large substantial manor, but by the time of the survey, the estate was listed as partial waste.

Pontefract

The earliest name for this West Riding of Yorkshire township existed as two separate Danish settlements, known as Tanshelf and Kirby, and despite the manor having been recorded as Pontefracto in 1070, the Domesday survey recorded the placename as Tateshale. Pontefract's contemporary placename comes from the Latin 'pons', meaning 'bridge', and 'fractus', meaning 'broken'. Hence, 'broken bridge'. The bridge in question is still open to debate; the nearest possible candidate being the one across the River Aire which lies some two miles distant from the present town.

Popplewell

The settlement at Popplewell began as a small collection of houses and farms on the edge of Hartshead Moor in Yorkshire. Its name comes from the Old English words 'popel', meaning either 'poplar tree' or 'pebble' – opinions vary. The additional affix 'wella', meant either 'well', 'spring' or 'fountain'. The name most probably means 'the spring or well near the poplar trees', from the Old English 'popple-waella'. However, the village has been interpreted by some as meaning 'the farm by the poplars'. At some time, probably in the late twelfth century, the hamlet was joined with nearby settlement of Scholes. The name Scholes is derived from an Old Norse word, 'skali', meaning 'shelter'. By 1254, Popplewell and Scholes comprised only fourteen families with a population of around seventy.

Portington

This placename in the East Riding of Yorkshire, is made up of three Old English elements: 'port', signifying a market, 'inga', meaning the people, family or followers, and 'tun', a farmstead. Hence the placename may be taken to mean 'a farmstead belonging to the people of a market town'. It was known in 1086 as Portinton and Portiton in the Howden Hundred, and recorded in the *Domesday Book* as being comprised of two carucates and three bovates of land belonging to the Bishop of Durham.

Romaldkirk

This township in County Durham was recorded in the *Domesday Book* as Rumoldescerce and Rumoldescherce, in the North Riding of land of Count Alan of Brittany in Yorkshire. The name is based on an Old English saint's name, St Rumwald and the Old Norse word 'krkja', meaning church. Hence, 'the church of Saint Rumwald'. Before the Norman Conquest, it belonged to Thorfin of Ravensworth and was valued at just three shillings. By 1086 it had been reassessed as 'wasta' (waste), thereby worthless for taxation purposes.

Raskelf

This North Yorkshire township's placename bears witness to the dominance of the Danes in the culture of north-eastern England during the Middle Ages. The name comes directly from the Old Norse words 'ra', signifying a roe deer, and 'skjalf', which means a shelf or a ledge. Hence, we may take the name to mean something like 'shelf or ledge where roe deer are found'. It was recorded in the *Domesday Book* thus: 'in Raschel, Knut [has] eight carucates to the geld, [with] land for four ploughs... [and] the king eight carucates'. It lay within the old Bulford Hundred of the North Riding, and in 1066 had belonged to Cnut, the son of Karli. By the time of the 1086 Survey it had passed to King William.

Redmire

Redmire means reedy pool, or more properly, a pool of reeds. The name of this North Yorkshire township comes from the Anglo-Saxon word 'hreod', signifying a reed or reeds, and mere, a small lake or pool. It was known in 1086 as Ridemare, in the North Riding of Yorkshire, no doubt a rather poor misspelling by the Norman French commissioners, and the land was owned by Count Alan of Brittany, and tenanted at that time by his brother Ribald. Before the Conquest there had been two Saxon Lords of the Manor – Gamal, the son of Karli, and Gillepatric of Spennithorne.

Reighton

The North Yorkshire township of Reighton derives its placename from two Old English words: 'ric', meaning a flat ridge, and 'tun', a farmstead. Therefore the name might translate as 'farmstead on a flat [or straight] ridge'. Domesday recorded it as Rictone, in the Hunthow Hundred of the East Riding at that time, when it was part of the king's land in Yorkshire, where Tholf and Gamal each held 'five carucates to the geld'.

Richmond

Still known as Hindrelaghe in 1086 and held by Count Alan, by 1110 this Yorkshire township had become known as Richemund. The placename originally comes from the Old Norman French words 'riche' and 'mont', meaning a 'strong hill'. Following the Conquest of 1066, William granted the honour of Richmond to Alan Rufus (known as Alan the Red on account of his flaming red hair), who built a stone castle on a hill overlooking the River Swale. In 1174, the castle was used to imprison King William (The Lion) of Scotland. The *Domesday Book* records 'in Hindrelaghe, one carucate'. By 1311, a defensive wall had been built around the settlement. Henry VII was also Earl of Richmond and renamed his palace at Sheen in Surrey, Richmond.

Ripon

The Saxons knew this Yorkshire township as Hrypis in the eighth century, and a monastery is known to have stood there for at least a century before that. In the Domesday Survey, it was entered as Ripum, and belonged to the soke of Aldfield owned by the Archbishopric of York in 1086. The placename comes from the ancient Celtic tribe called Hrype in whose tribal territory it lay. The exact meaning of that name is unclear, but the plural form of 'Hrypum' is the source of its present-day name, Ripon.

Rise

Recorded in 1086 by the name of Risun in the North Hundred of Holderness of Yorkshire, this settlement's placename refers to 'hris' (plural form: 'hrisum'), the Old English name for scrubland or brushwood. Hence '[place near, among or by] brushwood'. Before the Conquest it was held by Cnut, then passed to William Malet and after 1070 to Drew de Beuvrière, (sometimes Drogo de la Beuvrière), a Belgian supporter of William the Conqueror, who still retained it by the time of Domesday. The chief tenancy was held by the Archbishop of York and the survey assessed the entire estate as 'waste'.

Salton

Domesday lists this North Yorkshire township as Saleton, where 'St Peter has in demesne half a plough', and the king's abbot held another three carucates. Before the Conquest, Ulf held two manors on the estate, which in 1086 was worth ten shillings. The placename derives from the Old English words 'sahl' (or Sealh), and 'tun', which taken together mean 'farmstead where sallow trees grow'. Sallow is the old word for the willow tree, from the Latin word 'salix', and the prefix 'Sal' is common in English placenames where willows are found, eg. Salford, Salcombe, Salisbury, etc.

Saxton

This placename is another hybrid of the Old English and Norse languages, in that the 'Sax' element may well refer to a man called Seaxe or Saksi, possibly a Dane who founded the original settlement, plus the affix 'tun', indicating a farmstead of some kind. Alternatively, it may be a direct reference to Saxon occupation, in which case it could be translated as either 'settlement where Saxons live' or 'the settlement of a man called Saksi'. The *Domesday Book* records the place as Saxtun, in the Barkstone-Ash Wapentake of the West Riding of Yorkshire. The remains of Saxton Castle, a motte and bailey fortification with a medieval manor house, is a designated and scheduled Ancient Monument.

Scagglethorpe

Located at one time in the middle of the ancient territory known as Danelaw, the North Yorkshire village of Scagglethorpe betrays all of its Nordic heritage in its placename. First, the place is named after a Dane called Skakull or Skakli with the addition of the Old Scandinavian element 'thorp', which referred to an outlying or remote farmstead. Hence, 'Skakull's remote [or outlying] farmstead'. The survey of 1086 recorded the place as Scachetorp, and listed it in the West Riding Hundred of Ainsty, held at that time by Osbern d'Arques, having belonged to Ernwin the Priest before the Norman Conquest. It was a very small estate supporting just five households. There was sufficient land for three ploughs with three acres of meadow and half a league of woodland with '...four acres of mixed measures', possibly referring to arable land and a variety of vegetable produce that may have been grown there.

Scawton

Scawton was historically a parish in Helmsley district, in the North Riding of Yorkshire and is yet another example of the Scandinavian influence on English placenames. The word 'skal' or 'skali' are Old Norse for a hollow for sheltering livestock, and occasionally to a hut, a byre or shieling, built for that purpose. Hence, the placename translates as 'farmstead with an animal shelter or shieling'. In the Great Survey of 1086, three carucates of manor land were held by Robert Malet; before 1066, the Saxon tenant had been Archil. Another two carucates, previously held by Uctred, were in the possession of the Count of Mortain.

Scarborough

It is known that the Romans built a signal station on Scarborough Headland, as a warning against Saxon seaborne incursions. But the town is thought to have been founded by the

Danes in the tenth century, when Thorgil (also known as Skarthi, meaning 'hare-lip'), arrived in 996 and built a stronghold. The settlement became known as 'Skarthi's burh', or 'Skarthi's fort'.

Scotter

Scotter's placename harks back to a time when it was deeply embedded in Danelaw, and it comes directly from the Old Scandinavian words 'Scottar', meaning 'Scotsmen', and 'eyrr', which refers to a sandy or gravel bank. The placename may therefore be taken to mean 'gravel bank belonging to the Scots'. At the time of the Norman Conquest, the place was recorded as Scottere, and by 1086 had become Scotre.

Scrainwood

This Northumberland hamlet has a placename that means 'wood where shrewmice are seen'. The shrewmouse is a small mouse-like insectivorous mammal with a long snout that is related to moles and shrews. The placename comes from the Old English words 'screawa', a shrewmouse, and 'wudu', meaning 'wood' or 'woodland'. One of the earliest records of the placename was as Scravenwod in 1242.

Scremerston

Scremerston is a township partly in Ancroft Parish and also in the Tweedmouth Parish of Northumberland and is located about three miles from Berwick on Tweed. It was named after the Skermer family as Schermereton in 1196. The placename has had several variants over time, including Skremerston, Scrimmerstone and Skremerston.

Scriven

The name of the North Yorkshire village of Scriven comes from the Old English word 'screfen', meaning 'pits' or 'holes', a reference to the gravel pits and old quarries found around the village. Domesday recorded the place as Scrauinge, and listed it in the Burghshire Hundred of the West Riding, held in 1086 by King William as it had been by King Edward before 1066. The manorial estate was assessed at twenty ploughlands and valued at one pound, having been worth six pounds during the reign of King Edward.

Settle

The name of this Yorkshire town dates back to at least the seventh century, when Angles arrived and settled in the region. By the time of Domesday, it was known as Setel, in the ancient Parish of Giggleswick, from the Old English word 'setl', meaning a house or dwelling place, held by Roger de Poitou and described as 'wasta' or wasteland not liable for taxation.

Shilbottle

Another odd-sounding placename (known earlier as Shilbotel), this village in Northumberland means 'dwelling of the people of Shipley', and is thought to have been founded some time before 1267. The placename contains three separate elements, of which the first two, 'Shipley' and 'ingas' are somewhat truncated. The Old English 'ingas' element refers to people, followers or family, and the old Saxon word 'bothl' or 'botl' indicated a dwelling. Why the dwelling in question should have been earmarked for the people of Shipley, seven miles north, is curious.

Shincliffe

The village of Shincliffe in County Durham derives its name from the Old English words 'scinna', meaning 'phantom', 'ghost' or 'spectre', and 'clif', referring to a cliff or steep bank. Hence, the placename means '[place by a] cliff haunted by spectres'. The origin of this appellation is obscure, but the place was clearly regarded as haunted during medieval times when such superstitions were commonplace. Shortly before the *Domesday Book*, the placename was recorded as Scinneclif. The village name was also listed in the 1195 Charter Rolls as Sineclive.

Shipley

The West Yorkshire town of Shipley derives its name from the Old English word 'sceap' or 'sciep', meaning 'sheep', and the suffix 'leah', which refers to a woodland clearing. Hence, 'woodland clearing where sheep are kept', or more simply 'sheep fold'. It was known in 1086 as Scipeleia and it seems to have passed through several anonymous ownerships until the twelfth century, when the Lord of the Manor, Adam (known only as 'Adam, son of Peter'), granted grazing rights to Riveaux Abbey.

Skipton

The name of the Yorkshire township of Skipton is of Saxon origin and comes from the same origin as Shipley; it means 'sheep town' (or 'sheep farm'), 'sciep' or 'sceap', being the Old English word for a sheep, and 'tun', meaning a settlement or farmstead. Before the Conquest, it belonged to Earl Edwin, but after 1066 it was granted to a Norman baron, Robert de Romille, who was Lord of the Manor of Bolton Abbey. In 1086, the *Domesday Book* refers to it as Skipton-on-Swale (or Schipetune). De Romille built Skipton Castle in 1090 and in 1102, Henry I granted him further estates in Upper Wharfdale and Airedale.

Slaggyford

The Middle English word 'slaggi' meant 'muddy, and taken together with 'ford', signifying a shallow river crossing, the placename of this small hamlet in Northumberland can be interpreted as '[place by the] muddy river crossing'. The ford in question is likely to have been over the South Tyne river. By the thirteenth century, the placename had been written as Slaggiford.

South Shields

South Shields is an Anglo-Saxon name derived from 'scheles' or 'shiels', a Middle English word for a fisherman's hut or temporary shelter, specifically referring to those on the south bank of the River Tyne. The lesser known area on the northern bank is North Shields, or more commonly Tynemouth. South Shields was recorded in 1268 as Chelis, and by 1313 had been recorded as Suthshelis. For most of its early history, this was a small fishing village belonging to the priors of Durham Cathedral monastery and in medieval times it was Tyneside's most important port.

Spittal

Sometimes spelt Spittle, this small Berwick-upon-Tweed fishing village in Tweedmouth Parish began life as a leper hospital, dedicated to St Bartholomew and known as 'God's house' when it was established some time before 1234. The location of the hospital remains unknown but the village that sprung up around it gradually became known as Spittal.

Stainburn

The Stainburn placename contains two elements; first, the Old English word 'stan' (or the Scandinavian 'stein'), meaning 'stone'; second, the affix 'burna', which was the Anglo-Saxon word for a stream. Taken together they produce a meaning of 'stony stream'. Well before the eleventh century, the place was known as Stanburne, which by the time of Domesday had become Stainburne. The survey recorded it in the Burghshire Hundred of the old West Riding of Yorkshire, in the possession of King William at that time, with four thegns working five carucates 'to the geld'. There was land for two ploughs. Before the Conquest the estate had been valued at two pounds, but by 1086 it had been reassessed as waste, and thereby of little or no taxable value.

Staindrop
A village in County Durham, whose name contains two Old English elements: 'staener', meaning 'stony ground', and 'hop', a valley. Hence, the placename translates as '[place in the] valley of stony ground'. This eminently describes the topography of the village as it lies in a valley on a tributary of the River Tees. It has been recorded under several variant spellings over time, including Standropa and Stainthorp.

Stamford Bridge
This East Riding of Yorkshire township was recorded in 1075 as Stanford Brycg. The name is made up of two elements: 'Stanford', indicating the stony ford across the River Derwent, based on the Old English word 'stan', a stone, and 'ford', a shallow river crossing. Later, the aforesaid ford was replaced by a bridge – hence its modern placename. It was the site of the Roman settlement of Derventio.

Stockton-on-Tees
Although Stockton was initially an Anglo-Saxon settlement overlooking the River Tees, historically the Manor of Stockton dates from around 1138. Shortly thereafter, it was purchased by Bishop Pudsey of Durham, who built a castle there, or more probably a fortified manor house, and in the thirteenth century the village became a borough. The name derives from the Old English word 'stocc', related to logs or tree trunks, as in the word 'stockade', and 'tun', indicating a settlement. Hence, a 'settlement built of logs [or tree trunks]'. The 'on-Tees' element represents its location on the river of that name.

Sunderland
Sunderland in County Durham escapes all mention in the *Domesday Book* but is believed to have once been known as Asunderland or Sundered land, indicating a land mass that is separated or 'cut asunder' as it is by the River Tyne that runs through its epicentre. The first known settlement was at Monkwearmouth in 674 when Bishop Biscop founded Monkwearmouth-Jarrow Abbey, which was home to the Venerable Bede.

Thirsk
The North Yorkshire township of Thirsk in the Vale of Mowbray derives its placename from the Old Norse word 'thresk' or 'thraesk', which simply means marsh or bog land and may have indicated a settlement by a river, or on a flood plain. The township lies on Cod Beck, a tributary of the River Swale, which is thought to have caused marshy ground in early Saxon times – hence the placename. The *Domesday Book* records Thirsk under several different spellings, including Tresc, Tresch and Tresche. There were in fact two manors – one on land belonging to Hugh FitzBaldric in the Yarlestre Wapentake, where Thor rented twelve carucates of land, sufficient for six ploughs; the other amounted to six carucates and belonged to the king. The unfortunate FitzBaldric forfeited his estates following the rebellion against Henry I, who granted them to Neil Daubeney (sometimes Daubigny or d'Albini), whose son took the surname of Mowbray.

Thixendale
In 1086, this North Yorkshire village was recorded as Sixtendale, in the Ackham Hundred, held at that time by a man known as Odo the Bowman. Given the presence of Danish

settlers in eastern England at that time, it is not surprising that the placename originally derives from a Dane called Sigsteinn. The 'dale' element of the name comes from the Old Scandinavian word 'dalr', which represented a small valley (or a dale). Hence, 'small valley belonging to a man called Sigsteinn'.

Tickhill

Opinions differ as to meaning of the placename of this Yorkshire village near Doncaster. It was first recorded in the twelfth century as Tikehill. The first element has two possibilities: one is that it reflects the name of a man called Tica, and second that it derives from the Old English word 'ticce', meaning a young goat or kid. The second element of the placename, the Anglo-Saxon word 'hyll' is fairly self-explanatory. The placename might therefore mean either 'Tica's hill' or '[place on a] hill where young goats are kept'.

Tyne and Wear

Tyne and Wear is a Metropolitan County in north-east England, lying between its two main rivers, the Tyne and the Wear. Before 1974 those parts which lay north of the River Tyne (Newcastle upon Tyne and North Tyneside), were historically part of the County of Northumberland, while those to the south of the river (Gateshead, South Tyneside and Sunderland), were part of the old County of Durham. From 1974 these boroughs were incorporated into and administered by the new Metropolitan County of Tyne and Wear. After 1986 they became unitary authorities, and while Tyne and Wear retained a ceremonial status, it lost its administrative powers.

Tynemouth

As you might expect, the name of this town in North Tyneside means 'mouth' (or estuary) of the River Tyne. The Tyne is a name dating back to early Celtic times and simply meant 'river'. In 792 AD the placename was recorded as Tinanmuthe.

Wadsworth/Wadkin

Many first names come in and quickly go out of fashion and sometimes spellings change. Such is the case for the surname Wadkin which basically means 'child of Wad'. Back in the time of the *Domesday Book*, Wad (spelt various ways, including Waeddie and Waddes), was a popular first name. The surname Wadsworth is derived from the place of that name near Hebden Bridge, and originally meant 'Waeddi's enclosure'.

Wainfleet All Saints

'Waegn' is the Old Anglo-Saxon word for a wagon or large cart (as in the title of John Constable's famous painting *The Haywain*), and taken together with the Old English word 'fleot', which refers to a creek or stream, Wainfleet means '[place at the] stream where wagons can cross'. The final affix refers to the village church which is dedicated to All Saints and St Mary. In 1086, this Lincolnshire settlement was recorded six times as Wenflet, two in the Candleshoe Hundred of Lindsey South Riding, held by Gilbert of Ghent, having belonged to Ulf Fenman in 1066. Two more entries show Eudo, son of Spirewic as its Lord in 1086, having previously been in the possession of three Saxon men, Godric, Godwin and Toki de Burgh. Other parts of the manor estate were held by Jocelyn, son of Lambert and show its chief tenant as the Bishop of St Cuthbert's Church in Durham.

Wakefield

The first known documented reference to Wakefield occurs in the *Domesday Book*, where it is spelt Wachefeld and Wachefelt, from the Old English word 'wacu', referring to a wake or a festival, and 'feld' meaning 'field'. Hence, 'a field where festivals [or wakes], are held'.

Domesday records 'Wachefeld... in the demesne of King Edward, worth sixty pounds... now in the king's hand'. The survey listed nine berewicks, four villans, three priests, two churches, seven sokemen and sixteen bordars. In all, they possessed seven ploughs. It also recorded that there was a woodland measuring six by four leagues, valued at fifteen pounds.

Warter
This East Yorkshire village derives its placename from the Anglo-Saxon expression 'weargtrow', a term which translates as 'criminal tree'. The word 'wearg' meant 'criminal' or 'felon', and 'treow' was a tree. In common usage the expression specifically meant a gallows. The placename should therefore be interpreted as '[place with, or at the] gallows'. Domesday recorded the village as Wartre, a very small estate in the Warter Hundred of the East Riding, jointly held in 1086 by William de Percy and by King William.

Washington
Possibly the oldest record of this ancient County Durham placename occurred in 1112 in the Charter of Bishop Ranulf Flambard, when it was recorded as Wassyngtona, after an earlier Anglo-Saxon form, Hwaesingtun, itself derived from a man called Hwaesa (or Wassa), who may have been its founder or tribal chieftain. The 'ingas' element comes from the Old English, signifying the people or followers, and 'tona' (or 'tun') referring to an estate or settlement. Hence, 'the settlement (or estate) of the people of Wassa'. It should not be confused with the place of the same name in West Sussex.

Wharram-le-Street/Wharram Percy
The North Yorkshire village of Wharram-le-Street was recorded in 1086 simply as Warran in the Scard Hundred of the old East Riding of Yorkshire: the name came from the Old English 'hwer', meaning cauldrons or kettles, and translates loosely as '[place at] the kettles or cauldrons', possibly referring to a one-time local industry working copper. By the end of the thirteenth century, the settlement had divided into two estates and separate names emerged: Warram in the Strete, on account of its location on an ancient Roman road (from the Old English word 'straet'), and Wharrom Percy, which had come into the ownership of the de Percy family.

Whitby
Whitby was known to the native Brigantes tribes, before the arrival of the Romans, as Sinus Fari. It was later recorded in 1086 as 'Witeby... a Berewick in the land of Earl Hugh ... and William de Percy [holds it] of him'. The name comes either from the Old English 'hwit', meaning stone built, and the Old Norse suffix 'by', signifying a farmstead or village. An alternative view is that it comes from the personal name of a man called Hvitl. The latter would therefore translate as 'Hvitl's village'.

Woodmansey
This East Yorkshire village has been known since the late thirteenth century, when the placename was spelt Wodemanse. The first Old English element of the name, 'wudu-man', means exactly as it appears – woodman. The second, 'sae', indicates a pool. Hence, the placename might translate as '[the place at the] woodsman's pool'.

Yarm
The township of Yarm in North Yorkshire lies on a wide bend in the River Tees, a fact that is enshrined in its placename. It comes from the Old English word 'gearum' or 'gear', meaning 'dam' or 'weir', reflecting the ancient way that fish were caught in the region. The placename may be taken to mean '[place at the] fishing weirs'. Domesday referred to it as

the Manor of Iarun, and listed it in the North Riding Hundred of Allerton which was held by King William, having belonged to Hawarth of Stokesley before the Conquest.

York

York began as a small ancient Celtic settlement, known to them by the name Eborakon. Its exact meaning is contentious but there have emerged two possible translations – either as 'lands of a man called Eburos' or 'yew tree lands'. In 71, when the ninth Roman Legion arrived from Lincoln and set up their encampment, they named the place Eboracum. They ruled the city along with most of England for almost five hundred years. However, following Roman withdrawal from Britain in the fifth century, European migrants arrived, predominantly Anglo-Saxon and pagan Germanic tribes, who named the settlement Eoforwic. At that time it fell within the Northumbrian Kingdom of Deira.

Following numerous Danish incursions from Scandinavia, a Viking army led by Ivar the Boneless attacked the city in November 866 AD and took it into their possession, renaming it Jorvik. In order to stop the Danish advance, in 868 AD King Alfred made a truce with the Viking King Guthrum, a treaty whereby England was divided into the Anglo-Saxon southern kingdom and the northern and eastern territories that became known as Danelaw. In time, Danish settlers were absorbed into the native demographic, and by the time of the Norman Conquest of 1066, England was for the most part at peace. The *Domesday Book* recorded the placename as Euruic in 1086, in the possession of the Archbishop of York, Ulf Fenman and the Countess Godifu.

Yorkshire

An historic county in the north of England, based on the City of York, with the addition of the Old English word 'scir' (or the Old Scandinavian 'skyr'), meaning 'shire' or 'district'. The county is the largest in England and was formerly divided in three Ridings. Ridings (or 'thridings', meaning 'thirds', as the Vikings called them), were districts that were effectively counties in their own right. Before 1974, Yorkshire's three Ridings were North, East and West, of which only the East Riding remains.

Part Six

The North-West

Cheshire, Cumbria, Greater Manchester,
Lancashire, Merseyside, and Sefton

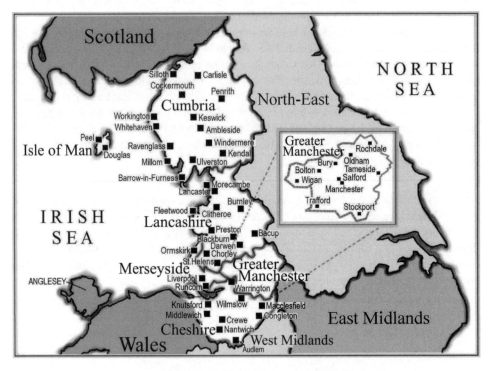

A map depicting the North-West region of England.

Accrington

Like many Lancashire towns, contemporary Accrington is a product of the Industrial Revolution, a time when it was transformed from a rural settlement into an industrial township where textile manufacture dominated the local economy. The name Accrington appears to be of Anglo-Saxon origin. In written records, from the twelfth century, it appears as Akarinton, Akerunton, Akerinton, Akerynton, Acrinton, Ackryngton and Acryngton. The placename may mean 'people of the acorn farmstead' from Anglo-Saxon 'aecern', meaning acorn, 'ingas' meaning the people or family, and 'tun', signifying a farmstead or village.

Aigburth

One interpretation of this Liverpudlian placename is from the Anglo-Saxon and translates as 'place of the oaks'. Other sources have it as referring to 'Aige's berth', the place where a Viking by the name of Aiges moored (or berthed) his boat. On balance, this latter explanation seems more likely, as Aigburth is located on the River Mersey. The variant spelling Aigburgh or Aighburgh sometimes occurs in old documents.

Ainstable
A Cumbrian village whose placename means '[place on a] slope where bracken grows'. The name comes directly from the Old Scandinavian word 'einstapi', which meant 'bracken' (or 'gorse') and 'hlilth', a slope. The name was recorded in around 1210 as Ainstapillith.

Ainsworth
This district in the Metropolitan Borough of Bury was named after a man called Aegen, who had an enclosure of some kind at this place – he may even have been personally responsible for the enclosing the land – we shall never know. The Old English word 'worth' referred to an enclosed plot or a paddock, before land enclosures and fenced-in land was commonplace. Hence, the placename means 'Aegen's enclosure'. In around 1200, the name was recorded as Haineswrthe.

Alderley Edge
Alderley Edge is an elegant, affluent village, with a history which dates back to the Bronze Age, with copper and lead mining taking place in the area since Roman times. At the time of the *Domesday Book*, Alderley Edge received two entries, as Aldredelic and Aldredelie: one as Over Alderley in the Hamestan Hundred held by William Malbank for Earl Hugh of Chester, and the other as Nether Alderley, held in 1086 by Bigod de les Loges. Several explanations of the placename derivation exist, but the most likely is that it originated from Aldred or Althryth, a woman's name, and 'leah', meaning 'Aldred's woodland clearing'. In the nineteenth century, the 'Edge' was added, reflecting the steep escarpment on which the township is located.

Aldford
Aldford means 'old ford' is an ancient township in the old Broxton Hundred which included part of the villages of Churton by Aldford and Edgerley, whose local church registers date back to 1639. The village gets its name from the river crossing over the River Dee. In the twelfth century, Robert de Aldford built the castle and, some time around the turn of the century, Richard de Aldford became Earl of Chester.

Aldingham
The Cheshire village of Aldingham is mentioned in the *Domesday Book* as belonging to a local man named Ernulf (or Alda), plus the Old English word 'ingas', meaning 'followers or family' and 'ham', signifying a settlement or homestead. Hence, the 'homestead of the family or followers of Alda'.

Allerton
Allerton appears in the *Domesday Book* as Alretune, though the current spelling has existed since the early fourteenth century. Its origins are two Anglo-Saxon words; 'alr', meaning 'alder' (the tree), and 'tun', signifying a village or enclosure where alder trees grew, testament to the rural nature of the original settlement.

Allithwaite
The name of this Cumbrian village illustrates the spread of Danish settlers and culture across the north of England, as it is made up entirely of Norse words. The first part is derived

from a Danish man called Eilifr, and 'thveit', the Old Scandinavian word for a clearing. Apparently, Eilifr made a woodland clearing, probably some time in the eighth or ninth centuries, and it has hereafter borne both his name and evidence of his land acquisition. The placename means 'Eilifr's clearing' and it was recorded as Hailiuethait by the end of the twelfth century.

Altrincham
Pronounced Alt-ring-ham (not Alt-rinch-ham), it is the Greater Manchester Borough of Trafford's charter town, whose placename first appears as Aldringeham, probably meaning 'homestead of Aldhere's people'. This is based on three Old English word elements: 'Aldhere', the probable name of its founder or earliest settler, 'ingas', meaning 'people, followers or family', and 'ham', a homestead or settlement. As recently as the nineteenth century it was being spelt both Altrincham and Altringham.

Ambleside
Located at the northern extremity of Lake Windermere, the town's name is derived from the Old Norse 'A-mel-saetr' which literally translates as 'river – sandbank – summer pasture'. Just south of Ambleside is the Roman fort of Galava, dating from around 79 and built to guard the road to the port at Ravenglass and defend the lower fells of South Lakeland from invasion by the Picts and Scots.

Anfield
Once common pasture land in the Walton on the Hill district of Liverpool, the Anfield placename is a corruption of the words 'hang field' or 'the hanging field', in reference to the steep sloping or 'hanging' characteristics of the local farmland terrain and not, as many might suppose, in reference to a place of public execution. In 1810, the area was advertised for sale as 'Hanging-fields behind Everton'. The name was also frequently written as Hongfield or Honghfield.

Anthorn
This Cumbrian hamlet derives its placename from the Danes as it is comprised of two Old Scandinavian word elements: 'einn', meaning 'one' and 'thorn', as the word implies, a thorn or a thorn bush. The placename means '[place by or near a] solitary thorn bush'. It was recorded as Eynthorn in 1279, and has a similar derivation to Aintree in Merseyside.

Arkholme
The Lancashire village of Arkholme's placename comes from the Old Scandinavian word 'ergum', and bears witness to Danish incursions and eventual settlements in northern England. In Norse, the word 'erg' meant 'hill pasture' or 'shieling', (that is, as animal shelter on a hill), and 'holmr' signified an island, (often higher ground surrounded by wetland or marsh). Hence, the placename means '[place on a] higher ground hill pasture'. The *Domesday Book* had an entry for Ergune, listed in the Amounderness Hundred, part of the North Lancashire area of Yorkshire at that time, held by King William, and having belonged to Earl Tostig before the Conquest.

Ardwick
The name of Ardwick is thought to have been derived from two old Saxon words: 'Ard', the abbreviated form of King Aethelred's name, and 'wic', a word for a specialised farm, a dairy or small hamlet. Therefore, Ardwick's placename translates from old Saxon as something like 'the dairy farm [or hamlet] of Aethelred'.

Armathwaite

This village in Cumbria lies on the River Eden and derives its placename from two sources, bearing witness to the influence of the Danes in northern England. The first element of the name comes from the Middle English 'ermite', meaning 'hermit', and the second from Old Norse word 'thveit', signifying a woodland clearing. The placename might therefore be interpreted as 'a hermit's [place in a] clearing'. Armathwaite was historically a chapelry in Hesket-in-the-Forest parish and the site of a Benedictine nunnery, built and endowed by William II (also known as William Rufus). The place was known in 1212 as Ermitethwaite.

Ashton Hayes

Ashton is a very popular placename in England, with at least a dozen other townships sharing it in common, but usually differentiated by other appended descriptions (like Ashton-under-Lyne, or Ashton upon Mersey, or some other topographical element). Ashton Hayes is a rural Cheshire village, originally in Tarvin Parish, in the Eddisbury Hundred. The Ashton element translates directly from Old English as 'settlement (or township) where ash trees grow'. The addition of the 'Hayes' element remains obscure, although it may have been named after the mansion of that name built by the Worthington family in 1780. The township recently changed its name from simply being called Ashton, owing to the many other Ashtons in England and residents' annoyance at frequently misdirected postal mail.

Ashton-under-Lyne

Opinions differ regarding the derivation of the name of Ashton-under-Lyne. The Ashton part is in itself straightforward and is derived from the Old English words 'aesc' and 'tun', together signifying a 'settlement surrounded by ash trees'. In 1160, the place was recorded as Haistune. However, the 'under-Lyne' part is most contentious. It possibly refers to the old boundary line (the 'Lyne'), between Cheshire and Lancashire which ran through the township. Another possibility is the Forest of Lyme (Lyme Park), which once covered the area, of which it may be a corruption. The 'under-Lyne' suffix was only attached to the town name in the mid-nineteenth century, to distinguish it from the nearby town of Ashton-in-Makerfield.

Aspatria

This Cumbrian township derives its placename from the Celtic Saint Patrick, and the Old Scandinavian affix 'askr', meaning 'ash tree'. Hence the placename translates as 'ash tree of St Patrick'. It was recorded around 1160 as Aspatric.

Aspull

The earliest record of Aspull is that contained in a survey of 1212, when, called simply 'One Plough-land', it formed part of the Childwall fee held by Richard, son of Robert de Lathom, under the Lordship of Manchester. The name comes from the Old English words 'aespe', referring to the aspen tree, and 'hyll', a hill. Hence 'hill where aspen trees grow'.

Astbury

A small picturesque Cheshire village located a few miles south of Congleton, Astbury was probably an important place before the Norman Conquest. Its name means 'eastern borough' or 'east defence'. Thus, the village was probably part of an outer defence network for the nearby town of Sandbach. The medieval Parish of Congleton comprised the townships of Buglawton, Congleton, Davenport, Eaton, Hulme Walfield, Moreton cum Alcumlow, Newbold Astbury, Odd Rode, Smallwood, Somerford and Somerford Booths.

Atherton

There are several possible explanations for Atherton's name, and none seem to be definitive. It may have been named after its possible founder, a man called Aethhere, or from the alder trees which grew there in great numbers, or perhaps from the Old English word 'adder', or 'elder', meaning chief, or else from the many small streams (or 'athers'), which run through it. So, the placename means either 'Aethelhere's farmstead', 'farmstead where alder trees are found', 'farmstead of the elders', or 'farmstead [surrounded by] small steams'. Take your pick.

Audenshaw

The origin of Audenshaw is probably from a Saxon personal name, Aldwine, a man who may once have owned the land. Evidence for the existence of Aldwine's shaw ('shaw' = a small copse or wood), dates from twelfth century records. Originally part of Ashton Parish, it became a separate Urban District in 1894, when it was still described as 'a pleasant and beautiful hamlet, lying in a wooded glen'.

Audlem

A small village, once in the old Warmundestrou Hundred, Audlem was recorded in the *Domesday Book* as Aldelime, held by Richard de Vernon, though it had been owned by Osmaer before the Norman Conquest. The placename probably translates as 'old lime', though it has also been suggested that it may have referred to a man called Alda who owned a lime tree in the settlement.

Bacup

Bacup is in the Borough of Rossendale on the boundaries of Lancashire and Yorkshire. The placename is derived from the Old English 'fulbaechop', comprising the words 'ful' meaning 'foul' or 'muddy', 'beac', a ridge and 'hop' a valley. The place was known around 1200 as Fulebachope, eventually, the prefix 'ful' was dropped and 'baechop' remained, possibly meaning 'ridge valley' or 'back valley', referring to its position in the Irwell Valley. The *Dictionary of British Placenames* translates the original placename as 'muddy valley by a ridge'

Bamber Bridge

Bamber Bridge was established when a bridge was constructed over the River Lostock in Lancashire in medieval times, and the place became known as Bymbrig. The name comes from two Saxon words, 'beam', which referred to a tree trunk or a timber beam, and 'brycg', a bridge. The bridge in question would have been a simple heavy wooden structure, and the placename means '[place near a] bridge made of tree trunks'.

Bardsea

Bardsea is located in the Low Furness area of Cumbria, two miles to the south-west of Ulverston, and was probably named from a person called Beornard or Bernhard. It was one of the townships forming the Norman Manor of Hougun held by Earl Tostig Godwinson, the half brother of King Harold; he held the whole of Lancashire north of the Ribble, and what was once part of the medieval Manor of Muchland. Known at the time of the Domesday survey as 'Berretseige ... in the land of the king in Yorkshire', it comprised just four carucates of land. By 1246, it was known as Berdesey, one of the manors of Hougun and of the de Bardsey family. According to some, the 'sea' component may suggest that it was in an area of coastal flooding and at one time a virtual island. The suffix 'sea', 'ey' or 'sey' is common in Scandinavian placenames and suggests a Nordic influence. Alternatively, Bardsea's origins may be related to its proximity to Birkrigg and its druid's circle; the 'bard' element of the placename suggests a druidic tradition, as does its possible derivation from 'berth-sig', an Old English name for a 'place of thickets'.

Barrow-in-Furness
By 1190, Barrow was originally that of an island known as Barrai, later renamed Old Barrow. It has had several variants over the years, including Oldebarrey in 1537, Old Barrow Insula and Barrohead in 1577. The former island was joined to the Barrow and Furness Peninsula and the town took its final name. The name synthesises the old Celtic British word 'barro' and Old Norse to mean 'an island with a promontory'. Although Barrow was not named as such in the *Domesday Book*, settlements like Hietun, Rosse and Hougenai (now Hawcoat, Roose and Walney), which are districts within the township, were recorded in the survey.

Bashall Eaves
At the time of the Great Survey of 1086, this small Lancashire hamlet was known simply as Bacschelf, a name derived from Anglo-Saxon times when 'baec' meant 'ridge' and 'scelf' referred to a shelf or a ledge. At that time the placename meant 'ridge by [or on] a shelf'. The second word of the placename, 'Eaves', comes from the Old English word 'efes', meaning 'edge', in this case the edge of a wood, (possibly the Forest of Bowland). The survey listed the place in the Craven Hundred of the West Riding of Yorkshire at that time, held by Roger de Poitou. Before the Conquest it had been a possession of Earl Tostig.

Bassenthwaite
Bassenthwaite is a village and civil parish in the Borough of Allerdale in Cumbria. It is an Old English name derived from the personal name Beabstan or Bastun, and from the Old Norwegian word 'thveit', a clearing. Hence, in modern English, 'Bastun's clearing'. Other variants of the name have existed over time, including Bastenethwait in 1208, Bastuntwait in 1274, and Bastenthwayt in 1358. Bassenthwaite Lake, earlier known as 'Bastun's Water', is named after the village. Technically, Bassenthwaite is the only lake in the National Park – all the others are, more properly, 'meres' and 'waters'.

Beckfoot
The hamlet of Beckfoot is in the civil parish of Holme St Cuthbert in Cumbria. The placename is derived from the Old Norse 'bekkr-futr', meaning 'the mouth of a stream'. A 'beck' is a local word for a stream in the Cumbrian dialect and the watercourse gives the settlement its name. Early names and spellings were simply Beck or Beckfoote.

Beeston
Beeston is known as a major surviving castle township, standing as it does on a sheer rocky outcrop overlooking the Cheshire Plain. It has a long history and began life as a Bronze Age hill fort. At the time of Domesday, it was recorded as Buistane, from the Old English words 'byge' and 'stan', signifying a stone or rock where commerce takes place.

Berrier
In 1166, this Cumbrian hamlet was recorded as Berghgerge, a name derived from the Old Scandinavian words 'berg', meaning 'hill', and 'erg', a pasture, shieling or animal shelter. The placename may therefore be interpreted as 'shieling on a hill'.

Beswick
Beswick is a small district located on the east side of the city and was incorporated into Manchester in 1838. Pronounced 'Bez-ick' (the 'w' is silent). Before 1066, it was

called Beaces Hlaw, with 'hlaw' being an old word for a small hill, often used as a burial mound. By the thirteenth century the placename had changed to Beaces Wic, indicating that the area was predominantly farm land. Who or what the 'Bes' element of the placename signified is open to interpretation, though the simplest and most plausible is that it belonged to a person called Bes or Bess.

Bickley Moss

Any English placename incorporating the word 'moss' invariably referred to a marshy place or a peat bog, as the word 'mos' meant exactly that in Old English. Similarly, the word 'bica' indicated a pointed hill or peak, and 'leah' meant a woodland clearing. The placename of this Cheshire village therefore translates as 'woodland clearing by a pointed hill near a peat bog'. The village was entered in the *Domesday Book* as Bichelei (the 'Moss' element having been added much later). It was listed within the Duddeston Hundred, held in 1086 by Robert FitzHugh having belonged to a man simply called Woodman in 1066.

Bickerstaffe

Bickerstaffe is a township located about three and a half miles south-east of Ormskirk in Lancashire. The placename may come from Anglo-Saxon 'bicera' or 'beocera stæth', meaning 'the beekeeper's landing place'. Other sources take an alternative view and maintain that the 'Bicker' element comes from the Old Norse 'by-kiarr', meaning bywater or village marsh. This last interpretation might therefore translate as '[the place by a] marshy village'.

Billinge and Winstanley

Formerly part of St Helens in Merseyside, in 1974 the Billinge Higher End ward and most of Winstanley ward became part of the Metropolitan Borough of Wigan. Billinge may mean the 'place of the people [who live] at the pointed hill', from the Old English 'billa', meaning 'ridge', and 'ingas', signifying 'the people or family '. The name was recorded as Bylnge in 1252.

Winstanley was named from the Old English personal name of an Anglo-Saxon settler called Wynnstan. This is itself composed of two elements, 'wynn', meaning joy or joyful, and 'stan', a stone. The precise nature of this conjunction is uncertain. Added to this is the suffix 'leah', indicating a woodland or forest clearing. Hence, 'Wynnstan's clearing'.

Birkenhead

Birkenhead is an ancient township in the Bidston Parish of the old Wirral Hundred. One of its earliest records dates from around 1150, when a priory was established on the west bank of the Mersey. In 1220, it was known as Bircheveth, derived from the Old English word 'bircen', meaning birch trees, and the Old Norse word 'heafod', signifying a headland or promontory. Hence, 'headland where birch trees grow'. By 1260, it had been recorded as Birkheued.

Blackburn

St Mary's Church in Blackburn is known to have existed since 596 AD. The name of the township dates from the Dark Ages, after a local stream known for centuries as 'Blakewater'. Situated as it is in a strategic position on the old Roman road from Manchester to Ribchester, it was an important stopover during Saxon and Viking times. Blackburn appears in the Domesday survey as Blacheborne. The origins of the name are possibly a combination of an Old English word 'bleac', together with 'burna', a stream, and almost certainly the placename means 'black(dark or bleak) stream'.

Blackley

Blackley (pronounced Blake-lee, and not Black-lee as outsiders understandably, though mistakenly, call it), comes from the Old English words 'blaek', meaning black or dark, and 'leah', a woodland clearing. Hence the name might mean 'clearing in a dark wood'. This is borne out by the fact that in medieval times the area was dense woodland, populated by deer and wolves, which made it a local hunting venue. Boggart Hole Clough and the River Irk which runs through it, were popular spots for catching eels or hunting rabbits.

Blackrod

This village is set on a hill due west of Bolton in central Lancashire. It is a small, predominantly residential township, overlooking open countryside with views across to Rivington Pike and the West Pennine Moors. The name probably comes from two Old English words, 'blaec' (or 'blaek'), meaning bleak, dark or black, and 'rod', another name for a clearing in a forest. This might refer to the fact that it was once part of the Forest of Horwich, which was subsequently cleared to create the Blackrod township. In 1201, the place was known as Blakerode.

Blencogo

On the face of it, an odd-sounding place, but the name of this Cumbrian village means '[place near the] summit where cuckoos are heard'. It is thought to come from the Celtic word 'blain', which is similar to the modern Welsh word 'blaen', meaning 'point' and 'cogau' (or 'cogow'), referring to cuckoos.

Bollington

A township in Prestbury Parish, in the Macclesfield Hundred, Bollington is a stone-built mill town of great character, lying south-east of Wilmslow near Macclesfield. The placename is straightforward, signifying a 'township or settlement of the people who live on (or beside) the River Bollin'. It was known as Bolinton in 1222, and as Bolynton by 1270.

Bolton

The Bolton coat of arms shows an arrow or 'bolt' through a crown, which local tradition has it referring to the key role which Bolton archers are said to have played in the defeat of the Scots at Flodden in 1513, and a possible explanation of the placename. The Crown itself represents the wooden stockade which surrounded the Saxon village, known as a 'tun', indicating a farmstead. Hence, 'bolt-tun'. However, as the township was named more than 450 years before Flodden, it seems more likely that the name derives from the Old English word 'bothl', which referred to a special building of some kind. Hence, 'settlement with a special building'. What that building might have been is unknown. In 1086, the *Domesday Book* recorded the place as Bodeltun.

Bootle

There are two places of this name in the north-west of England. Bootle is a Cumbrian township located a few miles south of Ravenglass, and a second was formerly a Lancashire township, but since 1974 boundary changes it has been in Sefton, Merseyside. There are two possible explanations of the derivation of this placename: either from an Old English word 'botl', meaning a building or a dwelling house, or simply after a person named Bota – opinions differ as to which is most likely. The former Lancashire township was recorded as Boltelai in the *Domesday Book* and by 1212 had become Botle. Other fourteenth century spellings include Botull, Bothull and Bothell. In the eighteenth century, it was known as Bootle cum Linacre.

Bosley

A Cheshire village whose placename means 'Bosa's (or Bot's) woodland clearing'. The name derives from a man's personal name plus the Old English 'leah', indicating a clearing or glade in a wood or forest. The Domesday entry for what it called Boselega, in the Hundred of Hamestan, had belonged to Godric of Lawton before the Conquest and valued at just one pound; in 1086, it was listed as held by Earl Hugh of Chester as Lord of the Manor and described as 'waste', and thereby worth nothing of value.

Bostock

The Cheshire village of Bostock derived its name from the Anglo-Saxon words 'Bota', which was probably a man's personal name, and the suffix 'stocc', (or 'stoche'), which usually indicated a special council meeting place of religious site. The placename may therefore be loosely translated as 'meeting place on Bota's land', or something along those lines. The village was entered in the *Domesday Book* as Botestoche, in the Middlewich Hundred, granted by King William to Richard de Vernon, it having been held by Osmaer of Shipbrook before 1066. The survey commissioners assessed the estate lands as 'wasta'.

Bowdon

One explanation of the placename is that it may be derived from two Saxon words, 'bode', meaning a dwelling, as in 'abode', and 'don' or 'dun', indicating a plain on a rise or down, which exactly describes its location on a sandstone edge. Another interpretation of the placename has it coming from the Anglo-Saxon 'boga-dun'. meaning a bow or brow, and a hill, and possibly signifying a bowed or curved hill. The Domesday survey records it as Bogadone, in the Bucklow Hundred, held by Hamo de Masci (sometimes 'Massy' or Massey), the first baron of Dunham Massey. Before the Conquest, it had belonged to a Saxon freeman called Alweard. It recorded one hide of land paying rent, of sufficient area for two ploughs, as well as 'a Frenchman having one plough'. There was already a mill and St Mary's Church with a priest, who owned half a hide for his own support and maintenance.

Bowness

Bowness-on-Windermere, now located within the Lake District National Park of Cumbria, was formerly in the old traditional county of Westmorland before boundary changes in 1974. One possible explanation is that the placename is derived from Old Norse words 'bogi' and 'nes', signifying a bow-shaped promontory. Another has it that Bowness (originally known as Bulnes), means 'the headland where bulls graze', from the Old English 'bula', and 'naess', signifying a headland, or perhaps referring to the keeping of a bull in the parish. The 'on-Windermere' element was added later, sometime around 1899.

Bradford

The placename of the suburb of Bradford, (in common with the City of Bradford in Yorkshire), was originally thought to have been Broad Ford, referring to a river crossing. In this particular case a ford over the River Medlock in Manchester. In medieval times the district was a place of pastures, streams and woodland, inhabited by deer and significant numbers of bees who added their honey to the local economy. It was reported that at one time wolves and eagles lived within its woodlands.

Bramhall

Domesday recorded this township, which now lies within the Metropolitan Borough of Stockport, as Bramale. Before the Conquest, the 'Mainou of Bramale' had belonged to two Saxon free men called Burn and Hacun, and there is an opinion that the placename may be a corruption of their combined names. However, a much more likely explanation is that it derives from the Old English 'brom', indicating a broom tree or shrub, and 'hahl', referring to a corner or nook of land. The translation of the placename may therefore be '[the] corner (or nook) of land where the broom tree grows'.

Bredbury
Bredbury is a village in the Metropolitan Borough of Stockport whose placename means 'fortified place made of planks'. The Old English affix 'burh' was applied to many such settlements that had been fortified in the tenth century against the ever-present threat of Danish incursions. The first element of the name comes from 'bred', which meant 'plank' or 'board', and was often used to describe wooden bridges. Domesday recorded the village as Bretberie and listed it in the Hamestan Hundred, then lying within the County of Cheshire, held in 1086 by Richard de Vernon, it having belonged to a Saxon called Wulfric before the Conquest.

Breightmet
The former township of Breightmet lies between Bradshaw and Blackshaw Brooks on the West Pennine Moors above Bolton. Its unusual name (impossible for any outsider to pronounce properly), is thought to be Saxon, and meaning a 'bright meadow'. Over the years there have been many different spellings of the placename, including Brihtmede, Brightemete, Breghmete, Brithmete and Brightmede. Pronunciation varies too. Some say 'Bright-met', others 'Brate-met', 'Break-met' or 'Brete-met'. Even locals disagree. There is a suggestion that Breightmet Hill may have at one time been a site for a fire beacon and therefore 'Bright-met' would seem to be the most likely correct pronunciation.

Brigsteer
The Cumbrian village of Brigsteer in the Civil Parish of Helsington derives its placename from the Old English word 'byricg', or the Old Scandinavian 'bryggja', both referring to a bridge. As for the second element of the placename, opinions differ. Some have it derived from the Stere family who may have occupied the estate at some time in its past, while others cite the Old English word 'steor', meaning 'steer' or 'bullock'. Hence, the placename might mean either '[place at the] bridge belonging to the Stere family', or 'bridge used by bullocks', what today we might call a cattle bridge. In the early thirteenth century the place was recorded a Brigstere.

Brindle
This Lancashire village gets its name from a combination of two Old English words, 'burna', meaning 'stream' or 'brook', and 'hyll', a hill. Hence, '[place at a] hill by a stream'. The stream in question would have been Lostock Brook. In 1206 the place was known as Burnhull.

Brinscall
The Lancashire village has a placename that is contentious. One argument has it meaning '[place by the] burnt huts', a name derived from the Middle English word 'brende', meaning 'burnt', and the Old Norse word 'skali', which referred to a hut, a shieling or an animal shelter, though the significance of the 'burnt' element is somewhat obscure. The village was known as Withinhull around 1160 and as Withinhulle in the Subsidy Rolls of Lancashire in 1332, which produces an alternative meaning of 'a hill where willow trees grow', which would seem to be a more likely proposition. The place was recorded as Brendescoles in around 1200.

Broxton
The name of this Cheshire village has a macabre origin in that the first part of the name may come from an Anglo-Saxon word, 'burgaesn', referring to a burial place or a graveyard. The second part comes from 'tun' meaning 'farmstead' or 'village'. Hence, 'village near a burial place'. In 1086, the name was recorded as Brosse, and listed in the Deddeston Hundred, held at that time by Robert FitzHugh, it having previously belonged to two Saxons called Brictmer and Raven in 1066. By the thirteenth century, the name was being recorded as Brexin and Broxun.

Bunbury
This small Cheshire village placename contains two Anglo-Saxon elements; first, probably the name of an early settler or founder called Buna, and second, the Old English suffix 'burh', indicating a stronghold or fortified place. Hence, 'Buna's stronghold'. The *Domesday Book* records it as Boleberie in the Rushton Hundred held in 1086 by Robert, son of Hugh d'Avranches, having belonged to Dedol of Tiverton before the Norman Conquest. By the twelfth century it had been recorded as Bonebury.

Burleydam
The 'bur' element of this Cheshire village placename is an Old English word meaning 'peasant'; the 'leah' element indicated a woodland glade or clearing, and the Middle English word 'damme' was added later, referring to an old mill race, or a dam that once existed there. In around 1130 the place had been recorded as Burley, and in 1643 in its present form as Burleydam. Hence, the village name means 'woodland clearing with a dam belonging to peasants'.

Burnage
This Manchester district placename is probably a corruption of 'brown hedge', from the old brown stone walls or 'hedges' which were common in medieval times. Burnage Lane still marks the path of the old road south to Cheshire.

Burnley
Burnley probably existed as a small hamlet as early as 800, but not until 1122 is it first officially mentioned, in a charter by which Hugh de la Val granted the church of St Peters to the monks at Pontefract Priory. The placename is believed to have been derived from 'brun lea', meaning 'meadow or woodland clearing by the River Brun'. Various other recorded spellings have existed over the years, including Bronley, Brunley and Bumleye.

Burscough
This Lancashire village placename bears witness to the advances made by Danish invasions of England in the eighth and ninth centuries in that it contains both Anglo-Saxon and Norse elements. The first is derived from the Old English 'burh', indicating a fortified place, and the second comes from the Old Scandinavian word 'skogr', meaning woodland or forest. Hence, taken together, they mean 'fort in [or by] a wood'. An early example of the name appeared in a late-twelfth century written form as Burscogh.

Bury
The name Bury was known earlier as Byrig, and later as Buri or Byri and comes from a Saxon word meaning a fortress or stronghold. In ancient times, the area was covered in woodland, marsh and moorland, and inhabited by nomadic herdsmen. The placename reflects the many 'burhs' and settlements fortified by King Alfred in the ninth century as a defence against Danish incursions. Several places share this name and others include

variations of 'bury', 'burg' or 'borough' elements as distinguishing prefixes or suffixes in their placenames, the likes of Bury in Cambridgeshire, Bury in West Sussex, Bury St Edmunds, Burscough in Lancashire, Bunbury in Cheshire, and many more.

Capenhurst
The village of Capenhurst on the Wirral Peninsular of Cheshire, gets its name from Saxon times when 'cape' meant 'lookout place' and 'hyrst' referred to a wooded hillside. In 1086, the *Domesday Book* listed the village as Capeles, a small estate in the Willaston Hundred, supporting three households and held by William FitzNigel, it having belonged to Arni of Neston before the Conquest.

Carlisle
A major city in north Cumbria, the name probably comes from a synthesis of the Old English 'Cair Luel' or the Welsh 'Caer Liwelydd' or may have been originally derived from the Latin 'Luguvalium', meaning 'fort of the God Lugus'. Historically in the old county of Cumberland, it was an early Roman settlement, established to serve the forts on nearby Hadrian's Wall. Archaeological excavations have revealed that Carlisle Castle was built on the site of a Roman timber fortress. In 1106, the town was known as Carleol.

Carnforth
Carnforth was originally settled by invading Danes and as a result, like many local placenames, it suggests a Scandinavian origin. It was once a main crossing over the River Keer, which some believe probably gave the town its name, over time corrupted from 'Keer-ford'. Another view is that the placename derives from the Old English words 'cran', meaning a crane or heron, and 'ford', a shallow river crossing. Hence, this interpretation might be 'a ford frequented by cranes or herons'.

Carrington
There are several possible derivations of the name Carrington - all from Old English. In the twelfth century, Carrington was known as Carrintona. The name may mean an 'estate associated with a man called Cara'. Alternatively, the first part of the name may be derived from 'caring', meaning 'tending or herding' or 'cring', which means 'river bend', so either 'place associated with herding', or 'settlement by a river bend'.

Cartmel
The South Lakeland village of Cartmel stands on a high sandbank overlooking Morecambe Bay, which gives a clue to the placename. It means 'sandbank by the rough stony ground'. The name is from the Old Norse word 'kartr', meaning 'stony ground' and 'meir', a sandbank. The name had emerged in its present-day form by the twelfth century.

Chadderton
The placename Chadderton, known as Chatterton in medieval times, is almost certainly derived from the Celtic 'cader' or 'cater', meaning 'a fortified place in the hills', with the Anglo-Saxon suffix 'tun' attached to indicate a settlement. The first record of the name dates from 1212, when Chadderton was under the control of the Asshetons, Chethams, Radclyffes and the de Traffords.

Chapel-en-le-Frith
When a chapel dedicated to the martyred St Thomas Becket was built in this Derbyshire township in the thirteenth century, the placename of Capella de la Frith was adopted. It comes from the Middle English word 'chapele' and the Old English word 'fyrhth', one of

several used by the Saxons for a woodland. The 'en le' element (meaning 'in the'), signifies the influence of Norman French on the development of the English language. The placename means 'chapel in the woodland'.

Cheadle/Cheadle Hulme

Cheadle in Greater Manchester (formerly in Cheshire) is really two words combined. Originally in Celtic it was 'ced legh'. The 'ced' element (pronounced 'ched'), meant 'wood', as did the 'legh' part, an Old English term added later. Therefore, technically the town name means 'wood wood'. By the time of Domesday, it was known as Cedde, in Hamestan Hundred, held by Gamal, a Saxon, for Earl de Gouville. Gamal's father had previously held it as a freeman. The whole manor was two leagues long and one league wide and contained woodland, an enclosure and a hawk's eyrie, as well as one acre of meadow. It was valued at ten shillings. By 1165, it had become known as Chedle.

Cheadle Hulme was known as Cheadle Moseley until the twentieth century. The word 'hulme' is derived from an old Danish word 'hulm' meaning 'island in the fen or water-meadow', therefore the whole placename might be reasonably defined as meaning 'a water meadow belonging to the town of Cheadle'. Alternatively, the name Cheadle may have been derived from the name of the Anglo-Saxon St Chad.

Chelford

There are two possible explanations for the meaning of the Chelford placename: one has it derived from a man called Ceola, whose river crossing it was; the other cites the Old English word 'ceole', meaning 'throat', but in this instance might represent a narrow gorge or channel. The place was recorded in the *Domesday Book* as Celeford in the Hamestan Hundred of Cheshire whose Lord of the Manor at that time was Earl Hugh of Chester. Before the Conquest, land for two ploughs in the estate had belonged to a man called Brun of Siddington. In 1086, it was assessed as waste ('wasta').

Cheshire

The name of this county in North-West England is based on the City of Chester, with the Old English affix 'scir', meaning 'district' or 'shire'. It appeared in the *Domesday Book* as Cestre Scire.

Chester

Chester was called Deva (or Deoua) around 150, after the river on which it stood (the River Dee). The Romans had another name for the place – they called it *Civitas Legionum*, which means 'city of the legion(s)'. By 735, the Saxons were referring to the place as Legacaestr, and by 1086, Domesday simply recorded the place as Cestre or Caestre, in reference to the remains of the Roman fort (or 'castle') that remained.

Chorley

Records show Chorley has held a market since 1498, which was the source of its early growth and prosperity. The placename comes from two Anglo-Saxon words, 'ceorl' and 'leah', a common placename element, signifying a clearing in a woodland. The word 'ceorl' refers to a person's status, usually a peasant, a freeman or a yeoman. Therefore, the placename probably means 'the peasant's clearing'.

Chorlton-cum-Hardy

Chorlton-cum-Hardy is derived from the old Saxon name Coerlatun-cum-Ard-Eea, meaning 'the dwelling [or township] of the coerls by trees and near water'. The Saxon word 'coerl', sometimes spelt 'churl' or 'chorl' represented a peasant or a freeman.

Church Minshull

It goes without saying that the many English townships and villages that include the word 'church' in their placename were invariably established around a religious building of some kind, and Church Minshull is stereotypical. The Minshull part of the placename is derived from a man called Monn and the Old English word 'scelf', meaning 'shelf', describing the topography of the village which is located on a broad shelf. Hence, the name means 'Monn's shelf near the church'. Domesday recorded the place as Maneshale in 1086, listed in the Middlewich Hundred and held by William Malbank, having belonged to two Saxons called Arngrim and Deorc before the Conquest. In the thirteenth century, part of the manor came into the possession of the de Vernon family and took the name Minshull Vernon, distinguishing it from the original part which was thereafter recorded as Chirchmunsulf.

Clitheroe

Clitheroe is an ancient market township in the Parish of Whalley within the ancient Blackburnshire Hundred. The placename is thought to come from the Anglo-Saxon words 'clider', meaning loose rocks or stones, and 'hoh', a hill. Hence, '[place at] the hill with loose stones', or more simply 'rocky hill'. Over time, the township's name has been variously spelt Clyderhow and Cletherwoode.

Cockermouth

Located at the confluence of the River Cocker and the River Derwent, this Cumbrian town is frequently listed among Britain's most unusual placenames, but Cockermouth, simply means 'the mouth of the River Cocker'. The river after which the town is named comes from the Celtic word 'kukra', meaning 'the crooked one', plus 'mutha', meaning mouth or estuary. It appears simply as Cocur in a document of 930, and by 1150 was known as Cokyrmoth.

Collyhurst

The name Collyhurst originally meant 'wooded hill' in Old English. This Manchester district placename appears in records as grazing or pasture land at the time of the Norman Conquest. The hill in question is actually largely made up of red sandstone – hence the area known as Red Bank.

Congleton

It is recorded that Godwine, Earl of Wessex, held Congleton in Saxon times. The township is listed in the *Domesday Book* as Cogeltone, in Middlewich Hundred, held by Bigod in 1086. Despite its land and woodland, it was rated as 'wasta' at that time, having no real value for taxation purposes. The next recorded reference was in 1282 as Congelton. The 'Congle' element could relate to the old Norse 'kang', or 'kung', meaning a bend or a hill, followed by the Old English 'tun', meaning farmstead or settlement. Hence, possibly, 'farmstead on the bend of a hill'. The town's origins date back to the Stone Age, with remains of a stone chambered tomb, known locally as the 'Bridestones', unearthed on the road to Leek. Bronze Age artefacts have also been found in the area.

Coniston

A civil parish in the Furness region of Cumbria which was historically part of Lancashire, until the mid-twelfth century, the place was spelt Coningeston. This almost certainly originated from the Scandinavian word 'kong' or 'konungr', meaning king, and the Old English 'tun', signifying a township or settlement. Hence, 'the king's town or estate'.

Crawshawbooth

This Lancashire village clearly had a strong medieval preoccupation with cows and crows, as the name implies. The Old English word 'crawe' meant 'crow' or 'crows', 'sceaga' was one of several words the Saxons had for a wood or woodland (in this case something like a copse), and the 'both' was Old Scandinavian for a cow house or herdsman's hut, or what in modern English we might call a 'booth'. The name translates in its totality as '[place by the] copse where crows are seen with cows'. The placename was recorded in 1324 as Crowehagh, and by the early sixteenth century had become Crawshaboth.

Crewe

The former Borough of Crewe and Nantwich played an important role in the development of Cheshire's industrial revolution. The placename Creu first appears in the *Domesday Book*, in Warmundestrou Hundred held by Richard de Vernon, having been previously owned by Osmaer, a Saxon. At the time of Edward the Confessor, it was worth ten shillings, but in 1086 valued as 'waste' worth just five shillings. The placename is probably derived from an even older Welsh word 'criu', meaning 'weir'.

Croxteth

A suburb of the City of Liverpool, the placename is believed to derive from an Old Norse contraction of 'Crocker's staithe', meaning 'the landing place of Crocker', a reference to a ninth century Viking who made a landing on the River Alt during the invasion of Britain from Ireland.

Crumpsall

Crumpsall derives its placename from Old English and means a 'crooked piece of land beside a river'. The original village of Crumpsall Green actually does lie on an oxbow bend in the River Irk and originally formed part of Blackley Forest. This valley often flooded and the resultant marshland was notoriously difficult to farm. It was known in the thirteenth century as Curmisole and two centuries later as Cromshall.

Culcheth

The township of Culcheth, part of Warrington in Cheshire, has a placename that means '[place near a] narrow wood'. It is a very old name, probably Celtic in origin and related to the Welsh words 'cul', meaning 'narrow', and 'coed', a wood or woodland. By the beginning of the thirteenth century the place had been recorded as Culchet.

Cumbria

Before 1974, the County of Cumbria was made up of two counties, Westmorland (meaning 'western moorland'), and Cumberland ('land of the Cymry'). Both of the names 'Cumberland' and 'Cumbria' are derived from the Welsh name for Wales. The two former counties were combined in 1974 and the Latinised name of the eighth century, Cumbria, was used for the newly combined county.

Darcy Lever

Darcy Lever was at one time a township or civil parish in Lancashire, in the Bolton-le-Moors Ecclesiastical Parish and in Bolton Poor Law Union. In 1212, it was known by its Latin name Parua Lefre (meaning Little Lever), and by 1590 as Darcye Lever. The name comes from the Old English 'laefer', referring to rushes or bullrushes, and has been interpreted as signifying '[the] place where rushes grow'. The Darcy affix came later as a result of the D'Arcy family, who owned the manor.

Darwen

The Lancashire town of Darwen dates back to Anglo-Saxon times, with an ancient burial ground uncovered in the Whitehall area. It takes its placename from the river of that name which runs through the town. In 1029, it was recorded as Derewent. The name of the river derives from the Celtic, meaning 'river where oak trees grow'.

Denton

Denton is a common English placename, with many such places in Cambridgeshire, Sussex, Lincolnshire and Norfolk. The origin of the name Denton has two possible explanations. One has it that it meant 'Dane town', a reference to the original Nordic setters, and another prefers 'valley settlement' from 'denu', meaning valley and 'tun', meaning town or settlement. As the township lies within the valley of the River Tame, the latter explanation seems most probable. By about 1220, the name Denton appears in contemporary documents relating to Lancashire.

Didsbury

The name of Didsbury is derived from the Saxon 'Dyddi's burh', probably referring to a man known by the name Dyddi, whose manor, stronghold or township it then was. Before Roman times, Didsbury was a pleasant wooded area close to the River Mersey south of Manchester. By 1246, it had become known as Dedesbiry.

Disley

In about 1251, the village was known as Destesleg, from the Old English 'dystels', meaning a mound or heap, and 'leah', a woodland clearing. Hence, '[place of the] mound in a clearing'.

Droylsden

Dating from the seventh century, Droylsden's origins are somewhat obscure, though some sources say that it was settled around 900. However, first mention of its name appears in the twelfth century when it was called Drygel's Valley, the word 'dryge' being Old English for 'dry', and 'denu', referring to a small valley, the whole name probably means 'dry valley'. In 1250 it was known as Drilisden.

Dukinfield

Evidence has been unearthed of Neolithic and Bronze Age flints around Dukinfield Hall, demonstrating a human presence in the area since prehistoric times. The name Dukinfield is generally taken to mean 'ducks [in] open land', or more commonly 'ducks in a field'. An alternative suggestion has been offered, in that the placename might mean 'raven of the field', supposedly derived from the Old English 'duce' and 'feld'. However, the Old English word 'duce', unequivocally refers to the modern word 'duck' (and is an alternative to the more commonly used Anglo-Saxon 'ened'), and not to a raven, rendering the former interpretation the most likely explanation of the placename.

Dukinfield received no mention in the Domesday survey, and it was some time after the Norman Conquest that the 'Mainou of Dokenfeld' was recorded within the Macclesfield Hundred of Cheshire. The original manor spanned two estates, part in the fee of Dunham Massey and part in Stockport, which was held by Matthew de Bramhall in about 1190. In the latter half of the twelfth century, when they became lords of the manor, some of his family took the name de Dokenfeld, and retained the manorial lordship until the mid-eighteenth century. It was during the twelfth (or early thirteenth) century that they began building the moated Dukinfield Old Hall, in a landscape which was still predominantly meadowland and pasture.

Dunham Massey

Dunham, in the Metropolitan Borough of Trafford, derives its name from the Old English words 'dun', a hill, and 'ham', a village or settlement. Hence, 'village on a hill'. The Manor of Dunham was recorded in the *Domesday Book* as Doneham, in Bowdon, in Bucklow Hundred, held by Hamo de Masci, having belonged to Aelfward, a Saxon thegn, before the Norman Conquest.

Eccles

A popular theory is that the Eccles placename denoted the site of a building recognised by the Anglo-Saxons as a church. 'Ecles' is proposed by some as the most likely source of the modern name. However, according to Denise Kenyon's *The Origins of Lancashire,* the derivation of the placename 'suggests that this may not be the case as there is not an exact correlation between Eccles placenames and pre-Domesday Hundreds in south Lancashire'. Its definitive origin remains obscure, but one possibility is that the Eccles placename is derived from the Romano-British 'Ecles' or 'Eglys', itself derived from the Ancient Greek word 'Ecclesia' (or Ekklesia), signifying a church. It was certainly known in its current name by 1200.

Edgeley

Edgeley is located centrally within the Metropolitan Borough of Stockport and was formerly in the Cheadle township. The name probably comes from the Old English meaning 'on the edge of the clearing' or possibly 'on the edge of a hill', which aptly describes this location. Edgeley, or Eddyshelegh, as it was known in former times, can be traced back to the early part of the thirteenth century.

Edgworth

Edgworth lies in the north-east corner of North Turton between Broadhead Brook and Quarlton Brook. The name Edgworth is of Anglo-Saxon origin and has existed in many forms, including Eggwrthe, Egewurth, Eggeswrth, Edgeword and Eggeworth. The name probably means 'a village on the edge of a hillside'. It is notorious for its seventeenth century 'folds' which refer to enclosures of a farmstead and cottages. Names like Isherwood Fold, Horrocks Fold, Thomasson Fold and Brandwood Fold are typical of the village.

Egremont

Egremont is a small Cumbrian market town, about five miles south of Whitehaven. Egremont Castle (now in ruins) was built about 1130, and stands on a mound above the River Ehen. The placename derives from the Old French 'aigre', meaning sharp or pointed (like a needle), and 'mont', a hill. Hence, '[place on a] sharp pointed hill'.

Ellesmere Port

Ellesmere Port is the largest of the townships on Cheshire's Wirral Peninsular, on the south bank of the River Mersey. It was recorded in the *Domesday Book* as Ellesmeles, the name derived from the Old English word 'mere', a pool or small lake, and the personal name of a man called Elli. Hence, 'Elli's pool or lake'.

Elswick

This Lancashire village was probably founded by a man called Aethelsige, after whom the original placename would have been made. The Old English affix 'wic' signified a specialised farmstead, like a dairy. The placename could therefore be reasonably interpreted to mean 'Aethelsige's [dairy] farmstead'. Domesday recorded the place as

Edelesuuic, in the Amounderness Hundred, listed at that time in Yorkshire, and held as a Crown possessison. Before the Conquest it had been overseen by Earl Tostig, the brother of King Harold.

Entwistle
The small village of Entwistle is located between the towns of Bolton, Darwen and Bury. It is surrounded by the villages of Edgworth, Quarlton and Turton and lies within the old Turton Urban District. The placename probably derives from Sir John Antwisel, who arrived with the Norman Conquest in 1066. The Entwistle township dates from the early thirteenth century, when it formed part of the Manor of Hennetwisel, which belonged to the Entwistle family of the Hospitallers.

Euxton
This Lancashire village was once a chapelry in Leland Parish in the Borough of Chorley. The correct pronunciation of the placename, according to its locals, is 'Ex-ton' and not as outsiders frequently say it – 'Yuke-ston'. The name means 'Arfric's farmstead', probably after its Saxon settler and founder. The township received no mention in its own right in the Great Survey of 1086, but fell within the Barony of Penwortham, whose overlord at that time was Roger de Lacy. He had leased two oxgangs of land to Evesham Abbey and a further two ploughlands to Robert Bussel. The remaining land was granted to a few other tenants. Over time the spelling of the placename has had many variants, including Euckeston in 1212, Eukeston in 1242, Euesketon in 1275, Euketon in 1276 and Eukestone in 1304.

Everton
The placename Everton is recorded as Evreton in 1094, Euerton in 1201 and Erton in 1380, but it has been known to have existed in its present form shortly thereafter. The name derives from the Old English words 'eofer', meaning wild boar and 'tun', a settlement. Hence, 'settlement where wild boars are found'.

Failsworth
The name Failsworth comes from two Old English words, 'fegels' and 'wrth', probably signifying an 'enclosure with a special kind of fence'. The township was not mentioned in the Domesday survey and its name does not appear in records until 1212, when it was recorded as Fayleswrthe.

Fallowfield
The name Fallowfield is not derived, as one might have supposed, because its fields lay fallow, but from an early owner of the area called Jordan de Fallafield. By the fourteenth century, the place was more commonly known as Fallafeld or Fallufeld.

Farnworth
Farnworth is located within the Metropolitan Borough of Bolton, about one mile south of the town centre. Its name comes from the Old English words 'fearn' and 'wrth', which together mean 'the enclosure among the ferns'. The Rivers Irwell and Croal flow though the township, which was known as Farnewurd in 1185, as Fornword in 1282, then later as Ferneworth.

Fazakerley
Fazakerley is thought to be an Anglo-Saxon placename derived from three words: 'faes', meaning 'on the border or fringe', 'aecer', signifying a field, and 'lea', 'leah' or 'lei',

meaning 'a clearing in a wood'. It may therefore be translated as 'the boundary near the woodland clearing'. The name has been in use since 1321. Other variants of the spelling include Fazakerly in 1321, Fesacrelegh in 1333 and Fasacre in 1325.

Formby
The Sefton township of Formby is likely to have been founded by Scandinavian settlers in the early ninth century. The village, originally spelt Fornebei, meaning either 'the old settlement' or a 'village belonging to a man called Forni'. The suffix 'by' is a common placename ending, derived from the Old Norse, signifying a settlement of some kind, possibly fortified.

Freckleton
The Lancashire village of Freckleton derived its name from a man called Frecla, who may have been its founder or an early chieftain or leader of the original settlement. The Old English affix 'tun' which is attached, signified an estate or a farmstead; therefore the placename translates as 'farmstead [or estate] belonging to a man called Frecla'. The survey of 1086 recorded the place as Frecheltun, in the Amounderness Hundred of North Lancashire (then part of the County of Yorkshire), held by King William at that time, and overseen by Tostig Godwinson, the Earl of Northumbria before the Conquest.

Frodsham
Frodsham's earliest settlers were Anglo-Saxons from the southern Kingdom of Mercia, and the two possible origins of the placename exist. One has it that 'ham' signifies a small village, or hamlet, and 'Frod' or 'Froda' was probably the name of the Saxon leader who founded it. Hence, 'Frod's hamlet'. An alternative suggests it is a corruption of 'ham on the ford' or 'ford ham', meaning, 'the hamlet on the ford' (across the River Weaver). In 1086, it was recorded as Frotesham, held by Earl Hugh, having previously belonged to Earl Edwin, a Saxon. It was assessed for taxation based on three hides of land paying 'geld', with land enough for nine ploughs. It also recorded one slave, eight villans and two bordars with two ploughs on the estate.

Garstang
The placename of the market town of Garstang may have come from the Saxon word 'gaerstung', referring to common or meadow land. Alternatively, it could be derived from the Old Scandinavian words 'geirr', meaning 'spear', and 'stong', signifying a post, possibly referring to a boundary marker or an ancient meeting place. In the Domesday survey, it is recorded as Cherestanc in Amounderness and listed as one of many 'vills' in Preston. It was assessed at six carucates of land belonging to Roger de Poitou, and 'inhabited by a few people, but it is not known how many the inhabitants are. The rest are waste'. It was some time around 1195 that it took on a semblance of its final name when it was recorded as Gairstang.

Gilcrux
The name of this Cumbrian village has strong Norse connections, as the first element of the placename is from the Old Scandinavian word 'gil', meaning 'retreat', and may have originally derived from the ancient Celtic language as 'cil' and 'crug', together meaning 'retreat on [or by] a hill'. There is even a suggestion that the 'crux' element might relate to the Latin word for a cross. If this were the case the name might mean 'retreat by [or with] a cross'. Around 1175, the placename was recorded as Killecruce.

Golborne and Lowton
These two districts of Wigan Metropolitan Borough were known in 1187 as the single entity of Goldeburn. The place probably began beside Millingford Brook and the name comes

from the Old English words 'golde', a marsh marigold, and 'burna', a stream. Hence the name may be interpreted as 'stream where marsh marigolds are found'. In days gone by, reputedly, yellow flowers grew there in abundance. In his *Historia Ecclesiastica Gentis Anglorum*, Bede recorded that the well in Goldborne had been blessed by St Oswald.

Until 1974 boundary changes, Lowton was a separate village. Its name derives from the Anglo-Saxon word 'hlaw', signifying a mound, (or sometimes a burial barrow), or in this case a typographical description of the village, which stands on raised ground surrounded by marshland. The affix 'tun' indicates a farmstead. The names therefore translates as 'farmstead on a hill (or raised ground)'. In 1202 the place was recorded as Lauton.

Goosnargh

This Lancashire village derives its placename from Old Irish and Scandinavian roots. The first element of the name was the personal name of an Irish immigrant called Gussan, and the second comes from the Old Norse word 'erg', meaning an animal shelter, a shieling or hill pasture. Hence 'Hill pasture [or animal shelter] of a man called Gussan'. In 1066, Goosnargh, Threlfall and Newsham each comprised the chapelry of Kirkham, and each was assessed as one ploughland, all held by Earl Tostig. It was recorded by Domesday as Gusansarghe in the Amounderness Hundred of North Lancashire, then part of 'the King's Lands in Yorkshire', and held at that time by King William.

Goostrey

Recorded as Gostrei and Gostrel in the *Domesday Book*, this village placename comes directly from the Anglo-Saxon English 'gorst-treow', which means 'gorse bush'. It was part of the Middlewich Hundred of Cheshire, and an old township and chapelry in Sandbach Parish which was granted to Ralph, with William, son of Nigel as its tenant-in-chief in 1086. There had been only one third of a ploughland to the estate when owned by a Saxon called Colben before the Conquest. At the time of the Great Survey it was assessed as 'wasta', and not liable for taxation. In 1119, the Lord of the Manor, Baron Hugh of Mold, gave the estates to St Werburg's Abbey in Chester. By 1200 the placename had been recorded as Gorestre.

Gorton

The district of Gorton was incorporated into the City of Manchester in 1909. The placename was known by the late thirteenth century and means dirty or grubby village or township, possibly on account of Gore Brook, a dark water course stained brown by the surrounding peaty land. In the event, however, the 'dirty' connotation was not so much real as perceived and the water itself seems to have been perfectly free from pollutants, such that by the beginning of the fourteenth century a water mill is known to have existed on the brook.

Grasmere

From the Old English 'graes mere', meaning a 'lake in pasture' or 'the lake flanked by grass'. Twelfth century spellings include Grys Mere and Grissmere. 'Mere' is an Old English name for a lake or pool. The poet William Wordsworth, who lived in Grasmere for fourteen years, described it as 'the loveliest spot that man hath ever found'.

Greasby

Greasby is a suburb of Birkenhead on the Wirral Peninsular of Cheshire. Originally the placename relied entirely on the Old English words 'graefe', meaning 'grove', 'copse' or 'woodland', and 'burh' a fortified place or stronghold. The end affix was eventually replaced with the Old Scandinavian element, 'by', meaning 'farmstead. The original placename meant 'stronghold by [or in] a copse', but its final version translates as 'farmstead in a copse [or grove]'. Domesday recorded the village as Gravesberie, in the Willaston Hundred, held in 1086 by Nigel de Burcy.

Great Harwood

Great Harwood is in the Parish of Blackburn. The origin of the town's placename has at least two possible explanations, with the 'har' element indicating 'grey'. Hence, 'grey wood'. Another possibility is that 'hara' comes from the Old English for a hare. Hence, 'a wood where hares are found'. The 'Great' element distinguishes it from Little Harwood, five miles west.

Grimsargh

More evidence of Danish incursions into Lancashire, as this village was named after a Viking settler called Grimr. The Old Norse affix 'erg', which completes the placename referred to a hill pasture (or shieling), which produces a meaning of 'Grimr's hill pasture' for the village name. Domesday recorded the place as Grimesarge, in the Amounderness Hundred, where two carucates of land were held by Earl Tostig before 1066 but at the time of the survey these were identified as part of 'the King's Lands in Yorkshire'.

Grizebeck

The Cumbrian village of Grizebeck derives its name entirely from Scandinavia, where the Old Norse words 'griss' referred to a young pig or piglet, and 'bekkr was their word for a brook or stream. Hence, the placename means 'brook [beside which] piglets are kept'. One of the earliest occurrences of the placename appears in the thirteenth century when it was recorded as Grisebek.

Haigh

Although little more than a village in the Borough of Wigan, Haigh has had a considerable influence in the history of the borough. The name Haigh is actually pronounced 'hay', and is derived from the Old English 'haga', signifying a hedge and signifies an area enclosed by hedges. The township was variously recorded as Hage, Hagh, Haghe and Haw in the sixteenth century.

Hale

A very common placename in England, the Cheshire township of Hale derives from the Old English 'halh', meaning a nook or a natural place of shelter, with overt reference to animal husbandry. It is a relatively small district, with spacious tree-lined roads, pleasant shopping facilities and parks.

Halliwell

The name of the old rural district of Halliwell in Bolton is thought to be derived from the words 'holy well'. Its name has appeared in many forms, including Haliwalle, Haliwell, Halliwoe and Hollowell. The exact location of the well in question is unknown but was probably the one in Moss Bank Park which was filled in after a young girl fell in and was drowned in 1740. One of the earliest records of the placename dates from 1289, when William de Pendlebury leased to Richard de Hulton 'the whole vill of Halliwell with its appurtenances... for an annual rent of a silver penny'.

Handforth

The district of Handforth, in the unitary authority of Cheshire East, derived its name from the Old English word 'hana', which represented a cockerel, and 'ford', a shallow river crossing. The placename therefore might mean something like '[place by the] ford where cocks are seen'. It has also been suggested that a viable alternative would be where the first element of the placename was 'han', another word which the Saxons used for a 'stone'. If this were the case, the placename might be better suited to '[place at the] ford with stones', suggesting stepping stones across the local river, the Dean, which is a tributary of the River Bollin. In the twelfth century the place was recorded as Haneford.

Harpurhey
The Manchester district of Harpurhey was named in the early fourteenth century after William Harpour, who enclosed some eighty acres of land that were formerly part of the Forest of Blackley. 'Haeg' is an Old English word for an enclosed area. Hence, 'Harpour's haeg'. At that time, it was pristine land, pleasant, fertile and watered by the River Irk which ran through it and was known to be plentiful with fish at that time.

Harwood
Harwood is located in the district of Bradshaw, a former township in the old Salford Hundred, located about two miles north-east of Bolton. In the thirteenth century, it was known by the name of Harewode. The origin of its name is ambiguous – two possible explanations exist. One is that it simply means 'the wood where hares are found'; the other maintains it is from the Old English 'har', meaning grey or hoary – therefore, 'the grey wood'. The word 'har', however, can also indicate a boundary, so the origin of the placename remains shrouded in uncertainty.

Haslingden
Haslingden is a small township in the Rossendale Valley of Lancashire, which was known in 1241 as Heselingedon; the placename comes from the Saxon words 'haeslen', referring to hazel trees, and 'denu', a dell or valley. Hence, the placename means 'valley of the hazel trees'. Along with that of the neighbouring towns of Rawtenstall and Bacup, it was once part of the Forest of Blackburnshire and the Forest of Rossendale, which was a hunting park during the late thirteenth and fourteenth centuries. Haslingden has the oldest recorded history of any of the borough towns of Rossendale, with its parish church, St James, having existed since 1284.

Hassall
The Cheshire hamlet of Hassall has a placename which means 'witch's corner'. The name derives from the Old English words 'haegtesse', meaning 'witch' (related to the word 'hag'), and 'halh', a nook or corner of land. The Domesday commissioners seem to have made a hash of the entry as it was recorded as Eteshale, and listed in the Middlewich Hundred, held in 1086 by William Malbank. Before 1066 it had jointly belonged to free men called Auti and Godric. The estate supported three radmen, two villans, one slave and four bordars. There was '...woodland one league long, and there is an enclosure and a hawk's eyrie'. The account concludes: 'At the time of King Edward it was worth four shillings; now five shillings'.

Haverthwaite
Haverthwaite was originally a small Viking settlement in the Furness region of Cumberland (now Cumbria), lying within the boundaries of the Lake District National Park. By 1336, it was known as Haverthwayt, from Old English words 'hafr' meaning 'oats', and the Old Norse word 'thveit' or 'thwaite', which signifies a clearing or settlement in a forest. Hence, 'a forest clearing where oats are grown'.

Hawkshead

Hawkshead is located just north of Esthwaite Water, in a valley to the west of Windermere and east of Coniston Water in the Lake District National Park of Cumbria. Originally granted in 1137 to the Cistercian monks of Furness Abbey by King Stephen, the village became an important wool market in medieval times. Its name in 1200 was Hovkesete, possibly from the personal name of a Norse man called Haukr and Old English 'heofod', or even the Old Norse 'saetr', meaning 'a summer farm belonging to Haukr'. An alternative explanation is that the placename translates as 'Hautr's hill [or mountain] pasture'. The placename was recorded as Hovkesete around 1200.

Hazel Grove

The Stockport district of Hazel Grove was known in 1690 as Hesslegrove or Hessel Grav, literally meaning '[the] hazel grove', due to the proliferation of the hazel trees in the vicinity.

Before this time it had been known as Bullock Smithy, as in 1560, Richard Bullock built a blacksmith forge (or smithy) on the corner of what is now Torkington Park on the main Manchester to Buxton Road. The Bullock Smithy placename survived until 1836, when the name Hazel Grove was revived.

Heaton Moor

Heaton is a common English placename, and comes from the Old English 'heah', meaning 'high', and 'tun', a farmstead or settlement. The addition of the word 'moor' produces a meaning for this village in the Metropolitan Borough of Stockport as 'farmstead on a high moor'. It was once agricultural land in Heaton Norris district and was part of the Manchester barony of the Grelley family. The 'moor' affix also distinguishes it from the nearby village districts of Heaton Mersey (located beside the River Mersey), Heaton Norris (after William le Norreys, an early owner or the manor), and Heaton Chapel (on account of the long since gone church that was built on a field known as Yarn Croft in 1758). There was also once a fifth 'Heaton', known as Heaton Reddish, but since the first name was dropped in the late nineteenth century it has been known simply as Reddish. (See: 'Reddish'.) In the eleventh century the place would have been known as Hetun or Heton.

Helmshore

Helmshore is a district of Haslingden in the Rossendale Valley of Lancashire whose placename comes from two Old English words, 'helm', meaning 'shelter' (for livestock), and 'scora', signifying a steep slope. The placename translates as 'cattle shelter on a steep slope', which eminently describes the village location of a tongue of land between the River Irwell and the River Ogden. The placename was written as Hellshour in the early sixteenth century.

Henbury

This Cheshire village was recorded as Hameteberie in the Hamestan Hundred in the 1086 survey. The first element of the placename is uncertain, but it may relate to the Old English word 'haemed', which means 'community'. The second element derives from 'burh' or 'byrig', indicating a stronghold or fortified manor house. Hence, possibly, '[the] community stronghold'. Before Domesday it had comprised land for sixteen ploughlands and contained two leagues of woodland – after King William's Conquest it was rated as 'wasta'. The Lord of the Manor at that time was Earl Hugh of Chester. Before 1066 it had been joint-owned by eight unnamed Saxon free men.

Heysham

The *Domesday Book* recorded the place as Hessam, a name derived from the Old English 'haes', meaning brush or scrubland, and 'ham', a village or settlement. Hence, 'a village surrounded by brushwood or scrubland'. In the Great Survey it was recorded as 'Hessam ... a vill belonging to Halton', assessed at three carucates of land, held by Earl Tostig Godwinson in 1066, but granted to the Abbey of St Martin in 1094.

Heywood

Midway between Rochdale and Bury lies the township of Heywood, surrounded by agricultural land, but still a thriving centre for industry and distribution. The name was spelt Heghwode in 1246 and probably derives from the Old English word 'heah', meaning 'high', and 'wudu', a wood, forest or woodland. Hence, 'high wood'. By the twelfth century, Heywood was recorded as a hamlet in the township of Heap.

High Hesket

This Cumbrian village has a placename that recorded the occupation of Danish settlers in the region and their preoccupation with horse racing. The name comes from the old Norse language, where 'hestr' meant 'horse' and 'skeith' referred to a racetrack or boundary. Hence, 'high boundary land where horses graze [or are raced]'. The first word of the placename distinguishes it from the nearby village of Low Hesket. Both are located on the edge of the Inglwood Forest. In 1285 the place was recorded as Hescayth, and soon thereafter the additional words 'in foresta' were appended to the name.

Hindley

Originally a farming community, the manor was first recorded as Hindele in 1212, the name of this Lancashire village probably derives from the Old English 'hind' and 'leah', meaning a clearing frequented by hinds or does. The town has been known variously as Hindeleye, Hyndeley, Hindelegh and Hyndelegh. The first recorded use of its current spelling, Hindley, was in 1479.

Holmes Chapel

Holmes Chapel, also once known as Hulme and later as Church Hulme, probably derived from the old Saxon 'hulm' or 'holm', meaning rising ground, or perhaps dry land surrounded by bog or marshland. On its northern boundary lies the River Dane, its name still bearing witness to Danish settlers who founded the settlement. After 1066, the lands were held by the Barony of Halton. The village is dominated by the old Parish Church of St Luke, which accounts for the Church Hulme name, which loosely translated as '[the] hill with the church'. Some time later this was corrupted to Holmes Chapel.

Hornby

Hornby, or more properly Hornby-with-Farleton, is a picturesque village in the Lune Valley, located between Kirkby Lonsdale and Lancaster, sitting astride the River Wenning. The name has two possible derivations: either a village on a horn-shaped piece of land; or from the personal name of a man called Horni, plus the Norse affix 'by', indicating a village settlement. In 1086, the *Domesday Book* listed Hornebi as originally one of three manors - Melling, Hornby and Wennington.

Horwich

The placename is thought to derive from two Old English words: 'har', meaning grey, and 'wice', a wych elm. Hence the placename may be taken to mean '[the place of] the grey wych elms'. The settlement was first documented in 1221 when the name was recorded as Horewic. At that time, it was a hunting chase for the barons of Manchester.

Hulme

The district of Hulme derives its name from the Old Norse word 'holmr', which signified a small island or land surrounded by marsh or a water meadow. In 1246, it was recorded as Hulm. In fact, modern-day Hulme is actually bounded by water on three sides – the Rivers Irwell, Medlock and Cornbrook – and historically would have been surrounded by marshes at times of river flood. Hence, its desirability as a defensive position on dry land and the origins of the placename.

Hutton Roof

There are twelve places in England which go by the name of Hutton. This particular Cumbrian village placename, originally recorded within the Amounderness Hundred of Westmorland, (counted as part of Yorkshire at that time), comes from 'hoh', meaning 'ridge' or 'hill-spur'', and 'tun', a farmstead or village settlement. Hence, 'village settlement [or farmstead] on a hill-spur or ridge'. In 1086, the placename was recorded as Hotun, assessed as 'waste' and held by King William, having belonged to Earl Tostig before the Norman Conquest. By the thirteenth century, the manor was held by a man (possibly a Dane) called Rolf or Hrolfr, and his name was attached to the placename. In 1278 the village was known as Hotunerof.

Hyde

The name of this Tameside township derives from 'hid' or 'hide', an Old English land measure, widely used in medieval England and in the Domesday survey as a basis for taxation. It was roughly equivalent to about one hundred and twenty acres, assessed at that time as the amount of land required to support a man and his family. Hence, it became a *de facto* unit of land measurement in the Middle Ages. The present spelling of Hyde occurred some time in the thirteenth century.

Huyton

Huyton was first settled about 600–650 AD by the Angles, migratory settlers from Western Europe. The township is mentioned in the *Domesday Book*, spelt Hitune, and held along with the Manor of Torboc, in the West Derby Hundred, by a nobleman named Dot. The placename comes from the Old English words 'hyth', referring to the landing place or jetty on the banks of the River Alt, in an area of land now known as Huyton Wetlands in Merseyside. The affix 'tun' indicated a settlement or village. Hence, 'settlement or farmstead at (or close to) a landing place'.

Ince

More properly, Ince-in-Makerfield, in the Borough of Wigan, the name was first recorded in the *Domesday Book* as Inise, from an old Welsh word 'ynys' or 'inis', meaning 'island'. The name refers to the village's position on a low marshy ridge around the Rivers Gowy and Mersey.

Kearsley

The name of the Bolton village of Kearsley is defined as 'a meadow of water grass', although some translate the placename as 'a clearing where water cress grows'. In 1187, it was spelt Cherselawe, and as Kersleie around 1220. The placename comes from the Old English words 'coerse', meaning cress (sometimes called watergrass), and 'leah', a woodland clearing or a glade in a forest.

Kelbrook

The small stream that flows through a ravine at the site of this Lancashire village is the source of its placename. The Old English word 'ceole', technically meaning 'throat', but here referring to the narrow ravine, and 'broc', meaning 'brook', combine to produce a placename that means '[place by the] stream that flows into the ravine'. The stream is now known as Kelbrook Beck (from the Old Scandinavian word 'bekkr', meaning 'stream'). Domesday called the place Chelbroc and listed it in the Craven Hundred, at that time falling within the West Riding of Yorkshire, jointly held by Roger de Poitou and William de Percy. It had been part-held by two Saxons called Bernwulf and Ulf during the reign of King Edward.

Kenyon

This district in the unitary authority of Warrington in Cheshire is thought to be a contraction of the Old Welsh 'Cruc Einion', where 'crug' meant 'mound' or 'hillock' and 'Einion' was the name of the man who may have been its founder or an early leader. Hence 'Einion's hillock [or mound]'. The mound is thought to have been an ancient Bronze Age burial barrow or tumulus. The place was known as Kenien in 1212.

Keswick

This Cumbrian township was first recorded as Kesewik in the thirteenth century. Scholars have generally considered the name to be from the Old English, meaning 'farm where cheese is made', the word deriving from 'cese' (cheese), with a Scandinavian word 'wic', meaning a specialised farm or dwelling, typically a dairy. However, not all sources agree. Some say that the derivation of townships in Viking-settled areas, as Keswick was, would not have been given a Saxon name and that the word is of probable Norse origin after a man called Kell. Hence, the placename might mean 'Kell's farm'.

Kettleshulme

This place has nothing whatever to do with kettles. At some time in its early medieval history, this small village in rural Cheshire had a Scandinavian settler called Ketil, apparently a man of some standing, whose name is enshrined in the village's placename. The second element of the name is also Norse: the Old Scandinavian word 'holmr' represented high ground or an island surrounded by a water meadow, marshland or a river flood plain. The placename translates as 'Ketil's island', and one of the earliest records of the placename was Ketelisholm in 1285.

Kirkby Lonsdale

Kirkby developed at a crossing point where several packhorse routes converged over the River Lune. It is one of the few Cumbrian towns mentioned in the *Domesday Book*, where it is described as Cherchibi, meaning a 'fortified village with a church'. It records 'In Kirkby near Ulverston, Lancashire, [a man called] Dubhan [has] six carucates to the geld (for rent)'. An earlier Saxon church was entirely rebuilt by the Normans, but the Neolithic stone circle on Casterton Fell and the remains of Celtic settlements at Barbon, Middleton and Hutton Roof suggest a much earlier occupation of the area. In 1093, Ivo de Taillebois, Baron of Kendal, gave the church at Kirkby to St Mary's Abbey in York. By the end of that century, the township had become known as Kirkeby Lauenesdale. The 'Lonsdale' affix translates as 'valley [or dale] of the [River] Lune'. This distinguished the township from other Kirkbys, such as Kirkby Stephen and Kirkby Thore, also in Cumbria, Kirkby in Ashfield in Nottinghamshire, Kirkby Malzeard and Kirkby Overblow, both in North Yorkshire.

Kirkham

The Parish of Kirkham was one of the largest in the County of Lancashire. In pre-Roman times, it was probably the main settlement of the Celtic Setantu tribe. Later, it was occupied by the Romans, as their military road ran through the district on its way from the fort at Ribchester. Kirkham's name is a combination of the Danish 'kirkja', referring to a church, and the Saxon word 'ham', meaning township or settlement. This is typical of the mixture of Saxon and Viking influences on the local culture. Hence, the placename means '[the] township with a church'.

Knock

Knock is an Old English word for a hillock and this is the origin of placename of this Cumbrian hamlet. The interpretation may be better expressed as '[place by a] hillock'. The hillock referred to is the nearby hill known as Knock Pike. In the twelfth century the placename was spelt Chonoc.

Knotty Ash

Knotty Ash is a small area on the eastern fringe of Liverpool that derived its placename from a gnarled ash tree, and by 1700 was simply known as Ash. The 'Knotty' prefix was added to the placename later – an old word for 'gnarled'. Hence, '[place by or at the] gnarled ash tree'.

Knutsford

The name of Knutsford is thought to derive from its connection to King Cnut, who supposedly forded the River Lily at this point in 1016. It appears under the name Cunetesford in the Bucklow Hundred in the Domesday survey, held by William Malbank. The Saxon, Erchenbrand, previously held it as a freeman and at the time of the survey was apparently a tenant on what had previously been his own land. Even though it was listed as half a hide, sufficient land for two ploughs, the account records that 'it was, and is, waste', but was still valued at ten shillings.

Lach Dennis

On the face of it this appears to be a very Scottish sounding placename, but Lach Dennis is actually a village in Cheshire. The first word of the name derives from the Old English 'lece', which referred to a stream or a bog. The second is the Middle English word 'danais', which is a corruption of 'Danish', as the manor was held by a Norse man called Colben at the time of the Great Survey of 1086. Hence, 'Danish man's estate by a boggy stream'. Domesday recorded the place as Lece, and by the mid-thirteenth century the estate had been recorded as Lache Deneys.

Lamplugh

The earliest inhabitants of the hamlet of Lamplugh, in the Whitehaven district of Cumbria, were probably people of the Neolithic, Bronze and early Iron Ages. The remains of one of their stone circles were still standing until the nineteenth century, in what is now known as School Field. The Roman road from Egremont to Cockermouth passed through Lamplugh. One explanation of the placename is that its ancient Celtic inhabitants named it Glan-Flough or Glan-Fillough, which translates loosely as 'wet dale'. Another cites the Old Welsh word 'nant', meaning 'valley', and the Middle Welsh 'blwch', meaning 'bare', which together produce Nant-blwch, which may be interpreted as 'bare valley'. By 1150, it had been recorded as Lamplou.

Lancashire

The name of the Palatine County of Lancashire is based on the City of Lancaster, and was known in the fourteenth century as Lancastreshire. To quote the *Friends of Real Lancashire*,

'Palatinate status was granted to Lancashire because of its strategic position in defending England from the Scots and conferred legal recognition of the extraordinary powers of the Duke within Lancashire'. (See: 'Lancaster'.)

Lancaster
The City of Lancaster derived its placename from the early Roman military settlement that was established there, and its location on the River Lune. The Old English word 'caester', meant 'Roman camp', and the name of the Lune comes from Celtic times, when it is thought to have meant 'healthy' or 'pure'. Domesday recorded the county as Loncastre in 1086. Her Majesty the Queen holds the ancient and customary title of Duke of Lancaster. The Duchy of Lancaster, which includes all the land from the River Lune in the north to the River Mersey in the south, currently provides income for the British monarch.

Langho
The name of the Lancashire village of Langho means '[place at the] long corner of land'. It derives from the Anglo-Saxon 'lang', meaning 'long, and 'halh', which refers to a corner or nook of land. It is thought to be a reference to the land between the River Ribble and the Calder. Historically, it was part of the Parish of Blackburn and was known in the thirteenth century as Langale.

Lees
The village of Lees in the Borough of Oldham dates back to the fourteenth century, when the name was recorded as The Leese. The word 'leas' or 'lees' is the plural form of the Old English 'leah', indicating woodland clearings. One of the earliest known residents of the manor was John de Leghes, a prominent landowner who took his surname from the township.

Leigh
Leigh is a common placename throughout England, with examples in Kent, Surrey, Somerset and Oxfordshire. The Lancashire township dates back well into the twelfth century and was recorded as Legh in 1276, derived from 'leah', meaning a meadow or a woodland clearing, similar in derivation as Lees (previously). It was famous until the nineteenth century for its dairy produce and its local cheese, known as the Leigh Toaster.

Levenshulme
The district of Levenshulme's placename is probably derived from two words, 'Leofwine' and 'hulm' or 'holm'. It is thought that this land belonged to Leofwine, a Danish settler, and it was an 'island' of dry land surrounded by marshland (a 'hulm'). Hence, 'Leofwine's hulm'. The spelling of the name has varied a great deal throughout the subsequent centuries, including Lywensholme, Leysholme and Lentsholme.

Linstock
Linstock is a small Cumbrian hamlet whose name comes from 'lin', the old word Saxons used for flax and is related to modern words like linen and linseed. The Old English word 'stoc' signified an outlying or remote farmstead. Hence, the placename means 'remote farm where flax is grown'. An early reference to the place spelt it as Linstoc.

Litherland
The placename is derived from Old Norse 'hlioar' or 'hlith-ar', signifying a slope, and the Old English 'land', whose meaning often referred to open or arable fields. Hence, 'sloping land (or fields)'. Referred to as Liderland and Liderlant in the *Domesday Book* of 1086, the first Manor of Litherland included the districts of Seaforth, Orrell and Ford.

Littleborough

Littleborough, on the edge of the Pennines, is one of the larger districts of Rochdale and has a history of both wool and cotton weaving. The name Littleborough is derived from the Old English 'lytel burh', meaning 'small fortified place', or some sources have it as 'lytel broc', meaning 'small watercourse', referring to the local stream that runs through the locality. Either is possible.

Little Lever

The once small village of Little Lever is located in the south-east of Bolton, in the old Parish of Bolton-le-Moors, in the Barony of Manchester, which was held by the Grelley family. It derives its placename from the Old English 'laefre', signifying a place where rushes grew, and was recorded as Parva Lefre in 1212, the Latin word 'parva' meaning 'little'.

Little Stanney

This Cheshire village derives its name from two Old English words, 'stan', meaning 'stone' and 'eg', an island. The 'Little' prefix came later to distinguish it from Great Stanlow near Ellesmere Port to its north. The placename may therefore be translated as '[the] little stone [or rock] island'. It was recorded in Domesday as Stanei, in the Willaston Hundred, thus: 'The earl [Hugh d'Avranches] holds Stanney and Little Stanney and Restald [holds some of it] of him. Regnvald held it as a free man'. There was land at that time for two ploughs, plus another in demesne, with the Church of St Werburgh (now Chester Cathedral) owning one-fifth of an acre. The survey goes on to add that this fifth acre 'ought to belong [to the church, and that] the canons claim it because they have lost it unjustly'.

Liverpool

As large and important a city as it now is, Liverpool began life as a small settlement beside a tidal pool next to the River Mersey. By 1190, it was called Lifer pol or Liuerpul, meaning 'muddy pool'. It is not mentioned in the *Domesday Book* – it was too small to merit an entry, as it would have been a modest little hamlet at the time.

Long Marton

Marton is a common English placename with places in Lincolnshire, Shropshire, Warwickshire and North Yorkshire. The name is Old English and derives from 'mere', meaning a pool or a lake, and 'tun', a farmstead or a village. Hence, 'village (or farmstead) by a pool'. The village of Long Marton in Cumbria was recorded as Meretun in the late-twelfth century, in reference to the length of the village.

Lostock

The derivation of this Bolton placename is vague, though it was already recorded as Lostok in 1205. It could have been derived from the Old English 'hlose', meaning pig or swine, and 'stoc' meaning sty or pig enclosure, although some translate this word as 'outlying or remote farmstead'. Another possible derivation may be from the Celtic 'llostog', the name for a beaver and may refer to the river where beavers were frequently to be found. In his *Dictionary of British Placenames*, A.D. Mills translates the name as indicating an 'outlying farmstead with a pig sty'. In 1205, the village name was spelt as Lostok.

Lunt

The small village of Lunt in the Sefton Borough of Liverpool derives its placename from an Old Scandinavian word, 'lund' or 'lundr', meaning 'small woodland' or 'woodland grove'. It was first recorded as Lund in 1251. Two places in Yorkshire shared a common origin and have the same meaning: Lund in the East Riding of Yorkshire, and Lund in North Yorkshire.

Lymm
The Cheshire town of Lymm was derived from the Old English, 'hlimme', a word that indicated a noisy stream or a fast-flowing or raging torrent. The placename may therefore be taken to mean '[place at, or by, the] noisy stream', almost certainly in reference to Slitten Brook that runs down a ravine through the town centre. Lymm's earliest record appears to be in the *Domesday Book* of 1086 when it was listed as Lime in the Bucklow Hundred, held by Gilbert the Hunter in 1086, having belonged to a Saxon man called Wulfgeat of Madeley before 1066.

Lytham St Anne's
Lytham is a seaside town on the Lancashire coast, whose early name was recorded as Lidun. At first glance, this would seem to bear scant resemblance to its origin, which was based on the Old English word 'hlith', which meant 'slope', or in its plural form as 'hlithum'. Hence, '[the place among the] slopes'. The slopes in question probably refer to the high sand dunes that are scattered along the coast. St Anne's (officially St Anne's-on-Sea), was a separate adjacent parish before 1922, based on its church of that name. From that date the townships of Lytham and St Anne's became the District of Lytham St Anne's.

Macclesfield
The earliest written reference to Macclesfield is found in the Domesday survey of 1086, where it is recorded as Maclesfeld in Hamestan Hundred. In 1183, it was referred to as Makeslesfeld. The English Place-Name Society gives its name as derived from the Old English 'Maccel', and 'feld', meaning 'Maccel's open country or field'. As a medieval town, its charter was granted to Earl Ranulf III of Chester by Prince Edward, the future king, in 1262, establishing it as a free borough with its own merchant guild.

Maghull
The township of Maghull in the Metropolitan Borough of Sefton in Merseyside is an old chapelry in the Parish of Halsall, which dates back to the Great Survey and was recorded as an agricultural settlement of six square miles which supported fifty people. The name Maghull could be derived either from the Old Irish word 'magh', the Old English 'maegoe' (which translates as may-weed), or the Celtic 'magos', followed by the Old English 'halh', which means 'flat land in a bend of the river'. However, some accounts have it as derived from the Anglo-Saxon word 'maegoehalh', which means 'nook on the land where mayweed grows'. There have been numerous variants of the placename over the centuries, including Magele, Maghhal, Mauwell and Maghell.

Malpas
Malpas is a small township in south-west Cheshire, which is typified by its distinctive half-timbered buildings. It was recorded in the *Domesday Book* as being held by Robert FitzHugh as his barony, set in the ancient Broxton Hundred, which included the hamlets of Bawbrook, Cross o'th' Hill, Ebnal, The Moss and Oathills. The name is derived from old French 'mal', meaning bad or poor, and 'pas', meaning passage or way. Hence, 'bad passageway'. The significance is obscure but may have been a reference to the path or track through the valley of Bradley Brook. It had been the original Roman road from Chester to

Wroxeter and would have become a muddy route that was prey to robbers and vagabonds. The 'mal' element might therefore have referred to either the condition of the road, or to its notoriety as a location for highwaymen.

Manchester

Manchester was founded in 79 AD, when Roman General Julius Agricola set up an encampment on a defensive promontory overlooking the confluence of the River Irk and the River Irwell in Lancashire. He called the new garrison *Mamuciam* (or Mamucia), based on a Latinised version of the Celtic word 'mamm', meaning 'breast-shaped'. Hence, the placename translated as 'a breast shaped hill'. By the time of Domesday in 1086 it had been recorded as Mamecester, in the Salford Hundred, held by Earl Roger de Poitou, its placename a reference to Agricola's long abandoned Roman fortress, known locally as 'the castle in the field', later corrupted to Castlefield. A brief reference in the town records shows that Edward the Elder took over the town in 920 and made repairs to the fortifications. At that time, it was little more than a small hamlet within the king's Manor of Salford.

Manley

The interpretation of the name of this village in Cheshire is '[place in a] common wood or clearing', or 'communal woodland clearing. It comes from the Anglo-Saxon words 'maene', meaning 'communal', and 'leah', a woodland glade or clearing. Domesday recorded the place as Menlie, in the Ruloe Hundred, held in 1086 by Earl Hugh of Chester (also known as 'Hugh the Wolf' and 'Hugh the Fat').

Marple

The township was known as Merpille by the early thirteenth century and there are at least two possible explanations of the placename. One is based on two Old English words, 'maere' and 'pyll', together meaning 'a pool or stream near the boundary'. Alternatively, Marple may have been derived from 'maere hop hyll' meaning 'the hill at the boundary valley'.

Mawdesley

Another rare settlement bearing the name of a woman. The Lancashire village of Mawdesley comes from the Old French personal name 'Matilde', or Old German 'Mahthildis' (which is frequently shortened as a diminutive to 'Maud'). The Old English word 'leah' represented a woodland glade or a clearing in a forest. Therefore, taken together the meaning of this placename is 'Maud's woodland clearing'. It was recorded as Madesle in 1219.

Meols, Great & Little

This village of Meols (sometimes referred to as Great Moels), located on the Wirral Peninsular of Cheshire, gets its placename directly from the Old Scandinavian word 'meir', and means 'sand dunes' It received two entries in the Great Survey of 1086, as Melas in Willaston Hundred, both held by Robert of Rhuddlan. One entry shows land for one and a half ploughs with one radman, two villans and two bordars. It was rated as worth ten shillings, and it concludes 'He (presumably the said Robert) found it waste'. The Domesday entry shows a second plot held by Leofnoth before the Conquest and apparently doing better than the first, with land for three ploughs and worth twelve shillings. The alternative prefix 'Little', was in use by 1361, and nowadays tends to refer specifically to the Little Meols Lighthouse.

Mere

There are places called Mere in Cheshire and Wiltshire, and both share a common origin. The name, Mere, is the Saxon word for a pool or a small lake. The Cheshire village was recorded in 1086 as Mera, and listed within the Hundred of Tunendune, held at that time by Gilbert (known as 'the Hunter'), it having belonged to Wulfgeat of Madeley in 1066. The estate comprised two acres of meadow, woodland half a league long and '...forty perches mixed measures'. This last is thought to refer to arable land with a variety of vegetable produce grown.

Merseyside

Merseyside came into being in April 1974, made up from a region that had previously been known as South West Lancashire. Self-evidently named because the boroughs of the Metropolitan County lie beside the River Mersey or within the Mersey Estuary. The word 'Mersey' is probably Old English in origin and is derived from 'maeres-ea' which meant 'border river'. The border in question would probably have been to that between the adjacent Saxon Kingdoms of Mercia and Northumbria. The present-day region is made up of North Liverpool, South Liverpool, Sefton, Knowsley, St Helens and Wirral. In 2017 Merseyside officially became part of an Liverpool City Region, with the election of a Metropolitan Mayor.

Mickle Trafford & Trafford Bridge

Two districts within the Greater Manchester Metropolitan Borough of Trafford, 'Mickle' and 'Bridge', distinguish themselves from the main centre. In fact, there is no such township as Trafford *per se* – it was an invention of 1974 when several small adjoining boroughs were amalgamated to create the new borough. Mickel Trafford gets its placename from the Old Scandinavian word 'mikill', meaning 'great', and Trafford Bridge from three Old English word elements, 'trog', meaning 'trough', 'ford', signifying a shallow river crossing (over the River Gowy), and 'byrcg', meaning 'bridge'. The 'trough' reference probably indicated that the ford may have become deeply worn, or troughed. In 1379, the first place was recorded as Mekeltroghford.

Middleton

A very common English placename, Middleton, in the Metropolitan Borough of Rochdale, was first recorded in 1194 and derives from the Old English 'middel-tun', meaning 'middlemost farm or settlement', probably a reference to its central position between the townships of Rochdale and Manchester.

Middlewich

Middlewich has been one of Britain's chief salt-producing towns since Roman times, when salt was regarded as a most valuable commodity. They named the town Salinae, from the Latin, meaning 'salt works'. Saxon invaders from Europe were quick to realise the importance of the resource and by the time of the survey of 1086, it was a highly prized commodity. The *Domesday Book* refers to it simply as Wich, in Middlewich Hundred, which at that time included the townships of Rode, Astbury, Kinderton and Witton, parts held by Gilbert de Venables (known as the Huntsman), by Hugh Delamere and by William Malbank. Most of these lands were previously in the possession of Saxons, including Godric and Hrafnsvartr. Later the township was spelt Mildestvich. The 'wic' or 'wych' suffix refers to a salt town, with Middlewich being the middle Cheshire town between Northwich and Nantwich. Unsurprisingly, the placename means 'middle salt works'.

Miles Platting

Miles Platting was incorporated into the City of Manchester in 1838. The origin of the name is unclear as there are no early records of the district at all. The derivation of the word 'platt' probably comes from an old word meaning 'a small piece of ground' and 'miles' is probably a corruption of the word 'mills'. Arguably, therefore, the placename might stand for 'mills on a small piece of ground', but this is purely speculative.

Milnrow

The name Milnrow is derived from Old English, though there are various explanations of where it originated. It may be a corruption of Millner Howe, a water driven corn mill at a place called Mill Hill, mentioned in documents dating from 1568. Another explanation is that it simply means a 'mill with a row of houses', combining the Old English elements 'myne' and 'raw'. Others have suggested that the name is derived from a local family with the surname Milne, who owned a row of houses in the locality. A map from 1292 shows Milnehouses at Milnrow's present location. Other variants include Mylnerowe and Milneraw.

Mobberley

This Cheshire township stands on a branch of the River Bollin and was recorded in the *Domesday Book* as Motburlege, from the Old English words 'mot', a meeting place, 'burh', a fortification or stronghold, and 'leah' a woodland clearing. Hence, 'the fortification in the woodland clearing where meetings take place'.

Moresby

This Cumbrian hamlet has both Old French and Old Scandinavian connections, as it was once in the possession of a man called Maurice, with the Old Norse affix 'by' attached to it and signifying a village or farmstead. Hence, 'Maurice's farmstead [or village]'. The village had been the site of an earlier Roman fort, known as Gabrosentum, a name which they took from the Celtic tribes who occupied the region, and which meant 'goat path', a reference to the steep path up the cliffs. The place was recorded as Moresceby around 1160.

Mossley

The name of the village of Mossley within the City of Manchester has two elements: 'mosi', from the Old Norse, indicating a bog or a swamp, and the Old English word 'lea' or 'leah', indicating a clearing in a wood. Hence, the placename may be taken to mean a 'woodland clearing by a swamp', perhaps on the flood plain of the River Tame. In 1309, according to records, the land was owned by Henry, son of William de Mossley, although by the nineteenth century, it was little more than a small hamlet included in the Manor of Ashton. In 1319, the placename was recorded as Moselegh.

Moss Side

The Manchester district of Moss Side, as the name suggests, was originally at the edge of a 'mosi', or 'moss', a peat bog moorland. In medieval times, turf or peat cut here would have been used as fuel for heating and cooking. The entry in the *Domesday Book* actually defined the area as 'wasta' (scrubland), and that a small village, or hamlet, was to be found there.

Moston

Moston is located on the northern limit of the City of Manchester, and would once have been open moorland, well away from the city centre. The placename is derived from two Old English words, 'mos', which generally referred to a place that was mossy, marshy or peat bog, and 'tun', signifying a settlement or farmstead. Hence, 'settlement in a mossy or boggy place'. It was already named by the early twelfth century having grown into a recognisable community near to the district known as White Moss. By 1195 the placename had emerged as Moston.

Mottram

More properly known as Mottram in Longdendale, this district of the Greater Manchester Metropolitan Borough of Tameside also includes Godley, Hattersley, Newton, Hollingworth, Tintwistle, Matley and Staley. The placename derives from the Old English word 'mot', 'motere' or 'moot', signifying a meeting or assembly place or a council, and was known in 1220 as Mottrum. The Longdendale affix was added at the beginning of the fourteenth century in order to distinguish it from the village of Mottram St Andrew in Cheshire. Longendale simply means 'dale of the long valley'. By 1308, the name had emerged as Mottram in Longedendale.

Mouldsworth

A Cheshire village whose placename means 'enclosure near a hill'. It comes from the Old English words 'molda', meaning 'crown of the head', and 'worth', signifying an enclosure. In fact, the village is located at the foot, not at the head of the nearby hill. In the twelfth century the placename was spelt Moldeworthe.

Mungrisdale

A small hamlet in Cumbria, whose placename is made from three separate elements; first, St Mungo (formerly known as St Kentigern), to whom the village church is dedicated and whose name was added later to the placename; second, the Old Scandinavian word 'griss', a pig; third, 'dalr', the Norse word for a valley. Hence, originally, 'valley where pigs are found', but perhaps nowadays it might more properly translate as 'St Mungo's valley where pigs are found'. The place was known in 1285 as Grisedale and by the beginning of the seventeenth century it had been recorded as Mounge Grieesdell.

Nantwich

This is one of the three 'wiches', the salt towns of Cheshire: Nantwich, Northwich and Middlewich. The 'nant' element of the placename may be from the Old Welsh word for a brook or stream, although some cite the Middle English word 'named' as meaning 'famous place'. The second element, 'wic' indicated a specialised farm like a dairy, or an outlying or remote farmstead. In 1194, there was a reference to the town as Nametwihc, which would indicate it was once the site of an ancient Celtic sacred grove. Whatever its derivation, by the time of the *Domesday Book*, Nantwich is recorded in Warmundestrou Hundred, as having eight salt pans, held jointly by Edward the Confessor and Earl Edwin before the Norman Conquest. In that 1086 survey, the township was recorded simply as Wich, being held by Gilbert de Venables and, along with Middlewich and Northwich, it rendered two shillings for each salt pan.

Nateby

The Cumbrian village of Nateby has decidedly Scandinavian connections, though opinions differ as to its definitive meaning. One view is that it comes from the Old Norse 'nata', meaning 'nettles' and 'by', a farmstead or village. Another has it as the name of a Danish settler called Nati, whose farm or village it was. We may never know which is true. The village's present name dates from 1242.

Nelson

Nelson came into being during the Industrial Revolution of the nineteenth century, when the two villages of Great and Little Marsden were combined. The placename 'Nelson' was taken in tribute to a national hero, Horatio Nelson, after the resounding success of the naval battle off Trafalgar in October 1805, in which he lost his life. The original village placenames were based on two Old English words, 'mearc', which marked a boundary, and 'denu', a valley. Hence, the placenames meant 'boundary in a valley' or 'valley boundary'. The valley in question refers to the deep valley of the River Colne which formed the historic boundary between the counties of Lancashire and Yorkshire.

Newton Heath
The Manchester district of Newton Heath takes its name, self-evidently, from Old English meaning 'the new town [or settlement] on the heath'. The heath in question stretched originally from Miles Platting to Failsworth and is bordered by brooks and rivers on all four sides: the River Medlock, Moston Brook, Newton Brook and Shooters Brook.

Newton-le-Willows
During Norman times, Newton became the chief town in the Newton Hundred. It was entered in the *Domesday Book* as Neweton. The first part of the placename comes from the Old English 'niwe', meaning 'new', and 'tun', a farmstead. Hence, 'new farmstead'. The 'le Willows' suffix was added later to distinguish it from some twenty-five other English towns, villages and hamlets of the same name, and means 'by the willow trees'. Domesday showed much of the lands were taken over by Robert de Banastre, whose family probably built a baronial mansion, but the site of it is uncertain. The manor was known as Newton-in-Makerfield well into the nineteenth century having been variously recorded after 1242 as Makeresfeld, Makefeld, Makerefeld and Makerfield. In 1897 the placename was recorded as 'Newton-in-Makerfield (otherwise Newton-le-Willows)'.

Newton Reigny
The 'Newton' part of this Cumbrian village placename has a meaning of 'new farmstead (or village)', as you might expect. Then, some time during the twelfth century the manor came into the ownership of the de Reigni family who attached their family name to the place. Whereas in 1185 the village name had been recorded as Niweton, in 1275 it had become Neutonreygnye.

Northenden
The south Manchester District of Northenden was entered in the *Domesday Book* as Norwordine in the Bucklow Hundred, then part of Cheshire, at that time held jointly by Ranulph de Briquessart (sometimes Ranulph le Meschin), and Bigod de Loges from Earl Hugh Gresford. Before the Norman Conquest it had been the possession of a Saxon thegn called Wulfgeat. The placename comes from the Old English words 'north', meaning (self-evidently), 'northern', and 'worthign', another Saxon word for an animal enclosure. Hence, 'northern enclosure'.

North Turton
As a placename, Turton, in the Metropolitan Borough of Bolton, comes from the Old Norse, meaning 'Thor's settlement (or farmstead)', bearing witness to its earlier Viking occupation. In 1185, it was recorded as Thirtun. The North Turton Parish Council came into being in April 1974, following the division of the former Turton Urban District Council and comprises the villages of Belmont, Chapeltown and Edgworth, along with Entwistle and Quarlton.

Oldham
Oldham is situated some eight miles north-east of Manchester, high in the Pennine Hills, overlooking the Cheshire Plain. The town can be dated from 865 when Danish invaders established a settlement and called it Aldehulme, possibly meaning 'old town or settlement'.

In 1215, much of the lands of Oldham were given to the Knights of St John of Jerusalem by Roger de Montbegon. By 1226, the place was recorded as Aldholm. An alternative explanation of the placename may be derived from the even older Celtic word 'alt' or 'ald', referring to a cliff or steep slope, with the addition of the Old Norse 'holmr', indicating an island or a place surrounded by marshy land. Hence, 'island on a steep slope', or 'island surrounded by marshy land', both of which eminently describe the township's location.

Openshaw

The Manchester district of Openshaw derives its placename from the Old English 'Opinschawe', based on the Old English words 'open' and 'sceaga', a small wood or copse. The word 'open' indicates that the wood was not fenced or enclosed. By 1282, the district was recorded as Opinschawe and by the fourteenth century it had become known as Oponshaghe. The wood was the private hunting domain of the Grelley barons of Manchester and was cleared in the early seventeenth century to make way for arable farmland and pasture, or possibly to provide timber for the emerging English navy.

Ormskirk

The Lancashire township of Ormskirk's first permanent inhabitants were probably Scandinavian settlers from Ireland and the Isle of Man who settled in northern England in the ninth century. Among their number was Orme, or Ormr, a Dane who settled near the River Ribble in around 840. Orme was an early convert to Christianity and built a 'kirkja', the Old Norse word for a church, in the settlement. By 1190, the place had become known as Ormeshirche, or 'Orme's Church', which over time became Ormskirk.

Orrell

The Orrell placename derives from the Anglo-Saxon words 'ora' and 'hyll', meaning 'a hill where ore is dug'. It has been variously recorded as Horul, Orel, Orhull and Orul and was earlier known as Orrell-in-Makerfield. It was in the Manor of Newton-in-Makerfield in Wigan before the Norman Conquest. In 1212, the manor was held by Richard de Orrell but became divided and was acquired by the Hollands of Upholland and descended to the Lovels and subsequently to the Earls of Derby.

Oswaldtwistle

The name Oswaldtwistle in Lancashire first appeared in the mid-thirteenth century as Oswaldestwisel. The name derives from a man called Oswald, and the Old English word 'twisla', which meant 'fork in a river'. Taken together they produce a meaning of 'fork in the river [belonging to] Oswald'. Some have argued that the man in question may have been St Oswald, the seventh century King of Northumbria, but this is entirely speculative.

Papcastle

The Cumbrian village of Papcastle was built on the site of a former Roman fort which they called Derventio, after the River Derwent on which it stood. The Roman connection is reflected in the Old English name element 'caester', which specifically meant 'Roman fort'. In 1260, the village was known as Pabecastr. The first element comes from the Old Norse word 'papi', which referred to a hermit. The placename may therefore be interpreted as 'Roman fort occupied by a hermit'.

Partington

The name Partington was first recorded in 1260 as being within the medieval Parish of Bowdon. The name derives from Old English, with the first element probably referring to a person called Pearta or Paerta. Alternatively, it might be 'part' (that is, land divided into partitions), followed by 'inga', meaning 'the people or followers', and the suffix 'tun' meaning a farmstead or settlement. The most likely explanation is that the placename means 'the settlement [or village] of Pearta's people'.

Patterdale

Patterdale probably derives from a Celtic source meaning simply the 'valley of a man called Patrick' or the 'valley of St Patrick'. Interpretations differ, but most authorities believe it to have been named after a man of that name, rather than from the dedication of its church to the Patron Saint of Ireland. That said, local tradition has it that St Patrick did indeed visit Patterdale in about 540, hence the name could be a corruption from 'Patrick's dale' to Patterdale.

Pemberton

Situated about two and a half miles south-west of Wigan town, but separated by the River Douglas, Pemberton has an old and long history. According to *British History Online*, Pemberton existed as an entity in its own right long before the Norman Conquest and afterwards probably formed part of a berewick in the Manor of Newton. The Pemberton placename derives from 'penn-bere-tun', which is believed to be a combination of the Celtic 'penn', meaning 'hill (or head of hill)', the Old English 'bere', meaning barley, and finally the suffix 'tun', meaning a farm or settlement. Hence, 'a hill settlement (or farmstead) where barley is grown'. The place was known as Penberton in 1201 and by 1212 had attained its modern form as Pemberton.

Pendlebury

The name Pendlebury probably comes from the Old English words 'penn', simply meaning 'hill' or 'hilltop', and 'burh' or 'buri', signifying a fortified settlement, manor or stronghold. Hence, 'a fortified settlement on a hilltop'. This may derive from the local geography, perched as it is on a ridge overlooking the River Irwell Valley. The township's name was variously recorded as Penelbiri in 1202, and as Pennilbure, Pennebire, Pennesbyry, Penilburi, Penulbury, Penhulbury and Pendulbury at various other times during its history. It is recorded that, in 1199, King John gave the land known as Peneberi as a gift to Ellis, son of Robert, who became Master Sergeant of Salford.

Pennines, The

The range of hills known as the Pennines, which run as a backbone down the length of northern England, is a relatively recent appellation, which though probably in common use, was not actually recorded as such until the eighteenth century. Two possible explanations exist for the origin of the name: one has it from the Celtic word 'penn', simply meaning 'hill', while another cites the Apennines, which similarly run down the length of Italy, as a likely source of the name.

Penrith

There are several possible derivations of the Penrith placename. The two Cumbric or Welsh words: 'pen' or 'penn', meaning either head, chief, or end (specifically of a hill), and 'rhyd' or 'rid', signifying a river ford. The placename interpretation may variously be either 'chief ford', 'hill ford', 'ford end', 'the head of the ford' or 'headland by the ford'. An alternative suggestion retains the 'pen' element but prefers the Welsh suffix 'rhudd' (meaning crimson). This red hill interpretation may refer to Beacon Hill to the north east of the town and the ford referred to in the placename is likely to have been a shallow river crossing over the River Eamont. There is also a place called Redhills to the south west near the M6 motorway.

Also, like many other places in the Eden Valley, Penrith is built largely with red sandstone and several buildings using this material can be seen around the town.

Penwortham

The Lancashire village of Penwortham in the present-day Borough of South Ribble betrays an ancient heritage in its placename, as the Celtic word 'penn' indicates a hilltop or end. The other two elements of the placename, 'worth' and 'ham' come from Old English and indicate an enclosed homestead or farm. Hence, we may take the name to mean 'enclosed homestead on a hilltop'. It was recorded as Penuertham in 1149, and had appeared earlier in the Domesday survey as Peneverdant, held by the king in 1086 and acquired by Roger de Poitou, before passing to Baron Roger de Lacy in 1205 as part of the Honour of Clitheroe.

Pooley Bridge

The small village of Pooley Bridge lies at the end of Ulswater in the Lake District of Cumbria, and like many places roundabout, it reveals the early presence of Danish settlers in the region in one of its placename elements. While the first comes from the Old English word 'pol', which simply means 'pool', in reference no doubt to the Ulverston lake it sits beside, the second part derives from the Old Scandinavian 'haugr', meaning 'mound'. The third modern English affix 'Bridge' completes the placename, which, all taken together, may be interpreted as '[the] mound by the pool with a bridge'. The mound in question is thought to be the ancient hill fort earthworks at Bowerbank to the west of the village, and the bridge is that over the Rive Eamont. It has had many variant spellings over time, including Powley-Bridge, Pulley and Pulhoue.

Poulton-le-Fylde

Poulton (perhaps originally Poolton), means 'the town by the pool'. Its name is derived from the River Wyre, situated at the bottom of the Breck at Skippool. In the *Domesday Book*, Poltun was counted in the ancient Parish of Amounderness Hundred, one of many parcels of Manor of Preston land held in 1086 by Earl Tostig Godwinson, brother of Harold II. The 'le-Fylde' affix was appended in 1842 to identify its location and to distinguish it from other places of a similar name, for example, nearby Poulton-le-Sands near Morecambe, Poulton in Gloucestershire and Poulton on the Wirral Peninsular. The Old English word 'filde' means a plain and refers specifically to the broad coastal plain of West Lancashire.

Poynton

The Poynton township, in the old Prestbury Parish of the ancient Macclesfield Hundred, derives its placename from three Old English words: 'Pofa', the name of the man who probably owned the land or founded the settlement, 'inga', meaning 'the people, family or followers', and 'tun', a farmstead or settlement. Hence, 'the settlement belonging to Pofa's family or followers'.

Prescot/Prestbury/Preston/Prestwich

The first element of these townships all have the same derivation, from the Anglo-Saxon word 'preost', meaning a priest or cleric, and indicate that at an early time in their history they all had priests residing within their settlements. The second elements of each placename provide the distinguishing factors. For example, the Merseyside township of Prescot, which was a large medieval parish in the West Derby Hundred, incorporated the Old English word 'cot', signifying a cottage into its placename. Hence, 'priest cottage'.

Prestbury, situated on the River Bollin in the old Macclesfield Hundred, inherited its name from the Old English words 'Preosta burh', which is sometimes translated as 'priest's manor', but more correctly signifies a priest's fortified enclosure of some kind. The timber-framed Priest's House still stands in the village, as it has done since it was built in 1448. It is now designated as a Grade II listed building and also serves as a local bank.

The City of Preston, which the *Domesday Book* identifies in the Hundred of Amounderness and part of 'the land of the king in Yorkshire', has a simple derivation: it is a combination of two Old English words, and literally means 'priest's town'. It was awarded city status by Her Majesty the Queen in April 2002.

The name of Prestwich in the Metropolitan Borough of Bury comes from the Anglo-Saxon meaning 'a priest's dwelling', based on the Old English 'preost', and 'wic', a house or dwelling.

Quernmore

The Saxon word 'cweorn' meant 'millstone, and 'mor' referred to moor or moorland. Therefore the meaning of this Lancashire hamlet's placename is '[place on the] moor where millstones are quarried'. It was spelt in 1228 as Quernemor.

Raby

This village on the Wirral Peninsular of Cheshire gives an insight into the extent of Danish territories in the region. The placename means 'farmstead at the boundary', and comes from two Old Scandinavian words 'ra', meaning 'limit' or 'boundary' and 'by', a farmstead. In the Great Survey of 1086 the place was recorded as Rabie, listed as a very small estate supporting just five households (including one slave), within the Willaston Hundred, and part-held at that time by William FitzNigel and the Canons of St Werburgh in Chester, the latter of whom had retained ownership following the Conquest and had shared it in 1066 with a man known as Arni of Neston.

Radcliffe

The Radcliffe district of Bury in Greater Manchester is located in and framed by the West Pennine Moors and was originally a coal and cotton district. It probably takes its name from the Old English 'read', meaning 'red', and 'clif', referring to the red cliff rock on the River Irwell. At the time of the Great Survey of 1086, the place was recorded as Radecliue or Radeclive, held by Edward the Confessor as a royal manor at the time of the Norman Conquest and by 1212 was held by Ranulf de Radcliffe, whose father William had taken the family name from the township.

Rainow

Rainow is a Cheshire village whose placename means '[place on a] hill spur where ravens flock'. The interpretation is based on two Anglo-Saxon words, 'hraefn', a 'raven' or 'ravens', and 'hoh', a shoulder, ridge or hill spur, which describes the village location on the ridge of a hill. It was recorded as Rauenouh in around 1285.

Rampside

This place in Cumbria has been known in many variations over the centuries, including Rameshede in 1292, Ramesheved in 1336 and Ramsyde in 1539. The name comes from two Old English words, 'ramm', signifying a ram (as in a male sheep), and 'heafod', meaning a head or a headland. It may therefore be interpreted as a 'headland in the shape of a ram's head'. The settlement was inhabited as early as 1292 and is recorded in documents related to Furness Abbey, but its origins are earlier still, with Viking and Roman artefacts having been found in the village church.

Ravenglass

Ravenglass is located at the estuary of the Rivers Esk and Mite. Historically, it lies within the old County of Cumberland. It was known by the thirteenth century as Rayenglass, with various spellings thereafter, including Renglas, Ranglas, Ravenglas and Ravenglasse. The name may be Celtic in origin, with the first element derived from the Gaelic word 'rann' or the modern Welsh 'rhan', meaning 'part' or 'portion'. The 'glass' element reinforces the suggestion that the name comes from the Welsh 'yr-afon-glas', meaning 'the blue river' or 'the blue harbour', and sometimes 'the green river', nothing whatever to do with ravens, as may be supposed. Others interpret it as signifying a small stream, an estuary or the mouth of a river. A.D. Mills has it derived from the Old Irish 'rann', in his *History of British Place-Names*, meaning a lot or a share, and Glas, the name of a person who may have owned the land at some time. Hence, according to his interpretation, '[the] lot or share of a man called Glas'. However, the exact meaning of the placename remains somewhat shrouded in ambiguity.

Ravenstonedale

An early written record of this Cumbrian village was as Rauenstandale in the twelfth century. The name derives from the Old English words 'hraefn' and 'stan', respectively meaning 'raven' and 'stone' (or 'rock'), along with the Old Scandinavian word 'dalr', meaning 'valley' (or 'dale'). Hence, 'valley of the raven stone', referring to the distinctive rock that is located there. The exact connection to ravens is unclear, but the bird is one of Denmark's national symbols, and was often thought to be an omen of evil in medieval Scandinavia. For much of its history, the place was known as Russendale. The Gilbertine Canons of Watton in Yorkshire were granted the village of Ravenstonedale, then in the County of Westmorland, by Thorpin, during the reign of Henry II, and established a small religious cell there some time in the late twelfth century. By 1336, this had developed into the Parish Church of St Oswald, and had been recorded as Rauenstandale.

Rawtenstall

Rawtenstall is the largest town in the Rossendale Valley of Lancashire and by 1323 was a part of the Royal Forest of Rossendale. The name Rawtenstall has two possible interpretations. One is a combination of the Middle English 'routen', meaning to roar or bellow, from the old Norse word 'rauta' and the Old English 'stall', meaning a pool in a river. Another interpretation relates to Rawtenstall's identification as a cattle farm in 1324 and combines the Old English 'ruh', meaning rough, and 'tun-stall', together meaning 'rough farmstead', referring to the site of a farm. The 'tun-stall' element may also be interpreted as 'cow stall'. Yet another translates the placename as 'buildings occupied when cattle were pastured on high ground'. In 1324 the placename was written as Routonstall.

Reddish

Reddish is located about one and a half miles north of Stockport town centre. It was known by 1212 as Rediche, from Old English words signifying a reed, a place by a reedy ditch or where reeds were gathered for thatching, and was once a thriving industrial centre with two old mills dominating its contemporary landscape.

Rivington

Rivington is a popular historic and scenic area located between the towns of Horwich, Bolton and Chorley, located below a high hill called Rivington Pike. The placename comes from the Old English words 'hreof', meaning rough or rugged, 'inga', the people or family, and 'tun', a farmstead or settlement. Hence, loosely translated, a 'settlement of people [who live] on a rugged hill'. Rivington was known in 1202 as Revingtun.

Rochdale

Rochdale appears in the *Domesday Book* as Recedham, and was part of the Salford Hundred. The placename comes from the River Roch, on which the town stands, and the Old Scandinavian word 'dalr', a dale or valley. Hence, 'valley of the River Roche'. The ancient name for the settlement dates back to early Saxon times, when it was known as Recedham, a name based on the Old English word 'reced', referring to a building or a hall, plus 'ham', signifying a village or homestead. The River Roche probably derives its name from this same source. By 1195, the placename had been recorded as Rachedal.

Romiley

Romiley lies in the north-east of Stockport on the edge of the Peak District and is located about four miles from the town centre. The Domesday survey called the place Rumelie ('roomy lea'), meaning 'a spacious woodland clearing', based on the Old English word 'rum', meaning wide, spacious or open. The survey recorded that Romiley was held by Earl Hugh, having one virgate in Hamestan Hundred, but assessed it as 'waste', and thereby not liable to be taxed. Before the Conquest, it had belonged to the Saxon Earl Edwin.

Royton

This Oldham district was known as Ritton in 1226, from the Old English 'ryge', meaning 'rye' (the cereal crop), and 'tun', a settlement or farmstead. Hence, a 'farmstead where rye is grown'. During the Middle Ages, this small township grew up around Royton Hall, a manor house owned by a long succession of dignitaries which included the Byron and Radclyffe families.

Runcorn

Runcorn has a long history and is first recorded in documentation in 916 AD, when Aethelflaed of Mercia visited to inspect the new fortifications. Around 1000 AD, it was recorded as Rumcofan, after two Old English words, 'rum', meaning wide, spacious or broad, and 'cofa', a cove, creek, bay or inlet. Hence, literally '[place by a] wide cove (or bay)'.

Rusholme

Rusholme was known in earlier times as Russum, probably from the Old English word 'ryscum', the plural form of 'rushes'. It was incorporated into the City of Manchester in 1885. The old Norse word 'holme' or 'hulme' signified marshy land or an island in a marsh. Hence, the placename may mean a 'marshy place where rushes are found [or gathered]'.

Sale

The Old English word 'salh', from which the Sale placename is derived, refers to the sallow, an old name for the willow tree. The Manor of Sale was one of thirty held by William FitzNigel, a powerful twelfth century baron. Eventually, land passed into the ownership of Richard de Massy, one of the Barons of Dunham. The placename first appeared in its present form some time around 1205.

Salford

As with Sale (above), Salford's name is a corruption of two ancient words: 'sal' or 'sahl', from the Latin 'salix', the old word for willow, and 'ford', a shallow river crossing. Hence, it could be translated as 'the willow ford'. For centuries, it was the only place to cross the River Irwell for many miles in either direction. The willow tree-lined banks of the Irwell still separate Salford from Manchester and the original river crossing is thought to be where Victoria Bridge is located today, near the corner of Blackfriars and Deansgate.

Salterforth
Salterforth is a Lancashire village, which as you might expect, has a salt connection. The placename means '[place by the] ford used by salt merchants'. It comes from the Old English word 'saltere', which stood for 'salt merchant' (a 'salterer'), and 'ford', a shallow river crossing, or ford. The ford in question crossed the Salterforth Beck at this place. The present-day placename is known to have been in use since the thirteenth century, but may have been around much earlier.

Sandbach
The place was known as Sondbache and Sondebache in 1260, and Sandbitch in the seventeenth and eighteenth centuries, names derived from the Old English words 'sand' and 'baece', which taken together signified a sandy valley stream or beck. Hence, 'sandy beck'.

Saughall Massie
In the fourteenth century this district of Wallasey on the Wirral Peninsular of Cheshire belonged to the de Massey family (sometimes de Masci), when they attached their family name to the Manor of Salghalle as it was then known. Saughall comes from two Old English words: 'salh', meaning 'sallow', an alternative name for the willow tree, and 'halh', which referred to a corner or nook of land. The complete placename may therefore be interpreted as 'corner of land where willows grow belonging to the Massey family'. The Massey family affix distinguished it from Great Saughall a few miles south-east. In the early fourteenth century the placename was recorded as Salghalle Mascy.

Scholar Green
This small Cheshire hamlet was first recorded as Scholehalc in the late thirteenth century and takes its placename from both Old Scandinavian and Old English sources. In Norse, 'skal' or 'skali', signified a corner or nook of land, while 'halh' was the Anglo-Saxon word for an animal shelter, hut or shieling. The placename therefore loosely means 'corner or land with an animal shelter'.

Sefton
Originally the small coastal village of Sefton in the north-west of England was entered as Sextone in the Great Survey of 1086, a name derived from the Old English words 'sef', meaning 'rushes', 'sedges' or 'bullrushes', and 'tun', a farmstead. Hence, 'farmstead where rushes grow'. By the thirteenth century it began to resemble its present-day name as Sefftun.

Shap
Located high in the Lakeland Fells of Cumbria, the placename of the village of Shap originated in the early twelfth century, at which time, before standard English spellings existed, it was probably known or written as Hep or Yheppe, from an Old Norse word 'hjap'. This is similar to the Old English word 'heap', signifying a pile of stones, probably referring to an ancient stone circle, or cairn, known locally as the Shap Stones.

Shevington
This Wigan placename has two possible interpretations: either based on a location or a person's name. It could mean 'a farmstead near a hill belonging to the people or followers of a man called Shevin', or 'people who live on the ridge of a hill called Shevin'. The first element of the placename derives either from the Celtic word 'cevn' or 'Shevin', a word related to the Welsh word 'cefn', meaning a ridge, the Old English 'inga' refers to people or followers, and 'tun' translates as a farmstead or settlement. In the early thirteenth century the place was known as Shefinton.

Shuttleworth

Shuttleworth is a village in the Metropolitan Borough of Bury whose placename comes directly from the Old English language, where 'scytel' meant a bar or a bolt (as in a gate or door fastening), and 'worth' signified an enclosure. Hence, '[place with a] barred or bolted enclosure', suggesting a securely gated and fenced-in yard, field or pasture. The village name was spelt Suttelworth in the early thirteenth century.

Skelmersdale

Skelmersdale is an old township near Ormskirk in Lancashire, which became a 'New Town' in the 1960s. Its name possibly derives from Old Scandinavian, meaning 'the valley of a man named Skjalmar or Skjaldmarr', although some have it that the meaning lies in three separate elements: 'skel', meaning 'hills'; 'mers', a small lake or mere; and 'dale', indicating a valley.

Skelwith Bridge

Skelwith, in the South Lakeland of Cumbria, in the old Lonsdale Hundred, is the site of a nearby waterfall, Skelwith Force, much visited by tourists. It was known in 1246 as Schelwath from two Old Norse words 'skjallr' meaning resounding or noisy, often referring to rapids, a cataract or a waterfall, and 'vad' meaning 'ford'. Hence, the placename may be taken to mean 'ford by a noisy waterfall'. It was a crossing place on the River Brathay, which was itself named from the Old Norse meaning 'broad river', before a bridge was built over it in the seventeenth century.

Slaidburn

Slaidburn is a Lancashire village located in the Ribble Valley whose ancient name comes from the Old English 'slaeget', meaning 'sheep pasture', and 'burna', a stream or a brook. Hence, 'sheep pasture by a stream'. The stream in question is thought to be the nearby Croasdale Brook. From early times, the Manor of Slaidburn formed part of the ancient Lordship of Bowland. It was recorded in 1086 as Slateborne, held by Roger de Poitou having belonged to Earl Tostig before the Conquest. At that time it would have been regarded as part of the king's lands in the West Riding of Yorkshire, and as such Slaidburn Parish Church remains officially part of the Diocese of West Yorkshire and the Dales.

Speke

Speke is a large township on the banks of the River Mersey. The placename probably derives from the Old English word 'spec', meaning brushwood, though some accounts have it as 'spic', meaning bacon, in reference no doubt to the swine fields that were common at one time in the area. It was known as Spek at the time of the *Domesday Book*, one of several forested manors belonging to Uctred, a Saxon thegn. Following the Conquest, the manor passed to the Molyneux family, who became the Earls of Sefton and lived at Croxteth Hall. The current spelling of Speke dates from the thirteenth century, despite other variations over time, including Specke in 1320, Speyke in 1500 and not uncommonly as The Speke in the sixteenth century.

Stalybridge

The name Stalybridge comes from the Old English word 'staef', a staff or stave, and 'leah', a clearing in a wood. The full meaning of 'Staly' is therefore 'a woodland clearing where staves are collected'. The 'bridge' part was added in the nineteenth century, when the town became an important market crossing point on the River Tame. Historically, the place was sparsely populated, and for the most part made up of farmers and weavers.

Standish

This Wigan district placename is derived from two Old English words: 'stan', meaning stone, and 'edisc', signifying a pasture or an animal enclosure. The placename may therefore be loosely translated as 'stony pasture or enclosure'. Its name was Stanesdis in 1178, and was subsequently spelt several different ways – as Stanedis, Stanediss, Standissh, Stanedich, Stanedissh and Standisch.

St Helens

St Helens, in the medieval Berewick of Hardshaw, and situated in the old West Derby Hundred of Merseyside, derives its placename from the chapel of ease, first recorded in 1552 and dedicated to St Elyn (the fourth century empress, Helen), mother of Constantine the Great. The township grew up around the chapel in the seventeenth century.

Stockport

Stockport is an old historical township located about seven miles south-east of Manchester city centre, at the confluence where the Rivers Tame and Goyt flow into the River Mersey. Two alternative explanations exist as to the origin of its name. One has it that, as a Saxon village, it was given the name Stockport, meaning 'the market place at the hamlet', perhaps because it is known to have had a market well before its charter was officially granted in 1260. Alternative authorities have it that there existed a fortified stronghold in the vicinity in ancient times and that even the Roman General Agricola recognised its strategic advantages when he fortified Stockport to guard the passage of the Mersey. The town's name, then, could have been derived from two alternative Saxon words 'stoc', meaning a stockaded place, a stronghold or castle, and 'port' meaning a wood. Literally, a 'castle in a wood'. Arguably, the latter explanation would seem to be the most plausible.

Stretford

The Trafford district of Stretford's Roman origins are borne out by the placename, which is derived from 'streta' or 'straet', meaning a paved road (invariably built by the Romans), and 'ford', a shallow river crossing. The place of the ford has been identified at the site of the aptly named present-day Crossford Bridge, where the original Roman road from Chester crossed the River Mersey on its way to Manchester. Stretford's placename may therefore be taken to mean 'ford on the Roman road'. The Metropolitan Borough of Trafford's name is itself derived from the same source as Stretford, and despite having the 's' omitted from the 'straet' element and a double-'f' added, it has exactly the same meaning.

Swinton

The name Swinton is derived from the Old English, Swynton, meaning either 'swine town' or 'pig farm'. During the Middle Ages, Swinton belonged to the religious order of the Knights Hospitallers at Whalley Abbey. Later, lands at Swinton were granted to Thurston Tyldesley, then of Wardley Hall. In a record of 1258 the placename was spelt Suinton.

Tameside

Tameside, as its title suggests, is named after the River Tame which cuts through the borough. Words like Tame, Thame and Thames (as in the London river) are ancient Celtic names simply meaning 'river', or in old Norse, 'dark river'. After the Roman withdrawal from Britain, various petty invasions and squabbles between local warlords took place and, by the seventh century, Anglian immigrants had moved in to occupy the region. Most of the placenames of Tameside reflect this influence. Werneth Low, for example, means 'a place growing alder trees', as well as Ashton and Denton, whose names contain the Scandinavian word 'tun', signifying a farmstead.

Tarbock
The small hamlet of Tarbock Green, in the Knowsley district of Merseyside, was once known as Thornebrooke, a name that from the earliest times signified a place where thorn bushes grew beside a brook, Domesday recorded the place as Torboc, in the West Derby Hundred (listed at that time in Lancashire), and held by Roger de Poitou, the Earl of Chester, it having belonged to King Edward before 1066.

Tarporley
The Cheshire township of Tarporley's earliest record is in the *Domesday Book*, when Torpelei was listed in Rushton Hundred. The placename could have come from one of two sources: either from the Old English word 'thorpere', meaning 'peasant' or from the Old Scandinavian 'thorp', indicating an outlying or remote farmstead. Either seem equally possible. Added to this first element is the affix 'leah', indicating a woodland glade or clearing. The placename would therefore suggest a meaning of 'a woodland clearing [or remote farmstead] occupied by peasants'. In 1281, the place was recorded as Thorperlegh.

Tarvin
The Romans called the original Cheshire settlement Tervyn, from the Latin word 'terminus', simply meaning 'end', possibly a place marking a tribal boundary, though it may have had an earlier origin in the Celtic 'teruen', or even from the Welsh 'terfyn'. Either way, Tarvin is the old name for the modern River Gowy, on which the township stands. Domesday marked the settlement as Terve, in the Hundred of Rushton, held jointly by William Malbank and the Bishop of St John's Church, Chester. The account lists eleven villans, ten smallholders, six others and three radmen. In total, the estate amounted to land for twenty-two ploughs and one and a half leagues of woodland. By 1185, the place had been recorded as Teruen.

Tilston
Tilston Parish was in the Tunedune Hundred of Cheshire which included the hamlets of Hob Hill and Lowcross Hill and lies twelve miles from Chester. It was a Romano-British settlement in the late second century and was probably known then as Bovivum. By 1086, it was recorded as Tilleston, the name derived from a man called Tilli or Tilla, who owned the land, and 'stan', a stone, usually a boundary marker. The placename may therefore be taken to mean 'stone of a man called Tilla'. Domesday recorded the manorial estate as Tillestone in Duddeston Hundred, held by Robert FitzHugh.

Tilstone Fearnall
The first word of this small Cheshire hamlet's placename comes from a man called Tidwulf, who may have founded then original settlement, and 'stan', a marker or boundary stone. Until the early fifteenth century, the place was known only by the first part of the name, which was recorded in Domesday as Tidulstane, and listed in the Rushton Hundred, held in 1086 by Robert FitzHugh. Later the Fearnall part was added to the placename. This comes from the Old English words 'fearn', a fern, and 'halh', which signified a nook or corner of land. The entire placename translates into modern English as 'Tidwulf's stone by a nook of land where ferns grow'. In 1427 the name was recorded as Tilston Farnhale.

Tockholes

The Lancashire village and civil parish of Tockholes, which now forms part of the Blackburn with Darwen Unitary Authority, was named after a Danish settler called Toca or Toki, and the Old English suffix 'ho', signifying a hollow. Hence, 'Toca's hollow'. The area was probably inhabited by the Brigantes, a Celtic tribe, as well as Anglo-Saxon settlers, and there is evidence of Bronze Age stone circles and barrows in the area. The village was known around 1200 as Tocholis when it was in the possession of the Pleasington family. It is recorded that Joice de Tocholis, who owned the manor at some time in its early history, took his family name from the place. Tockholes was once a joint township with Livesey, but has been a separate township since the late seventeenth century. It is located on the West Pennine Moors and also includes the hamlet of Ryal Fold.

Tonge

The Bolton district of Tonge is located south of Castle Hill. To the north lies Tonge Moor. The placename is thought to be derived from the Old English word 'tang' or 'twang', meaning a fork in a river, or a thin sliver or tongue of land. The supposed tongue in question lies between Bradshaw and Tonge Brooks.

Torver

This small Cumbrian hamlet derives its name entirely from its early Danish settlers. The placename comprises the Old Scandinavian word 'torf', which means 'turf', and 'erg', a shed or shelter. The placename therefore translates as 'turf [roofed] shed', or possibly from a man's personal name, as 'Thorfi's shed'. The shed concerned would almost certainly have been a shieling, or temporary field shelter for sheep.

Tottington

Tottington, in the Greater Manchester Metropolitan Borough of Bury, once included part of what is now Ramsbottom and as open farmland for centuries was regarded as good hunting land where traditionally deer and wild boar were common. Known as Totinton in 1212 and possibly meaning a 'settlement or estate belonging to the followers or people of a man called Tota', or more likely, given the elevated location of the township, from the Old English 'tot', meaning '[settlement on a] lookout hill'.

Toxteth

The Liverpool district of Toxteth appears in the *Domesday Book* as Stochestede, meaning 'the stockaded or enclosed place', from the Anglo-Saxon 'stocc', meaning stake, and 'stede', meaning place. One view is that it may have referred originally to a stockaded area that protected livestock. Another prefers it as named after a man called Toki, with the Old Scandinavian affix 'stoth', signifying a jetty or landing place; in which case the placename might be translated as 'Toki's jetty or landing'.

Twemlow Green

The Cheshire hamlet of Twemlow Green was known as Twamlawe in the twelfth century, a name that comes from the Old English words 'twegen' or ''twaem', meaning 'two', and 'hlaw', referring to a tumulus, a barrow or mound (typically an ancient burial mound). The name translates as '[place near] two tumuli'. In the nineteenth century at least five were found in the area. Later the village green was included as part of the village placename.

Tyldesley

The Wigan district of Tyldesley placename means 'Tilwald's clearing' and is derived from the Old English personal name Tilwald (its probable founder), and 'leah', signifying a woodland clearing. The placename has been variously recorded as Tildesleiha, Tildeslege, Tildeslegh and Tildesley. In 1210 the placename was recorded as Tildeslei.

Ulverston
From the Old English name Wulfhere, or the Scandinavian 'Ulfarr', meaning 'wolf warrior', and 'tun' signifying a farmstead or village. Hence, 'the village belonging to Ulfarr'. The wolf is still retained as an element on the Ulverston coat of arms. The township was listed in the Domesday survey as Ulvrestun and Ulureston, '...near Kirkby, in the Amounderness Hundred', where Dubhan and Thorulf, probably Saxons, were both recorded renting six carucates of 'land of the king in Yorkshire ...for geld'.

Urmston
A former Lancashire Urban District, Urmston is the largest township in the Borough of Trafford. Its name derives from Old English or Norse 'Orm', Wyrm' or 'Urm', an early owner – possibly Orme FitzSeward, the son of Edward Aylward – plus the Saxon affix 'tun', meaning farmstead or settlement. Hence, 'Orme's settlement'. In 1194 the placename was recorded as Wermeston.

Walkden
The district of Salford placename Walkden (sometimes Walkeden) derives from the Old English word 'denu', meaning a valley, possibly belonging to a man called Wealca or Walca. Hence, 'Wealca's valley'. Documents recording the name date back to 1246. By 1325 it had begun to resemble its present-day form as Walkeden.

Wallasey
Located on the Wirral Peninsular of Cheshire close to the Welsh border, the township of Wallasey was known as Walea in 1086. The name means 'island of the Britons', derived from the Old English word 'walh' (or 'wala' in its plural form), which could mean either 'Welshman' or 'Briton'; given that the border had not been fixed at that time and Wallasey might have been in either territory at various times in its early history. Then the affix 'eg' was added, signifying an island, or raised ground that was surrounded by marsh or wetlands, or prone to flooding at high tides, as was the case here. Domesday listed the manor in the Willaston Hundred, held at that time by Robert FitzHugh. Before the Conquest the manorial estate had belonged to a free man called Uhtraed.

Wardle
The Rochdale district of Wardle probably derives its name from the Old English word 'weard', meaning 'watch' or 'lookout', and the affix 'hyll', a hill. In modern English it might be expressed as 'ward hill', implying a 'fortified place on a hill'. The hill in question may have been the nearby Brown Wardle Hill. During the Middle Ages, Wardle was a small centre of domestic flannel and woollen cloth production; many of the original weaver's cottages survive today as listed buildings. Around 1193 it had been spelt as Wardhul.

Warrington
The Romans knew Warrington as Veratinum and following their withdrawal from Britain in the fifth century, a Saxon settlement was established. The *Anglo-Saxon Chronicles* referred to the Thelwall district of Warrington in 919 AD, when it recorded that 'King Edward went with troops, in the latter part of the autumn, to Thelwall, and ordered the borough to be built, occupied and manned'. By the time of the Domesday survey, it was already known as Walintune and a Saxon church dedicated to St Elphin was known to exist. The placename derives from two Old English words, 'wering', meaning a weir or a dam, and 'tun', a

farmstead or settlement. Hence, '[the] farmstead or settlement by the weir (or dam)'. The weir or dam in question would have been on the River Mersey. Domesday recorded the name as Walintune, and by 1259 it had been written as Warmincham.

Warton

Originally recorded as Wartun in the Amounderness Hundred of Lancashire in 1086, it derives from two Old English words 'weard', a watchtower or lookout post, (related to the modern English word 'ward'), and 'tun', meaning a farmstead or township. The placename may therefore be taken to mean 'the farm with a lookout post'. It was assessed at four carucates of land held by Roger de Poitou in the Domesday survey, having belonged previously to Earl Tostig Godwinson, brother of King Harold. The aforesaid lookout post seems likely to have been at a place known in the present-day as Warton Crag.

Wavertree

Bronze Age burial urns found in the Victoria Park district of Wavertree demonstrate that this area of Liverpool was an early prehistoric settlement. The placename derives from the Old English words 'waefre', meaning waving, unstable or restless, and 'treow', meaning 'tree', almost certainly referring to aspen trees that are common in the locality. Hence, the placename means '[place by] waving [or restless] trees'. The *Domesday Book* refers to the 'Mainou of Wauretreu', in the possession of a man called Leving, with land for two ploughs. It passed to the Walton family, who were Master Sergeants of the West Derby Wapentake and held the four oxgangs of land that came with the office.

Westhoughton

The township of Westhoughton is located about four miles south-west of Bolton, with the M61 Motorway running along its northern boundary. Earliest records show the small market town in the County of Lancashire, known by at least two other versions of the placename, including Westhalcton and Westhalghton. This is a conglomeration of three Old English words, 'west', plus 'halh', meaning a corner or nook of land, and 'tun', a farmstead. Hence, 'western farmstead in a nook of land'. The place was originally known simply as Houghton, but the 'West' was added later to distinguish it from Little Houghton near Eccles (now in Salford). Around 1210, it was simply known as Halcton, and by 1240 as Westalcton.

Whitefield

Whitefield, in the Metropolitan Borough of Bury gets its name from two Old English words: 'hwit', meaning 'white', and 'feld', signifying open or arable land (or what we would now call a field). There are at least two theories for the meaning of the placename. One is that it comes from the local weavers who used to lay out fabrics to dry and bleach in the sun – hence, 'white fields'. The other relies on the fact that, historically, Whitefield has been a farming community of open fields and that the name is a corruption of the word 'wheatfields'. It was already known by its present name by the end of the thirteenth century.

Whitehaven

The placename of this township in Cumbria was spelt Qwithofhavene around 1135 and probably derives from three Old Norse words, 'hvitr', meaning 'white', 'hofuth', indicating a headland or promontory, and 'hafn', a harbour. Taken together these three elements translate as 'harbour near the white headland', in reference to the white stone hill located beside the harbour. In 1278, the place was recorded as Witenhauen.

Widnes

There are two possible explanations of the derivation of the Widnes placename. One has its origin in the Danish words 'vid', meaning wide, and 'noese', meaning nose, referring to the promontory on the River Mersey. Another possibility is that the first part comes from the word 'wid', meaning wide or open and 'naess', referring a the headland or promontory, such as that on which the town is located beside the River Mersey. Hence '[place at the] wide promontory'. There are several older spellings, including Vidnes, Wydness and Wydnes.

Wigan

Wigan history began over 2,000 years ago, when Celtic warriors settled in the area. Later, the Romans built a fort and a settlement, known as Coccium. There is no reference to Wigan in the *Domesday Book*. It has been suggested that the placename dates from the seventh century and is of Celtic origin, named after a person actually called Wigan or Wiggin. An alternative explanation is that it derives from the ancient Celtic word 'gwig' and means 'little settlement' (or village), or 'wicum', meaning '[the place of] the dwellings', which effectively has the same meaning. Its spelling has been recorded in numerous historical documents variously as Wygayn and Wygan. The current spelling of Wigan dates from the end of the twelfth century.

Wigton

The Cumbrian placename Wigton is a corruption of 'Wicga's tun'. Wicga is thought to have been the place's founder, a chieftain or an early settler, and the word 'tun' being Old English for a farmstead, homestead or village. Therefore, Wigton can be interpreted as 'the hamlet (or farmstead) belonging to Wicga'. In 1163 it was recorded as Wiggeton.

Wilmslow

Wilmslow was not mentioned in the Domesday survey, and its placename is therefore difficult to define. One possible explanation is that it comes from the name of a man called Wighelm, who once owned the land, and the Old English word 'hlaw', meaning 'mound'. Hence, 'mound belonging to Wighelm'. Another theory is that it was the burial place of the first William de Bolyn (also known as Williams Lowe), who changed his name to Wilmslowe. In medieval times, the land was predominantly agricultural with extensive parklands and an ancient map shows that Fulshaw and Morley were once densely wooded. By 1250, the placename had been recorded as Wilmesloe.

Windermere

In the twelfth century known as Winandermere, from Vinandr, an Old Norwegian man's name (sometimes Winand or Vinand), and 'mere', the Old English word for a lake or large pool. Hence, 'Winand's Lake'. At ten and a half miles long, Windermere is the largest lake in England, although locals dispute the word 'lake', pointing out that it is a 'mere'. By the twelfth century the place was called Winandermere and until the nineteenth century, the name persisted as Winander Mere.

Winsford

Winsford's origins are uncertain, but two possible explanations exist. First, a derivative of 'Wainsford', a ford or shallow river crossing used in transporting hay carts (or 'wains'), across the River Weaver from Chester to Middlewich in Cheshire. Second, and more likely, someone called Wynn or Wine, lived by the ford and it became known as Wynn's Ford. In 1334 it was recorded as Wyneford.

Wirral

The Wirral is a peninsula in Cheshire that lies between the Dee and the Mersey estuaries. The name comes from the Old English word 'wir', meaning 'bog myrtle', and 'halh', a corner or nook of land. Hence, the name means 'corner of land where bog myrtle grows'. The bog myrtle is a flowering plant commonly found in western Europe and sometimes called 'Sweet Willow'. To describe the Wirral Peninsula as a mere 'corner of land' somewhat belittles its size, as it covers more than one hundred and fifty square kilometres. In the early tenth century the area was known as Wirheale.

Withington

The Manchester district of Withington was mentioned in the Domesday survey as little more than a wasteland ('wasta'). Later, in the twelfth century, the placename probably signified 'a settlement or farmstead near a willow wood'; a 'withy' was an old name for a willow branch or twig – hence, Withy Grove, a street name in Manchester city centre.

Withnell

The name of the small Lancashire village of Withnell appears in the early twelfth century as Withinhull. It comes from the Anglo-Saxon words 'withigen', meaning 'willow trees', and 'hyll', a hill. Hence the placename means 'hill where willow trees grow'. The name later appeared as Withinhulle, in the chapelry and Parish of Leyland. Initially, the manor was owned by the Whalley family, before passing to the Hoghtons, and by the end of the thirteenth century to one Adam de Withnell, who took his name from the village. There have been several variants of the placename over time, including Withenhull, Wythenil, Whytenhull and Wythenull. Locally, the village name is pronounced 'Winnell'.

Wrenbury

The Cheshire township of Wrenbury included the hamlets of Porters Hill, Wrenbury Heath and Wrenbury Wood. It was recorded in the *Domesday Book* as Wareneberie, in Warmendestrou Hundred, held by William Malbank. A freeman called Karli had held it before the Norman Conquest and it was recorded having woodland, enclosures and a hawk's eyrie, valued at five shillings and assessed as 'waste', thereby not liable for taxation. By 1230, the place was known as Wrennebury, from the Old English 'wrenna', a wren, and the affix 'burh', a stronghold or fortified place, which translates from Old English either as 'stronghold inhabited by wrens'. Alternatively, Wrenna may have been the original landowner's name, in which case 'stronghold of a man called Wrenna'.

Wythenshawe

The Manchester district of Wythenshawe takes its name from two Old English words: 'withy' or 'withigin', meaning a willow tree, and 'shaw' or 'sceaga', signifying a wood or a copse. Hence, a '[place in a] willow copse'.

Part Seven

The West Midlands

Herefordshire, Shropshire, Staffordshire, Warwickshire,
West Midlands, and Worcestershire

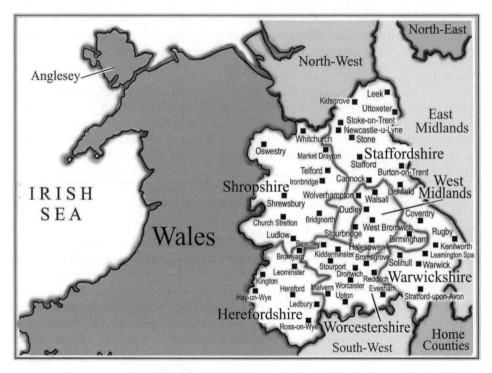

A map depicting the West Midlands region of England.

Acton Trussell

Originally known simply as Actone, this Staffordshire village derives its placename from two Old English words, 'ac', meaning 'oak tree', and 'tun', signifying a farmstead. Hence, Acton simply means 'farmstead [by the] oak trees'. Domesday recorded Actone, in the land of the Bishop of Chester, where Robert held an unspecified plot of land, most probably for rent. The account reads: 'There is land for four ploughs and in demesne is one plough, and ten villans and eight bordars with four ploughs'. There was a mill, eight acres of meadow and three by two furlongs of woodland. In the time of King Edward it had been valued at five shillings, but by the time of the survey it had been revalued at twenty shillings. From the fourteenth century, the estate was owned by the Trussell family, who appended their family name to the place, and the present-day placename, Acton Trussell, was well established by the late fifteenth century.

Alberbury

Almost certainly named after a woman called Aluburh, this Shropshire village arose out of the fortified manor house (or 'burh') that she established in the place. Hence, it became 'Aluburh's manor house'. Domesday recorded the place as Alberberie, in the Baschurch Hundred, in the possession of Earl Roger de Montgomery at that time, it having belonged to the Crown at the time of King Edward.

Albrighton

A village near Shifnal in Shropshire named after a man called Eadbeorht (or Aethelbeorht), and his 'tun', a farmstead or village. The place was recorded in the *Domesday Book* as Albricstone, in the Hundred of Baschurch, held at that time by Alchere de la Pin. Before the Conquest, it was held as two separate manors, one held by Algar (possibly the son of Earl Leofric and Godifu of Mercia), the other by a man called Godgyth (or Godhyte). The account reads: 'There is woodland for fattening one hundred pigs. But now it is in the king's hand... it was worth twenty-one shillings; now sixteen shillings. He found it waste'; in this instance 'waste' probably referred to cultivated land which had been allowed to fall fallow. By the late eleventh century the place had also been recorded as Etbritone.

Alcester

This Warwickshire township, located on the River Alne, with the addition of the Old English word 'ceaster', gives the clue as to the derivation of the placename, 'the Roman town on the River Alne'. The township had begun as a Roman settlement on Ickfield Street, and was known to them as Alauna, located in a strategic position on the road to Droitwich from Stratford-upon-Avon. The name of the River Alne probably came from a Celtic source meaning 'shining one'. In 1138, the township was recorded as Alencestre.

Alveley

Alveley is a small Shropshire village, one of the few named after a woman. Her name was Aelfgyth and the with the additional Old English suffix 'leah', indicating a woodland clearing or glade, the placename translates as 'Aelfgyth's woodland clearing'. In 1086, the Great Survey recorded the placename as Alvidelege, in the Cuttlestone Hundred, held by Earl Roger, it having belonged to Earl Aelfgar before 1066.

Areley Kings

The first part of this Worcestershire hamlet's placename comes from two Old English words, 'earn', meaning 'eagle', and 'leah', a woodland glade or clearing. Hence, '[place near the] woodland clearing where eagles are seen'. In the twelfth century the place was known as Erneleia, but it had earlier been known as Nether Arley, distinguishing it from nearby Upper Arley. As part of the Royal Manor of Martley, 'King's' was added so that by the beginning of the fifteenth century the placename had become Kyngges Arley.

Aston

There are more than a dozen places in England with the Aston placename. The ward of Aston, a suburb in the north-east of Birmingham, was first mentioned in the *Domesday Book* as Estone, from the Old English words 'est' and 'tun', simply meaning 'east village, farmstead or settlement'. The name reflects its location east of Birmingham, though it was formerly in the County of Warwickshire. By 1086, it had been granted to William FitzAnsculf, who held it for the king. It had previously belonged to Godmund the Saxon.

Astley Abbotts
The first element of this Shropshire village placename, Astley, derives from the Old English word 'est', meaning 'east' or 'eastern', and the affix 'leah', indicating a woodland glade or clearing. Hence, the word translates as 'eastern clearing in a wood'. In 1090, the placename was recorded as Estleia. By the thirteenth century, the manor and its estates had come into the possession of Shrewsbury Abbey, and the 'Abbotts' affix was appended and it became identified by its Latin name, Astleye Abbatis, which over time was Anglicised into Astley Abbotts, creating a placename which translates as '[place at the] woodland clearing belonging to the abbots'.

Atcham/Attingham
The Shropshire township of Atcham was known in 1086 as Atingeham, and its placename was probably based on the name of a man called Aetti, Etti or Eata. The original Old English element 'inga' indicated the 'people, tribe, or followers' or 'place associated with', and 'ham' signified a homestead or dwelling place. It is not clear at what point the 'ing' was removed and the placename shortened to Atcham, but it was known as such by the mid-nineteenth century, when it also continued to be locally known as Attingham. It has also been suggested that the final element may have been 'hamm', which signified a bend in a river, in which case we might interpret the placename as 'Aetti's dwelling on land at the bend of the river', or something along those lines. The *Domesday Book* refers to the place as being in the Wrockwardine Hundred, belonging to the cannons of the Church of St Alkmund in Shrewsbury, and tenanted by Godebold the Priest. It was valued at six shillings and eight pence and housed two villans and three smallholders.

Atherstone
Atherstone is a market town in North Warwickshire which dates back to Roman times, when a fortified settlement known as Manduessedum existed on nearby Watling Street, which ran through it. Domesday records it as Aderestone, belonging in 1086 to Bishop Odo of Bayeux, and held on his behalf by Corbin. The placename probably derives from the personal name of a man called Aethelred, with the Old English suffix 'tun', meaning 'the farmstead or village belonging to Aethelred'. It was in fields nearby that the Battle of Bosworth took place.

Avon Dassett/Burton Dassett
Avon is a common English river name found in several places around the country. Its origin was in ancient Celtic, where it simply meant 'river', or 'stream'. Hence, the River Avon technically means 'River River'. Both of the Warwickshire villages of Avon Dassett and Burton Dassett were commonly known as Derceto in the Great Survey of 1086. Their separation into two entities seems to have taken place sometime in the twelfth or early thirteenth centuries. Avon Dassett derived its second name from Old English words 'deor', a deer, and 'set' or 'cete', meaning a shelter or fold. Hence, '[place by] the deer fold on the [River] Avon'. In 1212 it was known as Auene Dercete. Nearby Burton Dassett derives its name the Old English words 'burh' and 'tun', respectively meaning 'fortified farmstead'. It was known as Magna Dercet in 1242 and Dassett Magna alias Burton Dassett in 1604. Domesday records Derceto in Stoneleigh Hundred of land belonging to the Count of Meulan, where three Saxon thegns 'held them and were free'. There was sufficient land for twelve ploughs with three more held in demesne. The manor estate was populated by twelve villans, ten slaves, five bordars and a priest. Its fifty acres of meadow were valued at eight pounds.

Aymestrey
The affix 'trey' generally comes from the Old English word 'treow', meaning 'tree', and this Herefordshire village has a placename that runs true to form. The tree in question belonged

to a Saxon man called Aethelmund, whose name is incorporated, so that placename means 'Aethelmund's tree'. In 1086, Domesday recorded the village as Elmondestreu, and listed it as a large manor in the Leominster Hundred. It merited two entries in the survey and belonged at that time to King William, it having been held by Queen Edith of Wessex, wife and widow of Edward the Confessor in 1066.

Baddesley Ensor

Originally known simply as Baddesley, this Warwickshire village was acquired by the de Edneshoure family in the thirteenth century, who appended their name to the place. The meaning of the placename derives from a man called Baeddi, whose woodland glade or clearing ('leah'), it was in Saxon times. Hence, 'Baeddi's woodland clearing'. The family name distinguished it from Baddesley Clinton, owned by the same family a few miles to the south. Domesday recorded the place as Bedeslei in 1086, and by 1327 it had been written as Baddesley Endeshouer.

Barlaston

This small village in Staffordshire was known by 1002 as Beorelfestun. The placename derives from the personal name of a man called Beornwolf, plus the Saxon element, 'tun', meaning 'farmstead'. Hence, 'farmstead belonging to Beornwolf'. Domesday records the place as Bernulvestone, in the Pirehill Hundred land of Robert de Stafford, where he personally held half a hide of land, which Helgot maintained on his behalf. Before 1066, it had belonged to Augustine, a free man. There were six acres of meadow and three acres of woodland, altogether valued at forty shillings.

Battlefield

Named after the Battle of Shrewsbury which took place nearby, this hamlet in Shropshire was probably first known as Hayteleyfeld, where the Old English element 'feld', signified the field of battle. In 1403, a college of secular canons was founded here and in 1410 the placename had been recorded as Bateleyfield. In 1410 the name had been written as Batelfeld.

Betton Abbots

This small Shropshire hamlet was recorded in 1086 simply as Betune, in the Condover Hundred, held at that time by the Bishop of Chester. The name is made from two Anglo-Saxon words, 'bece', meaning 'beech tree(s)' and 'tun', an estate or farmstead. Hence, 'farmstead where beech trees grow'. By the end of the thirteenth century, the manor had come into the possession of Shrewsbury Abbey and the affix 'Abbatis' was attached to the placename. This distinguished the manor from nearby Betton Strange which had been granted to Hamon le Strange in the twelfth century.

Bewdley

A small riverside township in Worcestershire, known in the thirteenth century as Beuleu, from the French word 'beau', meaning beautiful, and 'lieu', a place. Hence, a 'beautiful place'. At the time of the *Domesday Book*, it was called 'Wribbenhall... in the demesne of Kidderminster ... [and that] King William held it'.

Bicton

The placename of this small hamlet in Shropshire means '[place by the] hill with beaks'. The name comes from the Old English words 'bica', meaning 'bill' or 'beak', and 'dun', a hill. The settlement lies near to a long hill with pointed peaks, which is reflected in the placename. Domesday recorded the place as Bichetone, listed in the Baschurch Hundred, held in 1086 by a man called Wiger on behalf of the Canons of St Chad in Shrewsbury.

Biddulph

The *Domesday Book* lists this old Staffordshire township as Bidolf. The name may be derived from the Old English 'dylf', referring to a pit or quarry and the prefix 'bi', meaning 'place'. Hence, 'a place near the pit or quarry'. An alternative interpretation cites a corruption of the Old Saxon word 'bidulfe', meaning 'wolf slayer'. A rampant wolf still occurs on the family crest of the Biddulph family. Others prefer the Anglo-Saxon name Bydelph, where 'by' means 'near' and 'delph' signifies a 'digging place'. In which case, 'near or by a digging place', a possible reference to shallow mining.

Bilston

Little is known of the Black Country township of Bilston (in modern day Wolverhampton) before the tenth century, apart from the fact that in 996, the name was written as Bilsetnastum and Bilsetnatun. The Old English words 'bil' or 'bill', indicating a sharp edge or ridge, 'saete', meaning 'dwellers' or 'settlers', and 'tun', a farmstead, taken together complete the placename, which translates as 'farmstead of people who live at a sharp edge [of a hill]'. The 'bil' in question may refer to a local hill or escarpment, of which the nearby Sedgley Beacon is the favoured candidate. Alternatively, the name may derive from the personal name of a man called Bil, whose 'tun', or settlement it was. In 1086, Domesday listed the place as Billestune, in the Seisdon Hundred of Staffordshire, held at that time by the king.

Bircher

This Herefordshire hamlet's placename is derived from the Anglo-Saxon words 'birce', referring to a birch tree, and 'ofer', signifying a ridge. Therefore the name translates as '[place by a] ridge where birch trees grow'. An early spelling of the name was as Burchoure in 1212.

Birmingham

Derived from the Old English 'Beormingaham', the place was first known to be settled by the Beormingas tribe and literally means 'the settlement of Beorma's people'. Beornmund, after whom the township was named could have been a head man, perhaps its founder or leader at the time of the Anglo-Saxon settlement. The original settlement is believed to have begun close to the River Rea in what is now the Digbeth district. At the time of the *Domesday Book*, the 'Mainou of Bermingeham' lay within the Colehill Hundred of Warwickshire, and had been granted to William FitzAnsculf. At that time it was a very small settlement amounting to just nine households, supported by land for six ploughs and half a league of woodland. The manorial estate was valued at just one pound, revealing few clues as to its eventual emergence as England's second largest city. Nowadays, the city is locally known as 'Brum', short for 'Brummagem', a name that emerged in the seventeenth century, and which has come to mean 'cheap and showy' or 'shoddy'.

Bishops Itchington/Long Itchington

In 1001, both Bishops Itchington and Long Itchington were known as a single entity, as Yceantune. The name derives initially from the Riven Itchen, which pre-dates the Celtic era and whose precise meaning is a mystery. Add to this is the Old English affix 'tun', indicating a Saxon farmstead, and the original placename translates as 'farmstead on the River Itchen'. Following the Conquest, the manorial estate was granted to the Bishop of Coventry and Lichfield, and the 'Mainou of Bisshopoesychington' came into being. By the late twelfth centry, a part of the original estate, some five miles distant, became separated and was renamed as Long Itchington, the Old English word 'lang' indicating distance. Around 1185, it was recorded as Longa Hichenton. Domesday recorded Icetone in Stoneleigh Hundred, held by the Bishop of Coventry. Before the Conquest, the manor and its estates had been worth three pounds, and by 1086 had been revalued at twelve pounds.

Bitterley

The Shropshire village of Bitterley derived its placename from the Old English words 'butere', meaning 'butter', and 'leah', a woodland clearing, which taken together produce a placename that means 'woodland clearing where butter is made'. It has been suggested that the 'leah' element may more properly be interpreted as 'pasture', producing an alternative meaning of 'butter pasture', one that had good grazing and produced excellent quantities of milk for butter churning. Domesday recorded the place as Buterlie, in the Overs Hundred, held in 1086 by Robert de Lacy, having been a possession of Godwin before the Conquest.

Black Country, The

A name given to that region of central England lying between Birmingham and Wolverhampton, which due to heavy industrialisation during the nineteenth century and the smoke from blast furnaces and dirt from coal mining, rightly earned the region its name. At its epicentre is the town of Dudley, which houses the Black Country Museum, a major tourist attraction and local heritage site. The 'blackness' of the region's fabric has long since disappeared, but the term 'Black Country' is still proudly owned and vigorously defended by its resident population.

Blakemere

Blakemere in the County of Herefordshire derives its name from the Old English word 'blaec', meaning dark-coloured or black, and 'mere', a small lake, pond or pool. Hence, '[place by a] dark-coloured pool'. It is thought that pool in question would have formed part of the local River Wye. The present-day placename was first recorded in 1249 and in the nineteenth century it was sometimes referred to as Blackmoor.

Bourton on Dunsmore

Bourton on Dunsmore is a Warwickshire village which was known at the time of Domesday as Bortone in the Marton Hundred held by the Count of Meulan having belonged to Leofwin before the Conquest. The name comes from the Old English 'burh-tun', signifying a fortified place and a farmstead. Hence, 'fortified farmstead'. The 'on Dunsmore' addition was in reference to its location in the old district of Dunn's Moor, (itself named after a one-time owner), and in order to distinguish it from Burton Hastings a few miles away. The full placename therefore translates in full as 'fortified farmstead on a moor belonging to a man called Dunn'. Bourton and Burton are both variations with the same source and meaning.

Brampton Bryan

This Herefordshire village was first recorded in 1086 as Brantune, a name that was in place well before the Norman Conquest. It derives from 'brom' and 'tun', two Saxon words which respectively mean 'broom' (the shrub), and 'farmstead'. Hence, 'a farm where broom grows'. According to the Domesday survey, Brampton was listed as a settlement in Shropshire, lying within the Leintwardine Hundred in land belonging to Ralph de Mortimer. It had been held before the Conquest by a man called Gunnvarthr. Later, during the twelfth century the estate came into the ownership of a man called Brian, and from 1275 the place came to be known as Bramptone Brian, or 'farm belonging to Brian where broom trees grow'.

Bratton

There are several places in England called Bratton, including Bratton in Wiltshire, Bratton Clovelly and Bratton Fleming in Devon, as well as Bratton Seymour in Somerset. In general terms, the placename comes from two Old English words, 'brace', which referred to newly cleared, ploughed or otherwise cultivated land, and 'tun', a farmstead. The name therefore translates as 'farmstead with newly cultivated land'. However, the small hamlet of Bratton in the Wrekin district of Shropshire derives its name from a slightly different source - from 'broc', meaning 'brook' or 'stream'. In this case, the placename may be taken to mean 'farmstead by a brook'. This is thought to be a reference to the brook that flows nearby into the River Tern. Domesday recorded the place as Brochetone, in the Condover Hundred, granted to William Pantulf. Before the Conquest the manor had been valued at twenty-four shillings, but at the time of the survey it was declared to be waste ('wasta').

Bretforton

The medieval concept of a so-called 'plank ford' has long since fallen out of use, but it was at one time an efficient way of crossing a shallow stream and keeping the feet dry. Take the Old English word 'bred', which signified a board or plank of wood, together with 'ford', signifying a river crossing, and the combination perfectly fits this particular bill. Additionally, the Saxon word 'tun', which signified a farmstead, produces the complete interpretation of this Worcestershire village placename: 'farmstead near a plank ford'. The facility evidently existed well before the eighth century as the placename was recorded as Bretfortona in 709. By 1086, the name had been spelt Bratfortune and listed in the Fishborough Hundred held by Evesham Abbey, who had also held it at the time of King Edward.

Bridgnorth

In 895, Danes set up a camp, known to them as Cwatbridge, beside the River Severn in Shropshire. A few years later, Lady Aethelflaed of Mercia had a small castle built on the hilltop overlooking the river, which the *Anglo-Saxon Chronicles* recorded in 912: 'Aethelflaed, lady of the Mercians, on the Holy Eve of the Invention of the Cross, came to Scergeat and built a burh there, and in the same year, that at Bridgnorth'. In 1101, Robert de Belleme, the son of Earl Roger de Montgomerie (sometimes Montgomery), developed Bridgnorth Castle and became the Earl of Shrewsbury. By 1156, the township was known simply as Brugge (or Brugg), from the Old English 'brycg', meaning 'bridge' and, by 1282, as Brycg Norht and Brugge Norht. The township earned the 'North' element of its placename in view of another earlier bridge further south at Quatford, although its former whereabouts remain unknown.

Brierley Hill

The origin of the name reveals an Anglo-Saxon heritage, in that the Old English word 'brer', according to some, translates as 'brother', while others translate it as indicating a briar or bracken. The word 'leah' signifies a woodland clearing, plus the word 'hill'. The hill in question probably refers to the ridgeway that runs from Dudley to Wolverhampton. Hence, the placename might mean '[the settlement] on the hill in the woodland clearing', or 'woodland clearing on a hill where briars grow'. In the fourteenth century, the township was known simply as Brereley.

Broadwas

As early as the eighth century this Worcestershire village was known as Bradeuuesse. The first element of the name 'Broad' is a translation of the Old English word 'brad'. The second element comes from 'waesse' (related to the modern word 'wash', as in the area of East Anglia known as 'The Wash'), and referred to alluvial land, typical of flood plains or wetlands. This was the case here, as the River Teme is periodically known to flood and deposit rich alluvial soil over the landscape as it drains. Consequently, the placename means 'broad [stretch of] alluvial land'. Domesday recorded it a Bradewesham in the lands belonging to Worcester Cathedral, who had seven hides of land earning them revenue. The survey recorded the estate's assets as '...four slaves and two female slaves, and two mills rendering ten shillings, and a fishery rendering twenty sticks of eels and twenty acres of meadow and woodland one league long and one wide'.

Bromsgrove
Before the Norman Conquest, the Worcestershire village of Bromsgrove had been held by Earl Edwin. Even earlier, in 804, it was known as Bremesgrefan or Brommsgraf, from an Old English personal name of a man probably called Breme, with the addition of the suffix 'graf', signifying a grove or coppiced woodland. Hence, 'the grove of a man called Breme'. The *Anglo-Saxon Chronicles* called the place Bremesburh and Domesday recorded the place as 'the demesne of Bremesgrave'. A later spelling variant was Bromysgrove.

Bromyard
In 840, this Herefordshire township, located on the River Frome, was recorded when Bishop Cuthwulf established a monastery in a place known as Bromgeard. By the time of the *Domesday Book*, it had been recorded as Bromgerbe. The placename derives from the Old English words 'brom', signifying a broom tree and 'geard', meaning an enclosure. Hence, an 'enclosure where broom trees grow'. Before the Conquest, it had been owned by Earl Aelfstan.

Broseley
There are two possible explanations of the origin of this township in Shropshire. The first is that it may have been named after a man called Burgweard, whose 'leah', or woodland clearing it was. In the late twelfth century the placename was recorded as Burewardeslega. The second explanation is that the name derives from the Old English expression 'burh-weard', which meant 'warden' or 'fort-keeper', from 'burh', a fortified structure or stronghold, and 'weard', a guardian' or 'warden'. So the placename means either 'woodland clearing belonging to a man called Burgweard' or 'woodland clearing belonging to the fort warden'.

Bucknall
Bucknall is a district of Stoke-on-Trent in the County of Staffordshire, whose placename has at least two possible interpretations. On the one hand, it could be named after a man called Bucca; on the other, it may derive from the Old English word 'bucca', which referred to a he-goat (or billy goat). The second element of the placename comes from 'halh', which represented a corner or nook of land. Hence the placename could mean either 'corner of land belonging to a man called Bucca', or 'corner of land where billy goats graze'. Domesday recorded the place as Bucenhole and listed it in the Pirehill Hundred held by King William, having belonged to Ketil of Bucknall before the Conquest. There is another place of the same name in Lincolnshire.

Buildwas
The Shropshire village of Buildwas overlooks the flood plain of the River Severn in Shropshire. This goes some way to explain the second element of the placename ('-was'), derived from the Saxon word 'waesse', which referred to an alluvial marsh or flood plain. However, the 'build' element of the placename is more problematic; there is an opinion that

it relates to the Old English word 'bilde', which meant 'omen' or 'threatening'. Conceivably, the ever-present threat of flooding in the area might make this a reasonable assumption. So, in general terms the placename may be understood as '[place on] alluvial plain liable to flooding', or even more simply as '[place on] alluvial land'.

Burslem

A district of Stoke-on-Trent in Staffordshire, Burslem was recorded in 1086 as Bacardeslim. That name came either from the Old English expression 'burh-weard', meaning 'fort-keeper', or else a man called Burgweard – either is possible. The last element of the placename is also ambiguous; it could derive from the old district name 'Lyme', which itself could mean 'threshold' or 'lintel', or it may relate to Lyme Park in Derbyshire, whose vast parkland estate stretched right down to Staffordshire. So, the placename might mean either 'estate in Lyme belonging to a fort-keeper', or 'estate belonging to a man called Burgweard'. By the mid-thirteenth century, the placename had been written as Borewardeslyme.

Burton upon Trent

Burton is a common placename, with around sixteen other places of this name throughout England. However, this Staffordshire township's name was made specific by the addition of the river on which it stands. Hence, Burton-upon-Trent. The place was recorded in the Domesday survey as Bertone, from the Old English 'burh-tun', meaning 'a fortified farmstead'. It was held in 1086 by the Abbey of St Mary of Burton 'in the vill of Stafford'. The place was known in 1002 as Byrtun, had become Burtone by the time of Domesday, and by 1234 had been recorded by its Latin name, as Burton super Trente.

Bushbury

Bushbury is a district of the City of Wolverhampton in the West Midlands whose placename means 'bishop's fortified manor'. It was already known by the name Byscopesbyri in 996 AD, and comes from two Old English words: 'biscop', meaning 'bishop', and 'burh', a stronghold or fortified manor house. It is not known who was the bishop of the placename, nor where the manor house might have stood, as the area was overbuilt by extensive housing estates in the post-war period. Domesday recorded it as Biscopesberie in the Seisden Hundred which at that time stretched across parts of Staffordshire and Warwickshire and was part held by William FitzAnsculf and by the Canons of St Mary's, Wolverhampton. Before the Conquest, part of the estate had belonged to Countess Godiva of Coventry.

Cannock

Recorded in 1086 as Chenet in the Cuttlestone Hundred of Staffordshire, and by the twelfth century as Canoc, this rural settlement was held by Earl Aelfgar of Mercia before the Conquest, but taken over by King William thereafter and valued at just twenty shillings. The ancient parish also included the hamlets of Hednesford, Leacroft, Cannock Wood and Great Wyrley. The name derives from Old English and means 'a small hillock', possibly referring to Shoal Hill, north-west of the town. An area within the district known as Cannock Chase was originally land reserved for hunting and the breeding of animals. The 'Chase' element most probably comes from the Old English 'chace', itself derived from the French verb 'chasser', to hunt or chase.

Chatcull

This small Staffordshire hamlet relates its placename to a lime kiln once operated there by a man probably called Ceatta. The second element of the placename comes from the Old English word 'cyln', meaning 'kiln'. The *Domesday Book* records the place as Cetquille and

Ceteruille, in the Hundred of Pirehill, in the land of the Bishop of Chester, where there was only land for a single plough. The entry concluded that 'All these lands are waste'. In 1199 the place was recorded as Chatculne.

Cheddleton

Cheddleton is a Staffordshire village whose name derives from the word 'cetel', another Old English word for a valley, together with the affix 'tun', which signifies a farmstead. Hence, the placename may be taken to mean 'farmstead in a valley'. Domesday recorded the place as Celtetone, in the Totmonslow Hundred, held by Earl Roger of Shrewsbury, with William Malbank as its tenant-in-chief. Before the Conquest it had belonged to Godwin. It was then a small estate with just three villagers and one smallholder, with land for four ploughs and half a plough in demesne, and with a woodland of half a league. In 1202, the placename was written as Chetilton.

Chelmarsh

The marsh referred to in the name of this Shropshire village has long since ceased to exist, but nevertheless the Saxons identified the place as 'cegel-mearsc', where 'cegel', meant 'pole' or 'marker', and 'mearsc', a marsh. The name translates as '[place by the] marsh marked out with poles'. At a time before hard-metalled roads, such poles might have marked a safe passage through marshland. Domesday listed the village as Celmeres, in the Alnodestreu Hundred, held in 1086 by Ralph de Mortimer, it having belonged to Earl Edwin before the Norman Conquest.

Cheslyn Hay

This suburb of Cannock in rural Staffordshire was earlier known as Wyrley Bank, a name derived from the Anglo-Saxon words 'wir', meaning 'bog myrtle' (a species of flowering plant of the genus Myrica, also known as Sweet Willow), and 'leah', a woodland clearing. Hence, 'woodland clearing where bog myrtle grows'. Everything appeared to change some time in the late twelfth or early thirteenth century, when according to some accounts a coffin was found on a ridge nearby. Following that event, the place became known by a combination of three Old English words: 'cest', meaning 'coffin', 'hlinc', a ridge, and 'haeg', signifying an enclosure. In common parlance this might translate as 'enclosure on a ridge where a coffin was found', or even more simply, 'coffin ridge'. The place was recorded in 1236 as Haya de Chistin.

Cheswardine

A small Shropshire township whose name signifies 'enclosed settlement where cheese is made'. The name is derived from the Old English 'cese', and 'worthign', which referred to an enclosed or fenced settlement. It was recorded in 1086 as Ciseworde in Pirehill Hundred, of which two hides were held by Robert de Stafford, and leased to a man called Gilbert. Lady Godifu of Coventry had held it before the Conquest, '...but paid two shillings... to the Church of St Chad'. In 1160, the place was recorded as Chesewordin.

Chetwynd Aston

This village in the Wrekin area of rural Shropshire was recorded by Domesday as Catewinde in 1086. The name comes from a man called Ceatta and the Old English word 'gewind', signifying a winding path up a hill'. Hence, 'winding upward path (or ascent) of Ceatta'. The de Chetwynd family, who took their family name from the place, held the estate in the thirteenth century. Their appended family name distinguishes it from Church Aston a few miles away. Aston derives from 'east' and 'tun', together meaning 'eastern farmstead [or estate]'. In the seventeenth century, the village became known as 'Greate Aston alias Chetwynde Aston', and in the nineteenth century it emerged as its current name of Chetwynd Aston, though it was also known at that time as Field Aston.

Childswickham

A Worcestershire village whose placename translates as 'nobleman's place in a clearing or meadow', although some interpret it as 'young person's house in a woodland clearing'. The name might possibly derive from the Old English 'child' or 'cild', meaning 'young man', and 'ham', indicating a village, manor or estate, along with the Celtic word 'wig' or the Welsh 'gwig', signifying a lodge. The place was first recorded in 706 as Childeswicwon, and in the *Domesday Book* as Wicvene in the Greston Hundred, at that time located on the border of Worcestershire and Gloucestershire. It was held in 1086 by Robert, known as the Bursar, and had belonged to Baldwin, the son of Herelewin in 1066. The manor had a ten acres of meadow and two mills, and was valued at twelve pounds.

Chilvers Coton

The Chilver's Coton district of Nuneaton in Warwickshire gets its name from a man called Ceolfrith, who may have been an early settler or the founder of the settlement. The second word is from the Old English word 'cot, whose plural form is 'coten' meaning 'cottages'. Hence, the placename means 'Ceolfrith's cottages'. Domesday actually recorded the place a Celverdestoche in the Colehill Hundred, where the last element is from 'stoc', which referred to an outlying or remote hamlet or village. Later, the place was recorded as Chelverdescote.

Cholstrey

This Herefordshire hamlet is thought to be named either after a man called Ceorl, or else a 'ceorl', a Saxon name for a free man or a peasant – either is possible. The second element of the placename, 'treow', was Old English for a tree. Hence, either 'Ceorl's tree', or 'tree belonging to a free man or peasant'. Domesday recorded Cerlestreu, listed in the Leominster Hundred, a very large estate supporting over two hundred villagers, as well as eighty freemen smallholders, thirteen male slaves and twelve female slaves. It also had six priests. The manor was held in 1086 by King William, it having previously belonged to Queen Edith.

Churchover

In 1086 this Warwickshire village was known simply as Wavre, after the river on which it stood, which was subsequently renamed as the River Swift. In Old English 'waefre' means 'winding stream'. Later the Saxon word 'cirice', meaning 'church' was added, so that by the twelfth century the village name had become Chirchwavre, which over time developed into Churchover. The Domesday account placed the manor estate in the Bumbelowe Hundred (which at that time covered areas of Warwickshire and Northamptonshire) and assessed it as quite a large estate part-held by Earl Aubrey de Coucy, William FitzAnsculf and Thorkil of Warwick.

Church Stretton

This is an ancient Anglo-Saxon rural settlement near Watling Street, which ran from the Roman town of *Viroconium Cornoviorum* (Wroxeter), to Gloucester. The land had been occupied by the Celtic Cornovii tribe before Roman occupation and the Latin name which they gave the place meant 'the settlement of the Cornovii'. Later it was known simply as Stretton and recorded in 1086 as Stratune; before the Conquest had been held by Earl Edwin. This element of the placename translates as 'the settlement beside the [Roman] street'. The Saxon earls of Mercia had already built a church dedicated to St Lawrence in the settlement. By the mid-thirteenth century, the place had acquired a semblance of its present-day name, when it was recorded as Chirich Stretton and over time this became Church Stretton.

Clayhanger
The Clayhanger district of Walsall in the West Midlands was known as Cleyhungre in the thirteenth century, a name derived from the Old English words 'claeg', meaning 'clay' (related to the modern English word 'claggy'), and 'hangra', a wooded slope or hillside. Hence, 'clayey wooded slope'. There are places of the same name in the counties of Cheshire and Devon.

Clee St Margaret
A Shropshire village which, as the placename implies, lies near the Clee Hills and the Church of St Margaret. The hills take their name from 'cleo', an Anglo-Saxon word for 'rounded hill'. The 'St Margaret' element distinguishes the place from Cleeton St Mary, some five miles distant. Domesday identifies the village as Cleie, in the Patton Hundred, in the possession of Helgot of Holdgate in 1086. It was a relatively small estate of four ploughlands, with one mill, sustaining two villans, two smallholders and four slaves, altogether worth four pence. Before 1066, Aelfric held the manor as a free man. By the late thirteenth century, it was known by its Latin name, as Clye Sancte Margarete.

Cleeve Prior
This Worcestershire village name initially comes from the Old English word 'clif', which refers to a cliff or steep bank, a reference to its location on a prominent cliff edge ridge overlooking the River Avon. The second part refers to the Prior of Worcester who owned the manor. In 1086, it was known simply as Clive, but by the end of the thirteenth century it was recorded as Clyve Prior. The *Domesday Book* identified the village in Ash Hundred in the land of the Church at Worcester, attached at that time to Atch Lench, where there were ten and a half hides of land. It valued the estate thus: 'It was worth seven pounds [in 1066]; now six pounds. Of this land two hides, less one virgate, are waste'. In 1291 the placename was written as Clyve Prior and as late as the nineteenth century was referred to as Prior's Cleeve.

Clent
Before the Norman Conquest, the hamlet of Clent was held by Edward the Confessor, and after 1066 by William the Conqueror. At that time, it was recorded in the *Domesday Book* as annexed to Staffordshire, remaining so until 1832, when Parliament re-drew the county boundary to bring it into Worcestershire. The placename survives intact from the Old English and means a rock, or a rocky hill, amply describing its local topography. It was also known at one time as Klinter, from the Old Norse 'klint', meaning 'cliff'.

Cleobury Mortimer
Located on the Clee Hills of Shropshire, from which this village gets the first element of the placename, and taken together with the Old English second element, 'burh', it produces a meaning of 'fortified place in [or on] the rounded hill'. 'Clee' takes its name from the Saxon 'cleo', signifying a rounded hill. Before the Norman Conquest, the manor was owned by Queen Edith, Edward the Confessor's widow, but after 1066 it was given to Ralph de Mortimer, a veteran of the Battle of Hastings, whose family held possession for the next three hundred years, and attached their family name to the place. The *Domesday Book* records the village as Cleberie and Claiberie, in the Hundred of Conditre. It had a

population of forty-five households in 1086, very large for that time, with four hides of land suitable for twenty-four ploughs. The assessment recorded 'woodland for fattening five hundred pigs', and valued the manor at twelve pounds. The place was recorded as Clebury Mortimer in 1272.

Clifford Chambers
In the early tenth century, this village in Warwickshire was known simply as Clifforda, a name coming directly from Old English, where 'cliff' represented a bank, (as in a river bank), and 'forda' signified the shallow river crossing of the River Avon at this point. Hence, '[place at a] ford by a bank'. Domesday recorded the village as Clifort, in the Tewkesbury Hundred, (which at that time covered areas of Gloucestershire and Warwickshire), and belonged to King William, with Roger de Bully as its chief tenant. Before the end of the eleventh century the chamberlain of St Peter's Church in Gloucester was granted ownership of the manor, after which time it was known as Chaumberesclifford.

Clodock
A small Herefordshire hamlet named after the village church dedicated to the sixth century Christian martyr, King Clydawg of Ewias, or St Clydog, who was said to be grandson of Welsh King Brychan (as in the Welsh town of Brecon). Around 1150, it was known by its Latin name Ecclesia Sancti Clitauci. The twelfth century church is the traditional site of St Clydog's tomb, and became a destination for religious pilgrims.

Cockshutt
In medieval times, nets would be stretched across woodland glades and clearings to entrap woodcocks as they 'shot' or darted through. Such devices were called 'cockshoots', from the Old English words 'cocc', a woodcock, and 'sciete', to shoot or dart. This Shropshire village placename comes directly from that old practice, and was known in 1270 as La Cockesete.

Codsall
The Wolverhampton district of Codsall's entry in the *Domesday Book* places the small 'Mainou of Codeshale' in Seisdon Hundred within 'the Land of the King's Thegns', where three hides were leased by the king to Cynwine, who already held them before the Norman Conquest. The suggestion is that Cynewine swore allegiance to the Conqueror, or else offered some favour, as most Saxon eorls and thegns forfeited their lands after 1066. Only around twenty other Saxon thegns seem to have been so honoured by the time of the survey. There were only six inhabitants of the estate in 1086. The placename seems to come from an early founder or settler called Cod, whose 'halh', or corner of land it was. Hence, the placename Codshall might be interpreted as 'corner [or nook] of land belonging to a man called Cod'.

Colwich
Colwich is a Staffordshire village whose name means 'building where charcoal is made [or kept]'. It comes from the Old English words 'col', which could mean both 'coal' or 'charcoal', and 'wic', a specialised building or dwelling. The placename was recorded as Colewich in 1240.

Coseley
This district with the Borough of Dudley in the West Midlands derives its placename from two Old English words, 'colestre', meaning 'charcoal burner', and 'leah', a woodland glade or clearing. The name may be interpreted as meaning 'woodland clearing where charcoal burners work'. It was recorded as Colseley in 1357.

Coven

Not at all related to witches' covens and the like, this Staffordshire village derived its placename from the Old English word 'cofa', which means 'shelter'. The shelters in question exist as recesses in the local hillside and offered protection to sheep and cattle in inclement weather. The village received an entry in the *Domesday Book* as Cove, in the Cuttlestone Hundred, held by Earl Robert de Stafford and leased to Burgraed (identified as 'father of Edwin'). Before 1066 the manor had belonged to Alric, a Saxon free man. There were three acres of meadow, half a league of woodland reserved for the king in demesne. The survey entry concludes: 'The land is worth sixteen shillings'.

Coventry

The origin of this placename is contentious. One hypothesis has it derived from a man known as Cofa, who settled there and marked the boundary of his land with, or on a tree – in Old English, 'treow'. Hence its early name, Cofantreo, may be taken to mean 'Cofa's tree'. Another view has it that the settlement name comes from the local waterway, the River Sherbourne, once known as the River Couaen or Cune, which joined the Avon nearby and refers to the place where waters met. Yet a third cites the Celtic-Roman water goddess Coventina as the source of the placename and a fourth that it is derived from the word 'coven', an old word for a convent; given the existence of a Saxon abbey in the township, this is quite possible. In 1043, the placename was written as Couentre and in 1086 as Couentreu.

Cradley

More properly, the full placename is Cradley Heath, originally a clearing or heathland between Cradley and the nearby hamlet of Netherton, upon which residents had grazing rights, subject to payment to the Lord of the Manor. Hence the 'Heath' affix. The placename should be pronounced 'Crayde-lee', and not 'Crad-lee', as outsiders frequently mispronounce it. By the twelfth century, the Parish Church of St James had been built. The township was recorded in Domesday as Credelaie, part of the Came Hundred, meaning 'woodland clearing of a man called Croeda'. It was in the possession of William FitzAnsculf and held for him by a man called Pain. The Saxon, Wigar (or Withgar) had owned it before the Norman Conquest.

Cressage

The Shropshire village of Cressage denotes a place where religious meetings once took place beneath an oak tree. The name derives from the Anglo-Saxon words 'Crist', meaning 'Christ' (as in Jesus Christ), and 'ac', an oak tree. Hence, 'Christ's oak tree'. The place was known and recorded in 1086 as Cristesache, in the Condover Hundred, where 'Ranulph Peverel holds Cristache of Earl Roger. Eadric held it [at the time of King Edward] and was a free man'. The manor estate boasted a fishery that rendered eight shillings and woodland for fattening two hundred pigs. In 1066, the estate had been worth one hundred and ten shillings, but by the time of Domesday it had been assessed at six pounds.

Crudgington

A small village in the Telford-Wrekin area of Shropshire, Crudgington begins its name with a residual Celtic element related to the Welsh word 'crug', which signifies a hill-mound, hillock or tumulus. Added to this are the two Old English elements 'inga', meaning 'people or followers' and 'tun', a farmstead or estate. The three elements taken together produce a placename which means 'farmstead [or estate] of the people [who live on] a tumulus-shaped hill'. In the Great Survey of 1086 the village was listed as Crugetone, in the Baschurch Hundred, held by Robert FitzCorbet (known sometimes as Robert 'the Butler'), having been in the possession of Earl Edwin before the Conquest. The manorial estate was wealthy and had a fishery which rendered thirteen shillings and four pence in taxes, as well as a farm which rendered seventy-three shillings and four pence. It was valued at four pounds '...and one thousand eels'. By the twelfth century, the placename was being written as Crugelton.

Cubbington

The Warwickshire village of Cubbington derived its name from a man called Cubba, possibly its founder or chieftain, plus the Old English affixes 'inga', meaning 'people, tribe or followers', and 'tun', an estate or farmstead. Hence, 'estate belonging to the people of Cubba'. It was known in 1086 as Cobintone, Cubintone and Cubitone, in the Stoneleigh Hundred, held by the Abbey of St Mary in Coventry, as it had been before the Conquest. The account lists land for four ploughs and eight acres of meadow, supporting five villans, one smallholder and two slaves. The church held two hides of land, but a further three hides belonged to the Count of Meulan, it having been in the joint possession of Ketibiorn of Cubbington and Leofwin, uncle of Thorkil in 1066. The survey valued the manor estates at one pound and five shillings.

Ditton Priors

The name Ditton is fairly common in England, with others of this name in Kent, Surrey and Cambridgeshire. It comes from the Old English words 'dic' and 'tun', taken together to mean 'farmstead near a ditch [or dyke]'. The Shropshire village of Ditton Priors has a slightly different origin in that the 'Ditton' element probably refers to a man called Dudda, who once owned the farmstead. The 'Priors' element was appended when the manor came into the possession of Wenlock Priory. Domesday names the place Dodintone in 1086, in 'The Land of Earl Roger [of Shrewsbury]', divided between the Patton and Baschurch Hundreds, where its Lord in Chief was Earl Edwin who oversaw four berewicks within the manor. It was a very large settlement for its time, supporting thirty-eight households, including twenty villans and ten slaves. The manor also owned a salt pan in Droitwich. By 1346, the place had become known as Dodyton Prioris.

Droitwich

The Worcestershire town of Droitwich has long been celebrated as a salt town, on account of its underground brine streams which rise to the surface through artesian pressure. Salt was exported by pack horse throughout central and southern England for many centuries, having been organised into an efficient distribution network by the Romans. In common with many English salt-producing locations, in 1086 it was known simply as Wich. By the mid-fourteenth century it was known as Drihtwych, with the Old English prefix 'drit' or 'drith', meaning dirt, dirty or muddy, and 'wic', signifying some sort of specialised settlement. Hence, 'dirty [or muddy] salt town [or settlement]'.

Dudley

The West Midlands township of Dudley was formerly an enclave of Worcestershire, and probably derives it placename from a man called Dudda and the attached Old English element 'leah' indicating a woodland glade or clearing. Hence, 'Dudda's clearing'. The name appears in the *Domesday Book* as Dudelei, in the Hundred of Clent, a relatively small manor of sixteen households, boasting a woodland of two leagues, held by William FitzAnsculf, having been in the possession of Earl Edwin before the Norman Conquest.

Eardisland

In 1086, the Herefordshire township of Eardisland was known simply as Lene, based on 'Leon', the old Celtic name for the district. The Old English first element 'eorl' signifies a baron or nobleman, and the 'leon' element has been transformed into 'land'. The placename therefore translates as '[the] nobleman's estate in Leon'. At the time of the Domesday Survey, it was held by King William having belonged to Earl Morcar in 1066. The audit lists twenty-one villagers, nine smallholders, six slaves, two female slaves and eight others, and the manor estate was valued at twelve pounds. By the early thirteenth century the place had been recorded as Erleslen.

Edgbaston
The placename probably derives from a man called Ecghbeald (which means 'bold sword'), with the addition of the Old English suffix 'tun', signifying a settlement or farmstead. Hence, 'Ecghbeald's farmstead'. Apparently incorrectly spelt in the *Domesday Book* as Celboldeston in the Coleshill Hundred of Warwickshire, it was recorded as held by William Drogo de la Beuvrière, having previously been freely held by two Saxons, Aski and Alwig, and worth twenty shillings. By 1184, it was recorded as Edgabaldstone.

Edstaston
This hamlet in Shropshire takes its name from a Saxon man called Eadstan, who may have founded the original settlement, which probably began as a farmstead, as evidenced by the Saxon word 'tun'. Hence, 'Eadstan's farmstead'. For some reason the first part of his name was missing in the Domesday account, which recorded the place as Stanestune, and listed it as a very small estate supporting only three households in the Hodnet Hundred, held by William Pantulf (sometimes 'Pandolf') in 1068, it having belonged to Aelfeva and Ordwy before the Conquest. Its total assets amounted to two ploughlands and woodland for sixty pigs, valued in total at one pound.

Edvin Loach
This Herefordshire hamlet was recorded as Gedeuen in 1086, a name originally derived from a Saxon man called Gedda. The Old English word 'fenn', signifying marsh or fenland, was added and produced a placename meaning 'Gedda's marsh (or fen)'. Domesday listed the village within the Doddingtree Hundred, at that time spread across the three adjacent counties of Gloucestershire, Worcestershire and Herefordshire, and held by Osbern FitzRichard. Before the Conquest it had belonged to a man called Wulfheath. Then in the thirteenth century the estate came into the ownership of the de Loges family, whose name was attached to the village. Consequently, in 1242 the placename was recorded as Yedefen Loges.

Evesham
Located on the River Avon in Worcestershire, Evesham derived its name from a local swineherd called Eof (or Eoves), who reputedly had a vision of the Virgin Mary. This prompted Bishop Egwin of Winchester to build an abbey on the site in 709, at which time the place was known as Eveshomme or Eof's ham, which translates loosely as the 'land of Eof at the river bend' – (the River Avon has a long distinctive bend at this place). By the time of the 1086 survey, it was recorded in its present form of Evesham, held by Evesham Abbey. In 2008, the town erected a bronze statue commemorating Eof, its supposed founder.

Etruria
Etruria is a district of Stoke-on-Trent in Staffordshire, which was established and named by the internationally-famed potter and ceramicist, Josiah Wedgwood. Wedgwood built Etruria Hall where he lived; he established a pottery works there, and the township grew up around it. The name comes from the ancient land of the Etruscans, who lived in the Tuscany region of Italy, and whose pottery was a major influence of Wedgwood's work.

Fenny Compton

The Old English word 'fennig' meant 'muddy' or 'marshland', and this was the origin of this Warwickshire village placename. Compton is derived from two other Saxon words, 'cumb' and 'tun', which respectively mean 'valley' and 'farmstead'. Taken as a whole, the placename means 'farmstead in a muddy valley' or 'muddy farmstead in a valley' – either is possible. The description fitted the local topography as the village as it was originally located in a drain-off field below Compton Hill. Domesday recorded the place as Contone in 1086 and listed it in the Hunesberie Hundred, held jointly by the Count of Meulan and Thorkil of Warwick. In 1221, the place was recorded as Fenni-cumpton.

Fitz

This small Shropshire hamlet once belonged to a man called Fitt, who may have been its founder or an early leader of the settlement. In 1194, the name was recorded as Fittesho, a placename taken from his personal name plus the Old English word 'hoh', meaning a ridge or hill-spur. Hence, 'Fitte's ridge [or hill-spur]'. The last element of the name has long fallen into disuse and by 1255 the name was being written as Fittes.

Flash

The Old Scandinavian word 'flask' referred to a marshy place or swampy pool, and this name was probably applied to this village in Staffordshire some time way back in the eighth or ninth centuries. It was known in the late sixteenth century as The Flasshe.

Flyford Flavell

A Worcestershire village with an obscure placename origin, of which several quite different explanations have been given. There is a view that both the words 'Flyford' and 'Flavell' might have the same meaning, where the first may derive from the Old English 'fyrhth', meaning 'sparse woodland'. This is supported by its single eleventh century placename, Fleferth. The second word, 'Flavell', which may have been a Normanised version of the same word, could have been appended in order to distinguish it from the nearby village of Grafton Flyford. Another explanation is that the first part (Flyford), may have been a personal name of a local landowner. By 1420, the place continued to be known by a single word, Fleford, and it was not until the sixteenth century that it had been transformed to a recognisable form of its present-day placename – as Fleford Flavell.

Gailey

Gailey is a small hamlet in rural Staffordshire that was once known for the bog myrtle that grew there in abundance, a fact recorded in its placename. In Old English, 'gagel' referred to bog myrtle (sometimes known as 'gale'), and 'leah' was a woodland clearing. The placename therefore translates as 'woodland clearing where bog myrtle, [or gale], grows'. Domesday recorded it as Gragelie, in the Cuttlestone Hundred, held in 1086 by Robert de Stafford, it having previously belonged to Bodin of Gailey.

Ganarew

The fact that this Herefordshire village placename sounds Welsh is not surprising, given its proximity to the Welsh border. It is thought to be a Celtic name, similar to the Welsh words 'genau', meaning 'mouth' or 'opening', and 'rhiw', a hill. It is loosely interpreted as '[place by the] pass of the hill'. An alternative explanation has been offered in that it might have been a reference to St Gunguaui, (in Welsh: Gwynwarwy); if this were the case the name may be taken to mean '[place by the] hill of St Gwynwarwy'.

Grafton Flyford

At least ten other English villages and townships are named Grafton, which is a name derived from the Old English words 'graf', indicating a grove, and 'tun', a farmstead. Hence, Grafton means 'farmstead in [or near] a grove'. Examples include Graftons in Herefordshire, in Oxfordshire and North Yorkshire, amongst others. The Worcestershire township of Grafton Flyford was known as Graftone as early as the ninth century, and as Garstune in 1086, listed in the Hundred of Pershore, belonging to the Abbot of the Church of St Peter, Westminster and held for him by Walter Ponther. Before the Conquest it had belonged to Alwin and was held by Algar and Thorkil. The manor supported 'a priest and one Frenchman and six villans... [and] there are five slaves'.

Great Bolas

Great Bolas is a village in the Telford and Wrekin district of Shropshire that was known in 1198 as Belewas and in 1265 as Boulewas. The original placename was based on the Old English word 'waesse' (similar to the modern English word 'wash'), which referred to a river flood plain on the River Tern, or its marshland that is prone to seasonal flooding but quickly drains away. The first element of the second word, 'bo', may have referred to a small bend in a river (also known as a 'bogel'), in which case the word 'Bolas' might be translated as 'flood plain on a small river bend'. The 'Great' element came some time later to distinguish it from Little Bolas across the river.

Halesowen

Halesowen, in the ancient Clent Hundred, was held for the king by Earl Roger of Shrewsbury in 1086, when it was recorded as Hala. Before the Conquest, it had belonged to Sheriff Wulfwine, who also held salt pans in Droitwich. In 1276, it was known as Hales Ouweyn, after Owen (or Olwine), the Prince of Wales, who held it well into the mid-1200s, and the Old English element 'halh', signifying a corner or nook of land or a shallow hollow. Hence, 'Owen's [hollow or] corner of land'.

Hammerwich

Hammerwich is a Staffordshire village that began life as a blacksmith's forge, if the placename is to be taken at face value. The Old English word 'hamor' meant both 'hammer' and 'smithy' and 'wic' indicated a specialised building, in this particular case, a forge. Hence, the placename means simply 'blacksmith's forge'. Domesday recorded it as Humeruuich, listed in the Offlow Hundred, held by the Bishop of Chester who had retained it following the Conquest. By the end of the twelfth century the placename had been spelt as Hamerwich.

Hamstall Ridware

The Ridware element of this Staffordshire village placename is a combination of the Celtic word 'rid', meaning 'ford', referring to the shallow crossing over the River Blyth, and the Old English 'ware', meaning 'dwellers'. 'Ham-stall' is an old Saxon expression meaning 'village' or 'homestead'. The complete placename may be interpreted in its simplest form as 'dwellers at the ford'. It was known as Rideware before the Conquest and recorded in Domesday as Hamstal Rideware (or Riduare), in the Pirehill Hundred held by Earl Roger. In 1242 the place was recorded as Hamstal Ridewar. The Hamstall element of the placename was added in the thirteenth century to distinguish it from nearby Pipe Ridware which took its name from the Pipe family who had taken possession of the manor.

Handsacre

Put in the simplest of terms, the Staffordshire village of Handsacre was a plot of arable land once belonging to a Saxon man called Hand, and this is the meaning of the placename. The word 'aecer', which meant 'plot of land' has come down to us as 'acre', an area of land measurement. Domesday recorded Hadesacre (having failed to include the 'n' in the placename), and listed it as a very small estate supporting five or six households within the Offlow Hundred, held in 1086 by the Bishopric of Chester, who had also held it during the reign of King Edward. The estate amounted to forty-six ploughlands, had a fifty-two acre meadow and a mill.

Hanley Child

The placename of Hanley is a combination of 'heah' and 'leah', two Saxon words which taken together meant 'high woodland clearing'. In 1086 the place was listed as Hanlege, in the Doddingtree Hundred of Worcestershire (which at that time covered part of modern-day Herefordshire), in '...the Land of Gilbert FitzTurold', tenanted by a man called Hugh, it having been held by two Saxon men, Cyneweard and Ulfkil, before the Conquest. The survey accounts for '...one smith and a Frenchman with three ploughs'. By the mid-thirteenth century, the affix 'cild' had been added; technically this word applied to a child or children, but in this case the manor had become occupied by a young unnamed monk, and the description 'child' applied specifically to him – in other words, a young man. This distinguished the manor from Hanley William, two miles distant, which had come into the possession of William de la Mare in 1242, and thereafter it bore his name. In 1255, the placename was written as Cheldreshanle. The final placename translates as '[estate of the] young monk in the high woodland clearing'.

Hartlebury

This is a village in Worcestershire which once belonged to a Saxon man called Heortla who was probably its founder of chieftain, and the Old Saxon affix 'burh', indicating a stronghold or fortified manor. The placename therefore means 'Heortla's stronghold'. It was already known in 817 as Heortlabyrig, and by the time of the Domesday survey it had been recorded as Huerteberie, in the Cresslow Hundred, held by the Bishop of the Church of St Mary in Worcester, who had owned it before the Norman Conquest. It was a very large manor of forty-three households and valued in 1086 at thirteen pounds and five shillings.

Hay-on-Wye

Probably known best nowadays for its annual international book festival, the Herefordshire border township of Hay-on-Wye was simply known as Hagan in 958, as Haya in the early twelfth century and by 1259 had become known as La Haya. The name has a similar derivation to The Hague in the Netherlands as both may be derived from the Saxon word 'gehaeg', which means an enclosed field or a fenced-off hunting ground or chase. Due to boundary changes, the township lies on the border of Herefordshire and the Welsh County of Powys. The 'Wye' affix locates the town upon the river of that name. The township's name in Welsh is 'Y Gelli Gandryll', which means 'woodland of a hundred plots'.

Hereford

The placename is derived from the Anglo-Saxon word 'here', which signified an army or an armed force, and 'ford', a shallow river crossing place. Hence, loosely, 'a river crossing place suitable for an army' or '[place at the] army ford'. The ford in question would have been where the old Roman road crossed the Wye en route from Leintwardine to Monmouth, Earlier known as Herifs, by the time of Domesday it had become known by its present-day name of Hereford and was held by William the Conqueror.

Herefordshire
A unitary authority bordering Wales in central England, whose name is based on the City of Hereford, with the addition of the Old English word 'scir', meaning 'district' or 'shire'. The name translates as 'district based on Hereford'. It was recorded in the eleventh century as Herefordscir.

Himley
The Staffordshire village of Himley gets its name from the hop plants that were grown there in medieval times. The Old English word for the hop is 'hymele', plus the affix 'leah', which signifies a woodland clearing or glade, means that the placename means 'woodland clearing where hop plants are grown'. Domesday records Himley as Himelei, in the Seisden Hundred, in the land of William Ansculf, with one virgate rented from him by Gilbert of Englefeild and another 'two hides less half a virgate of land' leased to Arni. In 1066, the manor estates had belonged to three free man known as Lovet, Wulfstan and Ramkel.

Hodnet
This ancient Shropshire placename originated in the Celtic words for 'pleasant valley'. Given the village's very proximity to the border, it relates closely to the Welsh words 'hawdd', meaning 'pleasant', and 'nant', valley. The village overlooks the valley alluded to in the placename, through which runs the River Tern. Domesday referred to the place as Odenet, located in the Baschurch Hundred, belonging in 1086 to Earl Roger of Shrewsbury, it having belonged to King Edward in 1066. The account recorded nineteen ploughlands, three lord's plough teams and seven men's plough teams, and stated that '...there is a little wood rendering nothing'. There was a church in the manor and the estate was valued at eight pounds

Holmer
Holmer is a suburb of Hereford whose placename is derived from the Old English words 'hol', meaning 'hollow' (as in a narrow valley), and 'mere', a lake or pool. Hence, the name means '[place at the] pool in a hollow'. Domesday recorded the place as Holemere in 1086, listed in the Cutestornes Hundred, held by the Canons of St Peter's Church in Hereford, as it had been at the time of King Edward.

Hope Mansell
The Old English word 'hop', from which the first word of this Herefordshire village placename is derived, signified a valley, and the place was recorded as Hope by the Domesday Book in 1086. The survey listed it as a very small manor of just two households in Bromarch Hundred land which had been granted to William FitzBaderson. Before 1066 two Saxon men named as Leofric and Eadwulf '...held it as two manors'. The other manor might have been Long Hope, some four miles distant and now in the County of Gloucestershire. The estate passed to the Maloisel family some time in the late-eleventh century and their family name was attached to the place, so that by the twelfth century, the village had become known as Hoppe Maloisel.

Hopton Wafers
As in Hope Mansell, the 'hop' element of this placename refers to an enclosed valley, and Old English word 'tun' signifies a farmstead or village settlement. The second word of the placename comes from the Wafre family, who had taken possession of the manor

some time before the thirteenth century and attached their name to the place, thereby distinguishing it from nearby Hopton Cangeford and Hopton Castle. The name means 'farmstead [or village] in a valley belonging to the Wafre family'. Domesday listed Hopton, in the Conditre Hundred of Shropshire, held by Roger de Lacy in 1068, having belonged to Siward the Fat in 1066. In 1236 the placename was recorded as Hopton Wafre.

Hopwas

This Staffordshire village lies in the Tame Valley and has historically been prone to flooding, which begins to explain the last element of its placename. The Old English 'waesse', signifies alluvial or marshy land formed from sediment, and has a modern equivalent in the word 'wash' (as in The Wash region of East Anglia). The 'hop' element of the placename related to an enclosure, and sometimes to a valley. Hence, 'enclosure [or valley] on [or near] marshy or alluvial land'. Domesday recorded the name as Opwas in 1086, and listed it in the Pirehill Hundred, held by the Crown at that time.

Idlicote

Idlicote probably began as a single cottage which was established or built by a man called Yttel or Yttela during Anglo-Saxon times, as his name is embedded in the placename, as originally were the Old English words 'ing', generally taken to indicate an association, and 'cot', a cottage. Therefore, the placename could be translated as 'cottage associated with a man called Yttela'. The original settlement had developed into a very large manor and was recorded in 1086 as Etelincote, in the Fexhole Hundred of Warwickshire, in land belonging to Robert de Stafford. In the entry the original 'ing' element has been contracted to 'in' by the Domesday commissioners and over time this was diminished even further to a single 'i'.

Ightfield

The Shropshire village of Ightfield is named from the open land (or in Old English, 'feld' or 'felda') beside the River Ight, (now known as the River Ray), upon which the original settlement was founded. The Ight river name is so ancient that nothing is known about its meaning. In 1086 the place was recorded as Istefeld, in the Hodnet Hundred land held by Gerard de Tounai-sur-Dive, where the Saxon Wulfgeat had it as a free man before the Norman Conquest of 1066.

Ipstones

Ipstones derived its name from the Old English words, 'yppe', meaning 'upland' or 'highland', and 'stan', a stone (or stones). The placename therefore translates as 'stone [or perhaps even stony ground] in the upland', in recognition of its location on high ground near the River Churnet in rural Staffordshire. During the twelfth century the place was recorded as Yppestan.

Ironbridge

Located on the upper reaches of the River Severn in Shropshire, Ironbridge, as the placename implies, is named after the revolutionary cast iron bridge that spans the river in Ironbridge Gorge, near Coalbrookdale. Described as 'the birthplace of the Industrial Revolution', it is where Abraham Darby developed smelting using coke, thereby making the production of iron much cheaper. In 1779, Darby's grandson, also called Abraham, built the bridge, the first to be constructed entirely of cast iron, which had been designed by Thomas Pritchard. Unsurprisingly, the placename reflects its most distinctive feature, the iron bridge and the Gorge, which have been designated as a World Heritage Site.

Keele

This Staffordshire village was recorded in 1169 as Kiel, a name derived from two Anglo-Saxon words, 'cy', a cow or cows, and 'hyll', a hill. Taken together they mean 'cows hill' or 'hill where cows graze'. An alternative view is that the placename is of Scandinavian origin in that Keele is located on a ridge that looks like the keel of an upturned boat.

Kenchester

Like most other places with the 'chester' element in their placename, this small hamlet in Herefordshire would once have been the site of a Roman fort or military installation, which they knew as Magnis, which is itself of Celtic origin and means 'of the stones'. The first element of the name, 'Ken', refers to a man called Cena, who was probably its oldest known Saxon leader or the founder of the post-Roman settlement. The village name therefore means 'Roman fort or estate associated with a man called Cena'. Domesday recorded the place as Chenecestre, in the Stepleset Hundred, held in 1086 by a man somewhat disparagingly referred to as 'Hugh the Ass'.

Kenilworth

Recorded as Chinewrde in the Stoneleigh Hundred of the County of Warwickshire in the Great Survey of 1086 and held by Richard the Forester for King William, having belonged to Edward the Confessor before 1066. By the twelfth century it had been written as Chenildeworda. Its original name derives from a woman called Cynehild and the Old English 'worth' or 'wrth', meaning 'enclosure'. Hence, 'the enclosure belonging to Cynehild'.

Kerne Bridge

Kerne Bridge in the County of Herefordshire was named after the mill that once stood beside or near a bridge there. The Old English word 'cweorn' meant 'mill', (almost certainly a watermill), and 'byricg' meant 'bridge. The name was recorded in 1272 as Kernebrigges.

Kidderminster

Known in the ninth century as Chederminstre, this township occupies land lying between the River Severn and the River Stour in Worcestershire and began as a settlement on the Stour's left bank. The place is named after a man called Cydela plus the Old English word 'mynster', a word used in Saxon times to identify a monastery, church or other religious house. Hence, 'the monastery (or church) of Cydela'. There is evidence that King Aethelbald of Mercia granted the township a charter for the creation of a religious house in 736, on the site of the present-day Church of All Saints. No other significant records of the settlement exist before the Domesday survey, when it was recorded as 'Chideminstre ... held in the demesne of the king ... and of the same land Aiulf holds one virgate'. It is also recorded that the central manor had sixteen outlying farms or berewicks. In the mid-twelfth century, the place was recorded as Kedeleministre.

Kidsgrove

Located on the northern edge of the Borough of Newcastle-under-Lyme near the Cheshire border, Kidsgrove is a small township in the Wolstanton Parish of Staffordshire. It was not mentioned in the *Domesday Book*, but the placename was recorded in 1596 as Kydcrowe. It probably means 'a pen for young goats', from 'kyd' or 'kid', plus the Old Welsh word 'crau', or Old English 'crow' or 'crew', signifying an animal pen of some kind. Another explanation of the placename suggests that the original settlement way have been founded by a man called Cyda, which together with the Saxon word 'graf', meaning 'grove' or 'copse', might produce a placename meaning 'grove of a man called Cyda'.

Kilpeck

Located so close to the English border with Wales (which would not have been fixed at that time), it should come as no surprise that the first part of this Herefordshire village placename is of Welsh origin, and comes from the word 'cil', meaning 'corner' or 'nook'. And technically that is as far as any reliable explanation goes, for nothing authoritative is known about the remainder of the placename. The most obvious explanation is that it means '[place by the] corner'. However, in his book *A Dictionary of British Placenames*, A.D. Mills suggests that 'peck' (from the Old Welsh 'pedec'), might refer to an enclosure where animal snares, such as those used to hunt rabbits are placed. In this case, the name might mean 'corner enclosure where animal snares are set'. Domesday recorded the name as Chipeete, a very large estate for that time, in the Archenfield Hundred, held by King William. By around 1150 the name was written as Cilpedec.

Kings Norton

Norton is a common placename with around twenty other places of this name around England. The Kings Norton district of Birmingham is recorded in the *Domesday Book* as one of the eighteen berewicks or farms, thus: 'Kynges Nortune ... [in] the demesne of Bromsgrove ... held by the king', which had been owned by Edwin, Anglo-Saxon Earl of Mercia, before the Conquest of 1066. Edwin had fought alongside Harold at Stamford Bridge immediately before the Battle of Hastings. The township was known in Saxon times as Nortune in the Cme Hundred of Warwickshire, but when it was confiscated by William the Conqueror in 1068, the 'Kings' prefix was added.

Kingswinford

Located within the old County Borough of Dudley, though historically in the County of Stafford, Kingswinford is recorded in 1086 simply as Swineford, from the Old English 'swin', a pig, and 'ford', a shallow river crossing. Hence, 'Pig ford'. It was not until 1322 that the placename was written as Kyngesswinford, the affix 'King' having been added to mark it as a royal manor. Some records show it as Swinford Regis. Domesday records the land... 'in the Seisdon Hundred... [where] the king holds Kingswinford'; it goes on to record that King Edward had held it before the Conquest. The place was at one time known as New Swinford, distinguishing it from the nearby hamlet of Old Swinford.

Kinver

The Domesday commissioners recorded this little township as Chenefare and as Chenevare in the Seisdon Hundred of Worcestershire in 1086, as part of 'the king's lands in Staffordshire'. Well before the Norman Conquest the Saxons had known the place as Cynibre, from the Celtic word for a hill, or in part from Old English affix 'cyne', meaning 'royal'. A hill connection is borne out by Kinver Edge, site of an Iron Age hill fort and the fact that it was part of a Royal Forest in the eleventh century supports the regal association.

Knill

This small Herefordshire hamlet was recorded in the Domesday Book as Chenille, and listed in the Hezetre Hundred held by Osbern, identified simply as 'son of Richard', who had held it before the Conquest. The name comes from the Old English 'cnylle', meaning 'small hillock', a word we might nowadays call a knoll, and which eminently describes the place's location on a hill overlooking a stream.

Knyaston

This is a small hamlet in rural Shropshire, that was named after a man called Cyneweard, whose farmstead (or 'tun') it was in early Saxon times. Hence, 'Cyneweard's farmstead'.

Located as it is on the border with Wales, it is also known in Welsh as Tregynferdd (where 'tre' means 'farm', and Cynferdd is the man's name in that language). Domesday listed the place as Chimerstun, in the Merset Hundred, held in 1086 by Reginald the Sheriff.

Kyre

This small Worcestershire hamlet derives its name directly from the River Kyre on which it stands... and that is all that can be said about the meaning of the name, as its origins date back well into prehistoric times. Domesday did regard the place worthy of a mention however, and recorded it as Cuer and 'Chire', (Little Kyre and Kyre Magna), in the Doddingtree Hundred lands part-held by the Bishop of Hereford and part-held by Osbern FitzRichard.

Ladywood

The Birmingham inner city district of Ladywood almost certainly gained its name after the woodland dedicated to Our Lady, the Virgin Mary. Originally, it probably belonged to the medieval Priory of St Thomas in the township, but by 1565, when the name Lady Wood was first recorded, all trace of the woodland had gone. An alternative proposition is that in medieval times, local pasture land went by the name of St Mary Wood Field and may have been the origin of the placename. One thing is for certain; there is no longer a wood in Ladywood.

Leamington Spa

Leamington Spa was a small Warwickshire settlement on the River Leam and was known until the beginning of the nineteenth century as Leamington Priors. For centuries, it was owned and administered by Kenilworth Priory. The name Leamington means 'the farmstead on the River Leam', and the 'Spa' element came later. 'Leam', the name of the river, comes from the Old Celtic, meaning 'elm river', and the Old English word 'tun' signifies a settlement or farmstead. It was recorded as Lamintone in the Hundred of Stoneleigh by Domesday, in 'the Land of Earl Roger' (de Montgomery of Shrewsbury), held by him for King William. Wulfwine the Sheriff had held it before the Conquest.

Ledbury

The Herefordshire border town of Ledbury derives its placename either from the Old Welsh 'led', indicating the side of a hill, and the Old English word 'burh' or 'buri', indicating a fortified place or stronghold, or from the River Leadon, on which it stands. Hence, the placename translates as either a 'fortified place on the side of a hill', or a 'fortified place on the River Leadon'. Nobody seems quite certain which. The river name is itself derived from the ancient Celtic and means 'broad [or wide] stream'. The township was recorded as Liedeburge in the 1086 survey, in 'lands [which] belong to the Canons of Hereford' in the Wimundestreu Hundred. Before the Conquest, it had been held by the Saxon Earl Harold, but was apparently taken 'unjustly' by Godric, before '...the king restored it to Bishop Walter [of Hereford]'.

Leebotwood

The Shropshire village of Leebotwood might just have easily been written as 'Botswoodlee', as the two elements could have been expressed either way. The present name comes from the a man called Botta; he occupied the land some time in the eleventh century when his name was appended to the placename. Before that the placename would have been just based on 'leah' (the Old English word for a clearing), and 'wudu', a wood or woodland. Later the place was recorded as Botwood, then as Lee in Botwood and finally as Leebotwood. Hence, the name means 'Botta's clearing in a wood'. Domesday recorded the place as Botewde, in the Condover Hundred, held by Earl Roger of Shrewsbury, it having belonged to a man called Auti of Quatt before the Norman Conquest. The survey identifies two households on the estate and two riders (commonly known as radmen). It was a very small manorial estate, valued in 1086 at just three shillings. It was not until sometime around 1170 that the place became known as Lega in Bottewode, and the sixteenth century before it resembled its present-day name, when it was written as Lebotwood.

Lee Brockhurst

Lee translates from Old English as 'leah', meaning 'woodland clearing', and is a common element in English placenames. Most have distinguishing affixes to specifically identify them, of which the Shropshire village of Lee Brockhurst is typical. Brockhurst is made up of 'brocc', the old name for a badger, and 'hyrst', which signified a wooded hillside. Therefore, the entire placename may be taken to mean 'clearing on a wooded hill where badgers live, or are seen'. Initially, the village was simply known as Lee, and this was reflected in the *Domesday Book* entry where the village was recorded as Lege, in the Condover Hundred, held by a man known as Norman the Hunter. Three Saxons, Wulfgeat, Wihtric and Aelfheah, held the manor at the time of the Conquest. In 1086 the manorial estate was valued at three pounds, but declared to be 'waste'. It was towards the end of the thirteenth century that the placename was recorded as Leye under Brochurst.

Leek

Before the Norman Conquest, the hamlet of Leek in Staffordshire was in the possession of Earl Aelfgar of Mercia and, after 1066, William the Conqueror took it into his personal ownership. At the time of the *Domesday Book*, it was recorded simply as Lec, from the Old Norse word for a brook, probably meaning the '[place by a] brook'. The waterway in question is a stream that flows through the township to become a tributary of the River Churnet. The Great Survey accounted, '...[there is] land for twelve ploughs... three acres of meadow [and] woodland ... now worth thirty shillings'.

Leigh Sinton

In the thirteenth century, this Worcestershire village was recorded as Sothyntone in Lega. The second part of this placename translates from three Old English words: 'suth', 'in' and 'tun', which taken together mean 'south in the village'. The first part is derived from 'leah', which signified a woodland glade or a clearing. The placename therefore means either '[place in the] south of the village of Leigh', or possibly 'village south of the woodland clearing'.

Leinthall Earls/Leinthall Starkes

Originally, known as Lentehale, this Herefordshire placename comes from a long-lost Celtic river name, the Lent, meaning 'torrent' or 'raging stream' with the Old English affix 'halh', meaning 'corner [or nook] of land'. Hence, 'nook of land by a raging stream'. At some point in the township's history, the estate was divided into two – one part going to an earl and the other to a man called Starker – little else is known about the when or why of the arrangement. However, in 1275 Leinthall Earls (sometimes spelt 'Earles'), was known by its Latin name, Leintall Comites (the latter element translates as 'earl'), and Leinthale Starkare had also come into existence during that same century.

Leominster

Pronounced 'Lem-ster', this old Herefordshire market town probably began when King Merwald of Mercia founded a religious house around 660, on a site where St Ealfrid of

Northumberland reputedly performed a miracle, when he fed a lion from his hand. Hence the Latin affix 'Leo' to the placename, and the Old English suffix 'mynster' referring to a monastery, church or religious house. The placename may therefore mean 'monastery [church or convent] of the lion'. Another account cites an Old Celtic name for the district, 'leo', meaning 'place of (or at) the stream'. There is also an opinion that it may refer to Earl Leofric of Mercia who held land there. It is known that in 980, Danes sacked the settlement and destroyed the nunnery and it was Leofric who financed its rebuilding.

Letton
The name of this village near Eardisley in Herefordshire comes from an old Anglo-Saxon expression, 'leac-tun', which means 'enclosure where leeks are grown', or very simply 'leek field', although 'leac' was also sometimes used as a generic word for a herb or herbs. Domesday listed Letton as Letune, in the Leintwardine Hundred, held by Ralph de Mortimer in 1086 it having been in the possession of a man unflatteringly known as Wiward the Fat before 1066. There is another village called Letton near Walford in Herefordshire.

Lichfield
In the first century, the Romans built a fort called Letocetum two miles distant from the present city of Lichfield, at the crossing of two major Roman roads, Ryknild Street and Watling Street in Staffordshire. In 669, according to an account by Bede, when Bishop Chad moved from Northumbria to introduce Christianity to the Mercian tribes, it was known as Licidfelth or Lyccidfelth. By 720, the name was recorded as Lecitfelda, derived either from the Celtic, meaning 'grey wood', or a corruption of 'lece', a small stream, and 'feld', open land or fields. Hence, 'fields near a stream or a grey wood'.

Lilleshall
Lilleshall is a small village in the Wrekin region of Shropshire, whose placename comes from a man called Lilli, who may have been the founder of the original settlement or its leader. Added to that is the Old English prefix 'hyll', meaning 'hill', and we get an overall meaning of 'Lilli's hill' for the placename. Domesday listed it as Linleshelle, in the Wrockwardine Hundred where the Church of St Alkmund held ten hides with a further two in demesne. The estate was recorded with ten villans, five bordars and three French sergeants. Its chief tenant was identified as Godebold the Priest. In 1162, the name was recorded as Lilleshull.

Lingen
This Herefordshire village derived its placename from the River Lingen on which it stands. The river name originated in Celtic times and is thought to mean 'clear stream'. The township was recorded as such in 704 and was entered in the 1086 survey as Lingham, in the Leintwardine Hundred, listed as part of the County of Shropshire. It was in the possession of Ralph de Mortimer at that time; two Saxons called Gunnfrthr and Eadric held it as separate manors before 1066.

Longnor
The placename of this Shropshire village describes its location: '[place by the] long copse of alder trees'. The name derives from the Old English words 'lang', meaning 'long' (either as a description of length or of height), and 'alor', an alder tree, or trees. Hence, the name could equally be interpreted as '[place by the] long [or tall] alder tree[s]'. In 1155 the placename was written as Longenalra.

Ludlow

In 1086, the Norman knight, Roger de Lacy, began building Ludlow Castle on the Welsh-English border of Shropshire (an area known as the Welsh Marches), to hold back warring incursions into England. The place was known as Lodelowe, derived from the Old English words 'hlud' and 'hlaw', referring respectively to a mound and a noisy stream (the River Teme). Hence, '[place by, or on a] mound by a noisy stream'. In Welsh it was known as Llwydlo.

Luston

This Herefordshire village has a placename whose origin may be thought most unfortunate: it translates as 'farmstead full of lice'. The Old English word 'lus' meant 'lice' and 'tun' represented a farmstead. Domesday recorded the village as Lustone, quite a large estate for its day, supporting around twenty households in the Hundred of Leominster. Apart from some 380 residents it was also assessed with '... thirteen slaves, twelve female slaves, six priests and twenty other'. It had woodland measuring six by three furlongs and eight mills. In 1086 the manor was held by King William, having previously been a possession of Queen Edith, the widow of King Edward.

Madresfield

Two explanations have been offered for the meaning of this Worcestershire village placename; one has the Old English word 'maethere' representing a mower (that is, a man who mows a field or a lawn), and the other prefers it as the personal name of a man who owned the land. Hence, either 'open land belonging to or of the mower', or 'Maethere's open land'. The old word 'feld' or 'felda' not only represented what today we might think of as a field, but more generally of open land that had been cleared for arable farming. Maresfield received no entry in the *Domesday Book*, but was listed as Madresfeld in the *Westminster Cartulary* of 1086 as part of the Manor of Powick, belonging to Westminster Abbey, with Urse d'Abetot (sometimes known as Urse the Sheriff), holding one virgate and two carucates of the manorial estate. By the twelfth century, the name had been recorded as Metheresfeld.

Maesbrook

Maesbrook means '[the place by the] brook at the boundary'. The name probably comes from the Old English 'maere', meaning 'boundary' and 'broc', indicating a brook or a stream. However, it has been suggested that owing to the proximity of this Shropshire hamlet to the Welsh border, the first element may be derived from 'maes', a Welsh word meaning 'open field'. Domesday identified the place as Meresbroc, in the Wrockwardine Hundred held by Roger the Sheriff in 1086. By the end of the thirteenth century the place had been recorded as Maysbrok.

Mainstone

The Shropshire village of Mainstone gets its name from a combination of two Anglo-Saxon words, 'maegen' and 'stan', which respectively meant 'strength' (as in the modern expression 'might and main', often used to define strength), and 'stan', a stone. The name might be interpreted as either '[place by the] stone of strength' or '[place by a] stone that requires strength [to lift it]', or something along those lines. It is thought that in the early Saxon period such stones were traditionally used to test a young man's strength in competition with his peers. One such stone, which originally stood outside the village church, has now been installed inside it. In 1284, the village placename was recorded as Meyneston.

Malvern

In 1030, this township was known as Moelfern and by 1086 it had been recorded as Malferna, which translates as 'bare hill', from the Celtic 'mel' or 'moel', meaning bare or bald, and 'brinn', a hill. Long before the Conquest, an Iron Age camp had existed there. The description perfectly defines the topography of Worcestershire's Malvern Hills, in which the township is located. It is thought that Saxon Earl Harold Godwinson built another tier of earthworks on the original camp, but this was destroyed by Henry II in 1155.

Mamble

The name of this Worcestershire village originated in Celtic times, where the derived 'mamm' element (related to the modern English word 'mammary'), represented a 'breast shaped hill'. Hence, '[place on or by] a breast shaped hill'. Domesday recorded Mamele in the Doddingtree Hundred held in 1086 by Ralph de Mortimer, it having belonged to a Saxon man known as Saewold of Mamble in 1066.

Mansell Lacy

Before the Conquest, this place had been known as Maelueshylle, based on the Old English words 'malu', meaning 'sand', 'grit' or 'gravel', and 'hyll', a hill. Hence, '[place, or estate on a] gravel hill'. In 1086, the commissioners recorded the placename as Malveselle, in the Stepleset Hundred of Herefordshire, held by Gruffydd Boy, a man whose name shows a clear Welsh connection. The manor was held by the de Lacy family in the thirteenth century and they added their family name to the place some time before 1242, when it became known as Maumeshull Lacy. This manorial affix distinguished it from the nearby manor of Mansell Gamage, of which the Gamagis family had taken possession in the twelfth century.

Marchington

By the end of the tenth century, this village in Staffordshire was already known as Maercham and shortly before the Conquest the placename was recorded as Maerchamtune. The name contains three Old English language elements, of which the first, 'merece', signified the wild celery or smallage plant; the second, 'hamm', referred to a river meadow or flood plain, and finally, 'tun', meaning 'farmstead'. Hence, the name means 'farmstead at a river meadow where wild celery grows'. By the time of the Great Survey of 1086 the place had been recorded as Merchamtone, in the Offlow Hundred held by Henry de Ferrers, with its chief tenant being a free man called Wulfric.

Market Drayton

The word 'Drayton' comes from the Old English 'droeg', which means to drag (as with a sled), often used to describe places where sleds were used to move or porter material up a hill slope or incline. The affix 'Market' is fairly self-explanatory, that is, a place where markets were held. Both words used separately are common in English placenames where the local economy is predominantly based around farming communities and their produce, as is the case with this rural Shropshire township.

Martin Hussingtree

This Worcestershire village used to be two separate entities. The first part, 'Martin' has at least two possible derivations. One has it derived from the Old English words 'mere', a pool, pond or small lake, plus 'tun', which generally indicated a farmstead or smallholding of some kind. In which case, the place translates as 'farmstead by [or near] a lake'. An alternative contention is that the word 'Martin' derives from 'maere', meaning 'boundary', and may have signified the one which separates the Oswaldslow and Pershore Hundreds.

The second part of the placename is from an early settler called Husa, with the affix 'inga', referring to his followers, tribe or family, and 'treow', a tree. Hence, '[place at the] tree belonging to Husa's family'. Domesday refers to Husentre, in land belonging to the Church of St Peter of Worcester, where '...eleven villans have four ploughs and render annually one hundred cart-loads of wood for the salt-pans of Droitwich'.

Mathon

In Old English, the word 'mathm' meant 'treasure' or referred to a valuable gift, and this is thought to be the origin of this Herefordshire village's placename. That said, the significance is obscure. Many think it probably alluded to a valuable gift of land some time before the Norman Conquest, though this is somewhat speculative. Before 1066, the name was recorded as Matham, and at the time of the Great Survey as Matma and Matme, largely in the Doddingtree Hundred, part lying in Worcestershire, held by the Church of St Mary of Pershore, with Drogo FitzPoyntz and Roger de Lacy being the chief tenants of the manor.

Monkland

Originally known by its old Celtic name, 'Leine', this Herefordshire village received a name-change some time after 1066, when the land was formally recognised as a possession of the monks of Conches-en-Ouches Abbey of Saint-Pierre of Castellion in Normandy, though it seems that they laid claim to it long before the Norman Conquest. It was listed in the Hezetre Hundred, held by Ralph de Tosney, having belonged to Almer and Ulfkil before the Conquest. By about 1180, it had become known as Munkelen, a combination of the Old English word 'munuc', signifying a monk or monks, and the Celtic 'Leine' (later written as 'Leon'). Hence, the placename means '[the] monks' estate in Leon'.

Morville

The first element of this Shropshire village placename is uncertain, though it has been suggested that it may be a derivation of the Celtic word 'mamm', referring to 'a breast-shaped hill' (similar to the origin of Manchester, originally known as Mamuciam, and which has the same interpretation). Were this to be the case, the hill in question would be likely to have been the nearby Aston Hill. The second element of the placename, 'ville', was changed to the Old English 'feld' or 'felda', meaning 'open land' some time before Domesday. The survey listed it as Membrefelda, in the Alnodesteu Hundred, held by Roger, the Earl of Shrewsbury, with tenancies held within the manorial estate by Richard the Butler, the Abbey of St Peter in Shrewsbury, one man-at-arms and five other unnamed men. By the early twelfth century the name had been written as Mamerfeld.

Much Marcle

As with all placenames containing the word 'much', there is an implied reference to a greater or more important place, and the Herefordshire village of Much Marcle is no exception, as the name distinguishes it from the village of Little Marcle located some three miles distant. Marcle is a word derived from two Old English words, 'mearc', meaning 'boundary' or 'border', and 'leah', a woodland clearing. The placename may therefore be interpreted as 'greater [place by the] woodland clearing on the boundary'. Domesday recorded the place as Merchelai, a very large estate in the Wimundestreu Hundred, with parts held by King William, William FitzBaderon and the Abbey of Sainte-Marie of Lyre.

Much Wenlock

This small Shropshire township was originally known simply as Wenlock, and the 'much' element was added later to distinguish it from nearby Little Wenlock. The place was known from the seventh century as Wininicas and in the ninth as Wenlocan. By the time of the *Domesday Book* it was spelt Wenloch. The name has obscure origins and may have derived in part from the Celtic 'winn', meaning 'white', referring to the colour of Wenlock Edge's limestone, and the Old English 'loca', signifying an enclosed location. This might, perhaps, have been a reference to the monastery which had been founded in Wenlock by Merewalh, son of King Penda of Mercia, around 680. It contained the remains of St Milburga, the king's daughter and the monastery's one-time abbess.

Mucklestone

Mucklestone in the County of Staffordshire was probably established by a man called Mucel, whose personal name it took along with the Old English suffix 'tun' indicating a farmstead or dwelling. The place was therefore known as the 'farmstead belonging to Mucel'. In 1086 the village was recorded as Moclestone, 'In the Land of the King's Thegns', in the Pirehill Hundred, held by Lyfing (or Leofing) in 1086, having been tenanted by the Saxons Alric and Eadric before 1066. At that time it was a very small estate housing just three villans and a priest, and amounted to one acre of meadow and two furlongs of woodland, altogether valued at three shillings.

Naunton Beauchamp

The Worcestershire village of Naunton derives its placename from the Anglo-Saxon words 'niwe', meaning 'new', and 'tun', a farmstead or estate. Hence, 'new farmstead [or estate]'. The place was recorded as Newentune, in the Pershore Hundred, in the Great Survey of 1086, owned by the Abbey Church of St Peter, Westminster and held for them by Urse (Urso d'Abetot, sometimes referred to as 'the sheriff'). Three free men named as Alweard, Saewulf and (another?) Alweard held it at the time of King Edward. The estate amounted to ten hides in all, worth four pounds, with three hides leased to Herbrand de Pont-Audemer. The Beauchamp affix was added to the place some time in the eleventh century when the Beauchamp family became Lords of the Manor and in 1370, the placename was recorded as Newenton Beauchamp.

Neen Savage

This village is located on the River Neen in Shropshire (now known as the River Rea), and this is the origin of its placename. Neen is an old Celtic or possibly a pre-Celtic river name whose meaning has been lost in the mists of antiquity. In the thirteenth century the manor came into the possession of the le Savage family who attached their family name to the place in order to distinguish it from Neen Sollars, some four miles south, which had been held by the de Solers family since the late twelfth century. Domesday had recorded the place as Nene, in the Conditre Hundred in 1086, held by Ralph de Mortimer. Neen Solars was held by Osbern FitzRichard at that time.

Newcastle-under-Lyme

Known by its Latin name of Novum Castellum Subtus Lymam in 1173, it had no entry in the *Domesday Book*. The 'new castle' in question dates from the twelfth century; it had been built by Earl Ranulph of Chester. However, the relevance of the 'Lyme' suffix is contentious. One opinion is that it may have been part of the Lyme Park estate near Disley in the High Peak District of Derbyshire, or the vast Lyme Forest that covered north Staffordshire and south Cheshire, although this is supposition. Another is that it derives from the Latin word 'lymum', indicating an escarpment. A third and more obvious source is that it simply takes its name from Lyme Brook.

Norton Malreward

At least a score of places in England are known by the name 'Norton'; it derives from the Old English 'north', meaning 'northern' and 'tun' a farmstead or enclosure. Hence, 'northern farmstead'. The village of Norton Malreward was listed as Nortone in the Chew Hundred of Somerset in the 1086 survey, as a relatively small estate held at that time by Bishop Geoffrey of Coutances in Normandy, having belonged to a Saxon man called Alwold in 1066. The Malreward element of the placename is a degeneration of Malregard, a Norman family who became tenants of the manor in the early thirteenth century and attached their family name to the place. The neighbouring hamlet of Norton Hautville was combined with the estate and became a single parish in the nineteenth century.

Nuneaton

The Warwickshire market town of Nuneaton was listed in 1086 as the small hamlet of Etone in the Coleshill Hundred, signifying 'a place by the river or water', from the Old English 'ea', meaning river or water, and 'tun', a settlement or farmstead. By 1247, a Benedictine nunnery had been founded in the township by Robert, Earl of Leicester, which he rented to the nuns of Chaise-Dieu from France, and the affix 'nun' was added to the placename.

Ocle Pychard

This unusual Herefordshire village placename was known before the Conquest as Aclea, derived from 'ac', an oak tree, and 'leah', a woodland clearing. Hence, 'woodland clearing with oak trees', or something like that. Domesday recorded the place as Acle, and listed it in the Tornelaus Hundred held by Roger de Lacy. Then, in the thirteenth century the manor was taken into the possession of the Pichard family and their name was attached to the placename. In 1242 the name was recorded as Acle Pichard.

Onneley

Onneley's placename comes directly from a man called Onna (or possibly Ana), who may have been its founder, an early settler or chieftain. An additional Old English affix, 'leah', which indicates a clearing or glade in a woodland, completes the placename meaning as 'woodland clearing belonging to a man called Onna'. An alternative explanation is that the place derives from 'ana' and 'leah', which might translate as 'isolated woodland clearing'.

In 1086, the *Domesday Book* recorded the place as Anelege, in the Hodnet Hundred of Shropshire, held by William Malbank, the manor having previously belonged to a Saxon man called Eadric. In 1066, the estate had been valued at five shillings, but according to the survey 'now it is waste'.

Oswestry

The Oswestry placename derives from Oswald, a man's personal name, and the Old English suffix 'treow', meaning 'tree'. Hence, 'Oswald's tree', possibly named after King Oswald of Northumbria. Before 1066, this small Shropshire township had been held by Edward the Confessor. The *Domesday Book* names it Luvre, held for the king by Earl Roger de Montgomerie, who built Oswestry Castle; his tenant was a man called Reginald or Rainald. Its earlier Welsh name was Croes-Oswald and the Saxons knew it as Maserfield, a corruption of the Welsh, Mais-Oswald. For centuries, it was essentially a Welsh town, before eventually being annexed to the English Kingdom of Mercia.

Pedmore

This district of Dudley in the West Midlands at one time belonged to a man called Pybba, whose moorland, or marsh it was. Hence, the placename means 'Pybba's moor [or marsh]'.

Domesday recorded the place as Pevemore and listed it in the Clent Hundred of Worcestershire, held in 1086 by William FitzAnsculf having belonged to a Saxon man called Thorger in 1066. By the end of the twelfth century, the placename had been recorded as Pubemora.

Pensnett
Historically, Pensnett was a wooded hill area within the old township of Dudley in the West Midlands, which included Netherton Hill and Saltwells Wood. The name comes from 'pen', meaning 'hill' and 'snaed', an old word for a parcel of woodland. Hence, 'woodland on a hill'. By the thirteenth century it had become part of the Forest of Kinver and in the possession of the de Somery family, barons of Dudley Castle, who used the woodland as a hunting area, which became known as Pensnett Chase.

Perry Barr
Perry Barr, in the ancient Staffordshire Parish of Handsworth, (now a district of Birmingham), appears in the *Domesday Book* as Pirio, tenanted at that time by Drogo de la Beuvrière, who held it for William FitzAnsculf, Lord of Dudley Castle. It previously belonged to the Saxon, Leofwaru. The placename derives from the Old English word 'pirige', meaning 'pear' but is generally taken in a wider context to mean '[the place at the] pear tree[s]'. The adjacent district of Great Barr provided the second element of the placename, and was entered separately in Domesday, as Barre, from the Celtic, meaning 'hilltop'. This refers to the nearby Barr Beacon, the highest point in West Midlands region. It is thought that these two manors were combined some time during the fourteenth century.

Pershore
Situated on the River Avon in the Vale of Evesham in rural Worcestershire, Pershore was known as Perscoran in 972 and by 1086 as Persore. The name comes from the Old English 'persc', meaning 'a sloping bank', and 'ora', the osier (a small willow tree used in basket weaving). Hence, 'the sloping bank where osiers grow'.

Podmore
Podmore is a small hamlet in Staffordshire whose name means 'marsh frequented by frogs and toads'. The name comes from the Middle English word 'pode', meaning 'frog' or 'toad', and the Old English word 'mor', meaning 'moor' or 'marshland'. Domesday entered the hamlet as Podemore and listed it in the Pirehill Hundred, held in 1086 by the Bishop of Chester, who had also held it before the Norman Conquest.

Powick
This Worcestershire village was named from a man called Pohha, possibly an early settler or chieftain, plus the Old English word 'wic', which indicated a specialised farm or dairy. Hence, possibly, 'Pohha's dairy farm'. The placename had been recorded as early as 972 as Poincguuic, and by the time of Domesday as Poiwic. The Great Survey placed the village within the Pershore Hundred land belonging to the Abbey of St Peter of Westminster, as it had been part held before the Norman Conquest. It was a relatively wealthy manor, with four separate entries in the survey; one records the estate land overseen by Urso d'Abetot, having previously belonged to four Saxon men, Aethelward, Alwin, Brictmer and Saewulf; another shows the overlord as Gilbert, son of Turwold, with Alway and Kelibert of Crowle as its owners before 1066; finally, a fourth entry had Walter Ponther as its overlord, it having previously belonged to Godric. It was also a very large manorial estate, which supported eighty-two households, including four slaves, one female slave and a priest. In its entirety it was valued in 1086 at twenty pounds.

Prees

This Shropshire village is so near to the Welsh border, that unsurprisingly it gets its name from the Old Welsh Gaelic word 'pres', which means 'brushwood' or 'thicket'. Hence the placename simply means '[place near a] thicket of brushwood'. The Domesday account of the place records Pres, in Hodnet Hundred, in 'The Land of the Bishop of Chester', who held it before and after the Conquest. A Saxon man called Ansketil rented half a hide of manor lands from the bishop and Fulcher another two hides. The account goes on to report that 'The whole [at the time of King Edward] was worth fifty shillings; and afterwards it was waste; now what the bishop has is worth forty shillings'. Despite this, the survey counted 'woodland for sixty pigs'.

Quatt/Quatford

The origin of the name of this Shropshire village is a mystery. According to local parish tradition it may derive from the Celtic word 'coed', meaning 'wood', in which case the placename might possibly translate as '[place in or near] a wood'. The district was known to the Saxons as Cwat, but exactly what that meant remains open to speculation, but it is clear that there was a shallow river crossing, a 'ford', across the River Severn, before a bridge was built two miles north upstream that became known as Bridgnorth, rendering the ford redundant. Domesday recorded the village as Quatone, in the Steisdon Hundred, held by Earl Roger of Shrewsbury, and the ford as Quatford, in the Alnodestreu Hundred in 1086.

Quinton

Quinton, formerly in the County of Warwickshire, (now a district of Birmingham), translates as 'queen's town', from the Old English 'cwen' and 'tun', so that by the ninth century it was known as Quentone. The *Domesday Book* records the place as Quenintune and as being divided into Upper Quinton and Lower Quinton, held by Hugh de Grandmesnil, the son of Earl Ralph, and owned before the Conquest by Leofric.

Redditch

In 1138, a charter was granted to Cistercian monks to found an abbey at Bordesley in Worcestershire. A settlement grew up around it, at a place then called Red Dyche. By 1247, it was known as La Rededitch, indicating either a red ditch, or perhaps a reed ditch, from the Old English 'hreod' and 'dic'.

Ribbesford

This Worcestershire village derived its placename from a combination of three Old English words: 'ribbe', the ribwort plant, 'bedd', a flower bed, and 'ford', indicating a shallow river crossing. Hence, the entire name translates as '[place at a] ford by a bed of ribwort'. The ribwort is a common weed that is also known as the ribwort plantain or lamb's tongue, and is a species of flowering plant, a common lawn weed of the plantaginaceae family. The ford in question would have been across the River Severn at this location. Domesday recorded it as Ribeford and listed it in the Manor of Kidderminster in the Hundred of Doddingtree, held at that time by King William.

Ripple

The Worcestershire village of Ripple lies on a narrow strip or tongue of land, a fact that is reflected in its placename, which comes from the Old English word 'ripel', meaning 'strip of land'. It had been known as Rippell since the beginning of the eighth century and by 1086, Domesday had listed it a Rippel in the Oswaldslow Hundred held by the Bishop of Worcester, who had also possessed it at the time of King Edward.

Ross-on-Wye

Ross is a common placename throughout Britain, deriving from the Old Celtic 'ros', which indicated a moorland promontory or heathland. 'On Wye' was appended to the name in 1931, to identify it as the place located on the River Wye in Herefordshire. However, the origin of the river name predates all written records and its meaning is unknown. The *Domesday Book* records it simply as Rosse, one of three manors in Upton Bishop in the Bromsash Hundred, belonging to the Bishop of Hereford. Together, all three combined manors were valued at fourteen pounds. The survey also records the existence of a church and a corn mill.

Rous Lench

A Worcestershire village whose name relates to a man called Rous, who had an estate in Lench, a district to the north of Evesham. Lench derives from the Old English word 'hlenc', which means 'long hill slope', and appears in other local villages nearby, including Sherrif's Lench, Abbot's Lench and Church Lench, as well as Lenchwick (of which the 'wick' element denotes a dairy farm). Rous Lench owes its name directly to the Rous family, who held the manor in the fourteenth century, when their family name was appended to the placename. Before the time of the *Domesday Book* the place had been simply recorded as Lenc, and by 1086 it had come into the possession of the Bishopric of Worcester. At that time it was recorded as Biscopesleng, with some seven hides held by Urse (known as Urse the Sheriff), and tenanted by Alvred. The bishop held two hides personally in demesne, and a man called Frani also gave some kind of service to him for the use of five hides.

Rowley

The West Midlands township of Rowley derives from the Old English words 'ruh', meaning rough, and 'leah', a woodland clearing. Known in 1173 as Roelea, it is a small hamlet that formed part of a royal hunting ground, so that 'Regis' was added to the placename around 1140.

Rugby

The placename of Rugby in the County of Warwickshire has two possible derivations. The first is that it was a stronghold or fortified place belonging to a man called Hroca and in Saxon times may have been known as Hroceburh; the Old English suffix 'burh', or the Norse 'by', both signifying a stronghold. Hence, 'Hroca's stronghold'. Alternatively, it may be related to 'hroc', meaning rook; hence, 'a fortified place inhabited by rooks'. The place was recorded in 1086 as Rocheberie and in 1200 as Rokebi. It was one of many estates held by Thorkil of Warwick (also known as Hare Lip) at the time of the Domesday survey, and appears to have been leased to Eadwulf, a Saxon.

Rugeley

This placename comes from the Old English words 'hrycg', meaning 'ridge' and 'leah', a woodland clearing. Hence, 'the woodland clearing near [or on] a ridge'. It was recorded in 1086 as Rugelie, in the Seisdon Hundred of Staffordshire, held by King William, having been in the possession of Earl Aelfgar before the Conquest.

Salwarpe

This Worcestershire village has a placename that means '[the place on] dark-coloured silted-up land', from two Old English words, 'salu', meaning 'sallow' or 'dark-coloured', and 'wearp', which signifies 'silted' or 'clogged'. The place was known during Saxon times as Salouuarpe, and by 1086 had been written as Salewarpe, located in the Clent Hundred of land held by the Abbey Church of St Mary in Coventry. It was partly administered in 1086 by Urso (sometimes Urse) d'Abetot, who held it for the abbot. There were four burgesses and the manor owned six salt pans in Droitwich. Another part of the manor which had been in the possession of Alwin the Noble before the Conquest had Earl Roger of Shrewsbury as its overlord at the time of the survey. The two parts were valued at one pound and eight shillings, and six pounds respectively.

Sedgley
A district originally in Staffordshire, latterly in Dudley in the West Midlands, and finally part of the City of Wolverhampton, Sedgely was known in the tenth century as Secgesleage, and is named after an early settler or chieftain called Secg, whose 'leah', or woodland clearing it was. Hence, 'Secg's clearing'. Domesday recorded the village as Segleslei, in the Seisdon Hundred land where William FitzAnsculf held the manor on behalf of the king. Before the Norman Conquest, it had been partly in the possession of Earl Aelfgar (or Algar), and partly held by Geoffrey of Sedgley. The survey assessed sixteen acres of meadow and woodland two leagues long by one league broad, worth ten pounds, as it had been at the time of King Edward. It was a large estate supporting sixty households, three slaves and a priest. Sedgley also has the dubious distinction of being the author's birthplace.

Seighford
Seighford is a Staffordshire village that was known in the eleventh century as Cesteford, which gives a clue to the meaning of the placename. The 'ceste' element relates to the Old English word 'ceaster', which identified the place as the site of an earlier Roman fort. The second element, 'ford', signified the river crossing across the River Sow. Hence, the placename may be taken to mean '[place at the] river crossing by the old Roman fort'. Domesday had entered the manor as a very small settlement supporting just three households in the Pirehill Hundred. Its estate amounted to land for five men's plough teams, five acres of meadow and woodland measuring four leagues by two leagues. It was held in 1086 by the Bishop of Chester, as it had been before the Conquest.

Selly Oak
This Birmingham district appeared in the *Domesday Book* as Escellie, part of the Came Hundred, held by William FitzAnsculf of Dudley for the king and leased to Wilbert. Before 1066, it had belonged to the Saxon, Wulfwine, who was Sheriff of Warwick. By 1204, the township was recorded as Selvele. The placename derives from the Old English word 'scelf', meaning 'a ledge or a shelf [of land]', and 'leah', a woodland clearing. Hence, 'a woodland clearing on a ledge'. By the eighteenth century it was known as Sally Oak. The addition of the 'oak' element of the placename lies at Oak Tree Lane in the centre of the district, which was traditionally the location where John Rodway planted an oak tree in the grounds of Selly House sometime around 1710. This tree was not removed until 1909, when it had to be felled and the stump removed because its roots were damaging local houses. The stump was placed in Selly Oak Park, with a plaque identifying it as 'The Butt of the Old Oak Tree, from which the name of Selly Oak is derived'.

Shelsey Walsh/Shelsey Beauchamp
Originally, as just Shelsey, this village in Worcestershire gets its placename from an early settler or founder, possibly a chieftain called Sceld, and the Old English word 'leah', which means 'woodland clearing [or glade]'. Hence, 'Sceld's woodland clearing'. Then, from the thirteenth century, the Le Waley family took over the manor and appended their family name to the place, at which time it became 'Sceld's woodland clearing, belonging

to the Le Waley family'. This was done largely to distinguish their manorial estate lands from Shelsey Beauchamp, lying opposite across the River Severn, and belonging to the family of that name. At the time of Domesday, both were recorded as one and the same manor, as Caldeslei, in the Doddingtree Hundred, held by Ralph de Tosny, having belonged to Wulfmer before the Conquest. In 1275, the Manor of Shelsey Walsh was known as Seldesle Waleys.

Sheriffhales

The *Domesday Book* recorded this Shropshire village simply as Halas, and listed it in the Cuttlestone Hundred, which covered areas of Staffordshire and Shropshire at that time. The original placename comes from the Old English word 'halh', in its plural form meaning 'corners [or nooks] of land'. Some time after the survey, the manor was granted to the Sheriff of Shropshire and became known as Shiruehales. The word 'sheriff' comes from 'scir-refa', in medieval times known as a 'shire reeve', and the entire placename translates as 'nooks of land belonging to the shire reeve'.

Shifnal

This Shropshire township can be traced to the seventh century when it was called Idsall. In the twelfth century it was recorded as Scuffanhalch, probably named after a man called Scuffa, plus the Old English suffix 'halh', indicating a small valley, a nook or hollow. Hence, '[place at] a hollow belonging to Scuffa'. Domesday shows it as Iteshale in the Baschurch Hundred and records that Robert FitzTheobald rented seven and a half hides of land from Roger de Montgomerie, Earl of Shrewsbury.

Shilton

This village in Warwickshire derives its placename from the Anglo-Saxon words 'scylfe', meaning 'shelf' or 'ledge' [of land], and 'tun', a farmstead. The complete name means 'farmstead on a ledge'. Domesday listed Scelftone, in the Bumbelowe Hundred land of the Count of Meulan, where Waltheof of Hillmorton was a free man and tenant, as he had been during the reign of King Edward. There is also another village called Shilton in the County of Oxfordshire.

Shrawardine

In Old English the word 'scraef' (from which the first part of this placename is derived), meant 'cave', but was more generally applied to hollows or depressions in the landscape, also represented by the old word 'den'. Additionally, 'worthign' signified an enclosure of some kind. All these elements taken together produce a placename that means something like '[place in an] enclosure near a hollow or cave'. In 1086, the place was listed as Salueurdine, in the Shropshire Hundred of Baschurch, held by Reginald the Sheriff.

Shrewsbury

The Anglo-Saxons named this township Scrobbesbyrig, derived from the Old English 'scrobb', meaning scrub, and 'burh', a fortified place. Hence, 'the fortified place in the scrubland'. By the time of the Domesday survey, the Normans had named it Sciropesberie, recorded as being part held by the Church of St Alkmund and the remainder by Earl Roger de Montgomerie, 'including the whole shire, and all the demesne which King Edward had there'.

Shropshire

In the decades preceding the Norman Conquest, this county bordering Wales in central England was known as Scrobbesbyrigscir, and means 'district based on Shrewsbury'.

'Shrop' or 'Salop' is a shortened form of Shrewsbury, and its inhabitants are still known as Salopians. Domesday recorded the county name as Sciropescire and a century later it was known as Salopescira. The Old English word 'scir', signified a 'district', and became what we know as a 'shire'.

Snitterfield
The Warwickshire village of Snitterfield's placename comes directly from Old English, where the first element, 'snite', means a 'snipe', and the second 'feld', simply refers to a field or open land of some kind. Hence, 'open land where snipes are to be found'. The place was recorded in 1086 as Snitefeld, in Fernecumbe Hundred, held by the Count of Meulan having belonged to Saxi of Aylestone, a free man at the time of King Edward. It was quite a large estate with twenty-six households, comprising eleven villans, four borders (smallholders), ten slaves and one priest. The manorial estate was assessed at a value of five pounds.

Solihull
The Birmingham district of Solihull received no mention in the *Domesday Book* and little is known about the place until around 1220, when the Church of St Alphege was founded and a settlement grew up around it. At that time, it was known as Solhil, from the Old English 'solig', meaning 'muddy', and 'hyll', simply meaning hill. Hence, 'muddy hill'. By 1242, Solihull had been granted permission to hold a weekly market.

Stafford
Stafford has a long history dating back before Roman times and well into the Iron Age. Traditionally, the settlement was thought to be founded some time around 700 by a Mercian prince called Bertelin. However, its recorded history begins in 913, when Aethelflaed, who was married to the King of Mercia, had the area fortified against warring Danish invaders. The success of her measures was aided in part by the surrounding marshland, which later gave the settlement its name, Staithford, derived from the Old English 'staeth' or 'staith', meaning a landing place, and 'ford'. Hence, 'the ford by a landing place'.

Staffordshire
With the addition of the Saxon word 'scir', meaning 'district', or in modern English, 'shire', this midlands county name means 'district based on Stafford', its county town. In the eleventh century the name was written as Staeffordscir.

Stoke-on-Trent
As a placename, Stoke, is very common in England, deriving from the Old English word 'stoc', meaning an outlying district or farmstead. On account of its commonality, other identifying affixes are typical (e.g. Stoke Newington, Stoke Mandeville, Stoke Poges, etc). Stoke-on-Trent is similarly named, after the River Trent that runs through it.

Stourbridge
The township of Stourbridge gets its name, logically, from the bridge over the River Stour, where the settlement grew up. Bartholomew's *Gazetteer* of 1887 describes the place as 'a market township in the Oldswinford Parish of Worcestershire, on the River Stour, five miles south-west of Dudley'. The river name itself comes from the Old English or Celtic, probably meaning 'strong', with the Old English affix, 'brycg' or Old Norse, 'brugge', meaning bridge. It was recorded in the Worcestershire Assize Roll of 1255 as Sturesbridge and Sturbrug.

Stratford-upon-Avon
Known since the beginning of the eighth century as Stretfordae, and recorded in the *Domesday Book* as Stradforde, in the County of Warwickshire, this was a common English placename at that time, Stratford St Andrews, Stratford St Mary, Stoney Stratford and Stratford-on-Slaney being other examples. Its placename means the 'ford on a Roman road', from the Saxon words 'straet' and 'ford', with the affix 'upon Avon' attached later to identify it from the others. Avon is itself a common name for English rivers and in Celtic it simply meant 'water' or 'river'.

Sugnall
The village of Sugnall in Staffordshire has two possible explanations for the meaning of its placename. The first is that it was named after a man called Sucga, and the second is that it derives from the Old English word 'sugge', meaning 'sparrow' or 'suggena' (the plural form: 'sparrows'). Finally, the suffix 'hyll', signifying a hill. Hence, the placename means either '[place on a] hill belonging to a man called Sucga', or 'hill where sparrows are found', or something along those lines. Domesday recorded the place as Sotehelle and listed it in the Offlow Hundred land of the Bishop of Chester, whose main tenants were Frani and Fargrimr in 1086. The estate was valued at ten pounds, exactly as it had been at the time of King Edward.

Sutton Coldfield
Before the Norman Conquest, Sutton formed part of the Kingdom of Mercia and was held by Earl Edwin. After 1066, it was known as Sutone, from the Old English words 'suth' and 'tun', simply meaning 'south village or farmstead'. Sutton is a very common English placename – Sutton in Ashfield and Sutton Bonnington are other examples. The affix 'in Colefeud' was added in the mid-thirteenth century to distinguish it from the others and signified an 'open field where charcoal was produced'.

Talke/Talke Pits
The word 'talke' is of Celtic origin and was the ancient word for a cliff edge or ridge, as the one found in the vicinity of the Staffordshire township. In the Brittonic Celtic language, the word 'talcen' was more commonly referred to a brow ridge, such as the forehead, but had a wider usage to indicate the front end of an object or place. In 1086, it was recorded as Talc, in the Pirehill Hundred 'Land of the King's Thegns', held by Gamal, son of Gruffydd, having been a possession of Godric of Lawton before the Conquest. It was a small estate with just one ploughland to support four villans. There was an acre of meadow and another acre of woodland, altogether only worth two shillings to the Lord of the Manor. Talke Pits is a former mining village, whose Talk O' Th' Hill Colliery was part of the North Staffordshire Coal Field and lies close to the main village of Talke.

Tamworth
The Staffordshire town of Tamworth was founded in the sixth century by Anglo-Saxons at the confluence of the Rivers Anker and Tame. It was the ancient capital of Mercia, where King Offa lived and had coinage minted. By the end of the eighth century, the settlement was known as Tamouworthig, meaning 'enclosure on the River Tame', from the Old Celtic word for a river. Thames, as in the London river of that name, derives from the same source. In the 1086 survey, it had little more than a passing reference and it was recorded as belonging to the Manor of Drayton Bassett, known as Tamworde.

Tardebigge
The origin of this Worcestershire village's placename is somewhat obscure. The place was known as Taerdebicgan well before the Norman Conquest of 1066, and may have come from the ancient Brittonic Celtic words 'tarth', meaning 'spring' or 'well', and 'pig', signifying a peak or point, a feature of the local topography. By 1086, it had been recorded as Terdeberie and Terdesberie, in the Came Hundred, held by the Conqueror, as it had been by Edward the Confessor before him. There were nine hides of land with one ploughland held in demesne. The manor also owned seven salt-pans in Droitwich as well as two lead vats, '...[that] render twenty shillings and one hundred mittae of salt'.

Tenbury Wells
This Worcestershire settlement was known in the eleventh century as Tamedberie in the Doddingtree Hundred. Over the centuries, there have been many variants on the placename, including Tametburie, Themedebury and Teamburie. It was named after the River Teme, on which it stands, with the Old English suffix 'burh', indicating a fortified stronghold. Hence, the 'stronghold on the River Teme'. The name 'Teme' itself has the same derivation as 'Tame' and 'Thames' and is the old Celtic word for 'river'.

Tipton
The Black Country township of Tipton in the West Midlands was recorded at the time of the Domesday survey as Tibibtone in the Offlow Hundred. The name derives from the Old English personal name of a man called Tibba, plus the two affixes 'inga', meaning 'the family or people', and 'tun', a farmstead or settlement. Hence, it translates as 'settlement of the family or people of Tibba'.

Tixall
In Anglo-Saxon times this Staffordshire village must have been known for its goats, as the placename implies. 'Ticce' was the Old English word for a kid, or a young goat, and 'halh', referred to a corner or a nook of land. Hence, the placename means 'nook of land where kids are kept'. In 1086, Domesday listed Ticheshale in the Pirehill Hundred held by Earl Roger of Shrewsbury. Its lord in 1066 had been a Saxon called Almund, identified as the father of Alward.

Ullingswick
In 1086, this Herefordshire village was recorded as Ullingwic, probably after a man called Ulla, who may have been the founder of the original settlement. Two other Old English words are appended to the placename: 'ing', meaning 'associated with', and 'wic', a specialised farmstead or dwelling, typically a dairy farm. The entire placename may therefore be taken to mean 'Dairy farm (or dwelling) associated with a man called Ulla'. Domesday listed the village in the Tornelaus Hundred overseen by an unnamed man-at-arms on behalf of the Canons of Hereford Cathedral, who had also held it before the Conquest.

Upton-upon-Severn/Upton Warren
The small Worcestershire country town of Upton-upon-Severn, located beside the River Severn, derives its name from the Old English words 'upp' and 'tun', which together mean 'upper [or higher] farm or settlement'. It was known by the end of the ninth century as Uptune and by the time of the *Domesday Book* as Uptun and Uptune, held by the Bishop of Worcester, still possessing 'eight slaves and one female slave' at that time. The village of Upton Warren has a similar derivation, though it is located near Droitwich on the River Salwarpe. In 1254, William FitzWarren held the manor and by the end of the thirteenth

century the place had been recorded as Opton Warini, to distinguish it from a dozen other settlements with Upton as part of their placenames.

Uttoxeter
Long before the Romans came to Britain, it is thought that there was an ancient British settlement of the Cornavii tribe at Uttoxeter in Worcestershire. However, recorded history really begins when the *Domesday Book* lists it as Wotocheshede, where Wuttuc (or Wottuc) was probably the man who owned the land and the Old English suffix 'hoeddre' indicated a heath. Hence, the placename probably translates as 'heathland belonging to Wuttuc'.

Walsall
There are two possible explanations for this West Midlands placename. One is that it comes from the Old English, 'Walh', a man's name, and 'halh', meaning a corner of land. Hence, 'corner of land belonging to Walh (or Walla)'. Alternatively, the first element may equally indicate a Celt, a Welshman, or Welsh speakers, in which case 'corner of land belonging to a Welshman'.

Wappenbury
The Warwickshire village of Wappenbury located on the bank of the River Leam, began life as 'Weappa's stronghold [or fort]'. Weappa (or Waeppa), was the probable founder of the settlement, and lived in a fortified dwelling here, as the Old English affix 'burh', indicated a stronghold or fortified manor of some kind. The vestigial remains of an ancient trench still surrounds the village, which stands on an Iron Age hill fort, part of the original fortifications alluded to in the placename. In the Great Survey of 1086 the place was entered as Wapeberie, a large settlement of thirty-one households, valued at five pounds and five shillings, located in the Marton Hundred and held by Geoffrey de la Guerche (sometimes 'de la Wirce'), it having previously belonged to Leofwin, identified as the father of Leofric.

Warwick
By 1001, this township was known as Waerincwicum, and at the time of the *Domesday Book* as Warwic, in the Tremlowe Hundred, held by King William. The placename comes from 'waering' and 'wic', Old English words which together signified dwellings or a settlement by a weir or river-dam.

Warwickshire
A county in central England whose name means 'district based on Warwick'. It was recorded in the eleventh century as Waerincwicscir. The last element of the name, 'scir', is an Anglo-Saxon word meaning 'district' or 'shire'.

Wednesbury/Wednesfield
Wilson's *Imperial Gazetteer of England* described Wednesbury in 1870 as 'a town and parish in West Bromwich district of Staffordshire ... called by the Saxons Wodensbury, after the god Woden, [and] is now popularly called Wedgebury'. Domesday named it Wadnesberie, from 'Woden', the Norse god's name, and 'burh', signifying a stronghold or fortified place. Hence, 'Woden's stronghold', possibly referring to a burial barrow or a hill. It is known that in earlier times an Iron Age hillfort existed on the site and is probably the original source of the placename – one of the few places in Britain named after a pre-Christian deity. Nearby Wednesfield, (now a district of Wolverhampton), known earlier as 'Woden's field', was the site of a definitive battle where the Saxon forces of Aethelflaed of Mercia finally vanquished a concerted Danish attempt to conquer all of England and marks the place where their advance was halted.

Wellington

Although it was arguably an important Anglo-Saxon settlement before Norman times, the first record of this Shropshire placename is in the *Domesday Book* as Walitone, probably after a man called Weola or Weala, with the Old English affixes 'inga', meaning the 'people or followers', and 'tun', a settlement or farmstead. Hence, 'settlement of the people of Weola'.

Weobley

In all probability, this small Herefordshire village was founded by a man called Wiobba, whose 'leah' (from the Old English meaning 'woodland clearing') this was. The survey named the place Wibelai in 1086, located in the Stretford Hundred and held at that time by Roger de Lacy (sometimes 'de Laci'). In 1066, it was owned by a man referred to as Edwy the Noble. It was a large manor of some twenty-nine households, which included eleven slaves and two priests, and was valued at five pounds.

West Bromwich

The West Midlands town of West Bromwich, now in the Sandwell District, was entered in the *Domesday Book* as Bromwic, held by Ralph for Lord William Ansculf in the Upton Wapentake, the placename derives from the Old English 'brom', referring to the broom tree, and 'wic' meaning a dwelling or a farm. Hence, loosely, 'the dwelling where broom trees grow'.

Whitchurch

This Shropshire placename is probably derived from the Old English 'hwit' or Old Norse 'hvitr', meaning white. Hence, 'white church'. By 1086, it was still known by its Saxon name, Westune (meaning 'west settlement' or farmstead), in the Hodnet Hundred, held for Earl Roger de Montgomerie by William de Warenne, first Earl of Surrey, having previously belonged to the Saxon Earl Harold Godwinson.

White Ladies

A district of Aston in Birmingham, the place derived its name when it was occupied by the Cistercian nuns of Whitstones (the so-called White Nuns). It was not until 1481 that the name Whitladyaston appeared, as it had been formerly simply known as Eastune in the tenth century, and Estun by the time of Domesday. Commonly known as White Ladies Aston, the survey of 1086 places it within the Hundred of Oswaldslow, part-held by the White Ladies and with the Bishop of St Mary's Church, Worcester as its tenant-in-chief, as he had been before the Conquest. The placename Aston, means 'eastern farmstead', from the Old English 'east' (or 'est') and 'tun'.

Whittingslow

The Shropshire village of Whittingslow was named after its probable founder or an early chieftain by the name of Hwittuc. Taken together with the Old English affix 'hlaw', which signified a tumulus or burial mound, the placename means 'Hwittuc's burial mound'. Domesday recorded the name as Witcheslawe, in the Leintwardine Hundred, held at that time by Earl Roger of Shrewsbury.

Willenhall

The Saxons knew the Walsall district of Willenhall as Willanhalch or Willenhalgh, after an early founder of the settlement, a man called Willa, with the additional Old English suffix 'halh', which signified a small valley, a meadow or hollow. Hence, 'Willa's meadow or valley'. The earliest known written record is around 732, when a treaty was signed there by King Ethelbald of Mercia.

Wilmcote

The Warwickshire village of Wilmcote has the distinction of having been the home of Mary Arden, William Shakespeare's mother. The placename comes from Old English, with the first element derived from its probable founder, a man called Wilmund, with the additional affix 'inga', meaning the 'people or followers', and 'cot', a cottage dwelling. Hence, we may take the placename as meaning 'cottages associated with the people of a man called Wilmund'. In the early eleventh century, the place was recorded as Wilmundigcotan, and had been transformed into Wilmecote by the time of Domesday. It was recorded as a small settlement located in the Pathlow Hundred, which had been granted to Urso d'Abitot, with Osbern, son of Richard, as its chief tenant. Before the Conquest it had belonged to a Saxon known as Leofwin Doda.

Wolverhampton

Wolverhampton derives its name from Lady Wulfruna, the Anglo-Saxon woman who was granted the manor known as Heanetune in 985 by King Aethelred. This original name translates from the Old English as 'high town (or farmstead)'. In 1086, it was recorded as 'Hantone, [in] the land of the Clerks of Wolverhampton, of which the Canons of Wolverhampton hold one hide from Samson of Bayeux'. The placename signifies 'Wulfruna's high town [or farmstead]'.

Wooton Wawen

Wooton is a common English placename with at least ten other townships having it as part of their placenames. These include Wooton Fitzpaine in Dorset, Wooton Rivers in Wiltshire and Wooton St Lawrence in Hampshire, among others. The first element of the Warwickshire village of Wooton Wawen's name shares an origin in common with all the others, in that it comes from the Old English words 'wudu', meaning 'wood' or 'woodland', and 'tun', a farmstead. Hence, a 'farmstead in a wood'. Then, some time in the eleventh century, a Dane called Wagen (or Vagn) took possession of the manor and a version of his name was appended to its estate; thereafter the place became 'Wagens's estate in a wood'. The name went through several transformations over time, with its earliest known recorded spelling being Uuidutuun in 716, then Wotone by 1086 and not until around 1142 was it known as Wageneswitona. Domesday entered the settlement, at that time a very large manor, under the Pathlow Hundred, assessed at seven hides of land held by Robert de Stafford, its final words recording that its previous owner, 'Vagn held it freely'.

Worcester

The Romans founded Worcester some time around 50 AD and probably named it Cair Guiragon. The name in Old English was Weorgorna Ceaster, which meant 'the (Roman) fort of the Weorgoran people'. The name Weorgoran is thought to mean the 'people of the winding river', probably referring to the River Severn which describes a huge arc as it approaches the town from the north. By 717, it was known as Wigranceastre and in the *Domesday Book* it was recorded as 'Wirecestre ...[where] King Edward had his customary dues. Now King William has in demesne both the king's part and the earl's part, referring to King Edward and to Earl Edwin, a former lessee of part of the lands of Worcester'.

Wormleighton

For more than a century before the Norman Conquest of England, the Warwickshire village of Wilmanlehttune pointed to its probable founder, a woman called Wilma, who established a herb garden in the place. In Old Saxon English, the expression was 'leac-tun', where 'leac' actually signified a leek and 'tun' an enclosure. Technically, therefore, the expression means 'leek enclosure', though it is more widely interpreted as indicating a herb garden. Hence, the placename means 'Wilma's herb garden'. Domesday recorded it as Wimelstone and Wimerestone, in the Hunisberi Hundred of land belonging to Countess Godgifu of Coventry, with Geoffrey de Mandeville as it chief tenant. The entry concludes, 'Leofric held it freely at the time of King Edward'.

Wrekin, The
The Wrekin (pronounced 'reek-in'), is a hill which stands proud of the otherwise relatively flat surrounding Shropshire landscape at just over four hundred metres, and is one of the county's most distinctive landmarks. The precise meaning of the name is somewhat obscure, but is thought to have come from the ancient Celtic language, as its hill fort was the headquarters of the Celtic Cornovii tribe. The name may have descended through the Roman town of Wroxeter, which they knew as Viroconium. For a time the Normans renamed it Mount Gilbert after a local hermit, but the attempt was short-lived. In the eleventh century it was recorded as Wreocensetun, meaning 'the people of the Wrekin'.

Wroxeter
There is an opinion that this Shropshire township began as a Celtic settlement known to them as Virico, which the Romans occupied and fortified as a military establishment which they called Viriconium (sometimes 'Viroconium', 'Ouirokonion' or 'Uriconio'). The name Uriconio may be based on the nearby distinctive hill known nowadays as the Wrekin. By the time of the 1086 survey, it was recorded as Rochecestre, the last element derived from 'caestre', the Roman word for a fort. Hence, the placename may be interpreted as '[the] Roman fort at Uriconio (or the Wrekin)'. Domesday actually listed Wroxeter in the Wrockwardine Hundred of Staffordshire, held by Reginald the Sheriff, it having belonged to Thorth, a Saxon free man before the Conquest.

Yardley
The Birmingham district of Yardley's placename is derived from the Old English words 'gyrd', meaning a rod or a spar, and 'leah', indicating a woodland clearing. Hence, the name translates as a 'clearing where wooden spars are obtained'. It was referred to in the Charter of King Edgar the Peaceable of 972 as Gyrdleah (or Gerlei) in Warwickshire, when it formed part of the original endowment of Pershore Abbey. In 1086, it was recorded as Gerlei, within the district of Beoley and held by the Church of St Mary of Pershore.

Yarnfield
Yarnfield is a small village in Staffordshire whose earliest written record spelt the placename as Ernefield. The name comes from the Old English 'earn', meaning 'eagle', and 'feld', signifying open land or what in modern English we would call a field. Hence the placename translates as 'open land where eagles are found [or seen]'.

Yarpole
This village in Herefordshire derived its placename from the Old English words 'gear', meaning 'weir' or 'river dam', and 'pol', a pool. Hence, '[place by the] pool with a weir'. It was a fairly common practice in Saxon times to temporarily dam a river or stream to create a pool where fish may be caught. Domesday recorded the place as Iarpol, in the Wolfhay Hundred, held by Leofwin the Interpreter in 1086. The estate had been taken out of the possession of Queen Edith, who had held it before the Conquest.

Yockleton

In 1086, this small hamlet was recorded as Ioclehuile, in the Reweset Hundred of Shropshire, held by Robert (identified as the son of Corbet). The 'huile' element of the original name meant 'hill', but this was later replaced by the Old English word 'tun'. The first part of the placename derives from 'geocled', a word that referred to a small manor or estate. The original name would therefore have translated as 'small manor on [or by] a hill', which later became 'farmstead of a small manor or estate'.

Part Eight

The East Midlands

Derbyshire, Leicestershire, Lincolnshire, Northamptonshire, Nottinghamshire, and Rutland

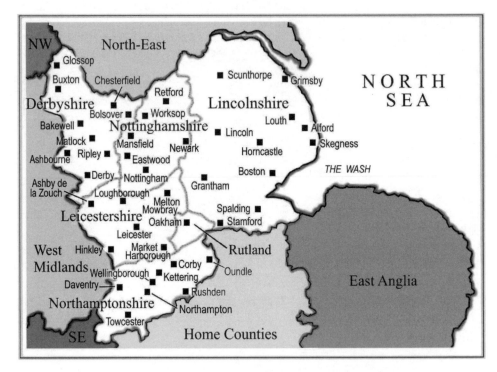

A map depicting the East Midlands region of England.

Alderwasley

This Derbyshire village has a placename that translates into modern English as 'woodland clearing on alluvial land where alder trees grow'. The name comes from a combination of three Old English words: 'alor', meaning 'alder tree', 'waesse' signifying alluvial land where nutrient-rich sediment is deposited following river flood, and 'leah', a woodland clearing. The chief candidate for such local floods would be the stream that runs close to Alderwas Hall. In 1251, the village was known as Alrewasleg.

Alfreton

One opinion is that the name of this small Derbyshire township is derived from a man called Aelfhere, whose farm or settlement it was before the Norman Conquest. In which case, the placename may be taken to mean 'the farmstead of Aelfhere'. An alternative view is that it may have been named after Alfred the Great, who founded the settlement. That said, two Roman military roads, Ryknield Street and Lilley Street, run very close to the township, indicating that there was probably some sort of settlement there long before Alfred's time. Whatever its true origin, in 1086 the place was recorded in the *Domesday Book* as 'Elstretune ... in the land of Roger de Bully', where Earl Morcar leased four acres of land from Ingram, who was holding it for de Bully.

Alsop en le Dale
This village was probably founded by a man called Aelle, who owned this small enclosed and somewhat remote valley in Derbyshire and this is the entire derivation of the placename. Technically the placename means 'Aelle's valley in the valley', as the 'en le Dale' element would seem on first sight to have the same meaning as the Old English element of the first word. Sounds complicated? Well yes, but most authorities explain it as a small enclosed valley (a 'hop'), within a larger valley (a 'dael'). The confusion highlights the problem with synthesising Norman French with Old Saxon English, and the kind of incongruities which that threw up. Hence, the translation should more properly be 'Aelle's small remote valley [lying] in a large valley'. Domesday had avoided this by simply recording the place as Elleshope, and it was not until the sixteenth century that the village was recorded as Alsope in le Dale.

Ashbourne
This Derbyshire township dates from Saxon times and was entered in the *Domesday Book* as Esseburn, from the Old English 'aesc', an ash tree, and 'burna', a small stream or brook. Hence, a '[place by a] stream where ash trees grow'. The 1086 record shows it in the possession of the Crown, having belonged to King Edward before the Conquest.

Ashby-de-la-Zouch
Usually shortened to Ashby, this small Leicestershire market town was known as Aschebi in 1086, when Domesday records it as part of the Goscote Wapentake held by Ivo for Hugh de Grandmesnil. In Old English, the word 'aesc', like the Old Norse 'askr' meant 'ash tree'. The suffix 'by' indicated a Danish settlement. Hence, 'the settlement where ash trees grow'. By 1205, it was known as Esseby la Zouch, after the Breton nobleman Alain de Parrhoet la Zouch, who became Lord of the Manor in 1160, at which time his family name was appended to the placename. The word 'Zouch' comes from an old Norman word 'souche', literally meaning a tree stump, but used then to describe a person of a stocky or thickset stature. The la Zouche family lived there until the reign of Henry IV in the fourteenth century, when it passed to the Earl of Ormonde, then to the Hastings family of Norfolk.

Ashby Puerorum
This Lincolnshire village has complex origins. First, 'Ashby' is a combination of the Old English word 'aesc', meaning 'ash tree', with the Old Scandinavian 'by', meaning 'village' or 'farmstead' (as in Ashby-de-la-Zouch, previously). Hence, 'village near ash trees'. Then, the second word is of Latin origin, where 'puerorum' meant 'of the boys' or 'belonging to boys'. The entire placename may therefore be taken to mean 'village [or farmstead] of the boys among the ash trees', or some combination thereof. Domesday merely recorded it as Aschebi, sokeland in 'the Land of the Bishop of Bayeux, where 'Othenkar and Ketillbert had four carucates of land to the geld'.

Aslockton
This Nottinghamshire village lay well within the Danelaw territory when it was founded by a Scandinavian settler called Aslakr, after whom the place is named. The addition of the Old

English word 'tun', signifying a farmstead, is evidence of the gradual assimilation of Saxon and Norse into the language. The placename may be taken to mean 'Aslakr's farmstead'. Domesday recorded the place as Aslachetune, in the Bingham Hundred held personally in 1086 by William the Conqueror, as it had belonged to King Edward before 1066.

Averham

Averham derived its name from its location on the River Trent and the tidal bore that frequently causes floods in the region. The Anglo-Saxon word 'egor' or 'egrum', from which the placename developed, referred to the flooding or high tides to which the village was subjected from the earliest days of its establishment. The word may indeed be related to the modern English word 'bore', and the placename may be interpreted to mean '[place by the] floods or high tides'. Domesday recorded the village as Aigrun in the land of Gilbert Tison in Nottinghamshire, where Swein had three carucates of land.

Aynho

The Northamptonshire village of Aynho stands high on a hilltop and means 'hill spur (a ridge or outcrop) of a man called Aega'. We may never known who Aega was, but he must have been a person of some importance to have stamped his name on the place. The final element of the placename 'ho' (sometimes expressed as 'hoo' or 'hoe'), indicated the spur of a hill, an outcrop or promontory. Hence, 'Aega's hill spur'. The place was recorded in 1086 as Aienho, in the Hundred of Sutton, held at that time by Geoffrey de Mandeville, having belonged to Esgar the Constable before the Conquest.

Bakewell

The Derbyshire town of Bakewell began as a Saxon settlement known as Baedeca's Wella, or Badecan welle, presumably after a man of that name who had a well or a spring in the township. It was recorded in the *Anglo-Saxon Chronicles* that in 920 Edward the Elder '…went into the Peak District, to Bakewell, and commanded a borough to be built in the neighbourhood and manned'. In 1086, it was recorded as 'Badequella … in the land of the king'.

Barlborough

In the years preceding the Norman Conquest this Derbyshire village was known as Barleburh, a name derived from 'bar', the Old English word for a boar, 'leah', a woodland clearing, and 'burh', a fortified place or stronghold. Hence, 'stronghold near [or in] a woodland clearing where boars are found'. In 1086, the place was recorded as Barleburg, listed in the Hundred of Scarsdale, held at that time by Ralph FitzHubert, it having been a possession of a Saxon man called Leofnoth, the brother of Leofric, before the Conquest.

Barnack

Barnack is a village and civil parish in Northamptonshire whose name means 'oak tree of the warriors'. It comes from the Old English 'beorn', meaning 'warrior', which some believe is related to the fighting Celtic tribes of the Kingdom of Bernica in Northumbria. The final element comes from 'ac', meaning 'oak tree'. The place was known as Beornican in the late-tenth century and by the time of the Great Survey it had been recorded as Bernac and was listed in the Upton Hundred, held in 1086 by William FitzAnsculf, it having belonged to Bondi the Constable before the Norman Conquest.

Barnetby le Wold

This North Lincolnshire village may have been founded by a Dane called Beornnoth (or Beornede), after which it took its name. This is especially reinforced by the village location within the territory of Danelaw, and the additional Scandinavian affix 'by', which meant 'farmstead' or 'village'. The 'le Wold' suffix identifies the place on the Lincolnshire Wolds. The placename in its entirety means 'Beornnoth's village on the Wolds'. In 1086, it was recorded as Bernedebi, in the Yarborough Hundred, held at that time by William de Percy.

Barnoldby-le-Beck
This North Lincolnshire village was an integrated part of the Danelaw territory of northern England, and its name reflects those Norse origins. The settlement was probably founded by a Dane called Bjornulfr. The affix 'by' was the Old Scandinavian word for a farmstead or settlement, and 'bekkr' was Norse for a stream (from which the modern English word 'beck', common in northern England, is derived). Hence, 'Bjornulfr's farmstead [or settlement] beside a stream'. By the time of the Domesday survey, the place had been recorded as Bernulfby, in the Havestoe Hundred, listed at that time in the North Riding of Lincolnshire, and held by Count Alan of Brittany. Before the Norman Conquest the manor had belonged to Earl Ralph 'the Constable'.

Barton in Fabis
Barton is a common placename with around twenty-seven villages and hamlets found of that name in England. It comes from the Old English expression 'bere-tun' (or 'baer-tun'), meaning either 'barley farm', simply 'farm', or signifying an outlying grange where grain was stored. This Nottinghamshire village had the Latin word 'fabis' attached some time before the fourteenth century, which meant 'in the beans', a reference to the beans that were grown in the locality. Thus the placename may have related to an outlying grange where beans were stored. At the time of the *Domesday Book,* the place was recorded as Bartone and listed in the Rushcliffe Hundred, held in 1086 by Saewin of Kingston, it having belonged to Algar Cida in 1066. In 1388, the placename was recorded as Barton in le Benes. Another place similarly noted for its bean crops is Barton-in-the-Beans in the County of Leicestershire.

Beeby
The name of this small Leicestershire hamlet further illustrates the gradual symbiosis of Anglo-Saxon and Danish culture in eastern England during the ninth and tenth centuries. It comes from the Old English word 'beo', meaning 'bee', and the Old Norse word 'by', signifying a farmstead or village settlement. Hence, the name may be taken to mean 'farmstead where bees are kept'. The Domesday entry for this place was as Bebi, listed in the Goscote Hundred, held in 1086 by the Abbey of St Guthlac in Crowland, who had also held it during the time of King Edward.

Belmesthorpe
Belmesthorpe is a small hamlet in the county of Rutland where a Danish man called Beornhelm probably established a farmstead, as the placename comes from Old Scandinavian and reflects his name and the word 'thorp', which signified an outlying or remote farm. The placename translates as 'Beornhelm's remote farm'. Around 1050, it was known as Beolmesthorp and in 1086, Domesday recorded it as Belmestorp, in the Witchley Hundred, which incorporated parts of the counties of Rutland, Lincolnshire and Northamptonshire at that time. The estate comprised sixteen acres of meadow, woodland four furlongs long and two broad, and it had three mills; the manor was held by Countess Judith of Lens, having belonged to Earl Waltheof before 1066.

Belper
Belper's placename is thought to derive from the Old French 'beau' or 'bel', meaning beautiful, and 'repaire', which translates as 'a retreat'. It received no mention in the

Domesday Book, but by 1231 it was recorded as Beurepeir, a manor held by Edmund Crouchback, Earl of Lancaster.

Bevercotes
This Nottinghamshire hamlet has a placename which translates loosely as 'beaver dwellings'. The name comes from 'beofer', the Anglo-Saxon word for 'beaver', and 'cot', which though technically meaning 'cottage', may have been more widely used to refer to a habitated dwelling – in this case a beaver 'lodge'. It harks back to a time when beavers were commonly found throughout Britain. The name was recorded as Beurecote in the mid-twelfth century.

Bitteswell
Wherever the word 'well' terminates an English placename it invariably derives from the Old English word 'welle' or 'wella', which signified not only a well, as you might expect, but also a stream or even a fountain, and this Leicestershire village placename runs true to form. The first element of the name comes from 'bytm', which indicated a broad valley. Hence, the placename translates as '[place by a] stream in a broad valley'. The Domesday survey listed it twice, as Betmeswelle and Betmeswel in the Guthlaxton Wapentake, lands part-held between Geoffrey de la Guerche and Earl Aubrey de Coucy, where Robert tended eight and a half carucates of land from the Earl and one carucate from Geoffrey.

Blankney
At some time in its early history this village in Lincolnshire was probably established by a man called Blanca, who built it on a plot of raised ground surrounded by fenland. Such settlements were common in the area, where marshes, swamps and wetlands offered a degree of defensive protection in turbulent times, when aggressive Danish incursions were commonplace. The placename means 'Blanca's island', from the Old English word 'eg', signifying such places as 'islands'. Domesday recorded Blachene in the Langoe Hundred lands of Walter d'Ainscourt it having been held by Hemming of Branston in 1066.

Blatherwyke
This Northamptonshire village has a placename that means 'farm where bladder plants are grown'. It derives from 'blaedre', an Old English word for meaning 'bladder', and 'wic', a specialised farm of some kind. Sometimes known as the Bladderwort, the plant included the Bladder Campion, a carnivorous plant, whose dried leaves were traditionally used to make a herbal infusion or medicinal tea. The village was recorded in 1086 as Blarewiche, and listed in the Corby Hundred, held at that time by Robert de Bucy.

Bole
Bole gets its name either from an Old English word, 'bola', or the Old Scandinavian 'bolr', both of which meant 'tree trunk', or in the plural form as 'bolum'. The placename may be interpreted as '[place by the] tree trunks'. Domesday recorded it as Bolun, listed within the Nottinghamshire Hundred of Oswaldbeck, held in 1086 by Roger de Bully, having belonged to Wulfmer in 1066.

Bolsover
The origin of the placename is somewhat obscure, but it has been suggested that it comes from the Old English 'Bula's ofer', 'Bull's ofer' or 'Boll's ofer'. It is thought to derive from a man called Boll, Bull or Bula, and 'ofer' meaning a ridge. Hence, it may be taken to mean either 'Bull's or Boll's Ridge'. By the time of Domesday, it was known as 'Belesovre... in the

land of William Peverel [in Derbyshire], once held by Leofric and now by Robert, made up of woodland and pasture and worth sixty shillings'.

Boothby Graffoe/Boothby Pagnell
This Lincolnshire village was known as Bodebi, in the Graffoe Wapentake, in 'The Land of Alvred of Lincoln' at the time of Domesday. The name 'Boothby' comes from the Old Scandinavian language, where 'both' meant 'booth' or 'shelter', and 'by' indicated a farmstead. Graffoe comes from the Old English words 'graf', meaning 'grove', and 'hoh', 'hoe' or 'hoo' indicating an outcrop or hill spur. Hence, 'farmstead with shelters in a grove on an outcrop', The shelters referred to were most likely for animals at pasture. The Graffoe element of the placename distinguishes it from Boothby Pagnell a few miles away, which was held by the Pagnell family in the fourteenth century.

Boston
Tradition has it that the town of Boston in Lincolnshire was named after its probable founder, the Saxon monk St Botolph, and is derived from the Old English 'Botolph's tun' (town or settlement). It got no mention in the *Domesday Book*, but was recorded as Botuluestan in 1130, which some suggest may indicate a different explanation, that its derivation is Botwulf, a man's name, and 'stan', a boundary stone marker or meeting place. Hence it may be taken to mean 'stone marker or meeting place of Botwulf'.

Bothamsall
Situated in a lofty position overlooking the valley of the River Meden and the River Maun in Nottinghamshire, this village placename perfectly describes its location. The name comes from two Anglo-Saxon words: 'bothm', meaning 'broad [or wide] river valley', and 'scelf', a shelf or ridge. Hence, the placename means '[place on a] ridge or shelf [overlooking] a broad river valley'. The village was recorded twice in 1086, as Bodmescel and Bodmescelf, 'Sokeland of this Manor' in the Bassetlaw Wapentake land of King William, where before the Conquest, Earl Tostig '...had twelve bovates of land to the geld'. The manor had one mill, forty acres of meadow, and '...woodland pasture half a league long and four furlongs broad'. In 1086, the estates were valued at sixty shillings, having been worth eight pounds at the time of King Edward.

Boultham
The first element of the name of this village in Lincolnshire comes from the Old English word 'bulut', which referred to the edible cuckoo flower (Latin name: *cardamine pratensis* - also known as lady's smock or mayflower). The second element could be either 'ham', signifying a village or a homestead, or 'hamm', an enclosure. Therefore the placename might equally translate as 'homestead where the cuckoo flower grows' or 'enclosure where the cuckoo flower grows'. The Great Survey recorded Buletham, a very small estate supporting just one family in the Graffoe Hundred, and held in 1086 by Robert de Stafford, it having been the property of Osmund Benz before the Norman Conquest.

Brailsford
The placename of the Derbyshire village of Brailsford translates into Modern English as '[place by a] ford near a burial place'. It derives from Anglo-Saxon times when the word 'braegels' signified a place of burial or a graveyard, and 'ford' referred (as it still does) to a shallow river crossing. In view of the fact that no graveyard has been found at the place, it has been argued that a more reliable alternative explanation of the placename's first element might come from ancient Celtic, and is similar to the Welsh words meaning 'hill court',

from 'bre', a hill, and 'llys' a court. This is borne out by the village location on the side of a hill. Whichever is the case, Domesday recorded the village as Brailesford in 1086 and listed it in the Appletree Hundred which then encompassed parts of Derbyshire and Nottinghamshire. The manor was held at that time by Henry de Ferrers and had belonged to Earl Waltheof in 1066.

Brassington
This Derbyshire village was named after a man called Brandsige, which together with the Old English expressions, 'ing', meaning 'associated with' and 'tun', a farmstead or estate, produces an overall meaning of 'estate [or farmstead] associated with Brandsige'. The Great Survey recorded the place as Branzinctun and listed it in the Hamston Hundred, held in 1086 by Henry de Ferrers having belonged previously to a Saxon man called Siward.

Brigg
A township in North Lincolnshire whose placename has a simple derivation from the Anglo-Saxon word 'byrcg', meaning 'bridge'. The place was originally called Glanford Brigg, based on the Old English 'gleam', signifying festivities or revelry, plus 'ford', a river crossing and 'byricg', referring to the bridge over the River Ancholme. Hence, 'bridge at the ford where festivities are held'.

Brigstock
The Northamptonshire township of Brigstock was recorded in 1086 as Bricstoc, from the Old English words 'brycg', meaning 'bridge', and 'stoc', signifying an outlying or remote village. Hence, 'remote village by a bridge'. Domesday listed it in the Corby Hundred, '... having land for three ploughs, and a mill rendering five shillings'.

Burgh le Marsh
During Anglo-Saxon times the settlement of Burgh le Marsh was simply called Burg or Burch, signifying a fortified manor or stronghold, one of many settlements fortified by Alfred the Great as a protection against Danish invasions. As it had been established on marshy land on the Lincolnshire coastal plain, it was natural that the 'le Marsh' element should be added to distinguish it from other places of the same name (e.g. Burgh in Suffolk, Burgh-by-Sands in Cumbria, Burgh on Bain, Great Burgh and Burgh Heath, also in Lincolnshire). The *Domesday Book* records the place as sokeland of Drayton with one and a half carucates of land paying rent and further land sufficient for twelve oxen. Part located in the Sokeland of Baradney, where the survey listed a church and five hundred acres of meadow, and another part lying with the Candleshoe Wapentake, where 'Godwine and Toki and Godric had ten bovates of land to the geld'.

Burton Latimer
Burton is a very common name in England with more than thirty towns, villages and hamlets sharing it as part of their placename. It derives from the Old English word 'burh', indicating a fortified place, farmstead, manor house or stronghold. The second part of this placename is connected with the Latimer family, who held it in the thirteenth century. The earliest known written record of the Manor of Burton Latimer in Northamptonshire was in the Domesday survey of 1086, which lists it as Burtone, part in the Orlingbury Hundred, whose chief tenant was Geoffrey, Norman Bishop of Coutances, with two hides and three virgates of land rented to Walkelin. In the reign of Edward the Confessor, Earl Ralph of Hereford held eight and a half hides of land. Another part of the manor lay within land belonging to Guy de Raimbeaucourt in Navisland Hundred. Before the Conquest it had belonged to

Burgred, the father of Edwin. Two-thirds of the township of Burton were assigned in the thirteenth century to the successors of Alan de Dinant and became known as the Manor of Burton-by-Thingden and the Manor of Burton Plessy (or Placy), before coming into the possession of the Latimers.

Buxton

The Romans established a Derbyshire settlement at Buxton towards the end of the first century and built baths, known as Aquae Arnematiae (meaning 'waters of the sacred grove'). They had been drawn to the region by the plentiful supply of fresh water and its strategic position on an important trading route. Later, Saxon burial mounds bear witness to the township's continued habitation. The origin of the placename is uncertain, but around 1100 it was known as Buchestanes, most likely derived from 'bucca', a male deer or buck, and 'stan', a stone, therefore perhaps 'buck stone', a possible reference to a boundary marker in an ancient royal hunting ground.

Caister

The Domesday entry for this Lincolnshire township states that before the Norman Conquest: 'In Castre and Hundon, Earl Morcar had three carucates to the geld'. By 1086 it had become a valuable possession of the king and worth fifty pounds. It was listed in the Yarborough Hundred as quite a large settlement with twenty-six and a half (?) households comprising forty villans, twelve free men and one priest. The placename is a direct translation of the Old English 'caester', signifying a Roman camp. There are two other English townships in Norfolk of the same derivation, but with distinguishing features: Caister-on-Sea and Caistor St Edmund.

Carlton Curlieu

This Leicestershire village placename is a combination of Old Scandinavian, Old English and Norman French. Taken respectively, 'karl' meant 'free man' or 'peasant', 'tun' signified an estate or a farmstead, and 'de Curly' was the name of the family who took possession of the manor in the thirteenth century. Hence, 'de Curley's estate [or farmstead] of the free men'. Domesday recorded it as Carletone, quite a large estate which included sixteen acres of meadow and land for seven plough teams, which supported more than thirty households in the Gartree Hundred and was held by Hugh de Grandmesnil as Lord of the Manor. By the late thirteenth century, the name had been recorded as Carleton Curly.

Chesterfield

Chesterfield began as a Roman settlement and its placename comes from the Saxon word for a Roman fort, 'caestre' and the Old English 'feld', meaning 'field' or 'open grazing land'. Hence, the 'field (or grazing land) near the Roman fort'. It was known in 955 as Cesterfelda and, by the time of the Domesday survey, it was recorded as Cestrefeld, one of six berewicks in Newbold in the Scarsdale Wapentake of Derbyshire, owned by King William.

Claypole

The name of this Lincolnshire village means '[place by the] clay (or clayey) pool'. It derives from two Anglo-Saxon words, 'claeg', meaning 'clay', and 'pol', a pool. The pool in question is thought to be part of the River Witham. It was recorded as Claipol in 1086, listed as a very large estate within the Loveden Hundred, supporting up to fifty households. There were fifty-five acres of meadow, a mill and a church and the estates were jointly held by Geoffrey Alselin and Bishop Odo of Bayeux. The manor was assessed as worth two pounds.

Cleethorpes

This Lincolnshire settlement was occupied by the Danes in the sixth century. The placename is a combination of the Old English word 'claeg', meaning clay, and the Old Norse word 'thorp', meaning a remote or outlying settlement. Therefore, it may be taken to mean 'outlying settlement near clay [deposits]'. Old Clee was recorded in the *Domesday Book* as Cleia, part of the sokeland of Great Grimsby, held by the Archbishop of York.

Corby

The Northamptonshire township of Corby is known to have been settled by Danes in the eighth century, its name probably deriving from 'Kori's by', where Kori was a man's name and 'by' is the Old Norse word for a farmstead or village settlement. Its name is recorded in 1086 as Corbei, in the Corby Hundred, one of many held by William the Conqueror. The town's emblem, the raven, probably originated in Norman times, as the French word for the bird is 'corbeau', from which the placename is derived.

Cotgrave

Despite appearances, the name of this Nottinghamshire village has nothing to do with graves or burials; the 'grave' element comes directly from the Old English word 'graf', meaning 'grove'. The grove in question belonged to (or was founded by) a man known to us as Cotta. Hence, 'Cotta's grove'. An error in recording the name by the Domesday commissioners saw it recorded as Godegrave, and listed in the Bingham Hundred, held at that time by Ralph de Buron, it having belonged to a Saxon man called Thorkil of Hickling before 1066.

Cowbit

The Old English word 'cu' referred to a cow or cows, and 'byht' signified a bend in a river (related to the modern English word 'bight'). Hence, this Lincolnshire village has a placename which means '[place by a] bend in the river where cows are pastured'. The river bend in question is that of the River Welland which flows around the village. The place was recorded as Coubiht in 1267.

Crick

The Derbyshire village of Crick traces its name back to a Celtic word 'creig', which is closely related to the Welsh 'craig', meaning 'hill'. The hill in question is thought to be the one on which the original settlement was established. Domesday recorded the name as Crice, and listed it as a very small estate supporting six households in the Morleystone Hundred and held in 1086 by Ralph FitzHubert, it having belonged to two Saxon brothers called Leofnoth and Leofric in 1066. There is a village of the same name in the County of Northamptonshire.

Cropwell Bishop/Cropwell Butler

These Nottinghamshire villages share the same ancestry, with the Old English word 'cropp', meaning 'hump', and 'hyll', a hill. Hence, 'rounded or hump-backed hill'. The hill referred to is known as Hoe Hill. Domesday recorded the place simply as Crophille, in the Bingham Hundred. Part of the original manor, Cropwell Bishop, acquired its distinguishing name when it was granted to the Archbishop of York. Before the Conquest it had belonged to the Canons of St Mary Southwell. Another part of the manor estate, Copwell Butler, was held in the twelfth century by the Butler family, whose surname was appended to the place. In the 1086 survey it had been granted to Walter d'Ainscourt, having previously belonged to the Saxon, Hemming of Branston.

Daventry
The Northamptonshire township of Daventrei appeared in the survey of 1086, and the placename may have come from pre-Conquest English and simply means 'tree of a man called Daffa'. It had been settled by Vikings under the leadership of Ivar (or Ivo) the Boneless, who called the settlement Danetre. An alternative explanation cites the Celtic phrase 'dwy-afon-tre', meaning 'the town of two rivers', as a more likely interpretation of the placename, given its location between the Rivers Leam and Nene, which have their sources nearby.

Derby
It was the Romans who first created a settlement called Derventio some time around 50 AD, when they constructed a fort on high ground overlooking the River Derwent at a place now known as Strutt's Park. The placename is a combination of the Old Norse words 'djur', meaning a deer, and 'by', a village or farmstead. Hence, 'a village or farmstead where deer are kept'. Derby was one of the newly created boroughs that were wrested from Danish occupation by King Alfred's daughter Aethelflaed. The *Anglo-Saxon Chronicles* recorded the account in 917 thus: 'Aetheflaed, lady of the Mercians, with God's help, before Lammas obtained the borough that is called Derby, with all that belonged to it. There also were killed four of her thegns, who were dear to her, inside the gates'. The township was known in the tenth century as Deoraby and in its present form by 1086, but at that time recorded as a borough in Nottinghamshire, probably held by Walter d'Ainscourt and previously belonging to a Saxon called Stori.

Dronfield
This placename probably derived from a local field where bees (or drones) were found in Anglo-Saxon times, and comes from the Old English words 'dran' and 'feld'. This Derbyshire township was recorded in 1086 as Dranefeld, in the Scarsdale Wapentake, held by the king, comprising 'one curucate of land sufficient for one plough'.

Edale
A village in Derbyshire, that nestles on the lower slopes of the Peak District, in what is commonly known as The Vale of Edale. The name means 'valley with an island', from two Old English elements, 'eg', an island, and 'dael', signifying a valley. The island in question is bordered by Grinds Brook, which is a tributary of the River Noe. Domesday recorded the place in 1086 as Aidele in the Blackwell Hundred, part of the Manor of Bakewell, in the possession of King William, as it had been by King Edward before the Conquest, and valued at that time at ten pounds and thirty pence.

Edensore
Domesday recorded this Derbyshire village as Edensoure, a name derived from a man called Eadin and the Anglo-Saxon word 'ofer', signifying a sloping bank or ridge, eminently describing the village location on a steep bank overlooking the River Derwent. Hence, the placename means '[place at] Eadin's sloping bank'. The 1086 account listed the village in the Blackwell Hundred, held at that time by Henry de Ferrers it having previously been a possession of two Saxons known as Ketil of Edensore and Leofnoth Sterre.

Egleton
Egleton, in the County of Rutland, was recorded in the *Domesday Book* as one of five berewicks held by the king and attached to the Manor of Oakham (or Ockeham). The name derives from Anglo-Saxon times and translates as the 'village or farmstead belonging to

a man called Ecgwulf'. By 1218, it was known as Egoluestun and by 1484, the Manor of Egleton was in the possession of Henry Grey, Lord of Codnor.

Egmanton

Egmanton is a village in Nottinghamshire whose placename reveals its earliest known settler, a man called Ecgmund, whose 'tun', village or farmstead it was in Saxon times. Domesday listed the village as Agemuntone, a large estate in the Bassetlaw Wapentake, held in 1086 by Roger de Bully.

Elmesthorpe

This Leicestershire village in what was known as Danelaw territory, derives its name from a settler called Aethelmaer and the Old Norse 'thorp', meaning 'outlying [or remote] farmstead'. Hence, loosely, 'Aethelmaer's remote farm'. An early record of 1207 shows the placename as Ailmerestorp. Some argue that Aethelmaer was the Bishop of Elmham in 1070, though this might be a reference to another man of the same name.

Fishtoft

The Lincolnshire village of Fishtoft gets its placename directly from the Old Scandinavian word 'toft', meaning 'building site'. The suffix 'Fish' was added sometime in the fifteenth century, suggesting either a connection with the fishing industry or else an influential local family of that name. The *Domesday Book* identifies the place simply as Toft, part in the Wolersty Hundred, part-held in 1086 by the Count Alan of Brittany, having been in the possession of Earl Ralph the Constable before the Conquest. Another part in the Fishtoft Hundred was a sokeland of Drayton, held by Guy de Craon and rented to Aethelstan, son of Godram, who had nine carucates of estate land in 1066. The survey concluded '[There is] land for many ploughs... there is a church and a priest, and one mill rendering ten shillings and sixty acres of meadow'. The entire manor was valued at ten pounds.

Fotheringhay

It was recorded as Fodringeia in 1086, in the Willowsbrook Hundred which was held for the king by Countess Judith of Lens. The placename was in use well before 1066, and one interpretation is based on the Old English words 'fodring' (grazing land, related to the contemporary word 'fodder'), and 'eg', an island or a place surrounded by water. Hence, possibly, 'grazing land surrounded by water'.

Friskney

A village in Lincolnshire whose name comes from Old English with Scandinavian undertones. The first element is from 'fresc', meaning 'fresh', and the second, 'ea', meaning river. Hence '[place at the] fresh river'. The 'sk' at the middle of the placename is a distinct Norse emphasis. The *Domesday Book* recorded the place as Frischenei in the Manor of Candlesby in the Candleshow Hundred, held by Ketilbiorn of Nettleton, having belonged to Swartbrand, son of Ulf before the Conquest. In 1086 it was a very small village, with just three households, amounting to a third of a ploughland with four acres of meadow.

Fulstow

The placename of this village in Lincolnshire has two possible explanations: the first element could relate to the Old English word 'fugol', meaning 'bird' or 'fowl', or else it could refer to a man called Fugol. The second element, 'stow', signifies a place of meeting or of religious significance. Hence, either 'meeting place where birds assemble', or 'Fugol's meeting place', although the former interpretation seems more probable. The place was recorded in the survey of 1086 as Fugelestou, in the Hundred of Haverstoe, whose chief tenant at that time was Roscelin of Fulstow, with Earl Hugh d'Avranches of Chester being lord of the manor. Before 1066 it had belonged to a Saxon man called Godric.

Gainsborough

Gainsborough is a traditional North Lincolnshire market town located on the River Trent, once famed for the manufacture of linseed cake, malt and cordage. The placename comes from Old English and means 'stronghold of a man called Gegn', or possibly 'stronghold of the Gaini tribe', the Old English suffix 'burh' indicating a fortified place of some kind. In 1086, is was recorded as Gainesburgh, in the Lindsey West Riding of the Corringham Hundred, in the lands of Geoffrey de la Guerche, where 'Reginald, Geoffrey's man, has two ploughs', which he rented from Nele d'Aubigny.

Glapwell

Glapwell is a village in Derbyshire which may once have had a well or a stream belonging to a man called Glappa. The Old English word 'wella' could refer to a stream or a well, and even a fountain. Alternatively, the name could come from 'glaeppe', meaning 'buckbean', another name for the bogbean, a perennial herbaceous plant that grows in wet areas. So the placename might translate as either 'Glappa's well [or stream]', or 'stream where the buckbean plant grows'. Domesday recorded the village as Glappewelle and listed it as a small manor supporting eight households within the Scarsdale Hundred and held by William Peverel. In 1066, the manor had belonged to Leofric, the son of Osmund.

Glentham

This Lincolnshire township in the ancient Parish of Caistor, now in the District of West Lindsey, derives its name from two Anglo-Saxon words, 'glente', meaning 'lookout place (or post)', and 'ham', which signified a homestead or dwelling. Hence, the placename may be taken to mean 'homestead by the lookout post'. The name indicates the location of the original settlement, sitting as it does on top of a hill. Another source translates the placename quite differently, as 'homestead frequented by birds of prey'. The village received three entries in the *Domesday Book*, as Glandham, Glantham and Glentham, in the Aslacoe Hundred. Before 1066, it belonged to the Bishop of Lincoln along with several Saxon earls and thegns, including Thorgisl, Rainfrid, Estan of Farningham, Wulfmaer and Wadard of Cogges. After the Conquest the manor was seized and granted to Bishop Odo of Bayeux and ten bovates rented to Aethelstan and Wulfmar.

Glossop

The former mill town of Glossop in Derbyshire is thought to come from the Anglo-Saxon 'Glott's Hop', and that Glott was a local man's name. 'Hop' signifies a small valley. Hence, 'Glott's valley'. By 1086, it was known as Glosop and received only a passing mention in Domesday where it was recorded that '...in Old Glossop Lyfing [had] four bovates of land'. By 1219 the village was recorded as Glotsop.

Gosberton

This Lincolnshire village was once known as Gosbertechirche, from Gosbert, a German man's personal name and the Old English 'cirice', meaning 'church'. Hence, 'Gosbert's church'. Some time during the fifteenth century, 'cirice' was replaced by the Middle English word 'toun', meaning 'village' or 'town', although the reason is unclear. Domesday recorded it under its original name, Gosbertechirche and Gosbertcherche, and listed the place in the Kirton Hundred lands belonging to the Bishop of Lincoln Cathedral, tenanted by Mauger of Gosberton having belonged to a Saxon man called

Asli (or Azur) before the Conquest. Part of the manorial estate was designated as a sokeland of Drayton, where Wulfbert had six bovates. Before 1066 Aethelstan held six bovates '...and Earl Ralph had the soke [of Drayton]'.

Gotham

A Nottinghamshire village whose placename comes directly from the Old English words 'gat', a goat, and either 'ham', a homestead or village, or 'hamm' an enclosure. Hence, the placename means either 'village where goats are kept' or 'enclosure where goats are kept' – either seems equally possible. In 1086 it was recorded as Gatham, in Rushcliffe Hundred, jointly held by the Count of Mortain and Saewin of Kingston.

Goxhill

This North Lincolnshire village placename is of Scandinavian origin, where the Old Norse word 'gausli' meant a gushing (or spouting) spring. In 1086, it was recorded as Golse, in the Yarborough Hundred, at that time listed in the Lindsey North Riding, part 'in the Land of Alvred of Lincoln' and part in the West Riding land of Drogo de la Beuvrière. By the twelfth century, the name had been written as Gousle and Gousel.

Grantham

The Lincolnshire town of Grantham is possibly named after a man called Granta. The Old English suffix 'ham' signifies that it may have begun as his settlement or village. It was known by its present name by 1086, when the *Domesday Book* recorded it as part of the Aswardhurn Wapentake and stated that '...in Grantham, [the] queen had twelve carucates'.

Grimsby

In pre-Roman times, Lincolnshire was home to the Celtic tribe of the Coritani. However, Grimsby as we know it was founded by the Danes, when they invaded eastern England in the ninth century. The placename derives from Old Norse suffix 'by', meaning 'village', and land that was probably founded and farmed in the ninth century by a fisherman called Grimmr or Grimm. In Norse mythology, 'grim' (a mask) and 'grimnir' (the masked one), are names adopted by the god Odin. Hence, 'Grimr's village'. Variations occur in many English placenames within what was known as Danelaw, examples being the numerous earthworks named Grimsdyke. By the time of Domesday, Grimsby had a population of a few hundred, which was a large settlement by the standards of the time. It was sometimes known as Great Grimsby, to distinguish it from Little Grimsby, some fourteen miles further down the coast. By 1086 the estate was known as Grimesbi and listed in the Bradley Hundred under the part ownership of Drogo de la Beuvrière, with Rolf, identified as the son of Skjaldvor, leasing four carucates of Great Grimsby land in Weelsby. Another part was held by Ralph de Mortimer, with a third in the possession of Bishop Odo of Bayeux. This last portion had belonged jointly to Erik, along with his brother Tosti and with Swein before the Conquest.

Gumley

Gumley's placename comes from its earliest known settler, probably a Saxon man called Godmund, as in the eighth century the settlement was known as Godmunesleah. Over time, the name seems to have become shortened to a single syllable, 'Gum', possibly as a recognised diminutive or affectionate form of the name. The Old English suffix 'leah' indicates a woodland glade or a clearing, so that the placename means 'Godmund's woodland clearing'. By 1086 the placename had been recorded as Godmundelai, in the Gartree Hundred of Leicestershire, held at that time by Robert de Vessey, and previously held by Aelric, son of Mergeat, in 1066.

Hagworthingham

This most complicated placename belongs to a village in Lincolnshire. It is made up of four Anglo-Saxon words: 'hagga', meaning 'hawthorn tree', 'worth', an enclosure, 'inga', signifying dwellers or inhabitants, and 'ham', a homestead. Taken together the name may be interpreted as meaning 'homestead belonging to the dwellers of the hawthorn enclosure'. The Domesday commissioners made a hash of recording the village name and entered it no fewer than nine times, as Hacherdingeham, Hacberdingham and Haberdingham, among others, and located in the Hill Hundred, part-held by Count Alan of Brittany, Earl Hugh (the Wolf) of Chester, Gilbert of Ghent and Drogo de la Beuvrière. In 1066, it had also been part-held, by Saxon men known as Holmketill, Ulf Fenman, Alnoth, Aethelstan, Tonni of Lusby and Earl Harold.

Hassop

This small Derbyshire hamlet's placename is derived from 'haegtesse' (from which the word 'hag' may have come), and 'hop', two Old English words which taken together respectively produce a name that means 'witch's valley'. It harks back to a time when witches, warlocks, ghouls, evil spirits and other similar superstitions were commonly believed and taken very seriously. Domesday recorded the place as Hetesope, listed in the Blackwell Hundred, held by King William in 1086 as it had been by King Edward until 1066.

Hemswell

Hemswell is a village and civil parish in the West Lindsey District of Lincolnshire. The name comes from a man called Hem or Helm, the settlement's probable founder, and the Old English suffix 'wella', indicating a spring, well or stream. Hence, the placename means 'Helm's spring (or well)'. In 1086, Domesday recorded it as Helmeswelle, in Aslacoe Hundred, held by Bishop Odo of Bayeux, having previously belonged to a Saxon called Alnoth. At the time of the survey, Losoard of Rolleston was leasing some of the estate lands.

Hibaldstow

The North Lincolnshire village of Hibaldstow derives its name from the Anglo-Saxon St Hygebald, (c 664–c.690), also known as Higbald, Hibald or Hygbald, who was buried there around 690 AD. The Old English affix 'stow' indicates a holy place, and there was a church in the township dedicated to him. Domesday records the place as Hiboldestou, Hiboldeston and Hiboldestone in 'the Land of the King' in the Manley Wapentake, listed with over two hundred acres of meadow and one hundred and twenty acres of scrubland. In 1086, Gamal had one and a half carucates, Brunier rented two bovates of land, ten bovates of the estate were rented to Rolf as well as, 'Gilbert, the abbot's man, [who] has two ploughs there'.

Hinckley

The Leicestershire township of Hinckley derives its placename from the Old English words Hynca or Hinc, a man's personal name, and 'leah', a woodland clearing. Hence, 'Hinc's clearing'. By the time of the Domesday survey it was recorded as 'Hinchelie ... in the land of Earl Aubrey in the Guthlaxton Wapentake'.

Holbeach/Holbeach St Marks/ Holbeach St Matthew

Holbeach derives its name from the Old English words 'hol' and 'baec' or 'bece'. Two explanations of their meaning have been offered: one has it that taken together the words translate as 'hollow [or concave] ridge'. Another varies somewhat in that the second element is suggested to be more properly read as 'bece', meaning 'stream' or 'beck', in which case this might translate as 'hollow [or deep] stream'. However, the original 'baec' element might better translate as rounded, raised or humped, which would support the first explanation. The township's entry in the *Domesday Book* has it as Holebech, in the Elloe Hundred, held by the Crowland Abbey of St Guthlac, who had also held it before the Norman Conquest of 1066. It was a very small vill at that time with just three villans and land for no more than one and a half plough teams.

Holbeach St Marks is a fenland village in the South Holland district, located about four miles north of Holbeach within Holbeach Marsh; its name comes from the church dedicated to St Mark, which was built in 1868–69. Similarly, the village of Holbeach St Matthew, which lies six miles north-east of Holbeach proper, derives its placename from the chapel of ease dedicated to St Matthew in the same year.

Hockerton

In Old English the word 'hocer' referred to a hump, or a hump-back, (typically a rounded hillock), and 'tun' signified a farmstead. Hence, 'farmstead on a rounded [or hump-backed] hill', which describes the hill on which the present-day village is located. Domesday recorded the village as Hocretone, in the Lythe Hundred of Nottinghamshire, part-held in 1086 by the Archbishopric of York, who had held it since before the Norman Conquest of 1066. Other parts were held by Walter d'Ainscourt and Roger de Bully. At the time of King Edward the manor and its estate had been held by the Canons of Southwell Abbey, as well as Saxons called Thori, the son of Roald, Thorkil of Hickling and Wulfsi.

Hucknall

Known as Hucknall Torkard until 1916, this Nottinghamshire township probably derives its name from a man called Hucca, with the Old English suffix 'halh', which translates as 'a corner or nook of land'. Hence, 'A nook of land belonging to Hucca'. It was recorded in the *Domesday Book* as Hochenale and Hukenhall, part held by William Peverel and part by Ralph de Burun (sometimes Byron).

Ible

This Derbyshire village name is derived from a man called Ibba, who may have been its founder or an early chieftain. Added to this is the Old English affix 'hol', meaning 'hollow' (as in a shallow valley or ravine). Hence, the placename means 'hollow of a man called Ibba'. In 1086 the place was recorded as Ibeholon, a very small manor supporting about three households and listed in the Hamston Hundred. The estate amounted to seven ploughlands, had thirty acres of meadow and woodland measuring four by two leagues. It was held by King William, having belonged to King Edward before the Conquest of 1066.

Ilkeston

The *Domesday Book* records the South Derbyshire township of Ilkeston as Tilchestune, in the land of Gilbert de Ghent, who in turn leased it to Malgar, of which, along with West Hallam and Stanton-by-Dale, Ulf Fenman (or Fenisc) leased six carucates and six bovates of land. By the time of the survey it was already known as Elkesdone, or Elchestane, derived from the personal name of a man called Ealac or Elka and the Saxon suffix 'dun', signifying a hill. Hence, the name can be taken to mean 'Ealac's hill'.

Immingham

The Lincolnshire town of Immingham derives its placename from a man by the name of Imma, plus the Old English suffixes 'inga', meaning 'people, tribe or family', and 'ham', a homestead or settlement. Hence, 'the settlement of the people of Imma'. By 1086, the place had been recorded as Imungeham, 'in the land of William de Percy' and that Alwine leased a small portion of it.

Ingoldmells
This small coastal village near Skegness in Lincolnshire has Scandinavian origins in that it comes from the personal name of a Dane called Ingolfr (or Ingjaldr), possibly its founder, and the affix 'meir', indicating a sand bar or sandbank. The placename may therefore be taken to mean 'Ingolfr's sandbank(s)'. The Great Survey named the place In Guldelsmere, in the Candleshoe Hundred of Lindsey South Riding.

Kesteven
This Lincolnshire village name means 'meeting place in a wood'. It is derived from the Celtic word 'ced' or Brythonic Welsh word 'coed', both of which mean 'wood', as well as the Old Scandinavian word 'stefna', which signified a meeting place or an important place of council, administration or assembly. The hotchpotch of different ethnic elements suggests it was a common assembly place in both Danish and Anglo-Saxon cultures. Before the Conquest, in about 1000 the place was listed as Ceostefne in the Pipe Rolls of Lincolnshire, and by the time of Domesday it had become Chetsteven. It was recorded as Ketstevene by 1194.

Kettering
In the tenth century, Kettering in Northamptonshire was known as Cytringan; shortly after the Conquest, it was being recorded as Cateringe. The name is based around a man's personal name, probably Cytra (or Ketter), with the addition of the Old English 'inga', meaning 'the people, followers, kinsfolk or family'. Hence, '[settlement of] the people or followers of Cytra'.

Kibworth Beauchamp
The first word of this Leicestershire village placename comes from Old English, where Cybba was a man who probably founded the original settlement or was perhaps its chieftain or leader, and 'worth', the old word for an enclosure or a paddock. Hence, 'Cybba's enclosure'. By the end of the twelfth or beginning of the thirteenth centuries, the de Beauchamp family had taken possession of the manor and in 1315 the village was named as Kybeworth Beauchamp, their family name having been appended to the place, thereby distinguishing it from the nearby village of Kibworth Harcourt, held by the de Harewecurt family. The survey of 1086 had recorded it simply as Chiburde, in the Gartree Hundred, held at that time by Robert the Bursar.

Kimcote
Kimcote gets its name from a man called Cynemund, who either built or possessed a cottage, (or in Anglo-Saxon English, a 'cot'), sometime in its dim and distant past. The earliest written record of this Leicestershire village was when it appeared in the Domesday survey as Chenemundescote, listed in the Guthlaxton Hundred, in land belonging to the Bishop of St Mary in Lincoln (now Lincoln Cathedral). Before the Conquest, Godric the Sheriff had been Lord of the Manor.

Kinder
The Derbyshire place called Kinder is best known for the high hill that bears its name, Kinder Scout. The name is old Celtic in origin and is thought to mean '[place with] wide views', a description which eminently describes its location. The later 'Scout' affix comes from the Old Scandinavian word 'skuti', meaning 'projecting cliff'. The entry in Domesday

records the name a Chendre in the Blackwell Hundred, held by King William in 1086, having belonged to a group of Saxons before the Conquest, including Aelmer, Brun, Godric, Leofing, Leofnoth, Ligulf and Swein. In 1275, the name was recorded as Kender and it acquired its present name, Kinder Scout, in 1767.

Knaith

This small Lincolnshire hamlet bases it name on two Anglo-Saxon words: 'cneo', meaning 'knee' or 'bend', and 'hyth', a river landing place or jetty. Hence, 'landing place on a [river] bend'. The river in question was the River Trent. Domesday listed the hamlet as Cheneide, a very small estate supporting three free men and their families in the Well Hundred, belonging at that time to the Bishop of Lincoln.

Kneeton

A rare village placename in Nottinghamshire, named after Cengifu, one of the few females so honoured. Little is known of her, other than she may have been the founder or leader of the 'tun', a settlement or farmstead which bore her personal name and that she may have built a church on her estate. Kneeton means 'farmstead [or settlement] of a woman called Cengifu'. Domesday recorded the village as Cheniuetone, in the Bingham Wapentake, part-held by King William, Roger de Bully and Count Alan of Brittany at that time. It had belonged to three Saxon men called Alwin, Wulfric and Alsi before the Conquest.

Langar

The Nottinghamshire village of Langar gets its name from two Anglo-Saxon words, 'lang' and 'gara', which taken together mean 'long point of land'. The place was recorded as Langare in 1086, a vary large estate in the Bingham Hundred which supported forty-nine households, which was held jointly by William Peverel and Walter d'Ainscourt. Before 1066 it had belonged to a man known as Hemming of Branston. Its value to the lord of the manor in 1086 was ten pounds.

Legborne

Legborne (sometimes spelt Legbourne) in Lincolnshire gets its name from two Saxon words: 'laec', meaning 'bog' or 'swamp', and 'burna', a stream or brook. Hence, '[place by a] swampy stream'. Domesday recorded the village as Lecheburne, and listed it in the Calcewath Hundred of the Lindsey South Riding, shared by Roger de Poitou and Earl Hugh of Chester. Before the Norman Conquest it had belonged to a man called Ambi and to Earl Harold. Altogether. the combined assets of the estate amounted to sixty acres of meadow and more than two hundred acres of woodland, in total valued at just one pound.

Leicester

The Romans knew Leicester as Ligera Caestre, the place where they set up a fortress some time after 43 AD. Their name came from the Latin 'Ligore', referring to 'people who lived by the River Legro' (now the River Soar), and 'caester' or 'castra', meaning 'camp' or 'Roman town'. Hence possibly, 'the Roman camp of the dwellers by the River Legro'. For most of the eighth and ninth centuries, Leicester fell under Danelaw, and it was not until 918 that it was reclaimed as Saxon territory by Lady Aethelflaed of Mercia, the daughter of King Alfred, as recorded in the *Anglo-Saxon Chronicles*: 'She (Aethelflaed) took the burh of Leicester under her rule, peacefully, early in the year, and the greatest part of the [Danish] force that belonged to it became subject to her'. In 1086, Domesday recorded the settlement as Ledecestre, and listed it in land of the Bishop of Lincoln, who held ten carucates at that time. The account reported that '...the king has in Ledecestre thirty-nine houses'. The estate included five ploughlands in demesne, twelve borders with four ploughs, three villans and a priest. There were twenty acres of meadow, two churches, and seven burgesses paying thirty-two pence a year in tax.

Leire
This Leicestershire village takes its placename from the River Leire on which it stands. The river name dates from before the very earliest of times and its meaning is lost to us, but it may be of the same or similar origin as that of Leicester, meaning 'Roman fort of the River Leire' (or the River Legro as they knew it), and also gave the county its name. Domesday recorded the village as Legre, in the Guthlaxton Hundred, part held in 1086 by the Bishop of Lincoln, Robert the Bursar and Robert de Bucy.

Leverton
This Lincolnshire settlement originated in Anglo-Saxon times when its placename meant 'farmstead where rushes grow'. The name comes from two Old English words, 'laefer', meaning 'rushes' (as in bullrushes), and 'tun', which could signify either a village or a farmstead, at a time when both were virtually indistinguishable. In 1086, the village was listed as Leuretune, in the Wolmersty Hundred, held by Count Alan of Brittany, having previously been a possession of the Saxon Earl Ralph (known as 'the Constable').

Lincoln
The Romans arrived in Lincolnshire in 48 AD and immediately set about building a fort which they called Lindum Colonia, later shortened to Lindum. The name is thought to be derived from the Old Celtic word 'lindon', meaning 'pool', and the Latin 'colonia', referring to a Roman garrison or colony. Hence, 'Roman colony by the pool'. The pool referred to is thought to be Brayford Pool in the River Witham, where the Normans later built the cathedral and castle.

Long Duckmanton
This Derbyshire village has nothing whatever to do with ducks or waterfowl, but took its name from a man called Ducemann, who may have established the original settlement. The Old English affix 'tun', implied a farmstead or a village, so the placename may be taken to mean 'farmstead or village belonging to Ducemann'. Originally there were two adjacent villages, of which one, the longest of the two, took the name Long Duckmanton. In more recent times both villages have been reunited as Long Duckmanton. Domesday recorded the place as Dochemanestun, in the sokeland of land belonging to Ralph FitzHubert, where '... Leofnoth had four carucates of land and two bovates to the geld'. It also recorded eighteen rent-paying tenants who between them had five ploughs.

Long Whatton
Whatton, as this Leicestershire village was originally known, comes from Old English, where two words, 'hwaete' and 'tun' combine to produce 'farmstead where wheat is grown'. The place was recorded in 1190 simply as Watton, and as it grew (presumably longer), the 'Long' word was attached some time in the fourteenth century.

Loughborough
Loughborough, in the County of Leicestershire, began life as a small Saxon settlement, and derived its name from a man called Luhhede, who established a fortified settlement or stronghold (a 'burh') in the place. Hence the placename means 'Luhhede's stronghold'.

In the 1086 survey, it was recorded as Lucyeburne, in the Guthlaxon Wapentake, where eight carucates of land were held by Roger de Bully for Earl Hugh de Gouville, it having previously belonged to Earl Harold.

Louth
The *Domesday Book* refers to this place as Lude, named after the River Lud in the East Lindsay district of Lincolnshire, whose name itself comes from the Old Saxon word for 'loud' or 'noisy'. The earliest record of the placename occurs when in 793, Aethelhard, the Bishop of Winchester, was made Archbishop of Canterbury, having previously served as the Abbot of Louth.

Lyddington
Lyddington, on the north-west slopes of the Welland Valley in the County of Rutland, was known in 1086 as Lidentone, with two possible derivations. It may signify a farmstead or settlement that once belonged to the family of a man called Hlyda, from the Old English suffixes 'inga', meaning 'the people or family', and 'tun', a farmstead. Alternatively, it might derive from 'hlyding', meaning 'noisy stream' and 'tun'. Hence, 'farmstead by the noisy stream'.

Mablethorpe
Mablethorpe combines Old Scandinavian and Old Germanic elements in its placename. The first part is thought to be the name of a man called Malbert, possibly a German settler, and the Norse 'thorp', a word used to describe a remote or outlying farmstead, Hence, 'Malbert's remote farmstead'. The place has three entries in Domesday, as Malbertorp, Maltetorp and Maltorp, in the Calcewath Hundred of Lincolnshire, a very large estate of some thirty-nine households and twenty acres of meadow. The manor was held by Gilbert of Ghent, having belonged to Tonni of Lusby before the Conquest.

Maltby le Marsh
This Lincolnshire village exemplifies the way that the Danes and later the Normans influenced the development of Middle English. Initially, the place took its name after a Dane known as Malti, which combined with the Old Scandinavian word 'by', to produce a placename that means 'Malti's farm'. Additionally, the 'le Marsh'; element combines the French word 'le', meaning 'the', and the Old English word 'mersc', meaning 'marsh' or 'marshland' to create an entire placename that means 'Malti's farm [on] the marshland', which eminently describes its low-lying coastal location. Domesday recorded the place as Maltebi, in the Louthesk Hundred, held by Earl Hugh of Chester, it having been in the possession of the Saxon Earl Harold in 1066.

Mansfield
The *Domesday Book* records this place three times – as Mamesfeld, Mamesfelde and Mammesfed, and listed it in the Broxtowe Wapentake of Nottinghamshire, and meaning 'open fields by the River Maun'. The Maun river name is probably a corruption of the Celtic word 'mamm' signifying 'a breast-shaped hill'.

Marefield
Nothing to do with mares or horses, the 'mare' element of this Leicestershire hamlet's placename relates to the marten, a bird of the swift family. The 'field' element has also slightly different connotations to the word in modern English, as the Saxon word 'feld' or 'felda' meant 'open land', at a time when land enclosures were not common. Open land also referred to scrubland and sometimes to woodland that had been cleared to produce arable

fields. Hence, Marefield means 'open land where martens are seen'. Domesday recorded the place as Merdefelde, and listed it in the Gartree Hundred lands which were held as a personal possession of King William in 1086, as they had been by King Edward before the Conquest.

Matlock

Domesday records the Derbyshire township of Matlock as 'Meslach ... in the land of the king, in the Winksworth Wapentake, [where] King Edward had two carucates of land to the geld'. By 1196, it was written as Matlack, based on the Old English 'maethel', meaning assembly or speech, and 'ac', an oak tree. Another possible derivation of the placename is a corruption of the Saxon for 'moot oak'. Hence, meaning 'oak tree where meetings are held'.

Mavis Enderby

Originally known simply as Endrebi, and recorded as such in the 1086 survey, this Lincolnshire village has Scandinavian origins. It was named after a Dane called Eindrithi, who had a farmstead or settlement which he established here (in Old Norse, a 'by'). The 'Mavis' part of the placename is a corruption of the name of the Malebisse family, who held the manor in the thirteenth century. Their name distinguishes it from the nearby villages of Bag Enderby and Wood Enderby. By 1229, the placename had been recorded as Malebisse Enderby.

Medbourne

The Leicestershire village of Medbourne's placename means '[place by the] meadow stream'. It comes from the Old English words 'maed', which signified a meadow, and 'burna', a brook or stream. Domesday recorded the place as Medburne and Metorne, in the Framland Wapentake, belonging to the king, who held two carucates of land and six and a half acres of meadow. Robert de Tosny held a further four carucates within the manor.

Monyash

The name of Monyash in Derbyshire has a simple enough meaning. It comes from two Old English words: 'aesc', referring to the ash tree, and 'manig', meaning 'many'. Taken together these two elements mean '[place of] many ash trees'. Domesday recorded the place as Maneis in 1086 and located it in the Blackwell Hundred, held by the Crown as it had been before 1066.

Morcott

Morcott is a village in the County of Rutland whose placename means 'cottage on moorland', from the Old English words 'mor' and 'cot', meaning respectively 'moor' or 'marshland' and 'cottage'. In 1086 the Great Survey recorded the placename as Morcote, and listed in in the Witchley Hundred which at that time covered part of Rutland and Northamptonshire, and was held by King William, it having belonged to Queen Edith of Wessex, Edward the Confessor's widow, before the Conquest.

Moulton/Moulton Seas End

Moulton is a common placename, with seven others of that name known in England, including villages and townships in Cheshire, Suffolk, North Yorkshire, Norfolk and Northamptonshire. The placename derivation has two possibilities: the first element may come from the name of an early settler or its founder, a man called Mula, or perhaps come from the Old English word 'mul', which means 'mule'. The last element comes from 'tun', signifying a farmstead or village. Therefore the name might translate into modern English as either 'Mula's village [or farmstead]' or 'farmstead where mules are kept' – either is equally possible. The village of Moulton, in the South Holland District of Lincolnshire, was known as Multune by the time of the 1086 survey, and fell within the Elloe Hundred, held by Guy de Craon. It had previously belonged to the Saxon, Aethelstan, who was identified as 'the son of Godram'. At that time it was assessed at having land for fifteen ploughs and supported six villans. The Fenland Parish of Moulton Seas End is a civil parish which includes the village of Moulton, as well as the villages of Moulton Chapel and Moulton Eaugate. Until 1885, Moulton Seas End was simply known as Seasend or Seaend.

Nether Langwith

The word 'Nether' occurs frequently in English placenames, sometimes integrated as part of a longer placename (like Netherton, Netherhampton or Netherfield), and at others complete in its own right, as is the case with this Nottinghamshire village. It comes from the Middle English word 'nethere', meaning 'lower', 'further down' or 'under'. The second word of the name, Langwith, comes from the Old Scandinavian words 'langr', meaning 'long', and 'vath', a ford or shallow river crossing. Hence, the placename means 'lower [place by a] long ford'. The village location is in fact 'lower' down the River Poulter than the nearby village of Upper Langwith. In the late-twelfth century, before the two villages separated, the place was simply known as Langath, and by the mid-thirteenth it had become Netherlangwat.

Normanby

There are more than a dozen places in England with a 'Norman' element to their placename, predominantly in Yorkshire, Lincolnshire and Nottinghamshire. This particular Lincolnshire placename is a combination of Old English and Norse elements. 'Northman' was the Saxon's word for Norwegian Vikings, and 'by' was the Scandinavian word for a farmstead. Hence, the placename interprets as 'farmstead of the Northmen', reflecting the influx of Scandinavian settlers in eastern England the eighth and ninth centuries. Domesday listed the place as Normanebi, in the Manley Hundred of Lincolnshire's West Riding, part in 'The Land of Drogo de la Beuvrière', and part held as sokeland by Guy de Craon.

Northampton

In 914, the township of Northampton was recorded as Ham tune, which translates as 'home farmstead', but shortly after the Norman Conquest the prefix 'North' was added to distinguish it from other places like Southampton. Domesday names it Northantone. The account continues, 'In the time of King Edward there were in Northantone, in the king's demesne, sixty burgesses, having as many dwellings. Of these, fourteen are now waste, forty-seven are left.'

North Hykeham/South Hykeham

The 'Hyke' element of this placename has two possible Old English derivations: one has it as 'hice', related to a small bird, and the second that it represents 'Hica', a man's personal name. The last element, 'ham' means 'homestead' or 'dwelling'. So the placename might mean either 'homestead of a man called Hica', or 'dwelling where small birds are found' – either is possible. The names of both North and South Hykeham appeared in Domesday as one village, described as Hicham, one of two manors in the Hundred of Graffoe of Lincolnshire within the Parish of Kestevan, held in 1086 by Kolgrim of Grantham with Count Alan of Brittany as its tenant-in-chief. Before the Norman Conquest it had belonged to Siward, a Saxon. The second part of the manor, South Hykeham, was held by Baldwin of Flanders, having belonged to Aelric, son of Mergeat in 1066.

North Kyme/South Kyme

Kyme comes directly from the Old English 'cymbe' or 'cimbe', meaning '[place at the] hollow, or at the edge'. The meaning of the North and South elements are fairly self-evident, but describe their locations at either end of a shallow depression in the local topography. The place was recorded as Chime in 1086, the northern part of the estate in the Langoe Hundred of Lincolnshire, held by Kilsveinn of Lincoln as Lord of the Manor, it having belonged to Auti in 1066. The southern part of the estate was listed in the Aswardhurn Hundred, held by Gilbert of Ghent from Egbert, who was Lord of the Manor. Before 1066, this had been in the possession of Tonni of Lusby.

North/South Scarle

This village, in the North Kesteven district of Lincolnshire, has a rather unfortunate origin, coming as it does from the Old English word 'scearn', meaning 'muck' or 'dung', and 'leah' a woodland glade or clearing. The name translates into modern English as 'northern [place at, or by a] dirty clearing', though the exact significance of the reference is obscure. The 'north' element of the placename distinguishes it from South Scarle a few miles further south. Domesday listed the place as Scornelei in 1086.

Ockbrook

At some time in its Anglo-Saxon past, there was a settlement beside a brook (a 'broc'), that was probably founded by a man called Occa, and this Derbyshire village placename reflects this history – 'Occa's brook'. The stream in question exists today and is still called Ock Brook. In 1086 the village was listed as Ochebroc, in the Morleystone Hundred, held at that time by Geoffrey Alselin, it having belonged before 1066 to Toki, son of Auti.

Peatling Magna

This Leicestershire village was simply known as Petlinge at the time of Domesday, a name derived from a man called Peotla and his associates or family (or 'ingas' in Old English). The placename means '[settlement or village of] Peotla's people'. The Latin word 'magna' was attached sometime later to distinguish it from Peatling Parva, (meaning 'Little Peatling'), a few miles to the south.

Pickwell

Pickwell acquired its placename back in Saxon times, when the word 'pic' meant 'point' or 'pike' and indicated a pointed hill (as in the Cumbrian mountain called Scafell Pike). The Old English word 'wella' indicated a stream, well or fountain. Therefore, the placename translates as '[place at or near a] pointed hill with a stream'. It was recorded in 1086 as Pichewelle, a very large manor in the Gartree Hundred of Leicestershire, held by Geoffrey de la Guerche, having belonged to Ordmer before the Norman Conquest.

Pinchbeck

The derivation of the Pinchbeck placename is ambiguous. Its first element could come from the Old English words 'pinc', meaning 'minnow', or perhaps 'pinca', the Saxon word for a finch. The second element is equally contentious. Is it 'baec', a ridge or ledge, or the Old Scandinavian word 'bekkr', a stream or brook? The possibilities are numerous: 'stream where minnows are found', 'stream where finches are found', 'ridge where finches are found' – difficult to say. The Lincolnshire village of Pincebec, near the River Glen, was entered twice in the Domesday Book as the very large village in the Hundred of Elloe, with one part in the Holbeach Manor estate held by Guy de Craon, having belonged to a Saxon called Aethelstan before the Conquest. The second entry is recorded in the Manor of Spalding, whose lord was Ivo Tallboys (sometimes de Taillbois) in 1086, it having previously been in the possession of Earl Algar.

Plungar
This Leicestershire placename means 'enclosure where plum trees grow' or 'triangular plot of land where plum trees grow'. It derives from 'plume', an Old English word for a plum, and 'gara' (or the Old Scandinavian 'garthr'), indicating a triangular plot of land. The name was first recorded in something like its present form as Plumgard, some time around 1125.

Quarndon
Quarndon gets its name from the Old English word 'cweorn', which meant 'millstone' and the affix 'dun', indicating a hill. The placename may therefore be taken to mean '[place on a] hill where millstones are quarried'. Typical of slipshod Saxon to Norman translations, the Domesday commissioners misspelt the placename as Cornum, and located it in the Litchurch Hundred of Derbyshire, which was held at that time by the Crown. By the end of the twelfth century, the name had been written as Querendon.

Ratcliffe on the Wreake
Ratcliffe is a fairly common English placename and translates directly from the Old English 'read' and 'clif' as '[place by or on the] red cliff (or bank)'. This Leicestershire township was recorded as Radeclive in 1086, in the Goscote Wapentake, land belonging to Robert de Bucy, where 'the wife of Robert Burdet... holds two carucates of land'. The manor supported three villans and two bordars who had one plough. There were twelve acres of meadow and a mill which rendered three shillings. The Wreake element of the placename is the river on which the estate stands. The River Wreake was given its name by Danish settlers when the area was part of Danelaw, and comes from the Old Scandinavian word meaning 'winding one', in reference, no doubt, to its meandering course.

Rempstone
A Nottinghamshire village named after a man called Hrempi, and the farmstead, or 'tun' he established there sometime in the eighth or ninth centuries. The Great Survey of 1086 recorded the placename as Rampestune and Repestone, in the Broxtowe Hundred, held by William Peverel.

Retford
The Domesday survey recorded Retford, one of the oldest boroughs in England, as Redforde in 1086 (simply meaning 'red ford'), in the sokeland of Bassetlaw Wapentake, belonging to the Norman Baron, Roger de Bully. It lists '...in Redforde are one and a half bovates of land to the geld. There is land for four oxen. The soke belongs to [a man called] Clumber. It is waste.' It has little more to add, other than there being one mill belonging to the Archbishop of York. The placename probably originates in the ancient ford across the River Idle which runs through a red clay bed that, disturbed by frequent crossing, made its waters run red.

Ripley
The township of Ripley in the Amber Valley Borough of Derbyshire was first recorded in 1086 as Ripelei, from the Old English 'ripel', meaning a narrow strip, and 'leah', a woodland clearing. Hence, a 'narrow strip of woodland clearing'. Domesday lists it as a sokeland in the land of Ralph FitzHubert, where Pentrich Leofnof (or Levenot) had two carucates of land for rent.

Rushden
From Saxon times, the area including the Northamptonshire township of Rushden, together with Higham Ferrers, Irchester, Raunds and Wollaston, was known as the Higham Hundred.

The placename comes from Old English 'ryscen', meaning rushes or bullrushes, and 'denu', a valley or dale, and together simply mean 'valley where rushes grow'.

Rutland

The small County of Rutland derived its name from a man called Rota, whose tract of land it once would have been. It was a small estate, and still remains Britain's smallest county, having been abolished and combined as a district in Lincolnshire following boundary changes in 1974, before it was re-established as a unitary authority in its own right in 1974 following innumerable public protests and requests for its reinstatement.

Saxilby

There is a view that the Saxilby placename may have come directly from the Old Scandinavian name meaning 'Saxulf's homestead'. Alternatively, it has been suggested it might translate more obscurely as 'the farmstead amidst the river mooring'. Until the nineteenth century, it was commonly known as Saxelby. In 1086, it was recorded 'Ad Saxebi in Lincolescira', granted to Bishop Odo of Bayeux, one of the seventy-six estates he held in Lincolnshire.

Scampton

This is another example of the influence of the Danes on emerging English culture. Scampton's placename probably comes from a Danish settler by the name of Skammr or Skammi (which translates as 'short'), probably its founder, whose 'tun', or farm it was. The village name could also be interpreted as 'short farmstead'. It demonstrates how the integration of Scandinavian and Anglo-Saxon played out in Danelaw, where Norse and Saxon English were often synthesised into what we recognise as modern placenames. Domesday lists the place as Scantone, in the Lawress Hundred of Lincolnshire. It was a large manor for its time with thirty-five households living on its estates, including sixteen villans, six smallholders and a priest. In 1086 it was owned by Gilbert of Ghent, and in 1066 it had belonged to Ulf Fenman.

Scrivelsby

The Manor of Scrivelsby in the Lindsey district of Lincolnshire was known in 1086 as Scrivelesbi and Scriwelesbi, in the 'Land of the King' in Aswardhurn Wapentake. It was assessed as three carucates and seven bovates of land and continued '...there are twenty sokemen, and twelve bordars have six ploughs, and two hundred and forty acres of meadow, and six acres of scrubland'. Much of the manorial estate came into the possession of Robert Despenser and was deemed a manor of 'Grand Sergeantry', whereby the holder performed the hereditary function of King's Champion in lieu of payment. The exact origin of the placename is somewhat obscure, but it may be related to the word 'scrivel', which is itself related to writing, or 'scrivening' (a 'scrivener' was a medieval scribe – a writer or calligrapher, at a time when most people, no matter how noble, could not write). The Scandinavian affix 'by' meant 'settlement' or 'farmstead'. Somewhat speculatively, therefore, the placename might mean 'settlement of the scriveners'.

Scunthorpe

The North Lincolnshire town of Scunthorpe derives its name from the Old Scandinavian, man's name Skuma, and 'thorp', signifying a remote or outlying farmstead or homestead. Hence, 'outlying farmstead of a man called Skuma'. In 1086, it was recorded as 'Escumetorp, in the land of the king', held by Earl Edwin in the Manor of Kirton in Lindsey. The account continues, that 'in Escumetorp [there are] twenty sokemen with two ploughs and three oxen, and eighty acres of meadow'.

Sempringham/Sempringham Fen
This is a small hamlet in the South Kesteven district of Lincolnshire which has been recorded under several placename variants, including Sempingham, Sepingeham, Spingeham and Sepingeham, as well as in its present-day form of Sempringham. The name is based on three separate Old English elements: 'Sempa', the personal name of the man who may have founded the original settlement in the ninth century, 'inga', which means 'the people or followers', and 'ham', signifying a dwelling of homestead. Hence, 'homestead of the people of Sempa'. In 1086, the place was recorded as Sepingeham and Spingeham, in the Aveland Hundred, in 'The Land of Robert de Tosney', amounting to ten acres of meadow and twelve acres of scrubland. The account continues that before the Conquest, '...in Spingeham, Morcar had four carucates of land and two bovates to the geld'. The manor was transferred to Jocelyn, son of Lambert in 1086; its tenant-in-chief as Gunfrid of Choques, and the estate was valued at forty shillings. Before 1066, the estate had been in the possession of Arnbiorn of Avethorpe. Sempringham was the home of Gilbert of Sempringham, the founder of the Gilbertines monastic order in 1131, and the son of the lord of the manor.

Shawell
Located on the boundary with Warwickshire, the Leicestershire village of Shawell's placename reflects the local topography, as the Old English word 'sceath', which made up the first part of the name, meant 'boundary'. Further, the second element, 'wella', signified a spring, a well or a fountain, producing a placename that means '[place by the] boundary spring'. Domesday recorded the original manor as Sawelle, a very large estate in the Guthlaxton Hundred, supporting forty households (including six slaves), and held at that time by the Count of Meulan, it having belonged to Saxi of Aylestone before the Conquest.

Shireoaks
The Old English word for a shire or county was 'scir', and 'ac' signified an oak tree or trees. As this Nottinghamshire village lies close to the border with Yorkshire, the placename may be interpreted to mean '[place by] oak trees on the county [or shire] boundary'. Its name was recorded in the twelfth century as Shirakes.

Shottle
The placename of this Derbyshire hamlet comes from the Anglo-Saxon words 'sceot', meaning 'steep slope', and 'hyll', a hill. Hence, 'hill with steep slopes'. Not untypically, the Domesday commissioners misspelt the placename as Sothelle, and listed it as a very small estate supporting three households in the Hamston Hundred, held in 1086 by Henry de Ferrers, having belonged to a Saxon man called Gamal during the time of King Edward.

Skegness
The seaside town of Skegness, in the East Lindsey District of Lincolnshire, probably began life as a Danish settlement. The placename derives from a Viking called Skeggi, meaning 'bearded one', from the Old Norse 'skegg', a beard, and 'ness', meaning a promontory or headland. Hence the placename may be taken to mean 'headland belonging to a man called Skeggi', or possibly, 'a beard-shaped promontory'. The place was in the ancient Candleshoe Wapentake of Lincolnshire but received no mention in the Great Survey of 1086.

Skirbeck
Skirbeck near Boston in Lincolnshire has clear Scandinavian overtones. The Old Norse word 'skirn' or Old English 'scir' means 'bright' or 'clear', and 'bekkr' is an old word

for a stream or brook, as in the word 'beck' which is still in widespread common usage in Cumbria. Hence, '[place by the] bright [or clear] stream'. Domesday recorded it as the very large Manor of Scirebec in 1086, and listed it in the Wolmersty Hundred, joint-held by Eudo, son of Spirewic, and Count Alan of Brittany.

Sleaford
This Lincolnshire township was known as early as 852 as Sliowaforda. The name comes from the Old English name for the River Slea, on which it stands, and its shallow river crossing – the ford. The original settlement belonged to the Celtic Coritanni tribe and became an important Roman settlement in the first century. It was at this place that they established the ford from which the town acquired its name; 'the ford over the River Slea'.

Spalding
One of the earliest written records of Spalding in Lincolnshire was a charter issued to the monks of Crowland Abbey by Aethelbald, who was King of Mercia from 716 until his death in 757. At that time, the township was referred to as Spaldelying. In 1086, the place was known as Spallinge and one view is that it may have derived its placename from the Old English word 'spald', meaning ditch or trench, and 'inga' or 'ingas', meaning the 'people, family or tribe'. Hence, 'people or tribes who live in [or beside] a ditch'. Such a ditch could have been created as a defensive feature of the settlement. Another view cites the Latin word 'spald', meaning shoulder, and the Celtic word 'yng', indicating marshland, bog or fen; therefore, this version might mean 'the people who live at the shoulder of marshland'. Yet a third and possibly better explanation is that it was named after the Spaldingas, an Anglian tribe who settled in the area in the sixth century.

Spondon
Spondon is a district of Derby whose placename means '[place by the] hill where woodchips are obtained'. The name comes from two Old English words, 'spon', meaning 'woodchip', and 'dun', a hill. Domesday recorded the place as Spondune, and listed it within the Morleystone Hundred, held in 1086 by Henry de Ferrers, it having belonged to Stori of Spondon before the Norman Conquest.

Staveley
This Derbyshire township, located on the River Rother, derives its name from the Old English words 'staf' and 'leah', respectively meaning 'stave' and 'woodland clearing'. Hence, the placename may be taken to mean 'woodland clearing where staves are found [or gathered]'. There are other towns of this name in Cumbria and North Yorkshire.

Stickney
This Lincolnshire village's placename means '[place on a] stick-like island'. It is derived from the Old English elements 'sticol' and 'eg'. The name comes about in view of the village location on a narrow sliver of land on an elongated island which falls between two streams.

Domesday records Stichenai in the Bolingbroke Hundred, whose Lord in 1086 was Ivo de Tailbois (sometimes 'Tallboys); before the Conquest it had belonged to Stori of Bolingbroke, and housed five villagers and thirty-three free men.

Stoke Bruerne
This Northamptonshire township was recorded in the *Domesday Book* as Stoche and Stoches, '...in the Land of Swein in Cleyley Hundred', where Swein held four hides of land sufficient for ten ploughs, from the king, an estate valued at three pounds in 1086. Stoke is a very common placename with several dozen places in England, including Stoke-by-

Nayland in Suffolk, Stoke Ferry in Norfolk and Stoke Giffard in Gloucestershire, among many others.

Stoke is derived from the Old English word 'stocc', meaning an outlying or remote farmstead. The second placename element, Bruerne, comes from the Briwere family (sometimes Briwerre), who took possession of the manor in 1254 and attached their family name to the place.

Stonton Wyville
This village in Leicestershire was originally known as Stantone, a name taken from the Old English words 'stan', a stone, and 'tun', which signified a farmstead or a village. Hence, 'farmstead on stony ground'. Then, some time in the thirteenth century the manorial estate came into the ownership of the de Wivill family, who attached their family name to the place and in 1265 it was recorded as Staunton Wyville. The Domesday entry had earlier listed Stantone in the Gartree Hundred, held at that time by Countess Judith of Lens, the niece of King William, it having belonged to Osbern de Brouay before the Norman Conquest.

Sutton-in-Ashfield
The name of this Nottinghamshire market township is derived from the Anglo-Saxon words 'suth' and 'tun', with the addition of the 'Ashfield' element signifying a 'southern enclosure where ash trees grow'. These large swathes of ash trees once formed part of Sherwood Forest. Sutton is a very common placename in England with other examples at Sutton Bonnington, Sutton Colefield and Sutton Bridge. At the time of the Domesday survey, it was simply known as 'Sutone, in the Soke of Mansfield in Broxtow Wapentake', and along with the neighbouring village of Skegby, was part of the king's manor of Mansfield.

Swadlincote
Swadlincote's entry in the *Domesday Book* records it as Sivaringescotes, a small manor in the Parish of Church Gresley, belonging to Nigel de Stafford, where Godric rented one carucate of his land. This Derbyshire placename is thought to derive from a man called Svartlingr (or Swartling), probably a Dane, who lived in a cottage there. Hence, 'Svartlingr's cottage'.

Tetford
This Lincolnshire placename derives from two Old English words, 'theod', referring to the people or the public, and 'ford', a shallow river crossing. Hence, the name may be taken to mean 'people's (or public) ford'.

Threekingham
It is thought that the name of Threekingham may have come from Tricingas, an ancient tribal name, though its precise connection has been lost in the mists of antiquity. The final element of the placename, 'ham', signified a homestead or settlement; hence, the complete placename may be taken to mean 'homestead [or settlement] of the Tricingas'. In 1086, the place was recorded as Trichingeham and listed as a very large estate supporting around fifty households in the Aveland Hundred of Lincolnshire. It merited no fewer than eight separate entries in Domesday, when it was part-held by Guy de Craon, the Abbey of St Benedict in Ramsey, the Bishopric of Durham, Gilbert of Ghent, Kolsveinn of Lincoln, Odo the Bowman and a man called Wulfgeat. By the late nineteenth century the placename had emerged as Threckingham.

Tonge
This small Leicestershire hamlet derives its placename from the Old Scandinavian word 'tunga', which translates directly into English as 'tongue'. It refers to a tongue or spur of land,

and evidently describes its location within the local topography. The *Domesday Book* lists the place as Tunge, in the Goscote Hundred, held by Henry de Ferrers in 1086, as it had been at the time of King Edward. The account records: 'Henry holds Tunge with all its appendages. There are twenty-one and a half carucates of land... six acres of meadow [and] woodland one league long and half a league broad. It was worth five shillings (in 1066); now ten pounds'.

Towcester
At that time, the township was known as Tofecaester, from the River Tove ('tove' is an Old English word meaning 'slow'), and 'caester', signifying a Roman fort. Hence 'Roman fort on the River Tove'. By 1086, it was recorded as Tovecestre, in the Witchley Wapentake of Northamptonshire, held at that time by King William.

Wainfleet
The Lincolnshire township of Wainfleet was recorded in 1086 as Wenflet, based on two Old English words, 'waegn', meaning 'wagon' or 'wain', and 'fleot', which represented a stream or a creek. Hence the original placename simply meant 'wagon stream'. The stream in question is the River Steeping and the placename may have referred to an ancient shallow ford where wagons may have crossed. Later, the name became Wainfleet All Saints, to distinguish it from the nearby village of Wainfleet St Mary. By the end of the thirteenth century the place had been recorded by its Latin name, as Weynflet Omnium Sanctorum.

Wellingborough
The Northamptonshire township of Wellingborough has been known since the sixth century, when the Anglo-Saxons called it Wendeling burh. It was named after a man called Waendel, with the suffix 'inga', meaning 'the people, family or tribe', and 'burh', a stronghold or fortified dwelling. Hence 'the stronghold of Waendel's people'. Domesday called it Wendleburie, part in Hamfordshoe Hundred, in the Bishop of Coutance's lands held by Crowland Monastery, as they had done since the time of Edward the Confessor.

Wigston
Also known as Wigston Magna, to distinguish it from Wigston Parva, this Leicestershire township derives its name from the Old Scandinavian personal name of a man called Wicing (or Wigca), with the Old English affix 'tun', signifying 'a farmstead belonging to Wicing'. The 'magna' element is Latin for 'great' or 'greater', and 'parva' means 'little'. Domesday records Wigston Magna as Wichingestone in Guthlaxton Wapentake, held by Hugh de Grandmesnil for the king. It had belonged to Earl Ralph before the Conquest. Wigston Parva was listed as Wicestan, in the 'almsland of the king', held for him by Aelfric the Priest. In this form, its name has a completely different derivation: Wicga and 'stan', a stone. Hence, 'stone of a man called Wicing or Wicga'. In the Middle Ages, Wigston was known as Wigston Two Spires (or Two Steeples), on account of its two medieval churches of St Wistan's and All Saints. Wigstan was a Mercian prince who was murdered and became a martyr, before becoming canonised as a saint.

Worksop
Worksop is located on the River Ryton, at the edge of Sherwood Forest, in the Bassetlaw district of Nottinghamshire. The name may come from two Saxon words, Weorc, a man's name, and 'hop'. Hence the placename may be translated with as 'Weorc's valley or enclosed field'; or else the Old English first element may be 'weork', meaning a workshop, or work's building, in which case it might mean 'workshop in a valley'. In the 1086 survey, it was recorded as 'Werchesope ...where Elsi, son of Caschin, has three carucates of taxable land'.

Wragby

Wragby betrays its Scandinavian heritage in the two Old Norse elements of its placename: 'Wraggi', the personal name of its probable Danish founder or early settler, and 'by', which refers to a farmstead or village. The placename may therefore translate as 'Wraggi's farm [or village]'. This Lincolnshire settlement was recorded in the Domesday survey in the Wraggoe Hundred of Lincolnshire, held by Waldin the Artificer ('skilled craftsman') in 1086, having previously belonged to Guthfrithr, a Saxon, in 1066.

Wrangle

A Lincolnshire village whose name has a similar meaning in both Old English and Old Scandinavian, as 'wrengel' and 'vrengill' respectively; both mean a 'crooked stream' or a 'crooked place'. The Great Survey lists the place as Werangle and Weranghe, in the Wolersty Wapentake, held by Guy de Craon in 1086, having belonged to Aethelstan, son of Godram, who had 'two carucates of land to the geld', before the 1066 Conquest. It records that '...in Weranghe [is] sokeland of Drayton. Ten carucates of land to the geld. [There is] land for five ploughs [and] seven sokemen have one plough there'.

Part Nine

East Anglia

Cambridgeshire, Essex, Norfolk, and Suffolk

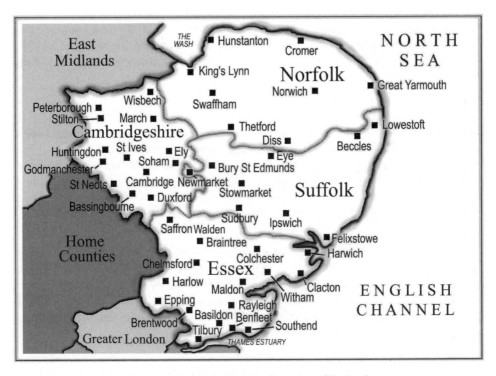

A map depicting the East Anglia region of England.

Acle

Acle is a village in Norfolk whose name derives from two Old English words, 'ac', meaning 'oak tree' and 'leah', a woodland glade or clearing. The placename therefore means either something like '[place near the] oak tree in a woodland clearing', or possibly '[place in the] oak wood'. The Great Survey recorded the place in the Walsham Hundred lands of the king, and that... 'Acle was held by Earl R[alph] the elder [as] five carucates of land at the time of King Edward'. A detailed account of its resources was entered for taxation purposes; these included woodland pannage for four hundred pigs, a mill, three horses, two head of cattle, one hundred and twenty sheep and eleven hives of bees.

Alby

Sometimes called Alby Hill, this Norfolk village has all the hallmarks of an early Danish settlement. It had probably been founded by a man called Ali, followed by the Old

Scandinavian affix 'by', which signified a farmstead or a village (at a time when both were virtually interchangeable). This produces a placename that simply means 'Ali's village or farmstead'. In 1086 the place was recorded as Alebei, and listed within the South Erpingham Hundred, held at that time by Roger Bigod (sometimes 'Bigot') it having been shared by several Saxons before the Norman Conquest, including Asford, Godwin of Scottow, Toki of Winterton, Withri of Hanworth and Wulfstan.

Aldeburgh

The Suffolk township of Aldeburgh derives its placename from the Old English words 'ald' or 'eald', meaning old or disused, and 'burh', meaning fortification or stronghold. Hence the placename might translate as 'old or disused fort or stronghold'. In 1086, the *Domesday Book* recorded the place as Aldeburc and that before the Conquest 'In Aldeburc, Wulfric, a sokeman of Eadric [of Laxfield], held... eighty acres as a manor [at the time of King Edward]'.

Anmer

The placename of this village in Norfolk means '[place by the] duck pond (or pool)'. It derives from the Old English words 'aened', meaning 'duck', and 'mere', a pond, a small lake or a pool. Domesday recorded the village name as Anemere, and listed it in the Freebridge Hundred, part-held by Count Eustace of Boulogne and by William de Warenne. The manor had previously belonged to seven unnamed free men and a Saxon called Ordgar, and was assessed with one acre of meadow, a fishery and one and a half salthouses. There were eight pigs and eighty sheep and the entire estate was valued at three pounds.

Ashbocking

It takes very little to see that this Suffolk hamlet had ash trees growing there at one time in its ancient history. In 1086, the survey simply recorded the place as Assa, and listed in the Bosmere Hundred, part-held at that time by St Etheldreda Abbey in Ely, Humphrey (known as 'the Chamberlain'), Richard FitzGilbert and King William. Then, in the fourteenth century the manor came into the possession of the de Bocking family, and their name was attached. In 1411 the village name was recorded as Bokkynge Assh.

Aythorpe Roding

There are eight villages in Essex with the name 'Roding', all derived from the River Roding, which was originally known as The Hyle. The name comes from an Anglo-Saxon tribe known as the Hrodingas who settled in the area in the sixth century. Each of the eight villages has a different supporting affix, most of them manorial. This particular part of the original manor was held the Aitrop family who attached their family name to the place some time before 1248 when it became known as Roeng Aytrop. Earlier, Domesday had recorded the placename as Rodinges, in the Dunmow Hundred, held in 1086 by Geoffrey de Mandeville.

Babergh

The original settlement of Babergh in Suffolk has an origin that is far from clear. The placename relies on the name of a man called Babba who may have been the founder of the village, and the Old English word 'beorg', which represented a hill or a mound, and might refer to a burial mound or tumulus where his remains were interred. However, despite the fact that the eventual name of the settlement also became that of the ancient Hundred in which it lay, suggesting that Babba was a person of some standing in his community, who he was remains something of a mystery. In 1086, the place was recorded as Baberga.

Bacton

Three places in England share the name Bacton – in Norfolk, in Suffolk and in Herefordshire. This Norfolk village reflects the name of the man who probably established the original settlement, a man called Bacca, who set up a farmstead here, (signified in Old English by the word 'tun'). Therefore, the placename means 'Bacca's farmstead'. The place was recorded in 1086 as Baketuna, and listed in the Tunstead Hundred, held at that time by Robert Malet, having belonged to Edric of Laxfield before the Conquest.

Badwell Ash

The placename of this village in Suffolk translates as 'spring (or stream) of a man called Bada in open land where ash trees grow'. The name was known as Badewelle Asafelde in the thirteenth century. The 'Ash' part of the placename is a shortened form of Ashfield, and relates to nearby Great Ashfield. It is assumed that Bada owned the land ('feld' or 'felda') through which the stream flowed. In Old English, 'wella' represented a stream, a well or a fountain.

Balsham

This is a village in Cambridgeshire that had already been recorded as Bellesham by 974. The name has two elements: the first is from a man's name, Baelli, who may have founded the homestead (or village). Hence, the placename means 'Baelli's village'. Domesday listed it as Belesham, in the Hundred of Radfield, part-held by Count Alan of Brittany and the remainder by the Abbey of St Etheldreda in Ely.

Bardfield Saling/Great Bardfield

Originally known simply as Bardfield, this Essex village gets its name from the Old English words 'byrde', meaning 'bank' or 'border', and 'feld', meaning open land. It translates as '[place on] open land by a bank (or on a border)'. The 'great' was added later to distinguish the village from Little Bardfield and latterly from Bardfield Saling, which gained its name from the neighbouring district of Great Saling. This name derived from the abundant willow trees (or 'sallows) to its south. Domesday recorded Bardfield as Byrdefelda and Great Saling as Salinges in 1086.

Barnham

The West Sussex village of Barnham was probably founded by a man called Beorna, whose homestead (or enclosure) may have formed the original settlement. The Old English word 'ham' signified a dwelling or homestead, while 'hamm' (with a double-'m'), indicated an enclosure of some kind – either are equally probable. Domesday recorded the place as Berneham, and listed it as quite a large estate supporting twenty-four households in the Binsted Hundred, held by a man called William for Earl Roger of Shrewsbury, it having belonged to a Saxon called Alnoth in 1066.

Barnham Broom

Domesday recorded this Norfolk village as Bernham in 1086, and located it in the Hundred of Forehoe, held at that time by a man called Starculf. The placename comes from the Old English word 'beorn', meaning 'warrior', or was perhaps named after a man called Beorna, and either 'ham', a homestead or dwelling, or 'hamm', an enclosure. Finally, the affix 'brom', which referred to a broom tree or shrub. Therefore, the placename may be taken to mean either 'dwelling of warriors by [or among] broom trees' or 'Beorna's enclosure among the broom trees' – something along those lines. The first part of the placename is identical to the village of Barnham in Suffolk.

Bartlow

The placename of the village of Bartlow in Cambridgeshire translates as '[place by the] mounds where birch trees grow'. It derives from the Old English words 'beorc', meaning 'birch tree', and 'hlaw', signifying a mound or a tumulus, a reference to the Roman burial barrows on the nearby Bartlow Hills. In 1232 the placename was recorded as Berkeslawe.

Basildon

The name of the Essex township of Basildon is of Anglo-Saxon origin, probably derived from a man called Beorhtel, with the Old English suffix 'dun' added, indicating 'Beorhtel's hill'. In 1086, the *Domesday Book* records it as Berlesduna and Belasduna, in the Barstable Hundred, owned by the Norman, Swein (or Sven, sometimes called Sven the Sheriff or Sven of Essex) and held as a tenant for him by Turold, who is said to have his portrait on the Bayeux Tapestry

Bassingbourn

This Cambridgeshire placename derives from an Anglo-Saxon man called Bassa, who settled by the local stream (known in Old English as a 'bourn' or 'burna'). The 'ing' element of the placename may refer to his family or followers. Hence, Bassingbourn probably means 'the stream of Bassa's followers'.

Bastwick

In the decade preceding the Norman Conquest, this village in Norfolk was recorded as Bastwic, and referred to a building where bast was stored. Bast is a bark of the lime tree that is used in ropemaking. The Old English word was 'baest', which is combined here alongside 'wic', which was the Saxon word for a building or a specialised farm. Domesday recorded the placename as Bastuuic, (there being no letter 'w' in the Norman French language at that time, and a double-'u' was used in its place). It listed the estate in the West Flegg Hundred, held in 1086 by Roger Bigot (sometimes 'Bigod'), valued at one shilling and having belonged to two unnamed free women at the time of King Edward.

Bawdrip

This Suffolk village was recorded as Bagetrepe in 1086, which gives a suggestion of the meaning of the placename. It comes from 'bagga', the Anglo-Saxon word for a badger, and 'trappe', a trap. Hence, 'place where badgers are trapped or snared'. Domesday recorded the village as a large estate supporting twenty-seven households, including six slaves, in the Hundred of North Petherton, held in 1086 by Walter de Douai, having been in the possession of Merleswein the Sheriff during the reign of King Edward. The manor was assessed with land for five men's plough teams, one cob, seven cattle and twenty pigs; the whole estate was valued at two pounds and five shillings.

Beccles

One explanation of this strange Suffolk placename comes from a time when there were plans for an early Christian church on this spot, known in Latin as the *Beata Ecclesia* and meaning 'blessed (or holy) church'. A crude wooden watchtower is thought to have been first erected here, facing out to sea to forewarn of hostile incursions by the Danes. By 960, an earth rampart and ditch surrounded the rudimentary settlement that was to become known by the time of Domesday as Becles. Another explanation is that it derives from two Old English words, 'bece' (a beck), and 'laes' (or leas), meaning pastures beside a stream.

Belchamp Otten

This Essex village placename means 'Otto's homestead with a beamed roof'. We have no idea who Otto was, but his possession of a homestead with a wooden beamed roof (recorded as early as 940), marked him out as a person of some status at a time when most had a simple that covering daub walls. The clue comes from the two elements which make up the first word of the placename, which were originally in Old English as 'belc', which meant 'beam' and relates to the modern English word 'balk', and 'ham', signifying a homestead or dwelling. Otto's name distinguishes the village from Belchampe St Paul and Belchamp Walter, held respectively by St Paul's Cathedral and a man called Walter. Domesday records the place as Belcham and Belcamp in 1086, listed in the Hinkford Hundred, part-held by The Canons of St Paul's Cathedral, Roger Bigod and Count Eustace of Boulogne.

Benfleet

This Essex township was known in the tenth century as Beamfleote and by the time of the *Domesday Book* as Benflet. The name derives from the Anglo-Saxon words 'beam', meaning a tree trunk, and 'fleot', meaning a river inlet or creek. Hence, the placename may be taken to mean 'tree-trunk creek' (or 'tree-stream'), probably referring to an old wooden bridge or pontoon across the inlet.

Benwick

There are two possibilities on offer for the meaning of this Cambridgeshire village placename. One has it derived from the Old English word 'bean', meaning as you might expect, a 'bean' or 'beans', and the other prefers 'beam', meaning 'tree trunk'. The second element of the placename, 'wic', referred to a specialised farm. The village name might therefore mean either 'farm where beans are grown', or 'farm by a tree trunk'. It was known in 1221 as Beymwich. On balance, the former seems most probable.

Billericay

This Essex township's placename probably comes from the Asian fruit, the myrobalan, whose Latin name is 'bellerica', and refers to a place where fabric dying or leather tanning took place. It was used extensively in Far Eastern fabric dying and batik and was imported into Britain for that purpose during the Middle Ages. The placename was recorded in 1291 as Byllyrica.

Bradfield Combust

Bradfield was a common name in Saxon England and three places of that name occur in the East Anglian County of Suffolk. The word generally meant 'broad [or wide] field [or open land]'. This particular village had the word Combust added following the burning down of the manorial hall in 1327. The Middle English word 'combust' meant 'burnt', and is related to the word 'combustion'. This addition to the placename distinguished the village from Bradfield St Clare nearby (owned by the Seyncler family), and Bradfield St George, named after the church in the village a few miles away. Domesday recorded the place as Bradfelda, and it was not until the mid-nineteenth century that it was listed as Bradfield-Combust and sometimes as Burnt Bradfield.

Braintree

Braintree is an ancient market town in north-east Essex which stands on the River Blackwater and was once the seat of the Bishops of London. In the *Domesday Book* the township was listed as Branchetreu, probably named after a man called Branca, who once owned the land, plus the Old English suffix 'treow', meaning a tree. Hence, 'Branca's tree'.

Brancaster

The Norfolk village of Brancaster began as a Roman military settlement which they called Branodunum, a name derived from the Celtic language and meaning 'fort of the raven'. The first name element is similar to the modern Welsh word 'bran', meaning 'raven' and the Old English word 'ceaster', which signified a Roman camp. In the decades immediately preceding the Norman Conquest the place was known as Bramcestria. Domesday recorded the village as Broncestra, a very large manor supporting over fifty households in the Docking Hundred, held in 1086 by the Abbey of St Benedict of Ramsey, who had also held it during the time of King Edward.

Brisley

Brisley is a village in Norfolk whose name means 'woodland clearing where gadflies swarm (or abound)'. It gets its name from an Anglo-Saxon word, 'briosa', the arcane name for any fly that bites livestock, especially a horsefly, warble fly or botfly. The Old English suffix 'leah' represented a woodland clearing or glade. The placename was recorded as Bruselea in the early twelfth century.

Bury St Edmunds

Originally an Anglo-Saxon settlement known as Bedric's Worth, the Suffolk township of Bury St Edmunds was named after a man called Bedric (or Beaduric), who had a farm enclosure (or in Old English, a 'wyrth'). A monastery was founded there by King Sigeberht of East Anglia in 630. By 945, it was known as Baederices Wirde and by 1038 in its Latin form, Sancte Eadmundes Byrig, meaning 'St Edmund's town', after the ninth century Saxon King Edmund of the East Angles. The 'byrig' element (or 'burh'), signified it was a fortified settlement.

Cambridge

By the mid-eighth century, the settlement was known as Grontabricc, meaning, 'the bridge on the River Granta'. The change in the placename from 'Grant' to 'Cam' is due entirely to Norman influence, though in 1086 it was still being recorded as Grantabrige, where Count Alan of Brittany had ten burgesses, with the lion's share of the manorial estates being reserved by King William, as they had been by Edward the Confessor before 1066. The placename gradually developed as Cantebrigge and eventually as Cambridge.

Caldecott

The village of Caldecott in Rutland has a name that comes from the Anglo-Saxon words 'cald', meaning 'cold', and 'cot', signifying a cottage, cottages or shelter. Hence the placename means 'cold cottage [or shelter]'. It is thought that the shelter in question was a temporary rest for travellers on the Roman road, Ermine Street. The placename has the same meaning as the village of Caldecote in neighbouring Cambridgeshire; there are places of this name (with various spellings) in Suffolk, Cheshire, Hertfordshire, Warwickshire, Buckinghamshire and Northamptonshire, among others. Domesday recorded this village as Caldecote, and listed it in the Witchley Hundred, which at that time covered areas of Northamptonshire and Rutland, and was held by the Bishop of Lincoln.

Cambridgeshire

A county in eastern England whose name means 'district based on Cambridge'. It was recorded in the eleventh century as Grantabrycgscir; 'the Old English word 'scir' meant 'district' and gives us the modern English word 'shire'.

Canewdon
The placename of the village of Canewdon in the County of Essex, means 'hill belonging to Cana's people'. It comes from the old Saxon words 'Cana', a man's name, probably referring to it leader or the founder of the settlement, 'inga', meaning 'people', 'family' or 'followers', and 'dun', a hill. The Great Survey of 1086 listed the village as Carenduna, in the Hundred of Barstable, held at that time in demesne by Swein of Essex.

Carleton Forehoe
The first element of this Norfolk placename comes from the Old Scandinavian word 'karl', meaning 'freeman', and bears witness to the lasting influence of the Danes on the local landscape. It is related to the Saxon word 'chorl' or 'coerl' and has the same meaning. The added affix 'tun' indicated an estate or farmstead. The Forehoe Hills also feature in the name, which in total may be taken to mean 'estate of the free men near the Forehoe Hills'. The hill name itself comes from the Old English word 'feower', meaning 'four', and the Norse word 'haugr', meaning 'hill'. Hence, 'four hills'. Domesday lists the village as Carletuna in the Forehoe Hundred. In 1268 it was being written Karleton Fourhowe.

Castle Rising
The castle of the Castle Rising placename was built by the Anglo-Norman noble, William d'Aubigny II (who owned the nearby Manor of Snettisham), some time after 1138. The name is a mixture of Old and Middle English, with the word 'castel' being fairly self-evident. However the older original name for the place, Risinga, derives from, two Old English elements: 'hris', meaning brushwood (or scrubland), and 'inga', signifying family, dwellers or followers. Hence, taken together, the placename might translate as '[dwelling] of the people who live near [or in] brushwood'. Yet another alternative has been offered – that the settlement's founder may have been a man called Risa, in which case the placename might be interpreted as '[settlement of] Risa's people'. Domesday records the very large Manor of Risinga, located in the Hundred of Freebridge in Norfolk, held at that time by Bishop Odo of Bayeux as Lord of the Manor, it having been in the possession of Archbishop Stigand in 1066. It was also a most valuable manor, and was assessed at a value to the Lord of the Manor at eighty-five pounds, which would have been an exceptionally large sum in the eleventh century.

Catworth
In all probability, the original Cambridgeshire settlement was established some time before the tenth century by a man called Catts or Catta, and was named Catteswyrth after him. The Old English word 'worth' signified an enclosure, either an enclosed paddock or an arable field. Therefore, the placename reads 'Catta's enclosure'. By 1086 the village had been recorded at Cateuuorde, in the land of William de Warenne in the former county of Huntingdonshire, where Aefic 'had three hides to the geld'. A substantial part of the manorial estates of Catworth had been held by King Edward before his death in 1066.

Chatteris
This Cambridgeshire town has two possible interpretations of its placename. The first is based on the premise that its founder and probable chieftain, perhaps an early Celtic man, who was called Ceatta. The second element of the placename may derive from the Old English word 'ric', meaning 'narrow ridge' or 'narrow strip of land', in which case it might mean 'Ceatta's narrow strip of land'. Alternatively, the first element may not be from a man's personal name at all, but from the Celtic word 'coed', similar to the Welsh word, meaning 'wood' or 'woodland'. Perhaps this version might be interpreted as 'woodland on

a narrow ridge (or strip of land)', or some variation on these themes. In 974 it was recorded as Caeteric, and in 1086 it had been written as Cietriz, listed in Ely Hundred, where three ploughlands of the manor were held by the Abbey of St Etheldrda in Ely, who had also held it before the Conquest. Another four ploughlands were held by the Abbey of St Benedict in Ramsey; they too had held it before 1066.

Chelmsford

Chelmsford began as a Roman settlement called Caesaromagus around 60 AD and was strategically placed midway between London (Londinium) and Colchester (Camulodunum). By the time of Domesday, the land was part of the Chelmsford Hundred and owned by Bishop Maurice of London, who had built a bridge across the River Can, bringing much passing traffic to the township. In 1086, the place was recorded as Celmeresfort, derived from a man called Ceolmaer, who once had owned the land, with the added Old English suffix 'ford', indicating a shallow river crossing. Hence, 'Ceolmaer's ford'. This crossing clearly pre-dated Bishop Maurice's bridge. By 1189, it had become known as Chelmsford.

Chignall Smealy

This Essex hamlet was known as Cingehala at the time of the Great Survey, possibly after a man called Cicca, who may have founded the original settlement. Then, the Old English words, 'halh', meaning 'corner [or nook] of land', along with 'smethe', meaning 'smooth' and 'leah', a woodland clearing. Taken together, all these elements produce a placename that means 'Cicca's corner of land in a smooth clearing'. By 1279 the name had been recorded as Chigehale Smetheleye.

Chigwell

In common with all other English placenames, the Old English affix 'wella' signified that there was a spring or a well, possibly a fountain, a stream or other watercourse in the original settlement. The well in question here belonged at one time, or may even have been sunk by a man called Cicca, for the name of this Essex township means 'Cicca's well [or stream]'. The place was recorded in Domesday as Cingheuuella, and listed in the Hundred of Ongar land belonging to Ralph de Limesy. The entry reads: 'R[alph] holds Cingheuuella in demesne, which Harold held of King Edward as a manor and as seven hides'. The estate was valued at ten pounds in 1086, having been worth eight pounds before the Norman Conquest.

Chipping Ongar

The Old English word 'ceping' indicated a township with a market, and 'angar' was a Saxon word for pasture or open grassland. Hence, the placename means 'pastureland with a market'. The 'Chipping' element distinguishes this Essex village from nearby High Ongar, which means 'high pastureland'. Before the Norman Conquest, the village was recorded simply as Aungre, presumably before the market had been established. Even in the 1086 Great Survey, it was being written as Angra. It was not until the outset of the fourteenth century that placename became known as Chepyngaungre.

Clacton

The placename of this township is more properly and officially, Clacton-on-Sea. The 'on-sea' element was added to distinguish it from Great Clacton and the nearby village of Little Clacton. But the placename had a much earlier beginning in the eleventh century, when it was already known simply as Claccingtune. The placename was derived from three Old English words, Clacc, the name of a man who it is thought once owned the land, 'inga', meaning the people, tribe or family, and 'tun', a farmstead or settlement. Hence, the name may be taken to mean 'the estate [or settlement] belonging to Clacc's family or tribe'. The *Domesday Book* identifies the place as 'Clachintuna... in Tendring Hundred [of Essex] ... in the Land of the Bishop of London', and that 'Great and Little Clacton was always in the bishopric as a manor and twenty hides'.

Claxton
This village in rural Norfolk may have derived its name from a Danish man called Klakkr, whose 'tun', or farmstead it was before the Conquest. Alternatively the second element of the placename might come from the Old Scandinavian 'thorp', signifying an outlying or remote farm. In which case, 'Klakkr's remote farmstead'. In 1086, Domesday recorded Clakestona, in the Lodding Hundred, a very large manor supporting forty-four households, and requiring four separate entries in the survey. The first and second entries show them held by Roger Bigot (sometimes Bigod), with Robert de Vaux leasing land from him. The second and third parts were held by Godric the Steward. Before the Conquest, various parts of the manorial estate lands were held by Archbishop Stigand, others by Edwin, Swetmann, Leofric, Ulfkil and Aslak of Rodenhala.

Coggeshall
Coggeshall is a village in Essex that is thought to have been once owned by a man called Cogg, the Saxon who may have established the original settlement. The second element of the placename is derived from the Old English 'halh', meaning 'corner or nook of land'. The *Little Domesday Book* recorded the place as Coghesshala, in the Hundred of Witham '...lands of Holy Trinity, Canterbury, for the sustenance of the monks'. At that time, three virgates were held by the church as they had been during the reign of King Edward. Additionally, Count Eustace of Essex held much of the estate in demesne. The account also records that one 'Theodoric Pointel held... two manors by exchange for [Great and Little] Coghesshala and now they are in the king's hands'.

Colne Engaine
This Essex village stands on the River Colne, which forms the first part of the placename. The name of the river, and the first element of the nearby town of Colchester, reputedly comes from Old King Cole of nursery rhyme fame. According to several ancient accounts a man called Cole-Brook was a nobleman, a Reading cloth merchant and Earl of Colchester in the early twelfth century, and may be the person referred to in the nursery rhyme (a 'factoid' frequently debated). Myth it may be, but it has long-since become enmeshed in oral tradition. What is certainly known is that in medieval times the Engayne family held the manor. In 1086, the place was recorded as Colun, and by 1254 it had been recorded as Colum Engayne, reflecting the family's manorial affix.

Colchester
This region of Essex was inhabited by the Celtic Trinovantes tribe before the twentieth Roman Legion arrived in Britain and called their Colchester garrison Colonia Camulodunum; the last element of the placename referred to the Celtic god Camulos. By the tenth century, it had become known as Colececastre, meaning 'Roman fort on the River Colne'. Of this, the Latin element 'ceastre', typical of many Roman military settlements, indicated a fort. By the time of the Great Survey in 1086 it had evolved as Colecestre (sometimes spelt Cole Casto), and was part listed in Tendring Hundred held by William, Bishop of London. It records 'In Colecestre the bishop has fourteen houses and four acres, which render no customary dues.' It also lists one house belonging to Count Eustace and two belonging to Richard.

Congham

Initially, Congham derives its placename from a Saxon word, 'cung', which referred to a steep round hill, taken together with 'ham', meaning 'homestead' or 'village'. The whole translates as 'homestead by a round-topped [or steep-sided] hill'. Domesday listed Congheham, in the Freebridge Hundred of Norfolk, two-thirds held by William de Warenne, and a third by a man identified as Berner the Bowman. Before the Conquest it had been in the possession of more than a dozen unnamed free men.

Copdock

A village in Suffolk whose name was recorded as Coppedoc inthe late thirteenth century. The placename comes from the Old English words 'copped', (from 'copp', meaning 'top'), which meant either 'pollarded', 'polled' or 'lopped', and from 'ac' an oak tree. Hence, the placename may be interpreted as '[place by a] pollarded [or lopped] oak tree'. A tree that has been lopped has had its top removed.

Corpusty

Opinions differ as the exact meaning of this Norfolk village placename. One has it derived from the Old Scandinavian word 'korpr', meaning 'raven', plus 'stigr', meaning 'path', which taken together produce an interpretation of the placename as '[place by the] path where ravens are seen'. Another cites a Dane called Korpr in whose territory the path in question lay. Either seem equally possible. Domesday recorded the place as Corpestih, Corpsty and Corpestig, in the South Erpingham Hundred, part-held by Bishop William of Thetford, William de Warenne and William d'Ecouis. Thirty acres had been held by Bishop Aethelmaer in 1066. Elsewhere it recorded that '...in Corpestih [there are] two free men, fourteen acres of land [and] there always has been one plough; and they are worth eleven pennies'. The remainder of the manorial estate was valued at four pounds and eight shillings.

Costessey

Costessey's placename came from an early settler, possibly a Danish man called Cost, which along with the Old English word 'eg', which stands for an island or dry ground surrounded by marsh or swamp. The name may be taken to mean 'island in the marsh belonging to a man called Cost'. The place appeared as Costeseia and Coteseia in the Great Survey, located in the Hundred of Foreloe, and held by Count Alan of Brittany, having belonged to Earl Gyrth before 1066. The account enumerates... 'four carucates of land; there have always been eight villans and eight bordars. Then [there were] four slaves, now one'.

Cromer

The North Norfolk township of Cromer received no mention in the *Domesday Book*. The placename is first recorded in the mid-thirteenth century as Crowemere, derived from a combination of the Old English words 'crawe', a crow, and 'mere', a lake. Hence the name means 'lake inhabited by crows'.

Dallinghoo

This Suffolk village was established on a hill-spur probably by a man called Dalla and his people, as that is exactly what the placename means: 'hill-spur of Dalla's people'. The placename components are all Anglo-Saxon, and include 'inga', which means 'people', 'followers' or 'family', and 'hoh', a hill-spur. Domesday recorded the name as Dallinghahou, in the Loose Hundred, held in 1086 by Count Alan of Brittany, it having belonged to an unnamed free man before 1066.

Dengie

This village in the County of Essex had already been named Deningei by the beginning of the eighth century. It probably derived its name from a man called Dene, who may have been the founder or the leader of the original settlement. The name comes from the Anglo-Saxon words 'ing', meaning 'associated with' or 'ingas', referring to followers, people or family, and 'eg', which signified an island, most typically high ground surrounded by marsh, water meadow or a flood plain. In this particular case the 'island' in question would have been the high ground that is surrounded by Dengie Marshes. Therefore the placename can be interpreted either as 'island associated with a man called Dene', or 'island of Dene's followers or people'. In 1086, the village was recorded as Daneseia, and listed in the Wibrihtesherne Hundred, jointly held by the Abbey of Saint-Valery and Bishop Odo of Bayeux, having belonged to Saxons called Siric and Thorkil, as well as two unnamed free men.

Dickleburgh

This village placename derives from a man called Dicel (or Dicla), who had established a fortified dwelling or stronghold of some kind in the place, or in Old English, a 'burh' (the origin of the present day 'borough' or 'burgh'). Hence, 'Dicla's stronghold'. The *Domesday Book* named the place Dicclesburc, in the Bliss Hundred of Norfolk, where the manor was in the possession of the Abbey of Bury St Edmunds, as it had done before the Norman Conquest of 1066. The manorial estate supported twenty-two households, which included four villans, twelve bordars, four free men and two priests. The survey accounted for seven acres of meadow, a woodland supporting sixteen pigs and one church which worked a quarter of an acre.

Diss

This Norfolk township has a name that means '[place by a] ditch', which comes from the Old English word 'dic', meaning 'ditch' or 'dyke'. Whatever or wherever the aforementioned ditch was, no trace of it seems to still exist, though the placename was in place well before the Conquest. Domesday recorded the name as Dice, and listed it in the Hartismere Hundred, at that time covering areas of Norfolk and Suffolk, and jointly held by King William and Robert Malet. Before the Conquest the manorial estates had belonged to King Edward and to an unnamed free man.

Ditchingham

Two equally plausible interpretations have been suggested for the origin of the Norfolk village of Ditchingham. The first cites the Old English word 'dic' which refers to a ditch or a dyke (as with Diss, previously), plus the two affixes 'inga', meaning people, family or followers, and 'ham', a dwelling of homestead. Hence, 'homestead of people who live by a ditch'. The second argues that the first element of the placename is derived for the personal name of a man called Dica (or Dicca), in which case we might translate the placename as meaning 'the people of Dicca's homestead'. In 1086, the place was recorded as Dicingaham, in the Hundred of Lodding, a very large settlement of thirty-six households, including twenty-two free men, held by King William, it having been a possession of Archbishop Stigand before the Conquest. The manorial estate included twenty-seven acres of meadow, woodland pannage for one hundred and four pigs, sixty-four sheep, fifty-five goats and two water mills.

Docking

A place named after a plant. In particular, the common dock leaf (*rumex obtusifolius*), also known as bitter dock. The original Norfolk placename is of Saxon origin, where the word was 'docce' with the affix 'ing' which meant 'a place characterised by' or 'known for'.

Docking therefore meant '[place] known for docks'. In the early eleventh century, it was recorded as Doccynge, and by 1086 had been listed as Dochinga.

Dunton Wayletts

The name of this small hamlet located in the Basildon Borough of Essex is entirely of Saxon origin. In Anglo-Saxon English the word 'dun', meant 'hill' and 'tun' was a farmstead or a village settlement. The second word comes from 'weylete', which indicated a place where roads met. Hence, 'the village settlement on a hill where roads meet'. Domesday records the place as Dantuna, held by Bishop Odo of Bayeux, half-brother of King William. The survey recorded that '...in Dunton [are] fifteen acres of land, which Wulwine held and they belong to the king undisputed'.

Elmsett

The Old English word for an elm tree or grove was 'elme' and 'saette' was a word used by Saxons for 'dwellers' or 'settlers'. Hence, this Suffolk village has a placename that means 'settlement of people who dwell among elm trees', or something very much along those lines. Well before the Norman Conquest the place was known as Ylmesaeton, and by the time of the Great Survey it had become Elmseta, a small estate listed in the Cosford Hundred supporting fourteen households, held by Roger d'Auberville. In the 1086 assessment its assets amounted to four cattle, twenty pigs and two hundred and forty sheep, with a total value of eight pounds.

Eltisley

Towns and villages whose placenames end in '-ley' or '-lea' invariably stem from Anglo-Saxon times, where that word element signified a woodland glade or a clearing made specifically to produce farmland. The village of Eltisley in Cambridgeshire was no exception. The clearing in question belonged way back in its early history to a man called Elti, whose name remains enshrined in the placename. In 1086, the place was recorded as Hecteslei and by the early thirteenth century it had become Eltesle.

Ely

This Cambridgeshire township was historically known as the 'Isle of Ely', owing to its situation among the ancient waterlogged landscape of East Anglia, before its fens were drained in the seventeenth century. Its original name was the Isle (or District) of Eels, from the Old English 'oel', or as it appears in the *Anglo-Saxon Chronicles*, as Elig, signifying an eel. Arguably, the placename might be taken to mean a place where eels are found, or more simply, 'eel island'.

Essex

A county in the east of England whose name means '[territory of the] East Saxons'. The name comprises two Old English elements, 'east' (which is self-explanatory), and 'Seaxe', meaning 'Saxons'. In the ninth century the region was known as East Seaxe, and by the time of the Great Survey of 1086 it had been recorded as Exsessa.

Farcet

As early as the tenth century, this Cambridgeshire village was known as Faresheued, based on the Old English words 'fearr', a bull, and 'heafod', which signified a hill, headland or promontory. The placename therefore translates as 'bull's hill', or 'headland shaped like a bull'.

Felbrigg

The Felbrigg placename means '[place by the] plank bridge'. It comes from a combination of Saxon and Norse words: the Old Scandinavian word 'fjol', meaning 'plank' (or board), and the Old English word 'brycg', a bridge. The name illustrates the influence of Danish culture on placenames in eastern England. The *Little Domesday Book* recorded it as Felebrug, and listed it within the Hundred of North Erpingham land of Roger Bigod in Norfolk, where it entered '...in Felebrug [there are] two free men of Gyrth's and they have two carucates of land'. It continued to assess the manorial estate as having woodland pannage for sixty pigs and four acres of meadow, with eight sokemen responsible for ploughing sixty-three acres of land.

Fen Ditton
The second element of this Cambridgeshire village placename is its original form and comes from two Old English words, 'dic', a ditch or dyke, and 'tun', signifying a farmstead. It was known in 975 as Dictunae. Hence, 'farmstead near (or in) a dyke'. The dyke referred to is Fleam Dyke. The 'Fen' affix had been attached by 1286 when it was known as Fen Dytton, in order to distinguish it from other places known as Ditton, including the nearby hamlet of Woodditton. Other Ditton placenames exist in Kent, Surrey and Shropshire.

Fingringhoe
This is a complicated Essex placename that is comprised of several Anglo-Saxon elements. The first part, 'finger' is self-evident; the second 'inga', in this specific instance meant 'people' or 'dwellers', and 'hoh'(or 'ho') indicated an outcrop or hill spur. Hence, 'outcrop of the people who dwell on a finger-shaped hill', or something along those lines. It is thought that the description referred to the narrow strip of land between the River Roman and Geeton Creek.

Fobbing
Fobbing is a village in the Thurrock area of Essex that was named after a man called Fobb or Fobba, who may have been its founder, an early leader or chieftain. The last element of the placename might come either from the Old English word 'ingas', meaning 'people', 'followers' or 'family', or from 'ing', which meant 'place'. These produce a placename that means either '[settlement of the] followers or family of Fobba' or simply 'Fobba's place'. It was recorded in 1086 as Phobinge, and listed in the Hundred of Barstable lands of Count Eustace, where five hides of the estate land had been held by the Saxon Beorhtmaer, described as a thegn of King Edward before the Conquest.

Fressingfield
This placename may possibly translate as 'open land of the people or followers of a man called Frisa, [or even a man identified as a Frisian]'. It comes from the Old English 'Frisa', plus 'inga', the people, family or followers, and 'feld', a word then signifying any stretch of open land, or what we would nowadays call a field. In 1086, it was recorded as Fessfelda, and in 1185, as Frisingfeld. Domesday placed the village in land belonging to Robert Malet in the Bishop's Hundred of Suffolk, where 'Alwine, a sokeman held six acres'. It was a very small estate, worth just one shilling in 1086.

Fring
Fring is a small hamlet in Norfolk, that probably belonged at one time to a man called Fera and his family, who may have been its original founders or early settlers. The additional Old English suffix 'ingas', meant 'family' or 'followers', which produced a placename which means '[settlement of] the family or followers of Fera'. The hamlet had three entries in the *Domesday Book*, which recorded its name as Frainghes, Fringe and Frenge, and listed it in the Docking Hundred, part-held by Bishop William of Thetford, Count Eustace of Boulogne and William de Warenne.

Frinton

More properly Frinton-on-Sea, this seaside resort may have been named after a man called Fritha, who founded a farmstead (or in Old English, a 'tun'), on the coast of Essex. Alternatively, the placename could have come from 'frithen', a word that meant 'protected' or 'safeguarded', in which case it could be interpreted as 'protected farmstead', suggesting that it may have been either heavily fortified or securely fenced. Domesday recorded the place as Frientuna, a small settlement in the Tendring Hundred held by Count Eustace of Boulogne. The 'on sea' was added in the nineteenth century to promote the place as an up and coming resort town as sea bathing began to grow in popularity.

Fyfield

The village of Fyfield in Essex was once an estate which measured exactly five hides of land if the placename is interpreted accurately. The name comes from the Old English words 'fif', meaning 'five', and 'hid', representing a hide of land. There are settlements in Berkshire and in Hampshire with the same name and meaning. The placename means '[estate comprising] five hides'. Domesday recorded the place as Fifhidam, in the Hundred of Ongar, land belonging to Count Eustace. The survey recorded the estate twice and in one entry stated that 'Richard holds Fifhidam of the count, which Beorhtmaer held as forty acres at the time of King Edward and as one manor'. Clearly, the aforesaid manor had been divided before 1086. In a second entry, the account recorded that 'Roger holds Fifhidem of John, which Leofric held... as one and a half hides and thirty acres' (that is, before the Norman Conquest).

Gamlingay

The name of this Cambridgeshire village has two perfectly possible interpretations. The first part of the name is straightforward – it comes from a man called Gamela, who may have been its founder. The second element of the name, however, is ambiguous, as it could relate to the Old English word 'ingas', meaning 'people' or 'followers', or it could come from 'ing', meaning 'place'. Finally, the last element comes either from 'haeg', meaning enclosure (think of 'hedge'), or from 'eg', signifying an island, or more technically, raised ground surrounded by water, fenland or marsh. So, the placename may be taken wither to mean 'enclosure associated with the people of Gamela', or 'Gamela's place on an land surrounded by water [or marsh]'. Domesday recorded Gamelingei in the Longstowe Hundred, part-held by Ranulf FitzIlger, Robert, the son of Fafiton and Eudo the Steward. It was a very large estate supporting sixty-two households, including four slaves. The entire manorial estate was valued at nineteen pounds and five shillings.

Garboldisham

Garboldisham in Norfolk was probably founded by a man called Gaerbald, whose homestead or village it was, along with the Old English word 'ham' signifying a village. In 1086, Domesday recorded the place as Gerboldesham, in the Guiltcross Hundred, in land belonging to King William. The survey lists 'Gerboldesham was held by one free man, Aelfric, at the time of King Edward for a manor [of] two carucates of land. There have always been three borders and one slave and four acres of meadow'. In 1086, the manor estate was valued at forty shillings.

Girton

Known in 1060 as Grittune and by the time of Domesday as Gretone, in the Northstowe Hundred, this small township, lying just over two miles from Cambridge, derives its placename from the Old English 'greot', meaning grit or gravel, and 'tun', a farmstead or settlement. Hence, 'farmstead on gravelly ground'. The Great Survey named Count Robert of Mortain as its owner and Judicael (known as 'the Hunter') as its overlord in 1066.

Glatton

The Cambridgeshire village of Glatton was recorded in the *Domesday Book* as Glatune, listed in the Normancross Hundred of the former County of Huntingdonshire and held at that time by Count Eustace of Boulogne. The name is comprised of two Old English words, 'glaed', meaning 'pleasant' and 'tun', a farmstead, and occasionally a village. Hence, 'pleasant farmstead'.

Glemsford

Glemsford was a place where games or entertainments were held in Anglo-Saxon times, which is demonstrated in its placename. The Old English word 'gleam', meant 'merriment' or 'games' and the 'ford' element locates this Suffolk village at a shallow river crossing. The placename is understood to mean '[place where] games are held by the river ford'. Immediately before the Norman Conquest the place was known as Glemesford and in 1086 Domesday recorded it as Clamesforda, in the Babergh Hundred, held jointly at that time by the Abbey of St Etheldreda of Ely and Ranulf Peverel.

Godmanchester

This placename derives from Godmund, a Briton who once owned the land, and the Latin suffix 'ceastre', indicating a Roman fortified settlement. Hence, 'Roman settlement associated with a man called Godmund'. Domesday places the township in the Leightonstone Hundred of Huntingdonshire (now Cambridgeshire), and describes it as a very large manor held by King William, as it had been held by Edward the Confessor in his day.

Gooderstone

Gooderstone is a village in Norfolk whose placename derives from two Old English words, 'Guthhere', a man who may possibly have been its founder, and 'tun' which means 'farm' or 'farmstead'. The placename may therefore be interpreted as 'Guthhere's farmstead'. The Great Survey listed the village of Godestuna, in the South Greenhoe Hundred, held in 1086 by Godric (known as 'the Steward'), with Archbishop Stigand having been its overlord in 1066. Its tenants had included ten free men and another named Asgot. It was a large estate with extensive meadows and woodland, supporting cobs, cattle and sheep. The whole manorial estate was valued at six pounds.

Great Henny

A small hamlet in Essex which stands on a hill which overlooks several brooks and streams. The word 'Henny' has two sources in Old English: one is 'heah', meaning 'high', and the other is 'eg', signifying an island. Hence, '[place on a] high island'. The first word of the placename distinguishes it from the nearby hamlet of Little Henny. At the time of the *Domesday Book*, these two hamlets appear not to have been separated, but were grouped under a single entry as Heni, in the Hinkford Hundred, then crossing both the counties of Essex and Suffolk, with Turolf holding most of the manorial estates and with Ranulf Peverel, Roger Bigot and Waleran being tenants-in-chief. Before the Conquest of 1066, according to the survey, the estate had belonged to five unnamed free men.

Great Hockham

The precise interpretation of the Norfolk township of Hockham is ambiguous. It may refer to its possible founder or chieftain, a man called Hocca, or derive from the Old English word 'hocc', a hock (the herb, also known as the marsh mallow). 'Ham' signifies a village, settlement or homestead. Hence, the placename might mean either 'Hocca's village', or 'homestead where hocks grow'. The 'Great' affix was added to distinguish it from the nearby village of Little Hockham, known in 1102 as Parvo Hocham. Domesday recognised the place simply as Hocham, in the Shropham Hundred land of Roger Bigod (or Bigot), which had belonged to Eadric, a thegn during the time of King Edward.

Great Yarmouth

The Norfolk coastal township of Great Yarmouth derived its placename from the River Yare, on which it stands. It comes from the old Anglo-Celtic language and probably means 'babbling stream', with the additional Old English suffix 'mutha', meaning 'mouth'. Hence, 'village [or settlement] at the mouth of the River Yare'. By 1086 it was known as Gernemwa (sometimes Yernemuth) and was already a flourishing herring fishing port with twenty-four fishermen and its own church. Domesday records Yarmouth in the East Flagg Hundred, having been held before the Conquest by King Edward. The affix 'Great' was added later to distinguish it from nearby Little Yarmouth, which was incorporated into the borough in 1668.

Grunty Fen

The origin of the placename is uncertain, but what evidence there is suggests the Old English word 'grund', which means 'bottom' ('foundation' or 'shallow place'), may be the clue to its meaning. This former parish in Cambridgeshire is indeed located on low-lying land in the middle of the Isle of Ely. Also, given that the Old Scandinavian word 'fen' described low or marshy land that was prone to seasonal flooding, the placename may reasonably be interpreted as 'a shallow place prone to frequent flooding'.

Guyhirn

Located on the banks of the River Nene in the Cambridgeshire fenlands of East Anglia, the name of the village of Guyhirn has a complex source. Most authorities have it coming from the Old French word 'guie', meaning a guide, specifically related to tides and the control of water flow, and the Old English 'hyrne', referring to a corner or angle of land. Taken together, these two references indicate a specific place, a corner of land where the tidal flow from the Wisbech river and the Nene floodbanks (which came inland as far as the township), was channelled in order to maintain water levels and control the inflow of salt water into the freshwater river beyond.

Halstead

This Essex town's placename means 'place of shelter [or refuge]', based on the Old English words 'heald' or 'hald', meaning 'protected' or 'held (safely or securely)', especially when related to the keeping of animals, livestock and cattle. The placename also exists in Kent and Leicestershire. Over time the name has undergone several changes, including Haltesteda and Hadstead. Domesday recorded the place as Halsteda and Haltesteda, in the Hinckford Hundred, a very large estate held in parts by Richard, son of Count Gilbert, by Waltheran, identified as the father of John, and part by William de Warenne. A man called Richard held sixty-four acres of estate lands from William, and twenty-two sokemen held a further half a hide and eleven acres. Before the Norman Conquest the manorial estates had belonged to thirty unnamed free men of Saxon birth.

Happisburgh

As with many other towns and villages whose placenames end in '-burgh' or '-borough' (which meant 'fortified manor' or 'stronghold'), the Norfolk village of Happisburgh was fortified during uncertain times when Danish incursions were commonplace. The placename actually means 'stronghold of Haep', the name of the man who may have established the original settlement on the Norfolk coast. Domesday recorded the place as Hapesburc, a very large estate in the Happing Hundred part-held by Count Alan of Brittany and part by King William.

Harlow

There are two prevailing theories as to the derivation of this placename; one has it from the Anglo-Saxon words 'here' and 'hlaw', meaning 'army hill', possibly referring to a Viking army who occupied it, and the other is based on 'here' and 'hearg', meaning 'temple hill or mound'. Either is possible. The former has been probably identified as Mulberry Hill, an ancient British meeting place and the latter associated with an Iron Age burial mound near the River Way, with all the religious implications that would suggest. The township was known as Herlawe before the Norman Conquest, and recorded later in the *Domesday Book* as the 'Mainou of Herlaua' (also known as Herlowbury), in Harlow Half Hundred, belonging to the Abbey of St Edmund.

Hartest

The 'Hart' element of this Suffolk village placename refers to the hart or stag, and would originally have been 'heorot' in Old English. The second element of the name, 'hyrst', meant 'wooded hill'. Therefore, the placename translates as 'wooded hill where stags live'. The place was recorded in 1050 as Hertest and in 1086 as Herterst.

Harwich

The township was not recorded in the *Domesday Book* but its placename pre-dates the Norman invasion, being derived from two Anglo-Saxon words, 'here' and 'wic', meaning 'army camp' or 'military settlement', a probable reference to a ninth century Viking encampment in the vicinity. By 1248, it was known as Herewic, in the Tendring district of Essex, and had developed from a small hamlet into a major town, due to the influence of the powerful Earl of Norfolk.

Hessett

This village in Suffolk derived its placename from the Old English words 'hecg', meaning 'hedge', and 'set', a dwelling or animal fold. Hence, 'animal fold surrounded by a hedge'. Such enclosures were not commonplace at this time, and Hesset appears to have been sufficiently unique to have the fact recorded in its name. Domesday entered the village as Heteseta, listed in the Thedwastre Hundred, part-held in 1086 by the Abbey of Bury St Edmunds and Frodo, identified as the brother of Abbot Baldwin. In 1066, the manor had been overseen by no fewer than sixty-six free men. Its estates amounted to six acres of meadow and a church and in total was valued at four pounds.

Hethersett

Hethersett's placename means '[settlement of the] dwellers who live among the heather [or on the heath]'. It comes from two Anglo-Saxon words, 'haeddre', meaning 'heather' or 'heath', and 'saete', meaning 'dwellers' or 'inhabitants'. This village and parish in the Henstead district of Norfolk was recorded in the Great Survey as Hederseta, and listed in the ancient Hundred of Humbleyard. The estate was assessed with eighty-seven sheep and seven hives of bees, which no doubt constituted a prosperous local industry thanks to the surrounding heathland. By the thirteenth century, the original estate had been subdivided into three manors, known as Hethersett Cromwells, Hethersett Hacons and Hethersett Woodhall, after the families who took their possession.

Hindringham

As with all places in England whose names end in 'ham', it refers to a homestead or settlement, and this Norfolk village is no exception. Two other Saxon elements define the placename, 'inga', meaning the 'people or dwellers of', and 'hinder', meaning 'behind'. Taken together, these elements produce a place whose name means 'homestead or village of the people who dwell behind'. It is thought that the 'behind' part of the explanation refers to the nearby hills behind which the village is located, although these are difficult to identify in a county as flat as Norfolk. Domesday recorded the name as Hindringaham, and listed it as a very large estate within the North Greenhoe Hundred, supporting around fifty households and held in 1086 by the Bishops of Thetford and of Exeter, as well as Drogo de la Beuvrière.

Hinxton

Hinxton was almost certainly named after the person who founded this Cambridgeshire settlement, a man called Hengist or Hengest. Earlier it had been known as Hengstiton, where the original element of the placename would have been 'ing', signifying his people or associates. Finally the Old English word 'tun', which referred to his estate or settlement, produced a placename that meant 'estate [or settlement] of the people of Hengest'. Domesday listed the village as Hestitona, a very large manor located it in the Whittlesford Hundred, and held jointly by four parties: King William himself, Picot of Cambridge, the Bishop of St Mary's Lincoln and Hardwin of Scales.

Hockering

The Old English word 'hocer' indicated a rounded hill, a hillock or a hump, and the affix 'ingas' referred to people, followers or family. Therefore the name of this Norfolk village translates as '[settlement of the] people who live by the rounded hill', or something along those lines. As usual, the Norman Domesday commissioners struggled with Saxon names and entered the village placename as Hokelinka. It was listed as a very large estate supporting over forty-seven households in the Mitford Hundred, held in 1086 by Ralph de Beaufour. The estate was assessed with fifteen acres of meadow, woodland with pannage for two hundred pigs, one hundred and thirteen sheep and nine cattle, altogether valued at five pounds.

Hockwold cum Wilton

The first part of this Norfolk village placename means 'woodland where hocks grow', based on 'hock', a plant of the hibiscus or mallow family, and 'wald', a woodland or forest. The final word translates as 'farmstead where willows grow'. The middle placename element, 'cum', is a Latin word meaning 'with'. Taken together the placename means 'woodland where hocks grow with a farmstead [or village] where willows grow'. While in 1086 these two villages in the Grimshoe Hundred were distinctly separate manors (Hockwold was recorded as Hocuuella and Wilton as Wiltuna), both were held by William de Warenne having previously belonged to Countess Aelfeva.

Hoxne

A most unusual placename. The Suffolk village of Hoxne's name relates to that part of leg sinew often known as the 'hock'. The whole word comes from Old English, where the two elements, 'hosinu' and 'hoh', respectively referred to the hock sinew and a hill-spur, outcrop or ridge. Hence, '[place on the] hock-shaped outcrop [or hill-spur]'. It was already known by its present name by the mid-tenth century and was recorded as Hoxana in the Domesday survey.

Hunstanton

The West Norfolk township of Hunstanton is probably named after a man called Hunstan, who once occupied the land, and the Old English affix 'tun', signifying a settlement or farmstead. Hence, 'the village settlement of Hunstan'. Another possibility suggests a reference to the River Hun which runs in Hunstanton Park, the ancestral home of the le Strange family, and the Old English word 'stan', meaning a stone. This may also be connected to the word 'Honeystone', a reference to the distinctive red carr stone of the region. The township was already known as Hunstanestun before the Norman Conquest. By the time of the Domesday survey it was recorded as Hunestanestuna, in Clavering Hundred, held at the time of King Edward by Bishop Stigand of Elmham (later Archbishop of Canterbury) and in 1086 it was in the possession of the Crown, held for King William by Ralph FitzHerluin.

Huntingdon

The first part of this Cambridgeshire placename comes from Hunta, possibly the name of its founder or chieftain, or even 'hunta', referring to a huntsman. The township was originally within the former County of Huntingdonshire, which was itself derived from the same source. The two other Anglo-Saxon elements of the placename, 'inga', signifying the family, people or tribe, and 'dun', meaning hill, are somewhat confusing, as no such hill seems to exist near the place. The township was known in 921 as Huntandun and by several different spellings in the *Domesday Book*, including Huntedone, Huntedun and Huntedune. The survey begins 'In the burh of Huntedone there are four ferdings', held by around one hundred and sixteen burgesses, including a bishop and a sheriff, as well as numerous earls and counts.

Huntingdonshire

This former historic County in East Anglia was based on the town of Huntingdon (now in the County of Cambridgeshire), with the appended Old English suffix 'scir', meaning 'shire' or 'district'. The county was abolished in 1974 and included in Cambridgeshire. In the eleventh century the name was recorded as Huntadunscir.

Ingoldisthorpe

This Norfolk village was probably established some time during the seventh or eighth centuries by a Dane called Ingjaldr, who established a remote farm whose placename came to mark his ownership. The name comprises two Old Scandinavian words: Ingjaldr (his personal name), and 'thorpe', a word that referred to an outlying or remote farmstead. Hence, 'Ingjaldr's remote farmstead'. Domesday twice recorded the village, as Torpe and as Evlvestorp, and listed it as a very large estate in the Smethdon Hundred, assessed with a meadow measuring fifty acres, two mills and one salthouse. It supported thirty-six households, and in 1086 the estate had four cobs (horses), fifteen pigs and four hundred and twenty sheep. In 1203, the village name was recorded as Ingaldestorp.

Ipswich

From the seventh century, the Suffolk township of Gipeswic (sometimes Gippelwich – the 'g' is silent), was an important port in the Kingdom of East Anglia. The placename may have derived from one of two possible sources: the first is that the land belonged to a man called Gip with the addition of the suffix 'wic', indicating 'the harbour belonging to Gip'; the second argues that the Old English word 'gip', meant 'gap', and may have referred to the wide estuary of the River Orwell. Either is plausible.

Ixworth Thorpe
A village in Suffolk which was originally simply called Torp and identified in the *Domesday Book* as Torpa and as Icsewrda, in the Hundred of Blackbourne. It was a relatively large settlement in 1086, supporting more than fifty households, in the lands of the Abbey of Bury St Edmunds and held by Robert Blunt (sometimes 'Blount'). It is uncertain who Ixworth actually was, but he was evidently a person of some standing as the place was named after him. The 'thorp' element of the placename comes directly from Old Scandinavian, suggesting that Ixworth was a Danish man, whose 'thorpe' or remote settlement, this was. By the beginning of the fourteenth century the place had become known as Ixworth Thorp.

Kelvedon Hatch
Many English placenames contain the word 'hatch; it derives from 'haecc', an Old English word which translates as 'hatch-gate', or in modern English, a 'gate'. The word was particularly significant because at a time before enclosed fields and pastures were commonplace, anything requiring a gate stood out as private land, demanding a degree of importance and potential status for its owner. In this particular case the gate is thought to have been placed at the entrance to a forest. The first word of the placename comes from 'cylu', meaning 'speckled' and 'dun', a hill. The entire placename therefore translates as 'speckled hill with a gate', but the significance of 'speckled' is somewhat obscure. In 1066, the place was known as Kylewendune, by 1086 it had become Keluenduna and it was not until the late-thirteenth century that it became known as Kelwedon Hacche.

Kessingland
This Suffolk village placename has hardly altered since it was first recorded as Kessingalanda in the *Domesday Book* in 1086. The name derives from a man called Cyssi or Cyssa plus the Old English elements 'inga', meaning 'people or followers', and 'open land'. Hence, 'open land belonging to Cyssi's people'. The survey lists the estate in the Lothing Hundred, in land belonging to King William, with Edric of Laxfield as its overlord. In 1066, it had been held by a Saxon man called Osfrith, and was valued at just one shilling.

Kettlebaston
Kettlebaston demonstrates the infusion of Scandinavian into Saxon society before the Norman Conquest. This small Suffolk village of just seven households was named after an early Danish settler called Ketilbjorn, whose 'tun', or farmstead it was. The placename therefore means 'Ketilbjorn's farmstead'. Domesday recorded the place as Kitelbeornastuna in 1086, and located it in the Cosford Hundred, part-held at that time by the Abbey of Bury St Edmunds and Gamas Humphrey. Before the Conquest it had belonged to four unnamed Saxons, listed as free men.

King's Lynn
At that time, the place was known simply as Linn, Lena, or Lun, from the Old Celtic word 'linn', meaning 'the pool', thought to be on account of the large tidal lake that frequently covered much of the area. The prefix 'King's' was added in the sixteenth century. Until that time it had become commonly known as Bishop's Lynn (in Latin Lenne Episcopi), part of the manor of the Bishop of Norwich. This name-change came about following the closure of the Franciscan priory under Henry VIII's Dissolution of the Monasteries, the estates passing into Crown ownership, at which point it was renamed Lynn Regis, or King's Lynn.

Kirtling

Kirtling is a Cambridgeshire village whose placename came from a man called Cyrtla, with the Old English affix 'ing', which signified an association. Hence, the name means 'place associated with a man called Cyrtla'. Domesday recorded it as Chertelinge, in the Cheveley Hundred, land belonging to Countess Judith of Lens, the niece of King William. There is a village of the same name in Norfolk.

Langham

The Old English word 'lang' meant 'long'. The second element of this Suffolk village placename could have been either 'ham', which signified a homestead or dwelling, or 'hamm', an enclosure. Hence, 'long homestead or enclosure'. Domesday recorded the place under its present name and listed it within the Blackburn Hundred, held in 1086 by the Abbey of Bury St Edmunds. Before the Conquest it had been jointly managed by seven unnamed Saxon free men.

Lavenham

The village of Lavenham in the County of Suffolk was known by the end of the tenth century as Lauanham and by the time of Domesday, recorded as Lauenham and Lauen. The placename probably derives from a man called Lafa or Lava, who may have been its founder or early chieftain, plus the suffix 'ham', indicating a homestead or farmstead. Hence, 'Lafa's farmstead'.

Leighton Bromswold

This township originally lay within the old County of Huntingdonshire and shortly after the Norman Conquest it was recorded as Lestona. By 1086 it had been recorded as Lectone, based on two old Saxon words, 'leac' and 'tun', together technically taken to mean 'leek farm', though probably describing a wider vegetable-growing farmstead. Some time in the thirteenth century, the Bruneswald affix was appended to the placename, the element 'wald' indicating a weald or woodland. It appears to have been an adjacent piece of land that belonged to a man called Brun. However, all trace of this separate connection has long since disappeared and both areas have become one and the same – as modern-day Leighton Bromswold.

Little Hautbois

On the face of it, Hautbois would seem to come directly from the Old French and translate as 'high wood'; however, many sources cite two Old English words as more likely: 'hobb', indicating a tussock or hummock, and 'wisc' or 'wisse', meaning 'marsh meadow'. Therefore, this last explanation might be interpreted as meaning 'marshy meadow with tussocks'. The 'Little' element of the placename was probably added as late as the mid-nineteenth century, to distinguish it from Great Hautbois, located some two miles away. Before Domesday the place was known as Hobbesse, and in 1086 as Hobuisse. In 1868 the village was known as Hautbois Parva.

Lowestoft

The placename Lowestoft is thought to come from a Dane called Lowe (sometimes Hlothver) who owned the land, and Old Norse word 'toft', meaning a settlement or village. Hence, 'Lowe's settlement'. Domesday records this Suffolk village as Lothuwistoft, held by Hugh de Montfort, tenanted by Roger Bigod, with one berewick and four carucates of land held by Earl Gyrth.

March

March is an ancient parish in the Isle of Ely district of Cambridgeshire and is currently the administrative centre of Fenland District Council. It was known and recorded as Merche and

Mercha at the time of the Domesday survey, the placename deriving from the Old English word 'mearc', meaning 'a place near or at the boundary or border'. Its meaning is very similar to its use in the Welsh Marches borderland between Shropshire and Wales.

Mark's Tey

Originally known as Tygan in the tenth century, this small village in Essex, gets its placename from the Old English word 'tiege', meaning 'enclosure'. Domesday recorded the place as Teia in 1086. In 1475, the manor was acquired by the de Merck family, who appended their family name to the place, when it was recorded as Merkys Teye. Their name distinguishes it from Little Tey and Great Tey, both lying a few miles away.

Meldreth

Meldreth is a Cambridgeshire village which was recorded in the *Domesday Book* as Melrede, a very large estate for its time in the Arringford Hundred, and held by several parties, including the Abbey of St Etheldreda of Ely, Hardwin of Scales, Count Alan of Brittany, Earl Roger of Shrewsbury and Guy de Raimbeaucourt. The placename come from the Old English words 'myln', meaning 'mill' and 'rith', meaning stream, which taken together produce a village name that translates as '[place by the] mill stream'.

Nazeing

The 'Naze' part of this Essex village placename is derived from the Old English word 'naess', which translates as 'promontory' or 'headland', and the last part comes from 'ingas', which referred to people, dwellers or followers. The name therefore translates as '[settlement of the] people who dwell on a promontory', referring to the village location overlooking the Lea Valley. In 1062, the place was known as Nassingan, and was recorded in 1086 as Nasinga, in the Waltham Hundred, part-held by Ranulf FitzIlger and the Canons of Holy Cross, Waltham, who along with several unnamed free men had held the manor before 1066.

Neatishead

In the years immediately preceding the Norman Conquest, this Norfolk village was known as Netheshird. The name comes from the Anglo-Saxon words 'geneat' and 'hired', which taken together respectively mean 'vassal's household'. Under the medieval feudal system a vassal would have been a subordinate person, a serf, or bondsman, who had obligations to the lord of the manor or to the monarch, often in menial tasks but also occasionally in military service. Clearly the French-speaking Norman Domesday commissioners found the name difficult to grasp and recorded the place in 1086 as Snateshirda, listing it within the Tunstead Hundred lands, held by the Abbey of St Benet of Holme, who had also had possession before the Conquest.

Newmarket

This Suffolk placename comes from its early Latin name, Novum Forum, as it was known by 1200, a name that translates directly as 'New Market'. It was not recorded in the survey of 1086 – it was the neighbouring village of Exning that had that distinction, recorded as Essellinge, after a man called Gyxen, and the Old English 'ingas', which together translates as the 'settlement of the family, followers or tribe of Gyxen'.

Norfolk

A county in eastern England, the name 'Norfolk' comes from two Saxon words, 'north', which is fairly self-explanatory, and 'folc', meaning 'folk' or 'people'. Hence, the county name means '[territory of the] northern people'. This distinguished them from the people of the south, in Suffolk. The northern people in question were the East Angles, a tribe who gave their name to East Anglia. Domesday recorded the county name as Nordfolc in 1086.

Norwich

The Norfolk township of Norwich began as the small Anglo-Saxon settlement of Northwic, on the north bank of the River Wensum. The settlement was subject to repeated Viking incursions, due in no small part to its exposed location on the North Sea coast; one such episode was recorded by the *Anglo-Saxon Chronicles* in 1004: 'Swein came with his fleet to Norwich, ravaged all the borough and burnt it down'. By the time of the Great Survey of 1086, it had been recorded as Noruic, Norwic and Norwici, from the Old English meaning 'north harbour'. It received no fewer than seven entries in the *Little Domesday Book*, as Noruic, Norwic and Norwici, listed under the Norwich Hundred, 'in the land of the king', where it notes a Frenchman, over eight hundred burgesses, around five hundred other households and six Englishmen and a priest. The account also recorded that at the time of King Edward, '...the town paid twenty pounds to the king ...and besides this twenty-one shillings and four pence [to certain] prebendaries, six sesters of honey, one bear and six dogs for the bear'.

Occold

Around 1050, this Suffolk village was recorded as Acholt, a name derived from two Old English words, 'ac', meaning 'oak tree', and 'holt', one of several names the Saxons used to denote a wood. Hence, '[place in the] oak tree wood'. Domesday listed the manor as Acolt, a very large estate in the Hartismere Hundred, with parts held in 1086 by Ralph de Limesy, Bishop Odo of Bayeux, Robert Malet, Hugh de Montfort and King William himself. Before 1066 a variety of Saxon men had possession of the estate, including at least twelve free men, Edric of Laxfield, a man called Bricthere and one Cyneric of Darmsden.

Offord Cluny

Originally known as Upeforde, this placename translates exactly as you might expect as 'upper ford (or river crossing)'. At the time of Domesday it was recorded as Opeforde, in the Toseland Hundred of the former County of Huntingdonshire. The Cluny affix was appended some time before the thirteenth century as it had come into the possession of Cluny Abbey in France, and in 1257 it was recorded as Offord Clunye. Part of the original Offord manor was divided at or around that same time and went to the de Dacy (or le Daneys) family, at which time that part of Offord was known as Offord Willelmi Daci.

Papworth Everard

Before the Norman Conquest, this East Anglian village was recorded simply as Pappawyrthe, after a man called Pappa, whose enclosure, or 'worth' it was. The survey of 1086 listed it as Papeuuorde (as there was no letter 'w' in the Norman French alphabet), and located it within the Papworth Hundred of Cambridgeshire, held by Picot of Cambridge. By the twelfth century, the manor was in the possession of as man called Evrard, who added his name to the place. Thereafter it was recorded as Pappewrth Everard, distinguishing it from the nearby village of Papworth St Agnes, whose manor was held at that time, not by the local church as one might have supposed, but by a woman called Agnes.

Peasenhall

Peasenhall in the County of Suffolk derives its placename from 'pisen', meaning 'peas' and 'halh', an element signifying a nook or corner of land. Hence, 'nook of land where peas grow'. In 1086, Domesday recorded the place as Pesehala, in the Blything Hundred, held at that time by Robert Malet and Roger Bigot (sometimes Bigod).

Peterborough

The ancient name given to Peterborough by Bede was Medeshanstede, after a man called Mede, who worked the land in Anglo-Saxon times, with the addition of the combined Old English words 'ham' and 'stede', indicating a dwelling with enclosed pasture, which taken together signified a farm or homestead. Hence, 'the homestead of Mede'. An alternative interpretation is that it translates more properly as 'Mede's well', and yet another explanation is that it might have derived from a Saxon word meaning 'whirlpool', possibly an occasional event on the nearby River Nene. From the time of the Norman Conquest it was known as Burg, meaning a stronghold or fortified township and later, following the foundation of an abbey dedicated to St Peter, as Burgh St Peter (or in its Latin form as Burgus Sancti Petri), before finally being known in the early fourteenth century as Petreburgh. It was listed in the *Domesday Book* in the County of Northamptonshire, but nowadays is located squarely in Cambridgeshire.

Pilgrims Hatch

This suburb of Brentwood in Essex derives its placename from a gate through which pilgrims passed to St Thomas's Chapel in the village. In Middle English the word 'pilegrim', meant 'pilgrim' and the Old English word 'haecc' signified a gate or hatch-gate. Hence, 'hatch-gate used by pilgrims'. The pilgrims in question would have been on their way to visit the twelfth century shrine of Thomas Beckett in Canterbury Cathedral. Until recently, a gate was also incorporated into the badge of local schools. The village name was recorded in 1483 as Pylgremeshacch.

Poringland

A Norfolk village named after its early settlers, probably called the Poringas, possibly the 'people of a man called Por', though this is an implied rather than a certain fact, as the Old English word 'ingas' refers to the people or followers, and sometimes of a tribe or family. The element 'land' usually referred to farmed or arable land. The placename may therefore be reasonably deduced as 'farmed arable land of the Poringas people'. The Great Survey of 1086 placed the manor in the Henstead Hundred, belonging to King William with Alnoth Grutt as its overlord, having been held by two Saxon free men before the Norman Conquest.

Potter Heigham

Before the Conquest, this village in Norfolk was simply known as Echam, and has two possible interpretations: either from the Old English 'hecg' or 'haecc', meaning either 'hedge' or 'hatch-gate', and either 'hamm' or 'ham', an enclosure or homestead. So the placename could mean either 'enclosure with a hedge', or 'hedge with a gate [or hatch]'. The 'Potter' element was added some time during the twelfth century, when the place was recorded as Hegham Pottere, a reference to the pottery or ceramics works that had been established there.

Potterspury

This Northamptonshire village was originally known simply as Perie at the time of the Domesday survey, a name derived from the Old English word 'pirige', meaning 'pear'. Hence it could be interpreted as '[place at the] pear tree'. At some point later, a pottery works was established and the prefix 'Potters' was added to the placename; in 1287, the name was recorded as Potterispirye.

Prittlewell

The name of this district in the Essex district of Southend-on-Sea means '[place by a] babbling stream'. The name began in Saxon times when 'pritol' meant 'babbling' or 'burbling', and 'wella', signified a stream, a well or a fountain. The stream or spring in question is thought to be that which still feeds the fishponds in Priory Park. Domesday identified the place as Pritteuuella, in the Rochford Hundred, held at that time by Swein of Essex, it having belonged to an unnamed Saxon free man before 1066.

Quendon

The placename of the Essex village of Quendon reflects the Old English word 'cwene', which means 'woman', but is related to the modern English word 'queen'. Added to this is the Saxon word 'denu', which signified a valley, and the placename works out as 'valley of the women'. The Great Survey listed it as Kuenadana, in the Hundred of Uttlesford, a small manorial estate held in 1086 by Eudo the Steward and tenanted by a man called Richard. The manor had been held by a Saxon called Ealdraed before the Conquest.

Rayleigh

The name derives from the Old English words 'raege', referring to a roe deer, and 'leah', a woodland clearing. Therefore, this Essex placename may be taken to mean a 'woodland clearing where roe deer live'. It is evident that the area was home to great numbers of deer, as in the sixteenth century, Henry VIII authorised the regular taking of deer stock from the region to replenish his own hunting grounds in Greenwich Park.

Rettendon

You might think that a village on a hill that was infested with rats might be a place to avoid, but that is the meaning of the placename of this Essex village. In Old English, 'raetten' meant 'rats' and 'dun' signified a hill. Perhaps such conditions were a fact of everyday life when the place was recorded as Rettendun around the first millennium. However, the manor of Ratenduna was still inhabited in 1086 when Domesday recorded it as a very large settlement supporting forty-five households in the Chelmsford Hundred of Essex, part-held at that time by Ranulf Peverel, Eudo the Steward and the Abbey of St Etheldreda in Ely, having been the property of Siward Barn, Leofson and Ely Abbey before the Norman Conquest.

Risby

Risby is a small village near Bury St Edmunds, which like many others in East Anglia bears the unmistakable imprint of Danish culture in its placename. The name is made up of two Old Scandinavian elements, 'hris', meaning 'brushwood' or 'gorse', and 'by', the word used by Danes for a village, settlement or farmstead. Hence, the name might mean 'farmstead or settlement among the brushwood'. It was recorded in 1086 as Risebi, in the Thingo Hundred of Suffolk, held by Roger de Poitou (sometimes Pictou or Potevin), with Archbishop Stigand of Canterbury as its overlord. Before 1066 it had belonged to Wulfmer.

Rishangles

The Suffolk village of Rishangles gets its original name from a combination of Scandinavian and Anglo-Saxon English, where 'hris' represented brushwood or gorseland, and 'hangra', a wooded slope. Therefore, the placename may be taken to mean '[place on a] wooded slope where brushwood grows'. Domesday recorded the village as Risangra, in the Hartismere Hundred, held in 1086 by Robert Malet, having belonged to Wulfeva of Thorndon and four unnamed free men before the Conquest.

Saffron Walden

Situated in the Upper Cam Valley in north-west Essex, Saffron Walden began as a small Roman garrison town near Cestreforda, now known as Great Chesterford. The Anglo-Saxons knew the settlement as Weala-denu, meaning 'valley of the Britons'. It was recorded as Wealadene in 1000 and as Waledana in 1086. The Middle English affix 'Safron' was added later to reflect the cultivation of saffron in the region and by the late-sixteenth century the township had begun to evolve into its present form as Saffornewalden. The local production of saffron established the township as a major supplier to the wider region of East Anglia. This highly prized and expensive commodity, derived from crocus stigmas, was used at that time in medicine and as a rare yellow dye.

Saham Toney
The Norfolk village of Saham Toney was originally known simply as Saham, a name derived from the Old English words 'sae', meaning 'pool' or 'pond', and 'ham', indicating a homestead, dwellings or a settlement. Hence, 'settlement by [or near] a pool'. The Great Survey identified the place as the very large Manor of Saham, in the Hundred of Wayland, part-held by King William and by Roger Bigot (sometimes Bigod), with a man called Robert as its chief tenant. Before 1066 it had been jointly owned by a Saxon free man, by King Edward and Earl Harold. Sometime in the twelfth century the manor and its estates came into the possession of the de Toni family, who appended their family name to the place. It was recorded under its present-day placename in 1498.

Sawtry
A Cambridgeshire village that was known as Saltreiam in the late-tenth century; its name means '[place by the] salty stream'. It comes from the Old English 'salt', whose meaning is self-evident, and 'rith', a stream, referring to the brackish water in the local stream that flows into the fens. Domesday recorded the village as Saltrede, in the Normancross Hundred (then in the former County of Huntingdonshire), part-held by the Abbey of St Benedict in Ramsey, Countess Judith of Lens, Eustace the Sheriff and Alwin (identified as 'the reeve's wife'). Before the Conquest it has been a joint-possession of St Benedict's Abbey, the aforementioned Alwin, Thorkil the Dane and Tosti (identified as 'brother of Erik').

Saxmundham
This Suffolk township is named after a Saxon called Saxmund, whose 'ham', or village settlement it was. In 1086, the place was listed as Sasmundeham, in the Plomesgate Hundred, held by Earl Roger Bigot (or Bigod), having been part-owned by at least ten Saxons before the Conquest, including men identified as Algar, Northmann the Sheriff and Wulfnoth, as well as seven other free men.

Scarning
According to its Anglo-Saxon name, this Norfolk village was a very dirty place. The Old English word 'scearn', referred to muck, mud or dung. Then the 'ing' element of the name implies an association of some kind; therefore the placename may be interpreted as 'dirty or muddy place', or 'place characterised by muck or mud', or something along those lines. Domesday recorded it as Scerninga, a very large manor in the Laundich Hundred with parts held by William de Warenne and Ralph Baynard; before 1066 it had belonged jointly to Archbishop Stigand, Fredegis of Scarning, Toki of Walton and an unnamed free man.

Scole
The Norfolk village of Scole had its origins at a time when East Anglia and much of England's east coast was part of the Danish-held territory known as Danelaw, and Old Scandinavian would have been a commonly heard language in the region. The name comes from the

Norse word 'skali', meaning 'temporary shed', 'shieling' or 'hut', of the type used to shelter animals that had been put out to pasture. Such sheds would have also provided overnight shelter for shepherds, a practice that survived well into the early twentieth century. In 1191, the placename was recorded as Escales.

Sea Palling

This Norfolk coastal village has a placename originally derived from a man called Paelli, who is likely to have been its chieftain or founder. The Old English 'ingas' element signified his family, tribe or followers, and the 'sea' element is self-explanatory. The placename may be interpreted as '[village of] Paelli's family (or followers) beside the sea'. Domesday listed the village simply as Pallinga. In the mid-nineteenth century it was recorded as Palling-near-the-Sea and by the late-nineteenth was known as Palling-next-the-Sea.

Shoeburyness

Shoeburyness is a district of Southend in the County of Essex whose placename somewhat improbably translates as 'promontory by a fortress providing shelter'. It derives from three Anglo-Saxon words: 'sceo', meaning 'shelter', 'burh', a stronghold or fortified place, and 'naess', a headland or promontory. The headland in question is at the northern side of the mouth of the Thames Estuary, and the fortress alluded to in the placename is thought to have been the remains of an ancient camp that once existed on the headland. By the tenth century the place was already known as Sceobyricg and by the time of the Great Survey it had been simplified to Soberia and Essoberia, listed in the Hundred of Rochford lands of Bishop Odo of Bayeux, which had been held in part before the Conquest by Robert FitzWymarc, but in 1086 parts held in demesne by Swein and valued at fifty-five shillings.

Sible Hedingham

Originally known and recorded as Hedringham in 1086, this Essex village placename comes either from the Old English word 'hythe', meaning 'jetty' or 'landing place' or from a man called Hytha – nobody is quite sure. The 'ingas' name element signifies 'the people or followers', and 'ham', means 'dwelling' or 'homestead'. Therefore, the placename could be interpreted as 'village of the people who live beside the landing place' or 'village of Hytha's people'. In 1231, the placename became Heyngham Sibille, after a woman called Sibil who inherited the manor, which over time derived its present name, Sible Hedingham. In the mid-thirteenth century the manorial estates were sub-divided and a second part became known by its Latin/Middle English name as Hengham as Castrum, or in modern English, Castle Edingham.

Snape

In Anglo-Saxon times, the word 'snaepe' signified a boggy or swampy plot of land, and this Suffolk village, is true to the word and lies in low land beside the River Alde. Domesday recorded the village name as Snapes and listed it as a very large estate for its time, supporting seventy households, which included twenty-one free men (who had held the entire manor before the Norman Conquest). It lay within the Plomesgate Hundred, held in 1086 by Robert Malet and valued at two pounds and one shilling. There is also a place in North Yorkshire of the same name.

Soham

The name of this Cambridgeshire township comes from the Anglo-Saxon word 'soeg' or 'sagt', meaning damp, soaked or drenched, in reference to its ancient watery landscape. The affix 'ham' indicates a village or homestead, hence the name means the 'damp (or wet) village'. The name is also reflected in the Icelandic word 'saggi', also meaning damp or moist. According to its entry in the *Little Domesday Book*, Soham was required to send 3,500 eels annually to feed the king's table, as well as fish three times every year.

Spaldwick

Any English placename ending in '-wick' invariably referred to a specialised farm or dwelling of some kind (e.g. a dairy or leek farm). In this respect the Cambridgeshire village of Spaldwick runs true to form. The first element of the placename comes from the Old English word 'spald', meaning 'ditch' or 'trench' and the second is from 'wic'. Therefore the entire placename may be taken to mean 'specialised farm near [or in] a ditch'. Domesday recorded it as Spalduice and Spalduic, listed in the Leightonstone Hundred of Huntingdonshire, held by Ely Cathedral who had also held it during the reign of King Edward.

Spexhall

The name of this small hamlet in Suffolk was recorded as Specteshale in 1197, and translates into modern English as 'corner of land where woodpeckers are seen (or heard)'. The word 'speoht' was the Saxon word for a woodpecker, and 'halh' referred to a small corner or a nook of land.

Stansted Mountfitchet

Stansted (or Stanstead) appears frequently as an English placename, including others like Stanstead Abbots in Hertfordshire, as well as places called Stanstead in Suffolk and Kent. The first part of this Essex placename comes from the Old English words 'stan', meaning 'stone' or 'stony', and 'stede' a place or location. Hence, '[settlement at a] stony place'. The Mountfitchet affix was applied to the estate in the twelfth century, when the Muntfichet family took possession.

Stilton

Famously known for its celebrated cheese the township of Stilton in Cambridgeshire was recorded in 1086 as Stichiltone, a name derived from the Old English 'stigel', meaning either a stile or steep incline, and 'tun', a village, farm or homestead. Hence, possibly, 'village by the stile'.

St Ives

St Ives in the County of Cambridgeshire has been inhabited since the Stone Age and was settled by the Romans in the first century. It was known to the Anglo-Saxons as Slepe, from an Old English word meaning a muddy or slippery place. This was on account of the frequent flooding of the low-lying landscape and the resultant silting up of the surrounding flood plain. In 1001, the stone coffin of St Ivo was reputedly discovered by a farmer in a ploughed field and the Priory of St Ivo was built on the spot. By 1110, the placename was known by its Latin name, *Sancto Ivo de Slepe* and became a site of pilgrimage. By the fourteenth century, the place had a shortened Latin name, Sancti Ivonis, before its eventual translation into the modern English name, St Ives.

Stock

The Old English word 'stoc' referred to an outlying or remote farmstead or settlement. Originally, this village in Essex was named after a man called Hereweard, and was known as Herewardestoc, or 'remote farm belonging to Hereweard'. His name was eventually dropped and Stock is what remains. The placename went through several variations over the years, including Herford Stoke in the late-fifteenth century, as Harrard Stock in 1608 and as Stoke alias Haverstocke in 1627.

Stonham Aspel/Earl Stonham/Little Stonham

Initially, these three contemporary villages were one single entity, recorded in 1040 simply as Stonham. The name comes from the Old English words 'stan', meaning 'stone' or 'stony', and 'ham', indicating a homestead or settlement. Hence, 'homestead on stony ground (or near a stone)'. In 1086, the place was entered in the survey as Stanham, in the Bosmere Hundred, held by Roger de Rames and overseen by Miled de Belefol, having belonged to Edric of Laxfield before the Conquest. The later affixes of Aspal and Earl were applied when the estate lands were separated and come into the possession of the de Aspale and the Bigod families.

Stowlangtoft

The Old English word 'stowe' represented a holy place, a shrine or a meeting place, and by the Middle Ages had come into common usage as the site of a church or a religious house of some kind. This Suffolk village placename is a typical example, and by the time of Domesday it was being recorded simply as Stou. Then, in the thirteenth century, the de Langetot family took possession of the manor and incorporated their family name into the placename, which became Stowelangetot. Later, the name developed into its present form of Stowlangtoft.

Stowmarket

In common with Stowlangtoft, the Old English prefix 'stow' indicated a holy place or a principal place of congregation. The addition of the word 'market' simply indicates that an important market was held there. Hence, the Suffolk township of Stowmarket, earlier known as Torneia, may be taken to mean a 'holy meeting place at a market'. By the time of the Great Survey, the place was known simply as Stowe, although some locals continued to call it Torneia (pronounced 'Thorney'), in the king's land of Stowe Hundred, sometimes referred to by the Latin name Stoe Mercatus, and the manor was held for King William by Roger Bigod (sometimes Bigot).

Sudbury

This ancient market town, in the Stour Valley of Suffolk, was known in Saxon times as Suthbyrig, which translates as 'southern stronghold (or borough)'. It appears in the *Anglo-Saxon Chronicles* in 798 as Suthberie, when Bishop Alfhun was recorded as dying in the town before being buried in Dunwich. By the time of Domesday, it was spelt Sutberia, located in the 'Hundred and a Half of Samford ... [in the] Land of Earl Morcar's Mother which William the Chamberlain and Otto the Goldsmith have custody of in the king's land'.

Suffolk

The eastern England county of Suffolk derived its name from Anglo-Saxon English, where 'suth' meant 'southern' and 'folc' meant 'people' or 'folk'. Hence, the county name may be taken to mean '[territory of the] southern people'. This distinguished them from the northern peoples of Norfolk. Both the northern and southern peoples in question were the East Angles, who gave their name to the region of East Anglia. In 895 the county name was spelt as Suthfolchi and by 1086 it had been recorded as Sudfulc.

Swaffham

This Norfolk town's placename is derived from the Swabians, the Anglo-Saxons who occupied the land after Roman withdrawal from Britain in the fifth century. In Old English, it was known as Swaefa ham, meaning 'the homestead or village of the Swabians'.

Swanton Morley

The Norfolk village of Swanton Morley was known in 1044 as Swane tonne, and by 1086 as Suanetuna, a name derived from the Old English 'swan', meaning 'herdsman', and 'tun', a farmstead. Hence, the placename means 'farmstead of the herdsmen'. Domesday places it as a very large village for the time, within the Laundich Hundred, and held by Ralph de Beaufour. Before the Conquest it had been held by Godwin and an unnamed free man. In the fourteenth century the de Morle family acquired the manor and appended their family name to distinguish it from other places of the same name, including the two other Norfolk villages of Swanton Abbot and Swanton Novers.

Teversham

This Cambridgeshire village placename may come from the Old English word 'tiefrere', which meant either 'painter' or 'sorcerer', or it was possibly the name of a man called Teofer, who may have founded the settlement. The additional suffix, 'ham', indicated a homestead or dwelling. Therefore, the placename means either 'homestead of the painter or sorcerer', or 'homestead belonging to Teofer'. Domesday recorded it four times, as Tueresham and Tevresham, quite a large estate for its time, supporting twenty-seven households in the Fleamdyke Hundred, part-held in 1086 by John (son of Waleran), Count Alan of Brittany and the Abbey of St Etheldreda in Ely. The abbey had retained its share of the manor since before the Conquest, but other parts had been held until 1066 by Edeva ('the Fair'), Earl Agar and Godwin ('the Noble').

Thaxted

The name of this Essex village comes from two Anglo-Saxon words, 'thaec', meaning 'thatch', and 'stede', a place. Hence, 'place where thatching materials are gathered', a reference to the profusion of reeds then found on the banks of the nearby River Chelmer. Domesday recorded the place as Tachesteda, a very large manor supporting over one hundred families in the Dunmow Hundred, held in 1086 by Richard FitzGilbert, having belonged to Wihtgar, the son of Aelfric, and an unnamed free man before the Conquest. The estate amounted to one hundred and fifty-four acres of meadow and woodland pannage for eight hundred and fifty pigs. Its population included fifty-four villans, thirty-four bordars, sixteen slaves and four free men. In 1086, its assets included two mills, four cob horses, thirty-six cattle, two hundred sheep and ten beehives, altogether valued at fifty-six pounds.

Thelnetham

This is a complicated placename in that its three Old English elements produce a placename that means 'enclosure where swans are seen near a plank bridge'. It comes from 'thel', meaning a 'plank' (a Saxon word which frequently referred to a wooden bridge), 'elfitu', a swan, and 'hamm', an enclosure. The plank bridge in question would have been across the Little Ouse river. In 1086, the village was recorded as Thelueteham, listed as a large estate supporting forty-two households (including three slaves), in the Blackburn Hundred of Suffolk, held at that time by Robert Malet, Frodo, the brother of Abbot Baldwin, and the Abbey of Bury St Edmunds. The Abbey had held part of the manor in 1066, shared with Acwulf and twenty-three unnamed free men.

Thorpe-le-Soken

This Essex village derives its placename from a time when the Danes held most of eastern England and the Old Norse language dominated the countryside. The word 'thorp', for example, is an Old Scandinavian term meaning 'outlying (or remote) village (or secondary settlement)', and together with the Old English word 'socn', which meant 'soke', a district with special jurisdiction (usually outside the control of the lord of the manor). This particular soke was formerly a Soke of Peterborough. The place was known in the twelfth century as Torp, and by the seventeenth had become known as Thorpe in ye Sooken.

Thundersley
The Old English affix 'leah' invariably referred to a woodland clearing, and this particular clearing in Essex was a sacred grove or glade which in ancient times was dedicated to the pagan god Thunor. Hence, 'Thunor's woodland glade'. The place was recorded as Thunreslea in 1086, listed as a very small manor supporting just twelve households, including two slaves, in the Barstable Hundred, held at that time by Swein of Essex having belonged to Godric before the Norman Conquest. At the time of Domesday the entire manorial estate was worth five pounds.

Tilbury
Tilbury was known as Tilaburg by 731, the name derived from a man called Tila, with the Old English suffix 'burh' added, signifying a stronghold. The placename may therefore mean 'Tila's stronghold'. By the time of the *Domesday Book*, it had been recorded as Tiliberia, in Barstable Hundred in land belonging to William de Warenne in Essex, held for him by Ranulf, having belonged before the Conquest to a Saxon called Sweting.

Titchwell
This ancient Norfolk settlement's placename reveals little of its meaning, as the Old English word 'ticce' actually signifies a young goat, or kid. Added to this is the 'wella' element, in reference to a well or a spring, and the placename can be interpreted as '[place where] young goats drink [at the well]'. It was known around 1035 as Ticeswelle, and by the time of Domesday as Tigeuuella, almost certainly because the letter 'w' does not exist in classic French (unlike in Anglo-Saxon), and the double-'u' may have been the only way that the survey commissions could represent the pronunciation. Whatever the vagaries of language, they listed it within the Docking Hundred, held by Roger Bigod (or Bigot), having been overseen by Earl Harold before the Norman Conquest.

Trunch
An extremely old placename harking back to Celtic origins, this village in Norfolk probably derives its placename from 'trum', meaning 'upland' or 'ridge', and 'coed' meaning 'wood' or 'woodland' (similar to the Welsh word of the same meaning). The name probably translates as 'woodland on a ridge'. This would fairly describe the village location on a plateau surrounded by valleys and woodland. Domesday listed the place as Trunchet, in the North Erpingham Hundred, held in 1086 by William de Warenne. By 1254 it had finally acquired its present placename as Trunch.

Tydd St Giles
The 'tydd' element of this Cambridgeshire placename probably comes directly from the Anglo-Saxon word for brushwood or shrubs, but could also be derived from 'titt', meaning 'teat', as used to describe a small hill or hillock. The place appended the dedication to the Church of St Giles in the village to distinguish it from Tydd St Mary in Lincolnshire, the latter being entered in Domesday simply as Tid.

Vange
The Basildon district of Vange in Essex began as a Saxon settlement which was called Fengge in the mid-tenth century; The name derives from the Old English words 'fenn', meaning 'marsh' or 'fenland' and 'ge', which meant 'district' or 'region'. Hence, '[place in a]

fenland (or marshy) district'. The marshland alluded to in the placename would have been Vange Marshes which were created by the creek that runs into the River Thames. Domesday recorded the place as Phenge, 'in Lands of the Bishop of Bayeux in Essex [in the] Hundred of Barstable [where] Ralph FitzTurold holds... Vange, which two [Saxon] free men held' before the Conquest.

Walsingham

The town of Walsingham, established on the banks of the River Stiffkey in Norfolk, was known as Walsingaham Parva at the time of the Norman Conquest; the placename derives from a person named Waels plus the two affixes, 'inga', signifying the followers, people or tribe, and 'ham', meaning homestead. Hence, 'Homestead of the people or followers of Waels.' The Parva suffix translates as little or small, in order to distinguish it from Walsingham Magna (meaning 'great') – both Little and Great Walsingham are now incorporated into a single entity.

Warboys

In 974, Archbishop Dunstan of Canterbury gave lands at what was then known as Wardebusc in the County of Cambridgeshire to Ramsey Abbey. The Warboys placename has two possible derivations; one is that it comes from 'weard', an Old English word meaning to watch or to keep watch (as in a sentry post), and 'busc', meaning a wood. Hence, possibly, 'a watch-post or lookout in a wood'. Alternatively, it may come from the name of a man called Wearda, in which case the placename translates as 'Wearda's wood'.

Wash, The

The Wash is a wide sea inlet that stretches across the coasts of the counties of Lincolnshire and Norfolk. Its name comes from the Old English word 'waesc', meaning 'sand banks washed by the sea'. It was originally an area of wetland that was fordable at low tides. The placename was recorded around 1545 as The Wasshes, and by the end of that century as Lincolne-Washes.

Watton

Watton is a village in Norfolk, whose placename reflects a man called Wada, its possible founder or chieftain, whose 'tun', or farmstead it once was. The name therefore means 'Wadda's farmstead'. The village was recorded in the Domesday Book as Wadetuna, in the Wayland Hundred, 'held by Ealdthryth (or Althryth), a free woman, at the time of King Edward...[and had] five carucates of land; now Ranulf FitzWalter holds it'. The tenant-in-chief was identified as Roger Bigot (or Bigod) at that time.

Wicken Bonhunt

This village in Essex has a complex placename that is made up of two separate names. The first is from 'wicken', a Middle English word meaning 'dwellings', and the second from the Old English 'bann', meaning 'to summons', and 'hunte', to hunt. All these elements taken together produce a meaning of 'place [or dwellings] whose people are summoned for hunting [or to the hunt]'. In 1086, the village was listed as Wicam, in the Hundred of Uttlesford, lands belonging to Gilbert FitzTurold. The survey recorded that 'Saxi, a free man, held Wicam at the time of King Edward as a manor and has three hides and thirteen acres'.

Wisbech

The Cambridgeshire settlement of Wisbech is the largest township in the Isle of Ely. The placename is thought to derive from two Saxon words, 'wisc', a meadow, and 'baec', meaning a river bank. Hence the 'meadow by the river bank'. A different interpretation of the first element is that it is derived from the River Wissey, whose name comes from Old English and means 'marshy stream or brook'. In 1086, it was known as Wisbece, according to Domesday, somewhat oddly recorded in 'So Far One Hundred. Now The Other', where twelve hides of land were held by the Abbot of Ely, 'who has soke over all the men of this vill'.

Wissett

In 1086, Domesday recorded this Suffolk village as Wisseta, a manor belonging to Count Alan of Brittany in the Hundred of Blything, and one of the 'Encroachments [or territories] of the King'. The original placename probably derived from a man called Witta, with the Old English suffix 'set', indicating an animal fold. Hence, 'Witta's fold'. The word 'sett' still survives as a place where badgers live.

Witham

The placename is a combination of the Brythonic Welsh word 'gwydd', meaning 'woods' and the Saxon suffix 'ham', indicating a township or settlement. Hence, 'the township in the woods.' An alternative suggestion is that it comes from the Old English 'wiht', signifying a bend in a river, in which case this Essex placename might be interpreted as 'homestead near a river bend'.

Wix

Wix is a derivation of the Middle English word Wikes, itself a plural form that comes from the Old English word 'wic', representing a specialised farm or dwelling (most typically a dairy farm). Domesday recorded the place as Wica and listed it in the Tendring District of Essex, part-held in 1086 by Hugh de Montfort and Walter (known as 'the Deacon'). In 1066, the manor had belonged in its entirety to Queen Edith of Wessex, the wife of King Edward.

Part Ten

The Home Counties

Bedfordshire, Berkshire, Buckinghamshire,
Hertfordshire, and Oxfordshire

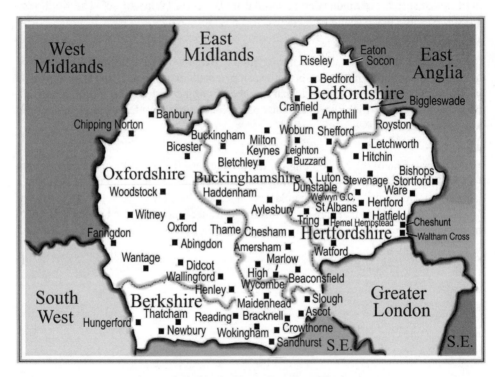

A map depicting the Home Counties of England.

Abingdon

The name is probably derived from a person called Abba, Aebba or Aebbe, who was one of its earliest settlers, with the addition of two Old English suffixes: 'inga', signifying the people, tribe or family, and 'dun', a hill. The placename may therefore be taken to mean 'the hill of Aebba's tribe or people'. Aebba was possibly the saint after whom St Ebbe's Church in Oxford was dedicated. Abingdon is actually located in a valley, not on a hill, prompting speculation that the township was moved when Abingdon Abbey was founded around 676. Reputedly, this was the first monastery to be established in Britain, though some argue that Glastonbury holds that distinction. King Edgar ('the Peaceable'), was educated at the abbey. In 989, a Saxon Parliament assembled at Abingdon, at which time it was known as Abbandune. Domesday spelt the placename as Bertune, locating it historically in the County of Berkshire, in the Homer Hundred, held by the abbey in 1086, and assessed before the Conquest at sixty hides – afterwards at just forty hides.

Aldermaston
The origin of this West Berkshire placename is derived from the Old English 'earldormann' (equivalent to a modern alderman), with the suffix 'tun' added. Hence, 'the alderman's estate or settlement'. It was recorded in the Great Survey of 1086 as 'the king's land of Aeldremanestone in the Theale Hundred', parts of which were held for him by various knights and nobles, including the Count of Evreux, Hugh Bolbec, Roger de Lacy, Robert d'Oilly, Bishop Osmund of Salisbury, Ralph Piercehedge, and many others, including several Saxon tenants.

Amersham
The placename is based on a man called Ealhmund, an early settler of the land, and the Old English suffix 'ham', signifying a homestead or settlement. Hence, the placename means 'homestead of Ealhmund'. It was recorded as Agmodesham in the County of Buckinghamshire in 1068 and held by Geoffrey de Mandeville for his master, Lord Bertram de Verdun, who was abroad on the king's service.

Amptill
The name of the Bedfordshire township of Amptill dates from Saxon times, when it was called Aemethyll, derived from the Old English word 'aenette', meaning 'ant', and 'hyll', a hill. Hence, the name means 'anthill', or 'ant infested hill'. The *Domesday Book* refers to it as Ammetelle, in the Redbornstoke Hundred, held by Nigel de la Vast for Nigel d'Aubigny. Before the Conquest, the manor had belonged to 'Alweard, a man of Aelfric, son of Goding', and was valued at four pounds.

Aspley Guise
The Old English word 'aespe' referred to the aspen tree, and the affix 'leah' meant 'woodland clearing'. In the mid-tenth century the placename was recorded as Aesplea. Hence, Aspley means 'woodland clearing where aspen trees grow'. The village entry in Domesday recorded it as Aspeleia, and listed it as quite a large estate supporting twenty-five households in the Manshead Hundred of Bedfordshire, held in 1086 by Hugh de Beauchamp, having been the property of Leofeva before the Norman Conquest. The manor came into the possession of the de Gyse family at some time in the thirteenth century, after which it became known as Aspeleye Gyse.

Aylesbury
Although the ancient Buckinghamshire settlement of Aylesbury is the site of an Iron Age hill fort dating from around 650 BC, it really began as a habitable township in Saxon times, when it was known as Aegelsburg. The name probably comes from an early settler called Aegel or Aegil, and the Old English suffix 'burh' or 'byrig', indicating a stronghold or fortified place. The placename may therefore be taken to mean 'Aegel's stronghold'. By 1086, it was known as Eilesberia, or Elesberie, in the Aylesbury Hundred, 'a demesne manor of the king, [which] has always been assessed as sixteen hides'. The *Domesday Book* also records a church within the estate lands, held by Bishop Remigius of Lincoln.

Ayot St Lawrence
In the years preceding the Norman invasion of England, this Hertfordshire village was known as Aiegete, the name coming from Aega, a man's personal name and the Old English word 'geat', meaning 'pass' or 'gap'. Hence, 'Aega's pass'. This pass was probably that which separated the village from Ayot St Peter a few miles south. Both villages had

dedications to their local church attached to their placename. Domesday listed the village as Aiete, in the Broadwater Hundred which appears to have been overseen and administered by a shire reeve.

Baldock
Tradition has it that the Hertfordshire village of Baldock was given its name by Knights Templar, who on returning from the Crusades around 1148, inexplicably called the place Baldoce (or Baldac), which was the Old French name for the Iraqi city of Baghdad. The place still has a thoroughfare called Templar Avenue.

Banbury
Banbury probably gets its name from a sixth century Saxon man called Banna, who built a fortified settlement, or 'burh', west of the River Cherwell in Oxfordshire. By the time of the *Domesday Book*, the place was known as Banesberie in the Dorchester Hundred, in land belonging to Bishop Remigius of Lincoln.

Barford St John
The Oxfordshire village of Barford was known simply as Bereford in 1086, the name derived from 'bere', meaning 'barley' and 'ford' or 'forda', a shallow river crossing. Hence, 'barley ford'. By the thirteenth century the name of the village church dedicated to St John was attached to the placename to distinguish it from the nearby village of Barford St Michael, at which time it was called by its Latin name, Bereford Sancti Johannes.

Barkway
The Old English word 'beorc' represented the birch tree, and this is the source of this Hertfordshire village placename. Add to this is the 'weg' element, meaning 'way', and the resultant placename literally means 'birch tree way'. This was a reference no doubt to a path or trackway that would have been lined with birch trees in Saxon times. The name was fully established before 1086, when it was recorded in typical Norman French as Bercheuuei, where there was no letter 'w', and the sound was phonetically spelt out as a double-'u', as it is still pronounced in modern English.

Barton-le-Clay
Barton is a common placename throughout England, with around twenty other townships bearing the title, deriving from the Old English 'bere-tun' or 'baer-tun', which translates as 'barley farmstead', a place where cereal crops were farmed or stored. The 'le-Clay' element of the name had appeared by 1536, when it was recorded as Barton-in-the-Clay in Bedfordshire, most probably to distinguish it from other places called Barton, and simply indicating that the township was built on a ridge of clay soil known locally as Gault Clay. Hence, the name may be loosely taken to mean 'the farm on clay soil where barley is grown or farmed'.

Beaconsfield
It's not too difficult to work out the meaning of the placename of the Buckinghamshire town of Beaconsfield – it derives its name from the Old English 'beacen', a signal or warning beacon, and 'feld', which in Anglo-Saxon times represented open land. The beacon in question stood on Beacon Hill at Penn, a few miles outside the present town. The modern English word 'field' clearly comes from this same source, with one essential difference. A 'field' is nowadays generally fenced or enclosed, but in Saxon times it referred to any form of open landscape, where forest or woodland had been cleared to create arable land. The placename should be properly interpreted as 'warning beacon in open land'. In 1184, the placename was recorded as Bekenesfelde.

Bedford

Bedford probably takes its name from Beda or Bieda, a Saxon chieftain who founded a settlement at a ford on the River Great Ouse. By the ninth century, the settlement was known as Bedanforde, which may be translated as meaning 'the ford belonging to Beda', or 'Beda's ford'. The Saxon King Offa of Mercia was buried in the town in 796.

Berkhamstead

This Hertfordshire township probably began as a dwelling or settlement founded by a man called Beorc, Beorth or Beorg. Added to his personal name are two Saxon suffixes; 'ham', indicating a village or a homestead, and 'stede', a dwelling or site of a building. We may confidently conclude therefore that Beorg had a dwelling in the settlement that was known by the tenth century as Beorthansteaedae. Domesday recorded it as Berchamstede and Berchehamstaed in 1086, listed in the Tring Hundred where some thirteen hides of land were held by the Count of Mortain. The account recorded: 'There six slaves and a certain ditchers have half a hide, and Ranulf, a sergeant of the Count, one virgate'.

Berkshire

The County of Berkshire is one of the few English counties not to be named after its county town, but is derived from a different source altogether. The first element of the name comes from a Celtic word, similar to the modern Irish Gaelic word 'barr', meaning 'hill', and the last element is from the Old English word 'scir', meaning 'district'. Hence, the county name may be interpreted as 'district in a hilly place'. It was known in 893 as Berrocscire, One of the 'hilly places' referred to might be that near Hungerford which was recorded as Berroc in the ninth century.

Bicester

This ancient Oxfordshire settlement is located on the ancient boundary between Saxon Mercia and Danelaw, and a fortified frontier guard post was built there. This is reflected in the placename, which means either 'Beorna's fort' or the 'fort of warriors'. The Old English word 'beorn' means 'warrior', but it may also have been the personal name of the man who built the fort. The suffix 'ceaster' indicated the site of a Roman military garrison. An alternative view is that Bi-cester means 'two forts', a possible reference to an earlier Roman fort and a second built in Saxon times. In the 1086 survey, it was known as 'Bernecestre, in Pyrton Hundred', and was in the possession of the Norman knight, Robert d'Oilly, who built Oxford Castle.

Biggleswade

The placename evolved as a ford across the river, probably owned by a Saxon called Biccel, Biceil or Biggel, and the Old English word 'waed', a shallow place where the river could be 'waded' across. The placename therefore means 'Biccel's ford'. The *Domesday Book* has it as Pichelesuuade, in the Biggleswade Hundred, made up of four small manors covering about nine hundred acres of Bedfordshire. By 1132, it was known as Bicheleswada.

Bisham

Bisham is a village in the Parish and Borough of Windsor in Berkshire, whose placename comes from a man called Byssel, who may have been its earliest known settler or founder. The second element of the placename could come from either the Old English word 'ham', indicating a dwelling or a homestead, or from 'hamm', an enclosure, possibly for animals. So, the name means either 'Byssel's village (or homestead)', or 'Byssel's enclosure'. Either are equally possible. In 1086, the village was recorded as Bistesham, in the Beynhurst Hundred lands of Henri de Ferrers, it having been held by Bondi at the time of King Edward.

Bishop's Stortford

Originally, known simply as Stortford, located on Stane Street, a major Roman road between London and Colchester, the name of this Hertfordshire settlement may have arisen from the personal name of a man called Steorta, which itself comes from an Old English word, 'steort', which translates as 'tongue', but in this instance probably referring to a spur or finger of land. Hence, either 'Steorta's ford', or 'ford at the spur of land'. Steorta may have been the leader or head of a small clan who lived near a ford in Saxon times and who controlled the crossing. Following the Conquest, King William gave the 'Mainou of Storteforde' to William, Bishop of London and consequently the 'Bishop's' affix was added to the placename. Stortford remained in possession of the London bishops until 1868.

Black Bourton

The Bourton element of this Oxfordshire placename comes from the two Old English words 'burh' and 'tun', which taken together respectively mean 'fortified homestead'. Bourton is a relatively common English placename element and exists in townships like Bourton-on-the-Water in Gloucestershire, Flax Bourton in North Somerset and the village of Bourton in Dorset. Black was appended to the placename when Augustinian canons, known as 'Black Canons', established Osney Abbey in the village in 1129; later the abbey became Osney Cathedral.

Bladon

Bladon was the old name for the river that flowed through the settlement of Bladon, and it is from this that the Oxfordshire village derived its placename, though the river is now known as the River Evenlode. The origin of the river name is most obscure due to its prehistoric age. Evenlode is a village in Gloucestershire in its own right, and comes from a man called Eowla, and the Old English word 'gelad', indicating a river crossing. Hence, 'Eowla's river crossing'. In 1086, Bladon was recorded as Blade, in the Lewknor Hundred land of the Bishop of Bayeux.

Bracknell

The Berkshire placename Bracknell derives from a man by the name of Bracca, and the Old English word 'halh', meaning a corner or nook of land. Hence, possibly, 'nook of land belonging to Bracca'. Alternatively, it may simply refer to a corner of land covered with bracken.

Bray

The village of Bray lies within the Berkshire district of Windsor & Maidenhead and comes either from the Old English word 'braye', meaning 'marsh', or from the Old French 'brai', meaning 'mud' – either is possible as they produce a similar placename, meaning 'marshy [or muddy] place'. Domesday recorded the place as Brai, Braio and Bras, listed in the Bray Hundred and held in demesne by King William as it had been during the reign of King Edward. The account recorded that '...there are eighteen hides and they did not pay geld', that is, not liable for rent or taxation. The estate supported fifty-six villans, seven bordars, four slaves and three knights. It amounted to fifty acres of meadow and woodland pannage for sixty pigs. It was all valued at seventeen pounds.

Brickhill/Great Brickhill

Brickhill's placename stems initially from Celtic roots, and is closely related to the Welsh word 'brig', meaning 'top' or 'summit', with an Old English word 'hyll', meaning 'hill' attached. This produces a name meaning 'hilltop' or 'hill summit'. The Great Survey of

1086 identified the village simply as Brichelle and Brichella, in the Bunsty Hundred of Buckinghamshire, belonging to Bishop Odo of Bayeux, where Turstin rented one hide. The first word of the placename, 'Great', distinguishes it from the nearby villages of Little Brickhill and Bow Brickhill. By the end of the twelfth century it was known by its Latin name of Magna Brikehille, meaning 'greater [place at the] summit of a hill'.

Brill

This Buckinghamshire village has a placename dating back to pre-Roman times, and is based upon the Celtic word 'bre' or 'brez', meaning hill, and also 'Bre' the name they gave to this hill. Later, the Saxons added 'hyll' to the word, (as if it were required), to produce a name that technically means 'hill-hill'. By the time of the Norman Conquest the place was known as Bruhells and in 1086 the survey recorded the place as Brunhelle.

Brize Norton

This Oxfordshire village was known simply as Nortone in Saxon times, and meant 'northern settlement, village or farmstead'. Then it came into the possession of one William le Brun at the start of the thirteenth century so that by 1266, the placename was recorded as Northone Brun, reflecting his family's ownership. Even later, the village church, dedicated to St Britius, probably gave its name to the village, which over time was corrupted to 'Brize'.

Broughton Poggs

There are around eighteen other villages and townships in England called Broughton. The name comes from the Old English words 'broc' and 'tun', which taken together mean 'farmstead beside or by a brook'. Domesday listed the village as Brotone, in the Bampton Hundred of Oxfordshire in the lands of Robert FitzMurdoch in 1086, it having been held by three unnamed Saxon free men before the Conquest. Some time before the late fifteenth or early sixteenth century, the manor came into the possession of the de Pugey family, who affixed their family name so that in 1526 the place was recorded as Broughton Pouges, which eventually became Broughton Poggs, which translates as 'farmstead by a brook belonging to the de Pugeys'.

Buckingham

The countryside surrounding Buckingham has been occupied since the Stone Age, with evidence of an Iron Age settlement. However, the township of Buckingham as we know it began in the seventh century, when immigrants arrived from the near continent and established a settlement near a bend in the Great Ouse river. Tradition has it that their leader was probably a man called Bucca. The additional Old English affixes of 'inga' and 'ham' respectively signify 'the people, tribe or family', and 'river bend'. Therefore, the placename translates loosely as 'land of Bucca's family at the river bend', though some accounts have it as meaning 'the meadow of Bucca's people'.

Bucklebury

In common with all the other English placenames ending in '-bury', '-burg' or '-borough' (which are derived from the Old English word 'burh'), Bucklebury was at some point in its early history a fortified stronghold or manor house. The first element of the placename identifies its earliest known settler, or a female founder (rare for that time), a woman called Burghild. Hence, 'Burghild's stronghold'. In 1086, this West Berkshire village was recorded as Borgeldeberie, a very large manor of fifty households in the Bucklebury Hundred, parts held by King William, by the Count of Evreux, by Walter FitzOther and by Hugolin (called 'the Steersman').

Buntingford

First recorded as Buntas Ford and Buntingeford in 1185, according to some accounts, the name comes from the Middle English 'bunting', referring to the bird, and 'ford', a shallow river crossing. Therefore, according to this version, the name would translate as the 'ford where buntings (or yellow hammers) are found'. An alternative view is that it does not relate to a bird at all, but to a Saxon chieftain called Bunta, and refers to the river crossing which his people controlled.

Burnham

This Buckinghamshire placename has a simple derivation, coming from the Old English words 'burna', meaning a stream (the word 'burn' is still widely used in Scotland in reference to a stream), and 'ham', indicating a farm or homestead. Hence 'homestead near a stream'.

Chalfont St Giles/Chalfont St Peter

Initially, the Buckinghamshire village of Chalfont would have been a single entity, whose name comes directly from Old English as 'cealf', meaning 'calf', and 'funta', a spring (or font). Hence '[place where] calves drink'. Domesday recorded the place as Celfunte, in the Burnham Hundred, part-held by Mainou the Breton and by Bishop Odo of Bayeux in 1086. Then sometime shortly before 1237, the village was divided with one part adding the name of the local church dedicated to St Giles and known thereafter by its Latin name as Chalfund Sancti Egidii, while the other, some two miles away, was named after the Church of St Peter as Chalfunte Sancti Petri. Hence, the two placename respectively mean '[place by the] Church of St Giles where calves drink', and '[place by the] Church of St Peter where calves drink'.

Charlton-on-Otmoor

The name 'Charlton' comes from the Old English 'ceorl', which meant 'free man', who, though still a fairly low class of peasant, was not bonded like a serf or a slave in medieval England. Therefore 'Charlton' signified a 'tun', or farmstead occupied by free men. The second part of the placename locates it on Ot Moor, marshy ground in Oxfordshire that once belonged to a man called Otta. Hence, 'Otta's moor'. Domesday recorded the village simply as Cerlentone in 1086, but by the early fourteenth century it was being called Cherlton upon Ottemour. In 1868 the name was recorded as Charlton-upon-Otmoor. Soon thereafter the 'upon' was contracted to 'on' and its present-day placename was in place.

Chenies

Until the late twelfth century, this Buckinghamshire village was known as Isenhamstede, after a Saxon called Isa (or Ysa) who owned the village or homestead ('hame-stede' in Old English). The placename actually meant 'Isa's homestead'. Then in the thirteenth century, the estate came into the possession of the Cheyne family, and it was renamed Ysenamstud Cheyne before being finally reduced to Cheynes in 1536.

Chesham

This village in Buckinghamshire was recorded as Caestaeleshamme in 1012, derived from the Old English 'ceastel', signifying a heap or pile of stones (sometimes known as a cairn), and 'hamm', meaning a river meadow or flood plain. Hence, 'river meadow by a heap of stones'. Domesday records Cestreham, in Burnham Hundred, part-held by Bishop Odo of Bayeux, of which one and a half hides had been previously held by Saxon Earls, Leofwine and Harold, four hides held for the king by Alsige, half a hide held by Turstin (or Toustain) Mantel, as well as the eight and a half hides in the possession of Hugh de Bolbec.

Cheshunt

At the time of Edward the Confessor, the original Manor of Cheshunt in Hertfordshire had belonged to his wife, Queen Edith (also referred to as Eddeva the Fair, Edith Swan-Neck and Edyth the Gentle Swan). The placename probably comes from two Old English source words, 'ceaster', signifying a stronghold or former Roman fort, and 'funta', a spring, which taken together mean 'the spring by the Roman fort'. By 1086, it had become known and recorded as Cestrehunt or Cestrehont, in Hertford Hundred, and included the Berewick of Hoddesdon, held by William the Conqueror's nephew, Count Alan Penthievre of Brittany (also known as Alan Rufus, Alain le Roux and Alan the Red).

Chiltern Hills

Often shortened to 'the Chilterns', this range of hills stretches across Buckinghamshire and Oxfordshire and probably received its name from the Celts, whose word 'cilte' or 'celte' meant 'hill slope'. In the early part of the eleventh century the range was known as Ciltern.

Chipping Norton

Norton is a common name throughout England, simply meaning 'northern settlement' or 'north town'. The 'Chipping' element of the placename came much later and was first recorded in the early thirteenth century as Chepingnorthona, from the Old English word 'ceping', signifying a market, distinguishing it from all other places of that name. A royal charter was granted for the market in 1244 and the full name of Chipping Norton dates from that time.

Codicote

This village in Hertfordshire was known in 1002 as Cutheringcoton. The name comprises three separate elements: the first referred to a man called Cuthhere, the second is an Old English word element 'ingas', meaning 'people, followers or tribe', and the third is 'cot', signifying cottages. Together they produced a placename that meant 'cottages of the people or followers of Cuthhere'. By the time of the Domesday survey, the Norman commissioners had contracted the placename to Codicote, and listed it in the Broadwater Hundred, held by the Abbey of St Albans. The survey recorded that 'Codicote and Oxwyce (Oxwick) were two manors at the time of King Edward, and now they are one'.

Cranfield

One of the earliest written references to the Bedfordshire township of Cranfield is in 969, when Cranfeldinga is recorded as a place on the boundary with Nottinghamshire. Some time before 998, the Manor of Cranfield was given to the Abbott of St Benedict of Ramsey Abbey. By 1060, the place had been recorded as Crangfeldae, and by 1086 as Cranfelle. The Old English words 'cran' and 'cranuc', signify a crane or a heron. Hence the placename translates as a 'field [or land] where cranes are found'.

Cuffley

The village of Cuffley, in the Welwyn-Hatfield district of Hertfordshire, was at one time part of the Manor of Northaw, which had been granted to the Abbey at St Albans in 793. In the survey of 1086 it was held by the Valognes family. The placename was based on a man called Cuffa, it earliest known settler or founder, and the Saxon word 'leah', signifying a woodland glade or a clearing. Hence, 'Cuffa's woodland clearing'. The village was recorded as Kuffele in 1255.

Cumnor

Cumnor is an Oxfordshire village that earlier lay within the County of Berkshire and was probably once a possession of a man called Cuma. It was known in 931 as Cumanoran, and translates from the Old English as 'Cuma's hill-slope'. The 'ora' element refers to a sloping hillside, which fits in with the local landscape, part of the extensive Midvale Ridge that drops gradually down towards the River Thames. Domesday identified the place as Comenore, in the Hundred of Hormer, held as a possession of the Abbey of St Mary's in Abingdon, as it had been before the Conquest.

Dacorum
Dacorum was the word commonly used in medieval England for the Danes, and meant '[the] hundred belonging to the Danes'. It referred to the Anglo-Saxon side of Watling Street, which was under Danish control. On the other side of the old Roman road was the Danish territory known as Danelaw. Nowadays Dacorum is a Hertfordshire council district. It was known at the time of the *Domesday Book* as Danais, and by the late twelfth century it had been recorded as Hundredo Dacorum.

Didcot
Didcot really began as a Saxon settlement some time in the seventh century, though archaeological evidence shows earlier traces of Iron Age and Bronze Age occupation in this region of Oxfordshire. The Anglo-Saxons knew the place as Wibaldeston, probably after an early settler called Wibald (or Wigbald) and the Old English suffix 'tun', indicating a farmstead or settlement. Hence, the placename meant 'Wibald's farm or settlement'. The present-day placename was recorded in 1206 as Dudecota, meaning 'Dudda's cottage'.

Dunstable
The Bedfordshire town of Dunstable was not mentioned in the *Domesday Book*, though it was probably included at that time in the royal estate of Houghton Regis. The settlement owes much of its medieval development to its strategic location at the crossing of two ancient roads; the old Roman military road of Watling Street and the even older ancient British road known as Ickneild Way. The area seems to have been otherwise an uncultivated area of open land and woodland, of little material value. Despite this, in 1109, Henry I had the woods cut down to protect travellers from what had been a notorious place for robbers and brigands. He also had a royal residence built there as a base for hunting in 1123. There is a suggestion that this gives a clue as to the origin of the placename, based on a local man called Dun, who is thought to have been a notorious robber and highwayman. Tradition has it that Dun defied the king and fixed a pole barrier and a ring on the highway by means of a staple driven into the ground, daring anyone to remove it. Hence, 'Dun's staple'. In the event, Dun was apprehended and hanged for his crimes, though he has the everlasting distinction of being recorded as a placename.

Elstree
In 785, this Hertfordshire village was known a Tithulfe's Treow, in the possession of a man called Tidwulf, whose name was corrupted over time to form the first element of the placename. The second element 'treow' is an Old English word meaning 'tree'. Hence '[place near] Tidwulf's tree'. The changing spellings of the name was marked over succeeding centuries: as Tidulvestre in 1188, as Idelestre in 1320, and as Elstre in 1598. It was not until the mid-nineteenth century that the place was finally called Elstree, though some still referred to the place as Idlestree.

Enborne
English placenames ending in '-borne' or '-bourne' invariably signify a stream or a brook, as the Anglo-Saxon word 'burna' always signified such a watercourse. In this respect the

village of Enborne in West Berkshire runs true to form. The first element of the name comes from the Old English 'ened', meaning 'duck' (as in the common water fowl). Taken together, these two elements produce a placename that means '[place by a] stream where ducks are seen'. The stream in question flows into the River Kennet nearby. Domesday listed it four times, as Aneborne and as Taneburne, a very large estate supporting forty households in the Kintbury Hundred. In 1086, the manor was part-owned by William Lovet, Roger de Lacy, Giles (the brother of Ansculf), and William FitzCorbucion. Before the Conquest, the estate lands had been jointly owned by Saxons called Tovi of Donnington, Edmund of Childrey and King Edward.

Faringdon
The Oxfordshire township of Faringdon (or more properly, Great Faringdon), in the Vale of the White Horse, was held by Harold Godwinson before the Conquest and assessed at thirty hides. The placename comes from the Anglo-Saxon words 'fearn', meaning a fern, and the suffix 'dun', referring to a hill. The placename may therefore be taken to mean a 'hill covered with ferns'. It was known in late tenth century as Faernedunae, and by 1086 as Ferenedone, which Domesday records as held in demesne in the king's lands in Wyfold Hundred.

Farnborough
This township in West Berkshire was known in the tenth century as Fearnbeorgan, from the Anglo-Saxon words 'fearn', meaning a fern, and 'beorg', signifying a hill or mound. The placename translates loosely as 'hill covered with ferns'. In 916, before the Conquest, Eadric (or Edric) and his descendants had been granted the manor by Aethelflaed, the Lady of Mercia. By 1086, it was recorded as Fermeberge, in Nakedthorn Hundred, held as the avowson of the Abbey and Church of Abingdon.

Fawley
Fawley's placename comes from two old words: 'fealu' (or 'fealg') and 'leah'. Together they produce a name that translates into modern English as 'fallow woodland clearing'. This often referred to woodland which had been cleared and ploughed to produce arable land. In 1086, Fawley was recorded as Falelie in the Desborough Hundred of Buckinghamshire and its estates sustained nineteen households (which included five slaves). There was sufficient land for two men's plough teams, it had four acres of meadow and a church. The manor was held by Walter Giffard at that time, having belonged to Earl Tostig before the Conquest.

Flitwick
The origin of this Bedfordshire placename is uncertain, though the 'wick' element derives from the Old English word 'wic', which signifies a farm, hamlet or homestead. It may be loosely taken to mean 'the hamlet or farm on the River Flitt'. There has also been suggested that the 'Flitt' element of the placename may have derived from the old word 'floet', simply meaning 'river'.

Gawcott
In 1086, this Buckinghamshire village was known as Chauescote and Gauecota, and was recorded in the Rowley Hundred, held at that time by the Bishop of St Mary's Church in Lincoln, who had held it long before the Norman Conquest. The placename is made up of two Saxon elements, 'gafol', meaning 'rent' or 'dues', and 'cot', a cottage or similar dwelling. Hence, 'cottage(s) for which rent is paid'.

Gerrards Cross

The South Buckinghamshire village of Gerrards Cross is located three miles east of Beaconsfield and did not exist as such until 1859, when a new ecclesiastical parish was created from parts of five other parishes; Chalfont St Peter, Fulmer, Iver, Langley Marsh and Upton. The placename comes from the Gerrard family who owned a manor in the district in the seventeenth century. Before their occupation, the place was known as Jarrett's Cross, which according to tradition was named after an infamous highwayman who frequented the area.

Goring

The village of Goring in Oxfordshire derives its placename from a man called Gara, who may have been the founder of the original settlement or an early chieftain, with the Old English affix 'ingas', signifying his people, family or followers. Hence, '[settlement belonging to] Gara's people'. The village entry in the *Domesday Book* was as Garinges, listed in the Langtree Hundred, held in 1086 by Robert d'Oilly having belonged to Wigot of Wallingford before the Conquest. There is another place of the same name in West Sussex.

Haddenham

The Buckinghamshire Parish of Haddenham is located in the Vale of Aylesbury, bordered on three sides by the River Thame, Dad Brook and Ford Brook. The placename is derived from the Saxon words 'haeda' and 'ham', together meaning 'homestead village'.

Hailey

This Oxfordshire village has a placename that means 'woodland clearing where hay is made'. It is derived from two old Saxon words, 'heg' and 'leah', which respectively refer to hay and a woodland clearing. The place was recorded as Haylegh in 1241. There is a village of the same name in Hertfordshire.

Hambleden

The word 'hamel' is Old English for 'broken' or 'crooked', and 'denu', meant 'valley'. This village in Buckinghamshire combines both in its placename, which translates into modern English as '[place in the] crooked valley'. It is thought to be a reference to the sharp bend in the valley at the village of Fingest in the Chiltern Hills. The place was known before the Conquest as Hamelan Dene, and by the time of Domesday it was recorded as Hanbledene, listed as an extremely large settlement for its day, supporting sixty-eight households, (including nine slaves), in the Desborough Hundred. The manor was held by Queen Matilda, the wife of King William, having been in the possession of Earl Algar before the Conquest.

Hampden

Hampden in the County of Buckinghamshire is a name that comes from the Old English words, 'hamm', signifying an enclosure, and 'denu', meaning 'valley'. The complete placename means 'valley with an enclosure'. It was recorded as Hamdena in 1086, listed within the Hundred of Aylesbury, held at that time by William FitzAnsculf, having been the property of Baldwin, the son of Herlewin in 1066. Later, the word 'Great' was attached to the placename, to distinguish it from nearby Little Hampden.

Hanslope

The name of this village in the Milton Keynes region of Buckinghamshire was recorded as Hamslape in 1086, a name that comes from the personal name of a man called Hamma together with the Old English word 'slaep', meaning 'slippery (or muddy) slope'. Hence, 'Hamma's slippery place'. Domesday listed the village in the Bunsty Hundred, held by Winemar of Flanders, it having previously belonged to a Saxon called Healfdene.

Hardmead
This is a Buckinghamshire village whose placename is derived from a man called either Heoruwulf or Herewulf, who possessed a meadow (or as the Saxons called it a 'maed'), way back in Anglo-Saxon times, and whose name forms the first element of the village name. The earliest known written record of the name was as Herulfmede in 1086, when it was listed in the Great Survey as a very large manor in the Moulsoe Hundred. The estate supported thirty-six families, and had a small meadow and woodland. It was held by Hugh de Bolbec and valued at one shilling.

Harpenden
This place in Hertfordshire was known before the Norman Conquest as Herpedene, and some think it translates as 'valley of the harp', from the Old English words 'hearpe', a harp, and 'denu' a valley. A somewhat fanciful explanation of this translation is that a local stream bubbled away so melodiously that it resembled the sound of a harp. Others maintain quite a different and more pragmatic explanation, where 'here-paeth' translates as highway or military road (a possible reference to the Roman road known as Watling Street), in which case the placename might be interpreted as 'military highway [through a] valley'.

Harrold
A village whose placename was not derived from a man's name as it might first appear, but from two Saxon words, 'har', signifying a boundary, and 'weald', high forest-land. Taken together these produce a name that may be interpreted as 'high forest-land near a boundary'. The high forest-land in question is rising ground above the valley of the River Ouse and the boundary is the place where the three counties of Bedfordshire, Buckinghamshire and Northamptonshire meet. The place was entered in the *Domesday Book* as Hareuuelle, located within the Hundred of Willy and in the possession of Countess Judith of Lens, having previously belonged to three unnamed thegns. In 1163, the placename was recorded as Harewolda.

Hazlemere
Little is actually known of the early history and it gets no mention in the Domesday survey of 1086, but by the thirteenth century, it had been recorded as Heselmere. The placename derives from the Old English 'haesel', meaning 'hazel' (as in the tree), and 'mere' a pool or small lake. Hence, 'a pool where hazel trees grow'.

Hemel Hempstead
There is an opinion that the first element of this Hertfordshire placename is from 'hamel', an old eighth century word meaning 'broken', and the Old English 'ham' and 'stede', signifying a place or a pasture - a corruption of the word 'homestead'. Hence it may be loosely taken to mean 'broken homestead' or possibly 'broken country'. An alternative view is that it derives from the German word 'Himmel' or the Dutch 'Hemel', both of which mean 'heaven'. Another cites 'Haemele', which was the name of the man who owned this district in the eighth century, in which case the placename means 'Haemele's homestead'. We may never known which is the actual source of the placename. In 1086, the settlement was recorded in the *Domesday Book* as Hamelamestede.

Henley-on-Thames
The earliest record of the township of Henley in the Chiltern Hills of south Oxfordshire dates from some time around 1140, when King Stephen is thought to have granted a charter for Henleiam. The name derives from two Old English words, 'heah', meaning 'high', and 'leah', a woodland clearing. This reflected the plentiful waterside meadows and upland pasture of

the region at that time. The 'Thames' affix came later to distinguish it from other places of that name (e.g. Henley-in-Arden in Warwickshire). The ancient name of the River Thames itself was known as early as 51 BC as Tamesis, probably a Latinised version derived from the Celtic 'tam', meaning dark, or the even earlier word 'ta', indicating 'turbulent flowing'.

Henlow

At the time of Domesday, the Manor of Henlow in Bedfordshire was held by Nigel d'Albini, after which it became known as Henlow Lanthony. The placename is of Old English origin, deriving from the word 'henn', a hen or other poultry bird, and 'hlaw', signifying a hill or mound. Hence, it means 'the hill where hens are found'. In the 1086 survey, it was recorded as Heneslau or Hanslaue, in Clifton Hundred, where d'Albini personally held five and a half hides of land, tenanted on his behalf by Erfast, of which three virgates were leased as almsland to the Abbey of St Nicholas in Angers, France.

Hertford

The Saxon township of Hertford, located at a crossing of the River Lea, was recorded as Herutford in Bede's *Ecclesiastical History of the English People* in 731. The placename comes from two simple Old English words, signifying a ford, or shallow river crossing, where harts, deer or stags are found.

Highnam

The Old English word 'higna' specifically referred to a religious community, and the affix 'hamm' signified a riverside meadow. Therefore the placename of this Gloucestershire village may be taken to mean '[place by the] riverside meadow belonging to a religious community [or monks]'. The monks referred to were those of the Abbey of St Peter in Gloucester, who owned the manorial estate. In 1086, the place was recorded as Hamme in the Langebrige Hundred, and by the twelfth century it had become Hinehamme.

High Wycombe

Although there are traces of earlier occupation, Wycombe was established in the second century when the Romans built a villa on the River Rye in Buckinghamshire. It was known as Wichama by the eighth century and Wicumun by the end of the tenth century. The placename is derived from the plural form of the Old English word 'wic', meaning a dwelling place or settlement, and 'cumb', a valley. The placename is commonly held to mean 'dwellings by a stream or in a valley'. By 1068, it was recorded as Wicumbe, in Desborough Hundred, held by Robert d'Oilly (sometimes d'Oyley, Doyley or de Oilgi), and assessed at ten hides.

Hinton Waldrist

Many places in England include Hinton in their placename, with at least a dozen on record. The word comes from the Old English meaning 'high farmstead'. Domesday listed Hentone in the Gainfield Hundred of Oxfordshire, held in 1086 by Odo of Winchester. Before 1066 the manor had belonged jointly to Wulfwynn of Creslow and two unnamed Saxon thegns. At some time in the twelfth century, the 'Mainou of Hentone' came into the possession of the de Sancto Walerico family, who attached their family name to the place. By the seventeenth century the placename had been recorded as Hinton Walruch and in 1868 it was recorded as Hinton-Waldridge.

Hinxworth

Domesday recorded the Hertfordshire village of Hinxworth in 1086 as Haingesteuuorde, and located it in the Odsy Hundred, a large manor estate held by Peter of Valognes, it having belonged to Almer of Bennington before 1066. The name comes from 'hengest', the Saxon word for a stallion, and 'worth', an enclosure or in this sense a corral or paddock. Hence, 'enclosure [or corral] where stallions are kept'.

Hitchin

The township of Hitchin, located on the River Hiz in Hertfordshire, was known in the mid-tenth century as Hiccam, which translates as 'territory belonging to the Hicce tribe', possibly derived from an even older Celtic source. By 1086, it was recorded as Hiz (pronounced 'Hitch'), in the Half Hundred of Hitchin, held by William the Conqueror and assessed at five hides of land suitable for thirty-four ploughs, which 'altogether... rendered one-hundred-and-six pounds a year assayed and weighed'. Before the Conquest, it had belonged to Harold Godwinson.

Holton

Holton is a village in Oxfordshire, whose name comes from two Anglo-Saxon words: 'healh', meaning 'corner' or 'nook' of land, and 'tun', a farmstead. It was already known as Healtun by the mid-tenth century. Hence, the name means 'farmstead in a corner of land'. The entry in the *Domesday Book* was for Eltone in the Headington Hundred, held by Roger d'Ivry. In 1066, it had belonged to a Saxon called Godfrey.

Houghton Conquest

Despite all indications to the contrary, this Bedfordshire village has little to do with the Norman Conquest of 1066, but refers to the Conquest family who owned the manor in the thirteenth century. The Houghton element of the placename derives from the Old English words 'hoh' (sometimes 'hoo', 'ho' or 'hooe'), meaning a ridge, outcrop or the spur of a hill, and 'tun' meaning 'farmstead' or 'settlement'. Hence 'settlement on the spur of a hill'. Domesday records the place as Houstone, a very large manorial estate in the Hundred of Redbornstoke, held in 1086 by Countess Judith of Lens, having previously belonged to Earl Tosti (sometimes Tostig).

Houghton Regis

Houghton is located in the Chiltern Hills of Bedfordshire; it is a common placename, with at least fourteen others known in England. The name is thought to derive from the Saxon words 'hoh' and 'tun', together meaning 'a farmstead on a ridge or the spur of a hill'. In 1385, the Latin affix 'Regis' appears for the first time on official documents. Meaning 'of the king', recognising its status as a royal manor. The *Domesday Book* records 'Houstone... a demesne of the king, is assessed at ten hides. There is land for twenty-four ploughs.'

Hungerford

Although there is evidence of Stone Age, Bronze Age and Roman occupation of the West Berkshire township of Hungerford, it received no mention in the *Domesday Book*, and did not appear in written documents until 1108. At that time, the church at Hungerford was assigned to the Abbey of Bec-Hellouin in Normandy. The placename is of Old English origin, indicating a ford or narrow river crossing, leading to poor quality or unproductive land. Hence, a possible origin of the 'hunger' element. However, this is somewhat speculative. An alternative and more credible explanation is that it derives from the Danish King Hingwar (sometimes known as Ivar or Ivo 'the Boneless'), who according to early manuscripts drowned at Hungerford in the late-ninth century. Hence, 'Hingwar's Ford'.

Iffley

Iffley is a district in the City of Oxford whose name comes from a combination of the two Old English words 'gifete' and 'leah'. The former refers to the lapwing or plover, and the latter to a woodland clearing. Hence, the placename translates into modern English as 'woodland clearing where plovers [or lapwings] are seen'. The place was already known as Gifetelea in the early eleventh century, and by 1086 appeared in the *Domesday Book* as Givetelei, listed in the Hundred of Headington held by Earl Aubrey de Coucy, having belonged to Azur, the son of Thorth, before the Conquest.

Ilmer

The Old English word 'il' referred to the leech or leeches, which were commonly used in medical practice in medieval England, and the word 'mere' represented a pond or a pool. The name of this Buckinghamshire village may therefore be taken to mean '[place by a] pool where leeches are gathered'. Domesday omitted the 'l' from its entry and recorded the placename as Imere, listed within the Hundred of Ixhill, held at that time by Bishop Odo of Bayeux, having belonged in 1066 to Godwin (identified as Earl Leofwin's man). The manor sustained eight villagers, one smallholder and four slaves and had land sufficient for three men's and two lord's plough teams. The entire estate was valued at four pounds.

Ivinghoe/Ivinghoe Aston

Archaeological excavations north of the village of Ivinghoe in Aylesbury Vale have revealed evidence of prehistoric settlements around the area known as Ivinghoe Beacon. At the time of the *Doomsday Book* of 1086, the place was known as Evinghehou, in the Yardley Hundred of Buckinghamshire, held in demesne by the Bishop of St Peter's & St Swithin's Church in Winchester - assessed for twenty hides and valued at eighteen pounds. The separate Manor of Ivinghoe Aston, which in Saxon times had belonged to Asgar (known as 'the Staller'), became part of lands in the possession of Geoffrey de Mandeville and later became attached to Quarrendon Manor. The Ivinghoe placename derives from Saxon times when it belonged to a man called Ifa and his people (indicated by the 'ingas' affix). The final Old English name element 'hoe', 'ho' or 'hoh', reflected the village location at the end of a heel or toe-shaped ridge. The placename has had several variants over time, including Hythingho, Yvyngho and Ivanhoe.

Kempston

Kempston stands on the River Ouse, a notoriously meandering river, and as such its name may be derived from the Celtic word 'camm', meaning crooked or bent. The added Old English suffix 'tun', indicates a farmstead or village settlement. Hence, the placename may mean 'the farm at the bend'. An alternative explanation has been suggested, based on the element 'Caemb', which may have been the name of the Saxon who founded the settlement, in which case, the placename could simply mean 'Caemb's farm or settlement'.

After the Conquest, the manor, then recorded as Camestone, was granted to Countess Judith de Balliol of Lens (also known as Judith of Rennes), the niece of William the Conqueror.

Keysoe

The Bedfordshire village of Keysoe has a name that combines two Saxon words: 'caeg', meaning 'key' and 'hoh', a ridge or hill-spur. Hence, '[place by the] key-shaped hill-spur'. The Great Survey entered the name as Caissot in 1086 and listed it in the Leightonstone Hundred which at that time included parts of Bedfordshire and Huntingdonshire, held by a man with the unfortunate name of Alwin Devil who had also held it during the time of King Edward. The whole estate was valued at just one shilling.

Kintbury

Kintbury derived the first part of its placename from the River Kennet on which it stands. The meaning of the river name, which is of Celtic origin, is lost in prehistory. However, the 'bury' element of the name comes from the old Saxon word 'burh', signifying a stronghold or a fortified manor. Taken together, these elements produce a placename that means 'fortified place on [or near] the River Kennet'. In the mid-tenth century the placename was known as Cynetanbyrig, and by the time of the Domesday survey it was being recorded as Cheneteberie, in the Kintbury Hundred of Berkshire, part-held by King William, by the Abbey of St Mary & St Melor in Amesbury and by William FitzOther.

Lambourn

The name of the West Berkshire village of Lambourn, as you might suspect, is related to lambs. The affix 'bourn' comes from the Old English word 'burna'. Meaning 'stream' or 'brook'. Therefore, the placename means something like '[place by a] stream where lambs are washed [or watered]'. The village was already known as Lambburnan by the end of the ninth century and by 1086 it had been recorded both as Lamborne and as Lanborne, and listed as an extremely large estate for its day, supporting one hundred and thirty-eight families (including fourteen slaves), in the Lambour Hundred. Domesday showed the manor estates part-held by Matthew de Mortagne, Hascoit Musard and King William. Before 1066 the land had been jointly owned by Wulfward White (known as 'the Noble'), a man called Brictheah and King Edward. In 1182 the additional word 'upp', meaning 'higher up stream' was added and it became known as Uplamburn.

Leighton Buzzard

Leighton Buzzard is known to have been occupied since Saxon times, with discoveries of sixth century artefacts and pottery. There are also ancient earthworks dating back before Roman times. The settlement was known at the time of the Domesday survey as Lestone, a name derived from the Old English 'leac', referring to leek (or garlic), and 'tun', a farmstead or enclosure. Taken together, the name might be interpreted as 'enclosure (field or garden) where leeks (or garlic) are grown'. The 'Buzzard' element of the placename comes from the Busard family who owned the estate in the thirteenth century, at which time it became known as Letton Busard.

Letcombe Bassett/Letcombe Regis

In 1086, this Oxfordshire manor was simply known as Ledecumbe, in the Eagle Hundred held jointly by King William and by Robert d'Oilly. The name comes from a man called Leoda, its probable founder or chieftain, and the Old English word 'cumb', meaning 'valley' Hence, the original placename translated as 'Leoda's valley'. Later the estate was separated, one part going to the Bassett family, which became Letcombe Bassett, and the other being retained by the Crown and was thereafter known as Letcombe Regis ('regis' meaning 'of the king').

Lillingstone Dayrell/Lillingstone Lovell

By 1086, the single entity that was the Buckinghamshire village of Lillingstone was recorded as Lillingestan, a small estate in the Stotfold Hundred held by Walter Giffard, having belonged to Queen Edith, the widow of King Edward, in 1066. The place was named after its probable founder, a man called Lytel. Additionally, the Old English affixes, 'inga', referred to the followers, family or people, and 'stan', a stone, usually a marker or boundary stone of some kind. The placename therefore translated as 'boundary stone of the followers of a man called Lytel'. Later, the estate was divided and the two new owner-families, the Dayrells and the Lovells, added their family names to the two adjacent manors.

Long Crendon
The 'Long' element of this Buckinghamshire village placename gives the clue as to its local topography – it is a 'long' village, and the affix was appended to the placename some time in the seventeenth century. The Crendon element refers to a man called Creoda, who was probably a Saxon chieftain, and 'dun', indicating a hill. Hence, 'Creoda's hill'. Domesday listed the place as Credendone, an extremely large estate for the time, in the Ixhill Hundred, held by Walter Giffard.

Loudwater
The Buckinghamshire hamlet of Loudwater lies within the Parish of Chepping Wycombe and gets its name from the nearby River Wye which flows on through High Wycombe. In 1241, it was recorded as Ludewatere. The name comes directly from the Old English, where 'hlud', meant 'loud' or 'noisy', and 'waeter' referred to any flowing water, whether a brook, stream or river. Hence the name means 'noisy water [or stream]'.

Luton
The township of Luton was established when Saxons created a settlement beside the River Lea in Bedfordshire in the sixth century. The Lea is thought to have evolved its name from a Celtic word, meaning 'bright river'. This, with the Old English affix 'tun', indicating a farm or a settlement, produced the placename Lygetun, meaning, the 'settlement by the River Lea'. By 1086 it was known as 'Loitune ... a demesne manor in the land of the king in Bedfordshire', assessed at thirty hides with sufficient land for eighty-two ploughs.

Maidenhead
The Berkshire township of Maidenhead was known to the Romans as Alaunodunum. Evidence of their occupation was unearthed in nineteenth century excavations carried out on Castle Hill and the remains of a Roman villa at Cox green. The origin of the placename is contentious and several possible explanations have been put forward. Originally, it was thought to have been named Maidenhythe, the Saxon 'hythe' or 'hithe' being the old word for a wharf or landing stage. This is an affix and placename that is common in south-eastern England, with examples like Rotherhithe and Greenhithe in London and the Kentish town of Hythe. In this case, the placename might be translated as 'landing stage of the maiden(s)'. The 'Maiden' element may refer to the nuns from nearby Cookham Monastery, who most probably used the wharf. An alternative and quite different version cites the old Welsh Celtic words 'Mawr-Din', meaning 'great fort'. Yet another and considerably less favourable explanation is that it comes from the Norman word 'midden', a rubbish dump. As an alternative, the 'head' element of the present placename may be related to the word 'hythe'. Landing stages and jetties are still widely referred to as pier 'heads'. It also appears commonly in contemporary English in placenames like Portishead, Peterhead and Leatherhead. Whatever the true explanation, Maidenhead was too small and unimportant a place to receive an entry in the *Domesday Book*, although it was known to have around fifty inhabitants and was held at that time by Giles de Pinkney (sometimes known as Giles de Sancto).

Mapledurham
The Oxfordshire village of Mapledurham derived its placename from the maple trees that once grew there. The name is a combination of the Old English words 'mapuldor', which

meant 'maple tree(s)', and 'ham', a dwelling or homestead. Hence, 'homestead (or dwelling) where maple trees grow'. The name was recorded by Domesday in the Langtree Hundred, held in 1086 by Miles Crispin, who had also held it before the Conquest.

Marcham

Marcham comes from the Old English word 'mearce', which represented the wild celery or smallage plant. The additional affix 'hamm' signified a water or river meadow, here referring specifically to the River Ock. The placename therefore translates as '[place at the] river meadow where wild celery grows'. It was known to the Saxons as Merchamme, and in 1086 to the Norman commissioners of the *Domesday Book* as Merceham, listed as a very large estate which they located in the Marcham Hundred of Berkshire at that time, and held by the Abbey of St Mary in Abingdon.

Markyate

The Markyate placename dates back to Anglo-Saxon English, where 'mearc' represented a boundary or boundary marker or fence, and 'geat' meant 'gate'. Hence, 'gate at the boundary'. The boundary in question was that between Hertfordshire and Bedfordshire, and the likelihood that a gate or portal of some kind would allow access to the old woodland at this location. The name as it exists today dates from the twelfth century.

Marlow

The placename of Marlow, in the Wycombe district of Buckinghamshire, was known by the beginning of the eleventh century as Merelafan, based on two Saxon words, 'mere', meaning a pool or small lake, and 'laf', signifying 'remaining land'. The name may be taken to indicate land that remains when a pool is drained. The Domesday survey recorded 'Merlaue, in the Land of Queen Maud in Desborough Hundred', assessed at fifteen hides, with twenty-six carucates in demesne, containing one mill, pasture, woodland pannage for a thousand pigs and a fishery annually producing a thousand eels.

Marston Moretaine

The placename Marston first appears in written records in 969 in connection with an early boundary dispute. The name derives from two Old English words, 'mersc', meaning a marsh, and 'tun', a farmstead or settlement. The name translates as 'farm in, or by, a marsh'. In 1086, the place was known as Merestone, in Redbornstoke Hundred of Bedfordshire, owned by Walter Giffard, and held for him by Hugh de Bolbec. The Morteyne name comes from 1383, when the manor came into the possession of the Morteyn family, and their name was appended to the place.

Meppershall

By 1086 this Bedfordshire township had been recorded as Maperteshale, in the Hitchin Hundred, at that time divided between the Counties of Hertfordshire and Bedfordshire, and held by Gilbert FitzSolomon. The name comes from Old English, where 'maepel-treow' meant 'maple tree' and 'halh' referred to a corner or nook of land. Hence the placename may be translated as 'nook of land where maple trees are found'.

Milton Ernest

Milton is a very common placename with around twenty villages, towns and hamlets of that name in England. It translates simply as 'middle estate or farmstead'. The Bedfordshire village of Milton Ernest was recorded as Middeltone in the survey of 1086. By 1330, the name appears as Middelton Orneys after being taken into the possession of a man probably called Ernels or Erneis, who appended his name to the placename.

Mogerhanger

Over the centuries, the placename of this Bedfordshire village has been variously spelt a: Moggerhanger, Mogerhanger, Muggerhanger and Morehanger. Its earliest record was in the twelfth century, when it was written as Mogarhangre. The first element of the name is somewhat obscure, but may be derived from an ancient Celtic word meaning a wall or a ruin; then with the Old English affix 'hangra', which signified a wooded slope or hillside, the entire placename may be taken to mean something akin to 'wooded slope with (possibly) a ruined wall'.

Much Hadham

This Hertfordshire village was known simply as Haedham in the mid-tenth century. The name comes from 'haeth', meaning 'heath', and 'ham', a homestead. Hence, 'homestead on the heath'. The Old English word 'mycel', meaning 'great', was added later to distinguish it from the nearby village of Little Hadham. Domesday recorded the village as Hadam, a very large manor in the Edwinstree Hundred, supporting sixty-six households and held by the Bishop of St Pauls, London. In 1373, the placename was recorded as Muchel Hadham.

Newbury

The history of the Berkshire township of Newbury began on the banks on the River Kennet some time after the Norman Conquest. By 1080, the place was already known as Neuberie, which translates from the Norman French as simply meaning 'new town or borough'. The original name of the settlement was Ulvritune or Ulvriton, possibly after its early Saxon founder, a man called Wulhere or Wulfweard, and meaning 'the township or settlement of Wulfhere'.

Newport Pagnell

This Buckinghamshire settlement was recorded in the Great Survey of 1086 as Neuport, in the land of William FitzAnsculf in Seckley Hundred. It had been held before the Norman Conquest by Ulf, described as a thegn of King Edward. The name comes directly from the Middle English words 'neu', meaning 'new', and 'port', which was a later reference to the Old Saxon word 'chipping' which referred to a market. Hence, Newport means 'new market [town]'. The Pagnell affix was appended when the Paynell family acquired the manorial estates in 1220.

Olney

The civil parish and old market town of Olney in the Borough of Milton Keynes in Buckinghamshire was known as Ollanege in the tenth century and derived its name from a man called Olla, who was possibly the founder of the original settlement. Added to this is the old affix 'eg', which meant either an island or dry land surrounded by wetland or marsh. The placename translates as 'dry land in a marsh belonging to Olla', or more simply 'Olla's island'. In 1086, Domesday recorded the placename as Olnei, in the Bunsty Hundred, which belonged to the Bishop of Coutances at that time. Before the Conquest, it was held by Burgred, identified as the 'father of Edwin', and by one unnamed free man.

Oxford

Oxford was known in the tenth century as Oxnaforda, a name which in Old English meant 'a river ford where oxen cross'. By that time, it was a sufficiently well-established township to possess a thriving market and at least four known moneyers producing coin for the Crown. Domesday recorded the place as Oxeneford, in the Headington Hundred, owned at that time by the Oxford Canons of St Frideswide, who had held it long before the Conquest.

Pangbourne

Pangbourne began as a small settlement belonging to a man called Paega, who gave his name to the place. The oldest spelling of the placename was Pegingaburnan in 844. This can be broken into three separate elements: 'Peg', referring to Paega personally, 'ingas', his people or family, and the final affix, 'burna', indicating a small stream. Altogether the placename can be interpreted a 'stream of Paega's people [or family]'. By 1086, the village had been recorded as Pangeborne and Pandeborne, in the Reading Hundred of Berkshire, held by Miles Crispin, it having been held by Baldwin at the time of King Edward. The record shows 'a mill rendering ten shillings and twelve acres of meadow... [and] of this land a knight holds one hide and there he has one plough and two acres of meadow'. The entire manorial estate was valued at four pounds.

Peasemore

Peasemore is a village in West Berkshire whose name is derived from the Old English words 'pise' and 'mere', meaning 'peas' and 'pond' respectively. The placename may therefore be taken to mean '[place by, or near a] pond where peas are grown'. At the time of the Great Survey the place was recorded as the 'Mainou of Praxemere', part in the Marcham Hundred held by Gilbert de Breteuil. Before 1066 it had belonged to two Saxon men called Godwine and Herlewin. Another part of the manorial estate lay within the Rowbury Hundred lands of Ralph de Mortimer in 1086.

Potten End

This Hertfordshire village was only established in 1894. It derived its name from 'pottern', a pottery, after the local pottery makers who had worked there in earlier times. The old expression 'end' (or 'ende') signified a place at the end or corner of a village or on its outskirts. Hence, 'pottery works on the outskirts of the village'.

Princes Risborough

This West Buckinghamshire township was recorded in 903 AD as Hrisanbyrge and belonged to King Harold. The placename derives from the Saxon 'hrisen', meaning 'hills', and 'beorg', which signifies brushwood. Hence, 'hills where brushwood grows'. In the thirteenth century the manor was in the hands of Edward, Prince of Wales, son of Edward III, known later as the Black Prince. As a result, the affix 'Princes' was attached to the placename, after which it became known as Princes Risborough.

Puckeridge

Puckeridge began near a Roman military settlement in the second century and was known to them as Ad Fines and was an important place with a temple dedicated to Minerva. The first element of this modern-day Hertfordshire village placename may be either 'puck', a possible reference to a mysterious sprite (as of Puck in Shakespeare's *A Midsummer Night's Dream*), or 'pucker', to wrinkle, fold or gather. Additionally, there is the Old English element 'ric' or 'hrycg', meaning 'ridge', or a raised outcrop or fold of land. The placename could therefore mean either 'a raised strip or ridge' or 'ridge where an imp or goblin lives'. Nobody seems quite clear which.

Quainton

Quainton gets its name from old Saxon words 'cwen', meaning 'queen' (and sometimes used as a generic word for 'woman'), and 'tun', a farmstead or an estate. Hence, 'queen's farmstead [or estate]'. Domesday listed this Buckinghamshire village as Chentone, a very large manor supporting forty-two households, (including at least eight slaves), in the

Ashendon Hundred, part-held by Miles Crispin and by Hascoit Musard, it having been shared by Wigot of Wallingford and Azur, son of Toti before the Norman Conquest.

Radlett
Radlett began as a settlement at an important crossroad at a junction with the Roman road of Watling Street in Hertfordshire. The Saxons used two words, 'rad', meaning 'road', and 'gelaet', meaning 'junction', to indicate a junction or a crossing, and this the origin of Radlett's placename.

Radnage
The name of this Buckinghamshire village translates from Old English as '[place at the] red oak tree', where 'read' meant 'red' and 'ac' meant 'oak tree'. Why a particular oak should have been red is open to speculation, but it was clearly distinctive enough to be recorded as such and to become the name of the settlement that grew up around it. It has been argued that the bark of the tree in question might have been unusually red in colour. It is also possible that it was subject to Melampsora, a fungus commonly known as 'rust' on account of its colour, although this is rare in oak species. In 1162 the village was known as Radenhech.

Royston
The Hertfordshire township of Royston was known for a time by its Latin name, Crux Roaisie, meaning 'cross of a woman called Rohesia'. The definitive origin is unknown but may be attributed to a Lady Rohesia (or Roisia), who is thought to have restored a much-revered Saxon or Celtic cross some time after the Norman Conquest. By the early fourteenth century, Roisia's Cross had become Roisia's Town and over time became corrupted as Royston.

Sandy
The township of Sandy is a parish in the Biggleswade District of Bedfordshire, located on the River Ivel and the Great North Road, the Roman road from St Albans to Godmanchester. The placename derives from the Old English words 'sand' and 'eg', the latter meaning 'island'. Hence, 'sandy island'. At the time of the *Domesday Book*, the 'Mainou of Sandeia' was held by Eudo (Le Dapifer) FitzHubert until his death in 1120.

Sarratt
The Sarratt name comes from 'sieret', an Old English word signifying a dry or barren place. The location of this Hertfordshire village is on a chalk landscape gave rise to the placename. It was known as Syreth at the time of the Domesday survey, yet merited no entry in its pages.

Shabbington
A Buckinghamshire village whose placename means 'estate or farmstead associated with a man called Scobba'. It was recorded in the *Domesday Book* as Sobintone, in the Ixhill Hundred, lands which had been granted to Miles Crispin. In 1086, the estate was assessed at ten hides with three more held in demesne. It had a fishery producing one hundred eels annually and there was woodland pannage for one hundred pigs. A man called Richard also leased four hides of land.

Shalstone
The Shalstone placename is derived from two Old English words: 'sceald', meaning 'shallow', and 'tun', indicating a farmstead or estate. Hence, 'farmstead at a shallow place', probably indicating a stream. The Great Survey recorded the place as Celdestone and

Celdestane, in the Stotfold Hundred of Buckinghamshire, lands belonging to the Bishop Lincoln at that time. The account concludes, 'This manor Aethelnoth Cild, a thegn of King Edward, held' (before the Conquest).

Sharnbrook

The origin of this Bedfordshire township's placename derives from Old English and technically means 'dung brook', based on two Saxon words, 'scearn', meaning dung or manure, and 'broc', a brook or stream, but might be more properly interpreted as 'dirty brook'. By 1086, it was recorded as Scernebroc in the Willey Hundred, in land belonging to the Bishop of Coutances, and that 'a certain Englishman, Thorgisl, holds half a hide of the bishop'.

Shenington

This Oxfordshire village has a placename that means '[place by the] beautiful hill'; it comes from the Saxon words 'scene' or 'scenan', meaning 'beautiful', and 'dun', a hill. Domesday recorded the place as Senendone, and listed it in the 'Land of the King' in Bloxham Hundred, which at that time stretched across Oxfordshire and Gloucestershire. The account stated that 'It is in the king's hand', but that Robert d'Oilly was its lord 'at farm' in 1086, and it had belonged to Brictric, the son of Algar in 1066.

Shiplake

An Oxfordshire village whose name means '[place at the] stream where sheep are washed'. It comes from the Old English 'sceap', meaning 'sheep', and 'lacu', a stream or pond, related to the modern English word 'lake'. The stream in question flowed into the River Thames at this point. In 1163, the placename was written as Siplac.

Shipton-under-Wychwood

There are a half dozen or so places in England called Shipton. The meaning is fairly straightforward, coming from the Old English words 'sceap', meaning 'sheep', and 'tun', a farmstead. Hence, 'farmstead where sheep are reared', or more commonly understood loosely as 'sheep town'. The particular Oxfordshire village distinguished itself from the others by the addition of 'Wychwood' (of Wychwood Forest, itself an ancient forest name) to the placename. The word 'Wychwood' comes from the Old English 'Huiccewudu', which translates as 'woodland of the Hwicce tribe', Anglo-Saxon peoples who settled the area in the sixth century. The original entry in Domesday was as Scipton.

Shottesbrooke

Opinions differ as to the interpretation of this district of Windsor in Berkshire placename. One is that it refers to a man called Scot, possibly the founder of the original settlement, and another cites the Old English word 'sceota', meaning 'trout'. Given that the second element of the placename is fairly self-evident, the village name might mean either 'brook belonging to a man called Scot' or 'brook where trout are found [live or breed]'. Either seem equally plausible. Domesday recorded the hamlet as Sotesbroc, in the Beynhurst Hundred, in 'the Land of Odo and Other Thegns', held by Alweard the Goldsmith, whose father had held it before him as a tenant of Queen Edith. In 1086, it listed 'a church, and two slaves [and] seven acres of meadow. It was worth seven pounds [in 1066]; now six pounds'.

Shrivenham

An interesting Oxfordshire placename which is derived from the Old English word 'scrifen', which means 'allotted', and 'hamm', an enclosure. In this case the land in question lay beside the River Cole and its rightful possession had been decreed by the church, following an ownership dispute. This dispute, about which little is known, took place long before the Norman Conquest, and was recorded as Scrifenanhamme around 950. In 1086, Domesday listed it as Scriveham, in the Shrivenham Hundred (then in Berkshire), in lands belonging to King William, as it had been held by King Edward before 1066.

Sibford Ferris

In the survey of 1086, the Oxfordshire village of Sibford Ferris was recorded simply as Sibeford, named after a Saxon called Sibba, who apparently controlled or owned the river crossing at this point (in Old English a 'forda'). Therefore the placename means Sibba's ford'. Later, the de Ferrers family took possession of the manor and it became Sibbard Ferreys. This distinguished it from Sibford Gowere, that portion of the original estate that went into the ownership of the Guher family.

Slough

The Berkshire town of Slough at one time was very much what it said on the label – a muddy, boggy or swampy place. The placename comes from the Old English word 'sloh', meaning 'mire' or 'bog', and the place was recorded as Slo at the end of the twelfth century. It has been suggested that the placename comes from the muddy land between Upton-cum-Chalvey and Eton.

Sparsholt

The name of the village of Sparsholt in the Vale of the White Horse in Oxfordshire was recorded in a tenth century Anglo-Saxon charter a Speresholte and in the *Domesday Book* of 1086 as Spersolt. The translates directly from two Old English words: 'spere' or 'spearre', a spar or a spear, and 'holt' a small wood or copse. Hence the placename may be interpreted as 'small wood where spars (or spear shafts) are gathered or cut'. It has also been suggested that it could also be a reference to a spear-trap in a wood where animals are caught.

Speen

This district in Newbury, West Berkshire, derives its name from the Old English word 'spene', which meant 'woodchip'. It was known in 821 as Spene. Hence, 'place where woodchips are found'. The word is thought to have come from the Latin name 'spinis', meaning '[place] near to thorn bushes'. Domesday recorded the name as Spone in the Thatcham Hundred, held in 1086 by Humphrey Visdeloup, having belonged to a Saxon known as Karli of Norton in 1066.

Spelsbury

An Oxfordshire village where a man called Speol built a stronghold or fortified manor house some time before the eleventh century, and the placename came to be known as Speolesbyrig, meaning 'Speol's stronghold'. In 1086, the place was recorded as Spelesberie, a very large estate in the Shipton Hundred, located at that time across the counties of Oxfordshire and Warwickshire, held at that time by the Bishop of Worcester.

St Albans

St Albans began as an Iron Age settlement on the River Ver, which the Romans named Verulamium. At that time, it was one of the largest settlements – and the oldest – in the lands that became the County of Hertfordshire. The township was destroyed by Boudicca in her revolt against Roman occupation in 60 AD. By 1007, the place was known as *Sancte Albanes Stow*, which translates from Latin as 'holy place of St Alban', 'stow' being Old English for a holy place or a church. St Alban was believed to be a Romano-British man who was executed by beheading for his faith some time around 250 and was reputedly the first Christian martyr in Britain.

Steeple Claydon

'Steeple' is a common English placename, with townships like Steeple in Dorset, Steeple Aston, Steeple Langford and Steeple Gidding in Wiltshire, Steeple and Steeple Bumpstead in Essex, and Steeple Morden in Cambridgeshire. The affix has two possible meanings: the Old English word 'stepel', indicating a steep place or a church spire, a tall tower or a steeple. The usage varied with each location. However, the use of the word in the placename of the village of Steeple Claydon in Buckinghamshire refers specifically to a tall tower or spire. The Claydon affix also comes from Anglo-Saxon, where 'claegig' meant 'clayey' and 'dun' signified a hill. Hence, the placename means '[place on the] clayey hill with a steeple'. Domesday recorded the place as Claindone in the Mow Hundred, a large manor whose chief tenant was Alric, known as 'the cook'. It was not until the thirteenth century that the village was known as Stepel Cleydon, in order to distinguish it from the nearby villages of East Claydon, Middle Claydon and Botolph Claydon.

Stevenage

The Saxons knew the North Hertfordshire settlement of Stevenage as Stithenaece, which meant 'place of the strong oak'. The placename derives from the seventh century Saxon words, 'stith', meaning strong or stiff, and 'ac', the old word for the oak tree. Domesday recorded the township as Stigenace, in the Hundred of Broadwater, held at that time by the Abbey of St Peter in Westminster.

Stokenchurch

By around 1200, this township was known as Stockenechurch, which translates from the Old English as 'church made of logs', though some prefer 'church within a stockade'. The old Saxon word 'stoccen' is related to a fortified wooden structure, or stockade.

Stotfold

Known at the time of the Great Survey as the 'Mainou of Stoffold Brayes', in earlier times this Bedfordshire township was known as Stodfald, from the Old English words 'stod', indicating a stud or horse breeding place, and 'fald', a fold or enclosure. Hence, 'stud enclosure for horses.'

Swerford

The Old English word 'sweora' meant 'neck, and 'forda' signified a shallow river crossing. Taken together they produced a placename meaning '[place at the] neck of land by a ford'. The River Swere took its name from the village. Domesday recorded the place as Surford, in the Shipton Hundred of Oxfordshire, and went on to state that 'These Lands Written Below Belong to the Fief of King William'. Robert d'Oilly leased five hides of the estate lands from Earl William FitzOsbern. By the end of the twelfth century the placename had been written as Swereford.

Swineshead

Swineshead is a Bedfordshire township that was known in 1086 as Suineshefet, which translates directly from the old Saxon words 'swin', a pig or swine, and 'heafod', a promontory or headland. It is not certain what the reference means, but most probably it described a feature of local topography where a local promontory or outcrop was shaped like a pig's head or snout.

Sydenham

This Oxfordshire village derives its placename from 'sid', an Old English word meaning 'broad', and 'hamm', an enclosure. Hence, '[place at the] broad enclosure'. Domesday entered the name as Sidreham, listed in the Lewknor Hundred, stating that... 'these lands written below belong to the Fief of Earl William', held in 1086 'at farm' by Gilbert de Breteuil, and further recorded that in 1066 'three thegns held it freely'.

Tackley

Two equally plausible explanations exist for the origin of this Oxfordshire village placename. On the one hand it could come from a man called Taecca, who may have been its founder or chieftain, or it might derive from the Old English word 'tacca', meaning 'young sheep'. The final element, from 'leah', signified a woodland glade or a clearing made in a wood to produce arable land for planting. Hence, either, 'Taecca's woodland clearing' or 'woodland clearing where young sheep are kept'. It was recorded as Tachelie in the 1086 survey, and located in the Wootton Hundred, held by Earl Hugh of Chester (sometimes called 'Hugh the Wolf' and 'Hugh the Fat'), having been a possession of Hugh the Chamberlain before the Conquest.

Taplow

It would be reasonable to suppose that at some point during Anglo-Saxon period a man called Taeppa might have been in the possession of, watched over, or had even been buried in a mound at this place in Buckinghamshire. Which of these, if any are true, we may never know. What is known is that the placename translates into Modern English as 'Taeppa's tumulus', from the Old English word 'hlaw', which signified a mound or tumulus, usually related to burial. Domesday recorded the name as Thapeslau in the Burnham Hundred, held in 1086 by Bishop Odo of Bayeux, it having belonged to Asgot of Hailes and one other unnamed man before the Norman Conquest.

Thatcham

The *Guinness Book of World Records* lists the Berkshire township of Thatcham as the oldest continuously inhabited settlement in Britain, with evidence of human occupation dating from prehistoric times (though several other English townships also claim this honour). The place was an important river crossing on Ermine Street, the Roman military road which ran from Cirencester to Silchester. By 954, it had been recorded as Thaecham, a name based on the Old English words 'thaecce' and 'ham', together signifying a thatched dwelling or homestead, or possibly a river meadow where reeds used in thatching were obtained. A popular local tradition has a quite different explanation, whereby a seventh century Saxon chieftain called Tace established the settlement. Hence, 'Tace's ham', which eventually evolved into Thatcham.

Therfield

In 1060, this Hertfordshire village was known as Therefeld, a name taken from the Old English words 'thyrre' meaning 'dry' and 'felda' meaning 'field (or 'open land', usually arable). The placename meant '[place by] dry open land'. Domesday listed the village as Derevelde and Furrewelde, in the Odsy Hundred part-held by the Abbey of St Benedict in Ramsey (as it had been held in demesne before 1066), and part-held by Hardwin de Scales.

Throcking

Throcking derived its placename from two Old English words: 'throc', meaning 'beam' (as in a wooden supporting or structural beam), and 'ing', referring to a place where they were obtained. Hence, 'place where beams are found (or obtained)'. Domesday recorded the village as Trochinge, in the Edwinstree Hundred of Hertfordshire, held at that time by Bishop Odo of Bayeux, having been in the possession of a Saxon called Aelfric Scova before 1066.

Thundridge
This placename comes from the Scandinavian god Thor (also known as Thunor), plus the Old English word 'hyricg' meaning 'ridge' or 'outcrop'. Hence, 'Thunor's [or Thor's] ridge'. Domesday refers to the place as Tonrinch, in the Braughing Hundred of Hertfordshire, held in 1086 by Bishop Odo of Bayeux.

Tingewick
Initially, this Buckinghamshire village gets its name from a man who was either called Tida or Teoda. Who he was is unknown, but he was of sufficiently high status to have himself enshrined in the placename. The other elements of the name include the Old English words 'ing', meaning 'associated with', and 'wic', which referred to a specialised farm or dwelling, most typically a dairy farm. Hence, the placename may be interpreted as 'dairy farm associated with a man called Tida'. The Great Survey of 1086 recorded the place as Tedinwiche, and listed it within the Hundred of Rowley, held at that time by Bishop Odo of Bayeux, having been in the possession of Alnoth (identified as 'the noble of Kent'). The estate was assessed at eight ploughlands with a meadow, woodland for eight hundred pigs and one mill, altogether valued at ten pounds.

Tring
The Domesday entry for the Hertfordshire township of Tring records Treunge, a name derived from the Old English words 'treow', a tree, and 'hangr', signifying sloping ground. Hence, '[place on a] wooded slope'.

Turville
Originally known as Thyrefeld at the end of the eighth century, just like the Herfordshire village of Therfield (previously), the Buckinghamshire village of Turville's placename translates as '[place by] dry open land', from the Old English 'thyre', meaning 'dry' and felda', meaning 'open land'.

Ufton Nervet
By the time of the Domesday survey, this West Berkshire village had been recorded as Offetune, probably named after a man called Uffa, who may have been its founder. The placename is a combination of Uffa's personal name plus the Old English affix 'tun', which could signify a farmstead or a village. The entry in the survey listed the village in the Reading Hundred, held at that time by Giles, the brother of Ansculf, having been a personal possession of King Edward before the Conquest. At some point during the thirteenth century the manor came into the ownership of the Neyrnut family who attached their name to the place, so that in 1284 the village placename was recorded as Offeton Nernut.

Waddesdon
Any English placename that ends in the suffix 'don' is almost certainly a reference to a hill, as it comes from the Old English word 'dun'. The first element of this Buckinghamshire village name comes from a Saxon man called Weott, whose territory it no doubt was. The placename is interpreted as '[the place near] Weott's hill'. It was listed as Votesdone in 1086, in the Waddesdon Hundred, held at that time by Miles Crispin, having formerly belonged to Brictric of Waddesdon and with Queen Edith of Wessex as its overlord in 1066.

Wallingford

Evidence of an early Saxon settlement at Wallingford in Oxfordshire dates from the sixth century, though it was not until the ninth century that King Alfred fortified it to resist frequent Danish incursions. At that time, it was known as Welingaforda, probably named after a man called Wealh, with the affixes 'inga', meaning 'the people, tribe or family', and 'ford', a river crossing. Hence, the placename might mean 'ford belonging to the people or family of Wealh'. The Normans recorded the place as Wallingeford and listed it 'in the Borough of Wallingford [where] King Edward (the Confessor) had eight virgates of land'.

Ware

The placename comes from the Saxon 'waer' or 'wer', indicating a weir or dam on a river. A clue to its origin can be found in the *Anglo-Saxon Chronicles* where they record that in 895, King Alfred's army sank Danish longships that had sailed up the Lea from the River Thames, and that he had a weir built at this place on the river to prevent further repetitions.

Watford

Watford may have derived its placename from the Old English word 'waet', meaning watery or marshy, or 'wath', meaning hunting, and 'forda', a river crossing. Opinions vary therefore as to its precise meaning – either 'marshy river crossing' or 'ford used when hunting'. The settlement which was to become Watford developed around the River Colne.

Watton at Stone

In 969, this Hertfordshire village was recorded as Wattun, and by the time of the Great Survey of 1086 it was being written as Wodtone. The placename comes from two Saxon words, 'wad', meaning 'wode' and 'tun' indicating a farmstead or settlement. The entire word means 'farmstead [or settlement] where wode is found'. Wode was a blue earth colour commonly used as a dye in early British cultures. In the early fourteenth century, the place was known as Watton atte Stone, the 'at stone' affix having been added, possibly a boundary marker stone.

Wendover

The placename comes from the Celtic name of a stream that once ran through this Buckinghamshire settlement and means 'white waters', probably on account of the chalk deposits of its bed. The *Domesday Book* lists the place as Wendoure, in the Hundred of Aylesbury, which had been two manors before 1066 (Wendover Borough and Wendover Forrens) held by King Edward.

Wigginton

Two places in the Home Counties go by the name of Wigginton, one in Hertfordshire and another in Oxfordshire. Both probably come from the same source, a man called Wicga. The final two elements of the placename, 'inga' and 'tun', taken together indicated 'people or family' and a farmstead or settlement. The placename therefore translates into modern English as 'settlement [or farmstead] of Wicga's people'. The Hertfordshire village of Wigginton was recorded by Domesday as Wigentone in the Tring Hundred, held by Count Robert of Mortain, while that in Oxfordshire was listed in the Bloxham Hundred, held in 1086 by Guy d'Oilly, having belonged to Leofric before the Conquest.

Windsor

The Windsor placename is derived from the Old English words 'windels', a windlass or boat winding gear, and 'ora', a river bank. It refers to a place where a windlass (or a windle) was used to draw boats up against the flow of a river. British canals still have 'winding holes', where specifically widened parts of a waterway allow long barges and narrowboats to be turned around, or 'winded'.

Winkfield

The origin of this Berkshire township comes from a Saxon man called Wineca, who owned the land which gave Winkfield its placename, 'Wineca's field'. It was known in 942 as Winecanfeld, when King Edmund (known as 'the Magnificent'), granted the manor to a holy woman called Saethryth; she in turn transferred it to the Abbey of Abingdon, who held it in 1086, when the Domesday commissioners recorded it as Wenesfelle, in the Ripplesmere Hundred.

Witney

Witney is the largest township in West Oxfordshire. It stands on the River Windrush and has been occupied since the Iron Age. By 969 it was known as Wyttanige, after a Saxon man called Witta and the Old English affix 'eg', 'ig' or 'ige', which referred to an island or a piece of dry land in a marsh. Hence, the placename might translate as 'land in a marsh belonging to Witta'. By the time of Domesday, it was known as Witenie, in lands owned by the Bishop of Winchester, having been held by Saxon Archbishop Stigand before the Norman Conquest.

Woburn

The original Saxon hamlet of Woburn in Bedfordshire derived its name from two Old English words, 'woh', meaning bent, winding or crooked, and 'burna', a small stream (which survives in Northern England and in Scotland as 'burn', with examples like Blackburn, and Bannockburn). Hence, the placename may be taken to mean at the 'crooked or winding stream'.

Wokingham

Wokingham, located on the Emm Brook in the Loddon Valley of central Berkshire, was probably founded by a Saxon man called Wocca. Taken together with the Old English affixes 'inga', meaning the people or family, and 'ham', a village or settlement, its placename might translate as 'the settlement of the people or family of Wocca'.

Woodperry

The Oxfordshire hamlet of Woodperry has a placename that combines two Old English words: 'wudu', meaning 'wood' or 'woodland', and 'pirige', a pear or pear tree. Hence, the placename means '[place in the] wood where pear trees grow'. Initially, the hamlet was known simply as Perie, a name recorded in Domesday, which listed it as a small manor in the Hundred of Headington, held in 1086 by Bishop Odo of Bayeux. The estate supported five villans, two bordars and four slaves, and was worked by two men's plough teams and one lord's plough team. Its taxable assets amounted to thirty acres of meadow, fifteen acres of pasture and a woodland measuring five by two furlongs, altogether valued at two pounds. The word 'Wood' was added later when it became known as Wdeperie, distinguishing it from the nearby village of Waterperry.

Woodstock

The name Woodstock probably comes from two Saxon words, 'wudu', a wood, and 'stoc', a place or a clearing, and might mean a 'clearing in the woods'. Alternatively, the Old English word 'stocc' or the Norse 'stokkr', signifying a tree trunk or stump, might refer to a specific tree or stump in a wood or woodland clearing, possibly a meeting place. Such places were common locations for local counsels. This latter explanation might be supported by the fact that King Aethelred is believed to have issued one of his three legal codes, which were probably drafted by Wulfstan II, Archbishop of Canterbury, at a witan (an assembly of councillors), at Woodstock. During Anglo-Saxon times, the settlement was known as Wudestoce, and may have been a royal hunting park. By the time of the Domesday survey, it was recorded as 'Wodestoch ... [one of] the king's demesne forests... nine leagues long and as many broad'.

Wroxton

The first element of this Oxfordshire village placename comes from the Saxon word 'wrocc', which signified a buzzard or some other bird of prey. The second element, 'stan', referred to a stone or stones. The name may therefore be taken to mean '[place by a] stone where buzzards are seen'. In 1086, the village was recorded as Werochestan, listed as quite a large estate in the Blozham Hundred, supporting twenty-four households, including two slaves, and held at that time by Guy de Raimbeaucourt, with his son Ingelrann as its tenant.

Part Eleven

Greater London

London Boroughs and Townships, including
those formerly in the administrative Counties of Essex,
Kent, Middlesex, and Surrey

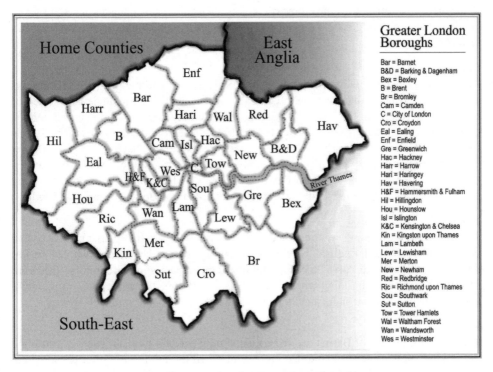

A map depicting the Greater London Boroughs & Townships.

Addiscombe

Addiscombe is a district of Croydon which at some time in its distant past belonged to a man called Aeddi. In 1229, the place was recorded as Edescamp, where the Old English word 'camp' represented an enclosed piece of land, (or what in modern English we might call a 'field'). Hence, the name means 'Aeddi's enclosed land'. It is thought that it was this same Aeddi who was also responsible for giving his name to nearby Addington.

Aldwych

This district was known in the seventh century as Lundenwic, meaning 'London port [or trading place]', after an early market probably established by the Danes in the late-ninth or early-tenth centuries. Later, it became known as the Old Market, where 'ald' meant 'old', and in 1211 it was recorded as Aldewich.

Arkley

The name of the Arkley district of Barnet comes from 'arc', an Old English word for a chest (at that time often called an 'ark'), and 'leah', which signified a woodland clearing. Hence, the name means 'woodland clearing where arks are made'. In the fourteenth century, the affix 'lond', meaning 'land', had been appended and it was recorded as Arkleyslond. It was in 1547 that it began to resemble its present day name when it was recorded as Arkeley.

Baker's Arms

A relatively recent placename, Baker's Arms lies on the boundary of Leyton and Walthamstowe and was named after a former public house of that name. It was first recorded in 1868, after the almshouses that were built between 1857 and 1866 by the Master Bakers' Benevolent Institution to relieve poverty in the township. These almshouses were given Grade II listed building status, purchased by Waltham Forest Council and refurbished as residential apartments.

Barking

Barking has been part of Greater London since 1963, when the former Municipal Boroughs of Barking and Dagenham were abolished. It was originally in the ancient Hundred of Becontree, formerly in the County of Essex, which was recorded in the *Domesday Book* as Beuentreu, after a man called Berica (or Beohha), and an old tree located at what is now Becontree Heath, where early council meetings are thought to have taken place during the Anglo-Saxon period. The placename simply meant 'Berica's tree'. In 731, it had been recorded as Berecingum, based on Berica, with the Old English affix 'inga', signifying 'the family, tribe or people'. This translates as 'settlement of Berica's people or family'.

Barnes

This district of Richmond was recorded as Berne in 1086, a self-explanatory placename derived from the Old English 'bere-aern', meaning 'barn'. The 'bere' element relates directly to barley, and 'aern' means 'building'. In ancient times, therefore, the word specifically implied a building where barley was stored, though later it took on the more general meaning that we understand today. In 1222, the placename was spelt Bernes.

Barnet

The London Borough of Barnet derived its name from the Old English 'baernet', meaning 'burnt land', and referred to land that had been cleared by fire, usually prior to ploughing and planting. In 1070, it was known as Barneto. It is thought that in earlier Saxon times, the settlement may have been known as Bergnet, part of the extensive woodland called Southaw, which belonged to the Abbey of St Albans.

Battersea

As early as 693, Battersea was recorded as Batrices eg (or Badrices ege), probably after a man called Baduric and the Old English affix 'eg', signifying an island or dry land surrounded by water or marshland. Hence, 'Baduric's island'. The island in question might have referred to higher land on the River Thames flood plain where Baduric established his settlement. By 1086, the place had been recorded as Patricesy, in land granted to the Church of St Peter of Westminster in Brixton Hundred. It was a large and wealthy estate amounting to seventy-two hides, with portions held by the Count of Mortain, the Bishops of Lisieux and of Bayeux and a man known as Gilbert the Priest, as well as King William himself.

Bayswater

Bayswater is a district in Westminster in Central London, and was historically a watering place for horses, which is the origin of the placename. Bay horses (and presumably horses of other colours) were literally watered there. The place in question was probably the River Westbourne, which was dammed in the early eighteenth century to create the Serpentine Lake in Hyde Park. In Middle English, what we now call a bay horse was originally known as a Bayard, and by the thirteenth century Bayswater was recorded as Bayards Watering Place. It was the mid-seventeenth century before the truncated form appeared as Bayeswater.

Beckenham

In 973, the name of this township in Bromley was recorded in its earliest form as Beohha Hammes Gemaeru. This somewhat complex placename has three elements: Beohha, the name of the man who may have established the first settlement here; then, either 'ham', meaning 'homestead' or 'hamm'; signifying an enclosure, and finally the Old English word 'gemaere', meaning 'boundary' or 'border'. The original name therefore translates as 'Beohha's homestead or enclosure at the boundary'. The place was recorded as Bacheham in 1086, the 'boundary' element having been dropped, and listed at that time in the Bromley Hundred of Kent, held by Bishop Odo of Bayeux.

Belgravia

Belgravia was owned and developed by the Dukes of Westminster in the 1820s and received its name from their Cheshire estate of Belgrave. The name Belgrave means 'beautiful grove', from the French word 'bel', meaning 'beautiful'.

Bermondsey

A district in Southwark, south of the River Thames, Bermondsey was known in the eighth century as Vermundesei. The place was named after a man called Beornmund, who might have been the founder of the first settlement, with the Old English suffix 'eg', meaning 'island' – a probable reference to high ground among the Thames flood plain or its marshes. Domesday called the place Bermundesye, and located it at that time in the Brixton Hundred of Surrey, parts held by the Count of Mortain and personally by King William.

Bethnal Green

Bethnal Green was an area within the ancient Parish of Stepney which now falls within Tower Hamlets Borough and dates from Saxon times when it was known as Blithehale (or Blythenhale). The name possibly derives from a man called Blitha, or from the Old English 'blithe', meaning 'happy', and 'health' signifying a corner or a nook. Hence the placename could mean either 'Blitha's corner' or 'happy corner'. Over time it became Beth'n'all Green and by the nineteenth century had become its present form of Bethnal Green.

Bexley

The oldest known documentation of the hamlet of Bexley was in a charter of 814, when according to some sources it was known as Byxlea, from the Old English 'byxe', related to the box tree, and 'leah', a woodland clearing. Hence, the placename means a 'clearing where box trees grow'.

Bloomsbury

The Camden district of Bloomsbury received its present-day name in the late thirteenth century, when it came into the possession of the de Blemund family who attached their family name to the manor. It became known and recorded thereafter as Blemondesberi. The 'bury' affix to the name comes from the Middle English word 'bury' or 'buri', or from the Saxon word 'burh' or 'byrig', meaning 'stronghold' or 'fortified manor'. The placename therefore means 'fortified manor belonging to the de Blemund family'.

Borough, The

This district in London's Southwark has a placename that comes directly from the Anglo-Saxon word 'burh', which represented a stronghold or fortified place. Its location may have been part of a defensive barrier to protect the City of London against Danish incursions from Kent and East Anglia across the River Thames. It was known by the mid-sixteenth century as Southwarke Borow.

Bow

By tradition, the district of Bow takes its name from an incident when Henry I's wife, Matilda, stumbled at the ford over the River Lea on one of her regular visits to Barking Abbey in 1177. The place had long been known as Stratforde, as a shallow crossing place on the river – hence 'straight ford'. Following the incident, the king ordered a bow-shaped bridge to be built across it for her future convenience, and the place became known as Stratforde-atte-Bow (at the Bow), and eventually was shortened simply to Bow.

Brent

In Anglo-Saxon times the place was known as Brente. There are two possible explanations for the origin of this placename; one has it derived from Brigantia, a Celtic goddess, and the other has it that the name Brent comes from the Celtic hill name or the Old English 'brant', meaning 'a steep or a high place'.

Brixton

The Greater London township of Brixton in the District of Lambeth was known before the Norman Conquest as Brixiges Stan. Which by the time of Domesday was recorded by the survey commissioners as Brixiestan. The Old English affix 'stan' indicated a stone, typically a boundary or road marker stone. The place probably began as a settlement whose chief or head man was called Beorhtsige, who may have erected a boundary marker here; it may also have marked an ancient meeting place.

Bromley

Originally in the County of Kent, this Greater London borough, ancient parish and market town has a charter going back to 1158 and a placename known since 862 as Bromleag or Brembel-lega. The name is of Anglo-Saxon origin and has arguably two meanings: first, as 'the place (or woodland clearing) where broom trees grow', and second as 'the place where brambles grow'. From the time of Domesday until the mid-nineteenth century, the manor belonged to the Bishops of Rochester in Kent and it was known for many years as Bromley St Peter and St Paul.

Brompton

This is a fairly common placename with at least a half dozen villages and townships of that name in England. The name comes from two Old English words, 'brom' and 'tun', respectively meaning 'broom' and 'woodland clearing'. Hence 'woodland clearing where broom trees are found'. The London Borough of Brompton, (which was formerly in the County of Middlesex), traces its placename back to the late-thirteenth century, when it was a rural area outside the city and apparently known for its plentiful broom trees at that time.

Camberwell

This place in the Southwark district of London is thought by some to have come initially from a man called Cantbeorht; others believe it originated in Latin as 'camera', meaning a room or a vaulted space. The second element of the name is from the Old English word 'wella', signifying a well or a spring. The vault alluded to in the second offering may have been the structure over the well, in which case the placename might translate as 'vaulted room over a well'. Conversely, the first alternative could be translated as 'Cantbeorht's well'. The jury is still out regarding which is the correct interpretation of the placename. In 1086 the place was recorded as Cambrewelle.

Camden Town

A relatively new district of London, Camden came into being in the mid-eighteenth century when, through an advantageous marriage, the First Earl Camden gained Kentish Town of which it formed a part. The Camden title came from Camden Place in Chiselhurst, itself named after the historian William Camden. In 1822, the place officially became Camden Town.

Canning Town

The district of Canning Town in the London Borough of Newham is a relatively recent appelation, and is named after Sir Samuel Canning, the wealthy Indian Rubber merchant who founded a company in the area in the nineteenth century. In 1868, the place was known as Canning New Town.

Canonbury

Canonbury is a district in Islington whose name means 'fortified manor of the canons'. The name comes from Middle English, where 'canoun' meant 'canon', a reference to the Augustinian Canons of St Bartholomew's who acquired this land in Smithfield in the thirteenth century, possibly some time before 1253. The 'bury' element of the name indicated a fortified manor or a stronghold. In 1373, the placename was recorded as Canonesbury.

Catford

No prizes for guessing the meaning of this placename in London's Lewisham district. It is known that here was once a woodland at a ford across the River Ravensbourne at this place and that wild or feral cats used to be found there. Hence, the placename has been known since 1254 as Catford.

Charing Cross

Known as Cyrringe before the Norman Conquest, this district of Westminster derived the first word of the placename from the Old English word 'cerring', which meant 'bend in the road', most likely referring to a bend in the River Thames rather than the old local thoroughfare. The Cross in question is the Queen Eleanor Cross erected by Edward I in memory of his widow in 1290, on a site that is the present-day forecourt of Charing Cross Station. It has also been suggested that the French expression *chère reine*, meaning 'dear queen', is another possible origin for the word 'Charing'. The place was known as Charryngcros by 1360.

Cheam

Cheam is a district of Croydon whose placename existed in the tenth century and is derived from two Old English words, 'ceg', a tree stump, and 'ham', a village or homestead. Hence, the name means 'village by tree stumps'. Domesday recorded Cheam as Ceiham, at that time listed in the Wallington Hundred of Surrey and held by the Archbishop of Canterbury.

Chelsea
Chelsea began in Saxon times as a small settlement beside the River Thames. The name is first recorded as Caelichyth in 767 and is derived from the Old English 'cealc', meaning 'chalk', and 'hyth', a 'landing place'. At that time, chalk and lime were common materials for wall washes or coverings. Therefore, the name may be taken to mean 'landing place for chalk or limestone', or even possibly a 'chalky landing place'.

Chingford
Historically part of Essex, Chingford was once known as Chingford Earls, after the Earl of Essex who owned the lands in the fifteenth century. By the mid-thirteenth century, the place was known as Chingelford, from the Old English 'cingel', meaning 'shingle', referring to a pebble river bed, and 'ford', a shallow river crossing. Hence, 'shingle ford'.

Chiswick
This district in Hounslow derived its placename from the medieval cheese-makers who once lived in the settlement. The place was known around the turn of the millennium as Ceswican, a name that comes from the Old English word 'cese' or 'ciese', meaning 'cheese' and 'wic'. In this context the 'wick' element refers to a specialised dairy or cheesery. Hence, 'farmstead specialising in making cheese'.

Clapham
There are places called Clapham in Bedfordshire, West Sussex and North Yorkshire. In common with the others, this district in Lambeth gets its name from the old word 'clopp', one of several words meaning 'hill', and 'ham', indicating a dwelling or homestead. Around 880, the place was recorded as Cloppaham, which by the time of Domesday had become Clopeham. The survey located it within the Brixton Hundred, at that time in the County of Surrey and in the possession of Geoffrey de Mandeville.

Clerkenwell
Clerkenwell in the district of Islington comes from the Middle English word 'clerk', meaning 'student' (or in its plural form, 'clercen'), and the Old English 'wella', which signified a well or a spring. The placename may be interpreted as 'spring (or well) where students meet (or gather)'. The spring in question has long since disappeared beneath the local thoroughfare.

Collier Row
The East London district of Collier Row is situated in the London Borough of Havering and its placename goes back to a time when charcoal burners worked there. The Middle English word 'colier' referred to charcoal burners (not as it later became, 'coal miners'), and a 'rewe' or 'rowe' signified a line or a row. Hence, 'row [of dwellings occupied by] charcoal burners'. In 1440, the placename was recorded as Colyers Rewe.

Covent Garden
There is thought to have been a Saxon settlement in Covent Garden since the seventh century, though little recorded history of the place exists from that time. The placename is a corruption of Convent Garden, which from the early Middle Ages was a vegetable garden owned by and supporting the monks attached to Westminster Abbey.

Cranford
Cranford was named after the River Crane on which it stands in the district of Houslow, and a shallow river crossing, or ford, that had existed there since well before the Norman

Conquest. The river name was almost certainly named after 'cran', the Old English word for a crane, (the water fowl), which evidently frequented the place. Domesday recorded it as Cranforde, in the Elthorne Hundred of Middlesex, held by William FitzAnsculf in 1086.

Cricklewood
By the end of the thirteenth century this district in Brent was recorded as Le Crikeldwode. The name is made up of two Middle English words, 'crikeled', meaning 'indented', 'crimped' or 'crinkled', and 'wode', a wood. Hence, 'wood with an indented edge'.

Crouch End
At some time in its history, this district in Haringey must have sported an important cross or crucifix, as 'crouch' is the Middle English word for a cross. The word 'ende' signified a district of an estate. Hence, the placename means 'district by [or of] the cross'. It was known as Crutche Ende in 1553,

Croydon
The Greater London Borough of Croydon appeared in the *Domesday Book* as Croindone, when it was a small agricultural settlement some ten miles south of London. In 809, it was known to the Saxons as Crogedene, derived from two Old English words, 'croh', their name for the herb wild saffron, and 'denu', a valley, making a placename that translates as the 'valley where wild saffron grows'.

Cubitt Town
This district in Tower Hamlets was named after William Cubitt, entrepreneur and one-time Lord Mayor of London. He was so honoured for his work in laying out housing estates for shipyard workers on the Isle of Dogs in the mid-nineteenth century.

Dulwich
This district in Southwark was known by the mid-tenth century as Dilwihs, and derived its name from two Anglo-Saxon words, 'dile', referring to the herb 'dill', and 'wisc', a water meadow or marsh. Hence, the placename may be taken to mean 'marshy water meadow where dill grows'. The placename eminently describes the contemporary topography of the area as Dulwich still abounds in many low-lying lakes and ponds.

Ealing
Known in the late seventh century as Gillingas, the name of this ancient township was originally derived from the name of a man called Gilla who began the settlement, plus the Old English affix 'inga', which refers to his followers, people or family. Hence, the placename means 'the settlement of Gilla's people'.

Edgware
Edgware, in the London Borough of Barnet, gets its name from a man called Ecgi and the Old English suffix 'wer', indicating a weir or a fishing pen or enclosure. Hence, 'fishing pen [or enclosure] of a man called Ecgi'. Who Ecgi actually was is open to speculation, but he was evidently the owner of a stretch of water or fish pond at some time in its early history.

Eltham
There are two possible interpretations of the placename of Eltham in the district of Greenwich. It could have been named after its founder or an early settler called Elta, plus the affix 'ham', indicating a homestead or a village, or it may be derived from the Old English

'elfitou', meaning 'swan'. So, either 'Elta's village' or 'village where swans are found' – either is equally plausible. The place was recorded in 1086 as Elteham, set in the County of Kent at that time and in the possession of Bishop Odo of Bayeux.

Enfield
Domesday recorded this place as Enefelde, the name derived from Old English, but with two possible derivations. First, after Eana, a man who may have founded the settlement, with the addition of the Old English affix 'feld', meaning a field or open land. Hence, 'Eana's field'. Alternatively, it may be based on 'ean', meaning a lamb, in which case the placename might translate as a 'field where lambs are born'.

Epping
The Manor of Epping was recorded in the *Domesday Book* as Eppinges or Epinga, in the Hundred of Waltham, in lands belonging to the canons of Holy Cross of Waltham, sometimes known as Crosiers or Cruzios, and formed part of the Manor of Eppingbury. The placename probably derives from the Old English 'yppe', meaning high ground or upland, and 'ingas', signifying a people or a tribal settlement. Hence, 'settlement of the people of the uplands'.

Erith
This township, formerly in Kent and located on the south bank of the River Thames, is now a district in Bexley, and derived its name from 'ear', and Old English word for gravel and 'hyth', a jetty or landing place. Hence, 'gravelly landing place'.

Finchley
Simple and to the point, the placename of Finchley in the London district of Barnet means 'woodland clearing where finches live'. The name comes from the Old English words 'finc', meaning 'finch', and 'leah', a woodland clearing. One of the earliest spellings of the placename was in the early thirteenth century when it was recorded as Finchelee.

Fulham
The placename of Fulham in the district of Hammersmith probably derives from two Saxon words, 'fullon', signifying birds or fowl, and 'ham', a home or settlement. Hence the name might mean, 'home [or place] of birds or fowl'. An alternative suggestion that it comes from a person called Fulla, and might translate as 'the homestead or dwelling of Fulla'. Yet a third explanation is that the name was originally 'Foul-ham', so named on account of its alleged dirtiness or muddiness. The place was known as Fulanham in the early eighth century, and by the time of Domesday it had been recorded as Fuleham, located at that time in the Ossulstone Hundred of Middlesex.

Greenford
Located on the River Brent in the district of Ealing, Greenford comes from the Old English word 'grene', meaning 'green', and 'ford', a shallow river crossing place. Hence, self-evidently, '[the] green ford'. It was known in 845 as Grenan forda and by 1086 had become Greneforde. The 'green' element may have referred to particularly grassy banks, or even green weeds at this place.

Greenwich
The original Saxon village of Greenwich was known in the tenth century as Grenewic, from the Old English words 'grene', self-evidently meaning green, and 'wic', a harbour. Hence, 'green harbour'. From its earliest days, East Greenwich as it was known, was a river port

and fishing village. By 1086, it had been recorded as Grenviz, or 'Grenuiz, in the Half-Lathe of Sutton, in Greenwich Hundred', held by the Bishop Odo of Bayeux for his half-brother, William the Conqueror.

Hackney
The name of the small hamlet of Hackney first emerged some time during the sixth century. It has been suggested that it derives from an island or raised bank in a marsh, known in Old English as an 'ey' or 'eg', and a man called Haca, or Hacon, who settled there. Others explain the word 'haca' as signifying a hook shaped spit or tongue of land. In the case of the latter, the placename might mean 'the raised bank shaped like a tongue'.

Hale End
There is an opinion that Hale End may have taken its placename from Walter de la Hale who was known to be living there in 1285. However, others cite the old words 'halh', meaning a nook or corner, and 'end', which signified a remote or outlying district. Hence, the name might translate as a 'remote corner of land'. There had been clearings in the Forest of Epping that had been known as North End and Wood End since the time of Domesday, but it was not until 1873 that the name Hale End came into being.

Hammersmith
Although evidence has been found for the Roman occupation of Hammersmith, it first emerged in historical records as a Saxon fishing village. The name derives from the old words 'hamor' and 'smitheth', a smithy or blacksmith's shop, which taken together mean 'the place of the hammer smithy [or forge]'.

Hampton Wick
The civil parish of Hampton Wick was created in 1831, separating it from Hampton by the creation of Bushy Park and establishing its own local administration. A 'wick' or 'wic' was an ancient landing or trading place. The landing place in question would have been beside the River Thames, and probably supplied goods and provisions to Hampton Manor House, which in 1527 became Hampton Court Palace, the palatial residence of the ill-fated Cardinal Wolsey.

Harefield
The name of this district in Hillingdon translates into modern English as 'open land used by an army'. It comes from the Old English 'here', meaning 'army' and 'feld', open land. The army in question is widely believed to have been a Viking army, and 'feld' could imply a battlefield or a military training ground. In the 1086 survey, the place was recorded as Herefelle, and listed in the Elthorne Hundred of Middlesex, held by Richard, the son of Count Gilbert, having belonged to Countess Goda (also known as Godifu or Gode, the sister of King Edward), before the Norman Conquest.

Haringey
Located on the banks of the River Lee, some evidence of early prehistoric and Roman occupation has been found in Haringey. The placename is of Anglo-Saxon origin and comes from a leader called Haering or Haring, who founded the settlement in the fifth or sixth century, plus the Old English 'haeg', meaning a grey wood, and translates roughly as 'Haering's settlement in the grey wood'. By the time of Domesday, the Manor of Harengheie was owned by the Bishop of London. In late medieval times it was known as Haringseye, which became shortened to Hornsey, and by the late sixteenth century the place had emerged as Haringay alias Hornesey.

Harrow

In the eighth century, the township that we now call Harrow was known as Gumeninga Herga, which by the time of the Domesday survey had been shortened to Herges and even later as Hareways. The Old English word 'hearg' referred to heathen people or pagans, and the name could be interpreted as 'the temple or shrine of the heathen tribe or people called Gumeningas'.

Havering

Havering probably derives its name from a man called Haefer, who, with his family, founded a settlement in what was then in the County of Essex. In Old English, the 'inga' element of a placename indicates the family or people of a person. Hence, the name means '[land of] the people of Haefer'. The *Domesday Book* records Haueringas and Havelingae, in the Hundred of Becontree, in 'Essex lands of the king', held by Harold. Later it was known as Havering-atte-Bower. The word 'atte' comes from Middle English and means 'at the' and is pronounced 'atty'. Tradition has it that Edward the Confessor built a country retreat, or 'bower' (Havering Palace) some time in the first half of the eleventh century. The appendage 'atte Bower', was added to the placename when it became the property of Queen Eleanor as part of the queen's dowry in 1267. The name therefore means 'Havering at the Bower'.

Hayes

Historically in the County of Middlesex, the Hayes district of Hillingdon in Greater London has a placename that means 'land overgrown with brushwood [or scrub]', and comes from the Saxon word 'haes', which referred specifically to a thicket or brushwood. It is assumed that at the time that the placename was established the area was indeed covered in scrub or brushwood. The placename was recorded as Hesa in 1177.

Hendon

Hendon was already known as Heandun by the late-tenth century, a name derived from the Old English words 'heah', meaning 'high', and 'dun', a hill. Hence, '[place on a] high hill'. The original settlement grew up around the Church of St Mary which stood atop a hill. Domesday recorded this district in Barnett as Handone in 1086, and listed it within the Gore Hundred of Middlesex, held at that time by Westminster Abbey, who had also owned the manor in 1066.

Highbury

The Islington district of Highbury's placename means 'high manor'; the name comes directly from the Saxon words 'heah', meaning 'high' and 'burh', a fortified place, stronghold or manor house. The name eminently describes its location on high ground. Formerly in the Parish of Stoke Newington, it was recorded in its own right as Heybury in around 1375.

Hillingdon

The ancient Middlesex Parish of Hillingdon lies on the River Colne, which formed its boundary with the County of Buckinghamshire. In medieval times, Hillingdon, Uxbridge and Cowley were one virtual entity and, as far as the Domesday commissioners were concerned, Hillingdon was within the Manor of Colham. By 1086, it was known as Hildendune or Hillendone, after a Saxon man called Hilda (or possibly 'Hille'), and the hill (or 'dun'), where he established the settlement. The Great Survey places it in Elthorne Hundred in land belonging to Earl Roger, having belonged to Ulf, a thegn of King Edward before the Norman Conquest.

Holborn

The name of this district in the London Borough of Camden means '[place by the] hollow stream'. It comes from 'hol', an Old English word meaning 'hollow' (as in a narrow valley or ravine), and 'burna', a brook or a stream, (or in Scotland, a 'burn'). The hollow in question is thought to be a dip in present-day Farringdon Road. Domesday recorded the place as Holeburne, a very small estate supporting just two households in the Ossulstone Hundred, held at that time by King William as it had belonged to King Edward until 1066.

Holloway

Holloway is located in the district of Islington and was first recorded as Le Holeweye in 1307. The name comes from the Old English words 'hol', meaning 'hollow', (as in a narrow valley), and 'weg', meaning 'way', an alternative to 'road', but having the same meaning. Hence, '[place by the] hollow way', or 'road in a hollow'.

Hounslow

The name has two suggested derivations; one has it derived from the Germanic word 'hund', a hound, and the other that it is named after a man called Hund who founded the settlement. The Old English affix 'hlaw', signifies a mound, possibly a burial barrow. Therefore, the placename may be taken to mean either '[burial] mound of the hound', or 'the mound belonging to [or of] a man called Hund'.

Isle of Dogs

The Isle of Dogs was known as such in 1520 and was mentioned in his diary by Samuel Pepys. The name may have been a corruption of the 'Isle of Ducks', given the surrounding marshland and its suitability as a habitat for water fowl. It cannot be truly said to be an island, except occasionally when high tides isolate it from the main river bank. It has also been suggested that the placename could also be a corruption of the 'Isle of Docks', given its proximity to the London docklands. Other possible variations include 'Isle of Dutch', 'Isle of Dykes' or 'Isle of Doggers'.

Islington

By the beginning of the eleventh century, the north London township of Islington had been recorded in an Anglo-Saxon charter as Gislandune, based on the name of a man called Gisla, and the Old English word 'dun', meaning a hill. Hence, 'Gisla's hill'. By 1086, the Domesday commissioners had written the placename as Isledone, in the Ossulstone Hundred of Middlesex, where the canons of St Paul's Church maintained two hides of land on the estate belonging to the Bishop of London.

Kennington

The Kennington district of Lambeth derived its placename from a man called Cena. The two additional Old English affixes 'inga' and 'tun' respectively relate to a family or people and to a farmstead or settlement. Hence, 'settlement of Cena's people'. Domesday recorded the place as Chenintune in the Brixton Hundred of Surrey, held in 1086 by a man known as Theodric the Goldsmith, who had also held it before the Conquest. By the thirteenth century, it was being written as Kenintone.

Kentish Town

The Kentish Town district of Camden has a fairly straightforward meaning. The Old English suffix 'tun' signified a farmstead or estate, and 'Kentish' is a Middle English expression meaning 'man of Kent', which may also have been used as a surname. Hence, the placename may be taken to mean either 'estate or farmstead [belonging to the] man [or men] of Kent', or 'estate of a man called Kentish'. Either is possible. In 1208, the place was known as Kentisston.

Kew

The precise explanation of this placename in the district of Richmond is still debated. In the early fourteenth century the place was recorded as Cayho, probably from the Saxon words 'caeg', meaning 'key-shaped', and 'hoh', 'ho' or 'hoe', indicating a projecting spur of land or a promontory. Alternatively, the name may come from the Middle English word 'key', meaning 'quay' or 'landing place'. So, either 'key-shaped promontory' or simply 'quay [or landing place]'.

Kilburn

Kilburn, is a district in Brent which was known in the early twelfth century as Cuneburna. Two different interpretations exist for the origin of the placename. The last element of the name is fairly straightforward, as the Old English word 'burna' signified a brook or a stream. It is the first element that is open to dispute: one has it derived from a man called Cylla, its probable founder (hence, 'Cylla's stream'); the other prefers 'cu', 'cuna' or 'cyna' as indicating 'cow' or 'cows', in which case the placename might translate as 'stream of the cows', even though no stream actually exists there today.

Knightsbridge

Knightsbridge was not mentioned in the *Domesday Book* and opinions vary as to the exact derivation of the placename. However, the most plausible explanation is that it originates in the Old English word 'cniht', which could signify a knight or simply a horseman or a young man, and 'brycg', a bridge. Hence, possibly, 'a bridge where young (horse) men congregate'. Other suggested variants include a tale concerning a knight who fought off and despatched a band of murderous thugs at the bridge, and another of two knights who fought to the death over some dispute at the site. Finally, it has been suggested that the bridge in question was solely used by knights and ladies and may have been prohibited to common folk. Which is true, we may never know.

Lambeth

Lambeth is thought to have derived its placename from the Old English words 'lamb' and 'hythe', suggesting a jetty, or landing place for lambs or sheep and was known before the Norman Conquest as Lambehitha. At the time of the Great Survey of 1086, the 'Manor of St Mary's which is called Lamhytha', in Brixton Hundred, originally in the County of Surrey, belonged to the Church of Lambeth, having been held before 1066 by Countess Gode, sister of King Edward. According to the survey, Odo, Bishop of Bayeux, also held a piece of arable land in the estate.

Lewisham

During his lifetime, Alfred the Great was Lord of the 'Mainou of Liofshema', which by late Saxon times was known as Lievesham. The placename may come from a man called Leofsa, Leof, or Laese, and the Old English suffix 'ham', signifying a homestead, village or settlement. Hence 'the settlement of Leofsa'. Alternatively, it has been argued that 'laes' or 'lase' is an old Saxon word for a meadow, which might suggest 'the settlement in the meadow' as a possible translation of the placename.

Leyton/Leytonstone

The township of Leyton in the Waltham Forest is thought to derive from Roman times and derives its name from the River Lea on which it stands, with the addition of the 'tun' affix, indicating a farmstead. Hence, 'farmstead on the River Lea'. The river name is of Celtic origin and is thought to mean 'bright one'. In the sixteenth century the place was called Low Leyton on account of its low-lying location beside the river, but the 'Low' was dropped in 1867. The place was recorded in Domesday as Leintune in 1086. In the first century the Roman tenth legion erected a mile marker stone on the road that ran through the district. The stone in question still stands. Over time, the place became known as Leyton-atte-Stone (Leyton at the stone), or Leyton Stone.

Limehouse
Limehouse was a name derived from the pottery-makers lime kilns or lime oasts that operated at one time beside the River Thames and was recorded in 1356 as Les Lymhostes.

Merton
When the Romans arrived in Britain, they built Stane Street through the district of Merton to link London with the port at Chichester. After Roman withdrawal from Britain, Anglo-Saxon settlers arrived from Germany and established what they called Mertone, signifying 'the farmstead by the pool', from the Old English words 'mere', meaning a small lake or pool, and 'tun', a farmstead or settlement. In 1086, the *Domesday Book* recorded Meretone, in Brixton Hundred of Surrey, held by the king. Before the Conquest it had been held by Earl Harald.

Maida Vale
The Maida Vale district of Westminster was created in the nineteenth century in commemoration of a British victory over the French at the Battle of Maida in Calabria, Italy, in 1806. Located as it is at the foot of Maida Hill, the 'Vale' element of the placename was appended as a description of the local topography.

Maldon/New Maldon
A district in Kingston upon Thames and historically part of Surrey, New Maldon was established in the nineteenth century, largely as a result of the opening of its railway station (which bore the name), that was opened in December 1846; thereafter it became an adjunct to the village of Maldon, which then became known as Old Maldon. The Maldon placename translates as 'hill with a cross or crucifix', from the Old English words 'mael and 'dun'.

Marylebone
This district in Westminster was named after the fifteenth century Church of St Mary. The 'bone' and 'le' elements were added in the seventeenth century. 'Bone' is a corruption of the Old English word 'burna', meaning 'stream' or 'brook'. Hence, the placename meant '[place at] St Mary's stream'. The stream in question was originally known as Tyburn, which derived from 'teo', meaning 'boundary', reflecting the fact that it marked the border between the Manors of Westminster and Ebury.

Mile End
Mile End was recorded as La Mile Ende in 1288, a name that comes from Middle English and translates as the 'hamlet a mile distant', in reference to its distance from London at that time.

Millwall
This district of Tower Hamlets was named after a mill which stood on or near a 'wall' in the eighteenth century; the wall in question is thought to have been a reinforcement of the Thames embankment.

Mitcham

Mitcham derives the first element of its placename from the Old English word 'micel', meaning 'large' or 'great', and 'ham', a dwelling place or homestead. Hence, 'large dwelling (or homestead)'. Domesday recorded the place as Michelham, in the Wallingford Hundred of Surrey, in the land of William FitzAnsculf, five hides of which were held at that time by the Canons of Bayeux in Normandy, having been held for King Edward by Beorhtric before the Conquest.

Mortlake

The second element of this placename is straightforward enough, coming from the Saxon word 'lacu', which referred to a pool of water or a stream. However, opinions differ as to the significance of the 'mort' element of the placename. One has it named after a man called Morta, and another cites the Old English word 'mort', which referred to a small salmon, one of several fish of this type at one time caught at this spot. The stream was probably Beverley Brook which enters the River Thames at this point. Domesday referred to Mortelage and Mortelaga, in the Brixton Hundred, held in demesne by the Archbishop of Canterbury.

Neasden

Neasden is a district in Brent and derives its placename from 'neosu', meaning 'nose', and 'dun', a hill. Hence, the best interpretation of the name would be '[place near or by a] nose-shaped hill'. It was known around the turn of the millennium as Neosdune. It seems probable that this was a reference to the nearby Dollis Hill ridge.

Newham

An Anglo-Saxon charter of 958 describes the area as Hamme, based on the Old English word 'hamm', indicating dry land between the rivers, or marshland. This almost certainly referred to a settlement bounded by the River Thames, the River Rosing and the River Lea. Domesday records the place simply as Hame, in the Hundred of Becontree, held by the canons of St Peter and belonging to Robert Gernon, a part having been in the possession of Aethelstan and another by Leofraed before the Norman Conquest. East and West Ham were partitioned some time in the twelfth century, when Westhamma was recorded in 1186. It would be more than eight hundred years before the two 'Hams' were reunited as Newham in 1965.

Notting Hill

There are several possible permutations of the meaning of the name of this district in the Borough of Kensington and Chelsea. The 'Notting' element of the placename could be either derived from the Old English word 'cnotta', which represented a knot or a lump, or else it might have referred to a man called Cnotta and his family or followers (which the old affix 'inga' indicates). In the mid-fourteenth century, the place was recorded as Knottynghull. The ancient 'hyll' element is fairly straightforward, but we are left with two schools of thought as to the exact interpretation of the placename: one has it as '[settlement on the] hill belonging to Cnotta's people [or family]'; another cites the township of Knotting in Bedfordshire as the most likely reference, and that Notting Hill's early settlers may have originated in that place.

Peckham

Peckham is a district on the south bank of the Thames in Southwark. The name derives from Saxon times when 'peac' meant 'peak' or 'pointed hill', and 'ham' signified a village, dwelling or homestead. Hence 'village on a peak'. In fact, there is no peak as such, though the district does lie on high ground. Domesday recorded the place as Pecheham, at that time in the Brixton Hundred of Surrey in land belonging to the Bishop of Bayeux, with part leased to the Bishop of Lisieux in Normandy.

Penge
The district of Penge in Bromley has a placename that means '[place at the] top of the wood'. It derives originally from Celtic and is related to the Welsh word 'pen', which means 'head', 'top' or 'summit', and 'coed', meaning 'wood'. Historically, Penge was an important area of woodland pasture. In the years preceding the Norman Conquest the area was known as Penceat.

Pentonville
Pentonville is a district of Islington whose name means 'Penton's town', from the French word 'ville', meaning 'town' or 'city', and the name of its founder, Henry Penton MP, who owned the land and began its development in the 1770s. It finally acquired the name Pentonville in 1822.

Pimlico
The source of the name of the Westminster district of Pimlico is ambiguous; for many years it was commonly held to have been named after Ben Pimlico, a local innkeeper, but more recently an alternative proposition has been mooted. It is suggested that the name was 'borrowed' from Pamlico in America, near to the place where Sir Walter Raleigh is thought to have attempted settlements in the 1580s. Whatever the truth of it, the placename, Pimlico, first appeared in its present form in 1626.

Pinner
Pinner is a district of Harrow whose placename means '[place by the] pointed bank'. It is derived from the Old English word 'pinn', meaning 'point' or 'peg' (similar to the modern English word 'pin'). The second element of the name is 'ora', meaning 'bank', thought to be a reference to the ridge that runs across what is now Pinner Park. By the early thirteenth century the placename had been recorded as Pinnora.

Poplar
Poplar has been a district in the London Metropolitan Borough of Tower Hamlets since 1965, when the former civil parish and borough were abolished. Poplar means what its says – it is the name of the tree. It's evident that there were poplar trees in the district from the earliest times. The word is first known in Middle English and underwent several different spellings in the fourteenth century, including Popeler and Le Popler.

Primrose Hill
The meaning of Primrose Hill, in the district of Camden, is easy to understand – a hill where primroses grew. In Middle English it was spelt as 'primerose', and carries the Old English affix 'hyll'. It is indeed located on a hill on the northern side of Regent's Park and its placename was first recorded in a popular song title of the late-sixteenth century.

Purley
Purley gets its name from the pear trees that were once abundant in the district. The name comes from the Anglo-Saxon words 'pirige', meaning 'pear tree', and 'leah', a woodland clearing. Therefore, the placename of this township in Croydon means '[place in a] woodland clearing where pear trees grow'. The district still possesses woodlands to its south and east. By the start of the twelfth century the placename had been recorded as Pirlee.

Putney

There are two possibilities for the meaning of this London district of Wandsworth's placename as the first element could be either a reference to a man called Putta, or else the Old English word 'putta', which signified a hawk or a bird of prey. The last element of the name comes from 'hyth', meaning 'landing place', a common term on the River Thames, where hythes were frequently makeshift jetties or wharfage quaysides (as in Rotherhithe). The placename may therefore mean either 'landing stage of a man called Putta' or 'landing stage where hawks are seen'. Domesday recorded the place as Putelei; in 1279 the name was written as Puttenhuthe and in 1474 as Putneth.

Redbridge

Redbridge derived its name from the red brick bridge that was built over the River Roding and was first recorded as the Red Bridge in 1746, having previously been known as Hocklee's Bridge. It was demolished in 1921 and replaced by a new bridge, but it survives in the placename.

Romford

Romford, in the London Borough of Havering, has long been said to derive its placename from the Old English word 'rum', meaning 'wide', 'spacious' or 'roomy', and 'ford', a shallow river crossing. Hence '[place by a] wide ford'. The ford in question lay on the River Rom (which was named after the settlement), and was an ancient Roman river crossing on the London-Colchester road. In more recent times, it has been suggested that the 'Rom' element of the placename may therefore have been a reference to the Romans, and the placename could possibly mean 'Roman river crossing [or ford]'. In 1177, it was written as Romfort.

Rotherhithe

The Rotherhithe district of Southwark gets its name from Anglo-Saxon times when 'hryther' signified 'cattle' and the word 'hyth' referred to a jetty, wharfage or landing place, in this case, beside the River Thames. It was here that livestock were unloaded on their way to market, resulting in a placename that means 'landing place for cattle'. The area was at one time known as Redriff, a name that still survives in Redriff Road. Consequently, in 1105 the name was recorded as Rederheia, and in 1127 it was recorded a Retherhith. It was not until the late nineteenth century that the place was known by two names, as Redriff and as Rotherhithe, the latter of which survives to the present day.

Ruislip

The explanation of the Old English meaning of this potentially confusing placename are two-fold: one suggests 'rysc-hylpe', which translates as 'rushy crossing'; the other is that it is 'rysc-slaep', meaning rushy slope or hillside. Both seem equally probable in that it could be interpreted as a slippery slope covered with rushes. Or 'slippery crossing place [across a river] where rushes grow'. Formerly in the County of Middlesex, this Greater London township appeared in the *Domesday Book* as Rislepe, 'In the Land of Ernulf de Hesdin, [in the] Elthorne Hundred', where he held twenty hides of land, worth twelve pounds, having been valued at thirty pounds at the time of King Edward.

Shadwell

The Shadwell placename has two possible interpretations. According to one, it derives from the old Saxon word 'fleot', meaning a creek or shallow inlet, and was known in the thirteenth century as Scadflet, from the adjacent churchyard of St Chad and the well that it filled. Hence, 'St Chad's well'. Another cites the Old English 'sceald', meaning 'shallow', and 'wella', meaning 'spring' or 'well'. Hence, '[place at the] shallow spring'. In 1222 it was recorded as Schadewelle, so either explanation seems equally probable.

Shepherd's Bush
Shepherd's Bush is a district in the Borough of Hammersmith and Fulham, and probably derived its placename from the Shepherd family who owned the bushy land thereabouts, and probably has little to do with sheep husbandry. However there is a contrary argument that it was originally common land used as an overnight resting point for shepherds and offered grazing as they drove their flocks to Smithfield Market in London. We may never know which is true. It was recorded in 1635 as Shepherds Bush Green.

Shooters Hill
This district in Greenwich has two equally plausible explanations of its placename. One thing is certain, the name is derived from 'sceotere', an Old English word meaning 'shooter' or 'archer'. This might suggest a hillside where archers practiced. However, another sees it as an area where thieves waylaid travellers on Watling Street which crosses the hill at this point. So, archers or thieves? Take your pick. One of the earliest known records of the placename was in 1226, when it was written as Shitereshell.

Shoreditch
The Old English word 'scora' signified a sloping bank and 'dic' meant 'ditch' Hence, the placename of this district in Hammersmith may have meant 'ditch by a bank [or on a slope]'. There is no record of the location of such a ditch. So, an alternative explanation has been proposed in the form of the old Brythonic word 'skor', meaning 'fort' or 'fortification', in which case the placename could be translated as 'fortified ditch', a possible reference to the Roman wall of the early city which they called Londinium. In the twelfth century, the place was recorded as Soredich.

Sidcup
Sidcup in the London district of Bexley derived its name from two Old English words, 'set', meaning 'seat', and 'copp', another name for a hill. The placename therefore means '[place on a] flat-topped [or seat-shaped] hill'. The hilltop on which the original settlement was eastablished has long since disappeared among dense urban sprawl. In 1254, the place was recorded as Cetecopp.

Snaresbrook
Snaresbrook is a district in Waltham Forest whose name may mean '[place where] snares are set by a brook', or something along those lines. It is by no means certain, but the word 'snare' was a Middle English word which signified animal or bird traps, and this is the most probable origin of the first element of the placename. 'Brook' is also a Middle English word, and means precisely what it says, and represents a brook or a stream. The name appears in its present form at the end of the sixteenth century, as Snaresbrook.

Soho
This district of Westminster was at one time used as hunting fields and the word Soho is thought to be a derivation of the hunting cry 'Talley ho', shouted loudly to alert the hunt that a quarry had been sighted. It was known as So Ho in 1632. Legend has it that the Duke of Monmouth, who lived in Soho Square, used it as his password during the 1685 Rising (known as the Monmouth Rebellion), when an attempt was made to overthrow James II.

Southall

Southall in the London Borough of Ealing has a placename that means 'southern corner of land'. The name comes from a combination of the Old English words 'suth', meaning 'southern', and 'halh', a corner or nook of land. In 1198, the placename was recorded as Suhaull, and by 1204 it had been written as Sudhale.

Southwark

Southwark (pronounced 'Suth-uck'), was known in the tenth century as Suthringageweorc, and was an important centre of government in Anglo-Saxon England. The name meant 'fort of the men of Surrey'. By 1086, the Domesday survey had shortened the name to Sudwerka, in the Kingston Hundred, of which the 'suth' element means 'southern', and 'weorc' signifies a defensive earthwork or fortress. Hence, 'southern fort'. As a fortified settlement it may have been an important defensive structure, protecting London from frequent incursions by the Danes who are known to be in the region in 1016.

Spitalfields

The 'spital' element of this Tower Hamlets district is the Middle English contraction of 'spitel', which stood for the word 'hospital'. In medieval times this often referred to a religious house or a leper hospital, frequently the only source of medical services available at that time. The 'fields' element is self explanatory. Originally, the field on which the settlement began was the property of the Priory of St Mary Spital and was founded in 1197; the place was recorded as Seintmariespitel in Shoreditch in 1394.

Stanmore

The Stanmore district of Harrow derives its placename from two Old English words: 'stan', a stone, and 'mere', a pool. Hence the name translates either as '[place at the] stone by a pool', or 'stony place by a pool', of which the latter is more widely accepted. In 1086, the place was recorded as Stanmere, in the Gore Hundred land of the Count of Mortain. The account reads: 'The same count holds Stanmere. It is assessed at nine and a half hides. There a priest has half a hide and [there are] four villans each on one virgate and three cottars on ten acres'. The estate assets amounted to pasture for livestock and woodland pannage for eight hundred pigs, altogether valued at sixty shillings. The audit concludes that before the Conquest, '...Eadmer Atule, a thegn of King Edward, held this manor'.

Stepney

Stepney may have been named after a man called Stybba, and was recorded at the turn of the first millennium as Stybbanhythe, where 'hyth' was the Saxon word for a landing place or a jetty. Alternatively, the first element of the placename may have come from the Old English word 'stybba', meaning a tree stump or wooden pile. Hence, the placename may mean either 'landing-place of a man called Stybba', or 'landing-place [or jetty] of wooden piles'. In 1086, Domesday recorded the place as Stibenhede, in the Ossulstone Hundred of Middlesex, held at that time by the Bishop of London.

Stockwell

The district of Stockwell in the London Borough of Lambeth gets its name from 'stocc' and 'wella', Old English words that respectively mean 'tree stump' and 'well (or 'stream'). Therefore the placename means 'well [or spring] near a tree stump'. In 1197 the placename was recorded as Stokewell.

Stratford

Of the eight places called Stratford in England, the name of this township in the London Borough of Newham reflects its location on the old Roman road from London to Colchester. The Old English element 'straet' was the word that Saxons used to describe the roads left behind following the Roman occupation of Britain, and 'ford' signified a shallow river crossing, in this particular case across the River Lea. The placename was recorded as Straetforda in 1067, and in its present form of Stratford as early as 1177.

Streatham

Like Stratford, this London district derives its name from 'straet', meaning 'Roman road', with the addition of 'ham', indicating a village or homestead dwelling. Hence, 'homestead on the Roman road'. Domesday recorded the name as Estreham and Stradham 'in the Two Hundreds of Ely Which Meet at Witchford', held by the Church at Ely in 1086.

Surbiton

Located in the Royal Manor of Kingston in Greater London, Surbiton derived its name from Anglo-Saxon times, when 'suth' meant 'southern' and 'bere-tun' related originally to a barley-growing farmstead, but often signifying an outlying farmstead, or sometimes translated as 'grange'. Hence, loosely, 'southern outlying (or remote) barley farm'. In 1179, the placename was recorded as Suberton. The nearby northerly place known as Norbiton has a similar derivation.

Swiss Cottage

An invention of the nineteenth century, the Swiss Cottage district in Camden is named after the Swiss Cottage Tavern, that had been built around 1840 to resemble an Alpine chalet. It stood at the junction of three major London roads and had been established on the site of a former tollgate keeper's cottage. It was later renamed the Swiss Inn and finally in the early twentieth century it became Swiss Cottage. Soon thereafter, the township adopted it as its placename.

Teddington

Despite numerous myths concerning the origin of this placename, including somewhat fanciful versions written by the likes of James Thorne and Rudyard Kipling, Teddington derived its name from an early settler called Tuda, its probable founder. The Old English affixes 'inga' and 'tun' respectively signify 'people', 'followers' or 'family', and 'estate' or 'settlement'. The placename therefore means 'settlement [or estate] of Tuda's people [or followers]'. It was already known by the end of the tenth century as Tudintun.

Tolworth

The Tolworth district of Kingston took its name from a man called Tala, who may have been the founder or leader of the original settlement. Tala evidently enclosed his land, as indicated by the Old English word 'worth', meaning 'enclosure'. Such enclosures were uncommon in Saxon England, where land tended to be farmed in long open strips and fences or hedgerows were hardly ever seen. Domesday recorded the place as Taleorde, and listed it in the Kingston Hundred, held in 1086 by Richard FitzGilbert. The account recorded that 'Eadmer held it, and could go where he would (before 1066)', identifying him as a free man who was not tied in servitude to the manor land. The estate also included six villans, one bordar and two slaves. In 1352 the name was recorded as Talworth and had evolved into its present form by 1601.

Upney

Upney was once a small hamlet in the County of Essex, but since 1974 has been part of the Borough of Barking in Greater London. The name comes from 'uppan' and 'eg' which translate respectively from Old English as '[settlement] upon' and 'island', generally referring to high or raised dry ground in marsh or fenland. Hence, the placename means '[settlement] upon dry ground [in a marsh]', or something along those lines. The present-day placename was recorded as early as 1456.

Walthamstow/Waltham Forest

By 1261, the Foresta de Wautham was known, having taken its name from Waltham Abbey of the Holy Cross, its own name derived from a venerated woman called Wilcume, with the added Old English suffix 'stow', indicating a holy place. Hence, 'the holy place of a woman called Wilcume'. The Waltham placename was recorded in the *Domesday Book* as Waltham Abbey, which had been established in 1060. The local forest was a royal hunting ground, known at one time as Wilcumestou, which some say translates as 'holy place where people are welcome', but this may be somewhat speculative. There are at least a half dozen other places in England called Waltham.

Wandsworth

The Borough of Wandsworth was named after a man called Waendel, whose enclosure, (or 'worth') it was. Hence, 'Waendel's enclosure'. The man and the place gave the name to the River Wandle which flows through the borough. Domesday recorded the place as Wandelsorde and Wendelsorde, in the Brixton Hundred, belonging to the Abbot of Saint-Wandrille and held on his behalf by an unnamed monk, it having been held by Swein for King Edward before the Conquest.

Wapping

Wapping traces its history back to Anglo-Saxon times and might have referred to the 'settlement of Weappa's family or people', after an early chieftain of that name, or it may have derived from the Old English 'wapole', signifying a mud-flat or marsh. Located as it is on the banks of the River Thames, this last interpretation makes perfect sense, though either is possible.

Wembley

The district of Wembley in the London Borough of Brent is named after its earliest known settler, a man called Wemba, who lived some time before the ninth century and owned a woodland glade or clearing, or as the Saxons knew such places, a 'leah'. Hence, the placename means 'Wemba's woodland clearing'. In 825, the place had already been called Wembalea.

Whitechapel

Whitechapel was named after a small chapel of ease dedicated in the thirteenth century to St Mary. The chapel was reputedly whitewashed with a lime and chalk mixture, a common practice on many medieval churches, prompting it to be referred to as the 'white chapel'. That original building, along with the church of St Mary Matfelon, was destroyed by bombs during the Second World War.

White City

White City is a district within the London Borough of Hammersmith and Fulham, whose name comes from the distinctive white stuccoed walls of the stadium built there to house the Imperial International Exhibition in 1909, on an area that had previously been open farmland. Its construction was accompanied by an exhibition centre and was known for a time as the Great White City due to the white marble which clad its pavilions.

Willesden

The district of Willisden in Brent was known to the Saxons as Willesdone, a name that comes from the Old English words 'wella', meaning a well, fountain or spring, and 'dun', a hill. The placename therefore means 'hill with a spring [or by a stream]'. Domesday recorded the placename as Wellesdone in 1086 in the Ossulstone Hundred of Middlesex, held by the canons of St Paul's as a demesne 'for their sustenance'.

Wimbledon

Wimbledon's original placename comes from Saxon times when a hill ('dun') belonged to a man called Wynnmann. It was recorded in the mid-tenth century as Wunemannedune. That version of the name was apparently completely unpronounceable to the Norman French tongue and the placename was shortened and written as Wimeldon in the early thirteenth century. By 1211, it had been written under its current name of Wimbledon.

Woolwich

Woolwich was recorded in 918 as Uuluuich. This looks ungainly to the contemporary eye, but given the letter we call 'w', is pronounced 'double-u', its origins are quite clear, and it's not much of a stretch to see the spelling of the name quite differently. The placename comes from the Old English word 'wull', meaning 'wool' and 'wic', a port, harbour or trading post. Hence, 'trading port for wool'. An even odder rendering of the placename occurred in the *Domesday Book* entry when it was recorded as Hulviz or Huluiz, '...in the Half-Lathe of Sutton in the Greenwich Hundred of Kent', in land belonging to Hamo the Sheriff.

Wormwood Scrubs

By the end of the twelfth century the place we call Wormwood Scrubs was known as Wormeholte. The name has two Old English elements: 'wyrm', meaning 'snake', and 'holt', which was synonym for 'wudu', meaning woodland or forest. Hence, 'woodland [infested with] snakes'. The addition later of the Saxon expression 'scrubb', meaning scrubland or brushwood somewhat complicates the translation, as some believe the placename might be better translated as 'scubland where wormwood grows'. By the fifteenth century, the name had changed to Wormoltwode and even in the early nineteenth century it was being recorded as Wormholt Scrubbs. It would be around 1865 before its present name of Wormwood Scrubs came into common usage.

Part Twelve

The South-East

East Sussex, Hampshire, Kent, Surrey, and West Sussex

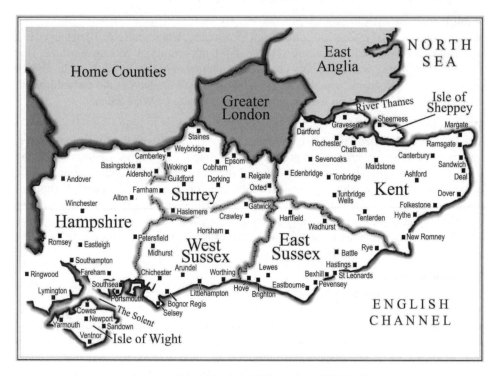

A map depicting the South-East region of England.

Abinger/Abinger Hammer

This Surrey Township was originally known simply as Abinger, until a forge or foundry was established at Hammer Hill within the township sometime around 1600, when the word 'Hammer' was added to the placename. The name was known in Norman times as Abingewurd. It comes from Old English and was held by a man called Abba. The affix 'inga' represented 'people', 'followers' or 'family', with the addition of 'worth', signifying an enclosure. Hence the full translation of the placename means 'the foundry enclosure belonging to the people of Abba'. Domesday recorded the place as Abinceborne, an apparent misspelling by the Norman French commissioner whose grasp of Anglo-Saxon was clearly rudimentary. The Manor of Abinger was held by William FitzAnsculf at that time; before the Conquest it had been held for King Edward by a man called Huscarl.

Aldershot

The first written record of the Hampshire Manor of Aldershot, in the ancient Crondall Hundred, was in 1171, when it was known as Halreshet. The name may come from the Old

English words 'alor', related to the alder tree, and 'sceat', a projecting piece of land or a promontory. Hence, the placename would mean 'a projecting piece of land where alders grow'. An alternative view is that the 'shot' element may be even older and simply refer to a wood or copse, in which case the name might translate as 'a wood where alders grow'. In the late twelfth century the placename was recorded as Halredshet.

Andover
The Hampshire township of Andover traces its history back to 950 when King Edred (or Eadred) had a royal hunting lodge built beside the River Anton in the Test Valley of Hampshire. By 962, it was called Andeferas and was a meeting place for a Saxon Parliament, the Witanagemot. The placename is based on 'Ann', the old Celtic name for the River Anton, and the profusion of Ash trees that grew around it, and 'dubrds', meaning waters. Hence, 'place of the ash tree waters.' Domesday recorded the place as Andovere in 1086, held by King William, having been a possession of King Edward before 1066.

Appledore
In the tenth century, this Kentish township was known as Apuldre, a name that translates from the Old English as '[place at] the apple tree'. It appeared in Domesday as Apeldres, in the Blackbourne Hundred, of which two sulungs of land belonged to the Archbishop of Canterbury. It was assessed with two acres of meadow, woodland to support six pigs, a church and six fisheries. There is a village of the same name in Devon.

Apuldram
There is some debate as to the exact meaning concerning the name of this West Sussex village. The first name element is fairly straightforward, as it comes from the Old English word 'apuldor', meaning 'apple tree(s)'. The second element however, could come from 'ham', meaning 'homestead', 'village' or 'dwelling', or from 'hamm', indicating an enclosure. So, the placename means 'village [or enclosure] where apple trees grow'. Either seem equally probable. The place was known in the twelfth century as Apeldreham and as recently as the nineteenth century it was being written as Appledram.

Ashford
Domesday referred to this Kent township as Estefort and Essetesford, a name based on the old name for the River Stour, known then as the Eshe or Eschet, which are variations on a pre-Saxon word for the ash tree. Consequently, the placename translates as either the 'ford, or shallow crossing, of the River Eshe', or possibly, 'the river ford of the ash trees'.

Bagshot
Bagshot is located in the north-west corner of Surrey and derives its placename from two Old English words, 'bagga', meaning 'badger', and 'sceat', which referred to a corner, a projecting piece or nook of land. Hence, 'corner of land frequented by badgers'. An alternative suggestion has been proposed, that the 'bag' element might have referred to its founder, a man called Bagg or Baga, and that the 'shot' element of the name is a corruption of the early Anglo-Saxon word 'scheatte', an alternative to the word 'inga', and roughly meaning 'the tribe or people of'. In which case, '[land of] Bacca's people'. The place was recorded as Bagsheta in 1164.

Barcombe
Barcombe derives its placename from two Old English words, 'bere', meaning 'barley', and 'camp', which signified an enclosed piece of land or a field. Taken together these produce a name that translates as 'enclosed land where barley is grown'. Domesday recorded it as

Bercham (mistaking the last element of the name to be 'ham', meaning 'homestead'), and listed it in the Barcombe Hundred in the area of Lewes in East Sussex. The entry shows quite a large estate supporting twenty-six households, with land for twenty ploughlands. It also recorded three and half mills (?) and a church, altogether valued at eight pounds and held in 1086 by William de Warenne. It had belonged to Azur of Slindon at the time of King Edward.

Basingstoke

Archaeological excavations have revealed that there were early settlements in the Basingstoke area of Hampshire as far back as the Stone Age, with other significant Iron and Bronze Age finds, as well as Roman pottery and coins. The place was known in 990 as Basingastoc and stems from a man called Basa, who founded the settlement on the banks of the River Loddon, at what is now Old Basing. The two affixes 'inga', meaning the people, family or followers, and 'stoc', a remote farmstead or hamlet, produce a placename that may be taken to mean 'the remote farmstead of Basa's people'. Domesday records it as Basingestoches, in the Basingstoke Hundred, a royal manor held in demesne by the king and as such it never paid any taxes or dues and was never hidated.

Battle

The history of the East Sussex township of Battle is inextricably bound to the Norman Conquest of England in 1066. The defeat of King Harold Godwinson marked a turning point in English history, as an Anglo-Saxon culture was overthrown and supplanted by a Norman French elite, that stamped its authority with brutal force and mercenary zeal upon the country. The battle after which the place is named actually took place on Senlac Hill, some six miles north-west of Hastings. The site is now the location of Battle Abbey, more properly called the Abbey of St Martin, which was erected by William the Conqueror as a monument to the event and to the eight thousand men, both Saxon and Norman, who perished there.

Battlesbridge

You could be forgiven for thinking that this village in Essex saw a battle taking place on its bridge at some time in its history, but nothing could be further from the truth. The name stems from the Bataille family who held the manor in the fourteenth century. The word 'bataille' does indeed mean 'battle' in French, but this is purely coincidental. The Old English word for a bridge was 'brycg', and referred to one on the estate which lay on the estuary of the River Crouch. The placename means 'the Bataille family [estate at the] bridge', and it was recorded in 1351 as Batailesbregge.

Bethersden

The Kent village of Bethersden was named after a man called Beauduric, who may have been its founder or leader. The additional Old English suffix 'denn' indicated a woodland pasture, either as a cultivated or meadow clearing or for foraging (often for pigs). The placename therefore means 'Beauduric's woodland pasture'. By the early twelfth century it had been recorded as Baedericesdaenne.

Betteshanger

An early settlement in Kent, known as Betleshangre in the late twelfth century, the placename has two possible interpretations, both derived from Old English. The first cites the word 'bytle' or 'gebytle', referring to a house or a building, with the second element of the name, 'hangra', signifying a wooded slope or a hillside covered with trees. Hence, 'house or building on a wooded slope'. Another explanation is that it might have been named after a man called Byttel, in which case the placename might mean '[place belonging to] Byttel on a wooded slope'.

Bexhill
In 772, the ancient East Sussex township of Bexhill, known then as Bexlea, was granted a charter to establish a church by King Offa of Mercia. The placename meant 'woodland clearing of box trees', from the Old English 'byxe', signifying a box tree, and 'leah', a woodland clearing. By 1086, the *Domesday Book* had recorded Bexelei, in the Bexhill Hundred, of which ten hides were held by Osbern for Count Robert d'Eu, who had been given the jurisdiction of the castle at Hastings by William the Conqueror.

Biddenden
By the end of the tenth century, this village in Kent was known as Bidingden. That early name contained three descriptive Old English elements: 'Bida', the man who owned or established the settlement, 'inga' referring to his people, followers or family, and 'denn', a woodland pasture. Therefore the original placename meant 'woodland pasture of Bida's people'. Over time the 'inga' element was dropped from the placename and it evolved in its present form as Biddenden.

Bognor Regis
Bognor claims to be one of the oldest recorded Saxon placenames in Sussex, on the basis of a document dated in 680, when it was recorded as Bucganora. The name stems from a female settler known as Bucge, with the affix 'ora', the Old English word for the shore, or a landing place. Hence, 'the shore or landing place of Bucge'. The Latin word 'regis', which means 'of the king', was added to the placename, in honour of George V who stayed there in 1929.

Bolney
The West Sussex village of Bolney was known in 1263 as Bolneye, and had belonged at some time in its distant past to a man called Bola. Who he was is not known, but he clearly carried sufficient status to be permanently recorded in the placename. The additional Old English element 'eg', signified an island, or raised ground surrounded by water or marsh, which perfectly describes the village location. The name simply means 'Bola's island'.

Borstal
According to some accounts, the name of this district of Rochester in Kent comes from two Old English words, 'borg', signifying safety or security, and 'steall', a place or stall. It has been suggested that the expression came about as a result of soldiers fleeing the battlefield near the River Medway, seeking a place of refuge. Others cite the word 'beorth', meaning 'hill'. Whichever is true, over time the name emerged as a local dialect word for a steep path up a hill. Domesday recorded the place as Borcstede and listed it as a small estate supporting a handful of households in the Rochester Hundred, which was held by the Bishop of Rochester, who had also held the manor at the time of the Conquest. Later, the name became synonymous with a correctional institution for young offenders.

Bransgore
The Middle English word 'gore' referred to a triangular plot of land. The 'Bran' element of this Hampshire village is less certain, though some have it belonging to a Saxon man called Bran way back in its early history. However, though somewhat speculative, it can reasonably be assumed that the placename means 'triangular plot of land belonging to a man called

Bran'. The plot of land in question is thought to be that at the bottom end of Burnt House Lane. In 1759 the place was recorded as Bransgoer Common and in 1817 as Bransgrove.

Bredgar
The name of this Kentish village translates into modern English as 'broad triangular piece of land'. It comes from 'brad', the Old English word for 'broad', and 'gara', which represented a triangular plot of land. The name appeared around 1100 as Bradegare.

Brighton
The placename stems from a man called Beorthelm, its Saxon founder, who created a 'tun' (a homestead, village or township), in what is now West Sussex. By 1086, it had been recorded as Bristelmestune and Brighthelmston, in the Welesmere Hundred, held by William de Warenne. As a placename, 'Brighton' was not used until the mid-seventeenth century, when it began to replace the full name of Brightelmstone (which remained the town's official name until 1810).

Broadstairs
The name of this place in Kent came about on account of the steps which were cut into the chalk cliff, the Chapel Stairs, that led up from the sea gate (York Gate), to St Mary's Chapel, a twelfth century shrine to Our Lady, and to the fortified township of St Peter's above. Local legend has it that John Buchan's book *The Thirty-Nine Steps* was based on those at Broadstairs, although there are in fact more than seventy actual steps at the place.

Burnham-on-Crouch
A potentially complex placename, which contains two water references: first, 'burna' was the Old English word for a stream or a brook, and second, the 'on Crouch' element refers to its location upon the River Crouch in Essex. Additionally, the 'ham' element signifies a homestead or a village, so that in its totality the placename means 'village by a stream on the [River] Crouch'. The stream in question runs a little way north of the village. The river name is thought to come from 'cruc', a word the Saxons used for a cross. Domesday listed the place as Burneham, in the Hundred of Dengie, where Ralph Bayard held the manor in 1086, it having belonged to Alweard, a Saxon free man at the time of King Edward.

Canterbury
When the Roman legions set foot in Kent in 43 AD, they were confronted by the local tribe, the Cantiaci. They seized and expanded the Celtic settlement and called it *Durovernum Cantiacorum*. This Latin placename is made up of several disparate sources; the first part, from the ancient British word 'duro', signifying a stronghold or a fortified enclosure, and 'vernum' or 'verno', probably a Latinised version of the old Welsh 'gwern', meaning a swamp, particularly of alder trees. The second part simply refers to the Cantiaci tribe. Hence, the Roman placename meant 'the fort, or enclosed settlement of the Cantiaci near the alder swamp'.

Chandler's Ford
This Hampshire township in the Borough of Eastleigh was originally named sometime before the tenth century, after a man called Searnaegel, who probably controlled the river crossing, or ford, where the Roman road crossed Monks Brook at Eastleigh. The placename was recorded as Searnaegles Ford in 909, and in 1280 as Sarnayylesford. The manor was taken over by the Chaundler family some time in the fourteenth century, and their family name superseded that of its earlier owner. The earliest record of their ownership was in 1759, when the place was registered under its present-day name of Chandler's Ford.

Chatham

The Saxons knew this Medway township as Cetham, a name some authorities maintain is derived from a synthesis of the Celtic word 'ced' or 'cet', meaning a wood, and the Old English 'ham', signifying a village or homestead. Hence, 'village near or in a wood'. Others cite the Saxon word 'cyte', meaning a cottage, thereby producing a placename that translates as 'village of cottages'. By 1086, the *Domesday Book* had it recorded as Ceteham in the Lathe of Aylesford, and that a farm, assessed at six sulungs, was rented by Robert Latimer, the son of Hamo or Hamon de Crevequer (known also as Hamo le Dapifer), from Bishop Odo of Bayeux.

Chertsey

This Surrey township began in 666, when Benedictine monks established the Abbey of St Peter, better known today as Chertsey Abbey, on the banks of the River Thames near Runnymede. The place was known at that time as Cerotaesei, after its founder, a man called Cerot (or Cirotis), plus the Celtic affix 'eg' or 'ey', signifying land surrounded by water, which together translate as 'island of a man called Cerot'.

Chichester

By the end of the ninth century, this Sussex township was known as Cisseceastre, named after a Saxon chieftain called Cissa, the son of King Aelle of the South Saxons, with the affix 'ceaster', signifying a Roman town or fortification. The placename may therefore be taken to mean 'the Roman town of Cissa'.

Chiddingstone

This Kentish village was at some time associated with a man called Cidd or Cidda, after whom it is named. Added to that are two Old English words, 'inga', which referred to his followers or people, and 'stan', a stone. The complete placename can be interpreted as 'stone associated with the people of Cidda' The stone in question was likely to have been a boundary marker or, typical of ancient Saxon tradition, a stone where councils met. In the early twelfth century the village name was known as Cidingstane.

Chilham

This village in Kent was probably named after a person called Cilla or Cille. We have no way of identifying this person as a man or a woman, but as the 'ham' element of the placename was Old English for a homestead, village or settlement, and if this is the case, then Cilla (or Cille) was clearly its leader or founder, as the village name translates as 'Cilla's village'. An alternative view is that the Old English word 'cille' might be more relevant, as it means 'a spring'; in this case the placename might be better translated as 'the village spring'. Domesday recorded the place as Cilleham in 1086, and listed it in the Felborough Hundred held at that time by Bishop Odo of Bayeux, the half-brother of King William and tenanted by a man called Fulbert.

Chipstead

There are villages called Chipstead in both the Counties of Surrey and Kent. The name is of Old English origin, where 'ceap-stede' simply meant 'market place'. Chipstead in Surrey was recorded as Tepestede in 1086, a large manor located in the Reigate Hundred and held by the Abbey of St Peter, Chertsey, having belonged to two Saxon men called Thorgisl and Ulf before 1066.

Chobham

The village of Chobham in Surrey gets its name from its earliest known settler, possibly its founder, a man called Ceabba. Additionally, the Old English word 'ham', meaning 'homestead' or 'village' – or 'hamm', indicating an enclosure (possibly an enclosed field, meadow or paddock), produces a meaning for the entire placename as either 'Ceabb's village' or 'Ceabba's enclosure'. Domesday recorded the name as Cebeham in 1086, a very large estate listed in the Godley Hundred and held by the Abbey of St Peter, Chertsey, who had held it since before the Conquest.

Coneyhurst
The West Sussex village of Coneyhurst includes the old word for a rabbit, as immortalised in the American seaside resort of Coney Island. In fact, this placename is of the same origin: the Middle English word 'coni', meaning 'rabbit'. Taken together with the Old English word 'hyrst', which signified a wooded slope or hillside, this produces a placename that means 'wooded hillside where rabbits are found'. The present name was probably first recorded and spelt this way in 1574.

Crawley
There is evidence of Stone Age, Bronze Age and Roman occupation of land around the West Sussex township of Crawley, but it was in Anglo-Saxon times that the settlement that they knew as Craweleah was established. The name comes from the Old English 'crawe', meaning crow (the bird), and 'leah', a woodland clearing. Hence, Crawley means 'a clearing frequented by crows'. In 1203, the place was known as Crauleia and was granted a charter by King John to hold a market every week.

Cuckfield
The origin of this West Sussex township requires no stretch of the imagination, as the first element stands for 'cuckoo' and is derived from the Old English spelling, 'cucu'. The second element does indeed refer to a field as we might understand it, but the Saxons intended their word 'feld' to encompass open land and pasture land, and sometimes in a more general sense, it could have been applied to a recently deforested area. Therefore, the placename should properly be interpreted as 'open land where cuckoos are found [or heard]'. Given that such an area would have probably still been surrounded by woodland, cuckoos were more likely than not to have been fairly common in the area. By the end of the eleventh century, the village had been recorded as Kukefeld.

Dartford
The Dartford township of Kent derived its placename from the River Darent on which it began, and an early river crossing, or ford, across it at this point. The river name is of ancient Celtic origin and means 'river where oak trees grow'. Domesday recorded it as Tarentefort, an extremely large estate for its day in the Axton Hundred of Sutton, and a property of the Crown as it had been before 1066.

Deal
Little is known about the Kentish township of Deal before the time of the Great Survey of 1086, except that it is widely accepted as the original landing place of Julius Caesar in his first failed attempt at the Conquest of Britain in 54 BC. The origin of the placename dates much earlier than Domesday, however, and is related to the Old English word 'dael', meaning a valley or hollow, and from which the modern words 'dale' and 'dell' are derived. In its earliest form, the place was known as Addelam (or Delam), the prefix 'add' (or 'at'), as the word suggests, means 'at the place of'. Hence the placename translates loosely as 'the place at the hollow, dale or valley'.

Debach

Debach is yet another potentially confusing placename, for there are two quite different interpretations of its meaning. On the one hand, some have it that this Suffolk hamlet's placename means '[place in the] valley of the deep river', yet there is no deep river here. It does stand, however, on a tributary of the River Deban (sometimes called the Deope), whose name does indeed mean 'deep river'. The second interpretation of the placename relies on the Old English word 'beac' or 'bece', meaning 'ridge', in which case the placename could mean 'valley or ridge near the river called Deope'. Domesday recorded the place as Depebecs, in the Wilford Hundred, part-held by eight nobles, including William de Warenne, Geoffrey de Mandeville, Count Alan of Brittany, Roger Bigod, Ranulf Peverel, Bishop Odo of Bayeux, Countess Adelaide of Aumale and Roger de Poitou, the whole of the manorial estates having belonged to several Saxon free men before the Conquest.

Dibden Purlieu

Domesday referred to the village of Dibden on the edge of the New Forest in Hampshire as Depedene, from the Old English words 'deop' and 'denu', which together mean 'deep valley'. The survey located the village in Redbridge Hundred held in 1086 by Oda. The second word of the placename, 'purlewe' is of Middle English origin and referred to land which removed from and lay outside the forest under boundary changes and was thereby not subject to the king's stringent forest laws, but which still lay partially under royal jurisdiction. The placename may be interpreted as '[place by the] deep valley on the edge of the forest'. In the late-fifteenth century the name was recorded as Dibden in Purlieu.

Ditton

There are at least a half dozen places in England called Ditton, including Ditton Fen in Cambridgeshire, Long Ditton and Ditton Thames in Surrey, as well as Ditton Priors in Shropshire. The village of Ditton in Kent is a large village and parish in the Tonbridge district and was important enough to receive a mention in the *Domesday Book*, as Dictune in the Larkfield Hundred, held by Bishop Odo of Bayeux with Haimo (or Hamo) the Sheriff as its overlord, it having previously belonged to Esbiorn Bicga before 1066. It was assessed as one sulung, and worth eight pounds in 1086.

Dorking

The origin of Dorking's placename is ambiguous; three explanations appear to exist. One has it derived from a man called Deorc, who may have been its founder or chieftain, plus the suffix 'ingas', signifying the people, family or followers. Hence, '[settlement of] the People of Deorc'. Alternatively, 'Deorc' may stem from an Old English word meaning dark or gloomy; hence '[settlement of] the dark people'. Thirdly, it may have come from an ancient Celtic word 'dorce', meaning 'bright, or clear stream'. Hence, '[settlement of] people who live by the bright stream'.

Dover

The Romans knew the town as Dubris, probably after the old Celtic word 'dubras', named from a local stream called Dour, and meaning 'waters'. They built a large harbour with two lighthouses and over time, three forts. The Saxons called the township Dofras and it continued to be an important cross-channel trading port with its own coinage and mint. Domesday recorded the place as Dovere in 1086, it having belonged to King Edward and Earl Godwin before 1066. Following the Conquest, the manorial estates were rented to several tenants, the most memorable of whom was a man unflatteringly referred to as Humphrey 'the Bandy-legged'.

Dungeness

According to some, Dungeness means 'promontory near Denge Marsh (or manured land)', from the Old English 'denge' or 'dyncge', meaning manure, dung or fertiliser, and 'naess', signifying a headland or promontory. The area had been reclaimed from the sea in the fourteenth century, and this may therefore be a reference to the fertility of the land. The placename was recorded as Dengemersc by 774. However, others have quite a different interpretation of this place in Kent: they cite the Old English 'denu', meaning 'valley', plus 'ge', meaning 'district', and finally 'mersc', a marsh. Hence, 'marsh in a valley district'. By the early fourteenth century, the place was being written as Dengenesse.

Dymchurch

This coastal township, located on Romney Marsh in south-east Kent, derives its placename from Anglo-Saxon times when 'dema' signified a judge, and 'cirice' represented a church. Hence, the placename means 'church of the judge'. The judge referred to was likely to have been the Lord of the Level, a governor of the marsh who administered and arbitrated the laws of passage across the marshes and monitored local smuggling. In around 1100, the name was written as Deman Circe.

Eastbourne

The Saxons called this East Sussex township Burne, from 'burna'. an Old English word for a stream or brook (still widely found in Scotland as the word 'burn'), and 'est', meaning 'eastern'. As a placename it more properly translates as '[the place by] the eastern stream'.

East Grinstead

The name of this township in West Sussex means 'eastern green place'. It comes from the Old English words 'est', meaning 'east, 'grene', meaning 'green, and 'stede', a place. The 'East' element of the placename distinguishes it from the village of West Grinstead a few miles away. In the twelfth century it was simply known as Grenesteda (green place), and by 1271 had been recorded as Estgrenested.

Eastleigh

This Hampshire township's name was already known as East Lea by 932 and simply means the 'eastern woodland clearing or glade'. At the time of the Domesday survey it was recorded as Estleie, in Mansbridge Hundred, whose tenant-in-chief was a man known as Henry the Treasurer. Before the Conquest, it had been held by Godwine for the king.

Empshott

Domesday recorded this Hampshire township as Hibesete in 1086, and listed it as a very small settlement supporting only four households in the Neatham Hundred and held at that time by Geoffrey the Marshal, it having belonged to Bondi (known as 'the Constable') and Saxi of Clatford in 1066. The name came from two Saxon words, 'imbe', meaning 'bee' and 'sceat', indicating a corner of land. Hence, 'corner of land frequented by bees'. In the late twelfth century the place was recorded as Himbeset.

Epsom

By the tenth century, the Saxons knew this North Surrey township as Ebbesham (or Ebbi's ham), the name possibly derived from a woman called Ebbe, who founded the settlement. An alternative origin suggests it stems from the Saxon word 'ebbe', to ebb, after a local spring that gushed and stemmed its flow intermittently. The *Domesday Book* named it Evesham in 1086.

Exceat

The former East Sussex township of Exceat, said to have been King Alfred's naval base, was located in the Cuckmere Valley. However, the Black Death and attacks by French raiders decimated its local population and in the fifteenth century the village was abandoned. The placename of this long defunct settlement was based on the Old English words 'aec' or 'ac', an oak tree, and 'sceat' a headland or promontory. Hence 'promontory where oak trees grow'.

Farnham

The place was known to the Saxons as Fearnham and translates as 'homestead where ferns grow', though some prefer it to translate as 'water meadow where ferns grow'. By Domesday, it was recorded as Farnham St Peter, in the Farnham Hundred of Surrey, owned by the Bishop of Winchester and assessed at sixty hides before the Conquest, with just forty hides after 1066.

Faversham

This Kentish placename is based on the Old English words 'foefer', referring to a blacksmithery or a forge, and 'ham', a homestead or village settlement. Hence, the name meant 'the village of the blacksmith (or the forge)' or perhaps 'village of the metalworkers'. In 811 AD, it was recorded as Fefresham, and was a royal demesne of King Coenwulf of Mercia. By the time of Domesday the place had been recorded by its present-day name and was a personal possession of King William, having belonged to Edward the Confessor before the Norman Conquest.

Folkestone

By the end of the seventh century, this Kentish fishing village was known as Folcanstan (or Folcestane), after a man called Folca who founded the settlement, and 'stan', a stone, that marked a meeting place or council. Hence, 'the meeting place stone of a man called Folca'.

By 1086, it was recorded in the Great Survey as Fulchestan, in the Limen Lathe of Folkestone Hundred, held by William d'Arques.

Gillingham

The Gillingham placename is derived from three elements; 'Gylla', the name of its first probable settler, 'inga', an Old English word meaning the family, people or followers, and 'ham', a settlement. Hence, 'settlement of the family or followers of a man called Gylla'. One of its earliest references occurs in 1016, in the *Anglo-Saxon Chronicles*, which recorded a battle being fought against the Danes led by King Cnut. The account recorded that: 'the king and ealdorman Eadric... fought with a force at Penselwood near Gelingeham, and ... many dead fell on either side'.

Godalming

By the end of the ninth century, the township of Godalming, in the Wey River Valley of Surrey was known as Godelmingum, after a man by the name of Godhelm, plus the Old English affix 'ingas', meaning the people, tribe or family. The Parish Church of St Peter and St Paul dates from this time. Hence the placename means 'the place of the people of Godhelm'. Godalming also had a vestigial Latin name, Godhelms Ingus.

Goodnestone

There are two places in the County of Kent that go by the name of Goodnestone – one is near Aylesham and the other near Farnham – both come from the same origin. By the end of the twelfth century they were being spelt Godwineston, based Godwin or Godwine, a Saxon man's name, and 'tun', which referred to a farmstead or settlement. Hence, 'Godwine's farmstead'.

Goudhurst

This village in Kent was named after a Saxon man called Gutha, who may have been its founder. Additionally, the Old English suffix 'hyrst', which signified a wood hill, produces a placename that means 'Gutha's wooded hill'. The place was known in the eleventh century as Guithyrste.

Gravesend

This Kentish township, contrary to all appearances, has nothing to do with graves or burial places. The first element of the placename comes from the Old English word 'graf', meaning 'grove' or 'copse'. The placename therefore more properly interprets as 'grove's end'. The grove in question is thought to be the Old Fort Gardens. Domesday recorded the place as Gravesham, where the second element meant 'homestead' or 'dwelling' in Old English, thought to be an error made by the Commissioners who compiled the survey. In 1157, the placename was more correctly spelt as Graussend.

Guildford

Evidence of Roman occupation has been found in this Surrey township, but it was in Saxon times that Guildford emerged as we know it today. It was one of a network of fortified townships and settlements created by King Alfred and Edward the Elder as a defence against Danish incursions into England. By about 880, it was known as Gyldeforda, from the Old English words 'gylde', meaning gold, or golden, and 'ford', a shallow river crossing. Hence, the name probably means 'the ford by the golden [or sandy] hill'.

Guston

A Kentish village named after a man called Guthsige, whose 'tun', or farmstead it was in Anglo-Saxon times. The Great Survey of 1086 listed the village as Gocistone, a small estate in the Bewsbury Hundred of Eastry held by the Canons of St Martin in Dover, having belonged to a Saxon called Alric before the Norman Conquest of 1066.

Hadlow Down

An early record of the placename of Hadlow Down in East Sussex was in 1254 when it was recorded as Hadleg, a name derived from the Old English words 'haeth', referring to heather, and 'leah', a woodland clearing. Finally, the Saxon word 'dun', meaning 'hill'. Hence, 'woodland clearing on a hill where heather grows'. By the early fourteenth century the name had been recorded as Hadledowne.

Hailsham

This Sussex placename is believed to derive from a Saxon called Heagel, Aella or Hella, who founded a settlement or hamlet. Hence the name may signify 'Haegel's settlement', or 'Haegel's ham'.

Halnaker

A most direct village placename near Chichester in West Sussex which translates as 'half an acre'. The name comes from the Old English words 'healf', meaning 'half' and 'aecer', the measurement of an acre, invariably of cultivated land, the size, no doubt, of the original settlement. Domesday recorded the place as Helnache, in the Hundred of Boxgrove, where forty-four households occupied and worked the lands belonging to Earl Roger de Montgomery.

Hampshire

This county in southern England initially derived its name from Hampton, the original name of the City of Southampton. The name means 'district based on Hampton', where 'scir' was the Old English word for a district, (from which he get the word 'shire'). In the ninth century the county name was written as Hamtunscir, and by the time of Domesday as Hantescire. Hampton is made up of two elements, 'hamm', meaning 'outcrop' or 'promontory', and 'tun', in this case meaning an 'estate'. The present name was shortened from Hamptonshire, and is often abbreviated to 'Hants'. Hence, the entire county name translates as 'district with an estate on a promontory', or something along those lines.

Hartley Wespall

The first part of the Hampshire village of Hartley Wespall's placename comes from 'heorot', an old Saxon word meaning 'hart' or 'stag' and 'leah', a clearing. The name therefore means 'woodland clearing where stags are seen'. Domesday recorded it as Harlei in the Holdshott Hundred, part-held in 1086 by Aelfric Small and Aubrey the Chamberlain. In 1066, it had been in the possession of Aelfric and another Saxon man called Alric. In the thirteenth century the manor and its estate came into the ownership of the Waspail family, whose name was attached to the place, so that in 1270, the village was named as Hertlegh Waspayl, distinguishing it from Hartley Wintney a few miles east.

Hartlip

This Kent village was known as Heordlyp in the eleventh century, a name that comes from the Anglo-Saxon words 'heorot', meaning 'hart' (a deer or stag), and 'hliep', meaning 'to leap'. It is assumed that the leaping place in question must have been some kind of fence or gate. Hence, the placename loosely means 'leaping place for deer' or 'gate or fence over which harts or stags leap', or something along those lines.

Hascombe

The name of the Surrey village of Hascombe translates into modern English as '[place in a] valley belonging to a witch'. It comes from 'haeste' a word related to the word 'hex', and meaning 'witch' or 'sorceress'. The Old English word 'cumb', common in many English placenames, signifies a valley. The place was recorded as Hescumb in 1232.

Hassocks

This was a relatively recent township in West Sussex, established during the nineteenth century in a field known locally as Hassocks. A railway station was built and took that name when the London to Brighton railway line passed through. The word comes from the Old English 'hassuc', referring to a clump of coarse grass. In modern English the word is spelt 'hassock', and is commonly found in English churches as a pad or cushion which is knelt on during prayers. In medieval times, these cushions would have been clumps of grass formed into cushion shapes for that same purpose.

Hastings

The Hastings placename came from a man called Heasta who had founded the settlement in Sussex centuries earlier, with the Old English affix 'inga', meaning the people, tribe or family. Therefore, the settlement was called Heastaingas, signifying '[the settlement of] the Haestingas tribe' or possibly '[the settlement of] Haesta's people'. It was also known as such to the French before the Conquest. Around 915 it had been known to the Saxons as Haestingsceaster, with the last element coming from the Old English word 'caester', signifying a former Roman military township or settlement. Therefore, at that time the meaning would have been the 'Roman town of Haesta's people'.

Headcorn

Headcorn is derived from the Old English word 'hruna', which referred to a tree trunk, and Hydeca, may have been the man who owned or had felled it. Hence, 'Hydeca's tree trunk'. This is would seem to be an unlikely name for a village in Kent, but it is thought that the tree trunk in question may have been felled (or to have naturally fallen) to make a footbridge over the local stream. The place was known in around 1100 as Hedekaruna.

Heathfield

The township of Heathfield, a parish in the Hailsham district of East Sussex in the Rape of Hastings and Hawkesborough Hundred on the River Cuckmere, was known as Hadfield or Hatfield in the twelfth century. The placename comes from the Old English 'haeth' and 'feld', together meaning 'healthy field', 'open field', or possibly 'field of heather'. In the twelfth century, the place was known as Hadfield.

Herringfleet

If you thought that the name of this Suffolk village had anything to do with herring fishing or fishing fleets, you'd be miles wide of the mark. It actually got its name from a man called Herela, about whom we know very little, except that evidently he was a person of some status, possibly the founder or the original settlement, and a man whose name is permanently recorded in the name of the place. Two Old English words complete the placename: 'inga', referring to his family, tribe or followers, and 'fleot', meaning 'stream' or 'creek'. Hence, the placename means 'stream or creek of the followers of Herela'. The place was recorded in 1086 as Herlingaflet, a small estate of just four households in the Lothingland Hundred lands held by King William. The estate had belonged to a Saxon called Wulfsi before 1066.

Herstmonceux

This East Sussex township was known simply as Herst at the time of Domesday. The name derived from the Old English word 'hyrst', meaning 'wooded hill'. The 1086 survey recorded Herste in Foxearle Hundred, held by 'Wilbert... of the count [of Eu] ... [and that] Eadmaer the priest held it [in the time of King Edward]'. In the twelfth century, the manor came into the possession of the Monceux family who appended their family name to the place. In 1287, the township was recorded as Herstmonceus.

Horsell

This suburb of Woking in Surrey gets its name from the old Saxon words 'horu', meaning 'dirt', 'dirty' or 'filthy', and 'sell' (or 'gesell'), which referred to an animal shelter. Hence, the placename has the unflattering meaning of 'filthy animal shelter'. In the thirteenth century the placename was written as Horsei and Horisell.

Horsham

There has been a settlement on the banks of the River Arun in the West Sussex township of Horsham since the mid-tenth century, when it was first recorded in a Saxon land charter granted in 947 by King Eadred. The origin of the placename has at least two possible explanations. In the first case, the 'ham' element, refers to a Saxon settlement, and the 'hors' element probably related to horses. In which case, Horsham may have been a settlement known for breeding or keeping horses. In the second case, it may have been named after a man called Horsa, its possible founder.

Horsmonden

The Anglo-Saxon name of this village in Kent comprises three elements: 'hors', meaning 'horse', 'burna', signifying a stream, and 'denn', a woodland pasture. The name may therefore be taken to mean 'woodland pasture near a stream where horses drink'. It was known at the beginning of the twelfth century as Horsbunenne.

Hurstpierpoint

By the middle of the eleventh century, this West Sussex township was known simply as Herst. The name is based on the Anglo-Saxon word 'hyrst', meaning 'wooded hill'. Then, in 1086 the manor was granted to Robert de Pierpoint and his family name was added to the placename. In 1279 it was recorded as Herst Perepunt.

Ickham

By the end of the eighth century, this village in Kent was already known as Ioccham, a name derived from two Old English words, 'geoc' and 'ham'. The former meant 'yoke', an ancient land measure amounting to about fifty acres and ploughed by a yoke of oxen; the latter signified a homestead or a village. Hence, 'village which comprises a yoke of land'. In 1086, Domesday listed the village as Gecham, a very large manor in the Downhamford Hundred, held by the Archbishop of Canterbury who had also held it at the time of King Edward.

Ightham

Ightham is a village in Kent whose name reflects its possible founder or early chieftain, a man called Ehta. The 'ham' element of the placename was the Saxon word for a homestead or village; the complete name means 'village [or settlement] of Ehta'. At the beginning of the twelfth century the name was spelt Ehteham.

Iwade

The Old English word 'iw' meant 'yew tree', and 'waed' meant 'crossing place' or 'ford', similar to the modern English word 'wade'. The two words came together to form the placename of this village in Kent. It translates as '[place by the] river crossing where yew trees grow'. The ford in question is thought to be that from the village to the Isle of Sheppey. In 1179, the place was known as Ywada.

Jevington

A village in East Sussex whose placename means 'farmstead of the people of a man called Geofa'. The name is based on the personal name of the man who was the likely founder or chieftain of the early settlement, plus the two Old English elements, 'inga', referring to his people, followers or family, and 'tun', a farmstead. Domesday recorded the place as Lovingestone and Lovringetone, in the Shoyswell Hundred, held in 1086 by Countess Gode (the sister of King Edward), with seven and a half hides rented from her by a man known as Ralph. At the time of King Edward it had been held by Cola, a Saxon and had been valued at three pounds. In 1086, it was revalued at four pounds and ten shillings. In 1189, the placename was recorded as Govingetona.

Kemsing

The village of Kemsing in Kent has been known since 822 when it was recorded as Cymesing. The name derives from a Saxon man called Cymesa with the Old English affix 'ing' attached, signifying 'place belonging to'. Therefore the village name translates as 'place belonging to a man called Cymesa'.

Kent

The name of the County of Kent in south-east England is of Celtic origin, similar to and related to the Welsh word 'cant'. It has been suggested that it may mean 'rim', based on its geographical location as a coastal district on the edge of Britain, but others prefer its meaning as 'land of hosts or armies'. In 51 BC, the region was known as Cantium. Canterbury gets its name from the same source.

Lewes

The placename of this East Sussex township was already established by 1086, but it had earlier been known as Loewe, a name either derived from Old English word 'hluews' and technically meaning a gash or a cut (but in this instance it probably simply meant 'gap'), or from 'hleow' meaning a mound or small hill. The placename has had several variants, including Loewes in 961, and even in the nineteenth century it was often spelt Lewis.

Maidstone

Evidence has been found of Middle Stone Age occupation on the River Medway around Maidstone, but it was the establishment of Watling Street, a Roman military road from Rochester to Hastings, that passed directly through the fledgling Kentish hamlet, which saw its emergence as an important settlement. By the late tenth century, the Saxons knew the place as Moegthanstan, a name taken from a combination of the Old English words 'moegden', meaning 'maiden, and 'stan', a stone. Hence, 'the maiden's stone' or 'the place where the maidens gather at the stone'. The Saxons frequently used significant standing stones as council meeting places. By the time of the *Domesday Book*, it had been recorded by the king's commissioners as Meddestane, in Maidstone Hundred, in the Lathe of Aylesford of Kent, where ten sulungs were assessed belonging to the Archbishop of Canterbury.

Malsanger

Malsanger is a small village in the Basingstoke district of Hampshire and listed as Gerlei in the Chuteley Hundred at the time of the Domesday survey, part-held by Walter FitzOther, who became governor of Windsor Castle. Also listed as Malshanter, another four acres of estate land were held by William d'Eu. The placename has undergone many name transitions over the years, including Mailleshangre, Maleshanger and Malsanger Yereley.

Marden

This Kent village has a placename that means either 'woodland pasture where mares are kept' or '[place at a] boundary in a woodland pasture'. The name comes either from the Old English word 'mere', a mare, or 'maere', signifying a boundary, and 'denn', meaning 'woodland pasture'. It was recorded around 1100 as Maeredaen. The same name is also found in the counties of Herefordshire and Wiltshire, though their derivations are completely different.

Margate

This traditional seaside town in the Isle of Thanet in Kent was known by the mid-thirteenth century as Meregate, from the Old English 'mere', referring to the sea or a pool, and 'geat', meaning gate. The placename therefore translates as 'the gateway [or possibly the landing stage] by the sea'. Its maritime significance was demonstrated when it became one of the 'limbs' of Dover, part of the Confederation of Cinque Ports in the fifteenth century.

Mottisfont

This Hampshire village lies at the confluence of the River Dunn and the River Test, a fact that is reflected in the placename. In Anglo-Saxon England the word 'mot' signified a meeting or a meeting place, and 'funta' meant 'spring' or 'fountain'. Hence, there was a spring at the place where the two rivers met, and that is exactly what the placename means. The spring in question is thought to have been that at Mottisfont Priory. Domesday recorded the village somewhat clumsily as Mortesfunde, in the Broughton Hundred, held in 1086 by Edwulf of Mottisfont, as it had been held by his father before the Conquest. In 1167, the placename was written as Motesfont.

Newhaven
This is a relatively new name for the East Sussex settlement of Newhaven. Formerly in the old Holmstrow Hundred, it was known in the twelfth century as Mechingas (or Meeching), a name some believe is derived from a man called Mece, plus the Middle English affix 'ingas', signifying the family or tribe. Hence, the old placename could be taken to mean '[village of] the family of Mece'. Others cite the Saxon word 'meces', meaning 'sword', in which case, there is a case for the translation as 'the settlement of the people [or tribe] of the sword'. By 1587, the place had been renamed Newehaven, following the creation of a new harbour.

New Romney/Romney Marsh
New Romney added the 'New' prefix to distinguish it from Old Romney, which is now known as Romney Marsh, and was originally known simply as Romney. The placename comes from 'rum', which is Old English for 'wide' or 'broad', and 'ea', a river. Hence '[settlement on a] broad river'. The name was known as Rumenea in 895 and by the time of Domesday as the small village of Romenel in Kent, whose chief tenants in 1086 were Bishop Odo of Bayeux and Hugh de Montfort.

Oxted
Oxted in the County of Surrey was recorded in the *Domesday Book* as Acstede, based on two Old English words: 'ac', meaning 'oak tree' and 'stede', meaning 'place'. The name therefore means 'place where oak trees grow'. The survey listed the village as a very large manorial estate supporting almost fifty households in the Tandridge Hundred, held at that time by Count Eustace of Boulogne, it having been a possession of Countess Gytha of Wessex before the Conquest.

Peacehaven
The village of Peacehaven in the Lewes district of East Sussex, was created in 1916 by Charles Neville, an entrepreneur who balloted readers of the *Daily Express* newspapers for a suitable name for the place. Initially, the winning entry was for the name of New Anzac-on-Sea, but Neville disliked the name and changed it to Peacehaven in 1917. He was immediately sued by the newspaper as a result for somewhat underhand land sales. Although the newspaper won the case, it was widely believed that Peacehaven was a more suitable placename, and augured the promise of better things when the Great War would be finally ended a year later.

Peper Harow
This village has a placename that suggests a musical connection way back in its early history as it means 'heathen temple of the pipers'. The name comes from the Anglo-Saxon words 'pipere', meaning 'piper' and 'hearg', which signified a heathen or pagan temple. Evidently pipe music played some role in the place's early religious or other rituals. In 1086, Domesday recorded the manor as Pipereherge, and listed it in the Godalming Hundred of Surrey, held at that time by Walter FitzOther, having previously belonged to Alward the

Noble. The estate was assessed with seven acres of meadow, with one mill, and altogether valued at five pounds. It had been worth only one pound and five shillings at the time of the Conquest.

Pevensey

When the Romans built a military settlement at Pevensey in East Sussex they called it Anderitum, which meant '[place at the] great ford', as it was the site of a crossing of a small tidal inlet there. By the mid-tenth century, the Saxons knew the place as Pevenesea, which comes from the name of a man called Pefan, who may have owned it or been the settlement's chieftain at that time. The additional Old English affix 'ea', meaning 'river' produces a translation of the whole placename as 'Pefan's river'. The *Anglo-Saxon Chronicles* describe the landing of William the Conqueror at Pevensey Bay on 28 September 1066: 'Then came William, Eorl of Normandy, into Pevensey on Michaelmas Eve, and as soon as they were prepared, they built a stronghold at the town of Hastings'. By 1086, the manor had been recorded as Pevensel in the possession of the Norman Count of Mortain. At the time of King Edward there had been twenty-four burgesses paying rent and tolls for the use of pasture and for harbour dues, which had increased to twenty-seven burgesses by the time of the survey, and a mint had been established in the town.

Pirbright

The name of this village in Surrey may be taken to mean 'sparse woodland where pear trees are found'. The interpretation relies on two Old English words, 'pirige', which meant 'pear tree', and 'fyrhth', a word used to describe scrubland on the edge of a forest or a sparse woodland. The placename was recorded as Perifrith in the mid-twelfth century.

Plaistow

The West Sussex district of Plaistow gets its name from Anglo-Saxon times when 'pleg-stow' meant a place where sports are played, probably indicating a local field or a village green. The name also occurs in the London Borough of Newham and in Bromley. It was known by the end of the thirteenth century as La Pleyestowe.

Pluckley

The village of Pluckley in Kent was once a settlement in a woodland clearing owned by a Saxon man called Plucca. At least, that is a literal translation of the placename. The survey of 1086 listed it as Pluchelei, in the Calehill Hundred of the Wye region, held by the Archbishop of Canterbury, and amounting to twelve and a half acres of meadow and woodland pannage for one hundred and forty pigs. The whole estate was valued at fifteen pounds at that time.

Plumpton/Plumpton Green

There are several places in England called Plumpton, with other villages of that name in Cumbria and Lancashire. All have a similar derivation from Anglo-Saxon times when 'plume' and 'tun' together signified a farmstead where plum trees grew. This village and civil parish in the Lewes District of East Sussex was recorded in the *Domesday Book* as the very large Manor of Pluntune, in the Straet Hundred, held at that time by William de Warenne having belonged to Earl Godwin before the Conquest. Nowadays, it is at Plumpton Green, some two miles away. that the majority of the resident population live.

Poynings

The name of this West Sussex settlement near Lewes was known to the Saxons as Puningas, and was recorded as such in 960. The name probably derives from a man called Puna and his family or followers (indicated by the Old English element 'ingas'). Domesday listed Poninges, in the Poynings Hundred in 1086 and held by William de Warenne.

Pyrford

The name of this village in Surrey translates into modern English as '[place at the] pear tree by a ford'. It comes from the Old English words 'pirige', meaning 'pear tree' and 'ford' or 'forda', initially referring to a shallow river crossing over the River Wey, though the present village of Pyrford is some distance away. Before the Conquest, the placename was written as Pyrianforda and by the time of the Domesday survey it had been recorded as Peliforde.

Ramsgate

The earliest known reference to Ramsgate is in the Kent Hundred Rolls of 1274, when it was listed as Ramisgate or Remmesgate, in the Ringslow Hundred. The name comes from the Anglo-Saxon words 'hraefn', which meant raven, but was also known as a man's personal name, Hraefn. The second element, 'geat', referred to a gap, probably in a cliff. The placename may therefore mean either 'raven's cliff gap', 'gap in the cliffs of the raven' or 'gap in the cliffs belonging to a man called Hraefn'. The township also appears as Raunsgate in the St Laurence parish records of 1290.

Reculver

The Romans built a military settlement at Reculver in Kent and called it Regulbium. Its later placename originated in ancient Celtic, where the prefix 'ro' (which technically translates as 'great'), in this instance is thought to mean 'great headland', even though none exists at the place. The reference is most likely to have been to the Isle of Thanet. Domesday recorded the place as Roculf in 1086, held by the Archbishopric of Canterbury, who had held it before 1066.

Reigate

This Surrey township appears in the *Domesday Book* as Cherchefelle, held in demesne by William the Conqueror in the Reigate Hundred, with Queen Edith (or Editha, King Edwards's widow), as its chief tenant, she having owned the manor in its entirety before the Conquest. Of its thirty-seven and a half hides of land, thirty-four were reserved for the sole use of the king. There were two mills, twelve acres of meadow with one hundred and forty pigs at pannage, and another forty-three from herbage. In all the manor estate was valued at forty pounds. The placename Cherchefelle is somewhat obscure but may have meant 'an open space by a hill', or possibly 'an open field next to a hill'. In 1088, the manor was granted to William de Warenne when he became Earl of Surrey. It was not until around 1170 that the name appeared as Reigata, a combination of two Old English words, 'raege', meaning roe-deer, and 'geat', signifying a gate. Hence, 'Gate of the roe-deer'.

Rochester

Shortly after their arrival in Britain in the first century, the Romans established a fort at a ford crossing of the River Medway in Kent, on the main road from Dover to London. They called the place Durobrivae, which meant 'the stronghold by the bridge'. By the early eighth century, the settlement had become known as Hrofaescaestir, a name they commonly abbreviated to Hroft. Bede recorded the place as Hrofaescaestre in his *Ecclesiastical History of the English People*, written in about 730. By 1086, the name had evolved as Rovecester, listed in the Bewsbury Hundred. At the time of King Edward it had been valued at one hundred shillings (equal to five pounds), but by the time of the survey it was assessed at being worth twenty pounds.

Runnymede

The name of this historic place near Egham in Surrey is derived from three Old English elements: 'run', meaning 'secret' or 'council' (related to the Modern English word 'rune'), 'eg', meaning 'island' or raised ground surrounded by wetland, and 'maed', a meadow. The placename in its entirety means 'meadow on the island where councils are convened'. It had long been a place of meetings and assemblies, and it was not coincidental that it was at Runnymede where disgruntled rebel barons convened to force King John to seal *Magna Carta* in June 1215. While the placename originally related only to the field or meadow, the name is now that of the local council and district.

Rusper

This village in West Sussex gets its name from the Anglo-Saxon words 'ruh', meaning 'rough' and 'spearr', indicating a beam of wood or a spar. Hence, we may take the placename to mean '[place by the] rough beam of wood'. The village name was written as Rusparre in 1219.

Rye

The East Sussex Cinque Port township of Rye has a history going back well before the Norman Conquest. King Ethelred had promised the 'Mainou of Rameslie' to the Benedictine Abbey of Fecamp in Normandy, but died before the promise could be fulfilled. It therefore fell to King Cnut, the second husband of his widow, Queen Emma, to confirm the gift. The Saxons knew the town as Rie (or Rameslie), possibly meaning 'bank', since it actually lay on an island which was flooded by marshes on the banks of the English Channel. The place was known as the Rye Camber, which in itself signifies a river bank on the Camber Sands. In 1130, it had been recorded as Ria.

Sandwich

Known in 710 as Sandwicae, this Kent township, located at that time on the River Stour, derives its name from the Old English 'sand' plus the affix 'wic', together signifying a 'sandy port or place'. By the time of Domesday the place had been recorded as Sandwice, Sanwic and Sandwic, listed in its own hundred within the land of the Archbishop of Canterbury.

Sevenoaks

In 1100, the Kentish township of Sevenoaks was still recorded by its ninth century Saxon name, Seouenaca, based on the Old English 'seofon' and 'ac', and somewhat self-evidently means 'the (place at) the seven oak trees'. The name derived from the oaks which once stood as part of the Manor of Otford and belonged to the Archbishops of Canterbury. Over the centuries, the eponymous oak trees (which are actually located in Knole Park), have been replaced several times, not least of which following the Great Storm of 1987 when six were blown down in hurricane-force winds, as well as subsequent vandalism which accounted for the demise of six of their replacements. Nowadays, eight oak trees are located at the Vine Cricket Ground, also known as Sevenoaks Vine.

Sheerness

The derivation of the Sheerness placename is ambiguous. It may have derived from the Old English 'scir', meaning 'bright', and 'naess', a promontory or headland, in which case, it means 'bright headland'. Alternatively, it might be 'scear-ness', in which case it signifies a plough share, related no doubt to the jutting beak-like shape of the headland on which it stands. Either explanation seems plausible. In 1203, it was recorded as Scerhnesse in the Lathe of Kent.

Shere

The name of this Surrey village means '[place by the] bright (or clear) stream', and comes from the Old English words 'scir'. The stream in question is the River Tillingbourne (also known as Tilling Bourne), which is a tributary of the River Wey. Domesday listed the village as Essira and Essire, in the Blackheath Hundred, in the possession of King William, it having belonged before 1066 to Queen Edith of Wessex, the widow of Edward the Confessor.

Sidlesham

This West Sussex village was named after a man called Sidel, who may have been its founder during the seventh century, or one of its early leaders. This, with the addition of the Old English word 'ham', which signified a homestead or a village, produced a placename meaning 'Sidel's village (or homestead)'. By 683, the place was already referred to as Sidelesham.

Sissinghurst

A village in Kent named after a Saxon called Seaxa. Two other elements occur in the placename, both of Old English origin: 'ingas', signifying his people, family or followers, and 'hyrst', which related to a wooded hill. The name may be taken to mean 'wooded hill of the followers (or family) of Seaxa'. At the end of the twelfth century the placename was written as Saxingherste.

Sittingbourne

This Kent township is thought to derive its placename from three Old English words, 'side', meaning a bank or a slope, 'inga' signifying the family, followers or people, and 'burna', a stream, brook or bourne. Hence, Sidingeburn, as it was known around 1200, may be taken to mean 'stream of the people who live on the bank'. Another explanation has been offered as to its meaning; it may come from a Saxon tribe, the Sydingas, the settlers who may have first built the township. One thing is certain – the original settlement grew up around the Roman military road known as Watling Street (now the A2 trunk road), along the banks of Milton Creek, a stream that ran through it, to join the Swale and on to the sea at Elmley Reach.

Shepherdswell

In 940, the Saxons recorded this place in Kent as Swythbrihteswealde. The name comes from two Old English elements; the first is derived from a man called Swithbeorht, with the second, 'wald' or 'weald', signifying a forest or woodland. Hence, originally it would have been understood to indicate 'Swithbeorht's woodland'. In 1086, Domesday recorded the township as Siberteswald and Siberteswalt in the Bewsbury Hundred, held by William de Poitou, with a man called Sigar holding half a plough in demesne; his father had previously held it as a prebend. In 1600, the placename was being spelt as Sibertwood, and in 1868 as both Sibertswold and as Shepherdswell, names which still continue in use to this day.

Smarden

In 1100, this village in Kent was known as Smeredaenne. The name derives from 'smeoru', which means 'butter' or 'grease', and 'denn', a woodland pasture. It means 'woodland pasture where butter is made or produced'.

Smeeth

The village of Smeeth near Ashford in Kent derives its name from the Old English word 'smiththe' or 'smidde', which meant 'a smithy' (a blacksmith's or farrier's forge). It was first recorded as Smitha in 1018. In his *History and Topographical Survey of the County of*

Kent in 1799, Edward Hasted suggested an alternative meaning: he recorded the placename as 'being written and usually called *Smede*, a name signifying an open smooth plain', citing King Offa who in 791 had given 'pasture for fifty hogs within Smede'.

Snargate
The Old English word 'sneare', from which the first element of this placename is derived, signified an animal snare, traditionally used to catch small animals like rabbits, foxes and hares, and the word 'geat' indicated a gap or gateway. Hence, one interpretation of the name of this village in Kent might be 'gate or gap where animals are snared', often referred to as a 'hatch-trap'. One of the earliest records of the placename was in the late-twelfth century when the name was written as Snergathe.

Snave
The small Kentish hamlet of Snave received its name from the Anglo-Saxons, who based it on the word 'snafa', which represented a spit or strip of land. Hence, '[place by] strips of land'. The name was being written as Snaue in 1249.

Snodland
In simplest terms, the name of this Kent village means 'land of Snodd'. More subtly, the Old English word 'land' specifically signified open unfenced cultivated land. As for Snodd, who or what he was is a mystery, apart from the fact that he had established his domain before 838 AD when the place was recorded as Snoddingland. The middle element comes from 'ingas', and referred to Snodd's people, tribe or family, but that element was later dropped. By 1086, the name had been corrupted and was recorded as Esnoiland, listed in the Larkfield Hundred of Aylesford, held at that time by the Bishop of Rochester, who had also held it at the time of King Edward. It was quite a large estate which supported over twenty households (including five slaves); there was sufficient land for six ploughs, it had thirty acres of meadow, woodland for four pigs, three mills and a church.

Staines
The Surrey township of Staines was known in the eleventh century as Stane, and derives its placename from the plural form of 'stan', an Old English word for a stone. It is thought that the stone or stones in question may either have been a Roman markers or milestones on the road from London to Silchester or possibly ancient territorial boundary stones. The Roman settlement at Staines was known to them as Pontibus, meaning 'place at the bridges', a reference to the River Thames crossing at this place. Domesday recorded the place as Stanes, and listed it as a very large estate supporting one hundred and forty households in the Spelthorne Hundred of Middlesex, held in 1086 by Westminster Abbey, who had held it since before the Conquest.

St Mary Hoo
Hoo (sometimes Hooe or Hoe) was an Old English word which signified a spur, outcrop or projection of land and is found in several other places in England, including Sutton Hoo in Suffolk and Hooe in East Sussex. In general terms, it means '[place at the] spur of land'. St Mary's Hoo in the Medway region of Kent gained its first affix when it was dedicated to the Church of St Mary in the village. The placename was recorded as Hoo St Mary in 1272.

St Nicholas at Wade
From the earliest times, this place in Kent would probably have been referred to simply as Wade, based on the Old English word 'waed', meaning a ford or river crossing, where it was possible to wade across. It was no doubt a reference to a passage over a stream leading to the

Isle of Thanet. By the mid-thirteenth century, the village had been renamed after the dedication of the local church to St Nicholas, and was known at that time by its Latin name, Villa Sancti Nicholai (meaning 'the village of St Nicholas'). By 1458, it had acquired its present-day placename as St Nicholas at Wade.

Surrey

The County of Surrey was known as Suthrige in 722, and by the time of the *Domesday Book* had been recorded as Sudrie. The name mean 'southerly district', based on the Old English words 'suther' and 'ge'. The Saxons viewed the region as southern relative to Middlesex (meaning 'middle Saxons'), in the north, and to Sussex (the 'South Saxons'), to the south.

Sussex

Sussex originally referred to the South Saxons, from whom from whom its name came. It derived from the Old English words 'suth', meaning 'south', and 'Seaxe', meaning 'Saxons'. In the ninth century the region was known as Suth Seaxe and by the time of the *Domesday Book* had been recorded as Sudsex, reflecting the Norman French language of the survey commissioners. In 1974, the historic county was divided into East Sussex and West Sussex, each acquiring county status, recognising a division that had long existed.

Thanet, Isle of

The name of the district of Thanet in Kent comes from ancient Celtic and means 'bright island'. By the third century it was being recorded as Tanatus, and by the time of Domesday it had become Tanet. The 'bright' element may have referred to some sort of warning beacon located on what is now Telegraph Hill. The Greek astronomer Ptolomy's map of Britain in his *Geographia* clearly shows Thanet as an island, which he called Tanatus. However, it became joined to mainland Britain as the Wantsum Channel ran dry as a result of falling sea levels and the Isle of Thanet became a peninsula; the term 'Isle' is nowadays more of an historical vestige than an accurate topographical description.

Tonbridge

This Kentish town located on the River Medway was entered in the Great Survey as Tonebrige, the name derived from the Saxon words 'tun', signifying an estate or a settlement, and 'brycg', a bridge. This interpretation of the placename may therefore be taken to mean either the 'settlement by the bridge', 'the town of the bridge' or 'the bridge of the settlement'. However, it has been suggested that the bridge in question may have been built or belonged to a man called Tunna, and that therefore the placename has quite a different significance.

Tuesley

It is commonly held that the name of this village in Surrey harks back to a dedication to the heathen god Tiw. The Saxon word 'leah', which forms the final element of the placename, indicated a clearing in a wood. Taken together, these elements produce an interpretation that means 'woodland clearing dedicated to Tiw'. A secondary, and quite different interpretation has Tiw as a man's personal name, possibly that of the founder of the original settlement or an early leader, in which case the placename means 'Tiw's woodland clearing'. The village had an entry in Domesday as Tiwesle, listed in the Godalming Hundred, held as a personal possession of King William and tenanted by Ranulf Flambard in 1086, having belonged to King Edward and overseen by a Saxon called Leofwin before the Conquest.

Udimore

The name of this East Sussex village translates as '[place by a] wooded pond'. It comes from 'wudig', meaning 'wooded' (that is, covered by woodland), and 'mere', the Old English word for a pond, a small lake or a pool. Domesday recorded the place as Dodimere, in the Babinrerode Hundred of Hastings, held by Reinbert the Sheriff for Count Robert d'Eu in 1086 having belonged to Earl Godwin and held for him by Algar in 1066.

Upchurch

No prizes for guessing the origin of this Kentish placename. It comes from the Old English 'upp' and 'cirice', which taken together mean 'upper church', or in better English, 'Church in a high place'. The description eminently describes the church and the village location, which traditionally stood as prominent landmarks for ships entering the Medway estuary. It was recorded at the start of the twelfth century as Upcyrcean.

Upwaltham

Upwaltham is a small hamlet in West Sussex, which was known simply as Waltham in the Boxgrove Hundred at the time of the Domesday survey. The name derived from 'weald' or 'wald', indicating woodland or a forest, and the Old English affix 'ham', which meant a homestead, village or small settlement. Hence, Waltham meant 'village or settlement in a forest'. The 'Up' element of the placename, meaning 'higher', was in place by 1371, when it became Up Waltham in order to distinguish it from Coldwaltham, a few miles to the east.

Weybridge

The name of the Surrey township of Weybridge simply means the 'bridge over the River Wey', a river name known as such since before Saxon times. Some time before 675, it was known as Waigebrugge and had been granted to the Benedictine Abbey of St Peter of Chertsey by Frithwald, the Subregulus of Surrey. It was known at the time of the *Domesday Book* as Webruge, in the Elmbridge Hundred, in land belonging to the Bishop of Bayeux.

Whitstable

The Whitstable placename translates as '[meeting place of] the white post', from the Old Saxon 'hwit', meaning 'white' and 'stapol' signifying a post or road marker, possibly an important meeting place. It was recorded in 1226 as Whitspl, in the Lathe of Kent, and not until the early seventeenth century was it finally known by its present name and spelling as Whitstable.

Wickhambreaux

Wickhambreaux in Kent was known to the Saxons as Wicham, which was a common English placename in early-medieval times, with others of that name in Hampshire, Berkshire, Essex, Suffolk and in Greater London. The name harks back to the Romano-British era of the first few centuries AD, when 'vicus' was the Roman name for a settlement, usually associated with or near a military fort. The 'wick' element of the placename is an anglicised corruption of 'vicus', and the Old English element 'ham' signified a homestead or settlement. Wickham may therefore taken to mean 'a settlement associated with a vicus' or 'homestead associated with a Romano-British settlement', or something along those lines. Domesday recorded the placename as Wicheham in 1086. In the thirteenth century the de Brayhuse family (sometimes de Braose) took possession of the manor and their family name was appended to the placename, so that in 1270 it had been recorded as Wykham Breuhuse.

Winchelsea

Winchelsea is a township in East Sussex, whose name translates from Anglo-Saxon as 'island at the bend [or corner] of a river'. The name has two distinct elements: 'wincel', meaning 'corner', and 'eg', indicating an island. Part of the settlement, known as Old Winchelsea, was swept away by the sea in the thirteenth century. Present-day Winchelsea was rebuilt on a nearby promontory and had become known by 1130 as Winceleseia.

Wingham

According to one interpretation, this village in Kent may have derived its placename from a man called Wiga. The attachment 'inga' and 'ham' in Old English signified 'people' or family', and 'homestead' or 'village' respectively. Hence, 'village of Wiga's family or people'. Another cites the Saxon word 'wig' which signified 'heathen temple'; in this case the name would translate as 'village of the people of the heathen temple'. In the ninth century the place was known as Uuigincggaham, and by 1086 Domesday had recorded it as Wingheham, held by the Archbishop of Canterbury, who had also held it before the Conquest.

Wittersham

Some time way back in its history, the village of Wittersham in Kent belonged to a man called Wihtric or Wittin. Thereafter, opinions differ as to the exact meaning of the remaining placename element. If it is 'ham', then it signifies a homestead or settlement in Anglo-Saxon times. However, if that affix had been 'hamm' (with a double-'m'), then it represented an enclosure or a promontory. The latter seems very probable as the village stands on high ground overlooking the River Rother and its levels. It might therefore be most properly interpreted as 'Wihtric's enclosure on a promontory'. The place was recorded before the Norman Conquest as Wihtriceshamme and in the *Domesday Book* of 1086 as Witdesham.

Woking

The Surrey township of Woking was known by the early eighth century as Wocchingas, named after a man called Wocc or Wocca with the added Old English affix 'ingas', which referred to a tribe, a people or family. The placename may therefore be interpreted as 'the [place or settlement of] the people of Wocca'. In the Great Survey of 1086 it was recorded as Wochinges, in the land of Bishop Osbern of Exeter, where King William held part of the farm previously owned by Edward the Confessor, which was assessed at fifteen and a half hides.

Worthing

The West Sussex township of Worthing (not to be confused with a place of the same name in Norfolk), derives from a Saxon man called Weorth or Wutha. The additional Old English suffix 'inga' referred to his family, his tribe or followers. Hence, 'Weoth's ingas' which translates as '[the settlement] of the family or people of Weorth'. It was recorded in 1086 as Ordinges and Mordinges, in the Hundred of Brightford, one of five grants of administrative Rapes in Sussex, held by the Norman knight, Robert le Sauvage, who became Sheriff of Norfolk and Suffolk.

Worting

Well before the Norman Conquest, this settlement in the Basingstoke region of Hampshire was known as Wyrtingas. The placename comes from the Old English word 'wyrting', which meant 'herbs' or 'vegetables'. The name may be interpreted as '[place with] herb or vegetable gardens'. Domesday listed the place as Wortinges, in the Chutely Hundred, held by the Abbey of St Peter in Winchester.

Part Thirteen

The South-West

Cornwall, Devon, Dorset, Gloucestershire, Somerset, and Wiltshire

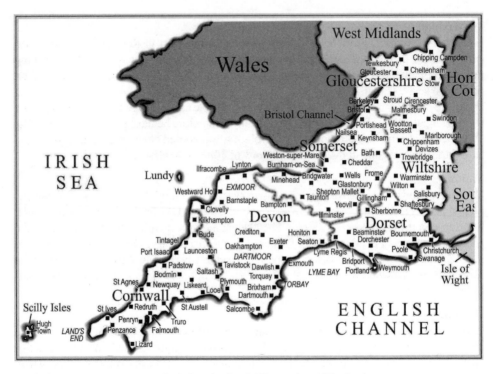

A map depicting the South-West region of England.

Abbas Combe

In 1066, there had been two estates in the Manor of Combe in Somerset, one known as Abbas Combe and the other as Temple Combe, on account of its association with the Knights Templar. The first word of this village placename, 'Abbas', is derived from the Latin 'abbatisse', which meant 'abbess', and referred to the Abbess of Shaftsbury Abbey who had early possession of the manor. The Old English word 'cumb', meant 'valley', and produces a placename that means 'valley of the abbess'. Domesday listed the manor as Cumbe, in the Horethorne Hundred, held by the Church of St Edward & St Mary of Shaftsbury as it had been before the Norman Conquest. In 1327 the estate was known by its Latin name, as Coumbe Abbatisse.

Abbotskerswell

Before the Normans came to England, this Devonshire village was known as Caerswylle, a name derived from the Old English words 'caerse', meaning 'cress' and 'wella', a stream, fountain or well. Hence, '[place near a] spring where water cress grows'. In 1086, the manor was recorded as Carsuella, in the ancient Kerswell Hundred, held at that time by the Abbot of Horton Abbey in Dorset. Then, at some time during the thirteenth century, the manorial estate came into the possession of the Abbot of Tavistock, and in 1285 the name was recorded as Karswill Abbatis. By the late seventeenth century the name had developed into Abbots Keswell, before finally settling as Abbotskerswell in 1868. At that time the placename was sometimes spelt Abbot's Carswell.

Affpuddle
Affpuddle is a small Dorset village whose name was recorded *Domesday Book* of 1086 as Affapidele in the Bere Regis Hundred, held at that time by Cerne Abbey, as it had been before the Norman Conquest. The placename contains two elements: first, a man called Affa or Aeffa, its probable founder or chieftain, and second, 'puddle', which was a later, and much more polite version of the name of the river on which it stands, the River Piddle.

Altarnun
The village of Altarnun, situated on Bodmin Moor on the North Cornish coast, is named after the Celtic St Nonna, a female holy woman, and the mother of the Patron Saint of Cornwall, St Piran or Pyran (in Cornish, Peran, and in Latin, Piranus), and an altar dedicated to her in the sixth century. Hence 'altar [of the church] of Nonna'. In the Cornish language, the village is known as Pluwnonn. The *Domesday Book* lists the place as Penpont, as it stands on Penpont Water, which is a tributary of the River Inney. The fifteenth century bridge over the river leads to the Church of St Nonna and a few hundred metres further to the Holy Well of St Nonna, which is traditionally believed to possess miraculous curative properties.

Ampney Crucis
This Gloucestershire village was originally known simply as Omenie at the time of Domesday, located in the Gersdones Hundred and held by Ralph de Tosny in 1086. By 1287, the village had acquired the name of the Church of the Holy Rood, known then by its Latin name, Ameneye Sancte Crucis (meaning 'Ampney of the Holy Cross' – 'rood' being an old name for a cross). Areas of the original settlement gradually took on similar dedications to the Christian saints to whom their churches were dedicated. These included Ampney St Mary (Ammeneye Beate Marie), and Ampney St Peter, (Amenei Sancti Petri). Another part of the township became known in 1205 as Dunamenell, probably after Ampney Brook, which as the name suggests lies downstream from Ampney. The two placename elements of the first word translate as 'Amma's stream', after an early founder or settler.

Angersleigh
Angersleigh's placename came from the Aunger family who owned the manor in the thirteenth century. Before that, this small Somerset hamlet had been recorded as Lega, a name derived from the Saxon word 'leah', which signified a woodland glade or a clearing. In 1354 the placename was known as Aungerlegh, which means 'woodland clearing belonging to the Aunger family'.

Avebury
This Wiltshire placename derives from a man called Afa, who is likely to have originally built the settlement as a fortified stronghold. Given that the Old English word for such a stronghold was 'burh', the place might be called 'Afa's stronghold'. The stronghold in question is thought most probably to have been a Bronze Age burial ground rather than having any defensive function. Domesday identified the place as Aureberie in 1086.

Awliscombe
The Devonshire village of Awliscombe stands at the place in a valley where a local stream joins the River Otter, and this is the origin of its placename. The name translates as '[place in a] valley at a fork in the river', from the Old English words 'awel', meaning 'fork', and 'cumb', a valley. The village had no fewer than six entries in Domesday, listed as Aulescome, Holescome, Horescome and Orescome, a very large estate for the time, supporting forty-eight households (including twelve slaves), in the Hemyock Hundred, in the lands of William Chevre ('the Goat'), with parts held by Ralph de Pomeroy and Gotshelm, the brother of Walter de Claville. Before the Conquest the manor had belonged as shares to various men, named as Kenias, Viking of Whipton, Alwin, Edmer and Alward, the son of Toki.

Banwell
The meaning of the placename of the village of Banwell in North Somerset has disturbing undertones, as the first element of the name comes from Old English word 'bana' and means 'killer' or 'poison'! The second element, 'wella', could signify either 'well', 'stream' or 'spring'. The placename may be interpreted as '[place by a] killer (or poisonous) spring', a probable reference to a contaminated local water source. It had evidently been so polluted since the early tenth century as the placename was recorded in 904 as Bananwylle. The Great Survey entered it as Banwelle, listed as an extremely large estate for its day, supporting eighty-six households (including ten slaves), in the Winterstoke Hundred, held in 1086 by the Bishopric of Wells, having belonged to Earl Harold in 1066.

Barnstaple
Known as Beardastapol in the late tenth century, the North Devon township of Barnstaple gets its name from two Old English words, 'bearde', meaning battle-axe, and 'stapol', a post or pillar. Hence, 'the post of the battle-axe'. In Anglo-Saxon England, stone pillars were often erected in places where religious or political meetings took place. It was an important fortified settlement, a borough created by King Alfred, as well as a major centre for commerce which had been established as a royal mint by King Athelstan.

Barrow Gurney
Neither a wheelbarrow, a funeral barrow, nor a hospital gurney were involved in the making of this North Somerset village placename! The first word comes brom the Old English word 'bearu', referring to a grove in a wood. The *Domesday Book* listed Nigel de Gurnai as Lord of the 'Mainou of Berue', in land belonging to the Bishop of Coutances, and after that time the place became known as Barwe Gurnay, which translates as 'de Gurnai's estate by a grove in the wood'. In 1086, the account recorded that '...Eadric held it at the time of King Edward and it paid geld for ten hides'.

Bath
In 796, this north Somerset township was known as Bathum and by the time of the *Domesday Book* as Bade, from the Old English 'baeth', a bath. This shortened version, commonly used in its plural form, derived from a longer Saxon placename, which translated as '[the place of] the [Roman] baths'. The aforementioned Roman baths were in the town they called Aquae Sulis (meaning 'the waters of Sulis'), part of the hot springs and spa in the Temple of Sulis Minerva, built around 50 AD. At that time, Bath was a recreational centre rather than the more typical Roman garrison town.

Beaminster
Written records of Beaminster (usually pronounced Bemm-inster), located on the River Brit in West Dorsetshire, go back to 862 when it was known as Bebingmynster. The name

comes from three Old English words 'Bebbe', probably a woman's name, 'inga', meaning 'the people, followers or family', and 'mynster', signifying a large church. Therefore, the placename translates as '[the settlement at] the large church belonging to the followers of Bebbe'. The settlement was part of a large estate and almost certainly the site of a large Saxon minster church. By 1086, the name was more recognisable, recorded in the *Domesday Book* as Beiminstre, belonging to Osmund, the Bishop of Salisbury, one of nine manors described as 'for the sustenance of the monks of Sherborne'.

Beechingstoke
The Wiltshire village of Beechingstoke was known simply as Stoke in 941, but by the time of the Great Survey of 1086 it had been recorded as Bichenestoch, in 'the Land of the Church of St Mary of Shaftsbury... [where] Turstin holds it of the abbess'. The placename is derived from two Old English words, 'bicce', meaning 'bitch' and 'stoc', a term used for an outlying or remote farmstead. Hence, the placename translates as 'outlying farmstead where bitches are kept'. Such pounds and kennels for dogs and bitches would commonly be kept for breeding and hunting in medieval England.

Beer Hackett
The Dorset village of Beer Hackett ought to be an alcohol-soaked place if its name were to be taken at face value. However, nothing could be further from the truth, as the Old English word 'bearu' represented a woodland grove, and 'baer' was another Saxon word for a woodland pasture. This bucolic setting was part of an estate held by a man called Haket in the twelfth century, and is the origin of the placename. It means 'woodland pasture belonging to a man called Haket'. Before Haket took ownership, the place was simply known as Beru, but after the acquisition it became known as Berhaket.

Bemerton
The placename of the Bemerton district of Salisbury in Wiltshire is potentially contentious – two quite different interpretations have been suggested. One cites the Old English word, 'bymere', meaning 'trumpeter' as the source of the first element of the name (which is a popular tradition, even though its relevance to the place is obscure), while another prefers it as meaning 'boomer', an alternative name for the bittern and the distinctive vocalisation that is associated with that bird. The final element, 'tun' refers to a farmstead. Hence, the placename could mean either 'farmstead of the trumpeters', or 'farmstead where bitterns are heard'. By and large, the latter explanation is widely accepted as the more probable. Domesday recorded the place as Bimertone, and listed it in the Branchbury Hundred, part-held by Aldred, the brother of Odo, and by Aiulf, known as 'the Chamberlain'. It was a small estate assessed with two and a half ploughlands, four acres of meadow and a mill, the two parts valued in 1086 at six shillings and at two pounds.

Bere Ferrers
'Bere' comes from the Old English word 'baer' or 'bearu' and signified pasture in a woodland. Hence, '[place in or near the] woodland pasture'. In 1086, Domesday recorded this Devonshire township as Birlanda, a large manor in the Roborough Hundred, held by Count Robert of Mortain. Then in the thirteenth century the estate came into the possession of William de Ferers and his family name was attached to the place. In 1306 the placename was recorded as Byr Ferrers.

Berkeley
The west Gloucestershire township of Berkeley is located two miles from the River Severn on the Little Avon river in the Vale of Berkeley. It was known in the ninth century as Berclea, a

name of Saxon origin, based on the words 'beorc', a birch tree, and 'leah', a woodland clearing. Hence, 'woodland clearing of birch trees'. The *Domesday Book* records it as Berchelai in the land of the king, where Edward the Confessor had five hides of land.

Berrynarbor

This Devonshire village was known in twelfth century simply as Biria, a name taken from the Old English word 'burh', meaning 'stronghold' or 'fortified place'. This is thought to refer to the site on which a medieval castle was built later. The manor had come into the possession of the Nerebert family in the thirteenth century, after which the place adopted their name and was recorded as Bery Narberd. Spelling varied over the centuries, with it recorded as Byry in Arbend in 1394 and as late as the mid-nineteenth century the name was being written as Berryn-Arbor. Altogether, the placename may be interpreted as '[place at the] fortified stronghold belonging to the Nerebert family'.

Berwick Bassett

The Old English phrase 'bere-wic' technically signified a farm where barley was grown, and translates directly as 'barley farm', but the Saxons used the term more generally to refer to any barn, grange or storage facility. This village in Wiltshire acquired the 'Bassett' appendage when the manor came into the possession of the Bassett family some time in the thirteenth century. Before their arrival, the manor had been known simply as Berwicha, but by 1321 it had become Berewykbasset.

Bibury

This village on the banks of the River Colne in the Cotswolds of Gloucestershire was known in the eighth century as Beaganbyrig, probably after Beage, a woman who first founded the place, with the added Old English suffix 'burh' or the Norse 'byrig', indicating a fortified settlement or stronghold. So the township's placename may mean 'the stronghold of Beage'. By the time of the *Domesday Book* it had been recorded as Begeberie, in land belonging to bishops of the Church of St Mary in Worcester.

Bicknoller

At some time in its dim and distant past the Somerset village of Bicknoller was associated with a man called Bica or Bican. The placename suggests that he owned an alder tree in the settlement, or an 'alor' as the Anglo-Saxons might have called it. The placename therefore means 'alder-tree of a man called Bica'. The name was written as Bykenalre at the end of the thirteenth century.

Bideford

Recorded as Bedeford in 1086, this North Devon township, located on the west bank of the River Torridge, may possibly translate as the 'crossing place at the stream called Byd', or else the first element may be from 'byden', an Old English word meaning 'hollow' or 'deep valley'. According to Domesday, Bideford had been one of several lands held by Beorhtric, who was King of Wessex from 786 until his death in 802 and was later held by Queen Matilda.

Binegar

The Somerset village of Binegar, located on the south-eastern edge of the Mendip Hills, may have derived its name from a woman called Beage, and the wooded slope on which she established a settlement (in Old English 'hangr' refers to a sloping hillside covered in woodland). In which case, the placename means 'Beage's wooded hillside [or slope]'. An alternative explanation has been offered, in that the first element of the placename may be related to the Saxon word 'begen', meaning 'berries', producing an interpretation of 'woodland slope where berries grow'. In the year before the Norman Conquest, the village name was recorded as Begenhangra.

Bishop's Cleeve

This Gloucestershire village was simply known as Clife in the eighth century, and by 1086 was being written as Clive. The name comes from the Old English word 'clif' meaning a cliff or steep bank, in reference to Cleeve Hill which overlooks the village. Domesday recorded the place in Tibblestone Hundred in land belonging to the Church of St Mary, Worcester (now Worcester Cathedral), part held as a tenancy by Durand the Sheriff. Most of the manorial estate had been held personally by the Bishop of Worcester, and by 1284 the placename had been recorded as Bissopes Clive.

Bishopstrow

The name of this Wiltshire village translates into modern English as 'bishop's tree', from the Old English words 'biscop' and 'treow'. The name comes from a legend that St Aldhelm placed his staff in the ground while preaching here and that from it ash trees began to propagate, and thereafter a church dedicated to the saint was established in the burgeoning settlement. For a while the place was known as 'ad Episcopi arbores', meaning 'at the Bishop's tree'. By 1086, the village had been recorded as Biscopestreu, and listed in the Warminster Hundred, held at that time by Edward of Salisbury, having belonged to a Saxon called Edred before the Norman Conquest.

Blackawton

The Old English word 'blaec' signified 'dark-coloured' or 'black', especially related to vegetation or soil, as was the case with this Devonshire village. It seems to have been a 'tun' or farmstead, established by a man called Afa, as the entire placename interprets as 'Afa's farmstead on dark soil', or something along those lines. Domesday recorded the place as Auetone and listed it within the Chillington Hundred, held by King William in 1086, having belonged to Esger the Constable before the Conquest. In 1281 the name was recorded as Blakeauetone.

Bleadon

The Old English word 'bleo' meant 'coloured' or 'variegated' and 'dun' meant 'hill'. The name of this North Somerset village near Bleadon Hill therefore translates as '[place by the] coloured hill'. Before the Norman Conquest, the place was already known to the Saxons as Bleodun; in the Great Survey of 1086 it was recorded as Bledone, in the Winterstoke Hundred which encompassed parts of the three neighbouring counties of Somerset, Buckinghamshire and Bedfordshire at that time, and was held by the Bishop of Winchester.

Bledington

This Gloucestershire village placename comes from the former River Bladon and the farmstead settlement, or 'tun', that was established there in Saxon times. Hence, 'farmstead on the River Bladon'. The origin and meaning of the Bladon river name is uncertain, and the waterway is currently known as the River Evanlode. Domesday recorded the village as Bladintun, in the Salmonsbury Hundred, held by the Abbey of St Mary Winchcombe in 1086 as it had been before the Conquest.

Blisland

The Cornish village placename of Blisland has an uncertain derivation, at least the first element. It has been suggested that it might have referred to an early settler by the name of

Blis or Bles, but this is pure speculation. The second element, 'land' is more straightforward; it refers to an estate, arable or open tract of land. Hence, 'open land belonging to Blis'. It was first recorded in 1284 as Bleselande.

Bodmin

Bodmin derives its placename from the Old Cornish words 'bod', a dwelling, and 'meneghi', signifying land belonging to a monastery or a church. Hence, 'a dwelling on church land' or 'dwelling by the sanctuary of churchmen or monks'. The name was recorded as Bodmine in the *Domesday Book*, in 'the Land of St Michael... [where] the Church of St Petroc holds Bodmine'.

Boscastle

Boscastle is named after the Norman French Boterel family, and was recorded at the end of the thirteenth century as Boterelescastel, which translates as 'the castle of the Boterel family'. The Boterels originally came from the village of Bottereaux in Normandy, and until the twelfth century, the name was frequently written 'de Boterillis'. It was beside the small harbour settlement which became known as Boscastle, that they built a castle during the reign of Henry I. However, nothing of the castle still exists.

Bolventor

A comparatively recent village settlement in Cornwall, Bolventor means '[the place of the] bold adventure', in reference to efforts made in the mid-nineteenth century to create a new farming community on Bodmin Moor. In 1844, it was first called Boldventure.

Bovey Tracey/North Bovey

First recorded as Bovi in the 1086 survey, this Devonshire village gets its name from the River Bovey. The river name is very ancient and its meaning is unknown. Domesday records the village in land belonging to the Bishop of Coutances in Normandy. This was a typical bequest from the Conqueror, who granted large tracts of the lands which he had seized to all the nobles and churchmen who had supported him in his conquest of England in 1066. The manor passed to the de Tracy family in the thirteenth century and by 1276 the village had been recorded as Bovy Tracy, to distinguish it from North Bovey a few miles away. In the mid-nineteenth century it was written as Bovey-Tracey,

Brampford Speke

The Old English words 'brom' and 'ford' came together in this Devonshire village to produce a meaning of 'ford where broom grows'. The ford in question is a shallow river crossing on the River Exe. Domesday identified the place as Branfort, Branford and Brenford, and listed it within the lands of the Bishop of Coutances and Walter de Claville, part-held by Drogo de la Beuvrière and by Baldwin, and where before the Conquest Wulfnoth had rented one hide, Brungar rented half a hide and Aelfgifu another half hide. The Espec family took possession of the manor in the twelfth century and in 1275 the placename was Bramford Spec, reflecting their ownership.

Brean

Brean is a village on the Somerset coast whose placename dates from 'brez', a derivation of an ancient Celtic word, similar to the Welsh word 'bre', meaning 'hill'. This probably referred to the nearby headland promontory which is known today as Brean Down. Domesday recorded it as Brien, a large estate supporting twenty-five households, ten cattle, four pigs and fifty-three sheep. The manor was listed in the Bempstone Hundred and held by Walter de Douai in 1086, it having been held by a man called Merleswein, identified as 'the Sheriff' in 1066.

Briantspuddle

Briantspuddle is a Dorset village whose name means 'Brian's [estate on the] River Piddle'. We know very little about who Brian was, except that he held the estate in the fourteenth century. Before that, Domesday had recorded the village as Pidele in 1086, and listed it in the Bere Regis Hundred, held by Godric the Priest. By the mid-fifteenth century Brian's personal name had been added and the place became known as Brianis Pedille. In the late-nineteenth century the village had acquired something approaching its present-day name, as Bryant's-Puddle. The nearby village of Puddle, based its name on the River Piddle, but adopted the more polite version of the form, as 'Puddle'.

Bridgwater

Bridgwater is a market town located at the foot of the Quantock Hills of Somerset that was first recorded in the Great Survey of 1086 as Brugie. By the end of the twelfth century it had become Brigewalter, a name that originated after the Conquest, when the manor, including the strategic bridge over the River Parrett, was given to Walter de Douai by King William and the affix 'Walter' was added to the placename. It became known as the Bridge of Walter, which over time was corrupted to Bridgwater.

Bridport

The Dorset town of Bridport began its recorded history as one of a line of fortified towns established in the ninth century by Alfred the Great as a defensive line against Danish incursions into the Kingdom of Wessex. By 1086, it had been recorded as Brideport, derived from a man called Bredy and the Old English suffix 'port', indicating a 'port or harbour belonging to Bredy'.

Brixham

Known as Briseham in 1086, this Devon fishing village in Torbay was named from a Celtic man called Brioc, with the Old English affix 'ham', together signifying the 'homestead or settlement of Brioc'. Domesday records it in the ancient Haytor Hundred, in land belonging to and personally held by Iudichael of Totnes. Before the Conquest it had belonged to a Saxon called Ulf.

Broadclyst

Broadclyst is a Devonshire village which is located on the River Clyst, and was originally known as Clistone, from the Old English 'tun', signifying a 'farmstead on the River Clyst'. Clyst was an ancient Celtic river name meaning 'sea inlet [or cove]'. The place was known at the time of Domesday by its old name, held at that time by King William, having been a possession of Ordwulf during the time of King Edward. The survey recorded: '...there is land for thirty-five ploughs and in demesne is one plough, and eleven slaves and seven coliberts; and thirty-five villans and thirty bordars with twenty-six ploughs'. With its extensive meadow, pastures and woodland it was a very large estate, valued then at twenty-four pounds. Its considerable size brought about a name change, and by the fourteenth century the Old English word 'brad', meaning 'broad' had been appended to the placename, so that in 1372 it was recorded as Brodeclyste.

Brokenborough

Unlike most places whose names end in '-borough', the Wiltshire village of Brokenborough is the exception. The final element of the placename comes not from the Old English 'burh' (which signified a fortified place), but from 'beorg', a word related to a barrow or burial mound. The first element, 'brocen', is what it sounds, and does mean 'broken'. The name is thought to refer to a tumulus, or ancient burial mound that was broken into or sacked some time before the tenth century when it was recorded as Brokene Beregge. The Great Survey recorded it as Brocheneberge, and listed it as a very large estate for its time in the Hundred of Cicementone. The estate supported fifty-four households, including eighteen slaves, and was assessed with land for sixty men's plough teams. There was a meadow measuring sixty acres, forty-five acres of pasture, a woodland measuring three leagues by two leagues and a furlong of mixed measures, as well as nine mills. In 1086, it was held by Malmesbury Abbey as it had been before the Conquest, and was valued at forty-one pounds and two shillings.

Buckfast/Buckfastleigh

The Devonshire township of Buckfast was recorded in 1046 as Bucfaesten and by the time of the Domesday survey as Bucfestre. The name comes from the Old English words 'bucca', referring to a male deer or goat, and 'faesten', meaning a shelter. Hence, 'Place of shelter for bucks'. Buckfastleigh simply adds the extension 'leah' indicating a woodland clearing. Hence 'a woodland clearing near Buckfast'. It was known in the thirteenth century as Lege Bucfestre.

Buck's Cross

The name of the Devonshire village of Buck's Cross is a corruption of the Old English words 'boc' and 'hiwisc'. The 'boc' element referred to what was known as 'bocland', an Anglo-Saxon expression which translates literally as 'charter land'. The second element, 'hiwisc', referred to land required to support a family. Bocland was granted by royal charter, carrying many privileges to those favoured by the Crown and usually required some oath of fielty. Many places in England have this as part of their placename, as boclands were useful administrative instruments of medieval royal authority. Domesday recorded the place as Bochewis, in the Hartland Hundred, held in 1086 by Theobald, identified as the son of Berner. Before the Conquest the estate had belonged to three unnamed Saxon thegns.

Bude

This small north-east Cornish seaside town on the River Neet (also known locally as the River Strat), in the Parish of Stratton, was formerly known as Bude Haven (or in Cornish, 'Porthbud'), on account of its sheltered harbour. The origin of the placename is uncertain, but is possibly taken from a river name, or may even be a corruption of 'bede' an Old Saxon word for a prayer or a bidding.

Budleigh Salterton

Budleigh may have been named after a man called Bud or Budda, with the affix 'leah', which referred to a woodland glade or clearing. Hence, 'Budda's clearing'. The Manor of East Budleigh was known in 1086 as Bodelie, held by the king in the County of Devon. Nearby, the salt industry blossomed and prompted an adjacent settlement, which Domesday recorded as Salterton. The name comes from the Old English 'salt-oern', which referred to a place where salt was processed or sold. In 1210, it was known simply as Saltre, but in time acquired the affix from the nearby settlement of Budleigh and became known by 1405 as 'Salterne in the Mainou of Buddeleghe'.

Burnham-on-Sea

This Somerset settlement was known to the Saxons in the ninth century as Burnhamm, where the Old English word 'burna' meant a stream, and 'ham' an enclosure or farmstead. Alternatively, 'hamm' may have signified a water meadow. Hence, possibly, the 'farmstead by the stream' or 'stream by the water meadow'. Burnham's northern boundary still follows the course of what little remains of a river, which was identified as the River Siger in 663. During prehistoric times much of the low-lying county of Somerset was under the sea and even in relatively modern times Burnham, along with neighbouring Highbridge, with whom it shared the manor in medieval times, has been prone to flooding. Drainage cuttings were made to deal with water flow on the Somerset Levels and make possible the gradual reclamation of the land. Such work is known to have begun at least a thousand years ago, possibly as early as Roman times.

Cadgwith

This coastal village in Cornwall derives its name from the Cornish language and means 'thicket'. As a sea port for most of its recorded history the place has had the 'porth' affix appended, to indicate that it was a port or a harbour. Historically, the placename has been translated as '[harbour near a] thicket'. In the mid-fourteenth century the place was recorded as Porthcaswith, by 1699 it was known as Por Cadgwith and it was not until the mid-eighteenth century that it became known as something approaching its present form, Cagewith.

Callington

The Cornish township of Callington (or in Cornish, 'Kelliwik'), located on the slopes of Kit Hill, was recorded in the Great Survey as Calwetone or Calwiton, a name based on the Old English words 'calu', possibly indicating a bare hill, and 'tun', a settlement. Therefore, the name may be taken to mean 'settlement on a bare hill'. Another interprets the placename as 'a settlement in a meadow'. Tradition suggests it may have been the site of Celliwig, a place associated with the legend of King Arthur. The survey of 1086 reported that 'The king holds Calwetone. There are four hides, but it pays geld for two hides. There is land for thirty ploughs'. There were three leagues of pasture and half a league of woodland, and it paid six pounds in tax.

Cam

This is a Gloucestershire village that is named after the River Cam on which it stands. The name is thought to have originated with the Celts, and is related to the modern Welsh word 'cam', meaning 'crooked' or 'bent'. It was recorded as Camma in the *Domesday Book*, and listed in the Berkeley Hundred, held in 1086 by King William as it had been by King Edward before 1066. An extremely large estate for its time, the manor supported two hundred and sixty-two villans, one hundred and forty-seven bordars, one hundred and thirty-six male slaves, fifteen female slaves and fifty-eight described simply as 'others'. There was land for one hundred and ninety-two men's plough teams. The manor boasted no fewer than ten mills and was valued at one hundred and seventy pounds, an unprecedented sum for the time.

Camborne

Camborne's placename comes from the old Cornish words 'camm' and 'bronn', which taken together mean 'crooked hill'. By the late-twelfth century, the name had been recorded as Camberon. Before the Industrial Revolution it was known as Camborne Churchtown,

Camelford

This place was almost certainly named after the River Camel, on which it is located. The river name itself comes from the early Celtic 'camm' or 'cam', and translates loosely as 'crooked stream'. Add to that the Old Celtic word 'alan', meaning beautiful, and the Old English suffix 'ford' and it produces a placename that simply means 'beautiful ford over the River Camel'. The place was already known as Camelford by the thirteenth century, though its placename is Reskammel in Cornish. Although the town has nothing to do with camels, the symbol of a golden camel was placed on the weather vane atop the town hall in 1806; the hall and the vane were both paid for by the Duke of Bedford, and the camel is also represented in the town's coat of arms.

Chagford
Chagford is a Devonshire township whose name means '[place near a] ford where chag grows'. The name comes from the Old English word 'ceacga', meaning 'chag', an old local dialect name for broom or gorse, and 'ford', a shallow river crossing or ford. In this particular case the ford would have been across the River Teign. The place was entered twice in the Great Survey, as Cageford and as Chageford, listed in the Wonford Hundred, part-held by the Bishop of Coutances in Normandy and part by Ralph Paynel. Before the Conquest the manor had belonged to Merleswein the Sheriff and a Saxon man called Doda.

Chaldon Herring
In the twelfth century, the 'Mainou of Chaluedon' in Dorset was in the possession of the Harrang family, who attached their family name to the place. Well before that, Chaldon's placename dated from Saxon times, when the first element of the name was derived from the Old English word 'cealf', meaning 'calf' (the young cow), and 'dun', signifying a hill. Hence, 'calf hill', or 'hill where calves graze'. The 'Herring' element was appended not only to claim ownership, but to distinguish the manor from Chaldon Boys, held by the de Bosco family. In 1243 the placename was recorded as Chaluedon Hareng.

Charlestown
The seaport of Charlestown lies on St Austell Bay in Cornwall. Originally, the village had been a small pilchard fishing community and had previously been known as West Polmear, a name derived from the Cornish 'porth meur', meaning 'great cove'. Then, at the end of the eighteenth century, the entrepreneur Charles Rashleigh was instrumental in the creation of its contemporary quays and wharfage from 1791–98; the modern village takes its placename from him – hence, 'Charles' town'.

Charlinch
The Charlinch placename comes from two Saxon words, 'Ceolred', a man's personal name, and 'hlinc', a ridge. Hence, 'ridge of a man called Ceolred'. Domesday recorded this Somerset village as Cerdeslinc, and listed as quite a small estate in the Cannington Hundred, held in 1086 by Roger de Courceulles (sometimes Courcelles) as Lord of the Manor. The estate supported six villagers and four slaves with land for two men's plough teams as well as two more of Courcelles. There was a meadow amounting to three acres, fourteen acres of pasture, two acres of woodland and one mill. Its livestock included a heavy cob horse, a cow, eleven pigs, eighty sheep and thirty goats. The entire manor and its estates were valued at two pounds.

Charlton Kings
The word 'Charlton' is derived from the Old English word 'ceorl', which represented a free man or a peasant, plus the affix 'tun', signifying an estate or farmstead. It was known in 1160 as Cherletone. Hence, the first part of the placename means 'farmstead or estate of free men'. The second part of the placename reflected it as a possession of the king in Gloucestershire, and this was incorporated to distinguish it from the nearby village of Charlton Abbots, held by Winchcombe Abbey. By 1245 it had become Kinges Cherleton, and not until the mid-nineteenth century did it take its form as King's Charlton, which was later reversed to produce Charlton Kings.

Chawleigh

This village in Devon gets its name from two Anglo-Saxon words, 'cealf', meaning 'calf' or 'young cow', and 'leah', a woodland glade or a clearing. Hence, 'woodland clearing where calves graze'. The manor was recorded in 1086 as Calvelie, and listed in the North Tawton Hundred, a very large estate supporting over fifty households (including twelve slaves), and held by Baldwin the Sheriff. The manorial estates were assessed at land for thirty ploughlands and ten men's plough teams, and had ten acres of meadow and twenty acres of woodland. Livestock included twenty cattle, ten pigs and two hundred sheep. Before the Conquest it had belonged to Siward of Hemington.

Cheddar

The history of the village of Cheddar located in the Mendip Hills of Somerset goes back to Roman times. The place was known as Ceodre around 880, the placename taken from the Old English word 'ceodor', which means 'ravine' – a clear reference to its most distinctive feature, Cheddar Gorge.

Cheddon Fitzpaine

The meaning of this Somerset village placename is 'Fitzpaine's estate in a wooded valley'. It derives from 'ced' or 'ched', the Celtic name for a wood (similar to the Welsh 'coed'), and the Old English word 'denu', meaning 'valley'. The manor was held by the Fitzpaines in the thirteenth century, at which time their family name was appended to the place. The Domesday entry for Cheddon was somewhat distorted as Succedene, and it was not until the end of the twelfth century that the placename was recorded as Chedene.

Cheltenham

Two possible explanations of Cheltenham's placename have been suggested: one has it as 'celte', an ancient name for a hill slope, with the old English affix 'hamm', meaning a river or water meadow – hence, 'river meadow on a slope called Celte'; another suggests it derives from Celta, a person's name, and therefore may be translated as 'water meadow belonging to a man called Celta'. This Gloucestershire township was known in 803 as Celtanhomme. The *Domesday Book* identified it as 'Chintenham in the land of the king... [where] there were eight and a half hides', and that 'one and a half hides belong[ed] to the church.'

Cheselbourne

Like the Dorset village of Chesil, the village of Cheselbourne derives the first part of its name from 'cisel', meaning 'shingle' or 'gavel', which together with the Old English word 'burna', which signified a stream, produces a placename that means '[place by a] gravelly stream'. It was known as early as the mid-ninth century as Chiselburne, and by the time of the Domesday survey it had been recorded as the Dorset 'Mainou of Ceseburne', in the Hilton Hundred land of the Abbey of St Edward and St Mary, Shrewsbury. It was assessed at that time at a value of sixteen pounds.

Chesil

The Dorset village of Chesil (previous), along with Chesil Beach (also known as Chesil Bank), gets its name from the Old English word 'cisel', meaning 'shingle', a pebble beach. The place was recorded as Chesille Bank in around 1540, and by 1608 it had become known as Chesill.

Chew Magna/Chew Stoke/Chew Mendip

The North Somerset village of Chew Magna takes its name from the River Chew, an old Celtic river name whose meaning has been lost in the mists of antiquity. Before the

Norman Conquest, it was known to the Saxons as Ciw, a name translated into Chiwe by the Domesday commissioners in 1086. They listed the village in the Chew Hundred of Somerset lands belonging to the Bishop of St Andrew in Wells, who also held the manor before the Conquest. It was a substantial estate at that time supporting over a hundred households, including forty-eight villans, thirty-six borders, twenty-two slaves and two swineherds. The much smaller adjacent estate of Chew Stoke was held by Serlo de Burcy, having been held by Aelfric before the Conquest. The 'Stoke' element was added to the placename, taken from the Old English word 'stoc', indicating a secondary or supporting settlement, and in order to differentiate the two estates from each other. It was recorded in the *Domesday Book* as Stoche. Chew Magna (sometimes known as Bishop's Chew) outstripped Chew Stoke in both size, value and productivity. The nearby village of Chew Mendip takes its name from its location on the slopes of the Mendip Hills.

Chippenham

In Saxon times, the Wiltshire township of Chippenham (not to be confused with the township of the same name in Cambridgeshire), was a royal forest and a king's hunting lodge by 853. The place was recorded as Cippanhamme in the *Anglo-Saxon Chronicles* in 878, when it records King Alfred's pursuit of Danish forces: 'The [Danish] force stole in midwinter, after Twelfthnight, to Chippenham. They rode over Wessex and occupied it'. The placename probably derives from its founder, a man called Cippa, with the added suffix 'ham' or 'hamm' which comes from the Old English and signifies a settlement, or a river meadow. Hence, 'river meadow or settlement belonging to Cippa'.

Chipping Campden

Known simply as Campdene at the time of Domesday, this Gloucestershire township in the Cotswolds derives its name from the Anglo-Saxon English 'camp-denu', where 'camp' meant a field or enclosure, and 'denu' referred to a valley. Hence the 'field in the valley'. After Henry II granted a market charter in around 1175, the 'Chipping' element was added, 'ceping' being the Old English word for a market. Hence 'the market [town in the] field in the valley'.

Chisbury

Chisbury means 'fortified place belonging to a man called Cissa', and was known to the Saxons as Cissanbyrig. The name comes from Cissa's personal name and the Old English affix 'burh', meaning 'stronghold' or 'fortified place'. Domesday recorded the Wiltshire hamlet as Cheseberie, and listed it in the Hundred of Kinwardstone, held in 1086 by Gilbert de Bretteville, it having belonged to a Saxon man called Edric during the reign of King Edward.

Chittelhampton

Chittelhampton is a Devonshire village whose placename means 'farmstead [or estate] of valley dwellers'. The name breaks down into three elements: the first comes from the Old English word 'cietel', meaning 'valley'; the second comes from 'hoeme', meaning 'dwellers' and the final part 'tun' indicates a farmstead or an estate. In 1086, it was recorded as Citremetona, in the Hundred of South Molton, held by Godwin of Chittlehampton, as it had been before the Conquest. It was a large estate supporting thirty-seven households, and had twelve acres of meadow, nine furlongs of pasture and one-and-a-half leagues of woodland, the whole manorial estate valued at seven pounds. At the end of the twelfth century the placename was recorded as Chitelhamtone.

Chitterne

The Wiltshire village of Chitterne received its placename long before the Norman Conquest of 1066. The name probably has Celtic origins, perhaps based on the word 'ced', meaning 'wood' or 'woodland', and 'tre', signifying a farm. In the later form of Old English, the word 'aern' meant 'house'. Hence, simply 'farm (or house) in a wood'. Domesday recorded it as Chetre, and listed it as a very large estate within the Heytesbury Hundred, with no fewer than four entries in the survey. At that time the manorial estates were divided between Edward of Salisbury and Earl Aubrey de Coucy. In 1268 the placename was recorded as Chytterne.

Christchurch

The earliest known record of Christchurch was in a grant of 939 made by King Athelstan to the monastery at Milton. By the twelfth century, Christchurch had already acquired a form of its present name – Christecerce, self-evidently meaning 'Church of Christ', in reference to the first religious house reputedly built on St Catherine's Hill. However, this Dorset township was much older, having been founded by St Birinus, the first Bishop of Dorchester, some time around 350. It was known earlier by its Saxon name, Twynham or Tweoxneam. That placename came from the Old English words 'betweoxn', meaning 'between', and 'eam', meaning 'rivers'. Hence, '[the settlement] between two rivers', in reference to the Stour and the Avon. Until 1974, the manor was in the county of Hampshire.

Cirencester

Following their invasion of Britain in the first century, the Romans built a military fort at Cirencester on the River Churn in Gloucestershire, which they called *Corinium Dobunorum*. A civilian settlement soon grew up around it to become the second largest town in England at that time, after London. By the third century, a strong stone wall had been built around the settlement. By 900 it was known as Cirenceastre, which in Old English meant 'Roman camp or settlement called Corinion'. The township's entry in the *Domesday Book* describes a large manor where at the time of King Edward '...[it] rendered three and a half modii of wheat, three modii of malt and six and a half sesters of honey... and three thousand loaves for the hounds'. These 'loaves' are thought to have been a kind of biscuit commonly fed to hunting dogs, similar in some ways to contemporary dog biscuits.

Clatworthy

A small Somerset hamlet, whose placename comes from the Anglo-Saxon word 'clate', referring to the burdock plant root, used for medicinal purposes, and 'worth' (later 'worthig'), an enclosed field. Hence, Clatworthy means 'enclosed field (or enclosure) where burdock grows'. It was recorded in 1086 as Clateurde, in Williton Hundred, held by the Abbey of St Mary, Glastonbury, with William of Mohun as its chief tenant. It had belonged to Aelfgyth of Clateurde before the Conquest. In 1243, the placename was recorded as Clatewurthy.

Clewer

A small hamlet located on the River Axe in Somerset, Clewer gets its name from the Old English words 'clif', which could mean either 'cliff' or 'bank' (as in river bank), and 'ware', which meant 'dwellers'. The placename translates therefore as '[place of the] dwellers on a river bank'. In 1086, the village was listed in the survey as Cliveware, in the land granted to the Bishop of Coutances in the Bempstone Hundred, where Fulcran and Nigel were named as tenants. There is a village of the same name in the County of Berkshire.

Clovelley

The small fishing village of Clovelly is situated on the north coast of Devon, clinging to a steep cliff which descends four hundred feet down a cobbled street to the fourteenth century harbour below. It was known in 1086 as Cloveleia or Clovelie and may have derived its placename from the old Cornish word 'cleath', meaning a dyke or a bank, possibly in reference to the ancient nearby earthworks known as the Clovelly Dykes. Another suggestion is that it refers to a man called Felec, who may have founded the settlement, possibly as Felec's legh. At the time of King Edward it had been assessed at three hides with thirty acres of meadow, forty acres of woodland and substantial pasture.

Codford St Mary/Codford St Peter

A Wiltshire village with an easily understandable placename – a ford, or shallow river crossing near the Church of St Mary, belonging to or overseen by a man called Codda. The ford in question was that across the River Wylye. It was known in the early tenth century as Codan Ford. Nearby is the village of Codford St Peter – at some time in their ancient history the two places would have been part of the same settlement, but by the time of Domesday they had become independent of each other and received separate entries. At that time both shared the placename Coteford, one part in land belonging to Osbern Giffard and another in the land of William d'Eu. In 1291, the placename was recorded in Latin as Codeford Sancte Marie.

Collaton St Mary/Colaton Raleigh

This small village in the Torbay district of Devon derived its placename from a man who was probably called Cola or Colla, and his farmstead, or in Old English, his 'tun'. The placename in its entirety means 'the farmstead belonging to Cola near St Mary's Church'. The village of Colaton Raleigh (Colaton spelt with one 'l'), some twenty miles north-east, was acquired by the de Raleigh family some time in the thirteenth century, and was recorded as the hamlet of Coletone in the Domesday survey of 1086, located within the Diptford Hundred and supporting only four households. At that time it was held by Iudichael (sometimes Judicael) of Totnes and leased to Thorgisl, it having belonged to Cola at the time of the Conquest. In 1316, the place was recorded as Coleton Ralegh.

Coombe Bissett

This Wiltshire village was in the possession of the Biset family during the twelfth century, at which time their family name was appended to the placename and it became Coumbe Byset. It had previously been known as Come or Cumbe, when it was recorded in the *Domesday Book*, based on an Old English word, 'cumb', which simply meant 'valley'. The survey listed it in 'the Land of the King', which had been held by a man called Gytha at the time of King Edward. In 1086, Leofric the Priest held half a hide of estate land on behalf of the manor church.

Congresbury

As with most, if not all English townships whose placenames end in 'bury', 'burg' or 'borough', it signifies that during Anglo-Saxon times this place was made a stronghold or a fortified manor house. Congar's 'burh' dates from the ninth century, when it was known in Old English as Cungresbyri. This North Somerset place also derives the first part of its name from St Congar, the sixth century saint who is thought to be buried in the village. Therefore the name translates as 'fortified place associated with St Congar'. Domesday recorded the manor as Cungresberie, in the land of King William, as it had been at the time of King Edward. At the time of the survey it was due to render '...twenty-eight pounds and fifteen shillings of blanch silver'.

Cornish Saints' Placenames

Cornwall has more than its fair share of townships which are named after saints and the religious sites dedicated to them, and while the origins of their placenames are largely self-explanatory, most have little else to distinguish them. A few of the more important are listed here.

St Agnes is named after the fourth century martyr and the church founded there in her honour.

St Anthony in Meneage is an Anglicised version of St Entenin, and the 'Meneage' element is a translation of the Old Cornish for '[place of] monks'. In 1269, it was known by its Latin name Sanctus Antoninus.

St Austell commemorates the sixth century monk, St Austol. Around 1150 the place was known as Sanctus Austolus.

St Blazey was named after the fourth century Armenian martyr St Blaise. It's earliest recorded name was in Latin, Sanctus Blasius, and it was recorded the mid-sixteenth century as Seynt Blazy.

St Buryan was dedicated to the female Irish St Beryan. The *Domesday Book* identifies it as Eglosberrie, it having been known earlier by its Latin name, Sancta Berriona (or Beriana).

St Cleer is dedicated to the ninth century St Clear. The village was known in 1331 as Seint Cler.

St Columb is named after the somewhat obscure female St Columba, an early Christian martyr who landed at the beach of Porth in Newquay from Scotland. However, two entites of this name exist, marking an early division of the old parish: St Columb Major and St Columb Minor.

St Erth is named after St Ercus, a Bishop of Slane in Ireland.

St Germans was possibly named after the fifth century St Germanus of Auxerre in France. The village name in Cornish is Lannaled.

St Issey is based on the church dedicated to St Idi, traditionally believed to be the son of a Welsh king. The place was recorded as Sanctus Ydi in 1195.

St Ives derives its name from the Irish St Ia (sometimes St La or St Ya) who arrived Cornwall in the sixth century. It had been earlier called Slepe, meaning 'slippery place', and by the late thirteenth century had been recorded as Sancta Ya. In Cornish the name was 'Porth la', or 'Porthia', meaning 'St La's Cove'.

St Just (in Cornish: Lannyust), sometimes called St Just in Penwith, is named after the third century St Justus of Beauvais in France.

St Keverne is named after the church dedicated to the obscure St Aghevran. It appears in Domesday as *Sanctus Achebrannus*. In Cornish, the placename is Lannaghevran, after the saint, who may have been otherwise known as St Kevin, an Irish missionary saint, the first abbot of Glendalough in modern day County Wicklow. He was probably a pupil of St Petroc.

St Levan is a hamlet dedicated to the Cornish St Selevan and is thought to be a corruption of the name 'Solomon', which later became 'Silvanus'. Consequently, it was recorded in the early fourteenth century as Sanctus Silvanus.

St Mawes is named after a chapel built there in dedication to St Maudyth, (sometimes St Maudez, St Maudetus, St Machutus or St Maudyth), who came to Cornwall some time around 550. Opinions vary as to his ancestry – some have him as a Welsh missionary and others as a bishop from Brittany in north-west France.

St Michael's Mount is a small rocky island dedicated to the Archangel Michael who is said to have appeared there in the early eighth century. The place was recorded in 1479 as Seynt Mychell Mount.

St Neot is named after a church dedicated to the saint, who is thought may have been a relative of Alfred the Great. The place is recorded in the *Domesday Book* as Neotestou and Nietestou, the last element of the name from the Old English 'stou', indicating a church or other religious site. Hence, 'church of St Neot'.

St Tudy is named after the sixth century monk and bishop of that name and the church dedicated to him. It was recorded in the *Domesday Book* as Hecglostudic, based on the Cornish word 'eglos', meaning church and the saint's name. Hence, 'church of St Tudy'.

St Winnow is a small hamlet dedicated to St Winnoc, an eighth century monk. Domesday recorded the placename as San Winnocus in 1086.

Cornwall

The County of Cornwall, in the extreme south-west of England, gets its name from the ancient Celtic tribe known as the Cornovii and the Old English word 'walh', meaning 'foreigner' or 'ancient Briton'. Hence, the county name means 'territory of the Cornovii Britons'. The word 'Cornovii' meant 'horn people', a reference to the horn-shaped geography of Cornwall, where they lived. In Cornish, the county name is Kernow, which is also derived from the Cornovii. In the early eighth century the county name was known as Cornubia, by the end of the ninth it had been recorded as Cornwalas, and the Great Survey of 1086 listed it as Cornualia.

Cotswolds, The

Initially a range of hills in Gloucestershire, Cotswolds has become a name of the wider region, known as 'the Cotswolds'. The name comes from 'wald', a word Saxons used to describe high woodlands or forests, and was probably a territory once owned or claimed by a person called Cod. Hence, 'Cod's high woodland'. The name was recorded as Codesuualt in the twelfth century.

Crediton

There had been a monastery in the settlement since the eighth century, and it was known in 990 as Cridiantune. The placename comes from the River Creedy in Devon, itself a Celtic name which meant 'dwindler', referring to a slow flowing river, with the added Old English suffix 'tun', signifying a farmstead, settlement or estate. Hence, the placename may be taken to mean the 'estate on the slow flowing river'.

Crewkerne

This Somerset village owes a great deal to the ancient Celtic tribes who occupied the territory, as the first element of the placename is thought to be related to the Welsh word 'crug', which means 'hillock'. The second element comes from either from another Celtic suffix, 'ern', or the Old English 'oern', referring to a building of some kind. Hence, 'building on a hillock (or hillside)'. By the ninth century it was already recorded as Crucern and in 1086 was written as Cruche, in the Crewkerne Hundred, which was part-owned by the Abbey of

Sainte-Etienne in Caen, Normandy, as it had been before the Norman Conquest. Another part of the estate had been granted to Robert, Count of Mortain, with Turstin the Sheriff and King William having significant interests in the estate. In 1066, a large portion of the manorial estate had belonged to Edeva the Fair, also known as Edith Swan Neck, the first wife of King Harold.

Cricket St Thomas/Cricket Malherbie

Yet another Somerset settlement with its roots in ancient British culture, as part of the placename is derived from the Celtic word 'crug', meaning 'rounded hill (or mound)'. Following the Norman Conquest, the Old French element 'et', which meant 'little' was applied to this small settlement. By the time of Domesday, the place was known and recorded as Cruche and Cruchet, marking a separation into two settlements, of which the smaller eventually became known as Cricket St Thomas, in the South Petherton Hundred, having adopted the local Church of St Thomas as part of its placename. It was held in 1086 by Count Robert of Mortain. One of his tenants was Ralph Lovel, whose descendants became overlords of Cricket. The other part of the estate, located in the Hundred of Abdick, came into the possession of the Malherbe family sometime in the thirteenth century, and their family name was thereafter appended to that placename.

Dawlish

The name of Dawlish had its origins in Celtic times when it was the name of the local stream, and meant 'dark waters'; it is closely related to the modern Welsh words 'du', meaning 'dark' or 'black', and 'glais', a stream or brook. Hence, '[place near] dark waters'. This seaside town in Devon was recorded in Domesday as Douelis, and listed in the Exminster Hundred as a very large manor supporting over forty households and held by the Bishop of Exeter, as it had been during the reign of King Edward.

Devizes

The Wiltshire town of Devizes originally gets its name from the old French word 'devises', meaning 'boundaries'. Hence the placename means '[place at] the boundaries'. The boundaries in question were at the place where the old Potterne Hundred and the Cannings Hundred met each other. It is known that some kind of Roman settlement originally existed and various coins and artefacts have been uncovered, but the township's recorded history began with the building of Devizes Castle by Bishop Osmund of Salisbury some time around 1080.

Devon

The County of Devon in south-west England derived its name from the Celtic tribe of the Devonians, earlier known as the Dumnonii, a word which meant either 'deep ones', a possible reference to their mining activities, or else a related to the god, Dumnonos, whom they are believed to have worshipped. The god's name, Dumnonus, might have meant 'mysterious one'. The county name is sometimes written as Devonshire, the Old English word 'scir' being attached to indicate 'district' or 'shire'. In the late ninth century the county name was written as Defene and Defenascir.

Dobwalls/Doublebois

This odd-sounding Cornish placename may be derived from a family called Dobb or Dobbs who lived or established the settlement somewhere in its distant past. It has been suggested that it may be a corruption of Doublebois, the next village along the A38 main road, whose name is derived from the French, meaning 'double wood'; given the heavily wooded landscape thereabouts, this is a plausible interpretation of the placename. In Old Cornish, Dobwalls is known as Fos an Mogh and was sometimes spelt Dubwalls. The name appears at the beginning of the seventeenth century by its present name and spelling, as Dobwalls.

Dolton

The precise meaning of this Devon village placename is speculative. What is certain is that the final element of the placename derives from the Old English word 'tun', which signified a farmstead. As for the remainder, it has been suggested that it comes from a contraction of 'dufe' and 'feld', respectively meaning 'dove' and 'open land'. The placename may be loosely interpreted as 'farmstead on open land where doves are seen', or something along those lines. Domesday recorded the village as Duueltone, and listed it as a very large estate in the North Tawton Hundred, supporting forty-six households and one slave, part-held in 1086 by Ansger (known as 'the Breton') and Baldwin the Sheriff, it having belonged to Saxon men called Ulf and Edric before the Conquest.

Dorchester

A settlement at Dorchester in Dorset, has been known since the fourth century, when it was named Durnovaria by the Romans. By 1086, the name had been corrupted to Dorecestre, which meant the 'Roman town called Durnovaria'. The name may be broken into two elements: first, 'durno' or 'dore', an ancient Celtic term which probably translates loosely as '[the place of] fist-shaped (or sized) pebbles'; the second element is from the Old English 'caestre', signifying a Roman fort or settlement. It its entirety the Dorchester placename may therefore be taken to mean 'Roman settlement at the place of fist-sized pebbles'. In the ninth century, the Saxons referred to themselves as Dorsaetas, 'People of Dor'.

Dorset

The southern English County of Dorset (sometimes but rarely referred to a Dorsetshire), derived its name from Dorn, itself a contraction of Dornwaraceaster, which was the old name for Dorchester. The Old English word 'saete', meant 'settlers' or 'dwellers'. Hence the county name means '[territory of the] people [or dwellers] of Dor'. In the ninth century the name was spelt Dornsaetum and Dorsteschire.

Drewsteignton

The Devon village placename reflects the ownership of a man called Drew or Drue, whose farmstead was located on the River Teign. Drew is believed to have owned the manor sometime in the thirteenth century. In 1086, before his occupation, the place was recorded as Taintone, in the Wonford Hundred of lands belonging to Baldwin the Sheriff, where there was land for twelve ploughs and a further two in demesne. There were six acres of meadow, sixty acres of pasture and woodland measuring one league long and three furlongs broad, the whole estate valued at fifty shillings. Before the Conquest, the manor had belonged to Osfrith of Okehampton. The River Teign, which is incorporated in the placename, derives its name from the Old Celtic word 'taenu', which meant 'to spread or expand', which reflected the river's tendency to flood at times. Drew evidently acquired the manor by the mid- to late-thirteenth century, as in 1275, the placename was recorded as Teyngton Drue.

East Lydford

This Somerset village has a placename that translates as 'eastern [place by the] ford across a noisy stream'. It comes from the Old English words 'hlyde', meaning 'loud or noisy one' (referring to a stream), and 'ford', a shallow river crossing. The addition of 'East' to the placename distinguishes it from the nearby village of West Lydford. The Great Survey recorded it as Lideford, in the Blachethorna Hundred, held by the Glastonbury Abbey of St Mary. Before the Conquest it had belonged to a Saxon called Alward.

Egloshayle

As with many south-west villages whose placenames contain the Cornish affix 'eglos', it signifies a church or religious site of some kind. This village name has the additional element 'heyl', which signifies a river estuary, in this case that of the River Camel. Hence, the placename may be interpreted as 'church on the estuary'. In 1166, the placename was recorded as Egloshail.

Egloskerry

A Cornish village whose name reflects its Celtic heritage in that, like Egloshayle, it comes from the word 'eglos', meaning 'church', and the name of the saint to whom it was dedicated, St Keri. The placename therefore means 'the church of St Keri'. An earlier spelling of the placename appeared around the middle of the twelfth century as EglosKery.

Enford

In Old English, the word 'ened', means 'duck', and 'ford' indicated a shallow river crossing, in this case on the River Avon. The placename of this Wiltshire village was recorded as Enedford as early as 934. Hence, '[place by the] river crossing where ducks are found'. Domesday listed Enedforde in the Elstub Hundred, held in 1086 by the Bishop of Winchester, who had retained it since before the Norman Conquest.

Englishcombe

One of the earliest written accounts of this North East Somerset village occurred in the *Domesday Book*, where it was recorded as Ingeliscumb and Engliscome, in land which had been granted to the Bishop of Coutances in Normandy. In 1086, it was held by a man called Nigel having been held by an unnamed thegn who had 'paid geld for ten hides' at the time of King Edward. The placename was probably derived from a man called Ingel, who owned or established the settlement in a valley, or as the Saxons would call it, a 'cumb'. Hence, the placename means 'valley of a man called Ingel'.

Evershot

The Old English word 'eofer' or 'eofor' referred to a wild boar, and the word 'sceat' signified a corner or nook of land. Therefore, the meaning of this Dorset village placename is 'corner of land where wild boars are seen [or possibly, trapped]'. In 1202, the placename was recorded as Teversict, and by the end of that century it was being written as Evershet.

Exeter

When the Roman Emperor Vespasian arrived in south-west England ahead of the Second Augusta Legion in 49 AD, he established a military fort in Devon which the Romans called *Isca Durnoniorum*; by the end of the second century it had become known simply as Iska. After their withdrawal from Britain there followed successive Saxon occupations, and by 656, Exeter had become a Saxon king's royal estate, known then as the Manor of Duryard in the Wonford Hundred. By 800 they called it Isca Chester.

Exmouth

The derivation of the Devon coastal town of Exmouth is fairly self evident: '[the township] at the mouth of the River Exe'. The last element of the placename derives from the Old English 'mutha', meaning 'mouth' or 'estuary'. However, a settlement at this place goes back to before the time of the Romans, for whom it was the most westerly place to appear on their maps.

Farrington Gurney
The first word of this North-East Somerset village placename is of Old English origin and comprises two elements: 'fearn', meaning 'fern', and 'tun', a farmstead or settlement. The de Gurnay family took the manor in the thirteenth century and attached their family name to produce a placename that means 'the de Gurnay's farmstead where ferns grow'. Before its acquisition, Domesday recorded the 'Mainou of Ferentone', in the Chewton Hundred, held in 1086 by the Norman Bishop of Coutances.

Fifehead Magdalen
Fifehead is a corruption of the Old English words 'fif', meaning the number 'five', and 'hide', represented a hide, a measurement of land area. Hence, 'five hides'. Domesday referred to the place as Fifhide, and located it within the Gillingham Hundred of Dorset, held in 1086 by Earl Hugh of Chester, and with Gilbert the Hunter as its overlord, it having belonged to Ednoth the Constable before the Conquest. Some time later, a dedication to the parish church of St Mary Magdalen was attached to the placename, and it was recorded as Fifyde Maudaleyne. This distinguished the village from nearby Fifehead Neville and Fifehead Quentin, which had been acquired by the de Nevill and the St Quintin families in the thirteenth century.

Fisherton de la Mere
This hamlet, located beside the River Wylye in Wiltshire, has a name that means 'farmstead of the fishermen belonging to the de la Mere family'. The de la Meres held the manor in the fourteenth century. Domesday recorded the place as Fisertone, in land held by Roger de Courcelles on behalf of the king. Before the Conquest a man called Bondi had rented ten hides and another five and a half hides were in demesne. The estate had a small mill, twelve acres of meadow, ten acres of woodland and '...pasture half a league long and as much broad. It was, and is worth twenty-five pounds'.

Fowey
The picturesque village of Fowey gets its name from the river on which it stands; the River Fowey placename comes from Cornish and means 'river of the beech trees'. At the time of the *Domesday Book*, Fowey was held by Richard, Earl of Mortain. By about 1223 it had been recorded as Fawi. Its first charter was granted by the Priory of Tywardreath in 1150, and confirmed by the Crown in 1245.

Frome
This Somerset township is named after the River Frome on which it stands. The name itself is probably of old Celtic origin, or possibly the Brythonic Welsh word 'frama' and translates as 'fair' or 'brisk-flowing', in reference to the river.

Galmpton
A village in Devon which in earlier times had been a farmstead rented by farmer-tenants, as the placename implies. The Old English expression 'gafol-mann' meant 'rent-paying man (or peasant)', and the 'tun' affix signified a farmstead. Hence, 'farmstead of rent-paying men (or peasants)'. The place was known as Walementone in 1086 and listed in the Kerswell Hundred, held by Ralph de Fougeres, having been the property of Countess Goda before the Conquest. The manor and its estates were valued at the very high value of thirty pounds in 1086.

Glastonbury
Known in 725 as Glastingburi, this ancient Somerset placename may be derived from the Celtic word 'glaston', possibly referring to a place where blue wode was found, or 'glastan',

a place with oak trees, or even from a man called Glast or Glasta. The addition of the Old English elements 'inga', meaning 'the people or family', and 'burh', a fortified settlement or stronghold, produce a placename which might mean 'stronghold of the people of Glaston'.

Gloucester

In the second century, the Romans called their settlement at Gloucester by its Latin name, Coloniae Nervia Glevensis, in honour of the Emperor Nervi; it translates as 'the Roman town of Nerva called Glevum'. This early form of the placename derives from three sources: the ancient Celtic name 'glevum', meaning a bright place, the Latin element 'ceastre', indicating a Roman town, and 'colonia', signifying a colonial settlement for retired legionnaires.

Great Bedwyn

Commonly known as Bedwyn, this Wiltshire village name comes from 'bedwinde', an Old English word for 'bindweed'. It may also have been the name of a local stream, whose name relates to an ancient Celtic word, similar to the Welsh 'bedw', meaning 'birch', and 'gwyn', meaning 'white'. The place was known as Bedewinde in the eighth century, and by the time of the *Domesday Book* had been recorded as Bedvinde, in the Kinwardstone Hundred, held personally by King William in 1086 as it had belonged to King Edward in his day. The word 'Great' in the placename was added later to distinguish it from nearby Little Bedwyn.

Grittleton

This Wiltshire village was known in 940 as Grutelington, a name derived from the Old English words 'Grytel', a man's name, 'ing', meaning 'associated with' or 'related to', and 'tun', a farmstead or estate. The name translates as 'estate associated with a man called Grytel'. Domesday recorded the village as Gretelintone, in land belonging to the Church of Glastonbury, who also held it before the Conquest. There were ten acres of meadow and eight acres of pasture, with five hides of the estate land held by the Bishop of Coutances and a further four and a half hides held by a man called Urse.

Goonhavern

The name of this Cornish village comes directly from the Cornish language, where the word 'goen' means 'downs' (rounded hills in southern England), and 'havar', which referred to land that was ploughed in summertime. Hence, '[place on the] downs that is ploughed in summer'. In 1300, the name was being written as Goenhavar, and by the mid-eighteenth century it had become known by its present name of Goonhavern.

Gunnislake

Gunni, or Gonne, seems to have been the Danish settler who established this Cornish settlement beside a stream in the Tamar Valley about ten miles north of Plymouth. The 'lake' element of the placename comes from Old English and means 'stream', rather than our contemporary English understanding of the word 'lake'. Hence, 'Gunni's [place beside a] stream'. The placename was recorded in 1485 as Gonellake.

Hammoon

A Dorset village whose name in 1086 was simply recorded as Hame, and listed in the Hundred of Sturminster Newton. The Old English affix 'hamm' in this case signified a bend in a river (though in other contexts it could mean 'enclosure'). The river in question is the River Stour which winds around the village on three sides. At the time of Domesday, the manor was held by William de Mohun (sometimes spelt 'Moion'), and his family name was appended to the placename. The estate supported fifteen households and it was assessed with four ploughlands, fifty acres of meadow, three furlongs of pasture and one mill.

The entire estate and its assets were valued at five pounds. By 1280, the village name had been recorded as Hamme Moun.

Haselbury Plucknett

The first word of this Somerset village's placename, Haselbury, comes from the Old English words 'haesel', meaning 'hazel', and 'bearu', signifying a wood grove. Hence, 'hazel wood grove'. Domesday recorded the place as Halberge, in 'Land of the King's Thegns', in the Houndsborough Hundred, held by Beorhtmaer (known as 'the Englishman'), just as he had held it at the time of King Edward. Later in the thirteenth century, the de Plugenet family acquired the manor and attached their family name, after which it was known as Haselbare Ploukenet. The entire placename translates as 'de Plugenet's [estate by the] hazel wood grove'.

Hasfield

Hasfield is another place whose name contains a reference to the hazel, coming from 'haesel' and 'feld', which taken together produce a placename that means 'open land where hazel grows'. Domesday recorded the place as Hasfelde in the Deerhurst Hundred of Gloucestershire, held by a group including Westminster Abbey, Winchcombe Abbey, Alfrith of Moreton, Gilbert (son of Turold), Reinbald of Cirencester, William (son of Baderon), and a man simply referred to as Gerard. It had extensive lands, sufficient for twenty-eight men's plough teams, as well as forty acres of meadow, woodland measuring one league by a half league, and four mills. The entire estate was valued in 1086 at forty pounds.

Hatherop

During Anglo-Saxon times, places whose name ended in 'throp' or 'thorp' invariably related to outlying or remote farmsteads, and the Gloucestershire village of Hatherop was no exception. The first element of its placename comes from the old word 'heah', meaning 'high', so that both elements taken together produce a placename which means 'high remote farm'. The name was recorded as Etherope in 1086, listed within the Hundred of Brightwells Barrow, held jointly by Arnulf de Hesdin and Roger de Lacy. One of the other 'thorps' of the region is Southrop, situated six miles to the south; its name means 'southern remote farm', and was recorded as Sudthropa around 1140.

Hawkesbury

This village in South Gloucestershire could either be related to a hawk (that is, the bird of prey), or to a man called Hafoc. The final element of Old English origin is 'burh', which signified a stronghold or a fortified manor house or other structure. Hence, the placename can be interpreted as either 'stronghold of the hawk' or 'stronghold of a man called Hafoc' – either seem equally possible. The Domesday Book account lists the village as Havochesberie, a very large estate in the Grimboldestou Hundred, supporting fifty-two households, including two slaves and seven free men. In 1086, the manor was held by the Abbey of St Mary in Pershore, who had continuously owned it since before the Norman Conquest.

Hayle/Helford

The South-West Cornwall coastal village of Hayle (in earlier records sometimes written as Heyl), located across the bay from St Ives, is named after the river which flows through it and comes from a Celtic word which means 'estuary'. The village of Helford shares a similar origin to Hayle in that it gets its placename directly from the river, and is derived from the same old Cornish word, along with the Old English 'ford', signifying a shallow river crossing. The placename therefore means 'crossing place on the estuary'.

Heanton Punchardon

This Devonshire village was earlier known simply as Hantone, and it was by this name that it was recorded in the *Domesday Book*. The survey listed the manor in the Braunton Hundred, held by Baldwin the Sheriff. It was assessed at a value of four pounds and had a mill and a fishery, besides extensive meadowland, pasture and woodland. The original placename came from the Anglo-Saxon 'heah', meaning 'high' (as in high rank), and 'tun', which referred to a farmstead, an estate or settlement. Hence, the placename translates as 'high [or chief] farmstead'. By the eleventh century, the manor had come into the possession of the Punchardon family and this was appended to the placename. By 1297, the village had become known as Heantun Punchardun.

Helston

Helston's placename is derived from the Cornish 'hen-lys' or 'helleys', meaning 'old court', plus the Old English suffix 'tun', indicating a settlement or estate. Hence 'settlement in an old court'. In 1086, the *Domesday Book* recorded Helston as Henlistone thus: 'The king holds Henlistone. There are six and a half hides... [and] there is land for forty ploughs'. The account lists the estate being maintained by twenty-three slaves, thirty villans and twenty bordars, with another forty tenants paying rent. Elsewhere it records a few hides of land in Heliston held for the king by the Count of Mortain, it having belonged to a man called Algar at the time of Edward the Confessor.

Hemyock

Hemyock probably derived its name from a local Celtic river-name meaning 'summer stream'. The placename should be interpreted as '[place by the River] Hemyock'. In fact, this Devonshire village lies on the River Culm. Domesday recorded it as Hamilhoc and Hamihock, in the Hemyock Hundred, lands belonging to King William. The account listed '...sixteen acres of meadow, pasture two leagues long and one and a half leagues broad, and eight furlongs of woodland'. There were also '... two cattle and forty sheep, rendering six pounds by weight'.

Herodsfoot

The name of the Cornish village of Herodsfoot (known in Cornish as 'Nanshiryarth'), translates as '[place at the] foot [of a stream] near Heriard'. Originally the nearby village was known as Heriard, but its name changed to Heriod in the seventeenth century and then to Herod in the eighteenth century. Heriard itself means 'long ridge', and derived its placename from the Cornish word 'hir', meaning 'long', and 'garth', signifying a ridge. Herodsfoot was recorded as Herriott Foote in 1613.

Hidcote Bartrim

The *Domesday Book* listed this Gloucestershire village as Hidicote, a name derived from a man called Hydeca or Huda, together with of the Old English word 'cot', meaning 'cottage' or 'cottages'. Hence, 'Hydeca's cottage'. In the thirteenth century, the manor was held by the Bertram family, and their name was attached to the place, after which it was known as Hudcot Bertram. This distinguished the manor from the nearby manor of Hidcote Boyce, named after the de Bosco (or de Bois) family who had acquired it at around the same time.

Hinton Ampner

Hinton was recorded in 1086 as Hentune, in the Mansbridge Hundred of Hampshire, land belonging to the Bishop of Winchester. The survey stated that '...it always belonged to the monastery'. It also listed fifteen villagers, fourteen smallholders and six slaves. There were eight acres of meadow, woodland supporting ten pigs, and the estate had one church. The placename comes from 'heah', meaning 'high', and 'tun', a farmstead. Hence, 'high farmstead'. Some time in the thirteenth century the estate came into the possession of the almoner of St Swithin's Priory in Winchester and thereafter the estate was known as Hinton Amner, which means 'high farm of the almoner'.

Honeychurch

It is thought that the Devonshire village of Honeychurch derived the first part of its placename from a man called Huna. The second part comes from the Old English word 'cirice', referring to a church. Hence, the placename means 'church belonging to a man called Huna'. An alternative interpretation raises the possibility that it could relate to bee-keeping and mean 'church where honey is produced', but this is largely discounted. Domesday recorded the village as Honecercha, and listed it in the Black Torrington Hundred, held in 1086 by Baldwin the Sheriff it having been the property of Alwin Blaec before the Norman Conquest.

Honeystreet

The 'honey' element in the placename of this Wiltshire hamlet has little to do with bees or honey and probably described the colour and consistency of an early track or ridgeway that crossed the Vale of Pewsey at this spot. The Old English word 'straet' has been attached here, somewhat optimistically, as it would originally refer to a Roman road, and one that would have been well-constructed and practically never muddy. However, the name may loosely translate as '[place on a] muddy road [coloured like honey]', or something along those lines. One of the earliest records of the name was as Honey Street in 1773.

Honiton

Little written history of the place exists before the *Domesday Book* of 1086, when it was recorded as Honetone and Hunitone in Devonshire, from the Old English, 'Huna', the name of its earliest known Saxon settler, and 'tun', a township or farmstead. Hence, 'township belonging to Huna'.

Huish Episcoli

Huish Episcopi, known in the tenth century as Hiwissh (meaning 'household'), is located in the Kingsbury East Hundred. The manor had been held by the Bishops of Wells Cathedral since Saxon times, and continued to be known by this name until the eighteenth century when the Latin affix 'episcopi' was added (meaning belonging to the bishop)..

Ilchester

The 'chester' element of this Somerset village betrays its Roman origins, as it signifies a Roman military settlement, fort or garrison. This was the settlement of Lindinis, a name derived from Celtic and similar to the Welsh word 'llyn', meaning 'pool' or 'small lake'. The 'Il' element refers to the River Gifl (which is now known as the River Yeo). The placename therefore means, 'Roman town on the [River] Gifl'. Domesday recorded the name as Givelcestre, and listed it in the Tintinhull Hundred, held by the Bishop of London in 1086, it having belonged to a Saxon called Britric in 1066.

Ilfracombe

This popular seaside resort on the North Devon coast is known to have been settled since the Iron Age when the hill fort called Hele's Barrow was constructed at nearby Hillsborough. It was known in 1086 as Alfreincome and was comprised of three separate elements: the first, after a man called Aelfred, the second Old English element, 'inga', meaning 'the people or followers', and third, 'cumb', meaning 'valley'. The placename therefore refers to the 'valley of the followers or family of Aelfred'.

Iron Acton

This is a village that began life as a farmstead where iron deposits were discovered in South Gloucestershire. The placename comes from the Old English words 'iren', meaning 'iron', plus 'ac', an oak tree, and 'tun', signifying a farmstead. The entire placename therefore translates as 'farmstead where iron was discovered by an oak tree'. The name suggests that there were iron workings here at some time in its early history. Domesday recorded the place (presumably before the iron was discovered) as Actune, and listed it in the Bagstone Hundred, held in 1086 by Humphrey the Chamberlain, it having belonged to Harold (described as Alwy Hile's man), in 1066.

Keevil

The meaning of the placename of this Wiltshire village is a widely disputed. It was known around 964 as Kefle, which some argue comes from the Old English words 'cyf', meaning 'hollow', and 'leah', a woodland clearing. Hence, 'woodland clearing in a hollow'. Others prefer a Celtic source word related to modern the Welsh 'cyfyl' or 'cyfle', meaning 'place' or 'district', in which case it may be interpreted as something like 'place (or district) in a woodland clearing'. By the time of the Great Survey, the name was written as Chivele, and listed as a very large estate within the Whorwellsdown Hundred, held in 1086 by Arnulf de Hesdin, having belonged to a man called Brictsi before the Conquest.

Keinton Mandeville

As a one-time royal manor, this Somerset village was recorded in 1086 as Chintune, a name taken from two Old English words, 'cyne', meaning 'king' and 'tun', a manor. Hence 'king's manor'. The Domesday entry for the village placed it within the Hundred of Blachethorna, held jointly by Roger de Courcelles and Count Robert of Mortain, having previously belonged to a Saxon man called Alstan of Boscombe. The Maundeville family took possession of the manor at some time during the thirteenth century and in 1280 it was recorded as Kyngton Maundevill.

Kilkhampton

The Cornish town and civil Parish of Kilkhampton (known locally as 'Kilk', and in Cornish as 'Kylgh'), dates from Saxon times when the settlement was known as Kilketon. The name is derived from the old Cornish 'kelk', possibly meaning a circle, ring, boundary or border, with two Old English affixes 'ham' and 'tun', signifying a farmstead or estate. This would produce a placename that means 'farmstead or estate by the border, or within the circle'. It has also been suggested that the estate of Kelk was granted by King Egbert of Wessex to the Bishop of Sherborne. By 1086, it had been recorded as Chilchetone and by the end of the twelfth century as an early form of its present name, Kilkamton.

Kilmersdon

Named some time in the mid-tenth century after its probable founder, the village of Kilmersdon in Somerset honours a man called Cynemaer in its placename. This taken together with the Saxon word 'don', which signified a hill, produces a village name that means 'Cynemaer's hill'. In 951 it was already known as Kunemersdon, and by the time it had been recorded in the Domesday survey it had become Chenemeresdone, listed as a very small estate within the Hundred of Kilmersdon, belonging to King William. Before the Conquest it had been a possession of the Bishop of Lichfield and valued at only five shillings.

King's Nympton

This Devonshire village began as a farm beside the River Nymet, which accounts for the second part of the placename, This is made up of the original Celtic river name, the Nymet (which itself means 'holy place'), and the Old English word 'tun', indicating a settlement or a framstead. The river is nowadays known as the Mole. Domesday recorded the village as Nimetone, in the Witherage Hundred, held by King William in 1086 – hence the prefix 'King's' to the placename. This distinguished the manor from Bishop's Nympton, located a few miles away and held at that time by the Bishop of Exeter. In 1254, the place was recorded as Kingesnemeton.

Knook

Probably originating in Celtic times, the name of this Wiltshire village may be related to the modern Welsh word 'cnwc', meaning 'hillock', a possible reference to a tumulus, or ancient burial mound near the local church. The name may be interpreted as '[place by the] hillock (or tumulus)'. Domesday listed the village as Cunuche, in the Heytesbury Hundred, part-held in 1086 by a woman called Leofgyth and a man called Alward Colling. Apparently, Leofgyth was a widow whose husband had held the manor at the time of King Edward.

Lamyatt

Should you think that the name of this Somerset village is in any way related to lambs, you'd be correct. The name comes from the Old English word 'lamb', and 'geat', meaning 'gate', Hence, '[place by a] gate for lambs', or even more simply, 'lamb's gate'. The village was already known as Lambageate by the late-tenth century, and by Domesday it had become Lamieta, listed in the Whitstone Hundred held by the Glastonbury Abbey of St Mary as it had been at the time of King Edward. It was a very large estate containing extensive meadows, pasture and woodland and had four mills. Little wonder that at the time of the assessment the manor and its estates were assessed with a high value of thirty-two pounds and five shillings.

Latton

At some time in its ancient history this Wiltshire village was notable for growing leeks, if its placename is to be believed. The name means 'enclosure or farmstead where leeks (or herbs) are grown', as the Old English word 'leac' could signify either a leek or more generally, a herb. The Great Survey listed it as Latone, a large estate in the Cricklade Hundred, supporting twenty households and part-held in 1086 by a man known as Humphrey the Cook, who had also held it during the reign of King Edward. Another part of the estate had been granted to Reinbald of Cirencester; his portion had been previously held by two unnamed Saxon thegns.

Launceston

The placename of Launceston on the River Kensey, is 'Lannstevan' in Cornish. It is comprised of three elements: 'lann', a Cornish word for a church, plus an abbreviation of St Stephen, and 'tun', the Old English Saxon word for a settlement or estate. Hence, the 'estate near the church of St Stephen'. The placename is pronounced 'Lawns-ton' and sometimes locally abbreviated to 'Lanson'. Domesday records it as Lanscaveton in the land of Robert, the Count of Mortain, the Earl of Cornwall and the half brother to King William.

Lechlade

This Gloucestershire village is located on the River Leach, which is reflected in the placename. The second element of the name is based on the Old English word 'gelad', which indicated a river crossing or a ford. The placename therefore translates as 'river crossing of the River Leach'. The Leach joins the River Thames a half mile or so to the south-east. The river name itself comes from 'laecc' and means 'boggy [or muddy] stream'. Domesday recorded the placename as Lecelade, a very large estate in the Brightwells Barrow Hundred, owned in 1086 by Henri de Ferrers.

Liskeard

By the beginning of the eleventh century, Liskeard, in the district of Caradon, was known as Lys Cerruyt, probably named after a man called Kerwyd, plus the Cornish word 'lys', meaning 'court'. Hence, the placename might translate as 'court of Kerwyd'. In the *Domesday Book* of 1086 it had been written as Liscarret, held by the Count of Mortain, it having belonged to Maerl Sveinn before the Conquest. The survey recorded twelve hides of land sufficient for sixty ploughs with three more in demesne. There was a market, a mill, four hundred acres of woodland and four leagues of pasture, altogether '...worth twenty-six pounds less twenty pence'.

Littleton Drew

There are a dozen or so places in England called Littleton, a name derived from the Old English words 'lytel', meaning 'little', and 'tun', which signified a farmstead or an estate. Hence, 'little farmstead or estate'. In 1086, this village in Wiltshire was recorded as Liteltone, in the Dunley Hundred, held by the Abbey of St Mary of Glastonbury and part-held by Bishop Geoffrey of Coutances in Normandy. Before the Conquest, Saxons named as Alward and Brictric had been Lords of the Manor. In the thirteenth century, the Driwe family took possession of the manor after which time it was known as Littleton Dru.

Lizard

Of course, there is a small village called Lizard, but the area is probably better known as a peninsula in the most southerly point of Cornwall – the Lizard Peninsula. According to some, the name comes from two old Cornish words: 'lys', which indicated a court, and 'ardh', a high point or clifftop. Hence, the 'court on the hilltop'. An alternative and more likely suggestion has it derived from the Cornish word 'liazherd' or 'lezou', which signifies a projecting headland. Domesday lists it as Lisart, in the Royal Manor of Winnianton in the Kerrier Hundred, at that time probably the largest manor in Cornwall.

Looe

The south-east coastal Cornish township of Looe is thought to have been an inhabited settlement for the best part of three thousand years. Until relatively modern times it was divided into two separate towns – East Looe and West Looe. They are joined by a bridge across the East Looe River (sometimes simply called the River Looe). The placename derives from the old Cornish 'loo', which meant 'pool' or 'inlet', in reference to the body of water known locally as the Mill Pool. Nearby is Looe Island, also known as St George's Island, which was settled by monks from Glastonbury Abbey from 1144. Its original Cornish name was Enys Lann-Managh, which translates as 'island of the monk's settlement'.

Lostwithiel

Lostwithiel's placename comes directly from the Cornish, Lostgwydeyel (sometimes 'Les Uchel'). It comprises 'lost', meaning 'end' or 'tail end', and 'gwydhye', a woodland or forest. Hence '(place at the) end of the forest'. In 1100, the Norman Lord Baldwin FitzTurstin built nearby Restormel Castle, which was rebuilt by Edmund, Earl of Cornwall, in the late thirteenth century. The place was known in the fourteenth century as 'The Port of Fawi' (Fowey), and was the capital of Cornwall, as well being one of the local stannary towns, assaying the purity of tin in its Great Hall.

Ludgershall

The name of this Wiltshire township has a complex meaning that is derived from an ancient practice whereby pits containing sharpened stakes (known as 'trapping spears'), were dug to impale animals. The Saxon word for such devices was 'lute-gar', from the Old English words 'lutuian', meaning 'to hide (or lurk)', 'gar', a spear, and 'halh' referring to a corner or nook of land. The placename may be interpreted as meaning 'corner of land where trapping spears are located'. The Domesday account of the village name was corrupted as Litlegarsele, while an earlier version of 1015 recorded it as Lutegaresheale.

Lymington

The settlement of Lymington in the New Forest region of South West Hampshire was founded by the Saxons in the sixth century, when it was known to them as Limentun, based on 'limen', the Celtic river name, meaning muddy or marshy river, and the Old English affix 'tun' indicating a settlement. Hence, 'the settlement by the muddy or marshy river'. Domesday recorded the place as Limington and Lentune, listed in Boldre Hundred, in the possession of Earl Roger Montgomerie of Shrewsbury (also known as Roger the Great), with Fulcwin as tenant-in-chief.

Lyme Regis

This township on the Dorset coast is named from the River Lim (or Lym) and was known as Lim in 774 when King Cynewulf of Wessex gave the land to the Abbott of Sherborne to set up a salt works. Later it passed to the Bishopric of Salisbury. By 1086, it was recorded as Lime, itself a Celtic word for 'stream' or 'river'. The 'Regis' affix was granted when Edward I declared it to be royal property in 1284. It was during his reign that a small harbour called the Cob was constructed.

Lyneham

The Wiltshire township of Lyneham, in the ancient Parish of Cricklade, derives its name from the Old English 'lin', meaning flax, and 'ham' signifying an enclosure or settlement. Hence, 'settlement where flax grows'. It has been suggested that there was an ancient British settlement nearby, supported by the area immediately to its north-west known as Barrow End.

Malmesbury

Malmesbury gets its name from an Old Irish man called Maeldub, which meant 'black chief'. The added affix 'burh' or 'byrig' indicated a fortified stronghold. Hence, the placename means 'Maeldub's stronghold'. The place had been known as Maldumesburg since Bishop Aldhelm built a chapel there in the late seventh century. By 1086, it had emerged as Malmesberie in the Cicementone Hundred, part-held by the Bishop of Coutances and by a man called Ketil, with the lion's share of the manorial estates being retained by the Crown.

Mappowder

This Dorset village placename means '[place by the] maple tree'. The Saxon word for the maple tree was 'mapuldor. Domesday listed the 'Mainou of Mapledre', a large estate supporting over thirty households (including fifteen slaves), in the Hundred of Buckland Newton, part-held in 1086 by King William, Bolla the Priest, Count Robert of Mortain and William d'Eu.

Marazion

The village of Marazion in west Cornwall derives its name from two Cornish words: 'marghas', signifying a market, and 'byghan', possibly meaning 'small' or 'little'. Opinions differ and the placename has been variously translated as 'Little Market' and as 'Thursday Market'. Whatever the true meaning, the Romans knew the place as Ictis, suggesting some form of market or trading post existed there long before their arrival in Britain. It was recorded as Marghasbigan in the mid-thirteenth century, and claims to be one of the oldest townships in Britain.

Marlborough

This Wiltshire placename has at least three possible explanations. First, it could be based on an early Saxon called Maerla (sometimes interpreted as 'Merlin'), with the addition of the Old English word 'beorg', meaning a hill or more probably a mound – hence, 'Maerla's [burial] mound'. Second, it may have derived from 'meargaella', signifying the gentian plant, a common ancient flavouring and colouring, in which case it might translate as the 'hill where gentian grows'. Third, it may have been named from the marl or chalk hills in the region. If the burial mound option is the case, it may have referred to a prehistoric funeral barrow that became the motte of Marlborough Castle which the Normans built in the late eleventh century. The latter interpretation is supported by the fact that it was locally recorded as 'The Mound'.

Meeth

Meeth either gets its name from the Old English word 'mythe', meaning 'confluence', or from 'maeth', meaning 'mowing' (as of grass). The former explanation would suggest a topographical origin, marking a confluence place where two watercourses or streams met, and the second, less probable suggestion is '[place where grass is] mown'. The 1086 survey listed the estate as Meda, a very small estate supporting just five households within the Merton Hundred of Devonshire and held by Baldwin the Sheriff, having belonged to Alnoth at the time of King Edward.

Mendip Hills

The Mendips are a range of hills in Somerset whose name may have had Celtic origins, probably related to the modern Welsh 'mynydd', meaning 'hill'. The second element may be 'yppe', meaning 'upland' or 'plateau', reflecting the wide plateau of its western region. The name in its entirety may therefore mean 'hill with a plateau'. In the late-twelfth century the hills were recorded as Menedepe.

Menheniot

A village and parish in the Liskeard district of Cornwall, located on the River Seaton. The placename is pronounced 'Men-en-yut', and in Cornish the name is written as Mahynyet. In the nineteenth century the placename was spelt Menhynnet. One of two possible translations of the placename has it as 'sanctuary of St Neot', from 'mihini' and 'Neot'. The *Penguin Dictionary of British Placenames*, based on the Cornish word 'ma', meaning plain, and the final element, 'nyed', presumably a reference to the aforementioned Cornish saint. In 1260, the place was recorded as Mahiniet. The current spelling of the name dates from the mid-nineteenth century.

Mevagissey

Until 1313, this small Cornish fishing village was called Porthilly in the old Parish of Lamorrick, part of the Manor of Tregear. The name became Meva hag Ysi, and first appears in something approaching its present form, as Meffagesy around 1400, named after the Irish Saints Meva and Issey, with the addition of the Cornish word 'ag' or 'hag', meaning 'and'. Hence '[the settlement of] Meva and Issey.'

Midsomer Norton

A north-east Somerset village which was known in 1246 as Midsomeres Norton. Norton is a very common English placename with around twenty other places called thisaround the country. 'Norton', comes from Old English and simply means 'north settlement' (or sometimes 'farmstead'). The Midsomer affix was added to commemorate the Feast of St John the Baptist, patron saint of the village church, which occurs on Midsummer Day.

Minchinhampton

Minchinhampton is a Gloucestershire village whose placename comprises three separate elements, all derived from Anglo-Saxon sources. The first element, 'myncen' translates as 'nun', 'the second, 'heah', means 'high' and the last, 'tun', signifies a farmyard or a settlement. These elements taken together mean 'high farmstead [or settlement] of the nuns'. The manor had been given to nuns from the Abbey of La Trinité in Caen, Normandy, in the eleventh century, having belonged to Countess Goda before the Norman Conquest. In 1086, the place had been recorded in the Great Survey simply as Hantone, a very large manor of over fifty households, held by the Abbey in the Hundred of Longtree. In 1221 the placename was written as Minchenhamtone.

Minehead

The seaside town of Minehead in Somerset was known as Mynheafdon in 1046; by the time of the Domesday survey it had become Manheve. The placename comes from two old Celtic words, 'monith' (sometimes appearing as Mohun, Manheve or Minheved in the town's civic documents), meaning 'mountain', and 'heafod', referring to a projecting spur of land. Hence, '[place of the[projecting mountain spur'. The mountain referred to is almost certainly North Hill, which overlooks the town and offers panoramic views of the Quantock, Brendon and Hopcott Hills.

Minions

Reputedly, the village of Minions on Bodmin Moor, part of Linkinhorne Parish, was known in Cornish as Menyon (probably meaning 'stone'), and is one of the highest in the county at three hundred metres above sea level. The place gets its name from the nearby Iron Age barrow known as Minions Mound, or Minions Barrow; its derivation is unknown but it was recorded in 1613 as Mimiens Borroughe.

Monksilver

The 'silver' element of this Somerset village name probably originally came from a watercourse whose Old English name was 'seolfor', meaning 'clear [or bright] stream'. Domesday listed it as Selvere in the Williton Hundred, part-held in 1086 by Roger de Courcelles and a man known as Alfred of Spain. Some time in the early thirteenth century the manor came into the possession of the monks of Goldcliff Priory and the affix 'manuc', meaning 'monk' was attached. The placename means 'monks [estate by the River] Silver'. By 1249, the place had become known as Monkesilver.

Morchard Bishop/Cruwys Morchard

Morchard Bishop is a Devonshire village which came into the possession of the Bishop of Exeter following the Survey of 1086 where it was recorded simply as Morchet, in the Crediton Hundred, held by the king. The Morchard element of the placename harks back to the Celtic 'mor', which compares with the modern Welsh word 'mawr', meaning 'big' or 'great', and 'ced' (or 'coed' in Welsh), which refers to a wood, a forest or woodland. Hence, '[the estate of the] bishop in the great wood'. The place was recorded as Bisschoppesmorchard in 1311, and by the mid-nineteenth had become known as Bishop Morchard, with the words reversed in modern times. The village of Cruwys Morchard, also in Devon, was recorded in the *Domesday Book* as Morchet in the Witheridge Hundred, held at that time by Bishop Geoffrey of Coutances. The Cruwys affix was attached around 1260, when the de Crues family took possession of the manor.

Morwenstow

In 1201, the coastal Cornish village of Morwenstow was called Morwestewe, referring to St Morwenna with the Old English affix 'stowe', indicating a holy place. The village name may therefore be interpreted as 'holy place of St Morwenna'. The most northerly parish and village in the county, it was known in Cornish as Logmorwenna. The Norman church of around 1296 stands on an original Saxon site and is dedicated to St Morwenna, an Irish saint from the early sixth century, and to St John the Baptist.

Newlyn

This seaport township is located in Mounts Bay near the end of the Cornish peninsula and has been known as Nulyn since the thirteenth century. By 1290, it had been recorded as Lulyn. The name derives from the old Cornish words 'lu' and 'lyn', respectively meaning 'pool' and 'fleet of boats' Hence, probably, 'pool for a fleet of boats'. In the thirteenth century, Newlyn was actually a collection of three small settlements, Newlyn Town, Street-an-Nowan and Tolcarne.

Newquay

As it suggests, this coastal town in Cornwall derives its name from the new quay that was built in the 1439. The township was known in 1602 as Newe Kaye; previously, it had been called Towan Blistra (or 'Blystra' in the Cornish language) and changed its name after Bishop Lacy of Exeter granted permission for the building of the new harbour. The word 'towan' meant hill or dune, and 'blistra' meant 'blown', as by strong winds that typically come from the north-east. Hence, 'wind-blown hill'.

Newton Abbott

Newton is a fairly common English placename, with around seventy places having some form of the name in Britain. It is based on the Old English 'niwe' and 'tun', which together mean 'new village, estate or settlement'. This Devonshire market township, located on the River Lemon in the Teignbridge District, close to Dartmoor National Park, was originally known as Teignwick. By around 1200, it had become Nyweton (or Nuietone), and when the Abbey of Torre was established in 1270, it was known by its Latin name, Nyweton Abbatis (the new town of the abbot).

Norton Malreward

The village of Norton Malreward was listed in the *Domesday Book* simply as Nortone. There are some twenty or so places called Norton in England, (places like Norton Bavant in Wiltshire, Norton Canon in Herefordshire, and Norton St Philip in Somerset). Norton derives from the Old English 'north', meaning 'northern', and 'tun', a farmstead or settlement. Hence, 'northern settlement'. It had been owned in 1086 by Geoffrey, the Bishop of Coutances. Typically, this village has an additional element affixed in order to distinguish it from all the others. In this case, when the Norman family of Malregard became tenants of the Manor of

Norton in the Chew Hundred of Somerset, a few miles south of Bristol, their family name was appended to the place. At that time the neighbouring hamlet of Norton Hautville was combined with it, Malregard was converted to Malreward, and the two were known thereafter as the village of Norton Malreward.

Nunney

This Somerset village was already known as Nuni by 954. The name either comes from the Old English 'nunne', meaning 'nun', or from a man called Nunna. Added to this is the suffix 'eg', signifying an island – dry or raised ground in a marsh or surrounded by wetlands. Therefore the placename could mean either 'Nun's island' or 'Nunna's island'– either is possible. It was recorded as Nonin in 1086, listed within the Frome Hundred, jointly held by William de Mohun and the Abbey of Sainte-Marie in Montebourg.

Offwell

This Devonshire village was listed in the Great Survey of 1086 as Offewelle and Offewille, a small settlement of eight households in the Colyton Hundred, held at that time by Baldwin the Sheriff, having belonged to Burgred of Aunk before 1066. It was valued at just seven shillings, despite its eighty acres of pasture and five furlongs of woodland. The placename comes from the Old English words, 'Offa', or 'Uffa', a man's personal name (possibly its founder or chieftain), and 'wella', signifying a well, stream or a spring. Hence, 'spring (or well) belonging to a man called Offa'.

Owermoigne

At the time of the Great Survey the name of this village in Dorset was recorded as Ogre, a name thought to derive from a Celtic word related to the Welsh 'oerddrws', meaning 'windy gap', in reference to places in the chalk cliffs and the strong sea breezes that frequently flow inland from channel. Domesday listed the manor in the Winfrith Hundred, held in 1086 by Matthew de Mortagne, it having been a possession of John, (known as 'the Dane'), before the Conquest. Some time in the thirteenth century the manor and its estates came into the ownership of the Moigne family who attached their family name, and in 1314 the placename was recorded as Oure Moyngne.

Ozleworth

This township in Gloucestershire was known as Oslan Wyrth in Saxon times, and had become Osleuuorde by the time of Domesday. It was listed as quite a large settlement in the Berkeley Hundred, held in 1086 by King William, having belonged to King Edward before the Conquest. The survey shows it as a potentially wealthy estate with ten mills and one hundred and ninety-two mens plough teams; it also lists ten radmen as tenants of the manor. The placename is ambiguous, in that it may derive from a man called Osla, whose 'worth', or animal enclosure it was, in which case the name means 'Osla's enclosure'; or it might equally translate as 'enclosure frequented by blackbirds'. This last explanation relates to the Old English word 'osle', meaning 'blackbird'. Either are equally possible.

Padstow

This Cornish fishing village was known in Cornish as Lanwenehoc, and by the eleventh century by its Latin name, Sancte Petroces Stow. The place was dedicated to St Petroc, a sixth century Christian saint, much venerated in Cornwall, and 'stow' indicated an assembly or council meeting place or a Saxon holy place. According to legend, St Petroc arrived from Ireland around 520 and built a monastery on the hill above the harbour. It has also been suggested that the placename may have had an association with St Patrick. In 981, the

Anglo-Saxon Chronicles recorded Padstow and the surrounding region attacked by Danish forces: 'St Petroc's in Padstow was ravaged, and in that same year much harm was done everywhere along the sea coasts in both Devon and Cornwall'. In 1318, the place was known as Patristowe, and by the early sixteenth century had been recorded as Padstowe, something approaching its present name.

Pancrasweek

This small Devonshire hamlet derives its placename from St Pancras, the village Church, and the Old English element 'wic', which translates as 'dwelling', 'small settlement' or 'hamlet'.

Hence, the name means 'hamlet of St Pancras'. By the end of the twelfth century, the placename had been written as Pancradeswike.

Peasdown St John

This was originally a small coalmining village in north-east Somerset, which really did not exist before the nineteenth century, and consequently, no early records of the place are known. However, the placename is apparently very old, and suggests a fairly straightforward interpretation, based on the Middle English words 'pese', meaning 'peas', and 'doun', a hill or rolling hillside. Hence. 'hillside where peas are grown'. The St John affix came later and relates to the dedication of the local church.

Penryn/Penzance

In the old Cornish language, Penryn simply refers to a headland, and the township was recorded by that name in 1216. It sits on a promontory, after which the township is named, and was a traditional subdistrict in Cornwall, located on the Penryn River that runs into the Fal Estuary of the English Channel at Falmouth. Penzance was known as Pensans at the end of the thirteenth century, located the old Hundred of Penrith and derives its name from the Cornish words 'pen', a headland, and 'sans', another name for a holy or sacred place. Hence, 'holy headland'. The reference is to the ancient chapel of St Anthony, first mentioned in records in 1284, which is thought to have stood on the headland to the west of Penzance Harbour.

Perranporth

Perranporth is a relatively new settlement, having been known at the latter end of the sixteenth century as St Perin's Creek, after the fifth century abbot and saint, St Piran or Pyran (in Cornish: St Peran), who was originally the patron saint of tin miners, though nowadays of the County of Cornwall. His flag, a white cross on a black background, has become the flag of the county. It was not until the nineteenth century that the village was known as Perran Porth. 'Porth' is an old word for a port or harbour. Hence, the 'Port of St Piran'.

Pitminster

A church in this Somerset village was at some time in its distant past associated with a man called Pippa, and by 938 was known as Pipingmynstre. The original Saxon name derives from three Old English elements, Pippa or Pipa, a man's personal name, possibly its founder or chieftain, 'inga', signifying his family, tribe or followers and 'mynster', meaning a large church or other religious house. Hence, 'church associated with the people or followers of Pippa'. The Domesday survey recorded the placename as Pipeminstre, in the Taunton Hundred, held in 1086 by the Bishop of St Peter's and St Swithin's Church in Winchester, as it had been before the Conquest.

Plush

An ancient Dorset settlement known by the Saxons as Plyssh since 891. It is situated within the civil parish of Piddletrenthide, about eight miles north of Dorchester. The placename comes from the Old English word 'plysc', which means 'shallow pool'. The reference may have been to that which still survives south of the village. Hence, '[place by a] shallow pool'.

Plymouth

The origin of the Plymouth placename is straightforward – it simply means '[the place at the] mouth of the River Plym'. It was recorded in 1230 as Plymmue, and as Plimmuth in 1234, its last element derived from the Old English word 'mutha', meaning 'mouth', referring to the place where the river flows out into Sutton Harbour. It had been given a passing mention in the *Domesday Book* as Sudone, meaning 'south farm', and developed as a township around the harbour to become the centre of medieval Plymouth.

Polyphant

Polyphant gets its name from the old Cornish language where the word 'poll' signified a pool and 'lefant' meant 'toad' or 'toads'. Hence, '[place by the] pool where toads are found'. Domesday recorded Polefand in the Rillaton Hundred of Cornwall, held by Count Robert de Mortain, it having been a possession of a Saxon man called Wulfric before 1066.

Ponsanooth

The name of this Cornish village comes directly from the ancient Cornish language and is comprised of three elements: 'pons', a bridge, 'an', which simply stands for 'the', and 'goeth', a drainage ditch or watercourse. The last element might also be a derivation of the Cornish word 'woodh', signifying a stream Therefore the translation of the placename into English might be: '[place at the] bridge at [or over] the watercourse', or even '[place at the] bridge by a stream'. In the early sixteenth century it was recorded as Pons an Oeth.

Porthleven

Porthleven grew at the mouth of a small stream called Leven, which translates from Cornish as 'smooth' and 'porth', meaning harbour. Hence 'smooth harbour'. It may also be related to St Elvan of Avalon, who was known to have preached Christianity to kings of the Britons.

Port Isaac

The placename of this northern Cornish fishing village has nothing to do with 'Isaac', but is taken from the old Cornish words 'porth', meaning a port or harbour, and 'izzick' or 'usek', meaning corn or chaff. Hence, 'corn port'. In Cornish the placename is Porthysek. Opinions vary as to the significance of the reference to corn, but possibly it may have been the result of harvesting in adjacent cornfields, with chaff blown into the sea and washed up on the beach.

Portwrinkle

A small one-time traditional pilchard fishing village on the western end of Whitsand Bay on the Cornish coast, Portwrinkle's placename is somewhat obscure. The first element, 'port', is straightforward, coming from the Cornish word 'porth', meaning 'cove' or 'inlet', but the second element, 'wrinkle', has left all-comers totally bemused and at a loss to give a satisfactory explanation of its meaning. The village is known in the Cornish language as Porthwykkel. In 1605, the place was recorded as Port Wrickel.

Praze-an-Beeble

An unusual village place name, Praze-an-Beeble comes directly from the Cornish language, where 'pras', means 'meadow', 'an' simply means 'the', and 'pibell' signifies a pipe or conduit, although some cite 'Beeble' as a direct reference to the River Beeble, on which the village stands. The placename may therefore translate as either 'meadow with a conduit', or more likely, 'meadow on the [River] Beeble'. The Beeble is a tributary of the River Hayle, which runs at the bottom of the village.

Priddy

A Somerset village whose placename is short, sweet and down to earth. Pun intended, as it comes from ancient Celtic and is related to two modern Welsh words, 'pridd', meaning 'earth', and 'ty', a house. Hence, 'earth house', referring no doubt to its basic mud or daub construction. In 1182, the name was recorded as Pridia.

Puddletown

This Dorset village stands on the River Piddle. The river name comes from Old English and means 'marsh' or 'fen'. Therefore the village placename translates as 'farmstead on the [River] Piddle', and therefore there are compelling reasons to call the place 'Piddletown'. However, when the local council attempted to convert the placename to Piddletown in the 1950s, better reflecting the township's location, local sensibilities were outraged and posed strong objections; the placename remained unchanged, despite the fact that it had been known by the name of Pideltown in the thirteenth century. The *Domesday Book* recorded it as Pitretone in 1086.

Puncknowle

The Old English word 'cnoll' is common in many English placenames and signified a hillock, a small hill or a knoll. This Dorset village is typical of such places, and was once owned or overseen by a man called Puma, whose name was incorporated into the village name, which means 'Puma's hillock'. In 1086, the name was recorded as Pomacanole, and listed in the Uggescombe Hundred, held by Hugh, 'the son of Grip's wife Hawise'. The estate had thirty-five acres of meadow, three furlongs of pasture and thirty acres of woodland. Its other assets included a mill, one cob horse, twelve cattle, thirteen pigs and one hundred and fifty-three sheep. It supported four villagers, five smallholders and four slaves and the whole estate was valued at five pounds.

Quantock Hills

The Quantock Hills in Somerset derive their name from the Celtic word 'cantuc', meaning 'border' or 'rim', which is related to the modern Welsh word 'cant' or 'canto', with an early form of the Old English word 'wudu', meaning 'wood'. The name appeared as Cantuctum in 880, and Cantoctona in 1086 and translates as 'rim or circle of hills'.

Quedgeley

The village of Quedgeley lies on the left-hand bank of the River Severn, some three miles south of Gloucester. The Parish of Quedgeley was established sometime before 1095 when St James Church was built, and is believed to have been formed by the amalgamation of several other parishes. The place was known in the early twelfth century as Quedesleya, and probably derived its placename from an early Saxon owner or founder named Cweod, with the addition of the suffix 'leah', indicating a woodland clearing. Hence, 'Cweod's clearing'.

Redmarley d'Abitot

This Gloucestershire village was known in 963 as Reodemaereleage, a name that comes directly from the Old English words 'hred', meaning 'reedy', or 'covered with reeds or bullrushes', 'mere', representing a pond or a small lake, and 'leah', a woodland glade or clearing. Hence, it translates as 'woodland clearing with a pond covered with reeds'.

Domesday recorded the place as Ridmerlege, in the Oswaldslow Hundred, held at that time by the Bishop of St Mary's Church in Worcester. In 1086, the tenancy passed to the Norman d'Abitot family who attached their family name to distinguish it from the village of Redmarley in Worcestershire. In 1324, the place was recorded as Rudmarleye Dabetot.

Redruth
This place name is derived from two old Cornish words, 'rid' meaning red, and 'rudh' or 'rhys', meaning a ford or river crossing. Hence, 'red ford'. The name comes from the stream that runs through part of the township, which is so discoloured by iron oxide that it has been known to run red since the fourteenth century, when the placename probably came into use.

St Austell
Little is recorded about the Cornish township of St Austell before 1150. It received no mention in Domesday, though the survey describes the Manor of Tewington as located near 'St Awstle situate not farr from the head of Tywardreth baye, nare unto Gwallon Downes'. The placename comes from the church dedicated in 1262 by Bishop Bronescombe to the Cornish saint, St Austoll (in Latin, Sancta Austolus). The church is nowadays dedicated to the Holy Trinity.

St Ives
Three townships in England are known by the name St Ives: in Cornwall, Cambridgeshire and Dorset. St Ives in Cornwall derived its name from St Ya (sometimes St La), a female saint, the daughter to an Irish chieftain who according to tradition, floated over the sea on a leaf and landed in Cornwall. It was there she founded an oratory in the mid-fifth century, which is now the local church that is dedicated to her. By 1284, it had been recorded as Sancta Ya. In Cornish the name was Porth la or Porthia, meaning 'St La's Cove'.

Salcombe
The placename means 'salt valley', from the Old English 'sealt', meaning 'salt', and the Cornish word 'cumb', meaning 'valley'.

Salisbury
The first evidence of human occupation of this Wiltshire township appeared some 2,500 years ago, when an Iron Age fort was constructed on what is now Salisbury Hill. It was there in 552, that Saxon invaders defeated native Celts, drove them westwards and occupied the area. The Celts had known it as Sorviodunum, a hangover from its former Roman name, where the Celtic 'duno' referred to a fort. The Saxons called it Searobyrg, based on two Old English words, 'Saero' or 'Sorvio', after the settlement's founder, and 'burh' or 'byrig', signifying a fortress or stronghold. Hence, 'stronghold of Sorvio'. The original site of the settlement was at Old Sarum, probably at the aforementioned Iron Age fort. The name Sarum is thought to have been a spelling error made by a medieval scrivener who made a bad copy from official documents. True or not, the misspelling stuck and the name was widely adopted.

Saltash
The township of Saltash was founded by Robert, Count of Mortain, Earl of Cornwall, half-brother to William the Conqueror and styled locally as Lord Trematon. The place was known by the beginning of the thirteenth century as Esse, from the Old English 'oesc', an ash tree. At that time the name meant '[the place at] the ash tree'. It was also known as Villa de Esse or Asheborough. When salt deposits were discovered in the area, 'salt' was affixed to the placename, so that by 1302 it was called Salteashe.

Sapperton

'Sapere' was the Old English word for a soap-maker and 'tun' represented a farmstead. Therefore the placename Sapperton simply means 'farmstead where soap-makers live (or work)'. In around 1075 the place was recorded as Sapertun, but in 1086 the Domesday commissioners misspelt the name as Sapletorne, listing it within the Gloucestershire Hundred of Tibblestone held by the Bishop of Worcester, as it had been before the Conquest. There are also places called Sapperton in the counties of Derbyshire and Lincolnshire.

Sennen

Sennen was named after St Senana, the patron saint of the local church; it was first dedicated in 1441 and recorded in its Latin form, as Sancta Senana, though the building is on a site that has been in use since the sixth century. St Senana was an Irish missionary, known to have established many churches along the Cornish coast, and thought to have founded the early Celtic church sometime between 410 and 1066 at Sennen, just one mile from Land's End.

Shaftesbury

The name of this Dorset township may be based on the old Saxon word 'sceaft' or 'sceapt', which referred to a sharp point or shaft, with the affix 'burh', signifying a fortified place or stronghold. Alternatively, it may have referred to a man called Sceaft. Therefore, two interpretations exist: either 'a stronghold of a man called Sceaft' or 'a stronghold on a shaft-shaped hill'. The Celts had called the hill on which the settlement was established 'Caer Palladur', because of its commanding position. The name translates as 'hillfort of spears', suggesting the latter interpretation as being the most likely. Local people refer to the town as 'Shaston'. It was recorded as Sceaftesburi in 877 and by the time of Domesday it was being written as Sceftesberie and Sceptesberie, where it was recorded that during the reign of Edward the Confessor, '...there were one hundred and four houses in the king's demesne... now there are sixty-six houses and thirty-eight houses have been destroyed from the time of Hugh the Sheriff until now'. The Hugh in question may have been Hugh of Warham or Hugh FitzBaldric – opinions differ.

Sharpness

Sharpness is located at the docks at Gloucester on the River Severn estuary, and was known at the time of Domesday simply as 'nesse', an Old English word meaning 'headland' or 'promontory'. The survey listed it in the Berkeley Hundred, held by King William. Some time after 1086, the land apparently came into the possession of a man called Scobba, so that by the mid-fourteenth century, it had been recorded as Schobbenasse.

Shaugh Prior

This once was a Devonshire village and civil parish in south-west Dartmoor, set in woodland or in a copse, a fact reflected in its Old English origin where the word 'sceaga' was one of several the Saxon used to describe woodland. Domesday listed the village as Scage, in the land of Iudichael (sometimes Judichael) of Totnes. The account recorded that 'Turgis holds Scage from Iudichael, [and that] Aelfric held it at the time of King Edward'. Later it came into the possession of the Augustinian monks of Plympton Priory, and this is reflected in the 'Prior' element of the present placename.

Shebbear

Shebbear is a village in Devon, that was known to the Saxons as Sceftbeara, which combines two Old English words, 'sceaft', which means 'shaft' or 'pole', and 'bearu', a grove or small wood. Together, the placename means '[place near the] grove where poles are gathered'. Domesday recorded the place as Sepesberie, a very large estate for its time, in the Merton Hundred, and held in the personal possession of King William.

Shepton Mallet

The original name of the township of Shepton, which stands on the Roman Fosse Way in Somerset, is derived from the Old English words 'sceap' and 'tun', respectively meaning 'sheep' and 'settlement' or 'township'. Hence, very loosely, 'sheep town'. As a Saxon settlement, Sceapton, in Whitstone Hundred, had a stone church by 1000, and before the Norman Conquest it was held by a man called Ulluert. It was recorded as Sepetone in the *Domesday Book*, which listed six and a half hides of land in the manor, held by Roger de Curcella (or de Courselles). The affix 'Malet' was added in the twelfth century, with reference to the Malet family who had been made Lords of the Manor by Henry I and by 1228, it had become known as Scheopton Malet.

Sherborne

This placename is common throughout England with examples in Gloucestershire and Hampshire, with several variations of the spelling, including Sherburn and Sherbourne.

The Dorset township of Sherborne on the River Yeo in Blackmore Vale derives its name from the Old English 'scir', meaning 'bright' or 'clear', and 'burna', referring to a brook or a stream. Hence, 'bright stream' or 'clear brook'.

Shrewton

The name of the Wiltshire village of Shrewton has nothing whatever to do with shrews, or small rodents of any description for that matter. It comes from the Old English expression 'scir-refa', which literally means 'shire reeve', the origin of the word 'sheriff'. Added to this is the word 'tun', which signified a farmstead or a manor. The placename may therefore be taken to mean 'sheriff's manor'. At the time of the Great Survey, the place was known by its earlier name of Winterbourne, after the stream that ran through the village (now called the Till). The survey listed Shrewton within the Dolesfield Hundred, held in 1086 by Edward of Salisbury. Before 1066, it had been jointly managed by Saxons named Alric, Alward and Wulfeva Beteslau. By 1232, the place had been renamed as Winterbourne Syreveton and in 1255 the Winterbourne part of the name had been dropped and it was recorded as Schyrreveton.

Sidmouth

The Devonshire township of Sidmouth lies in the old parish and district of Honiton, at the mouth of the River Sid, from which it derives its placename. The river name come from the Old English 'sid', meaning wide or broad, plus the Saxon 'mutha', meaning 'mouth', referring to the estuary. Hence, '[place at the] mouth of the broad river'. The name is briefly recorded in the *Domesday Book*, with 'one salt pan rendering thirty pence in Sedemuda to Mont-Saint-Michel land'.

Somerset

The name of the County of Somerset came about when the name of the township of Somerton was shortened and the Old English word 'saete', meaning 'settlers' was added, producing a placename which means 'district of the settlers of Somerton'. The town gets its name from 'sumor', the old word for summertime, and 'tun', a farmstead. Hence, 'farmstead [only] used in summer'. From earliest times the 'scir' element, signifying a 'district' or a 'shire', was frequently added to produce Somersetshire. In the twelfth century the name had been recorded as Sumersetscir.

Southampton
In the last quarter of the first century, the Romans established a township called Clausentum, near the modern-day city of Southampton, located on the outflow of the River Test and the mouth of the River Itchen in Hampshire. Later, in 690, Saxons built a new town on the opposite bank of the Itchen at what is now the St Mary's area, which they called Homtun, Hamwic or Hamtun. The placename was based on the Old English words 'hamm' and 'tun', which taken together mean 'the settlement or village on a promontory'. By 962, the prefix 'suth', meaning 'southern', had been added to distinguish it from the township of Northampton, and it became known as Suthhamtunam.

Staple Fitzpaine
In Saxon times, a 'stapel' or 'stapol' represented a post or pillar made of wood or stone, often a boundary or way marker. Domesday simply recorded the manor as Staple in 1086, quite a large estate which supported twenty-six households (including six slaves), located in the Abdick Hundred of Somerset and held by Robert, Count of Mortain. Before the Conquest, the manor had been held by two unnamed thegns. The Fitzpaine family took possession of the manor in the fourteenth century and added their family name to the place.

Stibb
This small hamlet near Bude in Cornwall is likely to have derived its placename from the Old English word 'stybb', which signifies a tree stump, though some prefer 'styb', which referred to a wooden weapon. The placename may therefore be interpreted as '[place by a] wooden stump'. By the early fourteenth century it was being written as Stybbe. The significance of the tree stump in question is unknown.

Stoodleigh
This small hamlet in Devon gets its name from Saxon times, when its elements comprised 'stod', an Old English term for a stud, that is a place where horses are bred, or sometimes for a herd of horses, and 'leah', a woodland clearing. Hence, we may take the placename to mean 'woodland clearing where a herd of horses is kept'. In 1086, the place was entered in the Great Survey as Stodlei, in the Witheridge Hundred, part-held by Ralph de Pomeroy and Bishop Geoffrey of Coutances. Its tenants included Drogo FitzMauger and a man called Robert.

Stow-on-the-Wold
In ancient times this Gloucestershire township was known as Stow St Edward (or Edwardstow), where 'stow' is an Old English word for a holy place, or commonly, a church. Hence, it translated as 'St Edward's holy place'. The saint in question is thought to have been St Edward the Martyr. By the time of Domesday, it had been listed, almost in passing, as in Salmonsbury Hundred which lay within the Manor of Maugersbury and belonged to Evesham Abbey. It recorded 'The Church of St Mary of Evesham holds Maugersbury near Eduuardes stou'. The 'Wold' part of the final placename comes from 'wald', a Saxon word signifying high ground that had been cleared of forest. Hence, 'holy place on the high ground'.

Stratfield Saye
Any English town or village with a 'strat' or 'straet' element to its placename is likely to have been originally a Roman road (which is related to the modern English word 'street'), and Stratfield Saye is no exception. The addition of the Old English word 'feld' or 'felda', which means 'open land', produces a meaning of 'open land by a Roman road'. In times

before land enclosures or fences were commonplace, the term 'open land' generally signified arable land or areas which had been cleared for farming. Immediately before the Conquest, the manor was known as Stratfeld, and in 1086 Domesday recorded it as Stradfelle, in the Holdshott Hundred of Hampshire, held at that time by Hugh FitzBaldric, Aelfric (identified as 'Small') and Gilbert de Bretteville. Then, in the thirteenth century, the de Say family took possession and in 1277, their manorial affix was added to the placename which was recorded as Stratfeld Say.

Stratton

In the late ninth century, Stratton was known as Straetneat, and may have derived from the Cornish word 'stras', meaning flat valley, and Neet, the river name. Hence 'valley of the River Neet'. Alternatively, the word 'straetneat', could mean 'road or way across a river'. By 1086, the Old English affix 'tun' had been added, signifying '[settlement in the] valley of the River Neet'. The township is one of the most northerly in Cornwall, and was actually mentioned in the will of King Alfred in 880. Its entry in Domesday recorded 'Stratone [in] the Land of the Count of Mortain', and continued, 'Bishop Osbern and Alvred the Marshal held it [at the time of King Edward] and it paid geld for one hide'.

Stroud

The Gloucestershire settlement of Stroud (or earlier, Strood), first appeared in documents as La Strode in 1221. The name referred to marshy land where the River Frome and Slad Brook met, at a place that was known as Stroudwater. This became an alternative name for the settlement at Frome and eventually for the whole of the Stroud Valley. Stroud is an evolution of the Old English 'strod', meaning overgrown or marshy land.

Swanage

The Dorset township of Swanage on the Isle of Purbeck derives its placename from two Anglo-Saxon words, 'swan' (meaning as it sounds – a swan), and 'wic', signifying a specialised farm. Hence the ninth century placename Swanawic, translates as 'farm where swans are bred, or reared'. By the time of Domesday, the name had hardly changed and was recorded as Swanwic or Sonwic, in land belonging to the wife of Hugh FitzGrip, held by Walter (sometimes called 'the Thunderer'), having been held in parage by Aethelweard before the Conquest.

Sydenham Damerel

The first part of this Devonshire village placename derives from two Anglo-Saxon words, 'sid', meaning 'broad' and 'hamm', an enclosure. Hence, 'broad enclosure'. Domesday simply recorded the place as Sidelham, in the Lifton Hundred, held in 1086 by Iudichael of Totnes (sometimes Judichael), it having been held by four unnamed Saxon thegns before the Conquest. Then in the thirteenth century, the de Albemarle family took possession of the manor and its estates, adding their family name to the place, at which time it became known as Sydenham Albemarlie, which over time transformed to Sydenham Damerel.

Taunton

Taunton is a township located on and named after the River Tone in Somerset and was already known by the early eighth century as Tuntun. The river name is of Celtic origin and translates loosely as 'sparkling stream' or 'fast-flowing river'. The Saxon word 'tun' signified a farmstead settlement, and taken together the complete placename means 'farmstead or village located on the River Tone'.

Tavistock
Known in 981 as Tauistoc, the placename comes from the Devonshire River Tavy, on which the original settlement was located; in Old English 'stoc' was another name for a farmstead. The river name is of Celtic origin; they knew it as Tau Vechan and it meant either 'dark' or possibly simply 'stream'. By 1086, the *Domesday Book* had listed the place as Tavestoc, in the land of the Church of Tavistock, held from the abbot by several tenants, including Ermenald, Ralph, Robert, Geoffrey and Hugh, as well as four unnamed Saxon thegns.

Tewkesbury
The Gloucestershire town of Tewkesbury, located at the confluence of the River Avon and the River Severn, appeared in the Great Survey as Teodekesberie and Tedekesberie after its probable founder, a Saxon called Teodec (or Theoc). The Saxons called it Theocsbury. The name is comprised of his personal name with the added Old English suffix 'burh' or 'byrig', signifying a fortified settlement or stronghold. Hence, 'stronghold of Teodec'.

Threemilestone
A Cornish village in the civil parish of Kenwyn, whose placename indicates exactly where it's to be found: three miles west from Truro. The village seems to have come into being some time in the nineteenth century and by 1884 had been formally named as Three Mile Stone.

Tintagel
In his *Historia Regum Britanniae* (History of the Kings of Britain), probably completed around 1138, Welsh cleric Geoffrey of Monmouth cited Tintagel as the place where the legendary King Arthur was conceived. The placename may have come from two old Cornish words, 'din' meaning fort or stronghold, and 'tagell', a promontory or neck of land. Hence, 'fort on a neck of land or promontory'. Alternatively, there is an opinion that its alternative name of Trevena (in Cornish: Tre war Venydh), would indicate that the name means 'settlement, or village on a mountain'. Another source has proposed 'dun (or din) tagell' as meaning in the Celtic language, 'a narrow place'. Given its location, either would seem appropriate. The site had almost certainly existed earlier as a stronghold of Devonian and Cornish rulers of the Dumnonia tribe of Celtic peoples. Tintagel received no mention in the *Domesday Book* in its own right, but was part of the Manor of Bossiney, which was recorded in the survey as the Manor of Botcinni, held by the Count of Mortain from St Petroc's Church in Bodmin.

Tintinhull
This Somerset village placename has distinct Celtic overtones in that the first element of the name, 'din', meant 'fort'. It is not at all clear why the 'tin' element has been repeated as it appears to have no real significance. However, the final element comes from the Anglo-Saxon word 'hyll', meaning 'hill'. It was already known as Tintanhulle by the tenth century. Hence, the placename can be interpreted as 'fort by [or on] a hill'. Domesday recorded the name as Tintenella in the Tintinhull Hundred, held by Count Robert de Mortain.

Tiverton
The Devonshire township of Tiverton stands on the River Exe and the River Lowman, and was known to the Saxons in the ninth century as Twyfyrde, Twyverton or Twyfordton. The placename derives from the Old English 'twi' and 'fyrde', respectively meaning 'two' and 'ford'. Hence '[the place at the] two fords', referring to crossings on the two rivers. Later the suffix 'tun' was added, to indicate a settlement or farmstead had been established there. The Normans recorded it as Tovretona in the Great Survey of 1086, part in the land of Ralph de Limsey, held by Garard and worth thirty shillings.

Tollard Royal

This Wiltshire village traces its name back to ancient Celtic, and is related to the modern Welsh words 'twill', meaning 'hole' or 'hollow', and 'ardd', signifying a hill. Hence, '[place by a] hollow hill'. Domesday recorded the place as Tollard in 1086, listed within the Stowford Hundred, held at that time by William d'Eu, having belonged to Tholf the Dane in 1066. Some time around 1200 the lands were acquired by King John and the 'Royal' affix was appended to the village name, distinguishing it from the nearby village of Tollard Farnham. In 1535 the placename was recorded as Tollard Ryall.

Tolpuddle

As with other villages and hamlets located on the River Piddle in Dorset, Tolpuddle adopted the more polite version of '-puddle' as the last element of its placename. The first element relates to a Scandinavian woman called Tola, who is recorded as having given the estate to the Abbey of Abbotsbury some time before the Conquest. The placename means 'Tola's [estate on the] River Piddle'. The *Domesday Book* recorded the estate simply as Pidele, and listed it in the Puddletown Hundred held by the Abbot of Abbotsbury.

Torquay

Torquay was known in Saxon times simply as Torre in the Kingdom of Wessex. In the south-west region, 'tors' were the name which Celtic peoples gave to rocky hills or outcrops. Later, the name might have been referred to as Torre Key. The Middle English affix 'key' was an early spelling of the word 'quay' (as in a landing stage or jetty), which came into use after fishing was developed by monks in the township. Hence, the placename means 'quay by a rocky outcrop'.

Totnes

Located on a promontory overlooking the River Dart in Devon, this ancient market town was known to the Anglo-Saxons as Totanaes, after its probable founder, a man called Totta, plus the Old English affix 'naess' or 'ness', which refers to a headland or a promontory. Hence, 'promontory belonging to Totta'. By 1086, it had been recorded as Toteneis and Totheneis, in the land of Iudichael of Totnes, a borough which Edward the Confessor held in demesne before the Conquest.

Treen

Treen is a small village in the Parish of St Levan, in the west of Cornwall, about three miles inland from Land's End. It should not be confused with the hamlet of Treen in Zennor Parish on the north coast of the county. In Cornish the name is Tredhin; one of its earliest records was in 1304 when it was written as Tredyn, and was spelt as Trethyn a few years later. Its name is from two Old Cornish words, 'farmstead' and 'fort'. Hence, 'fortified farmstead', reflecting its location near the cliff castle at the Logan Rock.

Tregadillett

Tregadillett (or Tregadylet in Cornish), is a small village which way back in the mists of antiquity either belonged to, or was founded by a man called Cadyled, with the Old Cornish affix 'tre', indicating a village or settlement. Hence, 'Cadyled's village'.

Trowbridge

This Wiltshire township's placename dates from Saxon times when it was called Treowbrycg, meaning 'tree-bridge' or 'tree-trunk bridge', referring to the first bridge built over the River Bliss. In 1086, Domesday recorded the place as Straburg, in the Melksham Hundred, in 'the Land of Oda and Other King's Thegns'.

Truro

There are at least four schools of thought concerning the origin of Truro's placename: one has it derived from the Cornish 'tri veru', where 'tri' means 'three' and 'veru' means 'roads'. Hence 'three roads'. Conversely, some have it as meaning 'three rivers', while another suggests 'tre uro', signifying '[the] settlement by the river', where the 'uro' element means 'river'. Truro does indeed have three major roads leading into its centre, and three rivers can be seen from certain places around the city. A fourth explanation cites Triueru, the name given to the town around 1174, as meaning '[place of] great water turbulence'. Whatever the actual meaning, it is lost in prehistory and thereby open to conjecture. What is known is that the earliest recorded use of the present placename appeared during Norman times.

Veryan

A small hamlet in Cornwall, known in 1281 by its Latin name, Sanctus Symphorianus, after the church was dedicated to St Symphorian, a second or third century French martyr. Over time Symphorian became corrupted to Severian and then Saint Veryan. Veryan was recorded in the *Domesday Book* as the Manor of Elerchi (or Elerky), owned by the Bishop of Exeter in 1086. The manor name was derived from 'elerch', the Cornish word for a swan, a swannery or a swan's house.

Wadebridge

The township of Wadebridge received no separate entry in the *Domesday Book*, but was included in the Manor of Pawton at that time. It was known in the mid-fourteenth century simply as Wade in the Parishes of Egloshayle and St Breock, each on either side of the river. In 1313, a market and two annual fairs were granted to the town. The placename comes from Old English and signifies a shallow ford. Before 1478, the shallow crossing on the River Camel could be waded across, which may be the origin of the 'Wade' element of the placename. Later the affix 'brycg' was added to reflect the three hundred and twenty foot long, seventeen arch toll bridge built in 1468 by the local vicar, Thomas Lovibond.

Warminster

Around 912, the Saxons knew the settlement as Worgemynster, based on the River Were in Wiltshire, itself an Old English river name meaning 'winding', and 'mynster', signifying a church. The placename translates quite simply as '[the] church on the River Were', the building in question being the Minster Church of St Denys. By the time of the *Domesday Book*, it had been recorded as Guerminstre, in land belonging to the Crown, and thereby had not been assessed for taxation purposes.

Wells

The placename means what it says; a place where water was found in 'wells' or 'springs'. It derives from the Old English 'wella' or 'wiells'. Before 1066, it was often written as Willan and by 1086, this Somerset township, which nestles among the Mendip Hills, had been recorded as Welle. The settlement actually had three wells which were claimed to have beneficial and curative powers. Two lie within the grounds of Wells Cathedral and were dedicated to St Andrew; the third is located in the town's market place.

Westbury

Sometimes known as Westbury-under-the-Plain, this Wiltshire market town lay within the largely agricultural Westbury Hundred, when it was recorded in the *Domesday Book* as Westberie. The placename simply means the 'westerly stronghold', where the element 'burh', 'buri' or 'burg', signified a fortified settlement, probably as part of Alfred the Great's reinforcement of the boundary of his Kingdom of Wessex, to offset the frequent Danish incursions of the ninth and tenth centuries. The ancient Parish of Westbury also included the civil parishes of Bratton, Dilton Marsh, Heywood and part of Chapmanslade.

Weston-super-Mare

There are around a dozen places in Britain by the name of Weston; the name means 'western township or settlement'. The place in North Somerset was simply known as Weston in the early thirteenth century and the *Super Mare* affix (Latin for 'on the sea'), only added in 1349 to distinguish it from other towns of that name. It was located in the Axbridge district and for most of its history it remained a small fishing village. In 1568, zinc ore was discovered, which turned the place into an important local industrial centre, and in the late nineteenth century it grew into a popular seaside resort.

Westward Ho!

This North Devonshire seaside village overlooking Bideford Bay is a relatively modern invention, having taken its name from the best-selling novel *Westward Ho!* published in 1855 by the author Charles Kingsley, who came to live in nearby Bideford. It is a rare placename, in that it intentionally terminates with an exclamation mark, the only place in the British Isles that does so.

Weymouth

This Dorset township was known in the early tenth century as Walmouthe or Walmutha, meaning the 'mouth of the River Wey'. The settlement developed as a port during Roman times for the access it offered via the river as far as Radipole, and thereafter on foot to the town of Durnovaria (Dorchester). In the twelfth century, what would become the town of Weymouth comprised two separate settlements: Weymouth on one side of the river and Melcombe Regis on the other. Both belonged to St Swithin's Convent in Winchester. They were not united until Elizabeth I granted a royal charter in 1571, as a result of which they became the Borough of Weymouth by Act of Parliament, and also included the former parishes of Preston, Radipole, Broadwey, Wyke Regis and Upwey.

Whimple

The Devonshire village of Whimple gets its name directly from the River Whimple, an ancient stream that ran through the settlement. The name comes from the old Celtic Cornish word meaning 'white pool', which is closely related to the modern Welsh 'gwyn', meaning 'white' and 'pwll', a pool or a stream. Domesday recorded Wimple, in the Cliston Hundred, held by Ralph de Pomeroy and tenanted by a man referred to as 'William the Goat'.

Wilton

The original settlement which would become Wilton was established by the Wilsaetes, a Celtic tribe, at a place where the Wylye and Nadder rivers meet in Wiltshire. One of Wilton's earliest known references in written records dates from about 838 when it was known as Uuiltune, from the Old English river name 'Wylye' plus the 'tun' affix, which translates as 'village or farmstead on the River Wylye'.

Wincanton

This Somerset village was known in Anglo-Saxon times as Wincawel. By the time of Domesday, it had been recorded as Wincaletone, based on three Old English elements: 'winn', meaning 'white', 'cale', after the River Cale on which it stood, and 'tun', a village settlement. Hence, the placename may be taken to mean '[the] village settlement on the white river'.

Winchester

The Hampshire township of Winchester, or Witancaester as the Saxons knew it, was the capital city of Alfred the Great's Kingdom of Wessex. It had been home to the Celtic Belgae tribe who knew the place as Caer Gwent, possibly meaning 'chief (or important) place'. Before that, Ptolomy had called the place Ouenta. When the Romans arrived in Britain and settled at a suitable crossing point on the River Itchen, they named their new settlement in Latin, Venta Belgarium, which translates as 'market place of the Belgae'. The Saxons referred to all fortified Roman settlements as a 'ceaster', and called the place Ouenta Ceaster, which by around 730 had emerged as Uintancastir, and by the ninth century it had become Wintonia, which later emerged as Winchester.

Winterbourne Abbas

There are at least a dozen places called Winterbourne or Winterborne in England. The name comes from 'winter' (which is self-explanatory), and the Old English element 'burna', a stream or brook, (or as is common in Scotland, a 'burn'). Hence, 'winter stream', possibly specifically referring to a local stream that was swollen and fast-flowing or flooded in winter. The place appeared in Domesday as Wintreburne, in the land of the Church of St Peter of Cerne, who earned revenue by renting out its ten hides of land. It was valued at sixteen pounds at that time. This Dorset township was finally known as Wynterburn Abbatis when the second part of the placename was attached sometime around 1244, in recognition of its ownership by the Abbot of Cerne.

Withiel Florey

The Withiel component of this Somerset hamlet is related to the Old English word 'withig', which signified the willow tree, similar to the modern (but now somewhat arcane) English word 'withy'. By the early eighth century, the place was already known as Withiglea. Then, in the thirteenth century, the manor came into the possession of the de Flury family, and their family name was appended to the placename. In 1305, the hamlet was recorded as Wythele Flory.

Wiveliscombe

Wiveliscombe is a Somerset township which was known in the middle of the ninth century as Wifelescumb. Opinions differ as to the explanation of the placename's first element. Wivel, or Wifel, may have been the founder or an early settler. Some argue that it represents the weevil and may have been a reference to a local valley where weevil beetles were common. The Old English affix 'cumb' signified a valley. Hence, the placename could mean either 'Wifel's valley' or 'valley of weevils'. The placename was recorded as Wivelscome, in the Kingsbury West Hundred, held in 1086 by the Bishop of St Andrew's Church in Wells, who had also held the estate before the Conquest.

Wookey

In the years immediately preceding the Norman Conquest this Somerset village was known as Wokey, a name derived from the Anglo-Saxon word 'wocig', which referred to a trap or snare for animals. Hence, '[place at the] animal traps'. It was probably a reference to Wookey Hole, recorded separately as Wokyhole in 1065 and where the trap in question may have been located. The Old English word 'hol' signified a hollow or a ravine.

Woolfardisworthy

This odd-sounding Devon village's placename is one of two places bearing the name, and although it sounds like a complex title, the meaning is fairly simple. At one time in its early history it was in the possession of a man called Wulfheard, possibly its founder. The second element of the placename, 'worthig', is an Anglo-Saxon word meaning 'enclosure', either for animals or arable land. Hence, the name means 'Wulfheard's enclosure'. Domesday listed it as Ulfaldeshodes in the Witheridge Hundred, held in 1086 by William de Poilley. In 1264, the placename was recorded as Wolfardesworthi, and by the early nineteenth century it was being rather formally written as 'Woolfardisworthy otherwise Woolsworthy'.

Wootton Bassett

Wooton is a common placename, with at least ten other places of that name in Britain. It derives from the Old English words 'wudu', meaning 'wood' or 'forest', and 'tun', signifying a village, farmstead or settlement. Hence 'village or farmstead in (or near) a wood'. The earliest known record of this North Wiltshire settlement was as Wdetun in 680, when the Saxon King Ethelred granted a charter to the Abbot of Malmesbury Abbey for ten hides of land. By the time of Domesday had become known as Wodetone. By the late thirteenth century, the Manor of Old Wootton belonged to Baron Alan Bassett, one of the twenty-seven counsellors named in the preamble to Magna Carta, whose family name was appended to the placename, and thereafter the township became known as Wootton Bassett. In October 2011, the township achieved Royal status and since that time has been officially known as Royal Wooton Bassett.

Yeovil

The South Somerset township of Yeovil is located on the River Yeo, which had been known as the Gifle in the ninth century, derived from an old Celtic river name, meaning 'forked river'. Until that time, the settlement had taken the river as its placename. It was only in Saxon times, some time around 880, that it became the River Yeo, from the Old English 'oe', simply meaning 'river'. The 'vill' element of the placename reflects the Norman French influence and means 'village'. Yeovil may therefore be taken to mean '[the] village on the River Yeo'. Even the *Domesday Book* reverted to the old name and recorded the place as Givele (or Ivle) in Stone Hundred land, part-owned by the Count of Mortain, where he held a small estate of just one hide of land, sufficient for two ploughs, and worth three shillings.

Zeals

The Wiltshire village of Zeals derived its placename from the surrounding ancient forest where willow trees abounded, which is reflected in the name. It comes from the Old English word 'sealh', meaning 'sallow', an ancient word for the willow tree. The placename therefore may be interpreted as '[place by the] willow trees'. Domesday recorded it twice, as Sele and Sela, in the Mere Hundred, part-held in 1086 by Alfgeat and by Jocelyn de Rivers. The manorial estates comprised land for three ploughs and one lord's plough team. There were around seven acres of meadow, more than forty acres of pasture land, and around one league of woodland. Its one mill supported thirteen villans, nine bordars, seven slaves and 'three other population' (which probably included craftsmen like blacksmiths or carpenters). The entire estate was valued at one pound and five shillings.

Zennor

Located on Cornwall's Atlantic coast three miles south-west of St Ives in the Parish of Penzance, the village of Zennor was named after its patron saint, St Senara, and recorded around 1170 in Latin as Sanctus Sinar. The saint is thought to have been the Breton Princess Azenor of Brest, the mother of St Budock, Bishop of Dol in Brittany. The present twelfth century Norman church is dedicated to her and stands on the site of an earlier sixth century Celtic church.

Part Fourteen

The British Islands

Including the Channel Islands, the Isle of Man,
the Isle of Wight, and the Isles of Scilly

Alderney

The earliest known name of this Channel Island was Riduna, which some believe was a Celtic name meaning 'before the hill', a name which was also adopted by the Romans who built a port there. The development of the placename during historic times was largely influenced by Danish occupation, when it was recorded as initially as Aurene, a word taken from the Old Scandinavian 'aurr', meaning 'gravel' or 'mud flats'. By the thirteenth century the word 'ey', meaning 'island' had been attached and it became 'island with gravel or mud flats'. In 1238, the place was recorded as Aureneie.

Alum Bay

This bay on the Isle of Wight is so named because of the large quantities of alum extracted from its rocks in the sixteenth century. The placename was first coined in 1720.

Bembridge

This place in the Isle of Wight was recorded in the early fourteenth century as Bynnbrygg, from the Old English words 'binnan', meaning 'beside' or 'this side of', and 'brygg', a bridge. Hence, 'the place beside [or this side of] the bridge'.

Binstead

By the time of the Great Survey of 1086, the village of Binstead had been recorded as Benestede in the Bowcombe Hundred, then listed in the County of Hampshire (now recognised as a county in its own right), and in the 'Land of the King in the Isle of Wight'. The name stems from Old English, where 'bin' or 'bean', and 'stede', a place. Hence, 'place where beans are grown'.

Bonchurch

Bonchurch is a small village on the Isle of Wight whose placename comes from the dedication of the local church to St Boniface, whose name is often shortened to Bona. It was recorded in the *Domesday Book* as Bonecerce, in the land held on the king's behalf by William FitzAzor. Before the Conquest, it had been held by Aestan for Earl Godwine.

Brading

The placename of the village of Brading on the Isle of Wight was known as Brerdinges as early as the seventh century. The name derives from the Old English words 'brerd', meaning 'hillside', and 'ingas', meaning the 'people, followers or family'. Hence, the name translates as 'people [who dwell on] a hillside'. The description eminently fits the location, situated as the village is at the foot of Brading Down. In 1086, the village was recorded as Berardinz, in land held by William FitzAzor and tenanted by his nephew.

Branstone

Branstone is a small hamlet on the Isle of Wight which was named after a Scandinavian man called Brandr plus the Old English suffix, 'tun', signifying a farmstead or a village settlement. Hence, 'Brandr's farmstead or village'. Domesday listed it as Brandestone in the Bowcombe Hundred, then lying within the County of Hampshire and held by William FitzAzur and his nephew. Before the Norman conquest the manorial estate had belonged to two unnamed free men.

Bryher

The island of Bryher, in the Isles of Scilly, gets its name from the Cornish 'bre', meaning 'hill', and 'yer' which makes it a plural (ie. 'hills'). Hence, '[place of the] hills', marking it as one of the hilliest parts of the archipelago. It was recorded in 1319 as Braer.

Carisbrooke

The Celts named the small stream which flowed through this Isle of Wight village as 'Cary', to which the Saxons added the word 'broc', signifying a brook or a stream. Hence, 'a brook called Cary' or 'Cary brook'. It has been suggested that the stream in question was the modern day Lukely Brook. In the twelfth century, the place was recorded as Caresbroc.

Chale

Chale gets its placename from the Old English word 'ceole', meaning 'throat'. In this sense it referred to a gorge or a ravine, such as the nearby Blackgang Chine. The place was recorded in 1086 as Cela, in the Bowcombe Hundred of the Isle of Wight, listed at that time in the County of Hampshire, held at that time by William FitzAzor. Its tenant-in-chief was a man called Wulfsi.

Channel Island Saints' Names

St Aubin

St Aubin is a port and old fishing village in the Channel Island of Jersey, located within the Parish of St Brelade. Its name refers to St Aubin, the sixth century Bishop of Angers in Western France, and the long-lost chapel that was dedicated to him.

St Brelade

The seaside resort of St Brelade on Jersey is named after a sixth century Celtic or Welsh saint named Branwalator or St Brelade (Broladre or Brelodre), who is thought to have been the son of the Cornish King Kenen. He was also known as the 'wandering saint'.

St Helier

St Helier is the capital of Jersey and is named after St Helier, a Frankish missionary who was reputedly martyred there in 555. He is celebrated in the Hermitage, a small twelfth century oratory on L'Islet, as well as in the Abbey of St Helier, which was founded in the mid-twelfth century by Robert FitzHamon, Seigneur de Creully and feudal Baron of Gloucester.

St Peter Port

St Peter Port is the capital and the main port of the Balliwick of Guernsey. In the Guernsey dialect and in French, the official name of the town is Saint-Pierre Port. The town grew around the church of St Peter some time in the eleventh century when it was known by its Latin name Ecclesia Sancti Petri de Portu, the port of St Peter.

Chillerton
Chillerton is a village on the Isle of Wight which was possibly named after an early settler called Ceolheard with the affix 'tun' indicating a farmstead. Hence, 'Ceolheard's farmstead'. Another explanation has been suggested in that the placename might have derived from three Old English words: 'coele', 'geard' and 'tun', which taken together mean 'enclosed farmstead in a valley'. Domesday recorded the small manor as Celertune, in the Bowcombe Hundred, held by William FitzAzur, having belonged to a Saxon called Blaecmann before the Norman Conquest.

Clatterford
In the way that pebbles on a beach clatter as you walk across or kick them make that distinctive clattering sound, so this small hamlet in the Isle of Wight has a placename that most aptly comes from the Old English word 'clater', meaning 'loose stones'. Additionally, the word 'ford', which referred to the shallow crossing at this point on Lookley Brook, produces a placename that means '[place by the] ford with loose stones'. It was known as Claterford by the mid-twelfth century.

Cowes
A coastal resort town and important anchorage on the Isle of Wight, Cowes derives its placename from the plural form of the Old English word 'cu', signifying cows, and the two sandbanks on the estuary of the River Medina that flows through the town into the Solent. They were recorded as the separate settlements of Estcowe and Westcowe in the early fifteenth century, and known traditionally as 'The Cows', due to what some think to be a resemblance to cattle. Later, they were consolidated to form the present-day town of Cowes.

Douglas
Douglas, or in the Manx language, Doolish, is the capital of the Isle of Man, having replaced Castletown as the island's seat of government. It is located on the south-east coast, at the confluence of the Dhoo and Glas rivers to form the River Douglas, which accounts for its placename. It is the outflow of the River Douglas that forms the town's harbour. The settlement was first recorded in 1192 by the monks of St Mary's Abbey. It appeared again, as Dufglas in 1257, the name having derived from the old Gaelic words 'dub' and 'glais', or the Celtic 'duboglassio', which roughly translate as 'black stream' or 'dark water'.

Gatcombe
The first placename element of this village in the Isle of Wight, is the Old English word 'gat', meaning 'goat', and the second, 'cumb', which stands for a valley. The placename was recorded in 1086 as Gatecome, and means 'valley where goats are kept'.

Godshill
The village of Godshill in the Isle of Wight has a placename that virtually speaks for itself, simply meaning 'hill associated with a god' (or 'god's hill'), from the Old English 'god' and 'hyll'. The place was known as Godeshella in the twelfth century. It seems probable that the village stands on an earlier pagan religious site that may have become a place of Christian worship later.

Grouville
Several hypotheses have been offered as to the meaning of the placename of the village of Grouville in the Channel Island of Jersey. It may be derived from a small settlement that grew up in what is now the parish by St Gerou (also known as Gervold or Geraldius), who was an

ecclesiastical scholar employed by Charlemagne in the ninth century. Others maintain that it is a corruption of the French 'gros villa' (which loosely translates as 'great farm'), while some cite Geirr, a Viking leader after whom the island and the township may have been named. The ecclesiastical parish and the local church are dedicated to St Martin de Grouville.

Guernsey
The earliest known name of the Channel Island of Guernsey was Lisia, thought to be a Celtic word and possibly referring to a man called Liscos. By the eleventh century, following successive Viking invasions and settlements, it was known as Guernesei, a name taken from Old Scandinavian 'Grani', possibly a man's name, and 'ey', signifying an island. It could be interpreted as 'Grani's island'. Alternatively the first element of the placename might come from 'granar', meaning 'pine tree', in which case 'island where pine trees grow'. In 1168, the place was recorded as Ghernesei.

Gurnard
This Isle of Wight village derives its placename from Saxon times, when the word 'gyre' referred to a marshy or muddy place, and 'ora', meaning either 'shore' or possibly 'flat-topped hill' referring to the hill behind the village. It was known as early as 280 as Gornore. Gurnard is also a breed of fish, and there is a remote possibility that the placename may have come from this source and that the fish may have been a popular catch at this coastal settlement since the earliest times.

Havenstreet
Two alternative explanations have been offered for the meaning of the placename of this village on the Isle of Wight. The second element of the name is straightforward, coming as it does from the Old English word 'straet', but the first element is problematic. It comes from 'haethen' and means either 'healthy' or 'heathen'. In which case the placename means 'healthy street' or 'heathen street', the latter either built by or used by heathens or pagans. Most authorities seem to prefer the first interpretation. The place was recorded as Hethenestrete in 1255.

Herm
Two alternatives have been suggested for the meaning of Herm (in the local Guernsey language spelt 'Haerme'); one is that it from the Old Norse word 'arm', due to the arm-shape of the island; another cites the Old French word 'eremite', meaning 'hermit', in view of the fact that during the sixth century, in its early medieval history, the island was occupied by monks. On this basis, Herm might be a shortened version of 'hermits'. It is the smallest of the Channel Islands and part of the Parish of St Peter Port in the Bailiwick of Guernsey.

Hugh Town
The name of this port in the town of St Mary's in the Isles of Scilly was first recorded in the seventeenth century, having been previously known in 1593 as the Hew Hill, the 'hew' element probably a corruption of the Old English word 'hoh', meaning 'spur of land' or 'promontory'. In 1868, the placename was spelt Heugh Town.

Isle of Man
The Crown Dependency of the Isle of Man (or in the Manx language, Ellan Vannin), is often referred to simply as Mann. The word 'ellan' is derived from 'mannin' and simply means 'island'. It was known to the Romans as Mona, and an early form the name was written as 'Manu'. However, local tradition has it that it was Manannan, the Brythonic and Gaelic sea god, who once ruled the island and gave it its name.

Isle of Wight
The Isle of Wight was known as Vectis in the mid-second century, a Celtic word probably meaning 'place of division' (although some translate it as 'course'), which is thought to be a reference to the two arms of the Solent that separate the island from the English mainland. Domesday recorded the island as Wit, then listed in the County of Hampshire, though it is now recognised as a county in its own right.

Isles of Scilly
Known as Sully since the earliest times, the Isles of Scilly, off the south-west coast of Cornwall, have a name pre-dating historical record, and began to be used some time during the first century. Its exact meaning and origin is unknown, but the Danes knew the islands as Syllorgar and the Romans called them Sully, from Sulis, the Roman Sun God, and possibly meaning the 'sun islands'.

Jersey
The largest of the Channel Islands, the Balliwick of Jersey is a Crown Dependency which was named after a Dane called Geirr or Gerr, which along with the Old Scandinavian word 'ey', meaning 'island', produces a place whose name means 'island of a man called Geirr'. In the eleventh century the place was variously spelt as Gersoi and Jersoi. Earlier, in the fourth century, the island had been known as Andium, a name fostered by its Roman occupants, but whose meaning is unknown. Jersey was invaded by Vikings in the ninth century and in 933, along with the other Channel Islands, it was annexed by the Duke of Normandy.

Le Hocq
Le Hocq is an area in the Parish of St Clement, in the south-east of the Channel Island of Jersey. It is a local Jersey dialect name, which is very similar to the modern French, and means 'the headland' or 'the cape'.

Merstone
Merstone is a village on the Isle of Wight whose placename comes from Saxon times, when 'mersc' meant 'marsh' or 'marshy ground', and 'tun' indicated a farmstead or village settlement. Hence, 'farmstead on marshy ground'. Domesday recorded the village as Merestone and Messetone, in the Bowcombe Hundred, land held by William FitzStur, it having belonged to Edward the Confessor before 1066.

Nettlestone
The placename of this Isle of Wight village means either 'farmstead near the nut pasture' or 'farmstead where nuts are found in a clearing'. It derives from 'hnutu', an Old English word meaning 'nut', followed either by 'laes', meaning 'pasture', or 'leah', a woodland clearing'. The Domesday record for the village was transcribed badly and entered as Hoteleston, listed as a very small estate in the Bowcombe Hundred of Hampshire. It supported just three smallholders with land for half a ploughland, held by King William in 1086 and valued at three shillings. Before the Conquest the manor had belonged to a Saxon called Alnoth.

Ningwood
This village on the Isle of Wight was recorded under the name Lenimcode in the Bowcombe Hundred by the *Domesday Book*, held by Gerwy de les Loges in 1086, and by the late twelfth century it had become known as Ningewode. The placename comes from the Old English 'niming' and 'wudu', which taken together mean 'enclosed wood', or 'wood in cultivation'.

Niton
This name of this village on the Isle of Wight comes from the Old English words 'niwe' and 'tun', which respectively mean 'new farmstead'. Domesday recorded the village in 1086 as Neeton, at that time lying within the Bowcombe Hundred of Hampshire, held by King William, as it had been by King Edward before him. The survey accounts for seven villagers, eighteen smallholders and nine slaves, with land for eight ploughs.

Peel
There are just over a thousand people on the Isle of Man who can speak the Manx language and often refer to Peel as 'Purt ny Hinshey', which means 'the harbour [or port] of the island'. The original Viking settlement was called Holmtown, from the Old Norse word 'holm' or 'hulm', meaning 'island' and the Middle English 'toun', a settlement. This name remained in use until the late seventeenth century. In 1392, a pele tower was built opposite the harbour, and the place was known in 1399 as Pelam. The name derived from the Anglo-Norman word 'pel', meaning a palisade or fortified enclosure. Thereafter, it was known as Peeltown. which by the mid-nineteenth century had simply become Peel.

Ramsey
The township of Ramsey is located in the Parish of Kirk Maughold at the mouth of the River Sulby, backed by the North Barrule Hills, on the north-east coast of the Isle of Man, and is the second largest town on the island. The placename stems from the Old English word 'ramsa' (or the Old Norse word 'hramsa'), which was the name for wild garlic and translates as 'the stream where wild garlic grows'. It was known in Manx in the mid-thirteenth century as Ramsa or Rhumsaa.

Rookley
It comes as no surprise that the name of this village on the Isle of Wight refers to rooks, or 'hrocs', as the Saxons knew them. This, together with the Old English element 'leah', which signified a woodland glade or a clearing, produces a placename that means 'woodland clearing where rooks are seen'. In 1202 the place was recorded as Roclee.

Ryde
There is scant written material in existence concerning the early history of the Isle of Wight township of Ryde before the mid-thirteenth century, when it was recorded as La Ride or La Rye, a name derived from the Old English 'rith', meaning 'a small stream'. The stream referred to was the Monktonmead Brook that enters the Solent at this point.

St Martin's
This northernmost of the Isles of Scilly was dedicated to the French saint, St Martin, Bishop of Tours and patron saint of France, who died in either 371 or 397. Initially the name was given to the local church but was eventually applied to the whole island. Around 1540, the placename was recorded in Cornish as Seynt Martyns, and appeared at the same time in English as St Martines Isle.

Samson
Nowadays this island, part of the Isles of Scilly archipelago, is completely uninhabited. Its name emerged as a dedication to a chapel on the island commemorating the sixth century St Samson, Bishop of Dol-de-Bretagne in Brittany. In fact, no chapel exists on the island, nor is there a record of one ever having been there, so apart from a reference in his biography, *Vita Sancti Samsonis* (Life of Saint Samson), written sometime between the seventh and ninth centuries, the attribution is a mystery. In 1160, the island was recorded as Sanctus Sampson.

Sark

The meaning of the name of the small Channel Island of Sark (in French: Sercq), is unknown, and may have come from the Veneti, an ancient Celtic tribe who occupied the island. However, some believe it came from Sargia, a corruption of the Roman settlement which they knew as Cesarea in the fourth century. Following the Roman withdrawal in the fifth century, and given the island's close proximity to the French mainland, it was probably settled by Breton-speaking peoples until 933, when it became part of the Duchy of Normandy.

Shalcombe

The village of Shalcome in the Isle of Wight gets its name from a combination of two Anglo-Saxon words, 'sceald', meaning 'hollow' or 'shallow', and 'cumb', a valley. Hence '[place in a] shallow valley'. In 1086, the place was recorded as Eseldecome, and listed in the Bowcombe Hundred of Hampshire, held at that time by the Church of St Nicholas, Carisbrooke, having preciously belonged to a Saxon called Alwin Frost.

Shalfleet

As in Shalcombe, Shalfleet derives its placename from the Old English words 'sceald', meaning 'shallow', and 'fleot', a creek. Hence, the name of this Isle of Wight village means '[place by a] shallow creek'. The creek in question flows into the stream known as Caul Bourne. The village was entered in the *Domesday Book* as Seldeflet, listed as a very large estate supporting forty households in the Bowcombe Hundred of Hampshire. It was held in 1086 by Jocelyn, the son of Azur, having belonged to Edric before the Conquest. The estate amounted to four acres of meadow, woodland for twenty pigs, a mill and a church, altogether valued at fifteen pounds.

Shanklin

This seaside township located on Sandown Bay on the south coast of the Isle of Wight was recorded in the Great Survey of 1086 as Sencliz and Selins, a name derived from the Old English 'scenc', a bank, and 'hlinc', a cup. Hence, 'bank by the drinking cup'. This referred to the local Chine waterfall which was a primary source of water in medieval times and appeared to come from a cup-shaped ledge. At the time of Domesday, the manor was recorded as Sencliz and belonged to Gosselin FitzAzor and eventually passed to the de Lisle family.

Shide

This district of Newport on the Isle of Wight derives its name from an Anglo-Saxon word, 'scid', meaning 'plank' or 'footbridge'. The placename may be interpreted as '[place by the] footbridge', a reference to an ancient bridge across the River Medina. In 1086, the place was recorded as Sida, in the Bowcombe Hundred of Hampshire,. The manor was jointly held at the time of Domesday by King William, and by Jocelyn and William FitzAzur.

Shorwell

Any English place with a 'well' element contained within its name, has a connection to water – the Saxon word 'wella' most typically referred to a spring, but equally it could have been a well or a fountain. The village of Shorwell on the Isle of Wight is no exception. Additionally, the Old English word 'scora' forms the first part of this placename, and signified a steep slope. Therefore, the placename translates as 'spring by a steep slope'. This eminently describes the village location, lying in a deep valley where the local spring rises and flows to the sea at Brighstone. Domesday recorded the place as Sorewelle, in the Bowcombe Hundred, part-held by King William and by Jocelyn FitzAzur, having belonged to a Saxon called Wulfnoth and three unnamed thegns before the Conquest.

Totland

The name of this village in the Isle of Wight means 'cultivated land [or estate] by a lookout place'. It derives from the Old English words 'tot' meaning 'lookout place', and 'land' which translates as cultivated land or an estate. It is thought that the lookout place may have been on Headon Hill where a warning beacon once stood. The original settlement may have been known as Totland Bay. In 1240, the place was recorded as Toteland and by the beginning of the seventeen century it had emerged as its present name, Totland.

Tresco

The small island of Tresco in the Scilly Isles derives its name from two old Cornish words, 'tre' and 'scaw', which together translate as 'farmstead of the elder trees'. The township was given by Henry I to Tavistock Abbey who established the Benedictine Priory of St Nicholas, whose prior, Alan of Cornwall, became Abbot of Tavistock in 1233. The original Cornish placename was Ryn Tewyn, meaning 'promontory among the dunes'; later it was known as St Nicholas's Island and in 1305 as Trescau.

Ventnor

Ventnor began as a small fishing village built on the Undercliff, a series of terraces located near Boniface Down on the south coast of the Isle of Wight. Around 1200, it was known as Holewela or Holeweye, based on two Old English words, 'hol', meaning hollow, and 'weg', the way. Hence, 'the way through, [or in], a hollow', or 'the hollow way'. This probably comes from the narrow road that leads up from the low-lying town centre to the downs above. The placename was replaced around 1617 by Ventnor, probably after the Le Vyntener family. Their family name is related to the vintner, or wine-grower, and it is possible that they owned the manor and were known for their vineyards, although many dispute this interpretation.

Whippingham

This Isle of Wight village was recorded in the eighth century as Wippingeham, a name taken from a man called Wippa, along with two Old English words, 'inga', meaning 'people', 'family' or 'followers, and 'ham', a homestead or village. Hence, 'homestead of the people (or followers) of Wippa'. Domesday listed the Manor of Wipingeham, in the Bowcombe Hundred, held in part by King William, by William FitzStur and by Wulfward. Before 1066, the estates had been part-held by the aforesaid Wulfward, along with two men called Bolla and Cypping of Worthy. The whole combined manorial estate was valued at just twelve shillings in 1086.

Wroxall

The Old English word 'wrocc' signified a buzzard or some other bird of prey, and the word 'halh' indicated a corner or nook of land. Hence, the placename of this village in the Isle of Wight translates as 'corner of land inhabited by buzzards [or other birds of prey'. Domesday recorded it as Wroccesheale, and listed it as a very large estate for its day, supporting over fifty households in the Bowcombe Hundred and held in 1086 by King William, having belonged to Countess Gytha of Wessex in 1066.

Yarmouth

Yarmouth derives its placename from its location at the mouth of the River Yar in the Isle of Wight, which means the 'muddy estuary'. The township settlement has been known for over a thousand years and was known as Ermud in the late tenth century, based on two Old English words, 'earen' and 'mutha'. It was an important port for the Isle of Wight during the time of King Ethelred, when Danegeld taxes were still being paid.

Part Fifteen

Novel, Odd, and Unusual Placenames

England abounds with unusual placenames. Many appear quaint, some are outrageous or downright rude, and on the face of it, others appear obscure or incomprehensible. In the end, all that can be said about some is that they are just odd. These are a few of the many.

Albright Hussey

The *Oxford English Dictionary* defines the word 'hussy' as a 'worthless woman', but it would be misleading to apportion such a characterisation to the name of this village near Shifnal in Shropshire. It was first recorded in the *Domesday Book* as Abretone and Elbretone, in the Baschurch Hundred, held in 1086 by Reginald the Sheriff. The first part of the placename is derived from a man called Aethelbeorht, who probably founded the original settlement or was at least closely associated with the place during the seventh or eighth centuries. Later, the manor came into the possession of the Hussy family, and in 1292, to avoid confusion with other placenames (like the nearby township of Albrighton), their family name was added.

Anton's Gowt

Anton's Gowt is a hamlet in Langriville Civil Parish of the East Lindsey district of Lincolnshire, once known as Wildmore Fen. The Anton of the placename referred not to a poor fellow who suffered from gout, but is thought to be a reference to Sir Anthony Thomas, who was instrumental in draining the Witham Fens sometime around 1631. The word 'gowt' is actually an old term for an underground water-pipe or sewer. The hamlet is located at the junction of the River Witham and the so-called Frith Bank Drain part of the Witham Navigable Drains system, the 'gowt' referred to in the placename. Guthram Gowt, a settlement in the South Holland district of Lincolnshire, is another example of the use of the term.

Aschelesmersc

A less English-sounding placename would be hard to find anywhere but in the County of Yorkshire, where the lasting influence of Danish culture and the Old Scandinavian language survive more-or-less intact in many townships. The oldest record of this placename appeared at the parliament held in Lincoln in the Spring of 1301, when a petition was made for subsidies to Edward I. The Old English word 'mersc' referred to a marsh or marshland, and all the places whose names end this way share a common topography. More information about the place is hard come by, except that the first element of the placename, Aschele, probably referred to a Danish man who owned the original settlement. Establishing townships in such unpromising terrain was not uncommon in the eighth and ninth centuries, where they provided excellent defensive positions against surprise attacks. A likely interpretation of the meaning would be 'Aschele's marsh'. The village was recorded in Domesday as Aschelesmersc, in the Dic Wapentake of the North Riding of Yorkshire.

Badger

Nothing whatever to do with badgers, this Shropshire village derived its placename from a man called Baecg; the additional Old English word 'ofer', meaning 'hill-spur' or 'flat-topped ridge', produced a placename that means something like 'flat-topped ridge belonging to Baecg'. In 1086, Domesday recorded the place as Beghesoure, in the Alnodestreu Hundred, where '...Osbern holds Badger of Earl Roger [de Poitou] and Robert holds of him. Bruning held it [before 1066] and was a free man'.

Barnacle
Barnacle is a Warwickshire village that according to contemporary sensibilities would seem a more appropriate name for a coastal fishing resort. However, nothing could be further from the truth. The placename comes from the Old English expression 'bere-aern', technically meaning 'barley building', but more commonly interpreted as 'barn'. The second name element, 'hangra', signified a wooded slop. The entire placename therefore means either 'barn on a wooded slope' or 'wooded slope near a barn'. Domesday recorded the place as Bernhangre, a very small estate in the Bumbelowe Hundred held in 1086 by the Count of Meulan, having belonged before the Norman Conquest to Hereward.

Beer
Several villages in England include the word 'Beer' in their placenames, and this seaside resort in Devon is one of them. Of course, the name has nothing to do with beer or ales of any kind, but in common with all others comes from the Old English word 'bearu', which represented a woodland grove or pasture. Hence, this placename simply translates as '[place by or in the] woodland grove'. Domesday recorded it as Bera and listed it in the Colyton Hundred, part-held in 1086 by Baldwin the Sheriff, Count Robert de Mortain and Horton Abbey.

Besses O' Th' Barn
Just to the north of Prestwich in the Metropolitan Borough of Bury lies Besses O' Th' Barn. This oddly named area, is known locally as 'Besses'. Many mistakenly believe that the placename was related to the highwayman Dick Turpin and his horse, Black Bess, and its possible stabling in a local barn. However, the place is actually an old industrial village whose name probably derives from an infamous pub landlady, Elizabeth 'Bess' Bamford, who ran the local Dog Inn from 1674–99. According to the BBC's *Domesday Reloaded* project in 1986, the pub originally resembled a barn, and the houses that were established around it came later. The Prestwich & Whitefield Heritage Society, suggest that Elizabeth became known as Besses o' th' Barn, and this became the eventual name of the pub and of the district. The district of Besses is probably best known nowadays for its celebrated brass band, one of the oldest in the world.

Birdlip
The Gloucestershire township of Birdlip was recorded in1221 as Bridelepe, derived from the Old English words 'bridd', referring to a young bird or birds, and 'hlep', a steep place or escarpment. Hence the name translates as 'steep place where young birds abound'.

Blubberhouses
This most unusual placename, located in the Washburn Valley, in the Borough of Harrogate in North Yorkshire, was known by the end of the twelfth century as Bluberhusum, a name taken from the Middle English word 'bluber', meaning 'bubbling (or fast-flowing) spring', and the Old English plural word 'husum', signifying dwellings or houses. Hence, [place at the] houses bubbling spring'. Over time the placename has been variously spelt as Bluburgh, Bluborrow and Bluburhouse.

Boarhunt
Based on its placename, you might assume that this Hampshire village was once an important hunting centre, perhaps part of a royal chase, but in fact it is neither related

to wild boars nor to hunting. The name is actually derived from two Old English words, 'burh', meaning 'fortified place' or 'stronghold', and 'funta', the origin of the modern word 'fount' or 'font' – one of several words used by the Anglo-Saxons for a spring. Hence, '[place by the] spring near a stronghold'. The spring in question has been identified as the one at Offwell Farm. In the tenth century the place was known as Byrhfunt, and it was recorded in Domesday survey of 1086 as Borehunt, listed in the Portsdown Hundred, part-held by Earl Roger of Shrewsbury, Hugh de Port and the Bishop of Winchester.

Britwell Salome

It is remotely possible that at some time in its past a resident of Britwell may indeed have danced the 'Seven Veils' in true Biblical fashion – but unequivocally that is not the derivation of any part of this Oxfordshire village placename. That comes from the de Suleham family who came into possession of the manor in the thirteenth century. The first part of the name comes from two Old English words, 'brit', referring to so-called 'Ancient Britons', and 'wella', meaning 'spring', 'fountain' or 'well'. The entire placename therefore translates as '[estate of the] de Suleham family by the spring of the Britons'. Domesday identified the village as Brutwell, in the Benson Half Hundred held by Miles Crispin in 1086. By 1320, the placename had become Brutewell Solham.

Bucklers Hard

In Old English, the word 'hard' was a south-west English dialect word which stood for a firm or secure landing place. The landing place in question was on the banks of the River Beaulieu in the New Forest of Hampshire. The village was named after the Buckler family who took possession of the village in the mid-seventeenth century. The placename was first recorded in 1789, and means 'firm landing place belonging to the Buckler family'.

Bugle

Apparently named after a local bugler, this Cornish village took its name from the Bugle Inn around which it sprang up in the 1840s. It seems that before this time the village was known as Carnrosemary, but locals began referring to the place as Bugle and the names appears to have stuck.

Bunny

This cute and cuddly Nottinghamshire village placename has nothing whatever to do with bunny rabbits or any other small mammals for that matter. The name comes from a combination of the Old English words 'bune', meaning 'reed' or 'rushes', and 'eg', an island, or more properly, a piece of raised ground surrounded by wetland, a seasonal flood plain or marshland. Hence, 'high or raised ground [or island] where reeds grow'. Domesday recorded Bonei, quite a large estate supporting twenty-eight households in the Rushcliffe Hundred, and held by Ralph FitzHubert in 1086, having belonged to Leofnoth, the brother of Leofric in 1066. The manorial estate amounted to one hundred and sixty acres of meadow, a woodland measuring ten furlongs in length and one furlong wide, one mill and a church; the entire estate and its assets were valued at three pounds.

Bures

In 1086, this Essex hamlet was recorded as Bure and Bura, a placename derived from the Old English plural word, 'buras', meaning 'the cottages' or 'dwellings'. Bures was later divided into three separate parishes: as Bures, (the original hamlet), Bures St Mary (identified with the local church), and Mount Bures in 1328 (Bures att Munte), due to its location 'at the mount' or (on a hill).

Burton Lazars

The apparently futuristic placename belongs to a village in Leicestershire, but has nothing to do with light-emitting rays or lasers. The 'Lazars' element of the name comes from the Leper Hospital of St Lazarus that was founded in the village in 1135. Burton is a common placename with fifteen or so others of that name in England. It derives from the Old English words 'burh', meaning 'stronghold' or 'fortified place', and 'tun', a farmstead. Hence, the whole village placename may be taken to mean 'fortified farmstead near St Lazarus' Hospital'. Domesday simply recorded the place as Burtone, in the Framland Hundred, part-held in 1086 by Geoffrey de la Guerche, Roger de Bully and Henry de Ferrers.

Catherine-de-Barnes

Catherine-de-Barnes is a relatively new district, having been heathland and once part of the Manor of Longdon which merged with the Manor of Ulverlei before incorporation into the Borough of Solihull in the West Midlands. The name derives from a twelfth century Lord of the Manor called Chetelberne, Ketelbarnus or Ketelberne, who founded the nearby Henwood Priory. The place has been locally known as Catney Barnes since the nineteenth century and is frequently abbreviated to Catney. In 1602, the placename was recorded as Katherine Barnes Heath. The village has also been recorded as Katherine at Barnes.

Chilmark

While this Wiltshire village placename would appear better suited to a measuring scale on the side of a chest freezer, in fact it translates from Old English as 'boundary mark in the form of a pole'. It comes from 'cigel', a pole, and 'mearc', a mark or marker. In the days before field enclosures and hedgerows, boundary markers, either of wood or of stone, were commonplace. In the late tenth century, the village was known as Cigelmerc, and by 1086, Domesday had recorded it as Chilmerc and listed it within the Dunworth Hundred, held at that time by the Abbey of St Mary in Wilton, as they had done before 1066.

Chimney

Chimney is a small hamlet in Oxfordshire, whose name comes from a person known as Ceomma, who may have been the founder of the original settlement on raised ground surrounded by marshland. In Old English, such places were called 'eg', which simply meant 'island'. This improbable sounding placename may therefore be taken to mean 'Ceomma's island'. The Normans recorded the place as Ceomannyg in 1069.

Chop Gate

The small North Yorkshire hamlet of Chop Gate (pronounced 'Chop Yat'), lies on the edge of the North York Moors National Park and traces its placename back to early medieval times. The name derives from the Old English word 'ceap', meaning 'market' or 'market place', which identified it as an important trading centre. The element is present in many other places with a market trading heritage (e.g. Chipping Norton in Oxfordshire, Chipping Camden in Gloucestershire, and Cheapside in London). The Old Norse word 'gat' indicated a road or carriageway. Hence the placename may be taken to mean 'market place on the road [or highway]'.

Christmas Common/Christmaspie

In the early seventeenth century, this Oxfordshire hamlet was known as Christmas Coppice and by the eighteenth it had been recorded as 'a village called Christmas'. Later that century it became Christmas Green. The coppice referred to in its earlier name was well-known for its abundant holly trees, and given that tree's association with the festive season, it was inevitable that sooner or later the name would emerge. In 1823, the village of Christmaspie was recorded in Surrey, a name coming from the local Christmaspie Farm, which was known in the sixteenth century.

Clutton

Clutton derives its name from two words, 'clud', one of many words the Saxon used for a hill, and 'tun', a farmstead or village settlement. Hence, 'farmstead by a hill'. Domesday recorded this Cheshire village as Clutone, a small manor in the Duddeston Hundred, held by William FitzNigel, it having previously been owned by Edward of Grappenhall (probably recorded as a Frenchman) and Wulfwin Chit. The manorial estates comprised sufficient land for two ploughs, half an acre of meadow and woodland half a league long, altogether valued in 1086 at just four shillings. There is a village of the same name in Somerset.

Compton Pauncefoot

Compton is a common English placename with around twenty other places sharing it in common. Most have other distinguishing affixes to avoid confusion, and the Somerset village of Compton Pauncefoot is no exception. The name 'Compton' comes from the Old English words 'cumb', meaning 'valley' (especially in south-west England where places with the 'coombe' or 'combe' element in their name are common), and 'tun', which signified a village or a farmstead. In 1086, the place was recorded as Comtone, in the Blachethorna Hundred, held at that time by Turstin FitzRolf (the son of Rolf). The Pauncefote family came into possession of the manor in the thirteenth century and their family name was attached, so that by 1291 the village had adopted the placename of Cumpton Paunceuot.

Copt Hewick

This North Yorkshire village has a placename that means 'high dairy farm with (or on) a peak'. It comes from the Anglo-Saxon word 'copped', which means 'having a peak', plus 'heah', meaning 'high', and 'wic', which signified a specialised farm (most typically a dairy farm). As its name implies, the village does stand, on a hill, and it was recorded in the Great Survey of 1086 as Heawic. Later, 'Copt' was added to distinguish it from the nearby village of Bridge Hedwick on the River Ure, and in 1208 the placename was recorded as Coppedehaiwic.

Cowpen Bewley

The name of this district of Stockton in County Durham has nothing whatever to do with cows, cattle or dairy farms. It derives its name initially from the Old English word 'cupe' (or in its plural form as 'cupum'), which represents a coop, a type of basket used locally to catch fish in the Tees estuary. The second word of the placename identifies it as part of the Manor of Bewley (which is a corruption of the old French word 'Beaulieu', meaning 'beautiful place'). In the early twelfth century, the village name was recorded as Cupum.

Crackpot

The North Yorkshire village of Crackpot may derive its name from the Old Scandinavian word 'kraka', a cow, and 'pot' or the Middle English word 'potte', meaning a deep cavity or hole, referring to the local rift or cleft in an area of limestone known as Scurvey Scar – not, as might first appear, a euphemism for a fool or an idiot. The placename could be translated as '[limestone] cleft frequented by cows'. No doubt in times past it was a frequent occurrence that grazing cattle found themselves trapped or marooned in the place.

Creeting St Mary

Creeting is a village in Suffolk that initially derived its name from a man called Craeta and his followers, implied by the Old English affix 'inga' which referred to people, family or followers. Domesday recorded the place as Cratingas, in the Bosmere Hundred, part-held by Aldgyth of Creeting as it had been before the Conquest. Other tenants of the manor included Robert Malet, Robert de Glanville, Walter de Caen, Bishop Odo of Bayeux and William de Warenne, as well as the Abbey of St Mary of Bernay and All Saints Church of St Mary of Creeting. Later, a dedication to the local village church was added to the name to distinguish it from nearby Creeting St Peter. In 1254, the village was known by its Latin name, Creting Sancte Marie.

Cross in Hand

This East Sussex village, sometimes known as Isenhurst, is reputedly where Crusaders from around the country assembled before proceeding to Rye and then on to the Holy Land to fight the Moors. This was supposedly marked by an inn sign which depicted a quarter standard held aloft by a mailed hand. What remains of that event now survives as the Cross in Hand pub in the village. In 1547 the place was known by its Latin name, Cruce Manus, and in 1597 as something approaching its present-day name, as Crosse in Hand.

Cruckmeole

Cruckmeole derives its name from the Meole Brook (the old name for Rae Brook), on which it stands. Taken together with the Old English word 'croc', which referred to a bend in a river, the placename of this Shropshire village may be interpreted as 'river-bend on Moele Brook'. The name of the brook is thought to derive from 'meolu', a Saxon word which technically meant 'meal', but in this particular case probably meant 'cloudy'. In the early twelfth century the place was simply known as Mele, but by the end of that century it had been recorded as Crokemele.

Dethick

The somewhat macabre name of this small hamlet in Derbyshire translates from Old English as 'death oak', where the meaning of the 'deth' element was self-evident, and 'ac' meant 'oak tree'. This was a term commonly used for oak trees from which criminals and murderers were hanged. In 1154 the placename was recorded as Dethec.

Dicker/Lower Dicker

The Middle English word 'dyker' meant 'ten', and was almost certainly derived from the Latin *decem*. This odd-sounding hamlet in East Sussex acquired the name 'Diker' in the early thirteenth century when it is said to have paid ten rods of iron by way of rent. Iron rods were a valuable commodity in medieval times, one rod being sufficient for a farrier to forge two horseshoes. Three related and adjacent settlements of this placename exist, Lower Dicker and Upper Dicker, while lying west of the River Cuckmere is the village simply known as The Dicker.

Didley

Didley is a small hamlet in Herefordshire whose placename derives from a man called Dudda, who owned or occupied a woodland clearing, or as the Saxons knew such places, a 'leah'. The placename translates as 'Dudda's woodland clearing'. Domesday recorded the manor as Dodelegie in 1086, located in the Stretford Hundred, and held at that time by the Bishop of St Mary's Church in Hereford, as it had been before 1066. The placename and its origin are identical to that of the town of Dudley in the West Midlands.

Doddiscombsleigh

Originally known simply as Leuga, from the Old English word 'leah', referring to a settlement or estate at or in a woodland clearing or a glade, the Devonshire village of Doddiscombesleigh first appears as Doddescumbeleghe in 1309. The extension of the placename arose when the manor came into the possession of the Doddescom family around that time. The Domesday record locates the 'Mainou of Leuga' in the Exminster Hundred of 'The Land of Godebold' (sometimes known as 'the Bowman'), who held it in 1086. Before the Conquest it had belonged to the Saxon, Alsige or Alsi of Castle Cary. It seems to have been a flourishing estate at the time of the survey, as between 1070 and 1086, the assessed value of the estate had risen from two pounds to three pounds.

Dowlish Wake

Dowlish is the name of the river on which this Somerset village stands; the name is of Celtic origin, and means 'dark stream'. Some time in the twelfth century, the Wake family took possession of the manor and attached their family name to the village, thus distinguishing their estate from the nearby village of Dowlish Ford. The placename may be interpreted as 'the Wake family [estate by the River] Dowlish'. Domesday recorded the placename in 1086 as Duuelis, in the South Petherton Hundred, held by Geoffrey, Bishop of Coutances. It was in 1243 that the place was first recorded as Duueliz Wak.

Drax

Drax is a name that is derived from the Old Scandinavian word 'draeg', and relates to the modern word 'drag', but was more properly used as a term for towing, hauling, drawing or portage. This North Yorkshire village is located on the River Ouse some way north of the River Aire and established itself as major centre for portage, transportation or dragging boats overland between the two rivers. Domesday recorded it as Drac, in the Barkston Hundred of the old West Riding, held by Ralph Paynel at the time of the survey, while Merleswein (known as 'the Sheriff') had been lord of the manor before the Conquest. In the eleventh century the placename was written as Drachs.

Drigg

The Cumbrian village of Drigg, a parish in the ancient Bootle district of what was then Cumberland, gets its placename directly from the Danes, and has the same meaning as the village of Drax in Yorkshire. In Old Scandinavian, the word 'draeg', means to drag or carry, in this case a place where boats were dragged overland, or perhaps manhauled up from the sea and portaged to the nearby River Irt. In the twelfth century the place was recorded as Dreg.

Duntisbourne Rouse

An apparently obscure Gloucestershire placename, which when broken into its component elements is remarkably straightforward. In 1055, the place was recorded as Duntesburne, which is based on an early founder or settler, a man known as Dunt, and the Old English word 'burna', meaning a small stream or a brook (similar to the Scottish 'burn', which has the same meaning). Hence, the original placename meant 'Dunt's stream'. In the thirteenth century, the manorial estate was split three ways, with one going to the de Rous family, who appended their family name to the place. Of the two other parts, Duntisbourne Abbots went to the Abbot of St Peter's Abbey in Gloucester, and Duntisbourne Leer came into the ownership of the Abbey of Lire in Normandy. In 1307, Duntisbourne Rouse was recorded as Duntesbourn Rus.

Edith Weston

This Rutland village holds no secrets in its placename, which means 'Edith's western estate'. The name comes from Queen Edith of Wessex, the widow of Edward the Confessor, and the western estate land which came to her as part of her marriage dowry. It lay to the west of the Royal Manor of Ketton. It was known in 1114 simply as Weston, but by 1275 had been recognised as Weston Edith.

Egg Buckland

Despite appearances to the contrary, this district of the City of Plymouth in Devon has nothing to do with eggs. It comes from an early possession or land granted to a man called Heca. The second part of the placename comes from the Anglo-Saxon expression 'boc-land', which translates literally as 'charter land'. Bocland was granted by royal charter, carrying many privileges to those favoured by the Crown and usually required some oath of fielty. Many places in England have this as part of their placename, as boclands were useful administrative instruments of medieval royal authority. This particular placename translates as 'bocland held by Heca'. It was recorded in 1086 as Bochelanda, and by 1221 as Eckebokelond.

English Bicknor

Bicknor is an old Saxon word made of two elements: 'bica', meaning 'point', and 'ofer', a flat-topped ridge'. It was recorded in 1086 as Bicanofre, a small manor in the Westbury Hundred of Gloucestershire, held by William FitzNorman. In 1248, the word 'English' was appended to the placename in order to distinguish it from Welsh Bicknor on the other side of the River Wye. The placename may be interpreted as 'English ridge with a point'.

Esh

Esh is a village in County Durham whose placename derives directly from the Old English word for the ash tree, 'aesc'. It was recorded as Esse in the twelfth century, and the placename means '[place by or near the] ash tree'.

Eye

This village in Suffolk derived its name from the Old English word 'eg', which simply meant 'island'. The island referred to in the placename would have been typical of settlements that were established on higher ground surrounded by wetlands, streams, marshes or river flood plains. Domesday listed this particular township as Eia, in the Hartismere Hundred of Norfolk/Suffolk (shire boundaries being rather flexible at that time); it was held by Robert Malet in 1086 having belonged to Swartrik before 1066. Another village of the same name exists as a suburb of Peterborough.

Fangfoss

Fangfoss is a village in the old East Riding of Yorkshire whose placename illustrates the inroads made by Vikings into Anglo-Saxon society, especially in the north-east of England. The first element of the name, 'fang', is an Old Scandinavian word for 'fishing', while 'foss' is Anglo-Saxon and means 'ditch'. Hence, possibly, the placename may mean 'a ditch used for fishing'. The Great Survey named the manor as Frangefos, and listed it in the Pocklington Hundred, held in 1086 by King William, it having belonged to Earl Morcar in 1066. By the twelfth century it had begun to resemble its present-day name and was written as Fangefosse.

Farewell

An early record of the placename of the hamlet of Farewell in the County of Staffordshire was in 1200, when it was written as Fagerwell, derived from two Old English words, 'faeger', meaning 'fair' or 'pleasant', and 'wella', which could refer to a spring, a well or a fountain. The name is commonly taken to mean '[place by the] pleasant stream'.

Feock

A small Cornish village whose name comes from the patron saint of its local church, St Fioc. In the twelfth century the placename was recorded as Lanfioc, the word 'lann' being Old Cornish for a church. Hence, 'the church of St Fioc'. Little is known about this obscure saint.

Follyfoot

This placename derived from an ancient practice that would be thought politically incorrect by today's standards. Although the name of this North Yorkshire village is derived from two Anglo-Saxon words, 'fola', a (horse) foal', and 'feoht', meaning 'fight', it actually allude to an old Viking sport, where two stallions were pitched against each other, often in savage and cruel combat, for the prize of mares who were in season, while the onlookers made wagers as to the victor. The village was evidently a place where this 'sporting' practice was held. In the twelfth century, the village was recorded as Pholifet.

Foulness

More 'fowl' than 'foul', this small Essex island has long been known for its wildfowl, and that is the origin of the placename. The name actually comes from two Saxon words, 'fugol', a generic word for 'bird', and 'naess', which signified a headland or promontory, which it once was, but due to land erosion and frequent damaging high tides, it is now separated from the mainland by narrow creeks and sea inlets. Hence, the original placename meant 'bird promontory'. In 1215 the place was recorded as Fughelnesse and listed in the Rochford Hundred.

Frenchay

In another life this could have been a derogatory term for a Frenchman, but it has little to do with anyone or anything from France. The placename of this suburb of Bristol in South Gloucestershire was recorded in 1248 as Fromshawe and it was not until the beginning of the seventeenth century that it had inexplicably changed to Frenchay. The original name from the River Frome on which it stands and the Old English 'sceaga', which referred to a small wood or a copse. The placename therefore could be translated as '[place by the] wood on the River Frome'.

Frog Firle/West Firle

The East Sussex of West Firle was recorded by the Domesday survey as Ferle (also known as Frog Firle), in the Flexborough Hundred of Pevensey, held by Count Robert d'Eu, and that Alan rented or leased four hides from him. The survey continues '...Almaer and Godwine held them of King Edward as two manors'. All trace of the 'frog' element has long since disappeared from the village placename. According to *Historic England*, the name survives now as '...dispersed medieval settlement remains at Frog Firle in the Cuckmere Valley' and in Frog Firle Farm. Nowadays the village is best known as West Firle. The name comes from 'fierel' and translates as 'place where oak trees grow', or 'oak forest', and latterly as 'western oak forest'. Oddly, there is no such place as East Firle.

Fryup

This North Yorkshire township derived its placename from a man called Friga, and not as some might suppose, as a euphemism for a full English breakfast. The second element of the placename, 'hop', is a Saxon word which signified a small enclosed valley. Therefore, the placename may be taken to mean 'Friga's small enclosed valley'. The place was known as Frehope in the twelfth century and as Frihop in the thirteenth.

Germansweek

This Devonshire village possesses an apparently improbable placename that has nothing to do with people of German nationality. It was originally recorded simply as Wica, and by the fifteenth century had acquired a dedication from the village church of St Germanus. The second element is Old English, where 'wic' signified a specialised farm, typically a dairy farm. Hence 'dairy farm near (or possibly belonging to) St Germanus's church'. Domesday recorded the 'Mainou of Wica', or Wiche, in the land of Baldwin the Sheriff, where Roger was its tenant-in-chief. It recorded that 'Eadnoth held it at the time of King Edward and it paid geld for half a virgate of land'.

Good Easter

It would be a natural confusion to think this a typographical error, for surely the expression should be 'Good Friday'? However, the name of this village in Essex is related neither to Easter nor Good Friday. In the eleventh century, the place was simply known as Estre, a name that comes from the Old English word 'eowestre', meaning 'sheepfold'. By the beginning of the thirteenth century, the fold in question had come into the possession of a woman called Godgifu, whose name became attached to the placename. Hence, 'Godgifu's sheepfold'. In 1200 the village was recorded as Godithestre.

Great Heck

Originally known simply as Hech, in the old Osgoldcross Wapentake of North Yorkshire, this village in derived its placename from the Old English word 'haece' or 'haecc', or from the Middle English 'heck', meaning 'hatch' or 'gate'. This may have been a gate on the main road which ran through the village or at the entrance to an enclosed woodland. The 'Great' part of the name distinguishes it from the nearby village of Little Heck.

Great Snoring

Nothing to do with noisy sleep patterns, the village of Great Snoring in Norfolk probably derives its name from a man called Snear and his followers, who probably arrived in East Anglia during the Saxon invasions which took place from around 450. The final element of the name, 'ingas', refers to people, family or followers. Therefore, the placename may be taken to mean 'village (or settlement) of the followers of Snear'. In 1086, the place was recorded as Snaringes, and listed in the North Greenhoe Hundred, held at that time by King William. Before 1066 the manor had belonged to a Saxon called Ketil. The 'Great' element of the placename distinguishes it from nearby Little Snoring.

Guiting Power

The Gloucestershire village of Guiting Power derived its name initially from the River Guiting on which it stands. That river is nowadays known as the Windrush, but its former name, (Guiting), meant 'running (or fast-flowing) stream', which came from the Old English word 'gyte', (technically meaning 'flood'). By the early thirteenth century the manor had become a possession of the le Poer family, and their name was attached to the placename. This distinguished it from Guiting Temple, which passed at that time to the Knights Templars. In 814 the placename was recorded as Gythinge and by the time of the Domesday survey it had been written as Gettinge, in the Holford Hundred, held in 1086 by William Goizenboded. In 1066, it had been the property of Alwin, the Sheriff of Gloucestershire.

Gweek
A most unusual placename for a small Cornish village, the meaning of which is surprisingly simple: it means 'hamlet' or 'village'. The word comes from the Cornish word 'gwig', or the Old English 'wic' – both are equally possible. It was recorded in 1201 as Wika.

Hog's Back
So named in 1823 to reflect the shape of its location, on a hill ridge in Surrey, which resembles a pig's back, the village of Hog's Back was known before that as Geldeedon (and Guildown), from the Old English 'gylde', meaning 'golden one' and 'dun', a hill. The 'golden' reference is thought to be to the sandy soil on the banks of the River Wey, which is also reflected in the name of the City of Guildford. The placename has undergone several transformations over time, including Geldedon in 1195, Gildowne in 1495 and Gill Down in 1744, before changing to its present form in the nineteenth century.

Hound
No dogs or hounds of any breed here. The name of this Hampshire village comes from the hoarhound (or horehound), a pungent plant of the mint family, traditionally used medicinally for the treatment of coughs and colds. Hound was a common abbreviation of the plant name, and comes from the Old English word 'hune'. Domesday recorded Hune, in the Meonstoke Hundred, of which three hides and four and a half acres of land were held by Hugh de Port. There was a mill, a church and twenty acres of meadow, worked by six slaves.

Howle
This small hamlet in the Wrekin region of Shropshire has little to do with a shriek or a crie de coeur, and more to do with the small hillock or mound on which the original settlement stood - what the Saxons called a 'hugol'. This is the derivation of the placename, which may be taken to mean '[place by the] mound or hillock'. Domesday spelt the placename as Hugle and listed it as a small manor in the Wrockwardine Hundred, held at that time by Turold de Verley. The account reported that '...Walter holds of him (Turold) [and that] Batsveinn held it before him at the time of King Edward'. It concluded, 'He found it waste'.

Huish Champflower
Huish Champflower is a small Somerset village, bordered by the Brendon Hills and Exmoor, whose earlier name of Hiwis comes from the Old English word 'hiwisc', meaning 'household'. There are at least seven places of this name in south-west England. Domesday places the early manorial estate in the Williton Hundred, held in 1086 by Roger Arundel, it having belonged to a Saxon man called Aelric in 1066. The manor came into the possession of Thomas de Champflur in the thirteenth century and his family name was appended to the placename, and by 1274 it was recorded as Hywys Champflur, indelibly marking his territory, and distinguishing it from the village of Beggearn Huish a few miles away.

Idle
The name of this suburb of Bradford in West Yorkshire should be taken to imply neither slothfulness, inoccupation nor idleness. It comes from an Old English word meaning 'empty', in this case a probable reference to uncultivated land. The place was known in the twelfth century as Idla, and in the thirteenth as Idel.

Indian Queens
The village of Indian Queens, located about ten miles from Bodmin, was named after the Indian Queen Inn in 1802, and according to local tradition this Cornish placename was derived from the Native American Princess Pocahontas, the youngest daughter of an Indian

chieftain. In the seventeenth century the inn was known as Red Indian Queen, and in the eighteenth as The Indian Queen. The inn was demolished in the 1960s and the inn sign is now on display in Truro Museum. There is still a street in the village called Pocahontas Crescent.

Inkpen

Foreign visitors to Britain must surely find the name of this village in West Berkshire to be a curiosity. The name actually comes from two old Saxon words, 'ing', meaning 'hill' or 'peak', and 'penn', an enclosure (related to the modern English word 'pen'). The hill in question is nowadays known as Inkpen Hill and the enclosure is thought to have been Walbury Camp, an Iron Age hill fort on the highest part of the hill. The place was already known as Ingepenne by the early tenth century, and was recorded by Domesday as Hingepene, listed as a very large estate supporting forty-five households in the Kintbury Hundred. It was held by William FitzAnsculf in 1086, having been a possession of two unnamed free men in 1066.

Itchingfield

No itching or scratching is necessary in any field around this West Sussex township. The placename comes from quite a different source to its apparently misleading title, in the name of a man called Ecci, who may have been the founder of the original settlement. The name was recorded in 1222 as Ecchingefelde, which comes from three Old English elements: Ecci, his personal name, 'inga' signifying his family, followers or people, and 'feld' or 'felda', meaning 'open land'. Hence, '[place in] open land belonging to the people or family of Ecci'.

Knockin

A small Shropshire village whose placename is not too dissimilar to the Herefordshire village of Knill, in that it has a similar meaning, coming from the Celtic word for a small hill. Hence, '[place by or on a] small hill'. Its earliest written record dates from 1165 when the name was written as Cnochin.

Limpley Stoke

Nothing limp about this Wiltshire village placename, as it derives initially from a sixteenth century chapel dedicated to Our Lady of Limpley. The meaning of Limpley is uncertain, and in 1333 the place was known simply as Stoke. The Old English word 'stoc' referred to an outlying or remote farmstead, making a complete placename that means something like 'remote farm associated with Limpley'. Prior to 1585 the village had been known as Hangyndestok, in the ancient Hundred of Bradford, which was granted by Aethelred II to Shaftesbury Abbey in 1001. The original placename derived from 'hangende', meaning 'hanging', probably referring to the village's location beside the River Avon and beneath a steep hillside. It was referred to as Hanging Stoke or Stook, in 1322.

Lower Peover/Over Peover

Peover is the Celtic name of the mid-Cheshire local river, whose origin translates as 'bright (or beautiful) one'. The river in question is now known as the Peover Eye, and forms one of the parish boundaries and gives rise to the words Over and Lower, reflecting the difference in elevation between the parishes. The placename is pronounced 'Pee-ver'. Lower Peover, the 'lower (part of the village of) Peover'. Other localities nearby are known as variants like Little Peover (sometimes called Peover Inferior, an alternative name for Lower Peover), Nether Peover and Peover Superior. It appears in the *Domesday Book* as Pevre, in the

Bucklow Hundred, held at that time by Ranulf; it had previously been held by Earngeat, listed as being 'free'. William FitzNigel is recorded holding Lower Peover, and Edward had held it in 1066. The record states: 'It was and is waste'.

Lydiard Millicent

You would be almost right to assume that this village in Wiltshire once belonged to a person by the name of Millicent, for so it was that a woman called Millisent held the manor during the late twelfth century. Before her acquisition of the estate the place was known simply as Lidgeard. The name is of Celtic origin and relates closely to the Welsh 'llwyd', meaning 'grey', and 'garth', a hill or hill ridge. Hence 'grey hill ridge belonging to Millisent'. By the time of Domesday it had been recorded as Lidiarde, in the Staple Hundred, held by King William at that time. Before the Conquest it had belonged to Godric the Sheriff. In 1275, the name was recorded as Lidiard Milisent. Her manorial affix distinguished the village from nearby Lydiard Tregoze, which had come into the possession of the Tregoz family at around the same time.

Mepal

In the twelfth century this village in Cambridgeshire was known as Mepahala, a name based on two Saxon words: the first is the personal name of a man called Meapa, who gave his name to the place, and the second the Old English word 'halh', which referred to a corner or nook of land. The placename therefore means 'nook of land belonging to a man called Meapa'.

Messing

An Essex village placename with unfortunate though erroneous connotations. The place has nothing whatever to with mess, but takes its name from a man called Maecca, one of its earliest settlers and possibly the founder of the original settlement. Additionally, the Saxon affix 'ingas' referred to his people, family or followers, so the placename means 'village of the people or family of Maecca'. In 1086, the place was recorded as Metcinges, in the Lexden Hundred, held by Ralph Baynard, having belonged to an unnamed (and rare) free woman before the Norman Conquest.

Minskip

A most strange placename – short and to the point. This village in North Yorkshire is a direct evolution of the Old English word 'maenscipe', which means 'community'. Domesday recorded the place as Minescip, a very small estate supporting three households in the Burghshire Hundred of the West Riding and in the personal possession of King William.

Moccas

This is yet another Herefordshire village whose close proximity to the Welsh border permeates its placename. In the Welsh language a 'moch' was a pig, and 'rhos' represented a moor or moorland. Hence, the placename might be interpreted as '[place on the] moor where pigs are kept'. Domesday recorded Moches, in the Dinedor Hundred, land granted to Nigel 'the Physician'. It also records that Ansfrid rented land from Nigel, just as Earnwine had done of the Church of St Guthlac before the Conquest. By 1130, the placename had become Mochros.

Mousehole

The fishing village of Mousehole in Cornwall was recorded as Musehole in 1284, and simply means 'mouse hole', possibly referring to a small hole in a local cavern. An alternative explanation has been suggested: it may derive its name from the Cornish word 'moeshayle', meaning the 'mouth of the river or stream', as a small stream runs through the village into the harbour. Mousehole was known even earlier as Porth Enys (the port of the island), in reference to St Clement's Isle which lies offshore.

Mow Cop
An oddly antiquated name for a hilltop place on the border of rural Staffordshire and Cheshire, it derived initially from the Old English phrase 'muga-hyll', a somewhat derogatory term meaning 'heap hill'. At the end of the thirteenth century the name was written as Mowell. The affix 'copp' was added, meaning 'hill top', so that in 1621, the place was recorded as Mowle-coppe. The original 'heap' alluded to is thought to have been a cairn or a pile of stones that marked the county boundary that ran, and still runs across the hill.

Much Hoole
This Lancashire placename gives no obvious clues as to its meaning or origin. It was originally known simply as Hulle. With the 'Much' added to the name it translates into modern English as 'bigger (or greater) place with a shed'. Still confused? Well, take into account that the Old English word 'mycel' means 'greater'. The modern English and Scottish words 'mickle' and 'muckle' both traditionally meant 'a large amount'. This is somewhat confused by the maxim 'many a mickle makes a muckle', where a 'mickle' has also come to mean 'a small amount'. Then, 'hulu' represented a shed or a hut. Taken literally, this placename means 'greater shed', but might be better understood as 'greater [place with a] shed'. The 'greater' element came into being in the early thirteenth century, when it was called Magna Hole, to distinguish it from the nearby village of Little Hoole ('magna' being the Latin word for 'great' or 'greater').

Mucking
At first sight, this would appear to be yet another Essex village with a disdainfully unfavourable placename. However, this hamlet actually got its name from a man called Mucca and his people or followers, as evidenced by the Old English suffix 'ingas' All evidence to the contrary, the placename means 'village [or settlement] of Mucca's people'. Domesday listed the village as Muchinga, in the Barstable Hundred, held in 1086 by the Abbey of St Mary in Barking.

Nappa
The placename of this North Yorkshire Hamlet does not very readily give up its meaning. It actually means 'enclosure in a bowl-shaped hollow' – all that in a two-syllable word! The name is derived from two Old English words, 'hnaepp', meaning 'bowl' or 'dish', and 'haeg', the possible origin of the modern word 'hedge', and referring to an enclosure (i.e. hedged in). In a typical confused manner, the *Domesday Book* commissioners recorded the placename as Napars, and listed it in the Craven Hundred of the former West Riding, held in 1086 by William de Percy, it having belonged to Bernwulf before the Norman Conquest.

Nately/Up Nately
Known simply as Nataleie in 1086, this Hampshire village's original placename translated as 'wet woodland or clearing', from the Old English 'naet', meaning 'wet', and 'leah', a woodland clearing. The affix 'upp', meaning 'higher up' appeared in 1274 when the village was named as Upnateley. Domesday listed the village in the Basingstoke Hundred, held by Hugh de Port, having belonged to Edwin the Hunter before 1066.

Nempnet Thrubwell
This is a most complex placename, with Old English elements like 'emnet', meaning 'plain' or 'level' and 'wella', indicating a well or a spring. Added to these is the Middle English

word 'atten', meaning 'at the'. Then there is the somewhat obscure 'thrub' element, that some think relates to the modern English word 'throb', which in this instance might mean 'gushing' (as in 'gushing stream'). Hence, somewhat speculatively, the interpretation of the placename might mean '[place by the] gushing stream on level ground', or something along those lines. Around 1200, this North East Somerset village was known simply as Emnet and in 1201 the name was recorded as Trubewel.

Nether Wallop

This Hampshire Village is located on Wallop Brook and gets its name from the Anglo-Saxon words 'wella', meaning 'well' or 'stream', and 'hop', a remote valley. Hence, '[place by the] stream in a remote valley'. The 'nether' addition came later and means 'lower', distinguishing the village from the other two 'Wallops', (Over Wallop and Middle Wallop). The Domesday survey identified Wallope, in the Broughton Hundred, held in 1086 by Alsi, described as 'son of Brictsi'.

Noctorum

A decidedly Latin-sounding placename which one might think is somehow related to the night, the Noctorum district of Birkenhead on the Wirral Peninsular of Cheshire actually derives its name entirely from the Anglo-Saxons and has quite different connotations. One of several Old English words for a hill was 'cnocc', and 'tirim' meant 'dry', two words which reflect significant Irish settlements in the area, and the virtually identical modern Irish words 'cnoc' and 'tirim'. The placename means '[place on a] dry hill', which describes the district's location on dry ground surrounded by marshes. Domesday recorded the place as Chenoterie in 1086, and listed it within the Willaston Hundred, held by William Malbank. In 1553 the place was recorded as Knocktoram.

North Piddle/Wyre Piddle

The Piddle placename has nothing whatever to do with urination, but comes from the Old English word 'pidele', which referred to a marsh or a fen. It was probably named after the nearby Piddle Brook, and means '[place on the River] Piddle'. The 'North' element of the placename distinguishes it from the village of Wyre Piddle, on the same river, but located some five miles distant on the edge of the Wyre Forest, from where it derives its name. At the time of the *Domesday Book*, they were one unified entity and recorded as Pidele, in the Oswaldslow Hundred of Worcestershire, in lands belonging to the Church of St Mary at Worcester, where five hides were held for them by Robert Despenser. There were four ploughs in demesne, and four male and two female slaves worked its twenty-four acres of meadow land. The Saxon, Cyneweard had owned the manor before 1066.

Owmby-by-Spital

The Lincolnshire village of Owmby-by-Spital may have derived the first element of its placename from the Old Scandinavian language, and could be translated as 'farmstead or village belonging to a man called Authunn'. The Danish element 'by' signified a farm or a homestead settlement. Alternatively, it has been suggested that it could come from the Norse word 'authun', which referred to uncultivated land or a deserted farm. The 'by-Spital' part of the name refers to the village location by, or near a hospital, (probably a leper hospital established by a religious order of monks or friars as was common at that time). The placename therefore translates either as 'Authunn's farmstead near a hospital' or 'uncultivated land [or abandoned farm] near a hospital' - either is possible. Domesday recorded the village as Odenbi in 1086 (that is, before the hospital had been established), and listed it within the Yarborough Hundred of the Lindsey North Riding, part-held by King William, Count Alan of Brittany and William de Percy.

Par

Par is a port and resort town in Cornwall, whose placename comes directly from the Cornish language as 'porth', signifying a port, landing place or harbour. The word is similar to the Welsh element 'porth' (as in Porth, Porthcawl, Porthmadog, etc), and has exactly the same meaning. The placename was recorded as Le Pare in 1573, as The Parre in 1665, and in 1748 it acquired its present name, simply as Par.

Pease Pottage/Peasenhall/Peasmarsh

Although the 'Pease' element of these three placenames would appear at first glance to all be references to peas, this is only the case with the village of Peasenhall in Suffolk, and with Peasemarsh in East Sussex. Pease Pottage was first recorded as Peasepottage Gate in the eighteenth century and was more probably referring to muddy ground than to a green edible pulse. However, the name of the village of Peasmarsh in East Sussex indicated marshy ground where peas grow, from the Old English 'pise', meaning 'peas', and 'mersc', indicating muddy or boggy ground.

Perranzabuloe

Probably one of the most unusual and least English-sounding placenames, the Cornish township of Perranzabuloe, like many others in Cornwall, derives from St Piran, the county's patron saint. The placename relies on the Cornish word 'Peran', the saint's name in Cornish, the affix 'lann', indicating the site of a church, and the Latin suffix 'in sabulo', which translates into English as 'in the sands'. Hence, the placename may be interpreted as 'Parish of St Piran's Church in the sands'. Domesday named the place a Lanpiran, in the Rialton Hundred. The survey recorded that 'The Canons of St Piran hold 'Perran' [Perranzabuloe], which was always free [at the time of King Edward]... [and that] when the Count [of Mortain] received it, it was worth forty shillings'. In 1535, the place was recorded as Peran in Zabulo and by the mid-nineteenth century was commonly known as Perran-in-the-Sands.

Pett

Known as Pette since the late twelfth century, this village in East Sussex gets its name from the Old English word 'pytt', meaning 'pit'. Evidently there was some kind of mining operation here at some time in its medieval history; what kind of pit the placename referred to, or where it was located is unknown, but the name means '[place by or near the] pit'.

Piddletrenthide

This Dorset township derives its placename from the River Piddle, which flows through it, and which was assessed for taxation purposes as containing thirty hides of land (or 'trente', from the Old French). The placename therefore translates as '[place or estate] on the [river] Piddle [assessed at] thirty hides'. The place had been known to the Saxons as Uppidelen before the Conquest, but Domesday recorded the place simply as Pidrie, in the Hundred of Cerne, Totcombe and Modbury in 1086. It was a very large manor supporting seventy households at that time and belonging to the Abbey of St Peter in Winchester. In 1212 the place was recorded as Pidele Trenthydes. The River Piddle is effectively little more than a stream, just a few feet wide, and may originally have been called 'Puddle', as some of the other villages on its course include Tolpuddle, Briantspuddle, Puddletown and Affpuddle. Local legend has the name changed from Piddle to Puddle in view of overly-sensitive and prudish Victorian attitudes, though it has reverted to its earlier form in more modern times.

Pidley

A Cambridgeshire village, originally in the old County of Huntingdonshire, that took its name from a man called Pyda, and the woodland clearing (or in Old English the 'leah'), he held. Little is known of the man except that his name had been included in the placename before the mid-thirteenth century, when it formed a single parish with nearby Fenton and was known as Pidele et Fenton. By the nineteenth century the place had been recorded as Pidley-cum-Fenton. Over the years, the placename has been variously spelt as Pidel, Puddle and Pydele.

Pity Me

Two traditions exist for the origin of the placename of this village in County Durham. One has it that it comes from the medieval monks who carried the remains of St Cuthbert to a place of perceived safety in the light of Danish invasions in Northumbria. It is said that on their arrival at this place they sang the fifty-first Psalm in Latin, which begins with the words *'Miserere mei, Deus'*, which translates as 'Pity me, O God'. Another is that it is a corruption of the French 'petit mer', meaning 'little pool', a name which early Norman monks gave to the place. Both seem equally compelling, and we shall probably never know the truth of it.

Potto

This North Yorkshire township was known as Pothow in the early thirteenth century and its placename contains two elements: the Old English word 'pott', suggesting a pot or pottery, and the Old Scandinavian word 'haugr', which meant a mound, a pit or ditch. Hence, the placename may be interpreted as 'a mound or pit where pots are found'. It typifies many places in the north-east, where Danish invasions and their subsequent occupation introduced such hybrid names.

Pratt's Bottom

Named after the Pratt family who were known to have lived there in the fourteenth century, Pratt's Bottom is a district in Bromley. The Old English word 'botm' refers to the bottom or end of a valley. The name may be interpreted as 'Pratt's valley'. The place was known towards the end of the eighteenth century as Sprat's Bottom and by the beginning of the nineteenth it had become Pratts Bottom.

Purston Jaglin

This unusual placename's derivation is similar to the Lancashire townships of Prescot, Prestwich, Preston and Prestbury, in that the first word incorporates the Old English words 'preost' and 'tun', signifying a settlement or farmstead run by priests. The second word, 'Jaglin', comes from an early occupant of the land by the name of Jakelyn. The settlement was known in 1086, simply as Preston and Prestone. It lay within the Parish of Featherstone in the ancient Osgodcross Hundred of the West Riding of Yorkshire, two miles distant from Pontefract. Domesday recorded that Ligulf was Lord of the Manor at the time of the Norman Conquest, and that by 1086 it had come into the possession of Ernwulf of Featherstone, with Ilbert de Lacy being its tenant-in-chief.

Ramsbottom

The placename was recorded in the early fourteenth century as Romesbothum, probably from the Old English word for garlic, 'ramsa', or the Norse word 'rhamsa', plus the affix 'bothm', meaning bottom, in reference to the garlic growing at the bottom of a field. In former times, the village was sometimes known locally (and disparagingly) as 'Tupp's Arse', a 'tupp' being the old word for a sheep or ram; in fact, the name may actually have little to do with sheep or bottoms, though some still translate the placename as 'a valley where rams graze or are pastured'. However, on balance the placename most probably means 'the valley of wild garlic'. The place is known locally and familiarly as 'Rammy'.

Rattery
Ought this Devonshire village be a place where vermin were kept? Its residents might take exception to that suggestion. Especially so because it has nothing to do with rats at all. The placename comes from the Old English words 'read', meaning 'red', and 'treow', a tree. Hence, '[place by the] red tree'. Domesday recorded it as Ratreu, in the Diptford Hundred, jointly held in 1086 by William de Falaise, an unnamed Englishman and two men-at-arms. Before the Conquest it had been in the possession of a Saxon man called Alwin.

Ripe
The village of Ripe in East Sussex gets its name from the Old English word 'rip', meaning 'strip', referring to a strip of land, but the placename is more appropriately interpreted as '[place by the] strip of land'. It was listed in 1086 by its present name of Ripe, a very large estate in the Edivestone Hundred of Pevensey, held by Count Robert d'Eu, parts having been held by Godwin and Earl Harold before the Conquest. There is another village called Ripe in the County of Kent.

Roos
Known in 1086 as Rosse in the South Hundred of Holderness, this old East Riding township takes its ancient name from the Celtic word 'ros', similar and probably related to the Welsh word 'rhos' indicating a moor or heathland. A somewhat speculative alternative suggests the Dutch or German word 'roos', meaning 'rose', may be another contender. The Domesday survey records its chief tenant as Drogo (also known as Drew) de la Beuvrière, with a man called Fulco as his sub-tenant, and that it had previously been held by two men, Murdoch of Hilston and Swartgeirr, Lord of Seaton.

Scratchy Bottom
Regularly voted as one of Britain's top ten rudest and unfortunate placenames, Scratchy Bottom (or Scratchy's Bottom), lies in a valley between Durdle Door and Swyre Head in Dorset. The place is a rough chalk deposited valley surrounded by cliffs, whose name indicates its location 'at the bottom' of the aforesaid cliffs. The placename is thought to translate as '[place in a] rough hollow'.

Sheepy Magna
Unusual and improbable as this placename may sound to some, it actually does have something to do with sheep. The name comes from 'sceap', the Saxon word for sheep with the suffix 'eg' appended, meaning 'island'. The Latin word 'Magna', meaning 'greater' distinguishes this Leicestershire village from nearby Sheepy Parva, where 'parva' is Latin for 'small'. The placename means 'greater island where sheep graze'. The island in question would have referred to higher ground surrounded by marsh, wetland or a seasonal flood plain. Domesday recorded the place as Scepehe, in the Guthlaxton Hundred, held in 1086 by Henry de Ferrers, who had also held it before the Conquest.

Shellow Bowells
Having a most unusual and apparently obscure placename, this Essex village was known in the eleventh century as Scelda and Scelga, and located by Domesday in the Hundred of Dunmow, held by Geoffrey de Mandeville, and part-held in demesne by Eudo 'the Steward', '...which Wulfmaer, a free man, held at the time of King Edward'. The placename comes

from 'sceolh', which meant 'winding' or 'twisted', referring to the River Roding. Hence, the name means '[place beside the] winding river'. The second word, 'Bowells', is a corruption of the family name of the de Bueles, who held the manor in the thirteenth century.

Shitterton

Widely regarded as one of the most unfortunate placenames in Britain, early records of the Dorset hamlet of Shitterton spell it as Scatera and Scetra, which comes from the Old English word 'scite', meaning dung (later in Middle English as 'schitte' and 'shit' in modern English). The 'tun' affix signified a farmstead or village settlement. Apparently, in medieval times, long before public conveniences or bathroom facilities existed, the stream that runs through the village was used as a public toilet. The placename translates as 'village or farmstead on an open sewer', or '[place where the] brook is used as a privy'. However, the authorities in contemporary Shitterton are at great pains to point out that nowadays the hamlet is a beautiful place of historic thatched cottages and surrounded by pastoral countryside.

Shudy Camps

The word 'Camps' comes from 'campas', a Latin-derived Old English word for a field or an enclosure. The first word of this Cambridgeshire village name comes from 'scydd', which referred to a hovel or a shed, and is related to the modern English word 'shoddy'. The placename could be said to mean 'enclosure or field with a hovel'. The first word distinguishes the village from Castle Camps, where there was a medieval castle that marked its superior status. Domesday recorded the place simply as Campas, and listed it within the Chilford Hundred lands of Robert Gernon. The account concludes '...Leofsige held this land under Earl Harold, and could depart without his leave', thereby defining him as a free man.

Sixpenny Handley

The Domesday survey valued this Dorset village as worth twelve pounds in 1086 - far more than sixpence. However, the 'sixpence' element of the placename has nothing to do with money, but comes from the Old English word 'seaxe', meaning 'Saxons'; this together with an ancient Celtic word, (similar to the modern Welsh word 'pen', meaning 'hill), translates as 'hill of the Saxons'. In 877 the place was known as Hanlee and even Domesday recorded it as Hanlege, listing it within the Sixpenny Hundred (from which it derived its name), a manor that was held in 1086 by the Abbey of St Edward & St Mary of Shaftesbury, who held it long before the Norman Conquest. It was not until the mid-sixteenth century that the village was recorded as Sexpennyhanley.

Slaughter/Lower Slaughter/Higher Slaughter

This village, set amongst the Cotswolds and on the River Eye in Gloucestershire, was recorded in the *Domesday Book* as Sclostre in the Salmonsburry Hundred, held in 1086 by King William himself, as it had belonged to King Edward before the Conquest. Contrary to popular conceptions, the place has nothing at all to do with death or slaughter, but is related to the modern English word 'slough'. Its derivation comes from the Old English word 'slohtre', which translates as either a 'deep ravine or channel' or possibly a 'muddy or miry place'. The settlement was established on the site of the present-day Old Mill, which by the fourteenth century had begun to be known as Slaughter Mill. The village is divided into Lower and Higher Slaughter by the Eye (which probably runs through the ravine alluded to in one interpretation of the placename), and the two are connected by a couple of small footbridges.

Sloley

The first element of this Norfolk hamlet's placename is not related to speed, and neither is it a measure of dim-wittedness, but refers to the blackthorn tree, or 'sloe'. Additionally, the Old English element 'leah', which signified a woodland clearing, produces a combined meaning of 'woodland clearing where sloe grows'. Domesday recorded it as Slaleia, in the Tunstead Hundred held by Reginald FitzIvo, it having belonged to a Saxon called Skeet before the Conquest.

Sock Dennis

You may be forgiven for wondering who Dennis was, and what this Somerset village has to do with his socks. Wonder no further. 'Sock' is an ancient word for a marsh or a flood plain (think of a 'soak'). In fact, this old parish lies on the alluvial flood plain of the River Yeo and the manor was held by the Dane family. Hence, the placename means 'marshy flood plain of the Dane family'. At the time of Edward the Confessor, the manor had been held 'in parage' by seven Saxon thegns and by 1086 it was tenanted by Robert FitzIves (sometimes known as 'the Constable'), who rented it from the Count of Mortain. It was listed as Soche in the Tintinhull Hundred, and assessed with seventy acres of meadow, supporting eleven households, five cattle, thirty-five pigs and twenty-five sheep. The entire estate was valued at three pounds and three shillings in 1086.

Sollers Hope

The de Solaris family owned this manor in the thirteenth century and with the addition of 'Hope', (from 'hop', meaning 'small enclosed valley'), the placename initially became Hope Sollers, and the name of his village in Herefordshire took on the meaning of 'the small enclosed valley of the de Solaris family'. Domesday had recorded the place simply as Hope in 1086, located in the Greytree Hundred, held at that time by Ansfrid de Cormeilles, having belonged to Hagu the Reeve before the Conquest.

Steeple Bumpstead

In 1086, this village was a large manor in Essex, and was simply recorded as Bumesteda and Bummesteda, in the Hinkford Hundred, where Count Gilbert held three and a half hides and thirteen acres of estate land, while substantial other amounts were held by the tenant-in-chief, Richard, Gilbert's son. The Domesday account continues: 'In Bumesteda one knight holds seven and a half acres, which one sokeman held under Eadgifu at the time of King Edward'. The placename comes three Old English words, 'stepel', referring to a church steeple, 'bube', which meant 'reeds' or 'rushes' and 'stede', a place. Hence, 'place where rushes grow with, or near a steeple'. In 1261, the village name was recorded as Stepilbumpstede. The first part of the placename distinguishes it from nearby Helions Bumpstead, held by Tihel de Helion at the time of Domesday.

Stelling Minnis

Then unusual placename of Stelling Minnis was recorded in 1086 as Stellinges, in the Bridge Hundred of Kent, held by Bishop Odo of Bayeux. Two possible explanations have been suggested for the origin of the name. First, that it referred to a man called Stealla, its probable founder, leader or chieftain, with the Old English affix 'ingas' signifying his followers, family or people. Hence, this might mean '[settlement of] the followers or people of Stealla'. Alternatively, rather than allude to a man's name, the first element could be derived from 'stealling', meaning 'stalls' (for cattle). The 'Minnis' element of the placename, might come from the Anglo-Saxon word 'maennes', indicating common land. In this case, the complete name could mean 'cattle stalls on common land'.

Stiffkey
Who at some time has not suffered a key which is too stiff to turn in a lock? Be that as it may, that is not the meaning of this Norfolk village placename. It comes from the Old English words 'styfic', meaning 'tree stump' and 'eg', an island. Hence, 'island with a tree stump'. The island in question would have been higher ground on the flood plain of the River Stiffkey (which was named after the village). The *Domesday Book* recorded the village as Stiukai, a very large estate for its time in the North Greenhoe Hundred, mostly held by King William, but part-held by Reginald FitzIvo. Before 1066 the manor had been jointly held by King Edward, by Toki of Walton, Ketil Alder and Earl Gyrth.

Stow cum Quy
This Cambridgeshire village has a name that combines the Old English words 'stow', indicating a holy place or a meeting place, 'cu', a cow, and 'eg', meaning 'island', along with the Latin word 'cum', meaning 'with'. The placename may therefore be taken to mean 'meeting place with a cow island'. A 'cow island' is thought to have been a raised piece of pasture land in marsh or fenland. In 1086, the Great Survey listed the place as Coeia, in the Staine Hundred lands of the Abbey of Ely, where '...Picot [of Cambridge] holds three hides and three virgates under the abbot'. At the time of King Edward, '...Aethelric the Monk and Godric, the men of the Abbot of Ramsey, held three and a half hides of this land... [and] could neither give nor sell them without the king's leave'. In 1316 the place was recorded as Stowe cum Quey.

Theydon Bois
The first word of this Essex village placename comes from the Old English words 'thaec', meaning 'thatch, and 'denu', a valley. Hence 'valley where thatching materials grow'. In the thirteenth century the manor came into the possession of the de Bosco (or de Bois) family who attached their family name to the manor. The French word 'bois', translates as 'forest', 'wood' or 'woodland'. Domesday referred to the place as Teidana in 1086, and by 1257 it had become known as Teidon Boys.

Thorngumbold
This apparently quaint placename has a simple derivation in that it comes from the Gumbald family who held the estate in the thirteenth century At that time it became known as Thoren Gumbaud, having been called Torne and Torn, from the Old English for a thorn bush in 1086, indicating '[place at the] thorn bush'. Domesday places the settlement in the South Holderness Hundred of Yorkshire, held by Drogo de la Beuvrière.

Tittensor
A small village in central Staffordshire, named after its possible founder, a man called Titten. Appended to his name is the Old English word element 'ofer', meaning 'ridge' (as in the topographical landscape feature). Hence, we may take the placename to mean 'ridge of a man called Titten'. In 1086, the village name was recorded as Titesovre and Titesoure, in the Pirehill Hundred, where three hides of the estate were granted to Robert de Stafford by the Conqueror, which he leased to Stenwulf of Sutton. Two Saxon free men, Wulfgeat of Madeley and Godric, held them before 1066. It was a small manor supporting eleven households, comprising eight villans, two borders and one slave, all valued at one pound and five shillings in 1086.

Toller Porcorum
If you thought that the second word of this placename was related to pork and to pigs you'd be perfectly right. The Latin word 'Porcorum' means 'of the pigs'. As for the first word, it

comes from the River Toller on which this Dorset village stands. Therefore this placename translates as '[estate on the River] Toller where pigs are kept'. The river name has now been changed to the Hooke, but the original name came from ancient Celtic and meant 'hollow stream', presumably long before the pigs were brought in. The 'Porcorum' element of the village name distinguishes it from nearby Toller Fratrum. The Latin word 'fratrum' means 'of the bretheren', referring to the Knights Hospitallers who had earlier held that part of the estate. Domesday recorded the place as Tolre in 1086, and in 1340 it was recorded as Tolre Porcorum.

Tow Law
This unusual placename near Wolsingham Moor in County Durham combines two Old English words, 'tot', meaning 'lookout or sentry post', and 'hlaw', a hill. Hence, 'lookout post on a hill'. The 'tot' element is fairly common throughout England, in places like Totnes in Devon, Tottington in Greater Manchester, Tottenham in London and Great Totham in Essex.

Ugglebarnby
A distinctively Scandinavian placename in North Yorkshire, and abiding evidence of the influence of the Danes in the north-eastern England. The original settlement was probably established by a Viking man called Uglubarthr, as indicated by the suffix 'by' at the end of the placename, which meant 'village' or 'farmstead'. Hence, 'village or farmstead of a man called Uglubarthr'. By the time of Domesday the placename had been recorded as Ugleberdesbi, in the North Riding Hundred of Langbaurgh, held by Earl Hugh of Chester (also known as 'Hugh the Wolf' and 'Hugh the Fat'). Its tenants were William de Percy and the Canons of St Peter in York, it having belonged to Earl Siward before the Norman Conquest.

Ugley
In fact, this village in the Uttlesford district of Essex is anything but 'ugly'; the placename is from quite a different source, and more likely to have been a corruption of the word 'Oakley', a name frequently used for the place, especially in the nineteenth century. The Saxon word 'leah' indicated a woodland glade or a clearing, so this explanation of the name would translate as '[place at the] oak tree in the clearing'. Alternatively, the name may have come from a man called Ugga, in which case, 'Ugga's clearing'. It has been known under several different variants over time, including Uggelle before 1066, as Ugghelea in the *Domesday Book* of 1086, as Oggeley in the early fourteenth century and as Ugley and Oakley at the end of nineteenth century.

Unthank
At a time in our history when it's possible to 'unfriend' a person on social media, it ought to be possible to 'unthank' someone too – no doubt that will happen in the fullness of time. However, for the present, the Cumbrian hamlet of Unthank holds this dubious distinction. The word 'unthanc' as it existed in Anglo-Saxon times, meant to bear ill-will, or to hold something 'against the will', in this particular case, land held without the consent of the owner. Some have suggested that it may also apply to land that is difficult or impossible to cultivate, possibly through bedrock, infertile or excessively stony ground. This small hamlet near Gamblesby was recorded by its present name in 1254.

Upper Slaughter
This Gloucestershire placename has nothing to do with murder or killing, as the name might suggest, but comes from the Old English word 'slohtre', which is related to the modern English word 'slough', and meaning a muddy or miry place. An alternative has been

suggested in that it may be related to the German word 'schlucht', meaning 'deep channel' or 'ravine'. In 1086, the place was recorded as Sclostre, a single manor in the Salmonsbury Hundred, held at that time by Emma, the mother of Robert de Lacy. The 'upper' addition, meaning 'higher', distinguishes it from the nearby village of Lower Slaughter.

Wackerfield

There exist two possible interpretations of the meaning of the name of this small hamlet in County Durham. The one cites the Old English word 'wacor', meaning 'watchers' or 'watchful ones', and 'feld' or 'felda', signifying open land. This was not quite the same as what we might think of as a field, as before land enclosures and hedgerows, the rural landscape was open and generally used for arable farming or pasture and would have required more-or-less constant surveillance. The second prefers it meaning 'osier' or 'willow', what we might call wicker, such as that used in weaving and basketry work. So the placename could mean either 'open land where osiers are found', or 'open land of the watchful ones', the latter possibly referring to people who watched over crops against thievery, as bird scarers or to drive off rabbits and other threats. Before the Conquest of 1066 the placename had already been recorded as Wacarfeld.

Weedon Bec

Known simply as Weodun in the mid-tenth century, this Northamptonshire village derived its placename from the Old English words 'weoh', meaning 'heathen (or pagan) temple', and 'dun', a hill. Hence, '[place by a] heathen temple on a hill'. It was recorded in the *Domesday Book* as Wedone, in the Gravesend Hundred, in land belonging to the Count of Mortain in 1086. Before the Conquest the manor had belonged to Estan of Farningham. Later, during the twelfth century, the manor passed to the Abbey of Bec-Hellouin in Normandy and 'Bec' was added to the placename, distinguishing it from Weedon Lois a few miles distant to the south. By 1379 the village had become known as Wedon Bek, and in 1868 it was recorded as Weedon-Beck. It was also sometimes known as Weedon-on-the-Street, a reference to its location on the Roman road of Watling Street.

Wem

Wem, in the County of Shropshire, was known to the Saxons as Wamm or Wemm, meaning marshland or a muddy place, referring no doubt to the frequent flooding of the River Roden that runs through the town. Following the Norman Conquest, King William gave the lands to Earl Roger de Montgomerie. In 1086, the *Domesday Book* records the place as Weme, held by William Pantulf (sometimes Pandolf), to whom Roger had granted the Barony of Wem. It goes on to state that two Saxons were allowed to hold manors; these included Wicga and Leofwine who paid for the privilege. The account also continues '...and Aelfgifu and [another] Aelfgifu held it as four manors and were free'. Confusingly, the two named persons were not specified as men or women, but given the prevailing culture of the time, they were most likely to have been men. Some translations of Domesday seem to prefer the name Aelfeva, and not Aelfgifu, which could easily be misconstrued as Aelfgifu of York, the first wife of Ethelred the Unready.

Wendy

The name of this Cambridgeshire village existed long before author J.M. Barrie used it as a name for a girl in the *Peter Pan* story – in fact it was already known as Wandei and Wandrie in 1086. The name derives from a combination of the Old English words 'wende', meaning 'bend', and 'eg', signifying an island or higher ground surrounded by water or marshland. The village is located on a bend in the North Ditch where it flows into the River Cam.

Domesday listed it in the Arringford Hundred, with four hides and three virgates of land held at that time by Odo on behalf of Count Alan of Brittany. The account recorded '...there is land for six ploughs. In demesne are two [ploughs]; and six villans and five bordars with four ploughs. There are four slaves and two mills rendering forty-five shillings'.

Westonzoyland

The village of Westonzoyland is possibly one of England's most alien sounding placenames. It is located on the Somerset Levels and the name is made from several Old English elements: the first two, 'west' and 'tun', respectively mean 'western farmstead (or estate)', and the second, 'zoy' is a corruption of 'Sowy' which is higher ground (at times effectively an island), an area not prone to flooding on the Levels between the River Cary and the River Parrett. The final element, 'land', is self explanatory. Taken together, these produce a meaning of 'western manor in the Sowi estate'. Domesday recorded the village as Sowi, and by about 1245 it was known as Westsowi, The Parish of Westernzoyland was created in 1515.

Wetwang

No amount of guesswork will help unravel the meaning of the placename of this village in East Yorkshire. To unlock its mysterious origin one needs to go back to Anglo-Saxon times and understand that the Old Scandinavian expression 'vaett-vangr' came from 'vaetti', which meant 'witness' or 'evidence', and 'vangr' meant 'garden' or 'field'. Therefore the placename should be interpreted as 'field where trials (or legal actions) take place (or evidence is given)'. Domesday recorded Wetuuangha, in the Warter Hundred, held in 1086 by the Archbishop of York, who had also held it before the Norman Conquest.

Wham

Wham is a village in North Yorkshire, whose name derives from the Old English word 'hwamm', which translates as '[place in a] marshy hollow or valley'. The place was known in the thirteenth century as Quane, and it was not until 1771 that the present day version of the placename came into being.

Whaplode St Catherine

This Lincolnshire village in the District of South Holland gets its placename from the Old English word 'cwappa', an eelpout or burbot (fish), and 'lad', a watercourse. Hence, '(place near the) watercourse where burbots are caught'. The St Catherine affix reflects the local village church which was built later. The place had been known a Cappelad since the early ninth century, and the Domesday survey names it as Copelade, in the Elloe Hundred, for the most part held in 1086 by the Crowland Abbey of St Guthlac, as it had been before the Conquest. Five carucates had been held by Count Alan of Brittany, before being taken as a Crown possession. The manor was assessed at a value of twenty shillings.

Wide Open

Sometimes spelt as a single word, Wideopen, this district of Newcastle upon Tyne in North Tyneside is a relatively recent placename, having been created sometime around 1863. As a mining district of the late Industrial Revolution (which had been sunk by Perkins and Thackrah in 1825), its exposed terrain was described as 'wide open' at the time, and the name stuck. The mine in question closed in 2011, and an extensive area was reclaimed to form Weetslade Country Park.

Wigwig

This odd-sounding place can be found in rural Shropshire and was probably established by a Saxon man called Wicga. Added to his name is the Old English affix 'wic', which referred to a specialised farmstead of some kind, most typically a dairy farm. Hence, the placename may be interpreted as 'Wicga's dairy farm'. The Great Survey listed the village as Wigewic, a very small estate supporting seven households in the Condover Hundred and held in 1086 by Turold de Verley, having belonged to a Saxon man called Almer in 1066.

Wing

Having an unusual and distinctive name, this Buckinghamshire village has two possible interpretations of its placename. It was recorded in the latter quarter of the tenth century as Weowungum, and may be related to a man called Wiwa and his family or followers, plus 'ham', meaning 'settlement' or 'village', in which case the place may be said to mean '[settlement of] Wiwa's people'. Alternatively, many believe the Old English word 'wig' or 'weoh' meaning 'heathen people' or 'pagans' is more fitting, and that the placename should more properly be said to mean 'homestead of heathen people'. By 1086, the name had been written as Witehunge, an extremely large manor for its day in the Cottesloe Hundred lands of the Count of Mortain. The account concluded: 'This manor Edward Cild, a man of Earl Harold (its former overlord) held and could sell' – this, of course, before the Conquest of 1066.

Bibliography

ACKROYD, Peter, *London: The Biography* (Penguin, 2001).

ALLEN BROWN, R, *The Normans and the Norman Conquest* (Boydell Press, 1968).

ANGUS-BUTTERWORTH, Lionel M, *Old Cheshire Families & Their Seats* (E. J. Morten, 1970).

ATKINS, Paul, *Seven Households: Life in Cheshire & Lancashire 1582–1774* (Arley Hall Press, 2002).

BAINES, Edward, *History of the County Palatine & Duchy of Lancaster* (1836).

BARDSLEY, Charles Wareing Endell, *A Dictionary of English and Welsh Surnames* (Franklin Classics Trade Press, 2015).

BARTHOLOMEW, John, *Gazetteer of the British Isles* (Harper Collins, 1977).

MCCLURE, Judith & COLLINS, Roger (eds.), *The Ecclesiastical History of the English People* (Oxford World's Classics, M2008).

BOYDELL & BREWER, *Victoria History of the Counties of England* (1953).

BROOKES, Stuart, *The Kingdom and People of Kent AD 400–1066* (History Press, 2010).

BUCHAN G. H, *A Brief History of the Duttons of Dutton* (The Academy/J Murray, 1901).

CAVENDISH, Richard, *Kings & Queens: The Concise Guide* (David & Charles, 2006).

COOPER, Glynis, *Illustrated History of Manchester's Suburbs* (Breedon Books, 2002).

CROSBY, Alan, *A History of Cheshire* (Phillimore 1996).

CROSBY, Alan, *A History of Lancashire* (Phillimore, 1998).

CROUCH, David, *The Normans: The History of a Dynasty* (Hambledon & London, 2002).

DALY, Mark & DAZELEY, Peter, *London Uncovered* (Frances Lincoln, 2016).

EMETT, Charlie, *Discovering County Durham & Teeside* (History Press, 2007).

FARRER, W and BROWNBILL J, (eds.), *A History of the County of Lancaster* (Victoria County History, London, 1907).

GLINERT, Ed, *Manchester Compendium* (Penguin 2008).

GREENALL, R, L, *The Making of Victorian Salford* (Carnegie Publishing, 2000).

GREENSLADE, M. W, *A History of Staffordshire* (History Press, 1998).

HALLIDAY, F. E, *A History of Cornwall* (House of Stratus, 2001).

HAMILTON, N.E.S.A, (ed.). *The National Gazetteer of Great Britain and Ireland* (Virtue, London, 1915).

HENSON, Donald, *The English Elite in 1066* (Anglo Saxon Books).

HIGHAM, N. J, *The Death of Anglo-Saxon England* (Sutton Publishing, 1997).

HILTON, R. H, *Medieval Society: The West Midlands* (Cambridge University Press 1983).

HEY, David, *A History of Yorkshire* (Carnegie Publishing, 2011).

HEY, DAVID, *Medieval South Yorkshire* (Horizon Press, 2003).

HOPE & SALMON, *English Homes and Villages* (Kent & Sussex), (1909).

KENYON, Denise, *The Origins of Lancashire: Origins of the Shire* (Manchester University Press 1991).

KIDD, Charles, (ed.), *DeBrett's Peerage and Baronetage* (DeBrett's Peerage Ltd).

LANCASHIRE FEDERATION OF WOMENS' INSTITUTES, *The Lancashire Village Book* (Countryside Books).

LEWIS, Samuel, *Topographical Dictionary of England* (1831).

LEWIS, William, *What's in an English Place-Name?* (Brazen Head Publishing, 2011).

LONG, Peter, *Hidden Places in East Anglia* (Hidden Places Travel Guides, 2008).

LYSONS, Daniel, *Magna Britannia: The County Palatine of Chester* (T. Cadell & W. Davies, 1822).

MARTIN, Prof Geoffrey, *Domesday Book: A Complete Translation* (Penguin 2003).

MAIS, S. P. B, *The Home Counties: the Face of Britain* (Batsford, 1947).

MILLS, David, *A Dictionary of British Placenames* (Oxford University Press, 2011).

MORRIS, Marc, *The Norman Conquest* (Cornerstone, 2012).

PIGGOTT & SLATER, *Directory of Manchester & Salford* (1841).

ORDERICUS VITALIS, FOSTER, Thomas (trans) *The Ecclesiastical History of England and Normandy* (Henry G Bohn, London, 1854).

ORMEROD, George, *History of the County Palatine and City of Chester* (revised by Thomas Helsby, 1882).

ROOM, Adrian, *The Penguin Dictionary of British Placenames* (Penguin Books, 2003).

SAVAGE, Anne, *The Anglo-Saxon Chronicles* (Book Club Associates, London, 1982).

SWANTON, Michael, (ed.), *The Anglo-Saxon Chronicles* (Psychology Press, 1998).

TAGGART, Caroline, *The Book of English Placenames* (Edbury Press, 2011).

WHITE, William, *History, Gazetteer & Directory of Devon* (David & Charles, 1968).

WHITE, William, *History, Gazetteer & Directory of Staffordshire* (1851).

WHITEMAN, Robin, *Wessex* (Orion Publishing, 1994).

WILSON, John Marius, *Imperial Gazetteer of England and Wales* (1870–72).

WOOD, Michael, *In Search of the Dark Ages* (BBC Books, 1981).

WHYNNE-HAMMOND, Charles, *English Place-Names Explained* (Countryside Books, 2005).

Online Sources

Domesday Book Online website (domesdaybook.co.uk).

Ford, David Nash, *Royal Berkshire History* website.

Fordham University, *Internet Medieval Sourcebook*.

Genuki website, *Cheshire Towns & Parishes* (ukbmd.org.uk/genuki/chs/parishes.html).

Historic UK History Magazine, *Historic UK* website (historic-uk.com).

Smith, Anna Powell, *Open Domesday* website (opendomesday.org).

The British History Online website (british-history.ac.uk).

The Institute of Historical Research/University of London/Boydell & Brewer, *The Victoria County History website* (victoriacountyhistory.ac.uk).

The Village Reference website (VillageNet.co.uk).

Thrush, Andrew and Ferris, John P (eds.), *History of Parliament Online* website (Crown Copyright and the History of Parliament Trust, 1964–2017).

University of Nottingham website, *Key to English Placenames*.

Libraries and Archives

Greater Manchester County Record Office.

Newspapers, Magazines and Periodicals

Kelly's Directory of Staffordshire (1896).

Hudson's Historic Houses & Gardens (Hudson Media Ltd, published annually).

Index